Larry M. Hyman and Frans Plank (Eds.)
Phonological Typology

Phonology and Phonetics

―
Edited by
Aditi Lahiri

Volume 23

Phonological Typology

Edited by
Larry M. Hyman and Frans Plank

DE GRUYTER
MOUTON

ISBN 978-3-11-068637-1
e-ISBN (PDF) 978-3-11-045193-1
e-ISBN (EPUB) 978-3-11-044992-1
ISSN 1861-4191

Library of Congress Control Number: 2018934237

Bibliografische Information der Deutschen Nationalbibliothek
The Deutsche Nationalbibliothek lists this publication in the Deutschen Nationalbibliografie; detailed bibliographic data are available on the internet http://dnb.dnb.de.

© 2019 Walter de Gruyter GmbH, Berlin/Boston
This volume is text- and page-identical with the hardback published in 2018.
Typesetting: Integra Software Services, Pondicherry
Printing and binding: CPI books GmbH, Leck
♾ Printed on acid-free paper
Printed in Germany

www.degruyter.com

Contents

Preface —— VII
Contributors —— IX

Larry M. Hyman
What is phonological typology? —— 1

Frans Plank
An implicational universal to defy: typology ⊃ ¬ phonology ≡ phonology ⊃ ¬ typology ≡ ¬ (typology ∧ phonology) ≡ ¬ typology ∨ ¬ phonology —— 21

Paul Kiparsky
Formal and empirical issues in phonological typology —— 54

Ian Maddieson
Is phonological typology possible without (universal) categories? —— 107

Jeffrey Heinz
The computational nature of phonological generalizations —— 126

Anthony Brohan and Jeff Mielke
Frequent segmental alternations in P-base 3 —— 196

Aditi Lahiri
Predicting universal phonological contrasts —— 229

B. Elan Dresher, Christopher Harvey, and Will Oxford
Contrastive feature hierarchies as a new lens on typology —— 273

Ellen Broselow
Laryngeal contrasts in second language phonology —— 312

Tomas Riad
The phonological typology of North Germanic accent —— 341

Carlos Gussenhoven
Prosodic typology meets phonological representations —— 389

Subject Index —— 419

Language Index —— 423

Author Index —— 426

Preface

This volume seeks to bring together two separate enterprises, typology and phonology, which have often gone their separate ways, even when apparently addressing each other. Although there has always been phonology in the many approaches to typology, there has always been far less of it than there has been of morphology and syntax. Particularly in recent times, during which phonological theory has flourished in many colours, the phonology in typological circles has centered either around segment inventories and basic phonotactics or limited itself to crudely categorising labels such as "syllable- vs. stress-timed languages", something which would barely pass muster with phonological theorists, whose concerns have been "deeper" and usually more formal. On the other hand, despite the numerous and diverse languages that would typically inform phonological theorising, typological questions as such were rarely of major consequence, if raised at all.

If one sees value or at any rate promise in typology, the research programme for discovering and accounting for order in diversity, and if you see no principled reasons to doubt that linguistic diversity is about as orderly in phonology as in syntax and morphology (or at any rate inflection), this state of affairs is regrettable. Since this is how we see it, we felt obliged to lend a hand towards improving relationships.

In organised typology, the success of our efforts was limited. Though long involved in various capacities in the Association for Linguistic Typology (ALT), it looks like we and a few fellow campaigners have not been able to significantly raise the profile of phonology at ALT's biennial conferences or in its other activities. The two of us hit rock bottom when a workshop to boost phonology in typology that we suggested as part of an ALT conference a few years ago did not find favour with the programme committee, for reasons we ourselves found unconvincing. Reassuringly, the phonological record of *Linguistic Typology*, the journal we have helped to run for two decades, is better, but still comparatively modest.

Perhaps we had gotten hold of the wrong end of the stick, trying to proselytise in typological circles. Changing tack, for the present volume we sought out linguists who define themselves and are perceived first and foremost as phonologists. Though rarely meeting at typological get-togethers and not so far published in *LT*, we were still expecting typological awareness rather than complete innocence, because our remit for them was as follows: Do typology! Present a sample piece of work appropriate for a workshop and subsequent publication as you think it can and ought to be done in state-of-the-art phonology!

And here we go. After two scene-setting and background-providing contributions from the editors (Hyman; Plank), the phonologists assembled here, typologically aware or indeed expert, address metatheoretical issues of what it means to do phonological typology (Kiparsky; Maddieson). Through different methodologies, they explore the possibilities of and limitations on segmental alternations (Heinz; Brohan & Mielke), seek system, not in segment inventories as such, but in featural contrasts, and find variability, though not randomness, of contrastive systems in language change and language acquisition (Lahiri; Dresher, Harvey, & Oxford; Broselow) and seek limitations on diversity and change concerning microvariation in tonal accent systems in North Germanic (Riad). An effort at conceptual clarification of what it is that can be typologised in prosodic typology – segments, constituents, their alignments – concludes (Gussenhoven).

Typology's subject matter is vast: for EVERYTHING about language – units, paradigmatic systems, rules for and constraints on forming prosodic constituents (syllables, feet ... anything syntagmatically complex without or with meaning) – we need to ascertain whether it is variable or invariable, and if it is variable we want to know whether it varies independently or co-varies with anything else. Despite the extensive knowledge accumulated in phonology over the past century, phonological typologists still have considerable work cut out for them for an unforeseeable time to come. The present collection will have served its purpose if it gives them encouragement and guidance. Naturally, phonological awareness or indeed expertise of none-too-basic a nature will be an asset for those planning to join in this enterprise: in phonology no less than in syntax and morphology, generalising is futile if the particulars over which one generalises are inadequately analysed.

This volume derives from a workshop in Somerville College, University of Oxford, on 11–13 August 2013 (funded by a European Research Council Advanced Investigator Grant to Aditi Lahiri). Subsequent to the preparation of this volume, a survey monograph of the same title appeared, by Matthew K. Gordon (Oxford University Press, 2016), adding another voice to the small chorus of performers striving to bring the adjective into harmony with the noun (or vice versa) of our shared title. A big thanks from all of us who were present goes to Aditi Lahiri, for there is no better host. There also is no better series editor for this sort of thing either, cruel but fair with her editors and authors: A thank you to our dear friend and colleague Aditi Lahiri in this capacity, too.

We might as well dedicate this collection to her on the occasion of a round birthday that must not go unmarked...

Larry M. Hyman
Frans Plank

Contributors

Anthony Brohan
Google, Mountain View, CA 94043, USA

Ellen Broselow
Department of Linguistics, Stony Brook University, Stony Brook, NY 11794-4376, USA
ellen.broselow@stonybrook.edu

B. Elan Dresher
Department of Linguistics, University of Toronto, Toronto, Ontario, Canada M5S 3G3
dresher@chass.utoronto.ca

Carlos Gussenhoven
Department of Linguistics, Radboud University, PO Box 9103, 6550 HD Nijmegen, The Netherlands
c.gussenhoven@let.ru.nl

Christopher Harvey
Department of Linguistics, University of Toronto, Toronto, Ontario, Canada M5S 3G3
c.harvey@mail.utoronto.ca

Jeffrey Heinz
Department of Linguistics and Institute of Advanced Computational Science, Stony Brook University, Stony Brook, NY 11794-4376, USA
jeffrey.heinz@stonybrook.edu

Larry M. Hyman
Department of Linguistics, University of California at Berkeley, Berkeley, CA 94704, USA
hyman@berkeley.edu

Paul Kiparsky
Department of Linguistics, Stanford University, Stanford, CA 94305-2150, USA
kiparsky@stanford.edu

Aditi Lahiri
Faculty of Linguistics, Philology and Phonetics, University of Oxford, Oxford OX1 2HG, UK
aditi.lahiri@ling-phil.ox.ac.uk

Ian Maddieson
Department of Linguistics, University of New Mexico, Albuquerque NM
ianm@berkeley.edu

Jeff Mielke
Department of English, North Carolina State University, Raleigh, NC 27695-8105, USA
jmielke@ncsu.edu

Will Oxford
Department of Linguistics, University of Manitoba, Winnipeg, Manitoba, Canada R3T 5V5
oxfordwr@cc.umanitoba.ca

Frans Plank
Somerville College, University of Oxford, Oxford OX2 6HD, UK
frans.plank@ling-phil.ox.ac.uk

Tomas Riad
Institutionen för svenska och flerspråkighet, Stockholms universitet, 106 91 Stockholm, Sweden
tomas.riad@su.se

Larry M. Hyman
What is phonological typology?

> Whatever typology is, it is on a roll at the moment and likely to continue.
> *(Nichols 2007: 236)*

Abstract: In this contribution I raise the question of what phonological typology is, can, or should be. I start by asking what linguistic typology is and then turn to the problem: despite the intellectual overlap, there is rare cross-communication in the study of sound systems by phonologists vs. typologists. Despite earlier contributions by Trubetzkoy, Jakobson, Martinet, Greenberg and others, and its inclusion in even earlier efforts towards "holistic" typology, phonological typology is often underrepresented or even excluded in typology textbooks. At the same time, many, if not most phonologists do not see a difference between phonological typology and crosslinguistic (formal) phonology. As a result, they often address issues of comparison without awareness of the field of typology and with little involvement in the foundational and methodological questions/controversies peppering the pages of *Linguistic Typology*, e.g., its concern with distributions, whether pre-established categories exist etc. I argue for a properties-based approach to typology, showing that phonology has always been – and should remain – basically typological in it concerns.

1 What is typology? What is phonology?

The purpose of this paper is to address the question of what phonological typology is, can, or should be. To do so, one has to consider its relationship both to typology and to phonology in general. Such a task is complicated by at least three factors. First, there is no agreement on what typology is, let alone phonological typology. In an article entitled "What, if anything, is typology?", the then president of the Association for Linguistic Typology wrote:

> Typology has the hallmarks of a mature discipline: a society, conferences, journals, books, textbooks, classic works, a founding father [Joseph H. Greenberg], and people who are called and call themselves typologists. (Nichols 2007: 231)

While most typologists would probably self-identify as studying the similarities vs. differences among languages, Nichols goes on to say that "despite these conspicuous identifying marks", typology should not be recognized as a subfield of linguistics, but rather as "framework-neutral analysis and theory plus some common applications of such analysis (which include crosslinguistic comparison, geographical mapping, cladistics, and reconstruction)" (p. 236). On the other hand, linguists who work in specific formal frameworks may engage in crosslinguistic comparison, but typically self-identify as syntacticians, morphologists, phonologists, etc. as they have less interest in issues of geography, language classification and history.

The second problem in characterizing phonological typology is that phonology is no longer the unified subfield that it once was. The following assessment appears in a recent review of the multivolume *Blackwell companion to phonology* (van Oostendorp et al. 2011):

> Phonology is changing rapidly [...] Some phonologists collect the evidence for their theories using introspection, fieldwork and descriptive grammars, while other trust only quantitatively robust experimentation or corpus data. Some test phonological theory computationally [...] whereas others prefer to compare theories on conceptual grounds [...] (Gouskova 2013: 173)

Gouskova goes on to observe that the diversification within phonology has become so great that "it is becoming harder for phonologists to talk to each other, for who can be a computer scientist, phonetician, neurolinguist and expert in adjacent fields such as morphology and syntax at the same time as having a command of the extensive literature on phonology-internal argumentation and phonological typology?" (p. 173).

Finally, whether typology and phonology are coherent subfields or not, there has been precious little interaction between the two groups of scholars. Most typologists do not work on phonology per se and usually cite phonological examples only en passant, if at all (there is for example no phonology in Whaley's (1997) *Introduction to typology*). For their part, phonologists frequently invoke typology, but without participation in the society, conferences, journals etc. referred to above. While typology is currently centered around crosslinguistic morphosyntax, phonology has been transitioning from a descriptive/analytical to experimental field. Slightly oversimplifying, "traditional" phonology from the time of the phoneme has been concerned with the underlying structures needed to account for the properties of sound systems. The methodology has largely consisted of phonological argumentation on how best to analyze a wide range of crosslinguistic phenomena. Given that phonology is part of grammar, this naturally includes the interfaces of phonology with both morphology and syntax, where the connection to grammatical typology should be even more clear. However, today's phonologist is more likely to be involved in laboratory techniques where the methodologies are instrumental, experimental, statistical, and computational. To the extent that the questions focus on how what is produced and how what is in the signal relates to the speaker's mind, ears, and vocal tract, the results may appear even more removed from the morphosyntactic core of the typology movement.

This non-intersection is highly atypical when compared with the interests of the founders of both fields. Joseph Greenberg's foundational work on typology and universals touched on virtually all aspects of phonology, e.g., syllable structure (Greenberg 1962, 1978), distinctive features (Greenberg, Jenkins, & Foss 1967), vowel harmony (Greenberg 1963), nasalized vowels (Greenberg 1966), glottalized consonants (Greenberg 1970), word-prosodic systems (Greenberg & Kaschube 1976), and so forth. His historical work on African languages also included phonological reconstruction, e.g., of tone in Proto-Bantu (Greenberg 1948) and labial consonants in Proto-Afro-Asiatic (Greenberg 1958). It is thus striking how few major morphosyntactic typologists show an active engagement with phonology today (but see Evans 1995, Donohue 1997, Haspelmath 2006, Plank 1998, among others).

On the other side, the non-involvement of phonologists with the field of typology stands in stark contrast to the fact that phonology has been typological from its very beginning. In fact, the very notion of the phoneme is a typological one, as evidenced in the following oft-cited passage:

> [...] it almost goes without saying that two languages, A and B, may have identical sounds but utterly distinct phone[mic] patterns; or they may have mutually incompatible phonetic systems, from the articulatory and acoustic standpoint, but identical or similar [phonemic] patterns. (Sapir 1925: 43)

The frequent comparison of allophonic aspiration in English with phonemic aspiration in Thai, Korean, etc. is inherently typological, a statement about how different sound systems can "phonologize" the same or similar phonetic substance. Ever since the introduction of the phoneme phonologists have been unified in recognizing that phonological representations are distinct from the observed phonetics. In the 1930s the Prague School developed the phonetics-phonology distinction further, emphasizing how phonological systems differ in their structural properties. Trubetzkoy's (1939) *Grundzüge der Phonologie* is both a highly theoretical and a thoroughly typological work. As any textbook in phonology would explain, a specific phonetic distinction may have a quite different status in different languages. A difference in voicing as in [t] vs. [d] may have a distinctive (paradigmatic) function in distinguishing between morphemes, e.g., *bit* vs. *bid* in English. It may instead have a demarcative (syntagmatic) function helping to determine where one is in the spoken chain. In Basaá there is a single set of underlying stops /P, T, K/, which are realized [p, t, k] in stem-initial position vs. [b, d, g] (~ [β, ɾ, ɣ]) stem-internally (Hyman 2003: 259). As a result, the prefixed word /ɓa-Tâ/ 'fathers' is pronounced [ɓatâ] while the suffixed word /ɓáT-â/ 'gather' is pronounced [ɓádâ] (~ [bárâ]). A third possibility is that the voicing difference is non-distinctive or allophonic. A well-known case of this comes from Korean, where /t/ is realized [d] intervocalically. Thus, when /su/ 'water' and /to/ 'way' are compounded, the result is [sudo] 'waterway, waterworks'. Among the other possibilities are free variation, as when the final /t/ of English *bit* is either released or not and what Trubetzkoy calls the expressive function, where differences indicate such things as social identity or attitude of the speaker, e.g. the "expressive" aspiration in the phrase *je t[ʰ]'aime* (Martinet 1960).

Once the phonological contrasts are established, a major component of Trubetzkoy's *Grundzüge* was to provide a typology of the contrasts found in one vs. another system. He classifies distinctive contrasts according to three different factors.

First, their relationship to the entire system of contrasts. This refers to the number of segments in the set. For example, the set of oral labial stops can be bilateral (/p/ vs. /b/) or multilateral (/p/ vs. /pʰ/ vs. /b/), depending on the language. The relationship to the system is said to be proportional, if other segments exhibit a parallel relation, e.g., bilateral /t/ vs. /d/ or multilateral /t/ vs. /tʰ/ vs. /d/. On the other hand, a contrast such as /l/ vs. /r/ is said to be isolated, since there is no other pair of phonemes which realizes a parallel contrast.

Second, the relationship between the contrasting segments, which can be privative, gradual, or equipollent. In a privative contrast one member has a "mark" which is lacking in the other. Thus in a /pʰ/ vs. /p/ contrast, /pʰ/ has aspiration, while /p/ lacks it. Gradual contrasts refer to scalar features such as the vowel height differences between /i, e, ɛ, æ/ or the pitch height differences between High, Mid and Low tone. In equipollent contrasts the segments are considered "logically equivalent". An example is labial /p/ vs. alveolar /t/, where each has a logically equivalent but different upper and lower articulator. Trubetzkoy is careful to distinguish "logically" vs. "actually" privative, gradual and equipollent, since it will depend on the system. While it makes no sense to think of /p/ vs. /t/ as differing on a continuous scale (they involve different articulators), Trubetzkoy might consider the relation to be privative if a language were to have only labial and alveolar places of articulation. In this case /p/ could be said to have a labial mark while /t/ lacks it.[1]

---

[1] In the UPSID database (Maddieson & Precoda 1992) I have however not found a language which only has the two places of articulation, labial and alveolar. For accessing UPSID I have used Henning Reetz's online interface: http://web.phonetik.uni-frankfurt.de/upsid.

Third, the extent of the contrast. This refers to whether the contrast is realized in all environments or whether there are contexts in which the contrast is neutralized. A well-known example of this is German final devoicing, whereby /rat/ 'advice' and /rad/ 'wheel' are both realized [rat] in isolation. Another is flapping in American English, e.g. *metal* and *medal*, both pronounced [mɛɾl] (cf. etymologically related *metallic* and *medallion* with [tʰ] and [d]).

The above examples not only establish that early modern phonology was heavily steeped in typology, but that the founders had two different ideas of phonological typology, depending on whether the starting point is substance vs. form. In the first approach one asks how different systems exploit a particular phonetic property. In the examples cited, it was seen that obstruent voicing can be distinctive, demarcative or allophonic. The possibilities can be more extensive, as in the case of nasality. As summarized in (1), there are at least five possibilities for how nasality may be underlyingly contrastive in a language (cf. Cohn 1993; Clements & Osu 2003):

(1) a. on consonants only: /m, n, ŋ/ e.g. Korean
    b. on vowels and consonants: /ĩ, ũ, ã, m, n, ŋ/ e.g. Bambara
    c. on vowels only: /ĩ, ũ, ã/ e.g. Ikwere
    d. on whole morphemes: /CVC/ᴺ e.g. Desano
    e. absent entirely: ----- e.g. Doutai

In addition to the above distinctions, languages may vary in whether they contain voiceless nasals, prenasalized or nasally released consonants, as well in whether the contrasts are found on all nasalizable consonants (e.g., including liquids and glides) and on all vowels. Similar substance-directed typology can be done with virtually any phonetic feature or property, e.g., voicing, aspiration, rounding, and so forth (cf. (1)). Still being substance-directed, a typologist will likely be interested in how one vs. another of these properties is distributed in the languages of the world, whether by genetic affiliation or by geography.

The second approach to phonological typology is form-directed: in this case the analyst explores the logical properties of a specific model. The above examples from Trubetzkoy fall into this category, as he was interested in the logical differences in the nature of the contrasts that his model of phonology recognized. It mattered less that /l/ and /r/ differed in laterality or rhoticity than the fact that they constitute an isolated bilateral contrast in any language which has only these two liquids. This second, form-directed approach finds reincarnation in virtually every model, if not every proposal in phonological theory. Since early generative phonology proposed ordered rules (Chomsky & Halle 1968), it was only natural that a form-directed typology should develop how these rules apply to forms and, in so doing, how they affect each other: a phonological rule could apply to a form left-to-right, right-to-left, simultaneously, and cyclically or non-cyclically. Earlier applying rules could be in feeding, bleeding, counterfeeding, and counterbleeding relationships, creating and/or taking away inputs to which later rules could apply (Kiparsky 1968; Kenstowicz & Kisseberth 1977). More recently, within optimality theory (Prince & Smolensky 1993), all of the possible rankings can be exhaustively computed in a "factorial typology" (cf. Gordon 2007). In short, almost any formal property can be "typologized" in terms of its logical parameters.

2 Phonology vs. typology

In both of the above approaches to phonological typology there has been a deep commitment to the idea that phonetics and phonology are distinct from each other. As Buckley (2000: 2) puts it, "becoming divorced from the phonetics is the very essence of phonology". The key goal of phonology has been to determine what is a possible phonological system. This has meant both determining the universal properties of sound patterns in languages as well as what is going on in the heads of speakers with respect to these sound patterns. While these goals are directed towards the quest for universals, the traditional approach has been to seek universals through the study of language particulars, which can be quite diverse. Determining how languages can vary within such confines has been the central goal of traditional typology, where there has been a distinction (confusion?) between two views of what typology is about. The first is that it concerns the classification of languages into "types". Thus, Hagège (1992: 7) defines typology as "a principled way of classifying the languages of the world by the most significant properties which distinguish one from another". While it is harder to find explicit definitions of phonological typology, Vajda's (2001) posting coincides with this view: "it is possible to classify languages according to the phonemes they contain [...] typology is the study of structural features across languages. Phonological typology involves comparing languages according to the number or type of sounds they contain".[2] The other view, which I have termed property-driven typology (Hyman 2009: 213, 2012: 371), is that typology is not about the classification of languages but rather the characterization of linguistic properties: "Typology, thus, is not so much about the classification of

---

2 Since submitting this chapter, Gordon (2016) has appeared who defines phonological typology as follows: "Phonological typology is concerned with the study of the distribution and behavior of sounds found in human languages of the world" (p. 1).

languages as about the distributions of individual traits – units, categories, constructions, rules of all kinds – across the linguistic universe; these distributions, not languages as such, are the primary objects of comparison" (Plank 2001: 1399). Although I will come back to the issue of distributions as a crucial ingredient of typology, note for now that Greenberg (1974: 14) also explicitly recognizes the above two views: "all synchronic typologies have this Janus-like nature in that the same data can be utilized either for a typology of linguistic properties or a typology of individual languages".

One reason why there has been so little interaction between typologists and other linguists has been common misconceptions. Nichols (2007: 233–234) debunks the following four misunderstandings about typology, presumably including phonological typology:

(i) typology deals with only superficial grammatical phenomena, while formal grammar deals with deeper abstraction
(ii) typology usually or often uses large surveys of hundreds of languages
(iii) in typology, explanations or theory are usually functionalist
(iv) the main theoretical constructs of typology are the implicational correlation and the implicational hierarchy

Concerning the first misconception, Nichols goes on to cite the following, to which I would add her own head- vs. dependent marking typology (Nichols 1986):

> I see no difference in analytic or theoretical profundity or abstraction between generative parameters and original contributions of typology such as direct object vs. primary object (Dryer 1986), verb-framed vs. satellite-framed lexicalization patterns (Talmy 1985, Slobin 2004), various aspects of alignment (e.g., Dixon 1994, Dixon & Aikhenvald (eds.) 2000), differential object marking (Bossong 1998, Aissen 2003), referential density (Bickel 2003), and others.

She concludes that most typologists do not exploit large databases, many (including herself) are not functionalists, and finally, implicational statements are "a convenient format for presenting and testing results [...] [but not] the be-all and end-all of typology".

In fact, typologists disagree on a number of issues, including these:

(i) whether typology is a field:

> what we call typology is not properly a subfield of linguistics but is simply framework-neutral analysis and theory plus some of the common applications of such analysis (which include crosslinguistic comparison, geographical mapping, cladistics, and reconstruction). (Nichols 2007: 236)

(ii) whether it has internal subfields:

> Linguistic typology includes three subdisciplines: qualitative typology, which deals with the issue of comparing languages and within-language variance; quantitative typology,

which deals with the distribution of structural patterns in the world's languages; and theoretical typology, which explains these distributions. (Wikipedia "Linguistic Typology")

(iii) whether typology necessarily involves the quest for universals (or is about diversity):

the goal of typology is to uncover universals of language, most of which are universals of grammatical variation. (Croft 2003: 200)

(iv) what the role of theory should be in typology:

The hypothesis that typology is of theoretical interest is essentially the hypothesis that the ways in which languages differ from each other are not entirely random, but show various types of dependencies (Greenberg 1974: 54)

A traditional typologist might embellish, but presumably not object to, Evans & Levinson's (2010: 2740) statement that "[...] the goal of linguistics is [...] to explain why languages have the properties they do" (vs. the goal of linguistics is to explain how a speaker with a finite and limited exposure can produce an infinite number of new sentences, how a child by the age of two can do such-and-such, etc.). Be this as it may, let me return to the view that typology is something which phonologists do all the time (Hyman 2007). As I pointed out above via the quote from Sapir (1925), phonology has always been explicitly crosslinguistic. Thus, both phonological theory and phonological typology are concerned with how languages encode the same phonetic substance into structured sound systems:

Phonological typology is a classification of linguistic systems based on phonological properties. There are four basic kinds of typology: 'areal' or 'genetic' typologies; typologies based on 'surface phonological properties'; typologies based on some 'underlying phonological property'; and 'parametric' typologies [...] In addition, phonological typology can refer to the classification of the elements that make up a phonological system. For example, articulatory descriptors like 'velar' and 'labial' form part of a typology of speech sounds. (Hammond 2006: 523)

The inseparability of phonology and typology continues unbroken right up to current optimality theory:

One of the most compelling features of OT, in my view, is the way that it unites description of individual languages with explanation of language typology. As a phonologist, I have always been impressed and sometimes overwhelmed by how the complexity and idiosyncrasy of each language's phonology is juxtaposed with the clarity and abundance of solid typological generalizations. Even though this is arguably the central research problem of phonology and of linguistic theory in general, progress in consolidating description and explanation has at best been halting and occasionally retrograde. (McCarthy 2002: 1)

The fundamental assumption of OT that constraint ranking varies from language to language has provided fertile ground for typological research in phonology. (Gordon 2007: 750)

Concerning the relation to phonetics, phonological analysis has always been concerned with levels of representation, specifically with establishing the nature of underlying representations and how these are brought to the surface (by rules, input/output conditions, etc.). While some take a single-level inventory approach to phonological typology, a meaningful PHONOLOGICAL typology must also be concerned with input-output relations and the notion of structural contrast. Typologies such as those found in Trubetzkoy (1939) or Hockett (1955) could not otherwise be possible.

> There is no clear division between phonological typology and phonological theory. Given their shared concern with the nature of phonological systems, one can't do insightful typology without addressing the same analytical issues that confront phonological theory. Throughout the history of phonology, the two have been inseparable both in principle and in practice. (Hyman 2007: 265)

In (1) above I provided a typology of the underlying representations nasality can have in different phonological systems. Similarly, (2) shows how different languages underlyingly systematize or "structure" Front and Round "color" contrasts:

(2) a. on vowels and consonants /i, e, u, o, a/, /k, kʸ, kʷ/ etc.
    b. on vowels only /i, e, u, o, a/, /k/ etc.
    c. on consonants only /ɨ, ə, a/, /k, kʸ, kʷ/ etc.
    d. on some vowels only /i, e, u, o, a, ɨ, A/
    e. on whole morphemes /.../ʸ, /.../ʷ

The systems in (2a, b) have triangular vowel systems with underlying front unrounded and back rounded vowels, while (2c) represents a vertical central vowel system with front and round features restricted to consonants (to which the centralized vowels typically assimilate). (2d) represents a vowel harmony system where some vowels are specified, others unspecified for Front and Round. Finally, as in the case of nasality, Front and Round can be prosodies on whole morphemes or words. Recall from (1) that some languages lack nasality entirely. The situation is different concerning Front and Round: while two languages (Qawasar and Yessan-Mayo) out of the 451 languages in the UPSID database (Maddieson & Precoda 1990; Maddieson 1991) lack a front vowel, both have the palatal glide /y/. Of the four languages (Jaqaru, Alawa, Nunggubuyu, and Nimboran) which lack a round vowel, only Nimboran also lacks the labiovelar glide /w/ and hence does not exploit the feature Round at all. (It is likely that a language will turn up that in parallel fashion does not exploit the feature Front.) No language has thus far been cited which fails to phonologize both Front and Round.

This does not necessarily mean that there will be a total lack of nasality, palatality, or rounding in phonetic outputs. Examples such as (1) and (2) illustrate that phonological typology cannot be about surface outputs alone (for which we might distinguish PHONETIC typology). One has to make a choice of level, which is particularly problematic in the case of tone systems. For example, Ik (Heine 1993) and Kom (Hyman 2005) both have underlying /H, L/ but a third [M] (mid tone) on the surface which they derive by the following rules:

(3) a. Ik   L → M / ___ H
     b. Kom H → M / L ___

Since the trigger H may drop out after conditioning L tone raising in Ik, and similarly, the trigger L can drop out after triggering H tone lowering in Kom, these languages have two underlying-contrastive tone heights /H, L/, but three surface-contrastive tone heights [H, M, L]. Are these 2- or 3-height systems? The only adequate approach is to typologize on the basis of the relation between underlying and surface contrastive elements, i.e., both Ik and Kom have a 2→3 tone-height system.

3 Property-driven phonological typology

In this section I want to present the arguments in favor of basing phonological typology on properties rather than (whole) languages. There are at least four reasons to resist the temptation to taxonomize languages into "types" (Hyman 2012, 2015). First, this gives the impression that the the labels are mutually exclusive. A good example is the stress- vs. tone language distinction, about which van der Hulst (2011: 12) writes: "Hyman [2009] [...] reduc[es] the typology of word prosodic systems to tone languages and stress languages". Although the work in question recognizes two independent properties Tone and Stress-Accent, which produce four situations, as in (4), what van der Hulst really meant to say is that I do not recognize a third prosodic property called "pitch-accent".

(4)

	stress-accent	no stress-accent
tone	Mayá, Usarufa, Fasu, Serbo-Croatian, Swedish-Norwegian, Ayutla Mixtec	Yoruba, Igbo, Kuki-Thaadow, Skou, Tokyo Japanese, Somali, W. Basque
no tone	English, Russian, Turkish, Finnish, Arabic	Bella Coola, French, Tamazight, Seoul Korean, Indonesian

A second reason to avoid labeling language types is that this gives the impression that there is a unique taxonomy. Consider the following hypothetical exchange over whether German should be classified with English vs. French on the basis of its vowel system. To illustrate, consider the hypothetical exchange in (5):

(5) Typologist #1: German should be classified with English as a "tense-lax vowel language", since both contrast /i, u/ vs. /ɪ, ʊ/ (etc.), as opposed to French.
Typologist #2: No! German should be classified with French as a "front-rounded vowel language", since both have /ü, ø/, as opposed to English.
Typologist #3 (e.g. me): No! You're both wrong. A property-driven typology would look like the following table, which allows us to also add Spanish:

	lax high vowels	no lax high vowels
front-rounded vowels	German	French
no front-rounded vowels	English	Spanish

An example of such an unproductive controversy arises in Beckman & Venditti who ask "Is typology needed?" (2010: 641) and argue against typologizing prosodic systems solely by function (e.g., tone vs. stress-accent) because Mandarin tonal L+H is allegedly like English intonational L+H*:

> [That one is a toneme and the other intonational] does not change the fact that these two languages are far more like each other in many other respects than either is to a language such as Japanese. (Beckman & Venditti 2011: 531)

While Beckman & Venditti find the Mandarin and English L+H similarities significant, compare the more usual view of Gussenhoven's (2007: 256) concerning the similar H+L in Japanese and English:

> While phonologically comparable, the pitch accents of Japanese and English have very different morphological statuses. In Japanese, they form part of the underlying phonological specification of morphemes, along with the vowels and consonants. Intonational pitch accents are morphemically independent of the words they come with, and are chiefly used to express the information status of the expression. The fact that the English example [...] seems to have an accentuation similar to the Japanese example [...] IS ENTIRELY ACCIDENTAL. (My emphasis; cf. Hyman 2012)

Related to this is the third argument: assigning a name to a system can give the false impression that something has been accomplished. On numerous occasions I have been approached with the comment, "I think my language may have pitch-accent, not tone". Upon probing such pronouncements further I find that this often means nothing more than the feeling that the tonal contrasts are more sparse in this language than in certain other languages which contrast tone on every syllable.

This brings us to the fourth reason to avoid whole taxonomies: the labels are often unclear. An "X language" can mean at least the following: (i) a language that has X, e.g., a "tone language" has tone, a "click language" has clicks; (ii) a language that lacks X, e.g., an "open syllable language" lacks closed syllables, an "intonation language" lacks tone or stress:

> **intonation language** *n*. A language which is neither a **tone language** nor a **pitch language**; a language in which the universally present intonation constitutes the only linguistic use of pitch. (Trask 1996: 184)

(iii) a language that marks X more than certain other languages, e.g., "tone language" vs. "pitch-accent language", "syllable language" vs. "word language":

> A pitch-accent system is one in which pitch is the primary correlate of prominence and there are significant constraints on the pitch patterns for words [...] (Bybee et al 1998:277)

> A syllable language is one which dominantly refers to the syllable, a word language is one which dominantly refers to the phonological word in its phonological make-up. (Auer 1993: 91)

(iv) a language which combines a specific set of linked properties into a "holistic" typology (see especially Plank 1998):

> there are obvious links between phonology and morphology; for example, it has been argued – most probably correctly – that vowel harmony is a phenomenon of agglutinating languages, or that fusional languages have more morphophonological rules than isolating ones. There may also be links between phonology and syntax, e.g. between head/modifier (operator/operand) serialization and the location of (sentence or word) stress. (Auer 1993: 1–2)

> Vowel harmony is a phonological process relating to the morphological word in syllable-timed languages, whereas vowel reduction is a phonological process relating to the phonological word in stress-timed languages. (Auer 1993: 8; cf. Donegan & Stampe 1983)

Such multi-property typologies invariably run into exceptions, and hence proposals of prototypes. A potentially useful deductive strategy is the canonical approach to typology:

> The canonical approach means that I take definitions to their logical end point, enabling me to build theoretical spaces of possibilities. Unlike classical typology, only then does one ask how this space is populated with real instances. The canonical instances, that is, THE BEST, CLEAREST, INDISPUTABLE (the ones closely matching the canon) are unlikely to be frequent [...] Nevertheless, the convergence of criteria fixes a canonical point from which

the phenomena actually found can be calibrated, following which there can be illuminating investigation of frequency distributions. (Corbett 2007: 9; my emphasis – LMH]

In prosody, canonical systems combine properties to meet a basic function (Hyman 2012). In Prague School terms, the definitional function of stress-accent is SYNTAGMATIC: it should unambiguously identify and mark off major category words within utterances. To best do this, canonical stress-accent therefore should be:

(6) a. obligatory: all words have a primary stress
 b. culminative: no word should have more than one primary stress
 c. predictable: stress should be predictable by rule ("fixed")
 d. autonomous: stress should be predictable without grammatical information
 e. demarcative: stress should be calculated from the word edge
 f. edge-adjacent: stress should be edge-adjacent (initial, final)
 g. non-moraic: stress should be weight-insensitive
 h. privative: there should be no secondary stresses
 i. audible: there should be phonetic cues of the primary stress

In other words, stress should be "biunique": One should be able to predict the stress from the word boundaries and the word boundaries from the stress. Stress is thus highly syntagmatic.

This contrasts with the definitional function of tone which, like segmental features, is to distinguish morphemes. Thus, for a two-height [H, L] system to best realize this function to distinguish the most morphemes, the properties of the canonical system should include:

(7) a. bivalence: both H and L are phonologically activated
 b. omniprosodicity: every tone-bearing unit (TBU) has a H or L
 c. unrestrictedness: all combinations of H and L occur on successive TBUs
 d. faithfulness: every /H/ or /L/ is realized on its underlying morpheme and TBU
 e. lexical: /H/ and /L/ should contrast on lexical morphemes (since there many more of them than grammatical morphemes)
 f. contours: HL and LH contours should be possible on a single TBU
 g. floating tones: H and L tonal morphemes and lexical floating tones should be possible

In contrast with the above, there is no canonical function for so-called "pitch-accent" systems. Each of the following possibilities either fails to provide a distinct function from that of stress-accent or represents an arbitrary criterion:

(8) a. a language which has an obligatory (but not necesarily culminative) H tone per word?
 b. a language which has a culminative (but not necessarily obligatory) H tone? (Hualde, 2006)
 c. a language which has either a culminative OR an obligatory H tone? (van der Hulst 2011)
 d. a language which has privative H tones (/H/ vs. Ø)? (Clark 1988)
 e. a language which limits tonal contrasts to the stressed syllable?
 f. a language which restricts its tones in whatever way?
 g. a language which has only two tone heights (H, L)?

[...] if we push the use of accents to its limits (at the expense of using tones), this implies allowing unaccented words (violating obligatoriness) and multiple accents (violating culminativity). In this liberal view on acccent, only languages that have more than a binary pitch contrast are *necessarily* tonal [...] (van der Hulst 2011: 13)

If systems can be as "liberally" typologized as van der Hulst entertains, as just quoted, then something is clearly wrong. I suggest it is the misguided notion that the goal of phonological typology is to taxonomize languages into pre-determined named "types". If we instead focus on the properties, rather than classifying languages or their subsystems, we will better be able to appreciate the richness of the variation found in the world's languages.

4 Where do phonology and typology part company?

So why should we distinguish phonological typology from phonology proper? After all, phonology has always been typological, developing its models on the basis of extensive crosslinguistic data (Chomsky & Halle 1968 cite over 100 languages, for instance). However, there are aspects of typology in which most phonologists have expressed little interest, e.g., mapping out phonological properties by geography, language family, or historical contact. (Some have little interest in linguistic reconstruction and language history as well.) Diverging from the traditional view of typology that I have been discussing is the distributional typology perspective "What's where why?":

> In the past century, typology was mostly used as an alternative method of pursuing one of the same goals as generative grammar: to determine the limits of possible human languages and, thereby, to contribute to a universal theory of grammar [...] that would rule out as linguistically impossible what would seem logically imaginable, e.g., a language with a gender distinction exclusively in the 1st person singular. Over the past decade, typology has begun to emancipate itself from this goal and to turn from a method into a full-fledged discipline, with its own research agenda, its own theories, its own problems. What has reached centerstage is a fresh appreciation of linguistic diversity in its own right, and the new goal of typology is the development of theories that explain why linguistic diversity is the way it is – a goal first made explicit by Nichols's (1992) call for a science of population typology, parallel to population biology. Instead of asking "what's possible?", more and more typologists ask "what's where why?". (Bickel 2007: 239)

To the theoretical phonologist it matters little that retroflex or ejective consonants cluster geographically in certain areas or occur only in certain language families. Instead, phonologists, like other formal linguists, have mostly been interested in the question of what is a possible phonology:

> Most theoretical linguists, from whatever camp, consider that it is a central goal of theoretical work on grammar to distinguish possible grammatical processes from impossible ones and – for the former – to explain why some possible processes seem more common [probable] than others. (Newmeyer 2005: 27)

Concerning this growing conception of typology, my impression is that traditional phonology has been less concerned with the "where" than the "how" (as in "how should we analyze this system?"). In this connection, what is the difference between a phonological typologist and a formal phonologist who works on languages? Is it a matter of goals ("research agenda"), emphasis, or initial assumptions? The following characterizations of Croft's (2007: 87) are reminiscent of the distinction I made between substance vs. form as the starting point in comparing phonological systems:

> [...] the structuralist and generative method assumes the same formal theoretical entities to exist across languages, and then looks for constructions with distribution patterns that appear to distinguish those formal theoretical entities in the language.
>
> Typological analysis proceeds very differently. A typologist uses a functional definition of a situation type, such as the Keenan-Comrie functional definition of relative clauses, and compares the different grammatical constructions used for that function across languages, and seeks relationships among the constructions (or grammatical properties of the constructions).

While such a distinction may be recognizable to many linguists, particularly non-phonologists, structural and generative phonologists who have done crosslinguistic studies and surveys differ in the degree to which they are concerned about geographic and genetic distributions. Thus, comparing the various crosslinguistic studies of stress-accent, compare the different weighting given to the "what" vs. "where" in Hyman (1977) and van der Hulst et al. (2010) vs. Halle & Vergnaud (1987) and Hayes (1995). These studies may even differ in how they answer the "why". (For an explicitly distributional typology of phonological properties conducted by two structuralist-generative phonologists, see Clements & Rialland 2008.)

This brings us to the role of historical explanation and the question of how to reconcile universals vs. diversity in phonological systems, which Kiparsky (2008: 52) addresses as follows:

> An increasingly popular research program seeks the causes of typological generalizations in recurrent historical processes, or even claims that all principled explanations for universals reside in diachrony. Structural and generative grammar has more commonly pursued the reverse direction of explanation, which grounds the way language changes in its structural properties. The two programs can coexist without contradiction or circularity as long as we can make a principled separation between true universals, which constrain both synchronic grammars and language change, and typological generalizations, which are simply the results of typical paths of change.

I think this sums up the non-contradiction in the fact that most phonologists both seek to determine what is universal AND at the same time appreciate the diversity that we find in the sound systems of the world's languages. In a rare article reflecting on the nature of phonological typology, Dressler (1979) applies Seiler's (1979) inductive vs. deductive typology to phonology:

> Work in the typology of process phonology is usually inductive. [...] The usual method of research is the sampling of similar phonological processes in different languages, the enumeration of frequent, general or exceptionless properties, of their clustering, of probable hierarchies and implications, and attempts at explanation by reference to phonetic data [...] Much less frequent are deductive process phonological typologies, although they are of primary importance, if typology should be based on language universals research [...]. (Dressler 1979: 261)

He goes on to point out the following apparently contradictory observations concerning phonological typology:

> Deductive research is easier in phonology than in grammar, since we simply know more about the phonologies of the languages of the world than about their grammars; on the other hand less deductive typology has been done in phonology than in grammar. (Dressler 1979: 262)

Of course this all depends on what one counts as "phonological typology". The original title of our workshop was "What is phonological typology – and why does it matter?" As a brief answer: We need to do phonological typology for the same reason we do general phonology, namely in order to understand why phonologies are the way they are. However, in the ever expanding, diverse field of phonology, we have the opportunity to incorporate the "What, where, why?" in a way that is harder in other subfields of linguistics. Phonologists can and should be involved in (i) looking at phenomena both in breadth (quantitatively) and in depth (qualitatively), (ii) identifying the geographical and genetic distributions of the phenomena, and (iii) considering a wide range of potential explanatory sources in addressing the "why?" It is only in so doing that we will attain a complete picture of what phonology can vs. cannot do and why.

References

Aissen, Judith. 2003. Differential object marking: Iconicity vs. economy. *Natural Language & Linguistic Theory* 21. 435–483.

Auer, Peter. 1993. Is a rhythm-based typology possible? A study of the role of prosody in phonological typology. *KontRI Working Paper* No. 21. University of Konstanz.

Beckman, Mary E. & Jennifer J. Venditti. 2010. Tone and intonation. In William J. Hardcastle & John Laver (eds.), *The handbook of phonetic sciences*, 603–652. Oxford: Blackwell.

Beckman, Mary E. & Jennifer J. Venditti. 2011. Intonation. In John Goldsmith, Jason Riggle, & Alan C. L. Yu (eds.), *The handbook of phonological theory*, 485–532. Oxford: Blackwell.

Bickel, Balthasar. 2003. Referential density in discourse and syntactic typology. *Language* 79. 708–736.

Bickel, Balthasar. 2007. Typology in the 21st century: Major current developments. *Linguistic Typology* 11. 239–251.

Bossong, Georg. 1998. Le marquage différential de l'objet dans les langues d'Europe. In Jack Feuillet (ed.), *Actance et valence dans les langues de l'Europe*, 193–258. Berlin: Mouton de Gruyter.

Buckley, Eugene. 2000. On the naturalness of unnatural rules. Proceedings from the Second Workshop on American Indigenous Languages. *UCSB Working Papers in Linguistics* 9. 1–14.

Bybee, Joan L., Paromita Chakraborti, Dagmar Jung, & Joanne Scheibman. 1998. Prosody and segmental effect: Some paths of evolution for word stress. *Studies in Language* 22. 267–314.

Chomsky, Noam & Morris Halle. 1968. *The sound pattern of English*. New York: Harper & Row.

Clark, Mary. 1988. An accentual analysis of Zulu. In van der Hulst & Smith (eds.), 51–79.

Clements, G. N. & Sylvester Osu. 2003. Ikwere nasal harmony in typological perspective. In Patrick Sauzet & Anne Zribi-Hertz (eds.), *Typologie des langues d'Afrique et universaux de la grammaire*, vol. 2, 70–95. Paris: L'Harmattan.

Clements, G. N. & Annie Rialland. 2008. Africa as a phonological area. In Bernd Heine & Derek Nurse (eds.), *A linguistic geography of Africa*, 36–85. Cambridge: Cambridge University Press.

Cohn, Abigail. 1993. A survey of the phonology of the feature [+nasal]. *Working Papers of the Cornell Phonetics Laboratory* 8. 141–203.

Corbett, Greville G. 2007. Canonical typology, suppletion, and possible words. *Language* 83. 8–42.
Croft, William. 2003. *Typology and universals*. Second edition. Cambridge: Cambridge University Press.
Croft, William. 2007. Typology and linguistic theory in the past decade: A personal view. *Linguistic Typology* 11. 79–91.
Dixon, R. M. W. 1994. *Ergativity*. Cambridge: Cambridge University Press.
Dixon, R. M. W. & Alexandra Y. Aikhenvald (eds.). 2000. *Changing valency: Case studies in transitivity*. Cambridge: Cambridge University Press.
Donohue, Mark. 1997. Tone in New Guinea languages. *Linguistic Typology* 1. 347–386.
Donegan, Patricia & David Stampe. 1983. Rhythm and the holistic organization of language structure. In F. Richardson (ed.), *CLS 19, Parasession on the interplay of phonology, morphology & syntax*, 337–353. Chicago: Chicago Linguistic Society.
Dressler, Wolfgang U. 1979. Reflections on phonological typology. *Acta Linguistica Academiae Scientiarum Hungaricae* 29. 259–273.
Dryer, Matthew. 1986. Primary objects, secondary objects, and antidative. *Language* 62. 808–845.
Evans, Nicholas & Stephen C. Levinson. 2010. Time for a sea-change in linguistics: Reponses to comments on "The myth of language universals". *Lingua* 120. 2733–2758.
Gordon, Matthew. 2007. Typology in optimality theory. *Language and Linguistics Compass* 1(6). 750–769.
Gordon, Matthew K. 2016. *Phonological typology*. Oxford University Press.
Gouskova, Maria. 2013. Review of Marc van Oostendorp, Colin J. Ewen, Elizabeth Hume, & Keren Rice (eds.). 2011. *The Blackwell companion to phonology* (Malden: Mass.: Wiley-Blackwell). *Phonology* 30. 173–179.
Greenberg, Joseph H. 1948. The tonal system of Proto-Bantu. *Word* 4. 196–208.
Greenberg, Joseph H. 1958. The labial consonants of Proto-Afro-Asiatic. *Word* 14. 295–302.
Greenberg, Joseph H. 1962. Is the vowel-consonant dichotomy universal? *Word* 18. 73–81.
Greenberg, Joseph H. 1963. Vowel harmony in African languages. *Actes du Second Colloque Internationale de Linguistique Negro-Africaine*, 33–38. Dakar: Université de Dakar, West African Languages Survey.
Greenberg, Joseph H. 1966. Synchronic and diachronic universals in phonology. *Language* 42. 508–517.
Greenberg, Joseph H. 1970. Some generalizations concerning glottalic consonants, especially implosives. *International Journal of American Linguistics* 36. 123–145.
Greenberg, Joseph H. 1974. *Language typology: A historical and analytic overview*. The Hague: Mouton.
Greenberg, Joseph H. 1978. Some generalizations concerning initial and final consonant clusters. *Linguistics* 18. 5–34.
Greenberg, Joseph H., James J. Jenkins, & Donald J. Foss. 1967. Phonological distinctive features as cues in learning. *Journal of Experimental Psychology* 77. 200–205.
Greenberg, Joseph H. & Dorothea Kaschube. 1976. Word prosodic systems: A preliminary report. *Working Papers in Language Universals* 20. 1–18.
Gussenhoven, Carlos. 2007. The phonology of intonation. In Paul de Lacy (ed.), *The Cambridge handbook of phonology*, 253–280. Cambridge: Cambridge University Press.
Hagège, Claude. 1992. Morphological typology. In *Oxford international encyclopedia of linguistics*, vol. 3, 7–8. Oxford: Oxford University Press.
Halle, Morris & Jean-Roger Vergnaud. 1987. *An essay on stress*. Cambridge, MA: MIT Press.

Haspelmath, Martin. 2006. Against markedness (and what to replace it with). *Journal of Linguistics* 42. 25–70.
Hammond, Michael 2006. Phonological typology. *Encyclopedia of Language & Linguistics*. Online. http://www.sciencedirect.com/science/article/pii/B0080448542000468
Hayes, Bruce. 1995. *Metrical stress theory: Principles and case studies*. Chicago: University of Chicago Press.
Heine, Bernd. 1993. *Ik dictionary*. Köln: Rüdiger Köppe Verlag.
Hockett, Charles F. 1955. *A manual of phonology*. Memoir 11, *International Journal of American Linguistics*.
Hualde, José Ignacio. 2006. Remarks on word-prosodic typology. *Proceedings of the 32nd Annual Meeting of the Berkeley Linguistics Society*, 157–174.
Hulst, Harry van der. 2011. Pitch accent systems. In van Oostendorp, Ewen, Hume, & Rice (eds.), vol. 2, #45.
Hulst, Harry van der, Rob Goedemans, & Ellen van Zanten (eds) 2010. *A survey of word accentual patterns in the languages of the world*. Berlin: De Gruyter Mouton.
Hyman, Larry M. 1977. On the nature of linguistic stress. In Larry M. Hyman (ed.), *Studies in stress and accent*, 37–82. *Southern California Occasional Papers in Linguistics* 4. Department of Linguistics, University of Southern California.
Hyman, Larry M. 2005. Initial vowel and prefix tone in Kom: Related to the Bantu Augment? In Koen Bostoen & Jacky Maniacky (eds.), *Studies in African comparative linguistics*, 313–341. Köln: Rüdiger Köppe Verlag.
Hyman, Larry M. 2007. Where's phonology in typology? *Linguistic Typology* 11. 265–271.
Hyman, Larry M. 2009. How (not) to do phonological typology: The case of pitch-accent. *Language Sciences* 31. 213–238.
Hyman, Larry M. 2011. Tone: Is it different? In John Goldsmith, Jason Riggle, & Alan Yu (eds.), *The handbook of phonological theory*, 2nd edition, 197–239. Oxford: Blackwell.
Hyman, Larry M. 2012. In defense of prosodic typology: A response to Beckman & Venditti. *Linguistic Typology* 16. 341–385.
Hyman, Larry M. 2015. Towards a canonical typology of prosodic systems. In Esther Herrera Zendejas (ed.), *Tono, acento y estructuras métricas en lenguas mexicanas*, 13–38. México: El Colegio de México.
Kenstowicz, Michael & Charles Kisseberth. 1977. *Topics in phonological theory*. New York: Academic Press.
Kiparsky, Paul. 1968. Linguistic universals and linguistic change. In Emmon Bach & Robert T. Harms (eds.), *Universals in linguistic theory*, 171–202. New York: Holt, Rinehart & Winston.
Kiparsky, Paul. 2008. Universals constrain change; change results in typological generalizations. In Jeff Good (ed.), *Linguistic universals and language change*, 23–53. Oxford: Oxford University Press.
Maddieson, Ian. 1991. Testing the universality of phonological generalizations with a phonetically specified segment database: Results and limitations. *Phonetica* 48. 193–206.
Maddieson, Ian & Kristin Precoda. 1990. Updating UPSID. *UCLA Working Papers in Phonetics* 74. 104–111.
McCarthy, John J. 2002. *A thematic guide to optimality theory*. Cambridge: Cambridge University Press.
Newmeyer, Frederick J. 2005. *Possible and probable languages: A generative perspective on linguistic typology*. Oxford: Oxford University Press.

Nichols, Johanna. 1986. Head-marking and dependent-marking grammar. *Language* 66. 56–119.

Nichols, Johanna. 1992. *Language diversity in space and time*. Chicago: University of Chicago Press.

Nichols, Johanna. 2007. What, if anything, is typology? *Linguistic Typology* 11. 231–238.

Oostendorp, Marc van, Colin J. Ewen, Elizabeth Hume, & Keren Rice (eds.). 2011. *The Blackwell companion to phonology*. Malden, MA: Wiley-Blackwell.

Plank, Frans. 1998. The co-variation of phonology with morphology and syntax: A hopeful history. *Linguistic Typology* 2. 195–230.

Plank, Frans. 2001. Typology by the end of the 18th century. In Sylvain Auroux et al. (eds.), *History of the Language Sciences: An International Handbook on the Evolution of the Study of Language from the Beginnings to the Present*, vol. 2, 1399–1414. Berlin: Walter de Gruyter.

Prince, Alan & Paul Smolensky. 1993/2004. *Optimality theory: Constraint interaction in generative grammar*. Malden, MA: Blackwell.

Samuels, Bridget D. 2011. *Phonological architecture: A biolinguistic perspective*. Oxford: Oxford University Press.

Sapir, Edward. 1925. Sound patterns in language. *Language* 1. 37–51.

Seiler, Hansjakob. 1979. Language universals research, questions, objectives, and prospects. *Acta Linguistica Academiae Scientiarum Hungaricae* 29. 353–367.

Slobin, Dan I. 2004. The many ways to search for a frog: Linguistic typology and the expression of motion events. In Sven Strömqvist & Ludo Verhoeven (eds.), *Relating events in narrative*, volume 2: *Typological and contextual perspectives*, 219–257. Mahwah, N.J.: Erlbaum.

Talmy, Leonard. 1985. Lexicalization patterns: Semantic structure in lexical forms. In Timothy Shopen (ed.), *Language typology and linguistic description*, volume 3: *Grammatical categories and the lexicon*, 57–149. Cambridge: Cambridge University Press.

Trask, R. L. 1996. *A dictionary of phonetics and phonology*. London: Routledge.

Trubetzkoy, Nikolai (1969 [1939]). *Principles of phonology*. Translated by Christiane A. M. Baltaxe. Berkeley and Los Angeles: University of California Press.

Vajda, Edward. 2001. Test materials dated August 17, 2001. http://pandora.cii.wwu.edu/vajda/ling201/test2materials/Phonology3.htm.

Whaley, Lindsay J. 1997. *Introduction to typology*. Thousand Oaks, California: Sage Publications.

Frans Plank
An implicational universal to defy: typology ⊃ ¬ phonology ≡ phonology ⊃ ¬ typology ≡ ¬ (typology ∧ phonology) ≡ ¬ typology ∨ ¬ phonology

Abstract: The purpose of this chapter is twofold: first, to assess how typology has been dealing with phonology, from early days to the present; second, focusing on phonology, to ask about asymmetries between phonology and syntax-inflection in general and about typological concerns in phonology itself. Looked at from both angles, the phonology–typology relationship is seen to be special, and the impression is confirmed that, in comparison especially with syntax, phonological typology as well as typological phonology are behindhand in the quest for system in linguistic diversity. Explanations are suggested in terms of the substance of subject matters and of the attitudes to description and theory in different subcommunities in linguistics.

1 Introduction

The purpose of this chapter is twofold: first, to assess how typology, unceremoniously introduced in §2, has been dealing with phonology (§3), from early days (§3.1) to the present (§3.2); second, focusing on phonology (§4), to ask about an imbalance of phonology and syntax-inflection in general (§4.1) and about typological concerns in phonology itself (§4.2). Looked at from both angles, the phonology–typology relationship is seen to be special, and the impression is confirmed that, in comparison especially with syntax, phonological typology as well as typological phonology are behindhand in the quest for system in linguistic diversity. (Though not all is well about the syntax–typology relationship, either.) Explanations are suggested in terms of the substance of subject matters and of the attitudes to description and theory in different subcommunities in linguistics.

2 The typological programme and where it is in arrears

In linguistics, typology is a research programme, not a subfield or a theory, and its remit is (i) to chart linguistic diversity, (ii) to discover order or indeed unity in diversity, and (iii) to make sense of what has been charted and discovered. Regrettably but perhaps understandably, given how this enterprise has usually been named after Gabelentz (1894, 1901) and given the meanings of this term in other fields, typology has sometimes been taken to be about the classification of the discipline's cherished cardinal individuals, namely languages, into types; but for linguistic typology "type" in this sense of "class" is really a secondary and indeed expendable concept. First and foremost typology's objective is to identify elementary variables where languages (or, to avoid this moot concept, mental lexicons and grammars) can differ, and then to examine whether these variables vary independently or vary together: when variables are found to co-vary, this means crosslinguistic variation is in this respect limited. It is not to be seriously expected that literally TOUT *se tient*, other than in a Saussurian logical sense of all sign values in a sign system being interdependent.

Since lexicons and grammars are as diverse and uniform as they have become over time – during the lifespan of individual speakers; across generations of language acquirers; through contacts between speech communities; in the evolution of our species – typology's closest association is with developmental linguistics. To the extent that linguistic diversity is limited and orderly rather than being without limit and random, and to the extent that any order that we are able to discover is not the result of non-linguistic contingencies of the histories of populations (itself a fascinating research field), patterns of diversity could be shaped (i) by timeless typological laws constraining states of mental lexicons and grammars and/or (ii) by laws of historical change and stability, constraining transitions between states. The evidence points to both being effective, although constraints are not always easily recognised as clearly being of one kind or the other.

By its very nature the typological research programme is all-inclusive: elementary variables from ALL structural domains should be examined for co-variation. It is an empirical issue, not one to be resolved a priori, whether some domains are in fact less tightly interconnected than others, showing independent variation rather than co-variation.

This is the lofty idea. Here we are asking about an imbalance in workaday practice: Within typology, on its own or in association with developmental linguistics, is phonology different? Contextualising the other way round: Within phonology, synchronic and diachronic, is typology different? And these are not quite the same question, notwithstanding the logical equivalence of the first two implications of the title when flipping antecedent and consequent in contraposition under negation. Is there too little phonological typology and/or too little typological phonology? Should, and could, there be more of either or both?

When diagnosing typology as phonologically deficient or healthy, or phonology as typologically challenged or up to the mark, what is phonology being compared with? Obviously the other structural domains into which grammar is compartmentalised: syntax and morphology, the latter with its subdomains of inflection and word formation. There is semantics/pragmatics, too, with the construction of complex meaning as the job of morphology and syntax. And there is the lexicon, storing the basic building blocks for all constructing, the material for grammar to work with (plus everything else that is non-compositional and therefore not taken care of by the grammar). Word formation as the lexical part of morphology, semantics/pragmatics, and the lexicon hardly compare any less unfavourably than phonology in their typological involvement. It is really only in explicit or tacit comparison with syntax and with the syntactic part of morphology, inflection, that phonology can possibly have grounds for complaint. To assess the situation correctly, phonology, as the grammar of sound, should perhaps be kept apart from phonetics; but then, typological contexts seem especially conducive to a blurring of this distinction, thereby strengthening the typological presence of the amalgamated domains.[1]

Now, ask around among experts – as I have informally done for years, working with an editorial board of a typological journal and helping with the programming of many a typological event, but sometimes also mingling with phonologists with or without typological sympathies – and they will very likely agree, especially when active in both phonology and typology, that, yes, the relationship between typology and phonology is special, namely less intimate or at any rate different, in comparison with syntax and inflection. Is this a misperception?[2]

3 The evidence

3.1 Early typology

In the past, as the typological programme was gaining momentum, inflection and syntax were distinctly in the limelight. Phonology was on the stage, too, but was more of a sideshow. Historically speaking, anybody complaining about an imbalance would have a point, then. Here is a bird's-eye view of the record.[3]

---

[1] As a test, consult the *World atlas of language structure (WALS,* http://wals.info/) and decide for yourself whether the variables labeled "Phonology" are phonological or phonetic, as you would draw the line.
[2] Syntax-and-inflection typologists will sometimes, upon reflection, express surprise that they had not noticed before how little phonology there was to be met with in their own circles. Perceptions similar to mine have been reported in Hyman (2007), and also in this volume.
[3] This whole subsection 3.1 draws on earlier historiographic writings of mine, in particular Plank (1991, 1992, 1993, 1998, 2001), where the reporting and referencing are more conscientious.

3.1.1 The pioneer years

The first typologist in my history was Tommaso Campanella (1568–1639). A Dominican monk, philosopher, astrologer, and utopian social theorist, he was the first to methodically do, among all his other activities, what today's typologists are doing, too – namely to take stock of linguistic diversity and to determine whether it is limited insofar as the values of certain grammatical variables, although logically independent of one another, co-vary rather than varying independently. Campanella's results, for the variables that he studied, were positive (or else they would presumably have gone unreported). His attention was attracted by parts of speech and "accidence", central to linguistic theory and descriptive grammars of the day. Universal or Philosophical Grammar took for granted that parts-of-speech grammar was in essence universally uniform; this was one of the dogmas Campanella doubted, and his doubt was not global and vague. He had evidence, coming from languages hitherto inaccessible (such as Vietnamese, as described by missionaries of his acquaintance) or neglected (such as the Romance vernaculars), that there was diversity where contemporary linguistic theory decreed uniformity; but in light of this evidence he could also identify specific constraints on diversity. Campanella discovered that nouns were not words which universally inflected for case and number, nor were verbs words which universally inflected for some such categories as tense and person-number. His crosslinguistic evidence suggested to him that although such inflection was an option, though not a necessity for either nouns or verbs, variation was yet not random. He was aware of languages where verbs inflected, but nouns did not (at any rate not for case: witness the Romance vernaculars), but not of languages where nouns inflected (for case), but verbs did not inflect. Thus, for all he knew, inflectional systems could not differ in all conceivable ways, given the elementary variables of word classes and inflectional categories: it looked like noun inflection implied verb inflection, but not vice versa. Further, turning from a connection between parts of speech to one between inflectional categories, nouns did not universally have to inflect for both case and number. They could (as in the Classical languages or also in Turkish); but they could also inflect only for number (as in the Romance vernaculars) or for neither (as in Vietnamese); but

---

My history is intended as an "inside narrative" (to borrow a term of Herman Melville's), and thereby differs from historians' histories of typology, which standardly begin with nineteenth century German Romanticism, a period that in my view produced little of substance that was novel or profound. Let me just emphasise that the typological speculations and insights referred to here were not private musings or only shared in private correspondence (subsequently buried in archives, if surviving at all), but saw contemporary publication.

there was no language in Campanella's smallish, yet diagnostically instructive sample where nouns only inflected for case. Hence, by inductive generalisation, diversity was limited here too, insofar as case inflection implied number inflection, but not vice versa.

There was no continuity of typological research into inflection after Campanella – which is not surprising because it would take a while before you could be a morphologist or indeed linguist by profession. Nonetheless, a wide range of individual inflectional categories as well as properties of inflectional systems were frequently on the agenda when diversity and its possible limits were examined, in whatever wider intellectual context. By the end of the nineteenth century the typological distinction between agglutination and flexion/fusion was well entrenched: a rich network of implications was assumed, on deductive as well as inductive grounds, to be connecting individual inflectional categories within and across word classes with regard to variables such as separation vs. cumulation of categories, invariance vs. variance of exponents, looseness vs. tightness of bonding between stems and morphological markers, distinction vs. non-distinction (syncretism) of term oppositions.

Words had always been principal units for linguistic theory and descriptive grammar, and the structure of constructions most obviously consisted in how words were ordered one after another. One did not have to be a serious polyglot to be able to observe that they were ordered differently in different languages, or also at different historical stages of one and the same language. Familiarity with the right kind of languages would soon suggest that there was indeed system to such differences. A traveller and diplomat with profound Oriental expertise, François (de) Mesgnien (or, Polish-style, Meninski, ca. 1620–98), apart from noting diversity in many grammatical particulars where current linguistic theory had decreed universal uniformity, discovered that different syntactic constructions did not have their constituent parts ordered randomly: across all kinds of constructions where one member was a head and the other a dependent (verb–object, noun–genitive, noun–attributive adjective, adposition–noun phrase, etc.), dependents would uniformly either precede or follow their heads. There were as many variables as their were kinds of head–dependent constructions; instead of varying independently, these variables all tended to co-vary.

Word order would remain at centre stage in the eighteenth century, although with a focus now on its relationship to inflection and periphrasis: rich inflection, notably for case and agreement, was hypothesised to license inversions, while impoverished inflection was hypothesised to necessitate rigid syntactic ordering, especially of dependents (or determiners) after their heads. This was how Abbé Gabriel Girard (ca. 1677–1748) and, a rare grammarian by profession,[4] Nicolas Beauzée (1717–89) had been elaborating the old Scholastic theory of a universal *ordo naturalis* of ideas and words expressing them. Publicised through the *Encyclopédie française*, such typological schemes (like also those involving inflectional systems, circulated by the *Encyclopedia Britannica*) were gaining currency, while Mesgnien's more discerning discovery that rigid word order itself permitted of orderly variation – head before dependent throughout, as per *ordo naturalis*, but also dependent before head throughout – was temporarily falling into oblivion.

Beginning with occasional early sightings in Greenlandic, Basque, and elsewhere of a special case (eventually called "ergative") which marked only transitive subjects, as opposed to intransitive subjects, which would receive the same case as direct objects of transitive verbs, the universal uniformity of such central syntactic concepts as subject and object came into question. But relational alignment would acquire typological significance only slowly, when it was realised that the potential for diversity was indeed vast here, because there were numerous patterns of relational identification across transitive and intransitive clauses, and alignments could in principle differ from verb to verb, from nominal to nominal, from tense/aspect to tense/aspect, and between different rules making reference to syntactic relations (e.g., case marking, verb agreement, constituent ordering, clause combining). At any rate, when Georg von der Gabelentz (1840–93), a professor of Oriental languages and general linguistics but originally trained in law and administration, set out a methodology for getting ahead with the typological programme (posthumously published in 1894), he used alignment and word order for illustration. His two variables were ergative vs. accusative alignment of case marking and the ordering (uniform or divergent) of genitives and adjectives relative to their heads. Of the four possible combinations of values, he found one underrepresented: ergative alignment and uniform ordering of genitives and adjectives; and for one he could presently cite no single attestation: accusative alignment and divergent ordering of genitives and adjectives. (In future, committees of experts, drawing up comprehensive checklists of variables and calculating the statistics

---

4 Beauzée was employed by the École Royale Militaire in Paris, where they still maintain a *centre linguistique* (http://www.rma.ac.be/clng/fr/index.html). Although, unlike his latter-day successors, Beauzée was a *grammairien* rather than a *grammatiste* (language teacher), his job was not to train future linguists of the kind he himself was one. Probably August Friedrich Pott (1802–87) – better known as a historical-comparative Indo-Europeanist despite his numerous Humboldt-inspired contributions to typology – was the first to have been trained as a general linguist (at least insofar as his doctoral dissertation at Göttingen was about general linguistics, dealing with the semantics of prepositions across languages), and whose academic responsibilities at the university of Halle an der Saale then included the training of future general linguists (Plank 1995).

of co-variation, would have to confirm such gaps and strikingly unequal value distributions.) The "conjunctures" to be inductively inferred thus were these: if a language has ergative-absolutive alignment for case marking, it will, with more than chance probability, also have divergent genitive and adjective ordering; if a language has divergent genitive and adjective ordering, it will, with considerably higher probability (if not certainty), also have ergative-absolutive alignment.

Gabelentz was optimistic that it would eventually be established, rather than continue to be merely decreed, that *tout se tient* – including even *das Lautwesen* (*Die Sprachwissenschaft*, posthumous 2nd edition of 1901: 481). But he did not live to flesh out how phonology was supposed to be internally and externally interconnected and to duly downscale his grandiose hope, for surely, unless you were thinking of Saussure's "values" of signs within a system, not EVERYTHING would turn out to cohere with EVERYTHING else.

3.1.2 Sounds different

Actually, languages had long been observed, if often dimly, to differ in their *Lautwesen*, and some such differences had begun to be presumed, if not methodically established, to be systematically interconnected.

Updating Biblical descent stories, languages were distinguished (most influentially by Bishop Isidore of Seville, ca. 560–636) depending on which classes of sounds or "letters" they featured as somehow the most prominent: guttural (the Semitic East), palatal (Greek and other Eastern Mediterranean), or dental (the Romance West). It likewise betrayed some awareness of sound inventories as harmonious and symmetrical systems of contrasts that sounds felt to be indispensable were occasionally deplored to be missing, such as the labial nasal in Iroquois; while, conversely, uncommon kinds of seemingly difficult-to-produce sounds would sometimes be reported from far-away regions, such as clicks from southernmost Africa.

Words were heard, and described, to be stressed partly similarly and partly differently, and sentences to be intoned and rhythmically organised partly similarly and partly differently, in different languages; but not much seems to have been made of this in early typology, when prosodic analysis was still in its infancy and hard enough to practise on even the most familiar languages closest to home. Once the awareness spread that pitch could not only be employed for intonation, but also lexically, "tone languages" would earn themselves a prominent place in galleries of linguistic curios. But these exhibits long remained something like monolithic erratic rocks of enigmatic provenance, obviously instantiating crosslinguistic diversity, but of little apparent significance for seekers of patterns of co-variation.

The length of words as measured in segments or syllables, and how sounds could and could not be combined to articulate them, were variables whose early typological standing was more assured. Although the words of a language would differ as to their length and composition, there seemed to prevail some consistency on both counts within languages, but not across them. Further, there seemed a prospect especially of word length correlating with something else, namely the richness or poverty (i) of sound inventory (including prosody) and (ii) of inflectional morphology. It was at something along these lines that such an early and inscrutable distinction as that between *naturales linguæ* and *grammaticæ linguæ* as championed by Guillaume Postel (1510–81), a Renaissance polymath with firsthand experience of languages of the East, appeared to be driving.

Going beyond inventories and phonotactics, it was noticed in early grammars of languages such as Turkish that certain similarity requirements were imposed upon the vowels of the constituent parts of words. That such vowel harmony conspicuously distinguished such languages from most others where words could ostensibly make free use of the entire inventories of sounds available to them was commented on at least as early as by Mesgnien-Meninski; but it was not suspected to be implicated in constraints on diversity. Elementary variables such as the dimensions for harmony (e.g., front–central–back, rounded–unrounded), its progressive or regressive direction, or vowels allowed to escape it, were not highlighted in early comparisons. Arguably this precluded the recognition that such phonological processes, regardless of the morphological and syntactic environments in which they were embedded, themselves gave ample room for variation – and that the empirical question was whether or not it was actually exploited by different languages.[5]

An early apogee of holistic typology was reached with the developmental scenario of James Burnett (1714–99, who as judge at the High Court of Scotland took the title Lord Monboddo). For him, as for other "conjectural historians" of the Scottish Enlightenment, language development from its first origins consisted in increasing "articulation", and "material" and "formal" articulation were proceeding in tandem: the extent of material articulation, pertaining in particular to (a) the elaboration of sound inventories, (b) the complexity of syllable structures, (c) word length, (d) accentual differentiation (as opposed to not-so-articulated tonal modulation), would therefore correlate with the extent of formal articulation, pertaining in particular to (a) the differentiation of parts of speech, (b) the elaboration of inflectional and derivational systems, (c) analytic syntax (as opposed to polysynthesis, where sentences are not yet articulated into words).

---

5 A "conjuncture" of vowel harmony and agglutinative morphology, where word cohesion is otherwise rather loose, was suspected by Jan Baudouin de Courtenay in the 1870's.

In Burnett's comprehensive scheme little remained of Latin-inspired Universal Grammar: just about all of morphosyntax and phonology/phonetics had become themes with variations. But for him, too, variation was not random but harmonious, and the reasoning was developmental: co-variation was the result of the co-evolution of all individual manifestations of ultimately one single fundamental human capacity, that of separating wholes into parts and imposing ever finer structure on the unstructured. Burnett's immensely influential Scottish contemporary Adam Smith (1723–90) had, in his occasional linguistic writings, preferred the term "analysis" to Burnett's "articulation" – whence the typological triad of analytic, synthetic, and polysynthetic (or "incorporating") languages to emerge soon after, finding equal favour among speculative and comparative grammarians. Burnett ventured further into the articulation of sound matter than others at his time, and he was also uncommonly well informed about contemporary languages, especially of North America, which were taken for representatives of different developmental stages of the human capacity for articulation. His inductive generalising about co-variation/co-evolution was not hastier than was customary; but in his case there were just too many languages, often ill described, and too many variables, material as well as formal, to keep under control.

3.1.3 Where sounds matter

Although the early protagonists of typology, from Campanella to Gabelentz, were doing, within their means, what typologists are still doing today, they were not academically trained professional linguists. Comparative linguistics as an academic discipline emerged over the nineteenth century, and what was being professionally compared then were sounds, words, and inflections among the languages of primarily one family, Indo-European.[6] The remit there was to work out the history of these sounds, words, inflections with the aim of reconstructing ancestral languages and the genealogical relationships between their descendents, preferably visualised through family trees. Sound matters couldn't have mattered more: sound laws (so-called) after all were the crowning achievements in this comparative enterprise, with the study of inflection and especially syntax taking a back seat. Despite its intellectual triumphs, academic historical-comparative linguistics remained precariously poised vis-à-vis the philologies; but it at least managed to eke out a niche for itself – and in the process marginalised

---

6 Morpurgo Davies (1997) is a masterful portrait of this century, an "inside narrative" in a class of its own. Morpurgo Davies (1975) highlights the relationship between historical and typological comparison. For further details also see Plank (1991, 1995).

typological comparison. Universal co-variations between variables, often morphosyntactic, rarely phonological, continued to be suggested, usually elaborating on old themes rather than breaking new ground; but they were no match for sound laws, too far were they lagging behind in the methodological rigour of their continuingly amateurish investigation. Obviously, detecting order in variation is more demanding the larger and the more diverse the set of languages to be compared – all languages ever spoken (well, a hopefully representative subset of them all) or only one family. Still, one can see why, at the end of the century, Gabelentz would issue his rallying cry for typologists to get their act together, at long last.

To do what the likes of Rasmus Rask, Jacob Grimm, Karl Verner, and the Neogrammarians were famously doing, likewise building on seventeenth and eighteenth century amateur predecessors, required phonological expertise. Morphology, syntax, even semantics were not wholly outside the scope of the new professionals; but practising the Comparative Method, the tool that gained historical-comparative linguistics the scholarly respectability that as yet eluded typology, at heart meant being a phonologist. The languages under comparison, for the purpose of ascertaining whether or not they had "sprung from some common source", had to be searched for words or morphemes that might be cognates;[7] then regular sound correspondences (more often differences rather than identities) had to be identified; then plausible stories had to be constructed for how a state of systematic difference, as between the daughter languages, could have resulted from a postulated state of uniformity, as in the proto-language, with regular sound change effectuating the transition. Latterly, reconstructed phonological systems and hypothesised phonological changes would sometimes be considered suspect if they were crosslinguistically uncommon or indeed unique: but how could typology convincingly serve as a control, when its own results were not beyond methodological doubt and what it delivered on the phonological front was so little to begin with?

3.1.4 Interim summary

At the heart of doing typology, as an amateur or eventually with an academic license, always lay the identification of elementary linguistic variables and their examination for co-variation or independent variation. There is no inherent reason why this enterprise should have disfavoured phonology, or, as the

---

[7] And sounds mattered even before one got started: there was an inbuilt historical limitation to the Comparative Method, insofar as cognates, if not lost, would at some point (after 8,000 years or so) become impossible to recognise, as the sound shapes of morphemes would inexorably change over time.

Comparative Method did in the case of historical-comparative linguistics, have favoured phonology.

If anything it should *ceteris paribus* have been easier to do phonological than morphosyntactic typology, because the methodological issue of the *tertium comparationis* is generally felt to be less of a problem here. Assuming that "genitives", "adjectives", or "direct objects", for example, are the same kinds of thing in all languages under comparison just because they bear the same name is riskier than taking crosslinguistic equivalence for granted for many descriptive terms in phonology, where they are often phonetically grounded, hence have a more solid claim to be universal.

Still, for the pre-academic times of typology as covered in the précis above, phonology was indisputably a runner-up to inflection and syntax. We have more than a century of phonology-in-typology and typology-in-phonology yet to size up to bring us up to date: Has the balance shown signs of shifting as typology was coming of age?

3.2 Typology these days

Easing the task of the historian, it was really only some sixty or seventy years into the twentieth century when the tide for typology turned rather dramatically from ebb to full flow. Still, instead of accompanying typology's march into modernity, with the typological programme advancing through wider and deeper knowledge of languages, through more penetrating linguistic analysis, and through refined typological methodology, let's zoom in on what we know best: ourselves. There are several kinds of indicators that, with us today, typology and phonology have remained the uneasy bedfellows that they had always been.[8]

3.2.1 Centers and projects

Typology's overdue rise to global prominence was heralded by several local research cooperations, usually gathering around a senior figure, focusing on selected structural domains, holding workshops, and publishing working papers and collective volumes.

In Prague the Linguistics Circle had a typological section, with Vilém Mathesius's pupil Vladimír Skalička (active from the 1930s to 60s) as the

---

[8] A similar point has been made on similar grounds by Hyman (2007) (and elsewhere, including in this volume).

eventual mastermind. From the 1960s onwards, the St. Petersburg/Leningrad school of typology produced a long series of collective monographs on grammatical categories, overseen by Aleksandr A. Xolodovič, Viktor S. Xrakovskij, and Vladimir P. Nedjalkov. Roughly concurrently, though with only modest interaction, there were the Language Universals Project at Stanford, directed by Joseph H. Greenberg (1967–76), and UNITYP ("Sprachliche Universalienforschung und Typologie unter besonderer Berücksichtigung funktionaler Aspekte") in Cologne under Hansjakob Seiler (1972–92). In Paris, a little later (1984), RIVALC got going, lead by Gilbert Lazard, and its remit was rather more specific: "Recherche interlinguistique sur les variations d'actance et leur corrélats".[9]

No phonology appears to have been on the typological agendas in St. Petersburg/Leningrad, Cologne, and Paris. In Prague, phonological traits, from segment inventories and phonotactics to rhythmic patterns, would be conjectured to be implicated in Skalička's "ideal" types, whose most conspicuous hallmarks were syntactic and morphological, but which were after all meant as holistic. However, the phonological typologising of Nikolaj S. Trubetzkoy and Roman O. Jakobson, earlier members of the Prague *Cercle*, would echo more resoundingly in Stanford, largely owing to Joseph Greenberg himself, where phonology was equally represented with syntax and morphology, each yielding one volume of the resulting book series, *Universals of human language* (4 vols., Stanford: Stanford University Press, 1978).

Eventually, funding was secured from the European Science Foundation for a large-scale international typological research programme.[10] From 1990–95, the nine theme groups of EUROTYP brought together over a hundred collaborators from Europe in the EU sense and beyond, eventually producing eight tomes, published in Mouton de Gruyter's series *Empirical Approaches to Language Typology* (forming its collective volume 20). One somewhat isolated group and one volume of EUROTYP were on a phonological theme, *Word prosodic systems in the languages of Europe* (coordinated/edited by Harry van der Hulst); the rest was syntax and inflection.

---

9 These research initiatives are instructively portrayed by group leaders in Shibatani & Bynon (1995). Paris did see groundbreaking research on phonological typology, namely work centred around André-Georges Haudricourt's *Phonologie panchronique* (1940 etc., with an interim summary in *La phonologie panchronique* by Claude Hagège & Haudricourt, Paris: Presses Universitaires de France, 1978); but it was only later that this attained formal project status.

10 Not without initial opposition: some reviewers of the programme proposal sought to block it as pointless; for them, the only respectable comparison was historical.

3.2.2 Results on record

The net results of the typological programme are instances of co-variation among particular variables: How many of those on record,[11] however confidence-inspiring or dubious, are phonological and how many syntactic and inflectional? Although incomplete and not updated over the last decade, the UNIVERSALS ARCHIVE at Konstanz (http://typo.uni-konstanz.de/archive/intro/) still gives an impression that should not be far off. Of the over 2,000 universals documented, some age-old, others novel, the domain Syntax accounts for 1129, Inflection and Morphology for 789 + 157 (with the intended domain distinction somewhat unclear), Phonology (including phonetics) and Prosodic Phonology for 543 + 62. (For completeness: Lexicon 158, Word Formation 51, Semantics, Pragmatics, and Discourse 142 + 14 + 11.) Without disentangling assignments to multiple domains, there are more than three times more syntactic and inflectional than phonological universals deposited in this archive. Discarding the possibility that far more phonological than morphosyntactic universals have inadvertently escaped archiving, this can mean two things: (i) crosslinguistic diversity is far more copiously constrained in syntax and inflection than in phonology; or (ii) typologists have strongly preferred syntax and inflection to phonology when prospecting for universals.

3.2.3 Conferences and journals

In typology, like in other academic enterprises, it is at conferences and in journals that new ground is broken. (Amateurs used to work in isolation or corresponded.) How does phonology stand its ground on these occasions?

The learned society devoted to the advancement of the scientific study of typology, the Association for Linguistic Typology (ALT; http://www.linguistic-typology.org/index.html), has held biennial conferences since its foundation in 1994. At ALT 1, in Vitoria-Gasteiz in 1995, 44 papers were given, and a mere two and a half (or two halves) of these were on phonology. (One by the present writer, eventually to mature into Plank 1998: not original research, but a historiographic piece meant as encouragement.) This was certainly not an auspicious start of phonology in organised typology. Subsequently phonology was to pick up slightly, but a modest 5–10% of presentations used to be the limit from ALT 2–10. Only most recently, at ALT 11, in Albuquerque in 2015, did phonology (and phonetics),

---

[11] Regrettably, over the centuries, negative results – demonstrations that variables do NOT co-vary – have continuously been deemed less worthy of reporting and recording.

while remaining a distant second to syntax and inflection, account for as many as 16% of the papers given (13 out of 81, including theme and poster sessions).[12]

This last figure is getting close to the routine proportion of phonology papers at the International Conferences on Historical Linguistics (ICHL), biennially organised by the International Society of Historical Linguistics. ICHL 22, convened in Napoli in 2015, had 29 phonology papers out of 246 papers accepted for general session as well as workshops; but 12% for phonology is relatively low for ICHL's, where the average over the years has been closer to 20%, a proportion that is also confirmed by the selections of papers published in the ICHL proceedings. Thus, the conference circuit does not see mass migrations of phonologists to either historical or typological fora of the kind of ICHL and ALT meetings. You are likely to meet quite a few typologists you know from ALT at ICHL, though, but what they have to say about the relationship between typology and diachrony typically concerns morphosyntax rather than phonology, even when their topic is grammaticalisation.

The figures for *Linguistic Typology* (*LT*), ALT's journal, show an imbalance, too, although less marked than at ALT conferences. As revealed in the five-yearly editorial reports published in *LT*, the period of 2006–11 saw 30 submissions on phonology and phonetics and (ca.) 80 on syntax and inflection, of which 15 and (ca.) 30 respectively were accepted; 2001–06 saw 20 submissions on phonology and phonetics and 64 on syntax and inflection, of which 11 and 23 respectively were accepted. Like at ALT conferences, phonology had a really poor start in this environment: 8 phonology and phonetics papers were submitted in 1995–2001 as against 100 for syntax and inflection, of which 2 and 30 respectively were accepted. Interestingly, these figures also show that phonology submissions had higher acceptance rates, reflecting superior quality or at any rate quality that it was easier to reach consensus on.

Spotchecks suggest that the proportion of phonology to syntax and inflection papers is somewhat, though not dramatically lower in *LT* than in historical linguistics journals such as *Diachronica*, *Journal of Historical Linguistics*, *Folia Linguistica Historica*, or *Transactions of the Philological Society*. (In traditional-style historical-comparative journals such as *Indogermanische Forschungen*, *Historische Sprachforschung*, or *Journal of Indo-European Studies*, on the other hand, phonology easily holds its own as of old.)

---

12 Only the programme committees will know how the rejection rates compared for phonological and morphosyntactic abstracts. There was probably never a bias against phonology at the stage of abstract selection; but there were very few acknowledged phonologists on these ALT committees, and common sense suggests that the perceived expertise of abstract selectors is a factor encouraging or discouraging abstract submission.

3.2.4 Databases

Since data collections are no longer jealously guarded as the collector's private property, an increasingly popular research tool in typology are online databases. Among the thirty or so world-wide typological databases I am aware of as recently active, the majority cover domains from syntax and inflection. But it is not as overwhelming a majority as one might have expected, since about a dozen are on phonology or include substantial phonological data:

- UPSID: UCLA Phonological Segment Inventory Database
  http://www.linguistics.ucla.edu/faciliti/sales/software.htm;
  http://web.phonetik.uni-frankfurt.de/upsid_info.html
- LAPSyd: Lyon-Albuquerque Phonological Systems Database
  http://www.lapsyd.ddl.ish-lyon.cnrs.fr/lapsyd/
- PHOIBLE Online: Phonetics Information Base and Lexicon
  http://phoible.org/
- P-base
  http://pbase.phon.chass.ncsu.edu/
- World Phonotactics Database
  http://phonotactics.anu.edu.au/
- StressTyp2
  http://st2.ullet.net/?
- XTone: Cross-Linguistic Tonal Database
  http://xtone.linguistics.berkeley.edu/index.php
- Metathesis in Language
  http://metathesisinlanguage.osu.edu/database.cfm
- Language Typology Database
  http://www.unicaen.fr/typo_langues/index.php?malang=gb
- tds: Typological Database System
  http://languagelink.let.uu.nl/tds/main.html
- WALS Online: World Atlas of Language Structures
  http://wals.info/
- SignPhon: A Phonological Database for Sign Languages
  http://www.ru.nl/sign-lang/projects/completed-projects/signphon/

Currently the most popular database is the *World atlas of language structures online* (*WALS*, http://wals.info/), created under the auspices of the now-defunct Linguistics Department of the Max Planck Institute for Evolutionary Anthropology at Leipzig. *WALS* examines numerous lexical and grammatical variables ("features") across large numbers of languages, with core and extended core samples of 100 and 200 languages and with more than 2,500 languages figuring in one survey or another. This database has been widely used to discover as well as to refute universals; but what you get from *WALS* directly are geographical patterns of value distributions, and these are of interest to historical linguists for all kinds of reasons. *WALS* is divided up into 192 chapters, which mostly cover one feature, but some cover several (last accessed 10 March 2016). Breaking down this number by "areas", there are 20 chapters devoted to phonological (or also phonetic) features – or 22 if "Writing systems" and "Para-linguistic usages of clicks" are added. Inflection (Morphology 12, Nominal Categories 29, Verbal Categories 17) claims 58 chapters, Syntax (Nominal Syntax 8, Word Order 56, Simple Clauses 26, Complex Sentences 7) 97. (The Lexicon gets 13 chapters, of which four are about the sound shape of pronouns, and one is about the sound shapes of the word for 'tea'.) In sum, almost eight times more morphosyntactic than phonological features were deemed worthy of (or also amenable to) *WALS*-style treatment, which is once again consistent with the underrepresentation of phonology in typology.

3.2.5 Teaching and texts

Unlike in the days of Campanella, Mesgnien-Meninski, and Gabelentz and indeed up to less than fifty years before present, most modern typologists will have been taught typology at some stage of their university training in linguistics. On the teaching side, practising typologists often design their own courses, with "learning by doing" as the chief didactic element, but there has also been a proliferation of typology textbooks. Concerning the specialist knowledge and know-how that textbook authors want to pass on to their readers, there are differences among them in selection and emphasis; but what virtually all share, with only one exception I am aware of (Moravcsik 2013), is that phonology is not emphasised, if selected at all:

– Haarmann, Harald. 1976. *Grundzüge der Sprachtypologie: Methodik, Empirie und Systematik der Sprachen Europas*. Stuttgart: Kohlhammer. – Some phonology, mostly phoneme inventories; but not really a textbook.
– Ineichen, Gustav. 1979. *Allgemeine Sprachtypologie: Ansätze und Methoden*. Darmstadt: Wissenschaftliche Buchgesellschaft; 2nd edn. 1991. – 3 pages "Zum Stellenwert der Phonologie", but it has no *Stellenwert* for the rest of the book.
– Mallinson, Graham & Barry J. Blake. 1981. *Language typology: Cross-linguistic studies in syntax*. Amsterdam: North-Holland. – No phonology: honest titling.
– Comrie, Bernard. 1981. *Language universals and linguistic typology: Syntax and morphology*. Oxford: Blackwell; 2nd edn. 1989. – No phonology: honest titling.
– Croft, William. 1990. *Typology and universals*. Cambridge: Cambridge University Press; 2nd edn. 2003. – Almost no phonology.

- Whaley, Lindsay J. 1997. *Introduction to typology: The unity and diversity of language*. Newbury Park: Sage. – No phonology.
- Cristofaro, Sonia & Paolo Ramat (eds.) 1999. *Introduzione alla tipologia linguistica*. Roma: Carocci. – 8 classic papers selected for didactic exposition: one, by Joseph Greenberg, half phonological.
- Song, Jae Sung. 2000. *Linguistic typology: Morphology and syntax*. Harlow: Pearson Education. – No phonology: honest subtitling.
- Moure, Teresa. 2001. *Universales del lenguaje y linguo-diversidad*. Barcelona: Ariel. – No phonology.
- Feuillet, Jack. 2006. *Introduction à la typologie linguistique*. Paris: Honoré Champion. – No phonology.
- Velupillai, Viveka. 2012. *An introduction to linguistic typology*. Amsterdam: Benjamins. – Ch. 4: Phonology, on segment inventories, syllable structures, tone systems: 27 of 517 pages, all exclusively based on *WALS*.
- Moravcsik, Edith A. 2013. *Introducing language typology*. Cambridge: Cambridge University Press. – Ch. 5: Phonological typology, on a par with chapters on lexical, syntactic, and morphological typology!
- Kahl, Thede & Michael Metzeltin. 2015. *Sprachtypologie: Ein Methoden- und Arbeitsbuch für Balkanologen, Romanisten und allgemeine Sprachwissenschaftler*. Wiesbaden: Harrassowitz. – No phonology.

For some time now, prospective typologists have also been able to benefit from summer (or autumn or winter) schools. Among the earliest I am aware of as exclusively devoted to this subject were the typology schools of the Deutsche Gesellschaft für Sprachwissenschaft at Mainz/Germany in 1998, of the Moscow Typological Circle in or near Moscow in 1998, 2000, 2002, and 2005, of ALT in Cagliari/Sardinia in 2003; the most recent, run by the Fédération Typologie et Universaux Linguistique of the CNRS, will be at the Ile de Porquerolles/France in the autumn of 2016. There have always been one or even two phonology courses at these schools, but one or two dozen were on offer for those typology students keener on other matters, such as inflection and syntax, methodology, and language/family surveys.[13]

Seeking guidance beyond the textbook level, apprentice typologists, and whoever else is in need of ready reference about this field, can now also consult specialised handbooks – currently these two:

---

[13] Details, so far as they could be recovered other than from memory, at: https://linguistlist.org/issues/9/9-874.html; http://listserv.linguistlist.org/pipermail/alt/2002-November/000039.html; http://typoling2016.sciencesconf.org/.

- Haspelmath, Martin, Ekkehard König, Wulf Oestereicher, & Wolfgang Raible (eds.). 2001/02. *Language typology and language universals*. 2 vols. Berlin: Walter de Gruyter.
- Song, Jae Sung (ed.). 2010. *The Oxford handbook of linguistic typology*. Oxford: Oxford University Press.

With its two weighty tomes, the first is almost a compendium of linguistics in its entirety; its section on "Phonology-based typology" (5 chapters), a chapter on syllable/accent-counting as one "salient typological parameter", and occasional passing references to sound matters add up to some 90 pages of phonology, out of 1,800. The second has one out of 30 chapters devoted to segment/phoneme inventories, which yields an even worse proportion of phonology (if this is what this chapter is, and not phonetics) to non-phonological typology.

A handbook of sorts, too, is this set of three volumes – with a great deal of morphology subsumed under "syntax", but with no companion set *Language typology and phonological description*:

- Shopen, Timothy (ed.). 1985. *Language typology and syntactic description*. Vol. 1: *Clause structure*. Vol. 2: *Complex constructions*. Vol. 3: *Grammatical categories and the lexicon*. Cambridge: Cambridge University Press. (2nd edn., co-edited by Matthew S. Dryer, 2007.)

3.2.6 Specialisation

Few linguists who see themselves and are seen by others as typologists, whatever further categorisations they might invite, are genuine all-rounders: some wholly devote themselves to methodology (and might in fact be statisticians), but most specialise in one structural domain or another – and inflection and/or syntax specialists far outnumber phonology (and phonetics) specialists. (Specialisation is not entirely novel in typology: the chief expertise of a pioneer such as Gabelentz, unlike that of most of his Neogrammarian colleagues at Leipzig, lay in syntax.) As crown witnesses I call the five previous presidents of ALT, Bernard Comrie, Marianne Mithun, Nicholas Evans, Anna Siewierska, Johanna Nichols: as typologists all are primarily known for their work in syntax and inflection, although most have a sound component to their work, too. Of the one editor and 27 associate editors who have so far overseen ALT's journal, *LT*, one was a phonologist (Larry Hyman, though also with morphosyntactic work to his typological credit), one a phonetician (Ian Maddieson), and one divided her time between phonology and morphosyntax (Joan Bybee); syntax and inflection were the main expertise of the rest, with one or the other on rare occasions moonlighting as phonologists (William Croft, Nicholas Evans, Frans Plank, Martine Vanhove). Further evidence pointing in the same direction is conveniently gathered from the ALT membership directory (http://ling-asv.ling.su.se/alt_filer/membership.html): as their "special interests" members do mention phonology or phonetics as such as well as particular phonological/phonetic topics such as tone, nasalisation and other phonological processes, phonotactics, prosody, sound change, speech perception; but these figures cannot compete with mentions of syntax and morphology and particular morphosyntactic topics. Phonologists might of course be doing their typology elsewhere – a question which we need to return to (§3.2) before we can conclude that among today's linguists with typological interests phonologists are comparatively rare.

4 Reasons why

4.1 Is typology special?

4.1.1 Phonology outside typology

Undeniably, then, however you look at it, typology has been, and continues to be, about co-variation and co-evolution in syntax and inflection much more so than in phonology. Now, what are the reasons for this imbalance? And is it desirable, and possible, to redress it in future?

A first step towards an answer is to raise a further question: Is typology special?

Above (§2.2.4) I compared typology to historical linguistics with regard to the amount of phonology one finds at specialised conferences and in specialised journals, concluding, if tentatively, that it is less than morphosyntax, too. It is probably only among those historical linguists active in comparative (and internal) reconstruction that phonological expertise will be at a premium. Making further comparisons with subfields within linguistics where languages are being studied from some sort of a selective perspective and with some special ulterior motives, the likelihood is that a similar imbalance will be encountered. Take psycho- and neurolinguistics, or sociolinguistics and anthropological linguistics, or computational linguistics, and syntax (but not necessarily inflection) will receive more attention than phonology, although the subject matter supposedly is languages as such and there would not seem to be inherent reasons for some structural domains being prioritised over others. Perhaps dialectology is a rare subfield where the preferences among syntax and phonology(-cum-phonetics) are reversed, with inflection possibly on a par with phonology (and with the lexicon ahead of both).

If phonology is pitched against syntax in linguistics as a whole, it will again emerge as the loser, although it will probably win second place before morphology. Relevant evidence are the contents of general linguistics journals (you name them) or the membership lists of learned societies catering for the discipline as a whole (to name some where I made spotchecks: Societas Linguistica Europaea, Linguistic Society of America, Linguistics Association of Great Britain, Philological Society, Deutsche Gesellschaft für Sprachwissenschaft, Société Linguistique de Paris, Società di Linguistica Italiana, Società Italiana di Glottologia, Australian Linguistic Society, Linguistic Society of India): more linguists specialise in, and publish on, syntax than phonology or also morphology.[14] As a subset of linguists, typologists thus are not ESPECIALLY averse to phonology, then: they are boringly average the way they like and dislike to specialise. If they are special, it is probably in their idiosyncratic partiality to inflectional morphology.

4.1.2 Quantum sufficit

The question is: Why? Is phonology felt by trainee linguists to be prohibitively difficult? Or too easy, too little of an intellectual challenge? Is the way phonology is being taught too forbidding, with the numbers of initiates and potential future teachers thus dwindling from generation to generation? Does phonology lack the allure of theoretical promise or practical usefulness or do phonologists lack charisma, and does syntax and do syntacticians have it? Whether or not these are plausible considerations, there is also a simpler answer, which is that there just IS less phonology to be studied in comparison with syntax and morphology.

As an approximation to what languages are about, take descriptive grammars (and dictionaries, but lexical typology is not our concern here). Framed by an introductory presentation of the language to be described and perhaps a core vocabulary and texts as appendices, they typically have three parts: phonology, morphology (or in fact only inflection, with word formation often set aside for separate treatment), and syntax, in this or more rarely reverse order. Here are a few specimens:
– Sweet, Henry. 1892/98. *A new English grammar: Logical and historical.* 2 volumes. Oxford: Clarendon Press. – Phonology 75 pages, out of over 600.

---

[14] Figures supplied upon request. These figures would be similar for organisations devoted to particular language families. In terms of specialised journals or also specialised conferences, however, syntax does not seem far ahead of phonology and morphology. Significantly, phonetics is the clear winner in this respect, essentially forming a professional world of its own. Even passable all-rounders in linguistics can yet be useless in phonetics (and vice versa).

- Jespersen, Otto. 1909–49. *A Modern English grammar on historical principles*. London: Allen & Unwin. – One volume on "sounds and spelling", six on syntax and morphology.
- Sapir, Edward. 1922. The Takelma language of southwestern Oregon. In Franz Boas (ed.), *Handbook of American Indian languages*, vol. 2, 1–296. Washington: Bureau of American Ethnology. – Phonology 43 pages, morphology 247 pages (with no separate syntax); Sapir's other grammar, of Southern Paiute (1930), almost doubles the share of phonology to one third.
- Bloomfield, Leonard. 1962. *The Menomini language*. Ed. [posthumously] by Charles F. Hockett. New Haven: Yale University Press. – "Sounds" and "morphophonemics" 46 pages out of 507 (plus 22 pages on "morphologic processes and constructions", many filled with attendant morphonological "modifications", to be distinguished from "morpholexical variation").
- Kibrik, A. E., S. V. Kodzasov, I. P. Olovjannikova, & D. S. Samedov. 1977. *Opyt strukturnogo opisanija arčinskogo jazyka*. 4 volumes. Moskva: Izdatel'stvo moskovskogo universiteta. – One volume lexicon, word formation, and phonetics, with the latter (the responsibility of Kodzasov) 160 pages out of 350, two volumes syntax, one volume texts and vocabulary.
- Heidolph, Karl Erich, Walter Flämig, & Wolfgang Motsch (eds.). 1980. *Grundzüge einer deutschen Grammatik*. Berlin: Akademie-Verlag. – Phonology (the responsibility of Wolfgang U. Wurzel) 95 pages out of over 1,000.
- Rice, Keren. 1989. *A grammar of Slave* (Mouton Grammar Library 5). Berlin: Mouton de Gruyter. – Seven chapters out of 48 (including an introduction to a typological character sketch of Slave as well as texts) on phonology.
- Rischel, Jørgen. 1995. *Minor Mlabri: A hunter-gatherer language of Northern Indochina*. Copenhagen: Museum Tusculanum Press. – One chapter on phonology (called a "sketch"), morphology, syntax each, of 18, 50, and 65 pages respectively.
- Rennison, John R. 1997. *Koromfe* (Lingua/Croom Helm/Routledge Descriptive Grammars). London: Routledge. – Syntax 137 pages, morphology 227 pages, phonology 97 pages, lexicon 57 pages (with the grammar structured according to the original LDS Questionnaire, devised by Bernard Comrie and Norval Smith, the latter responsible for the phonological questions: https://www.eva.mpg.de/lingua/tools-at-lingboard/questionnaire/linguaQ.php).[15]
- Evans, Nicholas, 2003. *Bininj Gun-Wok: A pan-dialectal grammar of Mayali, Kunwinjku and Kune*. 2 volumes. Canberra: Pacific Linguistics. – The two chapters on phonology and morphophonemics add up to 46 pages, out of over 700.

---

[15] In other grammars following this format, not written by phonologists, the phonology sections are substantially shorter.

- Hualde, José Ignacio & Jon Ortiz de Urbina (eds.). 2011. *A grammar of Basque* (Mouton Grammar Library 26). Berlin: Mouton de Gruyter. – Phonology (the responsibility of Hualde and Gorka Elordieta) 97 pages, morphology 249 pages, syntax 529 pages.
- Crane, Thera M., Larry M. Hyman, & Simon Nsielanga Tukumu et al. 2011. *A grammar of Nzadi [B.865]: A Bantu language of the Democratic Republic of the Congo.* Berkeley: University of California Publications in Linguistics – Two chapters out of ten on phonology (sound system, tone), plus one appendix on phonological reconstruction, a similar proportion as in a similar earlier collective grammar by Hyman on Aghem.

This sample is not entirely random: though differing in many respects, what my dozen grammars have in common is that they were written or co-written by recognised or in fact eminent phonologists.[16] They are a rather select group, because grammar-writing is not a common activity of phonologists,[17] and one could therefore suspect my sample to be biased in favour of phonology: grammar writers with no special phonological expertise could be expected to do worse on this count. But COULD one do worse, purely in terms of numbers of pages or chapters – if phonology experts themselves standardly get along with about a fifth or less of the space that they need for syntax and inflection to set out the phonology of the language they are describing?

Sometimes the contrast is even starker in abbreviation. Ten-or-so-page sketches or typological profiles of languages, as often prefixed to full grammars or also published separately as basic sources of information for a general audience, typically reduce phonology to segment inventory tables or omit it altogether, but rarely are quite as laconic in highlighting what is special (or not special, but typologically expected) about the syntax and inflection of the languages concerned. For example, unusual for an introduction to linguistics but true to its title, *How languages work* (edited by Carol Genetti and essentially the work of her department at UC Santa Barbara, Cambridge: Cambridge University Press, 2013) is accompanied by 13 "language profiles"; however, although the body of the book includes three expert chapters on phonetics, phonology, and prosody, twelve

---

16 Jespersen, Sapir, and Bloomfield were all-rounders, but had substantial phonetic or phonological work to their credit. Hyman has morphosyntax as a sideline. Evans is a part-timer, but the best to be had among Australianists for present purposes.

17 On current evidence, the contributors to the present volume, with a single exception (grammar-writing Hyman), are thus in the company of the likes of Jan Baudouin de Courtenay, Mikołaj Kruszewski, Ferdinand de Saussure, Nikolaj S. Trubetzkoy, Roman Jakobson, John Rupert Firth, Louis Hjelmslev, André Martinet, Kenneth L. Pike, Morris Halle (who did write and co-author what could have formed the phonology chapters of the grammars of two languages, Russian and English).

portraits give the impression that languages work without phonology, while one, on Kabardian (by the author of the phonetics and phonology chapters, Matthew Gordon), exclusively expands on the phonology of this language.

If such comparisons are something to go by, and if there are no languages reversing these proportions whether fully described or aptly sketched,[18] we can conclude that, given comprehensive grammars, purged of excessive verbiage and reduced to bare statements of units, paradigmatic systems, and rules for and constraints on constructions, the "Minimum Description Length" or "Kolmogorov Complexity" of any language will be substantially less for their phonology than their syntax and inflection.

Owing to this universal, as yet undisconfirmed, it will only be natural, then, if – like elsewhere in linguistics – more research into linguistic diversity and unity is about what there is more of to compare across languages: syntax and inflection.

The inferiority of phonology may not only be quantitative, but qualitative, too. Phonological patterns have been claimed to be less complex than syntactic patterns in terms of the Chomsky Hierarchy of formal objects: as pointed out by Heinz & Idsardi (2013),[19] syntax can be finite, regular, context-free, mildly context-sensitive, and context-sensitive, covering almost the entire spectrum from lowest to highest complexity (with computably-enumerable patterns the only ones unattested), while the grammar of sound is limited to its lower region, namely to finite and regular patterns. As such, this imbalance is unlikely to be behind the poorer performance of phonology in typology: context-free and context-sensitive patterns are not really what syntactic typology has primarily been thriving on, with instances of such higher complexity in short crosslinguistic supply even in syntax. However, Heinz & Idsardi's explanatory speculation that syntax and phonology draw on different learning mechanisms could have typological relevance. Though learnability has rarely been an issue in typology, any constraints on structural diversity clearly facilitate learning, just like constraints on formal complexity do, and the relative importance of co-variation detection in acquisition might be greater in one domain than in another. If it is at a premium in syntax, it could be the manner of its learning that ultimately accounts for the typological pre-eminence of syntax.

---

18 Don't be misled by dialect grammars: they tend to background what dialects supposedly do not much differ in, namely syntax. For example, *Die Kerenzer Mundart des Kantons Glarus in ihren Grundzügen dargestellt* by Jost Winteler (Leipzig: Winter, 1876), renowned for its innovative phonology, devotes 147 pages to this subject, 43 to inflection, and not one to the syntax of this Swiss variety of Alemannic, a dialect of High German.

19 Heinz' chapter in this volume is in the same spirit, but limits complexity comparisons to phonological patterns.

4.2 Is phonology different?

While the conclusion seems credible that there is less phonology to be investigated especially in comparison with syntax, or less complexity to be grappled with in phonology than in syntax, and hence there will be fewer phonologists to investigate it, in linguistics in general and therefore also, with a view to co-variation/co-evolution, in typology, it is not a wholly satisfying diagnosis. There are further symptoms of a deeper disparity that can hardly be accounted for through such quantitative or qualitative differences between subject matters as just mentioned. They become apparent when we turn around the question, from How much phonology is there in typology? to How much typology is there in phonology? Is there proportionally less than there is in syntax and inflection? While there are quantitative differences here too, they are not the full story.

4.2.1 Typology in phonology

Probably, although concrete figures are impossible to obtain, linguists who perceive themselves and are perceived by others as phonologists, of all persuasions combined, are proportionally less likely than syntacticians and morphologists to be members of typological associations such as ALT, to attend conferences advertised as typological, and to publish in journals of a typological profile (such as *LT*, *Studies in Language*, *Sprachtypologie und Universalienforschung*, *Linguistic Discovery*). But then, there is no monopoly on typology: journals and conferences dedicated to phonology itself (e.g., the Manchester Phonology Meeting, Laboratory Phonology, the journal *Phonology*) surely do not discourage or ostracise typological contributions. But do they get fewer of those than journals and conferences dedicated to syntax get (e.g., meetings like Syntax of the World's Languages, Wiener Morphologietagung, the journals *Syntax*, *Morphology*, *Word Structure*)? Categorising work as typological whenever its theme is the dialectics of diversity and unity and it specifically focuses on co-variation/co-evolution among structural variables, whether or not it has "typology" in its title, I would be surprised if differences turned out to be significant: my impression is that there is relatively little on the recent record that qualifies as typology for all three domains, allowing for certain variations depending on theoretical frameworks.[20]

---

[20] If you define typology as only being about diversity, as is sometimes done in phonological circles (and elsewhere), then matters are of course different. More on this point presently, and also in Hyman in this volume.

By contrast, fora for general linguistics, or indeed general science (such as *Science, Nature, PLOS ONE*), have seen a very tangible increase in typological studies over the last four or five decades, but again it does not look like phonology is conspicuously lagging behind morphology or syntax.

4.2.2 Teaching and texts

In introductions to phonology, to judge by teaching materials that are available on the internet, phonological typology has become an element at many institutions, which may or may not teach introductions to typology as such; morphology and syntax introductions also often have typology components, but perhaps more frequently this is taken care of in separate typology courses. The textbook market would seem to reflect the situation well: for example, picking out two popular series, in the *Cambridge Introductions to Language and Linguistics* both the phonology and the morphology texts, by Odden and Lieber, have chapters on typology, while the *Understanding Language* texts lack such separate chapters for phonology (Gussenhoven & Jacobs) as well as for morphology (Haspelmath (& Sims)) and syntax (Tallerman), but address typological issues in subsections and en passant, and more extensively for syntax and morphology than for phonology.

- Lieber, Rochelle. 2009. *Introducing morphology*. Cambridge: Cambridge University Press. (2nd edn. 2015.)
- Odden, David. 2005. *Introducing phonology*. Cambridge: Cambridge University Press. (2nd edn. 2013.)
- Gussenhoven, Carlos & Haike Jacobs. 1998. *Understanding phonology* London: Arnold. (3rd edn. 2011.)
- Haspelmath, Martin. 2002. *Understanding morphology*. London: Arnold. (2nd edn. 2010, with co-author Andrea D. Sims.)
- Tallerman, Maggie. 1998. *Understanding syntax*. London: Arnold. (4th edn. Routledge, 2015.)

4.2.3 Languages and linguistic theory

Over and above such similarities there is a curious and seemingly trivial difference between introductions to phonology on the one hand and those to morphology and syntax on the other: the former consistently serve up more languages. According to their indices, Odden's and Gussenhoven & Jacobs's phonology texts in one way or another make reference to some 150 languages, comparing to a little over 100 in Tallerman's syntax and in Haspelmath (& Sims)'s as well as Lieber's morphology texts. An early text such as Larry Hyman's *Phonology: Theory and analysis* (New York: Holt, 1975) had examples from and analyses for over 80 languages, at a time when introductions to syntax would make ends meet with one (often the author's own) and Peter Matthews' *Morphology*, the first *Cambridge Textbook in Linguistics* (Cambridge University Press, 1974), got along with a modest 20.

And such an imbalance is not encountered in textbooks alone. The language index, for example, of the Blackwell *Handbook of phonological theory* (edited by John A. Goldsmith, 1995) has 422 entries, while its companion *Handbook of morphology* (edited by Andrew Spencer & Arnold M. Zwicky, 1998), apart from missing the tag "theory" in the title, only has 159 entries for languages and families, incorporated in the subject index. Major theoretical works in phonology are routinely brimming with languages, too: to choose almost randomly, only think of Trubetzkoy's *Grundzüge der Phonologie* (Travaux du Cercle Linguistique de Prague 7, Prague 1939), Wolfgang Dressler's *Morphophonology* (Ann Arbor: Karoma, 1985), John Goldsmith's *Autosegmental and metrical phonology* (Oxford: Blackwell, 1990), Bruce Hayes' *Metrical stress theory* (Chicago: University of Chicago Press, 1995), or Robert Ladd's *Intonational phonology* (Cambridge: Cambridge University Press, 1996). Devoted to a single language, even Noam Chomsky & Moris Halle's *The sound pattern of English* (New York: Harper & Row, 1968) has a separate language index, with as many as 101 entries. Comparable language coverage in landmark monographs is hard to find in syntax: perhaps Guglielmo Cinque, with titles such as *Adverbs and functional heads: A cross-linguistic perspective* (Oxford: Oxford University Press, 1999) or *The syntax of adjectives: A comparative study* (Cambridge, MA: MIT Press, 2010), or Mark Baker, with *The polysynthesis parameter* (Oxford: Oxford University Press, 1996), *Lexical categories* (Cambridge: Cambridge University Press, 2005), or *The syntax of agreement and concord* (Cambridge: Cambridge University Press, 2008), come closest, but they are exceptions. Morphology is in between, as is suggested by the language counts for some works from the morphological Renaissance of the 1980s: Frans Plank, *Morphologische (Ir-)Regularitäten* (Tübingen: Narr, 1981) has 20+; Wolfgang Wurzel, *Flexionsmorphologie und Natürlichkeit* (Berlin: Akademie-Verlag, 1984) 75; Joan Bybee, *Morphology* (Amsterdam: Benjamins, 1985) 50+; Andrew Carstairs, *Allomorphy in inflexion* (London: Croom Helm, 1987) 48. The morphological counterpart to *SPE*, Mark Aronoff's *Word formation in Generative Grammar* (Cambridge, MA: MIT Press, 1976), is mostly about one language, English, but is livened up with tangential references to ten others.

What could seem an idle ranking of publications by language density arguably bears witness to a divergence of research traditions, and of an estrangement of professional sub-communities, between syntax and phonology.[21]

In syntax, and similarly in morphology, a tradition had developed of elaborating theories and frameworks on a narrow basis: at the expense of confronting crosslinguistic diversity, theorising would be informed by in-depth looks at selected structural phenomena in one or a few particular languages, and not just by utterances and texts, but also by native judgments about them. This was not only the policy in Generative Grammar: a collection such as *Syntactic theory 1: Structuralist* (edited by Fred Householder, Harmondsworth: Penguin, 1972), assembling 23 classic readings, accumulates a little over 100 languages and families, but most individual chapters make their theoretical points on the basis of individual languages, mostly English, with Ilocano (L. Bloomfield), Bilaan (K. L. Pike), Teleéfoól (P. Healey), Sundanese (R. H. Robins), Vietnamese (P. J. Honey), and Eskimo-Aleut (K. Bergsland) as sporadic co-stars and the rest as bit-part players. (The only multi-language exceptions in this reader are W. S. Allen, Transitivity and possession, and B. L. Whorf, Grammatical categories.) A pre-structuralist classic, Wilhelm Havers' *Handbuch der erklärenden Syntax* (Heidelberg: Winter, 1931), had limited itself to a subset of Indo-European, although with illustrations from spoken modern languages and with occasional comparisons of these "Kultursprachen" to none-too-specific "Natursprachen".

Eventually, from the 1960s and 70s onwards, as typology was beginning, through individual efforts like Joseph Greenberg's, to attract wider attention than ever before, languages in the plural would re-assert their right to be heard not only for their phonology, but also their syntax. With the Generative paradigm continuing to dominate, a misperception arose of syntax being done in two ways: "theoretically", engaging with single languages against the backdrop of Universal Grammar (largely taken for granted), vs. "descriptively", dealing with multiple languages and inductively inferring crosslinguistic generalisations about co-variation/co-evolution. When "theorists" were withholding the honorary epithet "theoretical" from the latter line, where theorising was primarily about finding and explaining inductive generalisations, they were probably encouraged by an occasional lack of subtlety in conceptualising syntactic

---

21 The admirable inside history of phonology by Anderson (1985) doesn't quite highlight this theme of languages and typology in phonology vs. syntax. Nor does the more recent collection of Honeybone & Bermúdez-Otero (2006), where similarities between phonology and syntax are emphasised, rather than possible differences in researching phonological and syntactic structures and architectures.

structures and processes and a reluctance to countenance abstract representations. Though far better informed crosslinguistically, syntactic typology as part and parcel of the "descriptive" approach remained theoretically indeed sometimes a bit basic.[22] It seemed like grammar was in bare essence to be conceived of as a checklist of variables, possibly with only two values, plus or minus – OV or VO? Adposition before/after NP? Genitive before/after head noun? Ergative or accusative or other alignment? A definite article, yes or no? Zero copula? Dual? Inclusive-exclusive? Gender, and where applicable: how many? Doing typology then typically meant searching for co-variation among such variables whose values the typologist could easily glean at a glance from lots of descriptive grammars.

In phonology, theory and framework development had never been divorced from crosslinguistic awareness to a similarly alarming extent. There were thus no grounds for a multilingual "descriptive" phonology to split off from a monolingual "theoretical" phonology à la syntax. Languages in the plural remained at the core of phonological theorising. In principle this meant that typology could have been done as part of theoretical phonology, rather than in a separate community where members defined themselves as typologists and where "non-theoretical" syntacticians were setting the agenda. And to some extent it was – namely to the extent that phonological grammar could be conceived of as a checklist and values could conveniently be checked for co-variation/co-evolution:[23] Does the language have this segment and that? Does it have quantity contrasts for vowels/consonants? Does it permit onset clusters, and if so which? How do its syllables go beyond CV? Does it enforce final devoicing? Does it have vowel harmony? Is it tonal? Level or contour tones, and how many? Which syllable of the word does it stress? However, this sort of thing – like listing segment inventories and phonotactic templates – was never considered all there is for phonological theory to address, and, when it was a point of departure, it did not represent a theoretical issue or conclusion. Hence, much of what was at the heart of phonological theorising, in variable frameworks

---

[22] This overly spartan mode of description arguably prevented such typological syntax from meaningfully engaging with diachronic syntax and from playing a more significant role in experimental psycho- and neurolinguistics.

[23] After Greenberg's "dynamicised" typology and Haudricourt's "panchronic phonology", the most determined single effort to explain co-variation as co-evolution in phonology was Juliette Blevins' *Evolutionary phonology* (Cambridge: Cambridge University Press, 2007). Characteristically, the impact of this book was felt more in phonology, theoretical as well as historical, than in typology, while similar evolutionary work in morphosyntax typically had stronger reverberations in typology than in syntax.

but invariably richly informed by diverse languages, has never translated into phonological typology of the checklist-based variety, a style so increasingly popular for syntactic and morphological typology and accounting for the latter-day bulk of it.

When phonology is seen as phonologists see it, aiming at adequate description and at the same time at making theoretical sense of what is being described, the grammar of sound is substantially growing in sheer volume. When syntax chapters in weightier descriptive grammars are compared with monographs on the syntax of the same languages, like those of the *Cambridge Syntax Guides*, there is no dramatic mismatch. The remit for authors of these *Guides*, of which a dozen have so far been published (mostly for European languages), is to be both descriptive and theoretical, while the editorial team itself (Peter Austin, Bernard Comrie, Joan Bresnan, David Lightfoot, Ian Roberts, Neil Smith), like the intended audience, is patently divided between "descriptive" and "theoretical" allegiances. The authors of the *Phonology of the World's Languages* series of Clarendon/Oxford University Press are likewise instructed, although by a single editor (Jacques Durand), to attend to both description and explanation, to the benefit of a single undivided body of intended readers, which should not be put off by differences between theoretical frameworks – and the resultant monographs, as yet 19, far exceed what would be found in even the most comprehensive of descriptive grammars. Intriguingly, several languages have both a Cambridge syntax guide and an Oxford phonology portrait devoted to them, and the Kolmogorov Complexity or at any rate book length is not necessarily less for the phonology: Arabic phonology (and morphology; author Janet Watson) 336 pages, syntax (authors Joseph Aoun et al.) 260 pages; Catalan phonology (Max Wheeler) 400, Spanish syntax (Karen Zagona) 300; Welsh phonology (S. J. Hannahs) 198, Welsh syntax (Robert Borsley & Maggie Tallerman) 412; Icelandic (& Faroese) phonology (Kristján Árnason) 368, syntax (Höskuldur Thráinsson) 580; Dutch phonology (Geert Booij) 218, syntax (Jan-Wouter Zwart) 418; German phonology (Richard Wiese) 368, syntax (Hubert Haider) 368; Hungarian phonology (Péter Siptár & Miklós Törkenczy) 336, syntax (Katalin É. Kiss) 292; Chinese phonology (San Duanmu) 382, syntax (James Huang et al.) 404.[24]

---

[24] The by far longest phonology, at 624 pages, is that of Danish, and you wonder whether to give credit to the language or the author (Hans Basbøll) for such unusual opulence. Portuguese phonology only needs 170 pages (from Maria Helena Mateus & Ernesto d'Andrade), almost as little as Chichewa syntax does (166, Sam Mchombo); and it is moot to speculate whether such frugality reflects on these languages or the describers of their phonology and syntax.

4.2.4 Languages and typology

Now, when phonology is being done with wide crosslinguistic awareness and with equal descriptive and theoretical poise, will the inevitable outcome be phonological typology – homemade, but like syntactic and morphological typology aspiring to chart diversity and to discover order or indeed unity? Is theoretical phonology, inseparable from descriptive phonology, methodically investigating whether variables co-vary or co-evolve, just like syntactic and morphological typology do, although not normally in communion with "theoretical" syntax and morphology?

Having many languages at one's analytic fingertips does not make one a typologist. Charting diversity is one thing, seeking order is another – and typology's remit includes both. In multilingual theoretical phonology it is often only the former which is on the agenda, and success consists in one's theoretical framework being able to insightfully deal with whatever can be found across languages, however diverse. The chief interest is in what there is and in its theoretical accommodation, rather than in what there isn't – in how diversity is constrained through variables systematically co-varying or co-evolving. Optimality Theory is an obvious framework to mention here, because it is sometimes considered "inherently typological", if only at the expense of redefining and narrowing typology's remit. But to also exemplify my point through a particular work: in metrical phonology a typology of feet was developed (prominently in Hayes' *Metrical stress theory*, a book hard to beat on language density), which indeed aims to constrain crosslinguistic diversity insofar as no language is supposed to employ further conceivable kinds of feet beyond these original types (essentially only iambs and trochees with variations). However, little comparative effort went into asking, further, whether single languages are free to employ different types of feet for different purposes (e.g., stress, all kinds of segmental processes affecting syllable structure, poetic meter) and for different lexical domains, or whether the choice of one foot type is a determinant for all foot-sensitive patterns of a language. Foot typology has only been taken in the direction of real co-variation/co-evolution typology by Elan Dresher & Aditi Lahiri (The Germanic foot: Metrical coherence in Old English. *Linguistic Inquiry* 22. 251–286, 1991), when they demonstrated that languages are "metrically coherent" – or at any rate the Old Germanic languages that they examined were, doing all their relevant business on the basis of just the resolved moraic trochee and no other foot type. Prosodic typology, where Hyman has long been arguing for co-variation among variables, rather than types of languages ("tone languages", "stress languages", "pitch-accent languages"), as the object of inquiry, is also moving in this direction, on such evidence as *Prosodic typology: The phonology of intonation and phrasing* (2 volumes, Cambridge: Cambridge University Press, 2005/2014), whose editor, Sun-Ah Jun, concludes by extracting, from two dozen language-particular accounts (all done in the same descriptive framework, ToBI), implicational generalisations about prosodic prominence and rhythmic or prosodic units such as these: "In stress languages (such as English, Arabic, Farsi, Swedish, Chickasaw), the prominence of a word is always marked by postlexical pitch accent (marking the head of the word), but not often by marking the edge of the word. [...] Languages that do not have any feature of lexical prosody (such as French, Bengali, Korean) mark the prominence of the word demarcatively at the postlexical level" (updated in the second volume through introducing the concept of "macrorhythm").

These are phonology-internal developments aligning phonology with morphosyntactic typology, but they have not found much resonance in typological circles. Other than a subject matter and theoretical angles unfamiliar, even impenetrable to many syntacticians and morphologists, there remains a difference in emphasis on methodology. Morphologists and syntacticians, often maligned as "non-theoretical", have made huge efforts since Georg von der Gabelentz to hone typological methodology: inductive generalisations are no longer arrived at as naively as in days of old, when assembling samples and determining statistical significance, if done at all, was amateurs' work. In phonological typology, theoretical accommodation, far above the level of checklist grammar, continues to be prized more highly than methodological sophistication, and cherry-picking continues to be preferred over sampling.

There are lessons to be learnt either way.

4.2.5 Is phonology hopeless?

I don't think typological phonology is hopeless, but I am less confident about phonological typology.

Intonation and prosody in general have variously been conjectured to be subject to intra-language variation of an extent unparalleled by syntax and morphology. However, as shown by the recent *Prosodic typology* collection which does recognise such variation, this does not seem an insurmountable obstacle for typological system-seeking. There is a methodological challenge here, insofar as the sampling points in (non-phonological) typology have typically been languages:[25] to cope with diversity of prosodic dimensions, it is dialects and idiolects –

---

25 Admittedly it has been recognised that often what has been sampled were really lower-level units such as "doculects", namely those varieties of a language that happen to have been documented (in a text or corpus, by a fieldworker, in a particular grammar).

individual mental grammars – that ought to be sampled, once typological phonology proceeds from cherry-picking to sampling.

The grammar of sound has been conjectured to be radically different from other grammar: "[phonology] is very complex; it does not seem to have any of the nice computational properties of the rest of the system" (Chomsky 2012: 40). If it is these "nice computational properties" of syntax and inflection which are responsible not only for unity, but also for orderliness of diversity, constrained by co-variation or co-evolution, then typologising in phonology would indeed be doomed. However, against such speculation, informed by a perhaps somewhat minimalistic outlook on syntax, stand arguments for rich parallels, like those collected in Honeybone & Bermúdez-Otero (2006): such structural and architectural parallels have all variously figured in both syntactic and phonological typology. Also, as touched on above (§4.1.2), the exact opposite case to Chomsky's has been made by Heinz & Idsardi (2013) for phonology being formally LESS complex than syntax, and different domain-specific learning strategies might have typological repercussions. If you are unconvinced by such theoretical reasoning and the body of work in phonology that is typologically minded, read on because the present collection is the best argument that typological phonology is not a dead loss.

Unlike typological phonology, it is phonology in typology that might be hopeless, albeit for extraneous reasons. It is to be feared that typologists, who as we saw are mostly syntacticians and inflectional morphologists by professional specialisation, will continue to lack the serious grounding that would enable them to appreciate what is going on in this (for them) hermetic field of phonology, once it rises above the checklist level of grammar and the going gets heavier than the tabulation of segment inventories. For the time being, there will probably continue to be two communities far apart and indifferent towards one another, phonologically challenged organised typologists here and phonologists as do-it-yourself typologists over there.

Acknowledgements: I can't seriously pretend to be telling an inside story of phonology, typological or otherwise; but without the many years of casual instruction from Aditi Lahiri and Larry Hyman, this work would have been pure science fiction (and I'm not sure whether utopian or dystopian). For contributing to my phonological education on frequent convivial occasions I'm also grateful to Elan Dresher, Carlos Gussenhoven, Paul Kiparsky, and Tomas Riad. Comments from Larry Hyman, Aditi Lahiri, and Edith Moravcsik have helped to improve the present chapter.

It took us ages to get our act together on this volume – which incidentally began with a failed attempt by my co-editor and myself to have phonology and typology discussed at an ALT conference. Thanks everybody for their patience: It's all my fault.

References

Note: Works dealt with as historiographical data are referenced in the body of the chapter.

Anderson, Stephen R. 1985. *Phonology in the twentieth century: Theories of rules and theories of representations*. Chicago: University of Chicago Press.

Chomsky, Noam. 2012. *The science of language: Interviews with James McGilvray*. Cambridge: Cambridge University Press.

Gabelentz, Georg von der. 1894. Hypologie der Sprachen, eine neue Aufgabe der Sprachwissenschaft. *Indogermanische Forschungen* 4. 1–7.

Gabelentz, Georg von der. 1901. *Die Sprachwissenschaft, ihre Aufgaben, Methoden und bisherigen Ergebnisse*. 2nd edn. Leipzig: Tauchnitz.

Heinz, Jeffrey & William Idsardi. 2013. What complexity differences reveal about domains in language. *Topics in Cognitive Science* 5. 111–131.

Honeybone, Patrick & Ricardo Bermúdez-Otero (eds.). 2006. *Linguistic knowledge: Perspectives from phonology and from syntax*. Thematic issue of *Lingua* 116(5).

Hyman, Larry M. 2007. Where's phonology in typology? *Linguistic Typology* 11. 265–271.

Morpurgo Davies, Anna. 1975. Language classification in the nineteenth century. In Thomas A. Sebeok (ed.), *Current trends in linguistics*, vol. 13: *Historiography of linguistics*, 717–827. The Hague: Mouton.

Morpurgo Davies, Anna. 1997. *History of linguistics*, vol. 4: *Nineteenth century linguistics*. London: Longman.

Plank, Frans. 1991. Hypology, typology: The Gabelentz puzzle. *Folia Linguistica* 25. 421–458.

Plank, Frans. 1992. Adam Smith: Grammatical economist. In Peter Jones & Andrew Skinner (eds.), *Adam Smith reviewed*, 21–55. Edinburgh: Edinburgh University Press.

Plank, Frans. 1993. Des Lord Monboddo Ansichten von Ursprung und Entwicklung der Sprache. *Linguistische Berichte* 144. 154–166.

Plank, Frans. 1995. Professor Pott und die Lehre der Allgemeinen Sprachwissenschaft. *Zeitschrift der Deutschen Morgenländischen Gesellschaft* 145. 328–364.

Plank, Frans. 1998. The co-variation of phonology with morphology and syntax: A hopeful history. *Linguistic Typology* 2. 195–230.

Plank, Frans. 2001. Typology by the end of the 18th century. In Sylvain Auroux et al. (eds.), *History of the language sciences: An international handbook on the evolution of the study of language*, 1399–1414. Berlin: Walter de Gruyter.

Shibatani, Masayoshi & Theodora Bynon (eds.). 1995. *Approaches to language typology*. Oxford: Clarendon.

Paul Kiparsky
Formal and empirical issues in phonological typology

Abstract: The word level in the sense of Lexical Phonology and Stratal OT, here referred to as the l-phonemic level, is a linguistically significant level of representation, which captures what was right about the structural phonemic level without inheriting its well-known problems. It does so in virtue of encoding non-contrastive but distinctive as well as contrastive but non-distinctive phonological properties. I show that phonological systems which appear marginal or aberrant from the perspective of structural phonemics and generative phonological underlying representations are normalized at the l-phonemic level, and that certain phonological universals become exceptionless only at this level. Dramatic instances include putative vertical and one-vowel systems such as those of Arrernte and Kabardian, and apparently syllable-less languages such as Gokana. I further argue that "external evidence" from change, dispersion, poetic conventions, and language games supports l-phonemic representations rather than classical phonemic representations.

The larger methodological point is that there are no theory-neutral grammars, and consequently no theory-neutral typology. In terms of Hyman's (2008) distinction, there are no "descriptive" universals of language. All universals are "analytic", and their validity often turns on a set of critical cases where different solutions can be and have been entertained. Therefore the search for better linguistic descriptions, more illuminating typologies, and stronger cross-linguistic generalizations and universals must go hand in hand.

1 Lexical representations

1.1 Problems with phonemes

Typological generalizations and universals are explicanda for linguistic theory, but they are themselves theory-dependent, for in order to be intelligible and falsifiable they must adhere to some explicit descriptive framework. This mutual dependency comes to a head at the margins of typological space, where reconciling typologies with descriptive frameworks and the analyses dictated by them can involve a labyrinth of choices. I explore a few of the tangled paths through it in the realm of syllable structure and vowel systems.

https://doi.org/10.1515/9783110451931-003

Phonological typology has been based on three distinct levels of representation: phonemic, phonetic, and morphophonemic (underlying, "systematic phonemic"). Most work on segment inventories is framed in terms of phonemic systems in the tradition of Trubetzkoy (1929, 1939), Jakobson (1958), and Greenberg (1978). A major resource is the UPSID collection of phonemic systems (Maddieson 1984, 2013, Maddieson & Precoda 1990), which has the virtue of being genetically balanced (to the extent possible), carefully vetted, and to some extent normalized to conform to a standard set of analytic principles.[1] The same resource has also been used by phoneticians to investigate the typology of speech sound inventories (Schwartz et al. 1997). Proponents of Dispersion Theory have attempted to model the UPSID vowel systems, even though the theory is strictly speaking about the phonetic realization of phonemes (maximization of perceptual distance and minimization of articulatory effort). A growing body of typology crucially relies on underlying representations (phonemes in the classical generative phonological sense), such as Dresher (2009) and Casali (2014). The analysis of Arrernte syllable structure that Evans & Levinson (2009: 434) cite as part of their argument that universals are "myths" is based on abstract underlying representations (Section 2.1 below).

Throwing abstract morphophonemic, phonemic, and phonetic inventories in the same bin is unlikely to produce coherent typologies and universals. So what kinds of categories and representations should typologists look at? At least two criteria follow from the nature of typology itself. We want typological categories that correlate with each other and show some historical stability. And we want the categories to be based on independently justified linguistically significant representations.

It is not obvious that the phonemic level satisfies either of these criteria. There is persuasive evidence for SOME level between abstract underlying representations and phonetics at which phonology is accessed in language use, including the classic "psychological reality" or "external evidence" diagnostics such as versification and language games, as well as language change, including sound change and phonologization, analogy, and borrowing. But phonemic theories do not converge on this level. Depending on how such fundamental issues as biuniqueness, invariance, linearity, and morphological conditioning ("grammatical prerequisites", junctures) are resolved, phonemic analyses diverge for all but the simplest textbook cases, and quite drastically for typologically challenging outlier systems of the sort I'll focus on here. For example,

---

[1] This useful work is often somewhat misleadingly called a "database" of "sound inventories". It contains phoneme inventories, which can be at considerable remove from the primary data. Really they are theories, just as grammars are not primary data but theories of languages.

if we require linearity (a phoneme cannot correspond to a sequence of sounds) Kabardian has seven vowel phonemes. If we don't require linearity, but do require biuniqueness, it has three vowel phonemes; otherwise it has two. Each of these phonemic analyses is currently advocated by researchers on Kabardian (Section 3.2).

I shall argue that what language users actually access, and what language change reveals, is not exactly the classical phonemic level, but the level of representations that emerges from the lexical phonology (in the sense of Lexical Phonology and Stratal OT). I'll refer to this as the level of LEXICAL REPRESENTATIONS and to its elements as L-PHONEMES. I will argue first that the classic diagnostics fit lexical representations rather than phonemic representations, where they differ, and then that the typology of syllable structure and phonological systems is best served by lexical representations. At this level phonological systems converge on significant common properties, and some important phonological near-universals turn exceptionless. The global factors of dispersion, symmetry, and naturalness, to the extent that they shape phonological systems, appear to take effect at this level.

Although I concentrate on unusual syllabification and vowel systems, these just highlight some inherent tensions between phonemics and typology that arise less conspicuously in most languages. They are due to the SPARSENESS and SEGMENTALISM of phonemic representations.

The point of phonemic representations is that they should be stripped of all predictable information. In Jakobson's words (1958 [1962]: 525): "A typology of either grammatical or phonological systems cannot be achieved without subjecting them to a logical restatement which gives the maximum economy by a strict extraction of redundancies." I'll defend the opposite view, that a specific class of redundant information is phonologically relevant,[2] and that its omission can lead typology astray – namely just that increment of information which accrues from the phonological computation in the lexical module. In particular, lexical representations include word stress, if the language has it, and word-level syllable structure, regardless of whether these things are predictable in the language or relevant to any phonological processes in it.[3] Lexical representations include this information for principled reasons, as we'll see directly. But they exclude postlexical feature specifications from sandhi processes and phonetic

---

[2] UPSID's convention of representing phonemes by their most frequent allophone, rather than by an invariant feature bundle, could be seen as a partial acknowledgment of this.

[3] This is inconsistent with the CONTRASTIVE HYPOTHESIS, according to which phonological generalizations can only refer to contrastive features (Currie-Hall 2007, Dresher 2007).

implementation rules. In this respect lexical representations are thus more like Praguian *Wortphonologie* than like *Satzphonologie*.

Besides sparseness, a second source of trouble for structural phonemics is its segmentalist commitment (criticized in Scobbie & Stuart-Smith 2008). It requires that a multiply associated feature be associated with exactly one contrastive segment in its span. Segmentalism is implied by such concepts as minimal pairs, the commutation test, and the view of a phonemic system as an inventory of abstract contrastive segments. Structural phonemics has no place for Harris' long components, Firthian prosodies, or Goldsmith's autosegments, not even those versions of it that take distinctive features as the basic units of phonology, such as Jakobson's. OT phonology has inherited segmentalism in its descriptive practice, and formalized it in correspondence theory, but nothing about OT inherently requires it. OT is a theory of constraint interaction, not a theory of representations. Lexical representations differ from phonemic representations in that they record the full cumulative effect of the stem-level and word-level phonological computation, including any redundant features assigned in those two lexical submodules, with one-to-many association of prosodies to segmental slots where appropriate, while still excluding allophones introduced in the postlexical module and phonetic implementation. This additional information turns out to be important for phonological typology and significant universals can be formulated over representations that incorporate it.

An example will help make these points clear. Gravina (2014: 90–94) describes Moloko (Central Chadic) as having a single underlying vowel /a/, and a second vowel /ə/ which does not appear in underlying forms and is predictably inserted where syllable structure requires.[4] In addition, a word may have one of two prosodies, palatalization and labialization (notated as ^{y}, ^{w}), which color its vowels to yield six surface vowels altogether:

(1)   No Prosody   Palatalization   Labialization
     /a/   a   ɛ   ɔ
     /ə/   ə   I   U

The prosodies spread leftward across a word, from suffix to stem and stem to prefix, but they do not cross word boundaries (e.g. (2g)).[5]

---

[4] Moloko allows as medial codas only the most sonorous consonants, the non-nasal sonorants /r/, /l/, /w/ or /j/. Violations are eliminated by inserting /ə/.
[5] I include the labial prosodies ^{y} and ^{w} within the phonemic representation, but they are not phonemically attached to the last segment.

(2) a. /mdga/   [mədəga]   'older sibling'
    b. /matabaɬ/   [matabaɬ]   'cloud'
    c. /mababakʸ/   [mɛbɛbɛk]   'bat'
    d. /gvaʸ/   [gɪvɛ]   'game'
    e. /gzaʷ/   [gʊzɔ]   'kidney'
    f. /talalanʷ/   [tɔlɔlɔŋ]   'chest'
    g. /na zmʷ ɗf/   [na zʊm ɗaf] (*[nɔ]..., *...[ɗəf]) 'I eat food'
    h. /aɬaɬaɗʸ/   [aɬɛɬɛɗ] (*[ɛɬɛɬɛɗ])   'egg'
    i. /ma-k̥r-akʷ/   [mɔk̥ʊrɔkʷ]   'we (excl.) kicked'

There are three special cases. The vowel of a pre-pausal syllable is neutralized to /a/, realized as [a], [ɛ], [ɔ] depending on the prosody, e.g. (2g)). Labialized consonants and /w/ color adjacent [a] to [ɔ], [ə] to [ʊ], and [ɛ] to [œ] (the only source of [œ]), and /j/ colors adjacent [ə] to [ɪ]. Finally, a word-initial vowel is always [a], regardless of the prosody, e.g. (2h).[6]

So how many vowel phonemes does Moloko have? Just /a/, for the epenthetic vowel is predictable, and the color prosodies are suprasegmental? Or six, since there are in principle six-way surface contrasts like CaCaC : CɛCɛC : CɔCɔC : CəCəC : CɪCɪC : CʊCʊC? The puzzle is that the epenthetic vowel is non-contrastive, therefore allophonic, but it is the bearer — in some cases the ONLY bearer — of the phonologically unpredictable and contrastive prosodies, therefore phonemic.

From the Stratal OT point of view, both answers are right. In this theory of grammar, three levels of representation naturally emerge from the phonological computation: (A) The STEM LEVEL is the innermost layer of morphology and phonology. Its constraint system characterizes the form of simple and derived stems, and derivatively via lexicon optimization the form of the roots and affixes from which they are built, so that there is no structural difference between underlying and derived representations at this level. (B) The WORD LEVEL constraint system generates words, and comprises constraints that apply in the span of a word, which in Moloko includes the spread of the palatalization and labialization autosegments to eligible slots. (C) The POSTLEXICAL PHONOLOGY applies to phrases and sentences syntactically generated by combining words, generating PHONETIC REPRESENTATIONS, the interface to speech production and perception.

At the stem level (whose representations I'll put between braces) Moloko has one vowel segment { a } and the autosegments { ʸ } and { ʷ }, formally the feature bundles [–consonantal, –back] and [–consonantal, +back] (hence mutually incompatible and compatible only with vowels). Epenthesis and the spread

---

[6] Perhaps through merger with an *a*-colored consonant inserted to satisfy ONSET.

of the prosodies at the word level produce a system of six vowels /a/, /ɛ/, /ɔ/, /ə/, /ɪ/, /ʊ/. Assuming that the structure-insensitive local assimilation processes that apply across word boundaries are postlexical, they add a seventh vowel [œ] to the repertoire. This is also where prepausal neutralization of height takes effect.

Now we have to settle a terminological matter. What shall we call the elements at the stem and word levels? The term "phoneme" is too handy to give up, but it becomes ambiguous now that we have two significant abstract levels of representation above the phonetic level, not just one as in classical generative phonology. Should we use it for input segments (as in Gravina 2014) or for lexical output segments, such as the six vowels of Moloko (as Gravina 2014: 153 does for the similar Mbuko language)? To avoid confusion I'll refer to the underlying elements as M-PHONEMES (morphophonemes) and to elements in lexical representations (the output of the word phonology) as L-PHONEMES, or LEXICAL PHONEMES. Phonemes in the traditional structuralist sense, not part of the proposed setup, are then S-PHONEMES.

L-phonemes are at once more concrete and more abstract than s-phonemes. As noted above, they are more concrete in that they incorporate redundant features and prosodic properties that are assigned in the lexical phonology. Consider syllable structure. Jakobson (1958) pointed out that all languages have CV syllables.[7] But in most languages syllabification is entirely predictable from the segmental chain, which means that it is not s-phonemic. At the s-phonemic level, such languages therefore have NO syllables, and in particular no CV syllables. More pointedly, some languages have completely predictable and unremarkable CV syllable structure that cannot be assigned at the s-phonemic level, even redundantly, because its segmental substrate is not present there. For example, Kalam words can contain long sequences of consonant phonemes, of which all but the word-final one are automatically syllabified with an epenthetic [ɨ] (for details, see Section 3.1 below), e.g. /pttt/ [ɸɨrɨrɨr] 'quivering' (Pawley & Bulmer 2011). In reality this language has a very strict syllable structure; indeed it is a textbook illustration of syllabic universals and preferences, but it violates almost all of them at the s-phonemic level, and a fortiori at the m-phonemic level.

In the face of such examples, one might consider framing syllabic typology at the phonetic level instead, where the regular syllable structure of a language such as Kalam is patent. But this is not a promising solution in general, for syllables are in general not phonetically characterizable. They are only definable over sequences of discrete phonological segments (see Section 2.2 below).

---

[7] See below for a defense of Jakobson's generalization against claims that some languages have only VC(C) syllables (Section 2.1) and that some languages have no syllables (Section 2.2).

Similarly, if stress falls predictably within words, it has no place in redundancy-free phonemic representations unless it plays a demarcative role at the level of the sentence. For example, if secondary stresses fall predictably on alternating syllables, they are absent from phonemic representations even if they play a role in morphophonology and selection of affix allomorphs. A consequence is that the theory and typology of stress (Hyde 2002, Alber 2005, Kager 2007, and many others) simply cannot be defined on s-phonemic or m-phonemic representations.

Conversely, l-phonemes are more abstract than s-phonemes in other respects. They do not register postlexical sentence-level processes, even when these neutralize contrasts or introduce new derived ones. In particular, the lexical form of a word is not necessarily the same as its isolation form, as we have just seen in Moloko. A better-known example is French, where final consonants, present in the output of the word level since they surface in liaison contexts, are dropped prepausally. Postlexical operations can mask word phonology with respect to syllable structure, lexical stress, and tone, to the point of altering its typological character. Ancient Greek is lexically a tone-to-stress system, while the postlexical component is a stress-to-tone system (Blumenfeld 2004). In preclassical Sanskrit, accent is culminative at the word level: a word has one and only one pitch accent. Postlexically, as a result of deaccentuation and glide formation across word boundaries, a word may be unaccented or have more than one accent. It is the culminative accentuation in the lexical phonology that is the phonologically important property because it is driven by constraints that lie at the core of the accentual phonology. Its loss in the postlexical phonology is the extraneous result of various processes that have no intrinsic connection to each other.

How do we identify the lexical representations of a language? The bottom line is that we have to work out its phonology and morphology. But there are some diagnostic shortcuts. Let us say that a constraint is ACTIVE at a given level if it ranked in such a way that it is visible in at least some derivation, i.e., that the output would be different if it were removed entirely. A constraint that is active at the word level has the following properties: (A) Its domain includes the entire lexical word, not only stems.[8] (B) It interacts transparently with all other word-level constraints. (C) It is asymmetrically bled and fed by stem-level constraints, and hence can render them opaque. (D) It can be rendered opaque by postlexical operations, resulting in derived surface contrasts. (E) It is sensitive to word-level morphology; when words are built recursively, it applies cyclically at each stage, which can lead to derived surface contrasts. (F) It is not sensitive to stem-level morphology. (G) Like all of lexical phonology, it operates on binary feature values

---

[8] Lexical words should be distinguished from postlexical words formed by syntactic processes such as cliticization, which are only subject to the postlexical phonology.

rather than gradient feature values, and its phonological context is defined in terms of binary feature values. Naturally not all these properties can be positively instantiated for every case, but whichever ones can be checked in a language should yield mutually consistent results.

The properties (A)-(G) are not stipulated arbitrarily. They are consequences of the principles of Stratal OT (Kiparsky 2000, to appear, Bermúdez-Otero 2012, 2015). (A) follows because the natural way of restricting a process to the word domain is to restrict the constraints that drive it to the word level ("level 2"). The interaction and non-interaction patterns (B)-(F) are implied by the architecture of the theory and basic OT. Binarity of feature specifications (G) is a property of the entire lexical phonology. Enhancement by new features is possible because Stratal OT has no principle of Structure Preservation, as originally adopted in Lexical Phonology, but soon abandoned in the face of a barrage of counterevidence (Harris 1987, 1990, MacMahon 1991, Borowsky 1993, Hall 1993, Martínez-Gil 1993, Kim 2001, Roca 2005). Structure-preservation in the lexical phonology was an attempt to reconstruct certain structuralist assumptions, with tenuous empirical support and no connection to the rest of the theory.[9] Finally, OT phonology has no constraints that prohibit syllabification. That is, building syllable structure does not incur faithfulness violations.[10] The empirical reason is that such faithfulness constraints would expand the factorial typology to predict nonexisting phonological systems, such as languages with arbitrary phonotactics. In particular, it would defeat the derivation of Jakobson's generalization that CV syllables are universal (Prince & Smolensky 1993).

1.2 Contrastiveness and distinctiveness

The basic concept of classical phonemics is that of phonological contrast, or opposition. A phoneme is defined as a class of non-contrasting sounds. Contrastiveness has been understood in two different ways. In American structuralism, it had to do with CONTRASTIVE DISTRIBUTION. Two sounds were held to contrast in a given phonological environment if they are neither in complementary distribution nor in free variation in that environment, i.e., if the occurrence of either of

---

[9] At the stem level, on the other hand, structure-preservation is a theorem of Stratal OT, because the phonological inventory and stem structure of a language derives from its stem-level constraint system. No special structure-preservation principle is needed. Note further that with the equivalent update, rule-based Lexical Phonology can provide essentially the same kind of rich word phonology as Stratal OT.
[10] REMOVING it by syllabification and desyllabification does; this will become important below.

them in a given context neither excludes nor implies the occurrence of the other in that context (Bloch 1953). Functional approaches (Trubetzkoy 1939, Martinet 1964) equated contrast with phonological RELEVANCE, or DISTINCTIVENESS, the potential of distinguishing utterances as revealed by minimal or near-minimal pairs and the commutation test. In Martinet's formulation (1964: 53), the function of "phonic elements of a language [...] is distinctive or oppositional when they contribute to the identification, at one point of the spoken chain, of one sign as opposed to all the other signs which could have figured at that point if the message has been a different one". The semiotic grounding of this view of the phoneme is apparent.

It has been clear for some time that the distributional and semiotic concepts of contrast don't converge. Two empirical insights led to this conclusion. One is that sounds which contrast in the distributional sense are sometimes perceptually indistinguishable. Labov (1994) documented the phenomenon of NEAR-MERGER, where speakers produce an instrumentally measurable contrast that they cannot perceive, either in the speech of other such speakers or when their own speech is played back to them. An example is the *source : sauce* opposition in some U.S. dialects (Labov 1994, Ch. 12).[11] Independently of this work, it was found that contextual neutralization can be incomplete (Port & O'Dell 1985, Port & Crawford 1989, Dinnsen 1985, Piroth & Janker 2004, Kleber, John, & Harrington 2010). For example, some German speakers pronounce underlying voiced and voiceless obstruents differently in word-final position, but not differently enough to enable hearers to distinguish them reliably. Port and his collaborators showed that German speakers can guess correctly whether a given instance of German [bunt] corresponds to /bund/ 'league' or /bunt/ 'colorful', with more than chance accuracy though far less well than a normal distinctive minimal pair. Berber speakers consistently articulate initial and final geminate voiceless stops longer than singletons, as in *ttut* 'forget him' : *ttutt* 'forget her' : *tut* 'she hit', even though this articulatory difference has no audible effect (Ridouane 2007). These are non-distinctive contrasts.

The second reason for separating contrastiveness and distinctiveness is that distributionally non-contrastive, redundant features can contribute to signaling phonemic distinctions ("the identification of signs" in Martinet's words) and are in that sense phonologically distinctive and relevant. Russian front /i/ and back /ɨ/ are allophones respectively triggered by palatalized and non-palatalized

---

[11] Such near-mergers had been reported in the earlier dialectological literature, though their significance remained unappreciated. For example, DeCamp (1958, 1959) notes near-merger of *four* and *for* in what was then old-fashioned San Francisco speech, since then replaced by complete merger.

consonants. But Jakobson, Fant, & Halle (1952) observed that the phonemic opposition between the consonants is more effectively cued by the vowel allophones that they condition than by the consonants themselves; in a noisy channel only the vocalic cues may be perceived. Moreover, the backness distinction between [i] and [ɨ] is phonologically relevant also in the sense that it actively participates in phonological processes. In the lexical phonology, velars are palatalized before /i/, but postlexically the direction of assimilation is reversed and velars back a following /i/ to [ɨ] like all other [+back] consonants (Rubach 2000, Padgett 2010). Russian /ɨ/ is a non-contrastive but distinctive segment.

One way of thinking of non-contrastive distinctive segments is that they ENHANCE lexical feature contrasts by redundant features, beyond what would result just from coarticulation (Stevens & Keyser 1989, Keyser & Stevens 2006). The enhancements can appear on the contrastive segments themselves or — what is more relevant here — on neighboring segments. They can be more saliently distinctive than the structurally contrastive segments they supplement, and historically more stable, often being precursors of new contrasts that arise by phonologization. Just as the realization of Russian /i/ as [i] or [ɨ] is a cue to the palatalization or velarization of the preceding consonant, English vowel quantity and its diphthongal reflexes (such as "Canadian Raising") are cues to the voicing distinction of coda consonants, Arabic vowel backing and lowering are cues to the pharyngealization ("emphasis") of consonants, etc. Such allophones have been called QUASI-PHONEMES (Ebeling 1960, Korhonen 1969, Liberman 1991, Janda 2003, Scobbie & Stuart-Smith 2008) or QUASI-CONTRASTIVE (Ladd 2006).[12]

Stratal OT separates the distributional property of contrastiveness from the perceptual/functional property of distinctiveness in the following way. Contrastiveness can be characterized at the input. Phonological derivations cannot differentiate identical inputs: they can enhance, neutralize, and displace contrasts, or translate prosodic or morphological differences into segmental oppositions, but they cannot create distinctness from identity. Featural contrastiveness is characterized by the dominant faithfulness constraints at the stem level, the innermost layer of the lexicon. These determine the availability of contrasts in lexical entries, and the extent to which markedness constraints affect the shapes of morphemes and of morpheme combinations at the stem level. Complexity and redundancy are minimized at this level. The sparseness of the input

---

[12] These terms have also been used to refer to contextually restricted contrasts, such as Spanish [r]:[ɾ] intervocalically (Hualde 2005), or Italian [ɛ]:[e] (only stressed syllables), as well as to marginal, "fuzzy" contrasts (Scobbie & Stuart Smith 2008). Currie-Hall (2013) sorts out these various uses.

representations and the invariant underlying form of morphemes presumably serve to facilitate the recognition, acquisition, and retrieval of the lexicon by making it easier to recognize morphological relationships among words.

The distinctiveness of a contrast, on the other hand, is dependent on the derivational level. At the word level, distinctiveness is characterized by the available stem-level inputs (no "freedom of analysis" here anymore!) and by the ranking of faithfulness constraints with respect to the markedness constraints at that level. The promotion of markedness constraints can optimize phonology for perception by enhancing lexical contrasts with redundant features that help the hearer identify them, or neutralize stem-level contrasts, or transpose them by a combination of contextual enhancement and neutralization of the original source of the contrast. Cyclic application or morphological conditioning can create new DERIVED feature contrasts which are not present in lexical representations, e.g., Belfast *winter* vs. *printer* (Wells 1982: 431, Borowsky 1993), British *holey* [hɒʊ.liː] vs. *holy* [hʌʊ.liː] (Harris 1990, MacMahon 1991, Borowsky 1993). The interface between the word-level and postlexical phonology is in principle analogous. Reduction and coarticulation in phonetic implementation minimizes effort in speech production at the cost of distinctiveness. Cases of near contrasts and incomplete neutralization probably arise here.

1.3 The argument from dispersion

We have seen that Moloko has one m-phonemic vowel and six l-phonemic vowels. ALL very sparse vowel systems appear to have a larger, typologically unremarkable symmetrical system of l-phonemic vowels due to the spread of vocalic features from prosodies or from adjacent consonants. The evidence will be laid out in Section 3. The l-phonemic systems usually resemble the reconstructed vowel systems of the languages' earlier stages or the current ones of related or neighboring languages, which suggests that they are more stable than the m-phonemic systems. Although the additional l-phonemic vowels are predictable, they are usually at least as perceptually salient as the site of the contrastive features that trigger them, if not more so, and can be as "psychologically real" to the speakers. In such cases, the segmentalist extraction of redundancies arguably obscures the way the language works.

Dispersion Theory holds that phonological systems maximize the perceptual distinctiveness of contrasts. At the s-phonemic level, so-called vertical vowel systems don't have this property. Lindblom (1986, 1990) and Flemming (1995) propose to reconcile vertical vowel systems with Dispersion Theory by appealing to a conflicting pressure for minimally complex articulations, which is best satisfied by central vowels such as /ɨ/ and /ə/ (see also Padgett & Ní Chiosáin 2001, Kaplan 2011 et al., among others). Factorial typology then predicts that there should be vocalic systems in which this markedness constraint dominates dispersion (MINDIST) constraints, consisting of only "minimally complex" central vowels. Such vowel inventories are however not attested either phonetically or in the output of the lexical phonology of any language.[13] In reality, all languages exploit the major dimensions of the vowel space, including the F2 dimension by distinguishing front and back vocalic l-phonemes (including Kabardian and Marshallese, see Section 4 below). What is special about so-called vertical vowel systems is that their peripheral vowels are derived in the word phonology rather than underlying; they are l-phonemes rather than m-phonemes.[14]

A more interesting class of apparent exceptions are certain Papua New Guinea languages, whose high vowels have been phonemically analyzed as underlying consonantal non-syllabic /y/ and /w/. I argue in Section 3.1 that they are underlyingly indifferent with respect to syllabicity and appear in both nuclear and marginal positions as required by the language's stringent syllable structure. When syllabification is taken into account, all these languages have /i/ and /u/.

For lexical representations, we may therefore remove the *if*-clause from Hyman's (2008) Vocalic Universal #5, quoted in (3).

(3) A vowel system may be contrastive only for aperture only if its vowels acquire vowel color from neighboring consonants.

We replace (3) with the categorical (4).

(4) All vowel systems have distinctive color and aperture.

---

13 There are of course vertical subsystems consisting of minimally complex reduced central vowels, such as English /ɨ/ and /ə/ (*Rosa's roses*). Irish has a subsystem of three short vowels /ɯ/, /ɵ/, /a/, plus six long vowels /iː/, /ɵː/, /uː/, /eː/, /aː/, /oː/ (Ó Siadhail 1989: 35–37). /ɯ/, /ɵ/ have back allophones [u] and [o] respectively before broad (velarized) consonants and front allophones [i] and [e] before slender (palatalized) consonants, e.g. /lʲɯm/ → [lʲum] 'with me', /lʲɯNʲ/ → [lʲiNʲ] 'with us'.
14 Even in vertical systems, when the non-low vowels are not colored by a consonant or prosody, they are often front rather than central. In the two-vowel system of Arrernte, the non-high vowel appears as [i] in initial position where there is no consonant to influence it, and Hale therefore set it up as /i/ (quoted in Green 1994: 35). Wichita has a three-vowel system /i/, /e/, /a/, with three degrees of length; phonetically also [o] and [u]. /i/ ranges between [i] and [e], /e/ between [ɛ] and [æ], and /a/ between low back unrounded [ɑ] and (when short) [ʌ] as in *but*, with rounding next to /w/, rarely [u] (Rood 1975). In the variety of Kabardian described by Colarusso (1992, 2006), the vowels transcribed as [ə] and [ɨ] are actually front vowels.

This means that at the level of lexical representations there are no one-dimensional vowel systems, whether vertical or horizontal. Minimal vowel systems are triangular, making use of both the front/back dimension and the high/low dimension. To this we can now add the more specific substantive generalization (5).

(5) All vowel systems have at least a low vowel and two non-low vowels. One of the non-low vowels is a front unrounded high vowel, the other is back.

An apparent counterexample to (4) and (5) is Qawasqar (a Fuegian language), which UPSID cites as having the phonemes /ə, o, a/. But Clairis (1977), UPSID's source, represents them as /e, o, a/, and says that /e/ has the allophones [i], [x] (devoicing?), [ɯ], [ə], [e], [æ], [a], of which [ə] is the most frequent (hence UPSID's /ə/). Clairis moreover says that [i] tends to be stable in certain words, and proposes that /i/ is a distinct phoneme in those words. If this is correct, Qawasqar has a non-minimal four-vowel system /i, e, o, a/ of a common type (as in Campa, Klamath, Malagasy, Mazatec, Nahuatl, Tacana).

1.4 The argument from symmetry and from the loss of generalization

When phonemics is integrated into a derivational morphophonemics, the divergence between contrastiveness and distinctiveness gives rise to a well-known formal problem. One of the first mentions of it in the literature occurs in Bloomfield's description of Menomini height assimilation:

> If postconsonantal y, w, or any one of the high vowels, i, ī, u, ū, follows anywhere in the word, the vowels ē and ō are raised to ī and ū [...] Since ū occurs only in this alternation, it is not a full phoneme. (Bloomfield 1939: ¶35).

So, ē → ī in (6a) and ō → ū in (6b) are parallel, but the former is morphophonemic and the latter allophonic, since ū is in complementary distribution with ō.

(6) a. /mayēček-waʔ/ → mayīčekwaʔ 'that which they eat'
    b. /ātɛʔhnōhk-uwɛw/ → ātɛʔnūhkuwɛw 'he tells him a sacred story'.

Bloomfield called Menomini ū a SEMI-PHONEME; other writers have used the term QUASI-PHONEME. We can now define these as l-phonemes which are not m-phonemes.

The phonemic level must mark the contrastive distinction between ī and ē and exclude the redundant, predictable one between ū and ō. But if we want the derivation from morphophonemics to phonetics to pass through a phonemic level, we must split raising into a morphophonemic rule ē → ī (solid arrow in (7)) and an allophonic rule ō → ū (dashed arrow), although they are obviously the same process.

(7)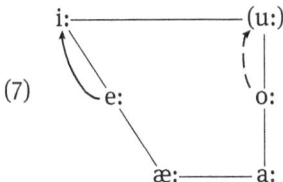

A formally identical English case was noted by Bloch (1941).

Although this duplication problem did not attract attention at the time, it led to a crisis in phonemic theory when it was raised by Halle (1959: 22) and Chomsky (1964) as an objection to any intermediate phonemic level (Anderson 2000). Crucially, THIS PROBLEM DOES NOT ARISE IN STRATAL OT. At any given level, the available contrasts are defined by the ranking of the relevant faithfulness and markedness constraints. Schematically, the asymmetric underlying vowel system of Menomini comes from a constraint — call it *ū — that dominates IDENT(High) in the stem phonology, thereby suppressing the height contrast between ū and ō. In the word phonology, both *ū and IDENT(High) are dominated by height assimilation, whose activation brings in the new l-phoneme. In this way the grammar formally characterizes both the neutralization of the contrast between ū and ō in the stem phonology (which makes the height specification irrelevant in input representations), and the derived distinction between them in the word phonology.

The activation of context-sensitive markedness constraints not only enhances feature distinctions and maximizes dispersion, but creates more symmetric inventories, and maximizes feature economy in the sense of Clements (2001, 2003). Like dispersion, symmetry and feature economy are tendencies of phonological systems, not absolute requirements, but they are quantifiable and statistically verifiable, as shown for feature economy by Clements (2003), and legitimate criteria for adjudicating between different phonemic solutions. I venture the following conjectures:

(8) a. L-phoneme inventories are never less symmetrical than m-phoneme inventories.
 b. L-phoneme inventories are never less dispersed than m-phoneme inventories.

Jimi (another Central Chadic language) makes an instructive comparison with Moloko. It has three basic underlying vowels, {i}, {ə}, {a}, plus long {i:} and {a:} (Gravina 2010: 134–139). Unlike Moloko, it has no general vowel harmony, and its vowels are not normally affected by adjacent consonants, e.g. (9a,b,c), EXCEPT that {ə} becomes [i], [u] after {j}, {w} or next to {ʔʷ}, {ʔʲ}, as in (9d-g), and {a} becomes [e] after {rʲ}, {lʲ}, as in (9h,i).

(9) a. {pʷabʷ-ən}   [pʷabʷ ən]   'baobab flower'
    b. {mʲəliŋ}   [mʲəliŋ]   'nine'
    c. {pətʲak-ən} [pətʲak ən]   'type of antelope'
    d. {jən-ən}   [jinən]   'head'
    e. {wənʲ-ən}   [wunʲən]   'to sleep'
    f. {bavəʔʷ-ən} [bavuʔun]   'scar'
    g. {tsʲigəʔʲ-ən} [tʃiⁿgiʔin] 'head (millet)'
    h. {lʲam-ən}   [lemən]   'to get into a state'
    i. {kərʲa-n}   [kərən]   'to bring'

Since {i} is an independent phoneme, whereas [u] and [e] are allophones occurring only in the contexts just mentioned, a split derivation would again be required to reconstruct an s-phonemic level. As in (7), the processes marked by dashed lines introduce new l-phonemes, increasing both symmetry and dispersion.

(10)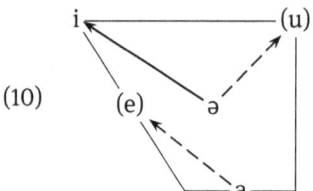

Unlike Menomini, Jimi does not achieve perfect symmetry. {a} is never raised to {o} due to a gap in the consonant inventory. Jimi has no labialized alveolars, so that the process that produces [e] after {rʲ}, {lʲ} has no corresponding labial triggers *{rʷ}, *{lʷ}.

1.5 The argument from diachrony: Sound change, analogy, borrowing

The concept of a quasi-phoneme originated in the literature on sound change and phonologization, as part of the effort to solve the problem why allophonic distinctions sometimes remain unaffected when their conditioning environments disappear, and become phonemic instead (Ebeling 1960, Korhonen 1969, Liberman 1991, Janda 2003). The idea was that this happens when they for some reason have acquired "quasi-phonemic" status before the environment changes — in Stratal OT terms, when they have become l-phonemes by the criteria (A)-(G) in Section 1.1. The allophones are already distinctive, but not yet contrastive. If sound changes are initiated postlexically (as must be assumed for many independent reasons) they do not affect lexical representations (Bermúdez-Otero 2015, Kiparsky 2015). This follows from the feed-forward relation between the strata.

When a phonological opposition first becomes distinctive at the word level, there is no contrastive input from the stem level to realize it. If it is instantiated at all, it is not by inputs from the stem level, but by types of lexemes that don't go through the stem phonology. This is where marginal phonemes can enter the word phonology. These are of three types: (A) non-lexical categories, including function words and interjections; (B) loan vocabulary, in so far as it is unassimilated, as is independently diagnosable by the unavailability of stem-level morphology for it; and (C) word-level derivatives, where opacity can arise through cyclic application of phonology ("analogy"). And these are indeed exactly the contexts where new distinctions in a language first appear. The Menomini quasi-phoneme [u:] appears out of its triggering context in interjections, loanwords, and for some innovating speakers by analogical generalization from raising contexts (Bloomfield 1962: ¶1.16). In English, phonological properties of simple words are almost always retained in their word-level derivatives; e.g., the lengthened vocalic nucleus of monosyllabic words is inherited by their polysyllabic word-level derivatives (*cart, carter* vs. *Carter*). Contrasts such as *bible* (short diphthong) vs. *libel* (long diphthong) have emerged in some varieties of English (Scobbie & Stuart-Smith 2008).[15]

I conjecture that all phonemes arise as l-phonemes. They remain when a sound change makes their conditioning environment opaque (whereas postlexical allophones disappear), and become contrastive ("phonologized", in Praguian terms) when their distribution can no longer be predicted. This is essentially equivalent to Hyman's (1976, 2008) proposal of an automatic → extrinsic → phonemic trajectory of phonological alternations. Correspondingly, we may suppose that all mergers pass through a near-contrast stage. The phenomenon of DISPLACED CONTRAST is a combination of merger and phonologization.

Adapting loanwords involves not only approximating their pronunciation with native phonetic resources, but rendering the donor language's contrasts as

---

15 These are nominal exceptions to Stieber's Law, which says that allophonic features cannot spread by analogy (see Manaster-Ramer 1994). But if Stieber's Law is taken as a generalization about l-phonemes, it may well be exceptionless.

best you can. In this task l-phonemes can be seen in action. Hsieh, Kenstowicz, & Mou (2009) (see also Kenstowicz & Louriz 2009) show that Mandarin Chinese borrowers, using "reverse engineering", privilege the salient allophonic (in my terms l-phonemic) vowel distinction over the less salient phonemic distinction between the nasal codas. With only one s-phonemic low vowel /a/, pronounced [æ] before /n/ and [ɑ] before /ŋ/, Mandarin cannot express the four-way English distinction *ran* : *rang* : *Ron* : *wrong*. It chooses to map it into the available two-way distinction as in (11a), giving up the /n/ : /ŋ/ contrast in order to maintain the [æ] : [ɑ] contrast.

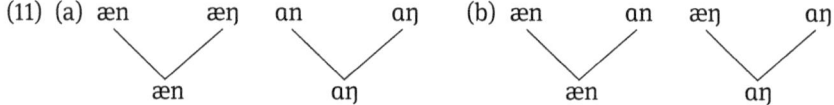

Thus *Dan* : *Don* would be rendered as [dæn] : [dɑŋ], while *ban* : *bang* would both be [bæn]. By the criteria laid out in Section 1.1, /æ/ and /ɑ/ are distinct l-phonemes in Mandarin, present in lexical representations just as /n/ and /ŋ/ are. The loan phonology privileges the front/back feature on vowels over the corresponding consonantal feature on nasal codas. Presumably the vocalic distinction is perceptually more salient than the consonantal distinction, as in the case of the Russian. Postlexical allophones are not used for such "reverse engineering" because they are not represented in the lexical phonology and unavailable for manipulation by speakers. For example, English borrowings from Chinese don't render tones by consonant voicing, although this might well produce approximations of at least some Chinese tonal contrasts.

1.6 The argument from poetic convention and language games

The artistic use of language, not just versification but also text-setting and language games, involves superimposing a second layer of constraints on already structured linguistic representations. In so far as it relates to phonology, the relevant level is obviously neither underlying representations and phonetics but somewhere in between.[16] The identity is not between s-phonemes, but l-phonemes provide the right representations, at least in many interesting cases. Here briefly are two telling examples.

---

16 For example, *artificial* and *beneficial* rhyme, even though they differ underlyingly ({-s-} vs. {-t-}), and *keep* and *coop* alliterate, even though their initial consonants differ phonetically in backness.

The classical rules of French versification, which remained normative into the twentieth century, stipulate that consonants that are deleted in word-final position count for purposes of rhyme, except that homorganic final voiced and voiceless obstruents are treated as equivalent. For example, *long* and *tronc* rhyme, but neither of them rhymes with *rond* or *pont*, which however rhyme with each other; none of them rhyme with *son*. Phonetically all five words end the same way, and traditional phonemics would reflect that: /tʁõ/ [tʁõ], /lõ/ [lõ], /mõ/ [mõ], /ʁõ/ [ʁõ], /sõ/ [sõ]. Morphophonologically they all end differently: {tronk}, {long}, {pont}, {rond}, {son} — the consonant shows up before suffixes, as in *tronquer, longue, ponter, ronde, sonner*. It is only in lexical representations that the two rhyming pairs match correctly: because of final devoicing at the word level, *long* and *tronc* both end in /-k/, and *dont* and *rond* both end in /-t/. The evidence that final devoicing of stops takes effect at the word level whereas final deletion is postlexical is that, in the classical *liaison* system (now as old-fashioned as the rhyming convention that reflects it) final voiced stops appear in devoiced form before a following vocalic word in close contact, e.g. *long hiver* [lɔ̃.ki.vɛʁ] 'long winter', *grand homme* [grã.tɔm] 'great man'. Therefore they must enter the postlexical phonology with the final consonant present but in devoiced form. In sum, traditional French versification conventions crucially refer to the lexical representation that is computed by the word phonology and forms the input to the sentence phonology:

(12) – Underlying (morphophonemic representation): {tʁonk}, {long}, {pont}, {ʁond}, {son}
 – Lexical representation: /tʁõk/, /lõk/, /põt/, /ʁõt/, /son/
 – Phonetic (and structuralist phonemic) representation: [tʁõ], [lõ], [põ], [ʁõ], [sõ]

That the rhyming conventions could outlive the sixteenth century pronunciation they reflect for centuries is presumably due to the fact that the living morphophonology of the language kept them intelligible.

Guimarães & Nevins (2013) used invented language games to probe whether Brazilian Portuguese nasal vowels are synchronically derived from vowel+nasal sequences, or underlying. Their experiments showed that the four nonlow nasal vowels [ĩ, ẽ, õ, ũ] are derived, whereas the low nasal vowel [ɐ̃] is an underlying segment. What accounts for this phonological difference? The phonetic difference between the plain and nasalized low vowel that G&N appeal to can hardly justify it. But there are some phonological processes, not mentioned by G&N, which show the low nasal vowel behaving differently from the non-low nasal vowels in a way which suggests that /ã/, unlike the other nasal vowels, is an l-phoneme. Stems in {-an-} regularly contract with a following ending {-a}, e.g. *sã* [sẽ] 'sane' (fem.), from /san-a/ (cf. masc. *são* [sẽw̃], from /san-u/). {-Vn-}stems where V is some other vowel than /a/ keep the stem form under these circumstances, e.g. *dona* [ˈdonɐ] 'lady', from /don-a/ (masc. *don* [dõ], from /don-u/), or in exceptional cases delete the nasal, e.g. *boa* [boɐ] 'good' /bon-a/ (masc. *bom* [bõ] /bon-u/). This distribution falls out if the low nasal vowel is formed at the stem level, whereas the other nasal vowels are formed postlexically.

(13) a. {san-} → /sẽ/ → /sẽ-a/ → [sẽ]
   b. {don-} → /don-a/ → [ˈdonɐ]

2 Syllabification

2.1 Arrernte

Arrernte (an Arandic language of Australia) has been claimed to have only VC(C) syllables (Breen & Pensalfini 1999 [B&P], Pensalfini 1998, Tabain et al. 2004). Evans & Levinson (2009: 434) cite B&P's work as "a clear demonstration that Arrernte organizes its syllables around a VC(C) structure and does not permit consonantal onsets [...] An initially plausible pattern turns out not to be universal after all, once the range of induction is sufficiently extended". VC(C) is indeed the most marked syllable type since it violates ONSET, NOCODA, and *COMPLEX, and contradicts the following generalizations (and Jakobson's CV universal):

(14) a. All languages have syllables with onsets.
   b. All languages have open syllables.
   c. All languages that have syllables with complex codas have syllables with simple codas.
   d. All languages have syllables with simple onsets.

B&P's claim that all Arrernte syllables lack onsets is about UNDERLYING representations. About 25% of words as actually pronounced begin with a consonant. Their analysis posits that they have an underlying initial /e-/, which is then deleted. Their claim that all Arrernte syllables are closed is likewise about UNDERLYING representations. According to Henderson & Dobson (1994: 23) "nearly all Arrernte phonological words end in a central vowel, though this vowel need not be pronounced, and is often absent in sandhi when another vowel follows". H&D's transcription implies a phonemicization that is consistent with all four universals in (14).

It has no underlying unpronounced initial /e-/, and posits final /-e/ where it is pronounced. (15) shows B&P's analysis in the first column, and H&D's in the second, with the actual pronunciation in the third.

(15) B&P   H&D
    /emp/   mpe   [mpɐ]   'let's go!'
    /em.eɳ/   meɳe   [mə́ɳə]   'food'
    /ekʷ.atʸ/ kʷa·tʸe [kʷáɟ(e)] 'water'
    /inəkə/   ineke   [e.nə́.kə] 'let's go!'

So Arrernte's syllable structure violates (14) at most in underlying representations, and then only under B&P's analysis which posits underlying forms with initial vowels and final consonants that undergo aphaeresis and paragoge, not under H&D's analysis.[17] Let us consider the evidence for B&P's analysis.

B&P's first argument for their morphophonological analysis is based on the generalization that the first syllable of a word is stressed, except if it is onsetless, in which case the second syllable is stressed. For if all words are assumed to begin with underlying V-, as in the first column of (15), stress can just be assigned to the second underlying syllable.[18] But an equally simple stress rule exploits the well-documented weakness of onsetless syllables, which causes them to be unstressable in some languages (Burzio 1994: 158, Downing 1998, Ryan 2014). Unambiguous evidence for this treatment of the Arrernte-type pattern comes from Iowa-Ota stress. In this language words are stressed on the first syllable, except if it has no onset, in which case they are stressed on the second syllable (Topintzi 2010: 58 ff., with other examples of this pattern).

(16) a. ˈpe.ce   'fire'
     b. ˈhe.ro.ta   'morning'
     c. a.ˈha.ta   'outtide'
     b. i.ˈtʰa   'there'

Iowa-Ota has the same stress pattern as Arrernte, but it cannot be reduced to second-syllable stress by positing deleted initial vowels. Finnish secondary stress

---

17 The same is true of the similar earlier claim about the syllable structure of the Kunjen dialects (Sommer 1970a, 1970b). As Sommer makes clear in the latter article, their output syllabification actually conforms to Jakobson's CV generalization.

18 Two other ways to simplify stress have been proposed, also with strange syllable structure. Topintzi & Nevins (2017) make initial consonants in Arrernte moraic, with stress falling on the second mora, so that [mə́ɳə] is /m_μə́_μ.ɳə_μ/ and [e.nə́.kə] is /e_μ.nə́_μ.kə_μ/. Schwartz (2013) assigned vowels a "vocalic onset node" (≈ null onset), with other onset consonants being excluded by *COMPLEXONSET.

exhibits the same pattern. Four-syllable words normally get a stress on the third syllable, except if it is onsetless, e.g. *á.te.ri.a* 'meal', *kómp.pa.ni.a* '(military) company' (Karvonen 2005). KiKerewe demonstrates the prosodic defectiveness of onsetless syllables in several different ways: they are light, tonally defective, and do not induce compensatory lengthening when desyllabified (Odden 1995). Regardless of how the unstressability of onsetless syllables is modeled,[19] it undermines the argument for abstract /V-/ in Arrernte.

The second argument adduced by B&P for VC(C) syllabification in Arrernte is based on the plural/reciprocal suffix. After a stem with an odd number of syllables, the suffix is *-err* or *-errirr*. After a stem with an even number of syllables, the suffix is *-irr*. Stems of more than one syllable can also have the optional allomorph *-ewarr*. The syllable count comes out right if an initial vowel is posited in words that begin with consonants, so that (17a) begins in /eʈ-/ and (17c) begins in /ekʷern/.[20]

(17) a. ʈ-**érr**(irr)   'poke'
     b. aʈ-**érr**(irr)   'grind'
     c. kʷérn-**irr**, kʷérn-**ewàrr**   'swallow'
     d. akʷérn-**irr**, akʷérn-**ewàrr** 'insert'
     e. alʷárerrn-**èrr**(irr)   'leave for later'

The obvious alternative is that the allomorphy is stress-conditioned: the allomorph *-err-* must head a foot, the allomorphs *-irr* and *-ewarr* cannot.[21]

B&P's third argument is that the reduplication pattern of the frequentative indicates VC(C) syllabification.

(18) empʷarr-em   'is making'   empʷarr**eparr**-em 'keeps making'
     akemir-em   'is getting up'   akemir**epir**-em   'keeps getting up'
     unt-em   'is running'   unt**epunt**-em   'keeps running'

For B&P, the frequentative suffix consists of a disyllabic foot, the first syllable pre-specified as *-ep-*, the second a copy of the final VC(C) syllable of the root. But this is a weak argument because prosodic morphology normally does not

---

[19] On one analysis onsetless syllables can be adjoined to an adjacent syllable to form a "sesquisyllabic" complex (Kiparsky 2003).
[20] Orthographic *rr* denotes an alveolar tap or trill, *r* a retroflex approximant [ɻ] (transcribed as ɻ in Pensalfini's and Breen's work). *rn*, *rt* are retroflex [ɳ], [ʈ]. The orthography uses *h* to mark dental place of articulation in *th*, *nh* etc. I have replaced them by the IPA symbols to prevent confusion with aspiration.
[21] Compare stress-sensitive root allomorphy in Italian, e.g. *vádo, andáte, andáre* (Kiparsky 1996).

involve copying prosodic constituents of the base. Rather, affixes are prosodic templates (defined by constraints) that get their unspecified segmental content from the base (McCarthy & Prince 1986). If the syllable structure of the reduplicant is fixed by the reduplication morpheme itself, then it can't tell us anything about the syllabification of the base. The argument is further undermined by Pensalfini's (1998) observation that the same type of reduplication exists in Jingulu, which uncontroversially has CV syllabification, and therefore in any case requires some such alternative analysis. A straightforward formulation consistent with the theory of Prosodic Morphology is that the suffix is /-epVC/, with VC filled by the closest part of the stem melody, e.g. /empʷarr/ → empʷarr-epVC → *empʷarr-eparr*.

The fourth argument, from the play language Rabbit Talk, is especially intriguing:[22]

(19) Ordinary speech   Rabbit Talk
     ampá**ŋkem**   **aŋkem**amp   'moan-PRES'
     iŋw**ę́nt̪**   **ęnt̪**iŋw   'tomorrow'
     (e)nʸtʸ**ę́n**ʸ**em**   (e)**nʸemen**ʸtʸ   'smell-PRES'

It looks like the initial syllable of the word, VC(C) in B&P's analysis, is moved to the end. But an unproblematic alternative is that the word rhyme (the portion of the word that includes the stressed vowel and everything that follows it, boldfaced in (19)) is flipped with the residue (prosodic circumscription), viz. (amp)(áŋkem) → *aŋkem-amp*.[23]

There is substantial positive evidence that Arrernte words do exhibit the universal preference for CV. One indication comes from the rendering of English loanwords. They insert a vowel after a final consonant, not before an initial consonant as the VC(C) syllable canon would predict.

(20) parrike   'paddock'   (*eparrik)
      t̪ay(e)te   'side'   (*et̪ayt)
      pʷelerte   'bullet'   (*epʷelert)

Arrernte songs categorically prefer CV. "In the Arandic [song] tradition, quite generally, the consonant of a line-final suffix [...] is transferred to the beginning of the line following, so that each line begins with a consonant, even if the actual Arandic word heading the line is vowel initial [...]" (Hale 1984). Turpin (2012) moreover observes: "All sung syllables have an onset. [...] creating a poetic line

---
22 The last two examples are from Breen; thanks to Toni Borowsky for passing them on.
23 The sources don't reveal the stress of the Rabbit Talk forms; my guess is that they stay on the same syllable as in the original word, e.g. *áŋkemamp*.

involves either deleting the line-initial vowel ([ɐˈn̪t̪əpə] → [ˈn̪t̪əpə] 'pigeon') or inserting a consonant ([ɐˈləmə] → [ˈwɐləmə] 'stomach')."

Postlexical syllabification shows CV preference as well. At the sentence level, ONSET and NOCODA are maximized:

(21) amp   eŋkʷiṉ   et̪   aṟek   aMeṟek → [am.peŋ.kʷi.ṉe.t̪a.ṟe.ka.Me.ṟe.kə]
      child   your   I   see-PAST camp-at
      'I saw your child at the camp' (Pensalfini 1998, from Green 1994)

Moreover, epenthesis is obligatory in phrase-final position and *e-* never occurs phrase-initially. This led Pensalfini (1998) to partially retract the B&P analysis at least for the phrasal level. However the arguments presented here seem to me to invalidate it for the word level too, and for any level of representation. Not only do Arrernte's lexical and postlexical phonological processes actively FAVOR CV syllables, but the claim that its output inventory of syllable types is derived from underlying representations that have exclusively VC(C) syllables is difficult to sustain.[24]

2.2 The universality of syllables

Hyman (1985, 2011, 2015) argues that Gokana has no phonological rules or constraints that must refer to syllable structure: its phonotactics and phonological alternations can all be stated in terms of segments and moras. Not all of them HAVE to be stated that way, and the assumption that Gokana has syllables would entail no complications, lost generalizations, or violations of typological expectations, such as anti-syllabic phonotactics. There might be cases where the syllabification is indeterminate, as Hyman notes, in which case the theory would dictate the least marked syllable structure.

Hyman's point, then, is not that Gokana cannot have syllables but that nothing is gained by positing syllable structure in it; all the action is in the moras. Gokana is not the only language where the syllable plays second fiddle to the mora: Japanese is another one, and the existence of syllables in Japanese has likewise been doubted (Labrune 2012, but see Kubozono 2003, Kawahara 2012).

As Hyman is careful to note, a language can have syllables even if they play no role in its phonology. Not every phonological property of a language need be

---

[24] Another case where theorizing has been led astray by a misconstrual of abstract phonemic and morphophonemic representations as phonetic transcriptions are Tundra Nenets word-final stops (Kiparsky 2006).

involved in its phonotactics and phonological alternations. It would be no more surprising for a language to lack phonological processes involving syllable structure than for it to lack phonological processes involving vowel height.

Like feet, syllables meet more scepticism and outright rejection than larger prosodic groupings such as phrases, both from linguists (Steriade 1999) and from phoneticians (Kohler 1966, Ohala 1990, Ohala & Kawasaki-Fukumori 1997). The main reason is probably that in many languages they are not phonetically demarcated, at least in casual speech, nor directly identifiable by some cross-linguistically invariant property. (The same is true of segments, as Hyman reminds me.) The syllable is not the sole domain of coarticulation, nor a "puff of air", nor a "chest pulse".[25] As Anderson (1982: 546) states, "the facts of acoustics and of articulatory co-articulation make it quite impossible to segment and identify the speech stream directly in terms of such units". Rather, syllables, their constituents, and the boundaries between them are manifested in multiple ways by their phonological effects, and it is the explanatory connections that can be based on this construct that justify it.

It is true that many generalizations involving syllables can be restated without reference to syllables, and doubters have sought to show that such restatements are in some cases as insightful or even more so. Certainly the early arguments for syllable structure in generative phonology, first as a feature (Chomsky & Halle 1968), then as a boundary marker (Vennemann 1972), and finally a constituent (Kahn 1976), were not conclusive. For example, the argument that syllable structure eliminates disjunctive environments such as "before a consonant or word boundary" is not sufficient because the generalization could be be equally well and possibly better addressed by sophisticated competitors to syllabic formulations. Some syllable effects can be expressed in terms of moras (Hyman 1985) or feet.

Even in languages such as Chinese, where syllables are well demarcated in speech, restrictions on codas and onsets could be reformulated in terms of postvocalic and prevocalic position.[26]

---

[25] This is not to say that syllabicity has no phonetic correlates. For example, Fougeron & Ridouane (2008) find that Tashlhiyt syllabic consonants are not longer than non-syllabic consonants, but they are less coarticulated.

[26] Tellingly, even Pāṇini, whose rich descriptive apparatus includes phonological and morphological features, ordered rules, constraints, blocking, Theta-roles, linking, and inheritance hierarchies, among others, did not use syllables, even though Sanskrit very clearly has them (Kessler 1994); they simply would not have made his grammar shorter. This is a case of the ICEBERG PROBLEM, fatal for the project of "describing each language on its own terms": a single language, however rich and precise the description, cannot reveal all aspects of UG.

The most persuasive argument for the syllable as a constituent is that it ties together a number of phenomena that competing syllable-less theories can only deal with separately in a disconnected way (Vaux & Wolfe 2009).

1. Distinctive syllabification, e.g. Finnish *hau.is.sa* 'in pikes' vs. *ha.uis.sa* 'in searches', English ˌ*ant.ˈac.id* vs. *fan.ˈtas.tic*, respectively with unaspirated coda *t* and aspirated onset *t*. These are predictable from the morphology, but syllabification can also be contrastive, as marginally in Sanskrit, where some words have inherent hiatus, e.g. trisyllabic *ti.ta.u-* 'sieve' (vs. disyllabic *da.dau* 'gave'). These pairs do not differ as to mora count.
2. Differences between onset and rhyme position, e.g. British aspiration or light vs. dark *l*, and ambisyllabicity in the corresponding American cases (Gussenhoven 1986).
3. Stressability. Polish ˈ*krvi* is monosyllabic. Polish has penult word stress, so if the word were disyllabic, we'd expect *ˈ*kr̩vi*. Serbo-Croatian *kr̩ˈvi* is disyllabic; in Serbo-Croatian, syllabic *r* can bear stress and pitch accent like vowels do.
4. Syllable counting, e.g., alternating stress, allomorphy dependent on even/odd parity.
5. Sonority sequencing: syllable boundaries as sonority troughs, nuclei as sonority peaks.
6. Restrictions on syllable size.
7. Differences between open and closed syllables (not reducible to syllable weight because heavy syllables can be open and light syllables can be closed).
8. Prosodic morphology: reduplication, infixation, truncation.
9. Language use: text-setting in song and chanting, language games, speech errors.

Obviously not all of these manifestations of syllable structure will exist in a given language. But when they do, they converge.[27]

---

[27] A caveat: syllable structure can change in the course of a derivation. The more careful formulation has to be that it must be consistent at any given level of representation. For example, in English *rhythm, spasm, plasm* are monosyllabic at the stem level. If the nasal were syllabic at this level, it would get stressed in words like *rhýthm-ic* (cf. *átom, atómic*), and words like *éctoplàsm, ángiospàsm, cýtoplàsm, cátaclàsm, hólophràsm*, would be stressed on the second part, on the pattern of *èctoparásite, àngiothlípsis, èndotóxin, cỳtocóccus, càtatónia, hòmophóbia, hòmomórphism*, rather than on the pattern of *éctomòrph, ángiospèrm, éndolỳmph, cýtocỳst, péricàrp, hómophòbe, hómomòrph*. Spanish [je] is a diphthong in the lexical phonology and behaves as a heavy syllable for purposes of stress, but postlexically [j-] is resyllabified from the nucleus into the onset, as shown by its allophonic realization (Harris & Kaisse 1999).

Suppose that Gokana has none of these things — no distinctive or contrastive syllabification, no audible syllable boundaries, no processes or constraints that distinguish onsets from codas, or count syllables, or are sensitive to syllable boundaries, or constrain the size of syllables, no evidence for syllables in versification or slogan-chanting, at least nothing that could not also be stated in terms of moras. Then is Gokana a language without syllables, or does it just not wear its syllable structure on its sleeve? In the absence of instrumental evidence, which might one day help decide the question (Fn. 25), we have to rely on phonological arguments. Let's consider the pros and cons.

Hyman's idea that Gokana does not HAVE syllables, only moras, is based on an *ex silentio* argument advanced in a more general context by Clements (2001: 72). The idea is that languages have syllable structure only when it is "activated", which is to say when it is "needed in order to express generalizations about the phonological system", such as phonotactic restrictions or phonological alternations (Hyman 2011). But this actually leads to an argument FOR syllables in Gokana: they explain many of its phonological properties that would otherwise remain arbitrary. Gokana obeys ALL cross-linguistic generalizations about syllable structure, including the ones in (14) and Jakobson's universal. Also, Gokana syllables are maximally bimoraic, and *COMPLEX is unviolated. Vowel-initial words get a predictable glottal stop, indicating that ONSET is active. It tolerates codas, but so do most languages. Gokana syllable structure is about as vanilla as can be. What makes it look odd is the frequency of hiatus, reflected in its long sequences of vowels, including identical vowels, apparently without rearticulation or other clues to syllable boundaries. Such examples don't per se argue against syllables, because they also occur in languages that unquestionable have syllables. For example, Finnish has hiatus, e.g. *vaa'an* [vaː.an] 'scale' (gen.) vs. *vaan* 'but, however', disyllabic *häät* [hæ.æt] 'carbon monoxides' vs. monosyllabic *häät* [hæːt] 'wedding(s)' (certainly contrastive, but probably not distinctive in normal speech), and long sequences of vowels such as *hääyöaie* [hæː.yø.ai.e] 'wedding night intention', but that doesn't warrant the conclusion that Finnish has no syllable structure — on the contrary, syllables are hugely important in Finnish phonology and allomorphy.

There are also a number of Gokana-specific facts that syllables help make sense of:

(22) a. Roots have the shapes CV, CVV, CVC, CVCV, but not *CVVV. Analysis: they are minimally a syllable and maximally a bimoraic foot, satisfying ONSET.

b. Derivational suffixes can have the shape -V or -CV. Analysis: they are minimal (light) syllables.

c. Prosodic stems may be of the form CV, CVC, CVV, CVCV, CVVCV, CVVCVV, CVVVV, but not *CVVVCV, *CVCVVV. They are maximally disyllabic (disyllabic trochees), as Hyman himself notes. Since Gokana syllables are maximally bimoraic, the restrictions follow.[28]
d. Gokana has CV-reduplication. Analysis: the Gokana reduplicant is a minimal (light) syllable, a very common type of reduplication as predicted by Prosodic Morphology (McCarthy & Prince 1986, 1993).

Such constraints are obviously helpful to hearers and learners in parsing the morphological structure of word. These data undermine even the weaker claim that Gokana CAN be analyzed adequately without syllables.

According to Hyman (2008), "imposing an arbitrary syllabification [on the word kẽẽẽẽẽẽ] adds nothing to our understanding of Gokana". I find this argument unconvincing for two reasons. First, the syllabification would NOT be arbitrary, for it would have to be compatible with the language's constraints, including the ones in (22). Secondly, it seems too much to ask that the syllabification of EVERY Gokana word should add something to our understanding of the whole LANGUAGE. We don't ask that of any other aspect of the phonological analysis of words. Rather, the analysis of the entire language has to be compatible with all its words and yield as many explanatory dividends as possible, within the language and across languages. A theory lives by the totality of its consequences.

A theoretical argument for the same conclusion follows from basic assumptions of OT. A constraint can be defeated only by a more highly ranked constraint. Prohibiting syllabification would require constraints that defeat syllable structure assignment. But syllabification per se violates neither faithfulness constraints or markedness constraints (although specific marked syllable structures violate such constraints as ONSET and *CODA, which can be ranked to yield the familiar factorial typology, and RESYLLABIFICATION does constitute a faithfulness violation). Such constraints are unmotivated and their adoption would expand the factorial typology in undesirable ways. For example, a language without syllables would not violate any constraints such as ONSET, *CODA, and *COMPLEX, and consequently not be subject to phonotactic constraints captured by those constraints.

---

28 Hyman suggests that this distribution could be due to the lack of inputs that would yield *CVVVCV, *CVCVVV (an accident or a conspiracy?). For example, *CVCVVV must be of the form Root + Derivational suffix + Inflectional suffix, and this can be neither /CVC-V-VV/, because this sequence would undergo vowel shortening, nor /CVC-VV-V/, because derivational suffixes must be minimal syllables of the form -(C)V.

This seems to me enough reason to reject the claim that Gokana has no syllables. Even if the symptoms of syllabicity in (22) are discounted, the very fact that the language is syllabifiable in conformity with typologically well-established constraints and preferences would be incomprehensible if it did not in fact have syllables. All in all Gokana speaks for rather than against the universality of syllables and CV syllables in particular, just as Arrernte does.

Japanese is a broadly similar case. It has the same kind of funny vowel sequences as Gokana, e.g., Bloch's example *oooóóo* 'let's cover the tail', and perhaps no syllable-conditioned phonological processes. Yet there is evidence for one-mora and two-mora syllables (McCawley 1968, Kubozono 1999, 2003, Itô & Mester 2003), possibly three-mora syllables, though Kubozono argues that these are divided into two syllables as /CV.VN/.

Labrune disputes the existence of syllables in Japanese, citing the three-way contrast in (23):

(23) a. *an.i* (three moras) /aNi/ [ˈãNi] 'ease'
      b. *ani* (two moras) /ani/ [ˈani] 'older brother'
      c. *anni* (three moras) /aNni/ [ˈãnni] 'implicitly'

The contrast cited by Labrune has a natural syllabic interpretation, however: *an.i* : *a.ni* : *an.ni*, with coda nasals counting as moras and causing nasalization of the tautosyllabic vowel.[29] Yet Labrune cites it as evidence AGAINST syllables in Japanese, on the grounds that (23a) violates the generalization that a closed syllable cannot be followed by a syllable that starts with a vowel. One might as well cite it as evidence against moras in Japanese, since it also violates the generalization that a consonant followed by a vowel is not moraic. Of course both generalizations are correct for the initial syllabification of unsyllabified segments, where onsets are universally favored over codas, but in morphologically derived words the syllabification of the base may prevail if faithfulness outranks these markedness constraints.[30] The moraic nasal in *an.i* 'ease', *an.itsu* 'idleness' is inherited from the root *an* from which they are formed (Itô & Mester 2015a: 296). This root can also be seen in words like *anraku* 'ease', *anshin* 'peace of mind', *anga* 'quiet rest', *heian* 'peace'. Therefore the data in (23) don't confute the syllabic analysis. In fact, they support it. For Labrune's alternative that moraic nasals are "special moras" which are "prosodic units in their own right which possess greater autonomy than syllabic codas" has nothing to say about this morphological connection.

---

29 I am grateful to Junko Itô and Stefan Kaufmann for information on Japanese.
30 Similarly the attempt to replicate the phonology of the source language in loanwords, as in Labrune's example *baiorin°* /baioriN/ 'violin'.

Labrune defines the class of "special moras" by enumeration as moraic nasals, second parts of long vowels, *i* after a vowel, first parts of obstruent geminates, which are exactly the weak (non-head) moras of heavy syllables. The fact that these fall readily under a unifying syllabic characterization constitutes further evidence for the syllable (Itô & Mester 2015b: 371).

Phonological descriptions of Japanese have found syllables useful to represent surface contrasts such as *kóo.o* 'likes and dislikes' vs. *ko.oo* 'response', and variation in the pronuciation of vowel sequences, e.g. *o.ó.i* (three syllables) and *óo.i* (two syllables) 'is much', 'are many', or *o.ó.u* (three syllables) and *oo.u* 'covers' (Martin 1975: 17). Syllable structure also plays a role in rules of accentuation and word formation, clearly productive since many of them involve the nativization of borrowed words (Kubozono 1999: 53). On balance, then, the universality of the syllable seems well supported.

The question whether all languages have syllables has a telling parallel in the syntactic question whether all languages are configurational. The claim that Gokana and Japanese lack syllables because they lack diagnostics for syllables is analogous to the claim that a language lacks a VP constituent because it has no diagnostics for it. In the absence of positive evidence for or against a VP, should we posit a minimal flat clause structure (Mohanan 1982, Austin & Bresnan 1996), or a VP?[31] The latter seems a better bet in view of previously overlooked evidence for a VP constituent, in some cases, interestingly, involving phonological phrasing (for Tamil, see Nagarajan 1995). Contemporary syntax leans towards the universality of VP.

3 Vowel systems

3.1 Kalam

The generalization that all languages have an /i/-type vowel is contradicted by analyses of some Papua New Guinean and Chadic languages. In these languages syllabic and non-syllabic semivowels (high vowels and glides) are in complementary distribution, but phonemicized as underlying /y/ and /w/ (Fast 1953, Laycock 1965, Barreteau 1988, Comrie 1991, Pawley & Bulmer 2011, Smith 1999).

---

31 Of course positive arguments against a VP constituent were sometimes adduced, one being that subjects and objects c-command each other for purposes of Condition C of Binding Theory. However, these arguments turned out to be fragile, and the formulation of Condition C on which it relies has itself been questioned.

This analysis reduces the phonemic vowel inventory to /e/, /a/, /o/, or just to /a/ (in some of the languages with an additional epenthetic /ə/ or /ɨ/).[32] Since *i, y* and *u, w* have the same segmental feature content, differing only in syllabicity,[33] this analysis amounts to specifying syllabicity in the phonemic inventory, despite its predictability, and despite the complementary distribution between the high vowels and glides. I believe that the need to specify semivowels as underlyingly non-syllabic in these languages is an artifact of segmentalist phonemics, and present a Stratal OT analysis in which all underlying segments are indifferent as to syllabicity, and the semivowels are derived from underspecified {I}, {U}. This yields exactly the same output as positing underlying /y/, /w/ or /i/, /u/, because the actual realizations are determined by the languages' strict syllable structure. I demonstrate this with a reconsideration of the exemplary analysis of Kalam by Blevins & Pawley (2010) and Pawley & Bulmer (2011).

In addition to the semivowels at issue, Kalam has the vowels /e/, /a/, /o/, plus an epenthetic vowel which is inserted predictably after unsyllabifiable consonants, realized as high central short [ɨ], with a word-final [ə] allophone. Underlying forms can have long sequences of consonants, and some words have no vowels at all. Only /y/, /w/, and /s/ (the language's only fricative consonant) occur as word-internal codas. Word-finally any type of consonant is allowed, including obstruents, nasals, liquids, and glides. Underlying forms are accommodated to a CV syllabic template where possible by inserting the nucleus /ɨ/, driven by the basic constraints ONSET and NOCODA.[34]

(24) a. /kn/ [ˈkɨn] 'sleep'
b. /kyn/ [ˈkiˑn] 'tree fern'
c. /an/ [ˈaˑn] 'who?'
d. /amy/ [ˈaˑˈmiˑ] 'mother'
e. /alw/ [ˈaˑˈluˑ] 'tree species'
f. /m/ [ˈmə] 'taro'
g. /b/ [ˈᵐbə] 'man'
h. /kay/ [ˈkaˑj] 'group, gang'
i. /key/ [ˈkeˑj] 'separately'

---

32 Or even to no vowels, as Barreteau (1988: 429–437) does for Mofu-Gudur, also a Chadic language. His analysis predicts the surface vowels just from the consonants, prosodies, and tone.
33 This has been generally accepted at least since Jakobson, Fant, & Halle (1952), irrespective of whether syllabicity is represented featurally as in Chomsky & Halle (1968), or by position in a syllabic constituent as in Kahn (1976), Gussenhoven (1986), and later work.
34 (24a-j) are from B&P, (24k, l) are from P&B.

j. /koy/   ['koˑj]   'blind'
k. /tdk-sp-m/   [tɨⁿdɨɣisiβɨ́m]   'you are trimming (branches)'
                                    (trim-PROG-2PL)
l. /md-n-k-nN/   [mɨⁿdɨnɨ́ɣinɨŋ]   'while I was staying' (stay-1SG-
                                    SUFF-while)
m. /ypd/   [yíβɨnt]   'be straight'
n. /pttt/   [ɸɨ́rɨrɨ́r]   'quivering'
o. /ym/   [ˈjiˑm]   'plant crops'
p. /wN/   [ˈwuˑN]   'hair, fur, feathers'

With respect to syllabification, Kalam phonemes can be divided into three classes:

(25) a. Consonants /p b m t s d n c j ñ k g ŋ l/ – always non-syllabic.
      b. Vowels /e a o/ – always syllabic.
      c. Semivowels /i u/ ~ /j w/ – syllabic and non-syllabic.

The epenthetic vowel [ɨ] ([ə] word-finally) is not in the underlying inventory, and is pronounced shorter than underlying vowels and vocalized semivowels:

(26) a. Epenthetic [ɨ], [ə] are short: /kn/ [ˈkɨn], /m/ [ˈmə]
      b. Phonemic vowels are half-long: /kay/ [ˈkaˑj]
      c. Including the syllabic allophones of the semivowels: /kyn/ [ˈkiˑn]

B&P give four arguments that the semivowels are always underlying consonants. Their first argument is that while /a e o/ are found word-initially in native words, no native words begin with /i/, /u/ or any central vowel. Instead, words may begin with [ji] or [wu]. B&P analyze them as beginning phonemically with /j/, /w/.

(27) a. /ym/   [ˈjiˑm]   'plant crops'
      b. /wN/   [ˈwuˑN]   'hair, fur, feathers'

P&B (2011: 31) describe the vowels in such words as predictably inserted "release vowels" colored by the adjacent semivowel. However, as reproduced in (27), B&P consistently transcribe them as half-long, like regular vowels and like the vocalized glides in words like (24b) /kyn/ [ˈkiˑn], but unlike the short vowel predictably inserted between two consonants in (24a) /kn/ [ˈkɨn].[35] That means that they are not release vowels, but vocalized glides, which for P&B's analysis means that the

---

[35] The length mark is inadvertently (I think) omitted by the authors in (24h,i,j), where I have inserted it.

semivowels are vocalized as [ji-], [wu-] before consonants, since no words begin with [i-], [u-]. P&B do not account for these data. A simpler alternative is that Kalam words are syllabified to have onsets where possible, so initial glides are [ji-], [wu-] before consonants and [j-], [w-] before vowels. Since semivowels can be both syllabic nuclei and margins, an initial semivowel followed by a consonant can satisfy the the CV preference by being syllabified as /ji-/, with the same melodic element serving as onset and nucleus. For example, underlying {Im} (or for that matter underlying {im} or {ym}) is then syllabified as /jim/, rather than as */im/, */jm/, or as */jm/. Since vowels cannot be affiliated with onsets, it also follows that underlying {Am} (or {am}) must be syllabified as /am/ rather than as */ɐam/. This derives the generalization that words can begin only with a consonant or with a true vowel but not with a semivowel or with an epenthetic /ɨ/.[36] There is then no need to specify the semivowels as underlyingly non-syllabic. This analysis is straightforwardly implementable in OT, as we'll see shortly in tableau (31) below. Before proceeding to that formalization, let us review B&P's remaining three arguments for underlying /y/, /w/.

B&P's second argument for underlying /y/, /w/ is that a word can end in a consonant or in a vocalized semivowel [-i] and [-u], but not in a vowel [-a], [-e], or [-o], e.g. (24d) /amy/ [ˈaˑmiˑ], but */ama/ *[ˈaˑmaˑ]. On their assumption that [-i] and [-u] are underlying consonants, this follows from the constraint that words cannot end in vowels. I assume the weaker constraint that words cannot end in non-high vowels.[37]

B&P's third argument is based on the distribution of the two allomorphs of the negative prefix or proclitic /ma-/ ~ /m-/ 'not, not yet'. The choice of allomorph is phonologically determined: /m-/ occurs before vowels: /m-ag-p/ 'he did not speak', /m-ow-p/ 'he has not come', /m-o-ng-gab/ 'he will not come'. /ma-/ occurs before consonants and before semivowels: /ma-pkp/ 'it has not struck', /ma-ɖan/ 'don't touch', /ma-ynb/ 'it is not cooked', /ma-wkp/ 'it is not cracked'.[38]

(28) a. /ma-ag-p/   [ˈmaˑⁱᵑgip]   'he did not speak'
      b. /ma-ow-p/   [ˈmoˑˈw(u)p]   'he has not come'
      c. /ma-d-an/   [ˈmaˑⁱⁿdaˑn]   'don't touch'
      d. /ma-wk-p/   [ˈmaˑwuˑˈɣɨp]   'it is not cooked'

---

36 Words beginning with a central vowel are excluded because the central vowel is only added after otherwise unsyllabifiable consonants.
37 On the other hand, it is conceivable that final high vowels are actually pronounced with an offglide, as in English, where a word like *bee* [biy] is transcribed as [biː].
38 The transcriptions in (28) are inferred from the information in P&B (2011: 30).

B&P's assumption that semivowels are underlying consonants explains this distribution. But so does my assumption that initial semivowels before consonants are syllabified as CV- to maximize onsets, as discussed in connection with the first argument.

B&P's fourth argument is that the only word-internal surface vowel sequences in Kalam are [i:a:], [i:o:], [i:e:], [u:a:], [u:o:], [u:e:]. These words have an alternative monosyllabic pronunciation in free variation (P&B 2011: 32), and P&B sometimes transcribe them with a bridging glide (see (29c)).

(29)	a.	/gyak/	[ˈ^{ŋ}giˑˈaˑk], [ˈ^{ŋ}giˑˈaˑk]	'they did'
	b.	/kyep/	[ˈkiˑˈeˑp]	'excrement'
	c.	/kyon/	[ˈkiˑˈyoˑn]	'insect species'
	d.	/kwam/	[ˈkuˑˈaˑm]	'tree species, *Garcinia archboldiana*'
	e.	/kwel/	[ˈkuˑˈeˑl]	'tree species, mango'
	f.	/kuok/	[ˈkuˑˈoˑk]	'bowl'

B&P reason that these are the only permitted word-internal vowel sequences because they are underlying consonant+vowel sequences, hence exempt from the prohibition against adjacent vowels. They would have to add some constraint to ensure that such hiatus sequences only arise after a consonant, in order to rule out such words as */yon/ *[ˈiˑˈyoˑn] in Kalam. On my account this follows automatically without any additional constraints. Since Kalam permits no tautosyllabic consonant clusters, and specifically no initial clusters, we know that *COMPLEX is undominated. ONSET forces syllables to have onsets where possible, so initial glides are [ji-], [wu-] before consonants and [j-], [w-] before vowels, e.g., /im/ = /ym/ = /Im/ is syllabified as [jiˑm]. Vowels must be syllabic, so /am/ = /a̯am/ = /Am/ is syllabified as /am/. This derives the generalization that words can begin only with a consonant or with a true vowel but not with a semivowel or with an epenthetic /ɨ/. We also know from such data as (24c,d,e) that ONSET is dominated. The ranking *COMPLEX ≫ ONSET forces the syllabification [ki.on] rather than [kyon].

All the pieces of our OT analysis are now in place. The constraints are listed in (30) and the derivations are illustrated in (31). In the representations, "v" stands for an empty nucleus (a syllable head with no affiliated phoneme), realized as [ɨ]. I give alternative inputs in the tableau in order to show the non-contrastive status of syllabicity in underlying representations.

(30) Constraints

a. $*V]_{\omega}$: A word can't end in a vowel.

b. SON: Consonants are non-syllabic, vowels are syllabic (see (25)).

c. NUC: A syllable has a nucleus.

d. IDENT(F): Input [αF] does not correspond to output [−αF].
e. DEP: Don't insert a segment.
f. MAX: Don't delete a segment.
g. *COMPLEX: A syllable does not have a consonant cluster.
h. ONSET: A syllable has an onset.
i. *CODA: A syllable does not have a coda.

(31)

		*V]_ω	SON	NUC	IDENT(F)	DEP	MAX	*COMPLEX	ONSET	*CODA
Input: /kn/, /kn̩/										
1a.	kn			*						
1b.	kn̩		*							
1c. ☞	kvn									*
1d.	kin				*					*
1e.	kv.nv	*								
Input: /kin/, /kjn/, /kIn/										
2a.	kvn					*				*
2b. ☞	kin									*
2c.	kn			*		*				
2d.	kij				*	*				*
2d.	ki	*				*				
Input: /im/, /jm/, /Im/										
3a.	vm					*			*	*
3b.	im								*	*
3c. ☞	jim									*
3d.	kim				*					*
3e.	ji.mv	*				*				
Input: /an/, /a̩n/										
4a. ☞	an								*	*
4b.	a̩an		*							*
4c.	kan			*		*				*
Input: /amy/, /ami/, /amI/										
5a.	a.mi	*							*	
5b. ☞	a.mij								*	*
5c.	a.mVj					*			*	*
5d.	a̩a.mvj		*							*
5e.	am						*		*	*

		*V]$_\omega$	SON	NUC	IDENT(F)	DEP	MAX	*COMPLEX	ONSET	*CODA
Input: /ama/										
6a.	a.ma	★							★	
6b.	a.maa̰		★						★	★
6c.	amak				★				★	★
6d. ☞	am					★			★	★
Input: /kjep/, /kiep/, /kIep/										
7a.	kjep							★		★
7b. ☞	ki.ep									★
7c.	kep					★				★
7d.	ki.tep				★					★

That monoconsonantal words such as (24f) /m/ ['mə] undergo epenthesis follows not from reranking the constraints for those derivations, as B&P suggest, but from standard constraints that are plainly unviolated in Kalam: lexical words are accented, accents fall on a syllable, and syllables contain a vocalic nucleus.[39]

Underlying forms are accommodated to a CV syllabic template by inserting a vocalic nucleus realized as [ɨ] where necessary, driven by the basic constraints ONSET and NOCODA. The insertion of the predictable [ɨ]-vowels can be regarded as part of the syllabification process. The evidence that they are epenthesized phonologically, rather than intruding phonetically, is that they are obligatory regardless of speech rate, provide a nucleus for syllables that would otherwise lack one, and carry word stress. Several strands of evidence show that they originate specifically in the word phonology rather than in the postlexical phonology. They are grouped into binary feet within the domain of a word: in a word consisting of such syllables, odd-numbered ones can get stressed (Pawley & Bulmer 2011: 30). Corroborating the lexical status of epenthetic vowels is the partial unpredictability, or perhaps morphological conditioning, of these stresses. For example, the second stress is on the fifth syllable in (24k) and on the third syllable in (24l), perhaps because of the different morphological structure. Finally, each member of a compound counts as a separate word for purposes of the syllable count and word-finality. The inserted nucleus [ɨ] is for these reasons an l-phoneme, not part of the s-phonemic representation because it is predictable.

---

39 B&P's remark in this connection that "technical problems within OT grammars can always be solved by invoking additional constraints" is unduly dismissive. Actually the data are predicted by the theory, in the sense that if monoconsonantal words did NOT undergo epenthesis, the analysis would require otherwise unwanted constraints, as the reader can verify.

Hence the regular CV syllable structure of the language cannot be represented at the s-phonemic level. P&B posit initial syllabifications with consonantal syllables like /t.d.k.s.pm/, /m.d.n.k.nŋ/, contrary to Jakobson's CV universal. The simple CV syllabification is, however, visible in lexical representations, where the l-phoneme /ɨ/ is present.

B&P say that Kalam ɨ does not neatly fit into Currie-Hall's (2007) typology of phonologically epenthetic vs. phonetically intrusive (excrescent) vowels, on the grounds that it has two properties of intrusive vowels in addition to the standard properties of epenthetic vowels: it does not repair illicit structures, and it is a central vowel ([ɨ], word-finally [ə]). Neither of these arguments hit the mark. The first argument overlooks the generalization that Kalam epenthetic vowels provide a nucleus for consonants that would otherwise have to be syllabified as codas but are prohibited in coda position.[40] But providing a nucleus for unsyllabifiable consonants IS repairing syllable structure. The second argument is based on the incorrect premise that inserted central vowels are always intrusive rather than epenthetic. There are many well-documented instances of epenthetic central vowels, for example in German (Wiese 1986, 2000: 245), Catalan (Wheeler 2005, Ch. 8), Armenian (Vaux 1998a, 1998b, 2003, Delisi 2015), Slovenian (Jurgec 2007), some dialects of Berber (Dell & Tangi 1993), Salishan languages (Parker 2011), and Mongolian (Svantesson 1995, Svantesson et al. 2005) — all demonstrably phonological cases of ə-epenthesis, some of them cyclic or morphologically conditioned, hence definitely lexical. The correct generalization is the converse: intrusive vowels are always central (unless of course they acquire peripheral features from their context). In other words, independent peripheral quality is a diagnostic for epenthetic vowels, but central quality is NOT a diagnostic of intrusive vowels. That being the case, Kalam epenthetic vowels fit perfectly into Hall's typology; they do not have "mixed properties".

Thinking that Kalam epenthetic vowels have mixed properties, B&P classify them as a third category which they call REMNANT VOWELS. They propose that remnant vowels arise from the historical loss of reduced unstressed vowels, followed by reanalysis of deletion as insertion in the complementary contexts

---

[40] This is not inconsistent with their formulation that vowels are inserted after consonants that require a release. It may be that syllable-final consonants must be released. Another question is whether it is justified to attribute the release property not only to plosives, but also to nasal stops and /l/, as B&P have to do; only the continuants /s/, /y/, and /w/ are licit medial codas. Phoneticians normally use the term "release" for the separation of articulators in plosives, and explain that plosives prefer syllable onsets because that is where their release burst is most easily preceptible. The prohibition of sonorant stops in word-internal codas in Kalam cannot be explained the same way, because they are not released with a noisy burst, and would be easily perceptible even in coda position, and are in fact common as codas across languages.

(rule inversion) and possibly generalization of the new insertion process, and that this origin explains their mixed properties. This is no doubt how the Kalam epenthetic vowels arose. However, even supposing contrary to fact that Kalam vowels had mixed properties, B&P's historical account would not explain that mixture, for there are numerous synchronic epenthesis processes that are extended inversions of original syncope and apocope processes and do NOT have mixed properties (see Andersen 1969 on the synchrony and diachrony of Ukrainian paragoge; on some analyses even the English schwa in the plural, genitive, and reduced copula is a case). In any case there are at present no known clear instances of epenthesis with mixed properties. The two-way distinction between phonologically epenthetic and phonetically intrusive vowels offers a sufficient typology of vowel insertion.

Comrie (1991) argues that of the seven Haruai vowels in (32), only /ə/ is phonemic.

(32)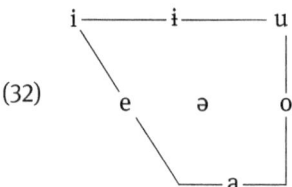

[ɨ] is an anaptyctic vowel predictably inserted after the first consonant in a sequence of consonants or in a word that consists only of consonants. Comrie analyzes the high vowels *i* and *u* as /y/ and /w/, on the basis of arguments that are similar to those of B&P for Kalam. He analyzes *a* as /əə/, and tentatively derives the mid vowels *e* and *o* from /əyə/ and /əwə/, respectively, with the reservation that some lexical items are exceptions to these contractions, and others undergo them only optionally. By strict structuralist methods this amounts to a contrastive distribution, leaving Haruai with a horizontal vowel system of three phonemes /e/, /ə/, /o/. My suspicion is that they may be reanalyzed as morphophonemically unspecified for syllabicity along the lines of what I proposed above for Kalam, emerging at the lexical level as vocalic and consonantal l-phonemes depending on syllable structure.

3.2 Kabardian

In the course of their argument that universals are "myths", Evans & Levinson (2009: 438) claim that it is "contested" whether all spoken languages have vowel phonemes at all, citing the Northwestern Caucasian languages, where "the quality of the vowel segments was long maintained by many linguists to be entirely predictable from the consonantal context (see Colarusso 1982; Halle 1970; Kuipers 1960)" (E&L 2009: 438). It must be said that there is no such debate about Northwestern Caucasian or any other languages; Colarusso (1982) and Halle (1970) demonstrated a minimum inventory of two contrastive vowels.⁴¹ And it is not accurate that "although most scholars have now swung round to recognizing two contrasting vowels, the evidence for this hangs on the thread of a few minimal pairs, mostly loanwords from Turkish or Arabic" (*ibid.*). Actually the majority of scholars recognize a THREE-VOWEL system, and to the extent that some have "swung round" to the two-vowel analysis, it is not from the vowel-less analysis but from the three-vowel analysis. Nor does the evidence particularly depend on Turkish and Arabic loans, or on minimal pairs. On the contrary, the strongest evidence comes from native words and the core vocabulary (Colarusso 1992: 22).

The history of scholarship on Kabardian phonology is worth reviewing as an example of the theory-dependence of phonemic analyses. Older reference grammars of Kabardian set up seven vowel phonemes: two variable short vowels /ə/ and /ɐ/, whose realization depends mostly on the following consonant, and five stable long vowels /ɑ: i: u: e: o:/, phonetically more peripheral than the variable ones (Jakovlev 1948, Turčaninov & Tsagov 1940, Abitov et al. 1957, Šagirov 1967, Bagov et al. 1970, followed by Maddieson 1984, 2013). Jakovlev (1923) discovered that the stable vowels can be derived by fusion of the short vowels with a glide. Most s-phonemic theories allow fusion (e.g., phonemicizing English [ɚ] as /ər/, or French and Portuguese nasal vowels as V+N sequences). In these it is straightforward to reduce Kabardian /i: u: e: o:/ to underlying /əy/, /əw/, /ɐy/, /ɐw/ respectively. Historically /ɑ:/ undoubtedly comes from an analogous fusion of /ɐh/, but synchronically it can't quite be reduced to that under the strictures of s-phonemics. So in addition to /ə/ and /a/, analyses typically posit it as a third s-phoneme. Its representation has been the subject of some debate. Currently favored is /a:/ (Choi 1991, Matasović 2006, Wood 1994, Gordon & Applebaum 2006, Applebaum & Gordon 2013). An older theory posits a vertical three-vowel system /ə/ /ɐ/ /a/ (Trubetzkoy 1925, 1929, 1939, Catford 1942, 1984, Kumaxov 1973, 1984). Abstract generative analyses, on the other hand, can

---

41 The two-vowel analysis is originally due to Kuipers (1960). After presenting it, he goes further by eliminating first /ɐ/ by doubling the consonant inventory with a set of ɐ-colored consonants, and then, in an extreme tour de force, eliminates the remaining vowel /ə/ by enriching the phonemic representation with an abstract juncture marker ":". In this analysis, not only were all phonemes consonants, but every consonant was a morpheme, and every morpheme was a consonant. It was conclusively refuted by Halle (1970), Kumaxov (1973), and Colarusso (1982), and has found no followers since.

easily derive the fifth long vowel [ɑː] from /ɐh/, in some cases ultimately from /hɐ/ and /ɐɣ/ by other processes. The result of that further analytic step is the two-vowel system of Kuipers (1960), Halle (1970), and Colarusso (1992, 2006).

It cannot be emphasized enough that the seven-vowel, three-vowel, and two-vowel solutions with its two variants do not reflect any disagreement about Kabardian, only the differences between phonological theories. The data and phonological generalizations of Kabardian are not at stake. Each analysis follows rigorously from exactly the same facts depending on the principles that it assumes. Even the choice between the two variants of the three-vowel phonemic system is a deep question of principle: what is at stake is whether phonemics should privilege phonetic criteria, or morphophonemic criteria and the overall simplicity of the grammar. The former in this case favor a qualitative opposition /ɐ/ : /ɑ/, the latter point to a quantitative opposition /a/ : /aː/. Far from being a dismaying free-for-all, this spectrum of analyses is heartening because it means that our understanding of Kabardian has reached a point where it can be advanced by sharpening phonological theory and typology by empirical work on other languages.

The upshot, then, is that Kabardian has at least three vocalic phonemes (s-phonemes), reducible to two underlying m-phonemes. With that and the failure of the refutation of the CV universal, E&L's case against phonological universals falls apart.

Even though Kabardian is not vowel-less, it remains, at the level of s-phonemic representations, an exception to the proposed universals on vowel systems in (14). A look at its phonology makes it likely that its lexical representations do conform to them. Phonetically, Kabardian makes full use of the vowel space, with unrounded and rounded front vowels and rounded back vowels, in three heights, ten vowels in all according to Colarusso (1992). In (33) I give examples of his phonetic and underlying forms, to which have added the phonemic representation according to the three-vowel analysis.

(33) a. [suwogʷɛpsɪˈsɑˑś] 'I was thinking of you' (p. 78)
　　　 /səwəgʷapsəˈsɑːś/
　　　 sə- w-　 a-　 gʷə+　psəsa-　 aɣ-　 ś
　　　 I- you- DAT- heart+ think- PAST- AFF

　　 b. [qʼɪzx̂ʷɪzɛteˈwuvæˈʔɑˑræræ] 'the reason why he stopped' (p. 86)
　　　 /qʼəzx̂ʷəzataywəvaʔaːrara/
　　　 Ø- qʼə-　　z-　 x̂ʷə- z-　 a-　 t-　 y-　 a-　 wəva+ ʔa-
　　　 3- INCEPT- what- for- self- DAT- SURF- DIR- DAT- stop+ there(upright)-
　　　 aɣ-　 ra-　 ra
　　　 PAST- PART- DEF

c. [wuzæpɪrɪsˈšaˑś] 'I led you' (p. 104)
   /wəzapərəšša:ś/
   wə- Ø- za- pə-   rə-   s- šə-   ay-   ś
   you- 3- all- sever- DISTR- I- lead (out)- PAST- AFF

d. [dɛriˑdɛˈzoˑk̓ʷə] 'we are going for a long walk' (p. 83)
   /darəydazawk̓ʷə/
   də- Ø- yə- rə-   yə- da+ zə-   a-   w-   k̓ʷə+   a
   we- 3- path- DISTR- DIR- out+ around-   PRES- PROG- move+   INTR

e. [sɪɖeːwɑˑś] 'I hit'
   /səɖaywahś/
   sə- ɖa- y- a-   w+   a-   ay-   ś
   I-   HOR- 3- DAT- strike+ at- PAST- AFF

This ten-vowel repertoire arises by assimilation in height, backness, and rounding to a following consonant, if there is one.[42] Vowels are fronted before [−high] coronals (alveolars, alveopalatals, palatoalveolars), fronted and raised before [+high] coronals (palatals and palato-alveolars), backed before plain uvulars and pharyngeals, backed and rounded before rounded uvulars, and raised and rounded before labiovelars (there are no plain velars). Onset consonants also color the following vowel, but in a variable and gradient manner at the level of phonetic implementation, as Colarusso (1992: 31) makes clear. Word-finally and before labials and the laryngeal /ʔ/, which lack a distinctive tongue position, the vowels are unraised and front (Colarusso 1982: 96, 1992: 30).[43] These assimilations, summarized in (34), generate ten surface vowels.

(34) Before consonants which are:

	$\begin{bmatrix}-\text{high}\\-\text{back}\\-\text{round}\end{bmatrix}$	$\begin{bmatrix}-\text{high}\\-\text{back}\\+\text{round}\end{bmatrix}$	$\begin{bmatrix}-\text{high}\\+\text{back}\\-\text{round}\end{bmatrix}$	$\begin{bmatrix}-\text{high}\\+\text{back}\\+\text{round}\end{bmatrix}$	$\begin{bmatrix}+\text{high}\\-\text{back}\\-\text{round}\end{bmatrix}$	$\begin{bmatrix}+\text{high}\\+\text{back}\\+\text{round}\end{bmatrix}$
/ə/ is realized as:	ɛ	ö	ə	o	ɪ	u
/ɐ/ is realized as:	æ	ö̞	ɑ	ɔ	ɛ	o

---

[42] It is always tautosyllabic, if Colarusso (1992: 15) is right that all intervocalic consonants are ambisyllabic, e.g. /dəda/ [ˈdɪ.dæ].

[43] E.g. /ʔa/ [ʔæ] 'hand', /psəʔa/ [ˈpsɛʔæ] 'wetness', [ˈpsɛ>ʔˑʔæ>] in Colarusso's narrower transcription. They are represented as central vowels [ə] and [ɐ] in Gordon & Applebaum (2006), which would be more consistent with the expectations of Dispersion Theory (Flemming 1995, 2016, Vaux & Samuels 2015). But in the samples I have heard they are definitely front in agreement with Colarusso's description: https://www.youtube.com/watch?v=gtuU5_U-gL4, https://www.youtube.com/watch?v=4-BY1vYfM_Q, https://www.youtube.com/watch?v=r_qQCUDaz-I.

The chart in (35) summarizes the assimilation patterns of backness and roundness, and (dashed arrows) of height; note that the mid vowels each have two sources.

(35)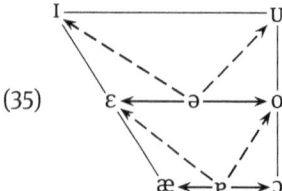

Before /ʔʷ/, which triggers rounding but not backing, /ə/ and /a/ are realized as ö, ɔ̈, not shown in the two-dimensional diagram. The long vowels /iː/ /uː/ /eː/ /oː/ originate by the same assimilation processes before /y/ and /w/, which are then deleted with compensatory lengthening. /h/ neutralizes /ə/ and /a/ without any other coloring effect, and deletes like the other glides, giving /aː/.

By the criteria (A)-(G) of Section 1.1, these assimilations are phonological processes, not coarticulation processes, and they take effect in the word-level phonology, everywhere within the word domain, but not across phonological word boundaries (Gordon & Applebaum 2010: 51). They are categorical and operate on discrete feature values. Note especially that [–high] consonants trigger a chain shift, so that [o] and [ɛ] represent either /ə/ and /ɐ/, depending on the following consonant.

The surface vowels of Kabardian are thus l-phonemes. The ten-vowel system that emerges at the word level is symmetric and dispersed. It is isomorphic to UPSID's ten-vowel system for Korean (Maddieson 1984: 283). Perhaps significantly, the four-way combination of the values of [round] and [back] that is its outstanding typological feature is also found in coterritorial Turkish and its relatives, and elsewhere in Eurasia (Uyghur, Selkup, Seto, Dagur, among others).

3.3 Marshallese

The other famous case of a vertical vowel system is Marshallese. Bender (1963) had posited the phonemic vowel system (36) (I have replaced the unrounded back vowels with their offical IPA symbols).

(36)

[–back, –round]	[+back, –round]	[+back, +round]
i	ɯ	u
ɪ	ɤ	ʊ
e	ʌ	o
ɛ	ɑ	ɔ

This is isomorphic to the Mofu-Gudur vowel system mentioned in Fn. 32. Bender (1968) reduced it to four vowels, taking the center series ɯ, ɤ, ʌ, a as basic (p. 20),[44] and deriving the other eight vowels by assimilation to adjacent consonants:

(37) a. [−back,−round] next to "light" (palatal or palatalized) consonants
    $p^y, t^y, m^y, n^y, l^y, j, y$
  b. [+back,−round] next to "heavy" (plain, or perhaps velarized) consonants $p, t, k, m, n, ŋ, l, r, h$
  c. [+back,+round] next to labialized consonants $k^w, n^w, ŋ^w, l^w, r^w, w$

When a vowel appears between consonants that differ in backness and rounding, it assimilates to both and is accordingly pronounced as a diphthong. This results in 24 diphthongs [iɯ], [iu], etc.

Bender further noted that the second row of vowels /ɪ ɤ ʊ/ can be eliminated from the inventory by deriving it from two sources: lowering of /ɯ/ before deleted /ʌ/, and raising of /ʌ/ before deleted /ɯ/:

(38) a. /bʷʌkʷɯ/ [bʷʊkʷ] 'bladder', cf. /bʷʌkʷɯ-nʸ/ [bʷʊkʷɯnʸ] 'his bladder'
  b. /wɯbʌ/ [ʊbʷ] 'chest', cf. /wɯbʌ-nʸ/ [ʊbʷʌnʸ] 'his chest'

He rejects this further reduction for the phonemic level because it would violate biuniqueness. Words like [bʷʊŋʷ] 'night' could be phonemicized either as /bʷʌŋʷɯ/ or as /bʷɯŋʷʌ/, unless one had access to the morphonological information about the underlying second syllable from suffixed forms, which is not available at the phonemic level. At the morphophonemic level, this objection falls away.

Nevertheless Bender's remarkable solution does not fully adhere to the principle of biuniqueness, and transcends structuralist procedures of segmentation and classification, for the context that triggers the vowel allophones is sometimes itself deleted, and the phoneme /h/, the "heavy" counterpart of /y/ and /w/, never surfaces at all. For example, the three-way contrasts in long vowel vowels seen in (39) are due to deleted intervocalic glides.

(39) a. /mayar/ mɛɛr 'to tell a lie', /mahaj/ maaj 'open field', /mawar/ mɔɔr 'bait'
  b. /mʌyʌj/ meej 'dark colored', /rʌhʌj/ rʌʌj 'bright colored', /tʌwʌj/ tooj 'conspicuous'

---

[44] Though in practice he writes the phonemes as /i,ɪ,e,a/.

The implication of these data for a Stratal OT analysis is that vowel coloring must take effect in the lexical phonology, and then made opaque by postlexical processes. So in the derivation /mayar/ → mɛyɛr → mɛɛr, lexical assimilation is masked by the postlexical deletion of its trigger.⁴⁵

Independent evidence that intervocalic glide deletion is postlexical is that Marshallese does not allow superheavy syllables (*CVVC, *CVCC), except for those that arise by just this deletion process. Thus postlexical glide deletion makes the syllable structure constraint opaque.

However, there is evidence that assimilation ALSO applies postlexically, as a coarticulation process. In rapid speech, consonant assimilation across word boundaries can feed vowel allophony, especially in sequences of identical consonants. For example, in (40b) /bek/ is pronounced like /bekʷ/ [bokʷ] 'sand' through assimilation to the initial /kʷ/ of the following word (Byron Bender, p.c.).

(40) a. /bek/ [bʌk] 'take'
b. /bek kʷeyet nʸ e/ [bokʷ kʷeet ne] 'take that octopus'

Phonetic implementation adds further color nuances to the vowels, which Bender interprets as due to "competing consonantal influences on a less fully specified vowel": the vowel in /tʸʌkʷ/ moves from front to back with increasing rounding, all at mid height: [tʸᵉᵒokʷ]. Similarly, /kʷʌtʸ/ is pronounced [kʷᵒəᵉtʸ].⁴⁶ It is not uncommon for constraints to be enforced at more than one level, with the respective applications obeying the ground rules at each level, as appears to be the case here.

I conclude that Marshallese vowel assimilation is a categorical word-level process operating on binary feature specifications, overlain by a gradient postlexical coarticulation effect.

Since the relation of levels in Stratal OT does not have to be biunique, the underlying three-height vertical system of three vocalic m-phonemes /ɯ ʌ ɑ/

---

45 The data in (39) undermine Hale's (2000) claim that the vowels of Marshallese are not only phonologically but PHONETICALLY underspecified for backness and rounding (he pointedly represents them at both levels with arbitrary dingbat symbols), and that the twelve vowels in (36) and their diphthongal combinations are introduced only in the acoustic/articulatory output. It would be hard to account for the contrasts in (39) as resulting from coarticulation (at least under standard assumptions about the phonology/phonetics interface). Deletion of glides would also have to be an acoustic/articulatory process, in counterbleeding order with acoustic/articulatory assimilation.

46 Choi (1992: 68) also concludes that the smooth transition between vowel qualities must be due to phonetic coarticulation processes: the F2 trajectory for Marshallese /tʸeap/ 'to return' shows no steady-state position for the tongue during the realization of the diphthong.

(or /i e ɑ/) that Bender (1968) entertained can be maintained. The fourth vowel height arises in the lexical phonology, where all vowels also assimilate to palatal and labial consonants. This yields the system of twelve vocalic l-phonemes (36), which is identical to the s-phonemic inventory of Bender (1963).

4 Conclusion

All putative phonological universals are framed in terms of theory-dependent categories, and defined on some theory-dependent level of representation, most often the phonemic level. Therefore the linguistic descriptions on which they are based cannot be theory-neutral or atheoretical. The approach of "describing each language in its own terms" is at best aspirational. With one exception, all grammars I am aware of draw heavily on existing descriptive frameworks.[47] Since there are no theory-neutral grammars, there is no theory-neutral typology. In terms of Hyman's (2008) distinction, there are no "descriptive" universals of language. All universals are analytic, and their validity often turns on a set of critical cases where different solutions can be and have been entertained. The choice between these is not a matter of taste or whimsy but of different assumptions, each one with testable empirical consequences in a multitude of other languages. It follows that the search for better linguistic descriptions, more illuminating typologies, and stronger cross-linguistic generalizations and universals should go hand in hand.

Stratal OT's word level representations encode the typologically significant phonological properties omitted in s-phonemic representations, including syllabification regardless of whether it is contrastive or not, and "quasi-phonemes". They also encode typologically significant abstract structural information that is missing in the phonetic record, such as metrical and prosodic structure and feature sharing, while omitting postlexical features and structurally irrelevant

---

[47] The exception is Pāṇini's Aṣṭādhyāyī, built from scratch strictly by using minimum description length as the sole criterion for establishing both the generalizations and the formalism in which these are expressed. This was done by defining the technical terms and conventions of the system in the grammar itself, so that minimum description length then requires that they are introduced if and only if they reduce the overall length of the grammar — that is, if the minimum possible cost of defining them is outweighed by the maximum possible grammatical simplification they allow. Autochtonous philologies such as that of the Japanese *kokugakusha* (Bedell 1968) and the Arabic tradition originating with Sibawayh (Versteegh 1997) also describe their respective object language in its own terms, but they were not comprehensive grammars in the modern sense. They were more concerned with settling points of usage and philosophical issues than with grammatical analysis per se.

coarticulation phenomena. This makes word phonology the sweet spot where typological generalizations appear at their tidiest: it seems likely that it obeys all phonological universals that phonemic representations do, and then some. The difference is most dramatic where phonemic theory imposes extremely abstract analyses, as in vertical and one-vowel systems. But the argument that the word level should replace phonemics in typological research can also be made in languages where lexical representations are fairly close to classical phonemic representations.

Since the lexical level of representation is empirically supported and formally anchored in Stratal OT and Lexical Phonology, it is a good candidate for replacing the classical s-phonemic level. That would remove an unmotivated residue of structuralism and replace it with a well motivated level of representation that serves some of the same functions. Our analysis of unusual syllabification and vowel systems shows it to be a Goldilocks level that is just right for typology, in that it conforms to some important generalizations that are obscured for technical reasons in structuralist phonemic representations, therby leading to cleaner typologies and turning near-universals into solid exceptionless universals.

Since lexical representations and l-phonemes were not defined with an eye on typology, its positive typological implications are a nice bonus that supports Stratal OT. In broader perspective, the outcome encourages the joint pursuit of linguistic theory and typology, where universals are not just inductive generalizations from putatively theory-neutral linguistic descriptions but hypotheses that at once guide analysis and are informed by it. It has the hallmark of a good theory, that it leads BOTH to better linguistic descriptions AND to stronger cross-linguistic generalizations and universals. Going beyond the typology of segmental inventories and syllable structure, the relevance of lexical representations is worth exploring further in dispersion theory, language acquisition, language use, and sound change.

Acknowledgement: Special thanks to Byron Bender for sharing his beautiful work on Marshallese, and to Larry Hyman for lively discussion and comments on a draft.

References

Abitov, M. L. et al. (eds.). 1957. *Grammatika kabardino-čerkesskogo literaturnogo jazyka.* Moskva: Izd-vo Akademii Nauk SSSR.
Alber, Birgit. 2005. Clash, lapse and directionality. *Natural Language & Linguistic Theory* 23. 485–542.

Andersen, Henning. 1969. A study in diachronic morphophonemics: The Ukrainian prefixes. *Language* 45. 807–830.
Anderson, Stephen R. 1982. The analysis of French shwa, or How to get something for nothing. *Language* 58. 534–573.
Anderson, Stephen R. 2000. Reflections on "On the phonetic rules of Russian". *Folia linguistica* 34. 11–27.
Applebaum, Ayla & Matthew Gordon. 2013. A comparative phonetic study of the Circassian languages. In Chundra Cathcart, Shinae Kang, & Clare S. Sandy (eds.), *Proceedings of the 37th Annual Meeting of the Berkeley Linguistics Society*, 3–17. Berkeley: BLS.
Austin, Peter & Joan Bresnan. 1996. Non-configurationality in Australian aboriginal languages. *Natural Language & Linguistic Theory* 14. 215–268.
Avery, Peter, B. Elan Dresher & Keren Rice (eds.). 2008. *Contrast in phonology. Theory, perception, acquisition*. Berlin: De Gruyter Mouton.
Bagov, P. M., B. X. Balkarov, T. X. Kuaševa, M. A. Kumaxov & G. B. Rogova (eds.). 1970. *Grammatika kabardino-čerkesskogo literaturnogo jazyka, 1. Fonetika i morfologija*. Moskva: Nauka.
Barreteau, Daniel. 1988. *Description du mofu-gudur: Langue de la famille tchadique parlée au Cameroun*. Paris: Editions de l'ORSTOM.
Bedell, George. 1968. *Kokugaku grammatical theory*. Ph.D. dissertation, MIT, Cambridge, MA.
Bender, Byron W. 1963. Marshallese phonemics: Labialization or palatalization? *Word* 19. 335–341.
Bender, Byron W. 1968. Marshallese phonology. *Oceanic Linguistics* 7. 16–35.
Bender, Byron W. 1971. Micronesian languages. In Thomas A. Sebeok (ed.), *Current trends in linguistics*, vol. 8: *Linguistics in Oceania*, 426–465. The Hague: Mouton.
Bermúdez-Otero, Ricardo. 2012. The architecture of grammar and the division of labour in exponence. In Jochen Trommer (ed.), *The morphology and phonology of exponence: The state of the art,* 8–83. Oxford: Oxford University Press.
Bermúdez-Otero, Ricardo. 2015. Amphichronic explanation and the life cycle of phonological processes. In Patrick Honeybone & Joseph Salmons (eds.), *The Oxford handbook of historical phonology*, 374–399. Oxford: Oxford University Press.
Bloch, Bernard. 1941. Phonemic overlapping. *American Speech* 16. 278–284.
Bloch, Bernard. 1953. Contrast. *Language* 29. 59–61.
Bloomfield, Leonard. 1939. Menomini morphophonemics. In *Etudes phonologiques dédiées à la mémoire de M. le prince N. S. Trubetzkoy*, 105–115. Travaux du Cercle Linguistique de Prague 8. Prague.
Bloomfield, Leonard. 1962. *The Menomini language*. Edited by Charles F. Hockett. New Haven, CT: Yale University Press.
Blumenfeld, Lev. 2004. Tone-to-stress and stress-to-tone: Ancient Greek accent revisited. *Proceedings of the 30th Annual Meeting of the Berkeley Linguistics Society*.
Borowsky, Toni. 1993. On the word level. In Sharon Hargus & Ellen Kaisse (eds.), *Studies in Lexical Phonology*, 199–234. New York: Academic Press.
Breen, Gavan & Rob Pensalfini. 1999. Arrernte: A language with no syllable onsets. *Linguistic Inquiry* 30. 1–25.
Burzio, Luigi. 1994. *Principles of English stress*. Cambridge: Cambridge University Press.
Casali, Roderic F. 2014. Assimilation, markedness and inventory structure in tongue root harmony systems. ROA 1319. http://roa.rutgers.edu/content/article/files/1319_casali_1.pdf.
Catford. J. C. 1942. The Kabardian language. *Maître phonétique*, 3rd Series 78. 15–18.

Catford, J. C. 1984. Instrumental data and linguistic phonetics. In Jo-Ann W. Higgs & Robin Thelwall (eds.), *Topics in linguistic phonetics: In honour of E. T. Uldall*, 23–48. Coleraine, N. Ireland: New University of Ulster.
Choi, John, D. 1991. An acoustic study of Kabardian vowels. *Journal of the International Phonetic Association* 21. 4–12.
Chomsky, Noam. 1964. *Current issues in linguistic theory*. The Hague: Mouton.
Chomsky, Noam, & Morris Halle. 1968. *The sound pattern of English*. New York: Harper & Row.
Clairis, Christos. 1977. Première approche du qawasqar: Identification et phonologie. *La Linguistique* 13. 145–152.
Clements, G. N. 2001. Representational economy in constraint-based phonology. In T. Alan Hall (ed.), *Distinctive feature theory*, 71–146. Berlin: Mouton de Gruyter.
Clements, G. N. 2003. Feature economy in sound systems. *Phonology* 20. 287–333.
Colarusso, John. 1982. Western Circassian vocalism. *Folia Slavica* 5. 89–114.
Colarusso, John. 1992. *A grammar of the Kabardian language*. Calgary: University of Calgary Press.
Colarusso, John. 2006. *Kabardian (East Circassian)*. München: Lincom Europa.
Comrie, Bernard. 1991. On Haruai vowels. In Andrew Pawley (ed.), *Man and a half: Essays in pacific anthropology in honour of Ralph Bulmer*, 393–397. Auckland: The Polynesian Society.
Currie-Hall, Daniel. 2007. *The role and representation of contrast in phonological theory*. Ph.D. dissertation, University of Toronto. *Toronto Working Papers in Linguistics*.
Currie-Hall, Kathleen. 2013. A typology of intermediate phonological relationships. *The Linguistic Review* 30. 215–275.
DeCamp, David. 1958. The pronunciation of English in San Francisco. Part 1. *Orbis* 7. 372–391.
DeCamp, David. 1959. The pronunciation of English in San Francisco. Part 2. *Orbis* 8. 54–77.
Delisi, Jessica L. 2015. *Epenthesis and prosodic structure in Armenian: A diachronic account*. Ph.D. dissertation, UCLA Indo-European Studies.
Dell, François & Oufae Tangi. 1993. Syllabification and empty nuclei in Ath-Sidhar Rifain Berber. *Journal of African Languages and Linguistics* 13. 125–162.
Dinnsen, Daniel A. 1985. A re-examination of phonological neutralization. *Journal of Linguistics* 21. 265–279.
Downing, Laura J. 1998. On the prosodic misalignment of onsetless syllables. *Natural Language & Linguistic Theory* 16. 1–52.
Dresher, B. Elan. 2009. *The contrastive hierarchy in phonology*. Cambridge: Cambridge University Press.
Ebeling, C. L. 1960. *Linguistic units*. The Hague: Mouton.
Evans, Nicholas & Stephen C. Levinson. 2009. The myth of language universals: Language diversity and its importance for cognitive science. *Behavioral and Brain Sciences* 32. 429–492.
Fast, P. W. 1953. Amuesha (Arawak) phonemes. *International Journal of American Linguistics* 19. 191–194.
Flemming, Edward. 1995. *Auditory representations in phonology*. Ph.D. dissertation, UCLA. (Published New York: Garland Press, 2002.)
Flemming, Edward. 2016. Dispersion theory and phonology. *Oxford Research Encyclopedias: Linguistics*. http://linguistics.oxfordre.com/view/10.1093/acrefore/9780199384655.001.0001/acrefore-9780199384655-e-110

Fougeron, Cécile & Rachid Ridouane. 2008. On the phonetic implementation of syllabic consonants and vowel-less syllables in Tashlhiyt. *Estudios de Fonética Experimental* 17. 139–175.

Gordon, Matthew & Ayla Applebaum. 2006. Phonetic structures in Turkish Kabardian. *Journal of the International Phonetic Association* 36. 159–186.

Gravina, Richard. 2014. *The phonology of Proto-Central Chadic: The reconstruction of the phonology and lexicon of Proto-Central Chadic, and the linguistic history of the Central Chadic languages*. Ph.D. dissertation, Leiden University. https://www.lotpublications.nl/Documents/375_fulltext.pdf

Green, Jenny. 1994. *A learner's guide to Eastern and Central Arrernte*. Alice Springs: IAD Press.

Greenberg, Joseph H., Charles A. Ferguson & Edith A. Moravcsik (eds.). 1978. *Universals of human language*, volume 2. Stanford: Stanford University Press.

Guimarães, Maximiliano & Andrew Nevins. 2013. Probing the representation of nasal vowels in Brazilian Portuguese with language games. *Organon* 28. 155–178. ling.auf.net/lingbuzz/001693/current.pdf

Gussenhoven, Carlos. 1986. English plosive allophones and ambisyllabicity. *Gramma* 10. 119–142.

Hale, Mark. 2000. Marshallese phonology, the phonetics-phonology interface and historical linguistics. *The Linguistic Review* 17. 241–257.

Hall, Tracy Alan. 1993. The phonology of German /R/. *Phonology* 10. 43–82.

Halle, Morris. 1959. *The sound pattern of Russian*. The Hague: Mouton.

Halle, Morris. 1970. Is Kabardian a vowel-less language? *Foundations of Language* 6. 95–103.

Harris, James W. & Ellen M. Kaisse. 1999. Palatal vowels, glides and obstruents in Argentinean Spanish. *Phonology* 16. 117–190.

Harris, John. 1987. Non-structure-preserving rules in Lexical Phonology: Southeastern Bantu harmony. *Lingua* 72. 255–292.

Harris, John. 1990. Derived phonological contrasts. In Susan Ramsaran (ed.), *Studies in the pronunciation of English: A commemorative volume in honour of A. C. Gimson*, 87–105. London: Routledge.

Henderson, John & Veronica Dobson. 1994. *Eastern and Central Arrernte to English dictionary*. Alice Springs: Institute for Aboriginal Development.

Hsieh, Feng-Fan, Michael Kenstowicz & Xiaomin Mou. 2009. Mandarin adaptations of coda nasals in English loanwords. In Andrea Calabrese & Leo Wetzels (eds.), *Loan phonology: Issues and controversies*, 131–154. Amsterdam: John Benjamins.

Hualde, José Ignacio. 2005. Quasi-phonemic contrasts in Spanish. In Benjamin Schmeiser, Vineeta Chand, Ann Kelleher & Angelo Rodriguez (eds.), *West Coast Conference on Formal Linguistics* 23. Somerville, MA: Cascadilla Press.

Hyde, Brett. 2002. A restrictive theory of metrical stress. *Phonology* 19. 313–359.

Hyman, Larry M. 1976. Phonologization. In Alphonse G. Juilland, A. M. Devine & Laurence D. Stephens (eds.), *Linguistic studies offered to Joseph H. Greenberg on the occasion of his sixtieth birthday*, 407–418. Saratoga, CA: Anma Libri.

Hyman, Larry M. 1983. Are there syllables in Gokana? In Jonathan Kaye, Hilda Koopman, Dominique Sportiche & André Dugas (eds.), *Current approaches to African linguistics*, vol. 2, 171–179. Dordrecht: Foris.

Hyman, Larry M. 1985. *A theory of phonological weight*. Dordecht: Foris.

Hyman, Larry M. 2008. Universals in phonology. *The Linguistic Review* 25. 83–137.

Hyman, Larry M. 2011. Does Gokana really have no syllables? Or: what's so great about being universal? *Phonology* 28. 55–85.

Hyman, Larry M. 2015. Does Gokana really have syllables? A postscript. *Phonology* 32. 303–306.

Itô, Junko & Armin Mester. 2003. *Japanese morphophonemics: Markedness and word structure* (Linguistic Inquiry Monograph Series 41). Cambridge, MA: MIT Press.

Itô, Junko & Armin Mester. 2015a. Sino-Japanese phonology. In Haruo Kubozono (ed.), *Handbook of Japanese phonetics and phonology*, 289–312. Berlin: Mouton de Gruyter.

Itô, Junko & Armin Mester. 2015b. Word formation and phonological processes. In Haruo Kubozono (ed.), *Handbook of Japanese phonetics and phonology*, 363–395. Berlin: Mouton de Gruyter.

Jakobson, Roman. 1931. Die Betonung und ihre Rolle in der Wort- und Syntagmaphonologie. In *Réunion Phonologique Internationale tenue à Prague: 18–21/XII 1930*, 164–183. (Reprinted in Jakobson, *Selected writings*, vol. 1: *Phonological studies*, 117–136. The Hague: Mouton, 1962.)

Jakobson, Roman. 1958. Typological studies and their contribution to historical comparative linguistics. In *Proceedings of the 8th International Congress of Linguists*, Oslo. (Reprinted in Jakobson, *Selected writings*, vol. 1: *Phonological studies*, 523–532. The Hague: Mouton, 1962.)

Jakobson, Roman, Gunnar Fant & Morris Halle. 1952. *Preliminaries to speech analysis*. Cambridge, MA: Acoustics Laboratory, Massachusetts Institute of Technology.

Jakovlev, N. F. 1923. Tablitsy fonetiki kabardinskogo jazyka. In *Trudy podrazriada issledovaniia severokavkazskikh jazykov pri Institute Vostokovedeniia v Moskve*, I. Moskva.

Jakovlev, N. F. 1948. *Grammatika literaturnogo kabardino-čerkesskogo jazyka*. Moskva: Izd-vo AN SSSR.

Janda, Richard D. 2003. "Phonologization" as the start of dephoneticization – or, on sound change and its aftermath: Of extension, lexicalization, and morphologization. In Brian D. Joseph & Richard D. Janda (eds.), *The handbook of historical linguistics*, 401–422. Oxford: Blackwell.

Jurgec, Peter. 2007. Schwa in Slovenian is epenthetic. 2nd Congress of the Slavic Linguistic Society. Berlin: ZAS. http://www.hum.uit.no/a/jurgec/schwa.pdf (accessed August 24 2007).

Kager, René. 2007. Feet and metrical stress. In Paul de Lacy (ed.), *The Cambridge handbook of phonology*, 195–227. Cambridge: Cambridge University Press.

Kahn, Daniel. 1976. Syllable-based generalizations in English phonology. Ph.D. dissertation, MIT.

Kaplan, Abby. 2011. Phonology shaped by phonetics: The case of intervocalic lenition. ROA 1077. http://roa.rutgers.edu/article/view/1107

Karvonen, Dan. 2005. Word prosody in Finnish. Ph.D. dissertation, University of California at Santa Cruz.

Kawahara, Shigeto. 2012. Review of Laurence Labrune, *The phonology of Japanese* (2012). *Phonology* 29. 540–548.

Kenstowicz, Michael & Nabila Louriz. 2009. Reverse engineering: Emphatic consonants and the adaptation of vowels in French loanwords into Moroccan Arabic. *Brill's Annual of Afroasiatic Languages and Linguistics* 1. 41–74.

Kessler, Brett. 1994. Sandhi and syllables in Classical Sanskrit. In Erin Duncan, Donka Farkas & Philip Spaelti (eds.), *The proceedings of the 12th West Coast Conference on Formal Linguistics*, 35–50. Stanford, CA: CSLI Publications.

Keyser, Samuel Jay & Kenneth N. Stevens. 2006. Enhancement and overlap in the speech chain. *Language* 82. 33–63.

Kim, Susan. 2001. Lexical Phonology and the fricative voicing rule. *Journal of Linguistics* 29. 149–161.

Kiparsky, Paul. 1996. Allomorphy or morphophonology? In Rajendra Singh (ed.), *Trubetzkoy's orphan: Proceedings of the Montréal roundtable "Morphophonology: Contemporary Responses"*, 13–31. Amsterdam: John Benjamins.

Kiparsky, Paul. 2003. Syllables and moras in Arabic. In Caroline Féry & Ruben van de Vijver (eds.), *The syllable in Optimality Theory*, 147–182. Cambridge: Cambridge University Press.

Kiparsky, Paul. 2006. Amphichronic linguistics vs. Evolutionary Phonology. *Theoretical Linguistics* 32. 217–236.

Kiparsky, Paul. 2015. Phonologization. In Patrick Honeybone & Joseph Salmons (eds.), *The Oxford handbook of historical phonology*, 563–582. Oxford: Oxford University Press.

Kiparsky, Paul. To Appear. *Paradigms and opacity*. Stanford: CSLI Press.

Kleber, Felicitas, Tina John & Jonathan Harrington. 2010. The implications for speech perception of incomplete neutralization of final devoicing in German. *Journal of Phonetics* 38. 185–196.

Kohler, Klaus J. 1966. Is the syllable a phonological universal? *Journal of Linguistics* 2. 207–208

Korhonen, Mikko. 1969. Die Entwicklung der morphologischen Methode im Lappischen. *Finnisch-Ugrische Forschungen* 37. 203–262.

Kubozono, Haruo. 1999. Mora and syllable. In Natsuko Tsujumura (ed.), *The handbook of Japanese linguistics*, 31–61. Oxford: Blackwell.

Kubozono, Haruo. 2003. The syllable as a unit of prosodic organization in Japanese. In Caroline Féry & Ruben van de Vijver (eds.), *The syllable in Optimality Theory*, 99–122. Cambridge: Cambridge University Press.

Kumaxov, M. A. 1973. Teorija monovokalizma i zapadnokavkazskie jazyki. *Voprosy jazykoznanija* 4. 54–67.

Kumaxov, M. A. 1984. *Očerki obščego i kavkazskogo jazykoznanija*. Nal'cik: Izdatel'stvo El'brus.

Kuipers, Aert H. 1960. *Phoneme and morpheme in Kabardian*. The Hague: Mouton.

Labov, William. 1994. *Principles of linguistic change*. Vol. 1: *Internal factors*. Oxford: Wiley-Blackwell.

Labrune, Laurence. 2012. Questioning the universality of the syllable: Evidence from Japanese. *Phonology* 29. 113–152.

Ladd, D. Robert. 2006. "Distinctive phones" in surface representation. In Louis M. Goldstein, D. H. Whalen & Catherine T. Best (eds.), *Laboratory Phonology*, vol. 8, 3–26. Berlin: Mouton de Gruyter.

Laycock, D. C. 1965. *The Ndu language family* (Linguistic Circle of Canberra Publications, Series C, 1). Canberra: Australian National University.

Liberman, Anatoly. 1991. Phonologization in Germanic: Umlauts and vowel shifts. In Elmer H. Antonsen & Hans Henrich Hock (eds.), *Stæfcræft: Studies in Germanic linguistics*, 125–137. Amsterdam: John Benjamins.

Lindblom, Björn. 1986. Phonetic universals in vowel systems. In John J. Ohala & Jeri J. Jaeger (eds.), *Experimental phonology*, 13–44. Orlando: Academic Press.

Lindblom, Björn. 1990. Explaining phonetic variation: A sketch of the H&H theory. In W. J. Hardcastle & A. Marchal (eds.), *Speech production and speech modelling*, 403–439. Dordrecht: Kluwer.

McCarthy, John & Alan Prince. 1986. *Prosodic morphology 1986.* http://scholarworks.umass.edu/linguist_faculty_pubs/13
McCarthy, John & Alan Prince. 1993. *Prosodic morphology I: Constraint interaction and satisfaction.* http://scholarworks.umass.edu/linguist_faculty_pubs/14
McCawley, James D. 1968. *The phonological component of a grammar of Japanese.* The Hague: Mouton.
MacMahon, April M. S. 1991. Lexical Phonology and sound change: The case of the Scottish vowel length rule. *Journal of Linguistics* 27. 29–53.
Maddieson, Ian. 1984. *Patterns of sounds.* Cambridge: Cambridge University Press.
Maddieson, Ian. 2013. Chapters in Matthew S. Dryer & Martin Haspelmath (eds.), *The world atlas of language structures online.* Leipzig: Max Planck Institute for Evolutionary Anthropology. http://wals.info/
Maddieson, Ian & Kristin Precoda. 1990. Updating UPSID. *UCLA Working Papers in Phonetics* 74. 104–111.
Manaster-Ramer, Alexis. 1994. On three East Slavic non-counterexamples to Stieber's Law. *Journal of Slavic Linguistics* 2. 164–170.
Martin, Samuel. 1975. *A reference grammar of Japanese.* New Haven, CT: Yale University Press.
Martinet, André. 1964. *Elements of general linguistics.* Chicago: University of Chicago Press.
Martínez-Gil, Fernando. 1993. Galician nasal velarization as a case against Structure Preservation. In *Proceedings of the 19th Annual Meeting of the Berkeley Linguistics Society*, 254–267.
Matasović, Ranko. 2006. *A short grammar of East Circassian (Kabardian).* Zagreb. http://mudrac.ffzg.unizg.hr/~rmatasov/KabardianGrammar.pdf
Mohanan, K. P. 1982. Grammatical relations and clause structure in Malayalam. In Joan Bresnan (ed.), *The mental representation of grammatical relations*, 504–589. Cambridge, MA: MIT Press.
Nagarajan, Hemalatha. 1995. Gemination of stops in Tamil: Implications for the phonology-syntax interface. https://www.ucl.ac.uk/pals/research/linguistics/publications/wpl/95paper
Odden, David. 1995. The status of onsetless syllables in Kikerewe. *OSU Working Papers in Linguistics* 47. 89–110.
Ó Siadhail, Mícheál. 1989. *Modern Irish: Grammatical structure and dialectal variation.* Cambridge: Cambridge University Press.
Ohala, John J. 1990. Alternatives to the sonority hierarchy for explaining segmental sequential constraints. In Michael Ziolkowski, Manuela Noske, & Karen Deaton (eds.), *Papers from the 26th Regional Meeting of the Chicago Linguistic Society.* Vol. 2: *Parasession on the syllable in phonetics and phonology*, 319–338. Chicago: CLS.
Ohala, John J. & Haruko Kawasaki-Fukumori. 1997. Alternatives to the sonority hierarchy for explaining segmental sequential constraints: In Stig Eliasson & Ernst Håkon Jahr (eds.), *Language and its ecology: Essays in memory of Einar Haugen*, 343–365. Berlin: Mouton de Gruyter.
Padgett, Jaye. 2010. Russian consonant-vowel interactions and derivational opacity. In W. Brown, A. Cooper, A. Fisher, E. Kesici, N. Predolac, & D. Zec (eds.), *Proceedings of the 18th Formal Approaches to Slavic Linguistics meeting*, 353–382. Ann Arbor: Michigan Slavic Publications.
Padgett, Jaye & Máire Ní Chiosáin. 2011. Markedness, segment realization and locality in spreading. In Linda Lombardi (ed.), *Segmental phonology in Optimality Theory: Constraints and representations*, 118–156. Cambridge: Cambridge University Press.

Parker, Aliana. 2011. It's that schwa again! Towards a typology of Salish schwa. *Working Papers of the Linguistics Circle of the University of Victoria* 21. 9–21.
Pawley, Andrew & Ralph Bulmer. 2011. *A dictionary of Kalam with ethnographic notes.* Canberra, A.C.T.: Pacific Linguistics, School of Culture, History and Language, College of Asia and the Pacific, The Australian National University.
Pensalfini, Robert. 1998. The development of (apparently) onsetless syllabification: A constraint-based approach. In M. Catherine Gruber, Derrick Higgins, Kenneth Olson & Tamra Wysocki (eds.), *Papers from the 32nd Regional Meeting of the Chicago Linguistic Society*, 167–178. Chicago: CLS.
Piroth, Hans Georg & Peter M. Janker. 2004. Speaker-dependent differences in voicing and devoicing of German obstruents. *Journal of Phonetics* 32. 81–109.
Port, Robert F. & Michael O'Dell. 1985. Neutralization of syllable-final voicing in German. *Journal of Phonetics* 13. 455–471.
Port, Robert F. & Penny Crawford. 1989. Incomplete neutralization and pragmatics in German. *Journal of Phonetics* 17. 257–282.
Prince, Alan & Paul Smolensky. 1993. *Optimality Theory: Constraint interaction in generative grammar.* RuCCS Technical Report 2, Rutgers University, Piscateway, NJ: Rutgers University. Center for Cognitive Science. Revised version published 2004 by Blackwell.
Ridouane, Rachid. 2007. Gemination in Tashlhiyt Berber: An acoustic and articulatory study. *Journal of the International Phonetic Association* 37. 119–142.
Roca, Iggy. 2005. Strata, yes, structure-preservation, no. In Twan Geerts, Ivo van Ginneken, & Haike Jacobs (eds.), *Romance languages and linguistic theory 2003*, 197–218. Amsterdam: John Benjamins.
Rood, David S. 1975. Implications of Wichita phonology. *Language* 51. 315–337.
Rubach, Jerzy. 2000. Backness switch in Russian. *Phonology* 17. 39–64.
Ryan, Kevin. 2014. Onsets contribute to syllable weight: Statistical evidence from stress and meter. *Language* 90. 309–341.
Šagirov, A. K. 1967. Kabardinskij jazyk. In V. V. Vinogradov (ed.), *Jazyki narodov SSSR,* vol. 4: *Iberijsko-kavkazskie jazyki*, 165–183. Moskva: Nauka.
Schwartz, Geoffrey. 2013. A representational parameter for onsetless syllables. *Journal of Linguistics* 49. 613–646.
Schwartz, Jean-Luc, Louis-Jean Boë, Nathalie Vallée & Christian Abry. 1997. Major trends in vowel system inventories. *Journal of Phonetics* 25. 233–253.
Scobbie, James M. & Jane Stuart-Smith. 2008. Quasi-phonemic contrast and the fuzzy inventory: Examples from Scottish English. In Avery, Dresher & Rice (eds.) 2008, 87–113.
Smith, Tony. 1999. *Muyang phonology.* Yaoundé: SIL.
Sommer, Bruce A. 1970a. An Australian language without CV syllables. *International Journal of American Linguistics* 36. 57–58.
Sommer, Bruce A. 1970b. The shape of Kunjen syllables. In Didier L. Goyvaerts (ed.), *Phonology in the 1980s*, 231–244. Ghent: Story-Scientia.
Steriade, Donca. 1999. Alternatives in syllable-based accounts of consonantal phonotactics. In Osamu Fujimura, Brian Joseph & Bohumil Palek (eds.), *Proceedings of LP 1998*, vol. 1, 205–246. Prague: Charles University and Karolinum Press.
Stevens, Kenneth N. & Samuel Jay Keyser. 1989. Primary features and their enhancement in consonants. *Language* 65. 81–106.
Svantesson, Jan-Olof. 1995. Cyclic syllabification in Mongolian. *Natural Language & Linguistic Theory* 13. 755–766.

Svantesson, Jan-Olof, Anna Tsendina, Anastasia M. Karlsson & Vivan Franzen. 2005. *The phonology of Mongolian*. Oxford: Oxford University Press.
Tabain, Marija, Gavan Breen & Andrew Butcher. 2004. VC vs. CV syllables: A comparison of Aboriginal languages with English. *Journal of the International Phonetic Association* 34. 175–200.
Topintzi, Nina. 2010. *Onsets: Suprasegmental and prosodic behaviour*. Cambridge: Cambridge University Press.
Topintzi, Nina & Andrew Nevins. 2017. Moraic onsets in Arrernte. *Phonology* 34. 615–650.
Trubetzkoy, N. S. 1925. Review of Jakovlev 1923. *Bulletin de la Société de Linguistique de Paris* 26. 277–286.
Trubetzkoy, N. S. 1929. Zur allgemeinen Theorie der phonologischen Vokalsysteme. *Travaux du Cercle Linguistique de Prague* 1. 39–67.
Trubetzkoy, N. S. 1939. *Grundzüge der Phonologie*. Prague: Travaux du Cercle Linguistique de Prague, No. 7.
Turčaninov, G. & M. Tsagov. 1940. *Grammatika kabardinskogo jazyka*. Moskva: Izd-vo Akademii Nauk.
Turpin, Myfany. 2012. The metrics of Kaytetye rain songs, a ceremonial repertory of Central Australia. http://linguistics.ucla.edu/event/icalrepeat.detail/2012/10/03/325/-/pho
Vaux, Bert. 1998a. The laryngeal specifications of fricatives. *Linguistic Inquiry* 29. 497–511.
Vaux, Bert. 1998b. *The phonology of Armenian*. Oxford: Oxford University Press.
Vaux, Bert. 2003. Syllabification in Armenian, universal grammar, and the lexicon. *Linguistic Inquiry* 34. 91–125.
Vaux, Bert & Andrew Wolfe. 2009. The appendix. In Eric Raimy & Charles E. Cairns (eds.), *Contemporary views on architecture and representations in phonology*, 101–143. Cambridge, MA: MIT Press.
Vaux, Bert & Bridget Samuels. 2015. Explaining vowel systems: Dispersion theory vs. natural selection. *The Linguistic Review* 32. 573–599.
Vennemann, Theo. 1972. On the theory of syllabic phonology. *Linguistische Berichte* 18. 1–18.
Versteegh, Kees. 1997. *Landmarks in linguistic thought*, vol. 3: *The Arabic linguistic tradition*. London: Routledge.
Wells, John. 1982. *Accents of English*. Cambridge: Cambridge University Press.
Wiese, Richard. 1986. Schwa and the structure of words in German. *Linguistics* 24. 697–724.
Wiese, Richard. 2000. *The phonology of German*. Oxford: Oxford University Press.
Wood, Sidney. 1994. A spectrographic analysis of vowel allophones in Kabardian. *Working Papers* 42. 241–250. Lund: Lund University Department of Linguistics.

Ian Maddieson
Is phonological typology possible without (universal) categories?

Abstract: Discussions of the sound structure of languages rely on a long tradition of categorization. In this chapter the question of whether it is possible to devise a continuous descriptive framework that does not rely on categories is considered and rejected. Complete identity between utterances does not occur and in any case cannot form the basis for generalization. Certain frameworks devised to compare rhythm types, sonority, and overall basic phonological complexity employ scalar variables, but these are in practise founded on categorical assumptions. Doing typological work in phonology without reliance on categories is considered unlikely to be possible.

1 Introduction

Phoneticians and phonologists have generally relied on a basic descriptive framework which presupposes a set of categories anchored in local and dynamic aspects of the speech production mechanism and in the auditory and perceptual systems and the mental processing capacities largely common to all humans, as well as in the nature of the acoustic signal that carries speech between the speaker and the listener. These include terms for places of articulation such as bilabial, velar, or pharyngeal, labels for categories of articulatory configurations and their auditory characteristics such as plosive, fricative, or nasal, and categories for acoustic properties such as burst, formant, and noise. Specific entities such as voiceless bilabial plosive ([p]) or low central unrounded vowel ([a]) are also referenced. In addition, higher-order categories such as consonant and vowel, liquid, sonorant and obstruent, coronal and guttural are customary. Categories such as the syllable and its component parts of onset, nucleus, rhyme, and coda, and other larger units such as the intonational phrase are also familiar. Analytical concepts such as tones, phonemes (or similar notions of contrastive elements), and stress, and inventories of these elements as well as categories that express relationships between variant forms, such as assimilation, gemination, or lenition, also form part of this framework. Comparison between the phonetic and phonological properties of languages has mostly been based on such categorical properties: this or that language has a similar vowel system to another but a distinct one from yet others; these languages allow limited syllable structures but others allow a larger range of structures; these languages require nasals before stops to assimilate in place but these others don't, and so on.

https://doi.org/10.1515/9783110451931-004

The most familiar body of work on phonetics and phonology from the nineteenth, twentieth, and twenty-first centuries (including, for example, Sweet 1877, Jespersen 1889, Trubetzkoy 1939, Hockett 1955, Catford 1977, Chomsky & Halle 1968, Maddieson 1984, Stevens 1998, Ladefoged & Maddieson 1986, etc., etc.) for the most part assumes that the categories established are more-or-less valid for any language without explicitly arguing the point. And much of this familiar conceptual framework and terminology has roots in considerably older traditions of scholarship in Greek, Roman, Arabic, Indian, or Chinese cultures which also imply that – even if the terms are used to describe properties of specific languages such as Latin or Sanskrit – the descriptive framework itself is not language-specific.

In other words, much of the terminology used in the phonetic sciences and applied in phonological analysis refers to categories that are determined outside the scope of an individual language. That is, they seem to fit the bill of being "pre-determined categories" of the sort that Haspelmath (2007) declared "do not exist". Haspelmath (2010) argues that cross-language comparison, and hence any form of linguistic typology, cannot be based on "descriptive categories" but must instead be based on "comparative concepts". This seems like a distinction without a difference. The notion of a category is of course widely discussed in philosophical literature and in many specialized fields, and is open to divergent interpretations, but by-and-large anything that can be called a concept can be interpreted as a category. Harnad (2005) in a trenchant (and entertaining) article argues that any cognitive act is necessarily an act of categorization. The very name "typology" implies recognition of types, that is, categories. But purely physical scales can be non-categorical. As an example, Harnad mentions the categorical set of colors as opposed to the continuous property of electromagnetic wavelength/frequency which human perceptual and cognitive systems divide up in colors.

In this chapter I consider whether it is conceivable (or useful) to discuss within- and between-language similarities and differences without forming categories, i.e., without appealing to any discrete variables (not necessarily the familiar ones) that are taken to be language-independent. That is, can we insightfully compare languages or their phonological attributes without establishing types? In particular the foundation of various continuous-seeming scales proposed in the literature will be discussed.

2 Commensurability

Any kind of linguistic analysis, most especially typology, depends on being able to say that some tokens are exemplars of the same "entity" or can be placed in a commensurable space: otherwise each speech act is *sui generis* and no generalizations are possible.

"Sameness" could be physical identity; in which case it would not be necessary to form any kind of over-arching category to subsume any differences. But no two utterances, even by the same speaker of the same lexical string in the same language, are ever identical. Hence, IDENTITY can never provide a basis for grouping of phonetic/phonological samples. Repetitions of the same utterance by the same speaker even under similar conditions differ in many details. Consider the two spectrograms in Figure 4.1. These show two repetitions by a female English speaker of a string of digits which form a familiar telephone number. The speaker is very habituated to saying this string and the two repetitions are so similar that listeners cannot reliably say if they have heard two playings of the same recording or two different recordings.

These two utterances have almost identical overall timing and very similar F0 contours – but nonetheless they differ in many details of timing, amplitude, and spectral composition, some of which are indicated in the annotations provided on the figure.

Note that for convenience the differences are mostly described here using categorical labels, e.g., vowel, nasal, burst, formant, etc., since these terms are familiar. However, in principle it is possible to largely avoid these categorical labels by using circumlocutions referring only to continuous variables, such as

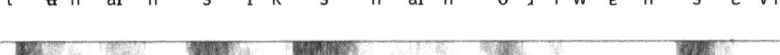

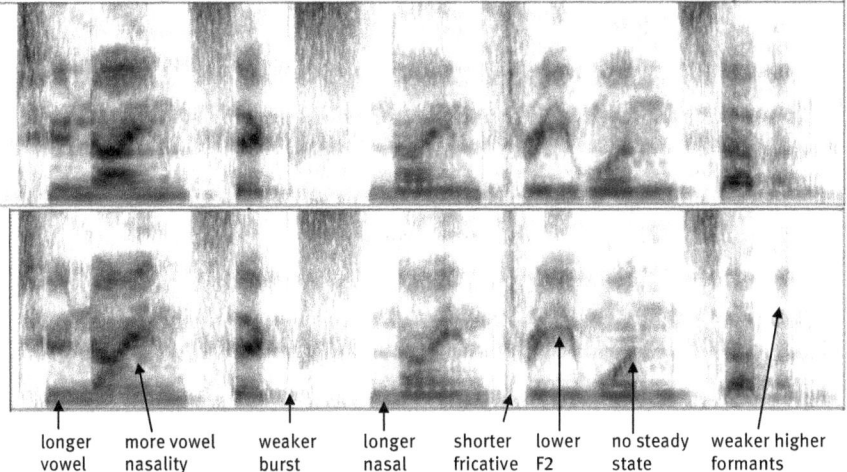

Figure 4.1: Spectrograms of two repetitions of a digit string by the same speaker. Differences between the two repetitions are noted on the lower spectrogram.

"the time interval between the first major increase in signal amplitude and the following salient reduction in amplitude" instead of "first vowel".

A non-categorical alternative to identity is therefore to rely on such continuous variables which can provide a space within which comparisons of a scalar nature can be made. Work in the phonetic sciences, including in the Laboratory Phonology paradigm, frequently measures properties of utterances in terms of continuous variables in spatial, temporal, amplitude, frequency and other dimensions. These are typically employed to quantify differences between samples considered to exemplify different categories. But can typology be done using continuous variables? That is, could we do comparison between languages – the sorting out of similarities and differences between them – without using "types"? Some work appears to attempt to do this, for example, the extensive amount of work devoted to quantitative studies of rhythm.

3 Scalar measures of rhythm

This research tradition is inspired by the rhythmic typology proposed by Lloyd James (1940), and popularized by Pike (1946) and Abercrombie (1967). This approach proposed a division into "syllable-timed" and "stress-timed" languages based on whether syllables or stresses are are believed to be closer to being isochronous. Later, "mora-timed" languages, with Japanese as the prototype, were added as a third major class. The clearly categorical nature of this typology was challenged by Dauer (1983) who compared English, Spanish, Italian, and Greek. In all four of these languages the inter-stress interval increases LINEARLY with an increase in syllable count, despite a consensus that English and Spanish (at least) belong to different rhythm categories. Moreover, the slope of the line fitting inter-stress interval and syllable count is similar in all languages and mean syllable duration is very similar, as shown in Figure 4.2 (data replotted after Dauer 1967).

Dauer did not conclude that languages cannot be grouped by rhythmic properties (though some readers interpreted her data that way). Instead, she suggested that a variety of factors lead to judgments of rhythmic difference, and that these place languages on a continuum rather than in discrete categories. These factors concern (at least) syllable structure, the role of stress, and vowel reduction. She argues that "stress-timed" languages have more closed syllables than "syllable-timed" ones, calculating that closed syllables constitute 56% in English, versus 30% in French and 26% in Spanish. "Stress-timed" languages have more heavy syllables than "syllable-timed" ones, and heavy syllables tend to attract stress and hence have more stresses per unit time. "Stress-timed" languages have more reduction of vowel quality in unstressed syllables than "syllable-timed"

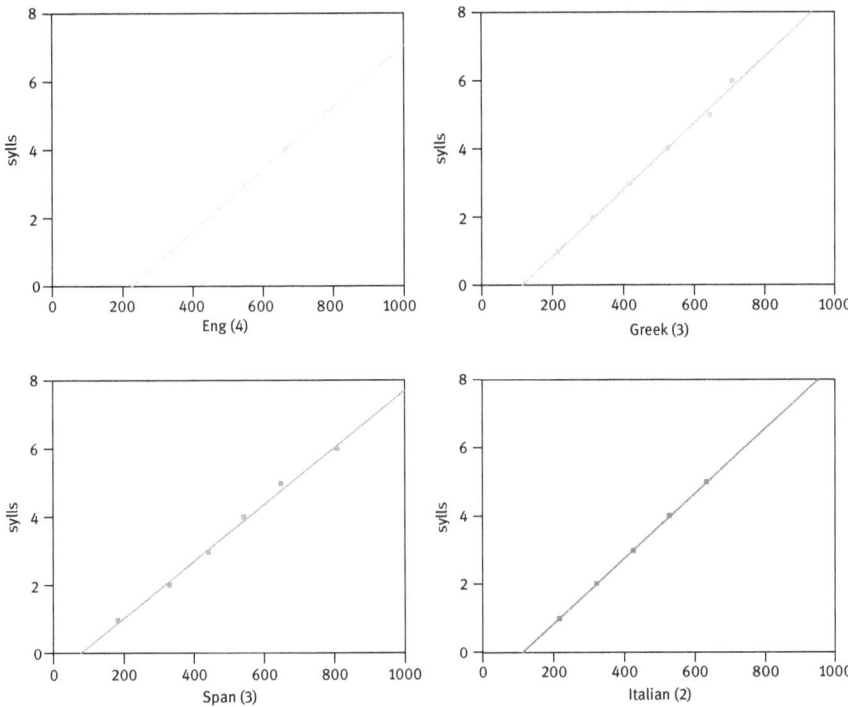

Figure 4.2: Utterance duration by syllable count in four languages (average of data from 2–4 speakers).

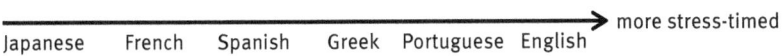

Figure 4.3: Dauer's exemplification of a continuum of "stress-timedness".

ones and "stress-timed" languages have a more important contrastive function for stress and therefore are more likely to allow alternative stress patterns syntagmatically. Dauer illustrates a partial continuum as in Figure 4.3.

Ramus et al. (1999), motivated, inter alia, by Dauer's suggestions, proposed that it would be possible to make continuous measures which reflect the linguistic impressions of rhythm type. Specifically they suggested measuring the following three parameters in a sample of connected speech for any given language:
- %V proportion of speech that is vocalic (the inverse is %C)
- ΔV standard deviation of vocalic intervals
- ΔC standard deviation of consonantal intervals

Of these three measures, %V reflects how much of the speech is vocalic, ΔV reflects the variability of vocalic intervals, and ΔC reflects the variability of consonantal intervals.

Ramus et al. (1999) made measurements of sample sentences in data from eight languages: English, Polish, Dutch, French, Spanish, Italian, Catalan, and Japanese. In the traditional rhythmic typology, the Germanic languages are considered "stress-timed", the Romance languages are considered "syllable-timed", and Japanese is considered "mora-timed". Polish has no agreed classification. Figure 4.4 plots the two-dimensional grouping of these languages on the %V and ΔC variables. This pair of variables groups languages into the traditional categories: English and Dutch are grouped together, the four Romance languages are grouped together, with Japanese distant from both these groups. Polish is classified with "stress-timed" languages in the space defined by these two variables.

Figure 4.5 plots mean %V vs ΔV. This pair of variables also groups the expected languages into the traditional categories, with the two Germanic languages together, the four Romance languages together, and Japanese apart. However, here Polish is in a group of its own.

In principle, thus, these languages can be placed in a continuous multidimensional space, which supports – but does not depend on – a classification based on intuitive impressions of rhythmic similarity/difference that was originally based on assigning them to categories.

Substantial subsequent work inspired by the original study by Ramus et al. has measured data on more languages, suggested modified indices, tested if perceptual similarity estimates match measured distances, examined the effects of variables such as speech rate and text type, as well as other factors. For example, Grabe & Low (2002) provide data on 18 languages, as shown in Figure 4.6.

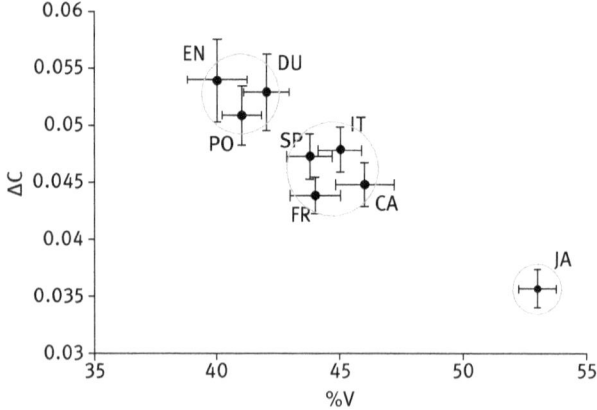

Figure 4.4: Mean values of ΔC vs %V by language, after Figure 1 in Ramus et al. (1999).

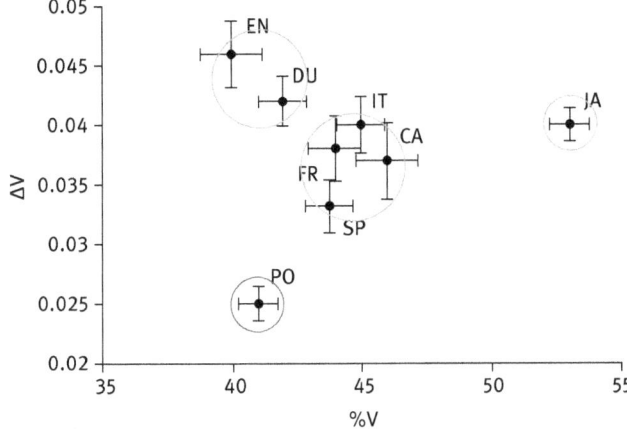

Figure 4.5: Mean values of ΔV vs %V by language, after Figure 2 in Ramus et al. (1999).

At first glance it may appear that this work is a promising effort to do phonological typology with continuous rather than categorical variables. However, this is not really the case, for both pragmatic and principled reasons. First of all it doesn't work in practical terms: the proposed measures turn out to be highly variable across individual speakers, speech rates, language samples, etc. (see, for example, Dellwo et al. 2012, Arvaniti 2012). Very strikingly the languages in common between the Ramus et al. (1999) and Grabe & Low (2002) studies are placed quite differently

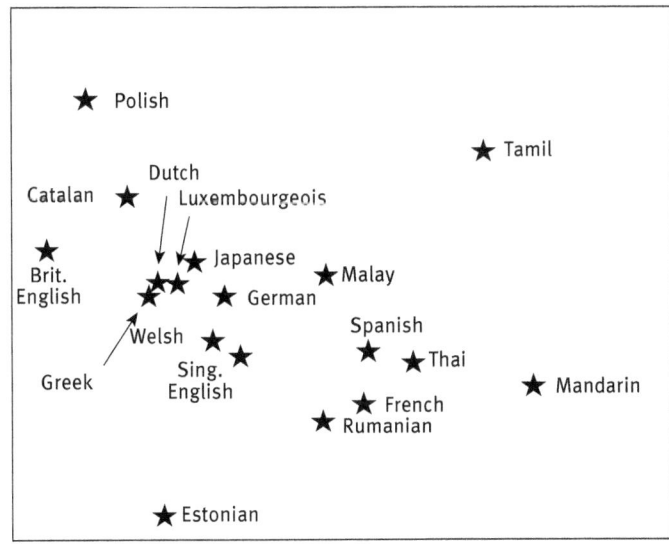

Figure 4.6: Mean ΔC vs %V over 18 languages after Figure 3 in Grabe & Low (2002).

in ΔC / %V space as can be seen by comparing the results in Figures 4.4 and 4.6. In Figure 4.4 Catalan is close to the other Romance languages, whereas in Figure 4.6, Catalan is distant from French and Spanish (and Rumanian) and close to the Germanic languages in the sample. Polish is close to English and German in Figure 4.4 but distant from all other languages in Figure 4.6. Japanese is distant from all other languages in Figure 4.4 but falls with the Germanic languages in Figure 4.6.

These inconsistencies could be due to various causes, in particular, the fact that measurements of these parameters on individuals speaking the same language vary considerably, as illustrated in Figure 4.7 showing variation among eight speakers of Swiss German on the %V parameter. The means for these different individuals range from about 38% to about 47%, which is greater than the difference between English and French in Ramus et al. (which is about 5%) or between French and German in Grabe & Low (which is about 4%), and each individual also varies over a considerable range within the speech samples used.

Another major source of within-language variability comes from the fact that measurements on the same language at different speech rates vary. Dellwo (2009) provided ΔC measurements from five languages from speakers speaking a varying rates. The results are shown in Figure 4.8 with the data divided into five speech-rate "bins". The left panel shows the raw data. In all five languages the variability of

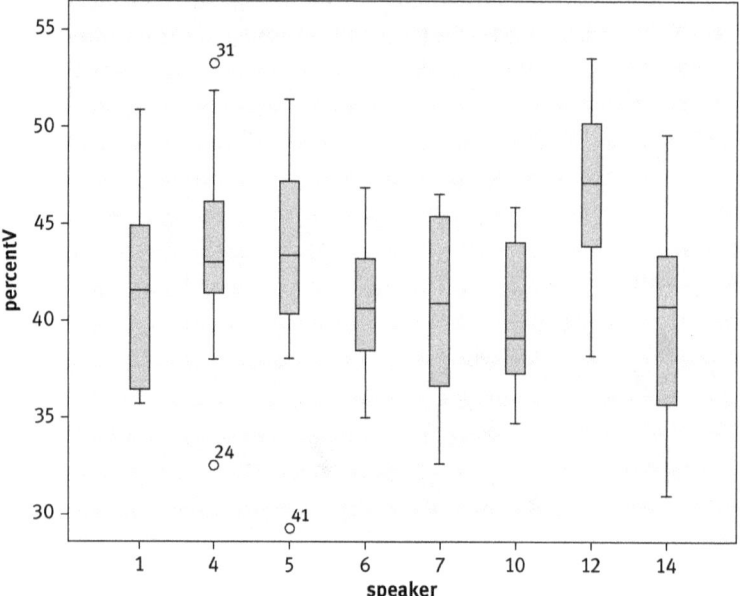

Figure 4.7: Individual speaker means and variation of %V for 8 Swiss German speakers from Dellwo et al. (2012).

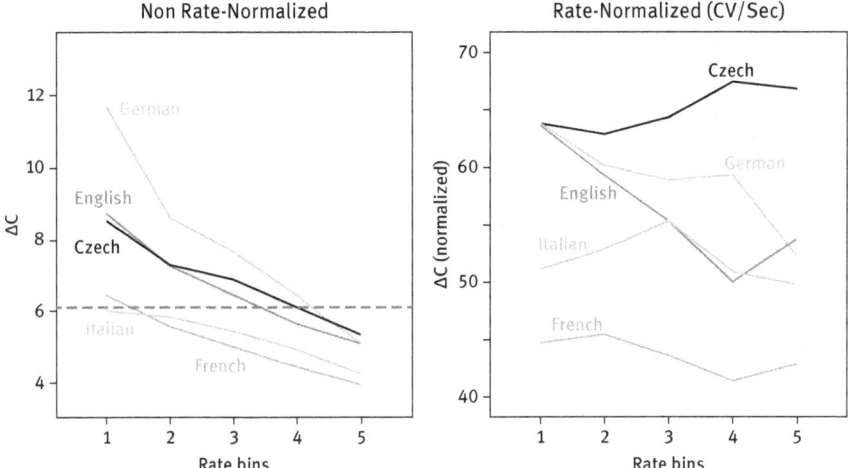

Figure 4.8: Raw and rate-normalized measures of ΔC in five languages by speech rate (from Dellwo 2009).

consonant intervals declines as speech rate increases, but more sharply for those languages with higher variability at slow rates. Hence fast-rate German overlaps with slow-rate French (as highlighted by the dotted line). Applying a rate-normalization which standardizes speech rate according to the local CV alternation rate, as in the right panel, to some extent stabilizes the data from Czech, Italian, and French. Normalized ΔC in these languages at the fastest rate is similar to that at the slowest rate. However, English and Italian are now confounded at faster rates.

These practical problems illustrating the instability of the proposed rhythmic parameters are compounded by one of principle. Obviously, the calculation of indices such ΔC or %V relies on a prior categorization of the speech data into intervals labeled as Consonants and Vowels. These are presumably precisely the kind of "pre-established categories" whose existence was questioned in Haspelmath (2007). The resulting metrics are continuous variables, which enable languages to be compared in a multi-dimensional continuous space, but they depend on an assumption of categoriality.

4 Phonological complexity scales

There are parallel problems for other seemingly continuous metrics which have at times been put forward as ways to place languages along a continuous scale or in a multi-dimensional non-categorical space. One example is the measure labeled TPD (for "Total Phoneme Diversity") by Atkinson (2011). Atkinson proposed a single

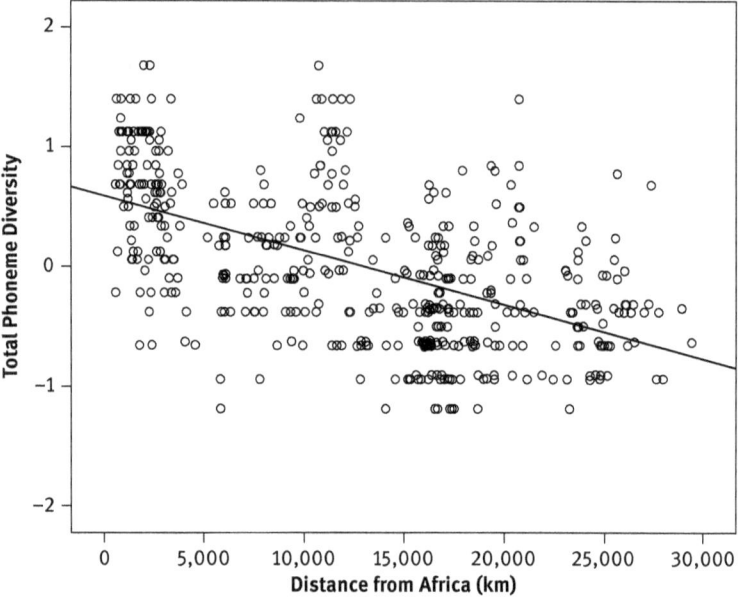

Figure 4.9: TPD vs distance from a hypothesized origin in (West) Africa (Figure 3 in Atkinson 2011).

index designed to reflect phonological complexity in order to test his hypothesis that phonological complexity broadly declines with distance from humanity's original African homeland (analogically with the established decline in genetic diversity, due to the founder effect). Figure 4.9 shows the fit between TPD and distance from a hypothesized origin in Africa to the present location of a large sample of languages. When languages are grouped into his choice of six major geographical areas, Africa has the highest mean TPD value, and South America and Oceania the lowest, as shown in Figure 4.10. Thus these language groups can be compared along a single continuous variable. However, the TPD score, itself continuous, is calculated from counts of consonants, (basic) vowels and tones – founded on traditional categories, and the assumption that such entities take part in categorical contrasts. Improved (but still simple-minded) phonological complexity scores (e.g., Maddieson et al. 2011) can be proposed, but these remain derived from categorical data.

5 Sonority scaling

Similarly, work by cultural anthropologists examining the relationship between cultural/environmental factors and phonological structures is based ultimately on categorical data, even when a continuous scale is used. This work seems to be little known among linguists, so will be summarized in some detail here.

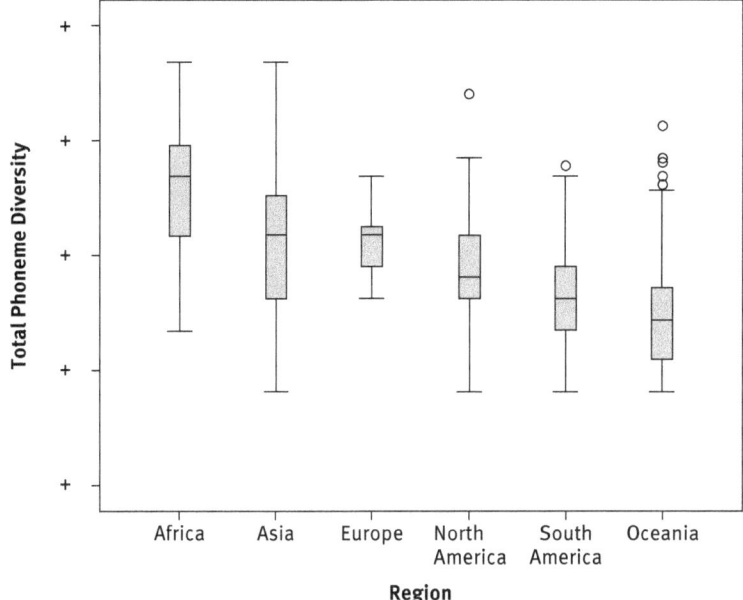

Figure 4.10: Mean and range of TPD scores for languages grouped into six regional clusters (after Figure 4 in Anderson 2011).

Munroe et al. (1996) proposed that there is a major influence of climate on phonological structure. Their hypothesis was that people in warm climates spend more time outdoors than those in cold climates. This means that they are often communicating over larger distances under poorer transmission conditions (because they are outdoors). Hence, there is a greater need to optimize the sound transmission characteristics of the language. They interpreted this (originally) as predicting that warm climate languages will show a preference for simple CV syllables.

Munroe et al. counted the proportion of CV syllables in up to 200 words of the "basic" lexicon of 60 languages chosen to represent the 60 major cultural areas recognized in the Human Relations Area Files (current version at http://hraf.yale.edu). Their basic result was that languages situated in warm climates did indeed generally have a higher proportion of CV syllables in the wordlists. (Their dividing line between "warm" and "cold" was that a cold climate has mean winter temperature of 10°C (50°F) or lower for 5 or more months per year.) In a follow-up study Munroe & Silander (1999) examined if the effect can be found within language families (as a check on whether it is an artifact of where language families with different inherited prototypical syllabic patterns are located).

The findings by Munroe and colleagues were challenged by Ember & Ember (1999) who proposed that "baby-holding" rather than climate was a better predictor of the frequency of simple CV structures across languages. And this prompted Munroe's team to counter that calculating a continuous "sonority score" and making climate a multi-valued, rather than binary, variable re-affirmed climate as a significant predictor of cross-language structural differences in their phonology. Their result is shown in Figure 4.10, which plots a sonority score against the number of cold months per year.

The debate continued, with Ember & Ember (2007) pointing to the large variation in sonority scores among languages in warm climates seen in Figure 4.11, and looking for further factors that might explain this. They proposed three additional factors: (i) degree of sexual freedom (which correlates with higher sonority); (ii) degree of plant cover (correlates with higher sonority); (iii) degree of "mountain-ness" (correlates with lower sonority). Their figure relating scores

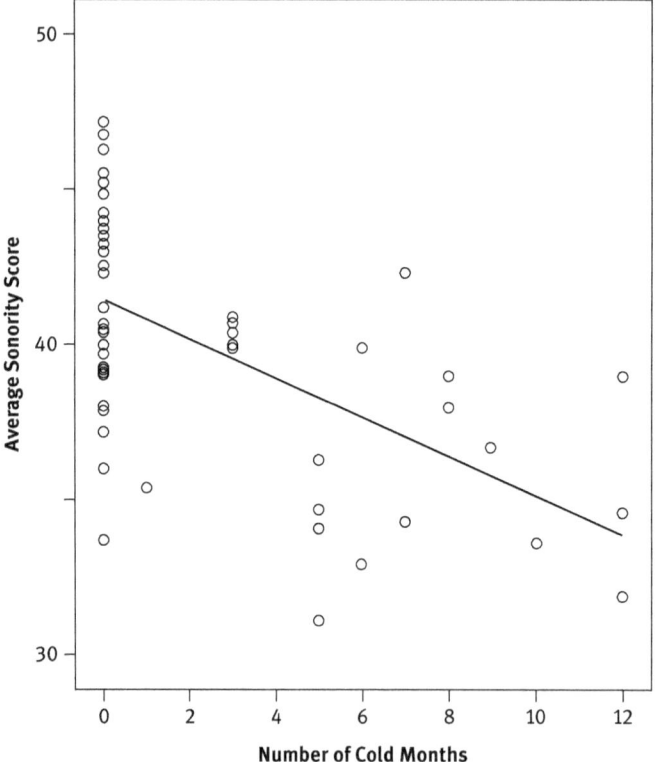

Figure 4.11: Plot of "sonority score" vs number of cold months, after Ember & Ember (2010), using data from Fought et al (2004). Linear fit shown, $R_2 = .329$.

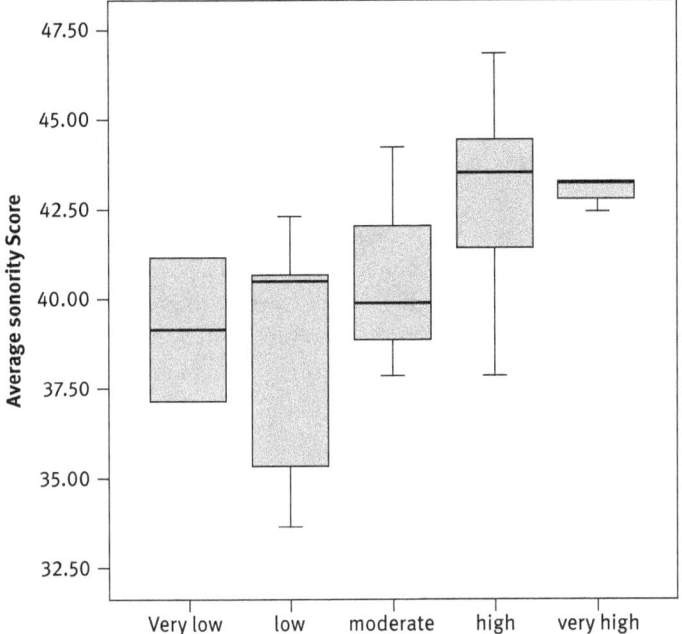

Figure 4.12: Boxplot of mean sonority score by sexual freedom (after Ember & Ember 2010, based on data in Fought et al 2004, and Huber et al 2004).

for extra-marital sex (taken from Huber et al. 2004) to the sonority scores provided by Fought et al. (2004) is shown in Figure 4.12. Very broadly, the higher sonority scores occur in languages spoken by what are reported as more sexually free societies.

The correlations found in these studies are intriguing, and in all probability some relationship between phonological characteristics and climatic and ecological variables is real (e.g., Maddieson & Coupé 2015). However, here the interest is primarily in the effort to place languages along a continuous scale of sonority. But note that in this case also, as with the work on rhythm types, the constructed continuous scale used to compare the languages is one based on categorical values. The sonority score was calculated by assigning a value between 100 and 2 to phonetic classes such as low vowels (scored 100), nasals (scored 9), and stops (scored 2). A score is constructed for each word in word-lists from each language by summing the values for each segment in the word and dividing by the number of segments counted (affricates, for example, count as two segments) and the mean word-score per language is then calculated. This procedure evidently depends entirely on the prior recognition of the categories of individual segments to which sonority values are assigned.

6 Non-categorical sonority scaling?

The fact that efforts to place languages on a continuous sonority scale seem to yield interesting results suggests that it could be worth considering the construction of a purely continuous scale of sonority that does not depend on a prior categorical labeling.

It is possible to imagine a scale that depended only on a measure of the intensity of recorded speech samples, either of a list of words as in Fought et al. (2004) or of continuous speech. The higher the proportion of speech duration that consists of high-intensity sound the more sonorous it would be considered. This could in principle be measured as the mean intensity found in the samples being compared. (Note that intensity is a measure of the integrated and rectified instantaneous amplitudes throughout a sample.)

There are, however, considerable problems in implementing such a comparison, both of a practical and a theoretical nature. The major practical problem revolves around the fact that amplitude values in a recording depend not only on the speech power itself but on the conditions and equipment used in the recording and on potential moment-to-moment variations in the orientation of the speaker to the microphone. Also individual speakers speak louder or more quietly than others. All these factors mean that a crude measure of mean amplitude of individual samples might not be representative of characteristics of a language. Possible normalization schemes could be proposed, such as scaling amplitude values in relation to the maximum observed in the sample, or to an average of the maxima recorded in the tokens of the low central vowel /a/ which is present in most languages and generally assumed to be the most sonorous segment. Note that the latter strategy would depend crucially on identifying the category of /a/ tokens, and would fail for languages that did not have a comparable segment.

Amplitude also varies as a function of such factors as utterance type and position in an utterance. In many languages, for example, amplitude typically diminishes over the duration of an utterance. Consequently a given word occurring late in an utterance would have lower amplitude than the same word occurring early in the utterance. If a hypothesis of cross-language relative sonority differences is based on the relative frequency of more versus less sonorous segments in the LEXICON (rather than in running speech), then this is a potentially serious confound. An unguided comparison of mean speech intensity across samples is thus unlikely to be informative.

Despite these problems it is certainly possible to conceive continuous scales of language-level sonority. Rather than a purely algorithmic procedure a preliminary test of a scoring using a minimally categorical classification guided by local amplitude peaks and valleys has been conducted. Speech samples are divided into sonorant and non-sonorant intervals. Sonorance is defined by two properties: presence of a (quasi-)periodic fundamental frequency and presence of a formant-like structure in the mid-frequency range for speech (c. 300–3000 Hz). In general there is on the order of 10 dB difference between peak amplitude in a sonorous interval and the amplitude valley in a non-sonorous interval. A language's score is the percentage of a speech sample's duration that is sonorous according to these criteria.

The test data for this project is a subset of the language materials used in Easterday et al. (2011). That study was designed to examine – regardless of any attempt to assign languages to rhythm classes – whether the factors suggested by Dauer (1983) as influencing rhythmic type judgments, such as syllable structure and vowel reduction, actually correlate with the metrics put forward by Ramus et al. (1999). The speech samples used are drawn from those created by the Global Recordings Network (see http://globalrecordings.net/en/), an evangelical Christian organization that makes recordings of proselytizing materials in a wide range of languages publicly available online. Although it is not the intended purpose of these materials, they provide a potentially valuable tool for cross-linguistic research, particularly of the kind that simply examines acoustic properties without any need for a transcription of the content. The recordings are well-matched in terms of style and content since they are based on the same set of prepared didactic texts and pictures.

Easterday et al. (2011) segmented the recordings used in their study into Consonant and Vowel intervals, similar to the process in the work on rhythmic typology discussed earlier. These analyses are being relabeled so as to calculate the percentage of duration in running speech which is periodic and broadly falls above a (locally-defined) intensity threshold. Samples are of monologues of running speech spoken fluently but in a moderately careful style. Pauses between sentences or other utterance units are excluded from the duration calculation. The actual speech duration measured in each sample varies between about one half and one minute in length (range 27.3–52.3). Voiceless stop closures following a pause are included as part of the pause duration. To date this re-analysis has been completed for one speaker of each of 13 languages. The results are shown in tabular form in Table 4.1 and graphed against distance from the Equator in Figure 4.13.

The results of this analysis show that the range from highest to lowest sonorant percentage is quite wide, but strikingly the majority of the languages cluster around being about two-thirds composed of sonorous material in running speech, at least in these samples. This suggests that this is an approximate norm for languages. The results remain too meager so far to draw strong conclusions, but they do provide a further hint in support of the suggestion that some aspects

Table 4.1: Sonorous percentage in sample of 13 languages.

	% SONORANT
Qiang	62.4 %
Nez Perce	64.4 %
Thaayore	64.9 %
Tamazight	65.7 %
Chukchi	66.8 %
Sheko	67.0 %
Sgaw Karen	67.1 %
Mixtec	68.4 %
Pohnpeian	68.5 %
Maori	69.1 %
Ekagi	71.2 %
Towa	76.9 %
Maung	93.4 %

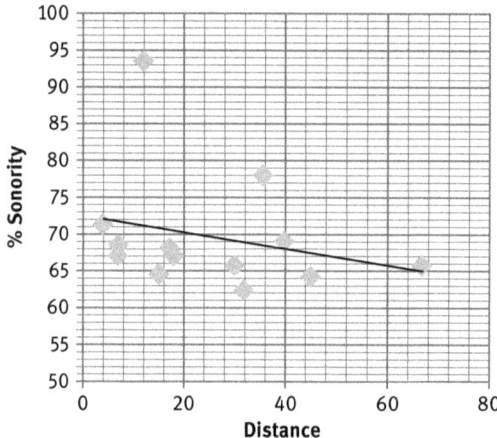

Figure 4.13: Sonorous percentage against absolute distance in degrees from the Equator.

of linguistic structure have links to climate and environment. The distance of a language's location from the Equator can serve as a very rough proxy for warmer vs. cooler climate. Figure 4.13 plots the sonority score against the language's point location as shown in the LAPSyD database (Maddieson et al. 2013). There is indeed some correlation between lower sonority and distance from the Equator. This aligns with the proposal in Fought et al. (2004) and other suggestions that sound patterns in languages are in part designed in response to environmental factors (e.g. Maddieson et al. 2013, Maddieson & Coupé 2015).

However, once more, the basis for constructing this particular continuous variable depends on a categorization of speech intervals, in this case one that is functionally equivalent to establishing the binary categories of sonorous and non-sonorous. The languages themselves are neither sorted into categories, nor said to possess or lack particular categorical properties, so the role of categorization in this exercise is minimal, but it is still there.

7 Final remarks

It has been shown that several proposals to characterize aspects of phonological typology along continuous scales that are found in the literature turn out to be based on a prior step involving categorical classifications. A thought experiment to devise a sonority measure that was entirely free of non-categorical assumptions seemed to founder on practical and theoretical difficulties. However, one that makes only a minimal appeal to prior established categories shows some promise of providing interesting differentiation between languages, and a potentially intriguing connection to hypotheses suggesting adaptation to aspects of the environment. This perhaps shows that cross-language comparisons using scalar variables, albeit derived from categorization, may nonetheless be of some interest.

Is the failure to devise purely continuous scales for typological properties simply a failure of imagination, due to over-familiarity with the traditional way of observing phonetic and phonological characteristics through the lens of established categories? Quite possibly. It seems also possible that Harnad is right: "To cognize is to categorize". Any attempt to distribute languages along a parameter seems to entail defining some property which is present or absent either in an absolute or a gradient fashion in each language examined. A property is necessarily a categorical entity. This does not mean that the categories that are familiar in the established traditions in the phonetic sciences are necessarily the most useful we can devise, or that they are applicable to all languages. But to this phonological typologist, it does not seem practicable to compare languages in the absence of categories.

References

Abercrombie, David. 1967. *Elements of general phonetics*. Edinburgh: Edinburgh University Press.
Arvaniti, Amalia. 2012. The usefulness of metrics in the quantification of speech rhythm. *Journal of Phonetics* 40. 351–373.

Atkinson, Quentin. 2011. Phonemic diversity supports serial founder effect model of language expansion from Africa. *Science* 332. 346–349.

Catford, J. C. 1977. *Fundamental problems in phonetics*. London: Longman.

Chomsky, Noam & Morris Halle. 1968. *The sound pattern of English*. New York: Harper & Row.

Dauer, Rebecca. 1967. Stress-timing and syllable-timing re-analyzed. *Journal of Phonetics* 11. 51–62.

Dellwo, Volker. 2009. Choosing the right rate normalization methods for measurements of speech rhythm. In *Proceedings of AISV*.

Dellwo, Volker, Adrian Leemann, & Marie-José Kolly. 2012. Speaker idiosyncratic rhythmic features in the speech signal. In *Proceedings of Interspeech 2012*, Portland OR.

Easterday, Shelece, Jason Timm, & Ian Maddieson. 2011. The effects of phonological structure on the acoustic correlates of rhythm. ICPhS Hong Kong.

Ember, Carol R. & Marvin Ember. 2007. Climate, econiche, and sexuality: Influences on sonority in language. *American Anthropologist, New Series* 109. 180–185.

Ember, Carol R. & Marvin Ember. 2007. Rejoinder to Munroe and Fought's commentary. *American Anthropologist, New Series* 109. 785.

Ember, Marvin & Carol R. Ember. 1999. Cross-language predictors of consonant-vowel syllables. *American Anthropologist, New Series* 101. 730–742.

Fought, John G., Robert L. Munroe, Carmen R. Fought, & Erin M. Good. 2004. Sonority and climate in a world sample of languages. *Cross-Cultural Research* 38. 27–51.

Grabe, Esther & E. L. Low. 2003. Durational variability in speech and the rhythm class hypothesis. In Carlos Gussenhoven & Natasha Warner (eds.), *Papers in laboratory phonology* 7, 515–546. Berlin: Mouton de Gruyter.

Harnad, Stevan. 2005. To cognize is to categorize: Cognition is categorization. In Henri Cohen & Claire Lefebvre (eds.), *Handbook of categorization in cognitive science*, 19–43. Amsterdam: Elsevier.

Haspelmath, Martin. 2007. Pre-established categories don't exist: Consequences for language description and typology. *Linguistic Typology* 11. 119–132.

Haspelmath, Martin. 2010. Comparative concepts and descriptive categories in crosslinguistic studies. *Language* 86. 663–687.

Hockett, Charles. 1955. *A manual of phonology* (Indiana University Publications in Anthropology and Linguistics, Memoir 11). Bloomington IN: Indiana University.

Huber, Brad R., Vendula Linhartova, & Dana Cope. 2004. Measuring paternal certainty using cross-cultural data. *World Cultures* 15. 48–59.

Jespersen, Otto. 1889. *The articulations of speech sounds represented by means of analphabetic symbols*. Marburg: N. G. Elwert.

Ladefoged, Peter & Ian Maddieson. *Sounds of the world's languages*. Oxford: Blackwell.

Lloyd James, Arthur. 1940. *Speech signals in telephony*. London: Pitman.

Maddieson, Ian. 1984. *Patterns of sounds*. Cambridge: Cambridge University Press.

Maddieson, Ian, Tanmoy Bhattacharya, Eric D. Smith, & William Croft. 2011. Geographical distribution of phonological complexity. *Linguistic Typology* 15. 267–279.

Maddieson, Ian & Christophe Coupé. 2015. Human language diversity and the acoustic adaptation hypothesis. *Proceedings of Meetings on Acoustics* 25, 060005. http://dx.doi.org/10.1121/2.0000198

Maddieson, Ian, Sébastien Flavier, Christophe Coupé, Egidio Marsico, & François Pellegrino. 2013. LAPSyD: Lyon-Albuquerque Phonological Systems Database. *Interspeech* 2013, Lyon.

Munroe, Robert L., R. H. Munroe, & S. Winters. 1996. Cross-cultural correlates of the CV syllable. *Cross-Cultural Research* 30. 60–83.

Munroe, Robert L. & Megan Silander. 1999. Climate and the consonant-vowel syllable: A replication within language families. *Cross-Cultural Research* 33. 43–62.

Pike, Kenneth L. 1946. *Intonation of American English*. Ann Arbor: University of Michigan.

Ramus, Franck, Marina Nespor, & Jacques Mehler. 1999. Correlates of linguistic rhythm in the speech signal. *Cognition* 73. 265–292.

Stevens, Kenneth L. 1998. *Acoustic phonetics*. Cambridge, MA: MIT Press.

Sweet, Henry. 1877. *A handbook of phonetics*. Oxford: Clarendon Press.

Trubetzkoy, Nikolai S. 1939. *Grundzüge der Phonologie*. Travaux du Cercle Linguistique de Prague 7.

Jeffrey Heinz
The computational nature of phonological generalizations

Abstract: This chapter studies the nature of the typology of phonological markedness constraints and the nature of the typology of the transformation from underlying to surface forms from a computational perspective. It argues that there are strong computational laws that constrain the form of these constraints and transformations. These laws are currently stated most clearly in terms of the so-called subregular hierarchies, which have been established for stringsets (for modeling constraints) and are currently being established for string-to-string maps (for modeling the transformations). It is anticipated that future research will reveal equally powerful laws applicable to non-string-based representations. Finally, this chapter argues that these laws arise as a natural consequence of how humans generalize from data.

1 Illuminating the phonological component of grammar

Wilhelm von Humboldt's phrase "language makes infinite use of finite means" (1836/1999) is oft-cited by Chomsky because not only does it encapsulate an important characteristic of natural language, but it also highlights why GENERATIVE grammars play an important role in understanding this aspect of language. In brief, generative grammars are the finite means, but the linguistic knowledge they represent can be applied to unboundedly many linguistic forms. The psychological reality of generative grammars is the powerful scientific hypothesis which underlies all work in generative linguistics.

In this chapter, we will study generative grammars from both a typological and computational perspective. The same Wilhelm von Humboldt is reported (Frans Plank, p.c.) to have suggested that in order to do linguistic typology, two encyclopedias are necessary. The first is "an encyclopedia of categories" and the second is "an encyclopedia of languages". The encyclopedia of categories provides an ontology with which the encyclopedia of languages — and the generalizations about them — can be studied. The object of inquiry is natural language and the linguistic generalizations. But the light we shine on them comes from the encyclopedia of categories.

This chapter will argue that the theory of computation provides a meaningful and insightful encyclopedia of categories, with which linguistic generalizations ought to be studied. (My discussion is limited to phonological generalizations, though much important work in a similar vein exists for other kinds of linguistic generalizations (Chomsky 1956; Gazdar & Pullum 1982; Shieber 1985; Rogers 1998; Kobele 2006; Graf 2013).) I will endeavor to explain that when phonological generalizations are studied in this light, there are computational laws which govern important aspects of their nature. I will also argue that current phonological theory does not account for these laws, and I will make suggestions as to how phonological theory might be modified to do so.

In this way, the goals of this chapter are similar to the goals of Charles Kisseberth in his 1970 paper "On the functional unity of phonological rules":

> I will show [. . .] that a rather rich set of diverse phenomenon is related in a complex, but quite coherent way. The theory of phonology has hitherto been blind to phenomena of this sort [. . .] and I will attempt to make some suggestions about the kind of apparatus the facts [. . .] seem to require that a theory of phonology contain. I am not, however, principally interested in proposing detailed formalism; instead I would like to encourage phonologists to *look* at the phonological component of a grammar in a particular way. (Kisseberth 1970: 239, emphasis in original)

Kisseberth argued that important generalizations in languages were missed by not paying attention to the functional unity of phonological rules. The introduction of surface constraints into phonological theory followed, and later became one of the cornerstones of Optimality Theory (OT; Prince & Smolensky 1993, 2004).

Similarly, I am arguing that important generalizations in languages are being missed by not paying attention to the computational nature of phonological generalizations. Yes, I am talking about computational generalizations of phonological generalizations. I argue that these meta-generalizations are important because they too suggest a conspiracy of sorts: phonological generalizations across languages are distinct, but they exhibit a very strong tendency to exhibit particular computational properties.

I will argue that, when phonological generalizations are studied under this light, the hypothesized computational laws are SUFFICIENTLY EXPRESSIVE to account for the impressive range of cross-linguistic variation, and are simultaneously VERY RESTRICTIVE in the sense that strong predictions are made about which logically possible phonological generalizations are not humanly possible ones. I will argue that in this respect these computational laws better match the attested typology than what is predicted by classical OT (and many of its variants), which, I will argue, is NEITHER sufficiently expressive NOR restrictive. I will also argue that the restrictive nature of the computational laws help answer questions about how such phonological generalizations can be learned.

The arguments that I am making in this chapter are not novel. They have previously been published in articles and conference proceedings. This chapter thus provides a roadmap for phonologists of this literature, and attempts to present a unified, overarching perspective on both the importance of this computational encyclopedia of categories and its implications for a theory of phonology.[1]

2 What is phonology?

The fundamental insight in the twentieth century which shaped the development of generative phonology is that the best explanation of the systematic variation in the pronunciation of morphemes is to posit a single underlying mental representation of the phonetic form of each morpheme and to derive its pronounced variants with context-sensitive transformations. This development, present in Chomsky (1951) and Halle (1959), was perhaps stated most fully and completely with Chomsky & Halle (1968), and persists in OT (Prince & Smolensky 2004) today.

Thus there is a point of agreement between different theories of phonology, which is stated in (1).

(1) There exist underlying representations of morphemes which are transformed to surface representations.

As a result of this fundamental insight, every particular theory of phonology grapples with three fundamental questions:

(2) a. What is the nature of the abstract, underlying, lexical representations?
 b. What is the nature of the concrete, surface representations?
 c. What is the nature of the transformation from underlying forms to surface forms?

I would like to give some examples of how phonological theories aim to answer these questions. It is not possible in this chapter to comprehensively survey the range of answers that have been offered. Therefore, I only highlight some answers (and only in very broad strokes).

---

[1] The roadmap is not exhaustive. Notable earlier research which examines the nature of phonological generalizations from a computational perspective but which will not receive as much discussion as it should includes Potts & Pullum (2002) and Graf (2010b), which also come from an intellectually similar perspective.

Rule-based theories, as exemplified by Chomsky & Halle (1968), for example, have argued that the abstract underlying representations are subject to language-specific morpheme structure constraints (MSCs). The transformations from underlying forms to surface forms are due to language-specific rules, which are applied in a language-specific order. Constraints on surface representations were, generally speaking, not part of the ontology of these theories, and therefore were not posited to have any psychological reality. Such generalizations — the phonotactic generalizations — were derivable from the interaction of the MSCs and the rules.

On the other hand, in classical OT (Prince & Smolensky 1993, 2004), there are no constraints on underlying representations (richness of the base), but there are psychologically real, universal constraints on surface forms (markedness constraints). The transformation from underlying forms to surface forms is formulated as an OPTIMIZATION over these markedness constraints, in addition to constraints which penalize differences between surface and underlying forms (so-called faithfulness constraints). While both the markedness and faithfulness constraints are universal, their relative importance is language-specific. So in every language the surface pronunciation of an underlying representation is predicted to be the optimal form (the one that violates the most important constraints the least), though what is optimal can vary across languages because the relative importance of the constraints can vary across languages.

These two theories are radically different in what they take to be psychologically real. The ontologies of the theories are very different. Perhaps this is most clear with respect to the concept of phonemes (Dresher 2011). Phonemes exist as a consequence of the ontology of rule-based theories, but they do not as a consequence of the ontology of OT. This is simply because phonemes are a kind of MSC; underlying representations of morphemes must be constructed out of them, and nothing else. In OT, there are no MSCs and hence there are no phonemes. Consequently, generalizations regarding complementary distribution are explained in a very different manner in the two theories, and they promote different views of the notion of CONTRAST. Despite these differences however, there is an important point of agreement: in both theories, complementary distribution of speech sounds in surface forms is the outcome of a transformation of underlying forms to surface forms.

This is the point I wish to emphasize: neither theory abandons the fundamental insight stated in (1).[2] The theories offer radical different answers to the questions in (2), but THEY AGREE ON THE QUESTIONS BEING ASKED.

---

[2] It is true that periodically some work is published in that direction, for example the work on output-to-output correspondence (Benua 1995, 1997, and others).

Like earlier research in generative grammar, research in computational phonology agrees with the insight in (1) and the questions being asked in (2). In this chapter we ask three derivative questions. In theories like SPE, which posit morpheme structure constraints, what does the theory of computation bring to the nature of these generalizations regarding underlying representations? In theories like OT, which posit markedness constraints, what does it bring to the nature of these phonotactic generalizations? And for ALL theories of phonology, What does it bring to the study of the nature of the transformations?

The theory of computation provides a way to answer these questions. The encyclopedia of categories it provides allows these different generalizations to be classified according to computational criteria. What makes this approach valuable is that it is about as atheoretical as one can get. This is because it explicitly separates the intensional descriptions of the generalizations from their extensions. The intensional description of the generalization is the one given by a phonologist in their grammatical description of the generalization. It is the "finite means" in Humboldt's sense. The extension of this intensional description is one that typically describes an infinite-sized object. It is the "infinite use" in Humboldt's sense. Mathematically, this infinitely-sized object exists. It is like a perfect circle, a set of infinitely many points each exactly the same distance from a center. But we can never see the object in its entirety. We cannot see an infinity of points, even if we know they are there. The situation with linguistic generalizations is similar. The extension is there, but they cannot be written down in their entirety since they are not finite. But we can write down a grammar which can be understood as generating the infinite set, in the same way that a perfect circle can be generated by specifying a center point and a distance, the radius.

The same perfect circle can be described in other ways as well. If we employ the Cartesian plane, we could generate a circle with an equation of the form $(x - a)^2 + (y - b)^2 = r^2$ where the r is the radius of the circle and (a, b) is its center. The equation is interpreted as follows: all and only points (x, y) which satisfy the equation belong to the circle. The equation is an intensional description and the set of points, the circle, is its extension.

We can also describe a circle on a plane with polar coordinates instead of Cartesian ones. Recall that polar coordinates are of the form (r, θ) where r is the radius and θ is an angle. The equation $r = 2a \cos(\theta) + 2b \sin(\theta)$ provides the general form of the circle with the radius given by $\sqrt{a^2 + b^2}$ and the center by (a, b) (in Cartesian coordinates). The polar equation is interpreted like the Cartesian one: all and only points (r, θ) which satisfy the equation belong to the circle.

There are some interesting differences between these two coordinate systems. Each point in the Cartesian system has a unique representation, but each point in the polar system has infinitely many representations (since the same angle can be described in infinitely many ways, e.g. 0° = 360° = 720° = . . .). If the center of the circle is the origin, the polar equation simplifies to $r = a$ whereas the Cartesian equation remains more complicated $x^2 + y^2 = r^2$. Thus, the polar equation $r = 4$ and the Cartesian equation $x^2 + y^2 = 16$ are different equations with different interpretations, but they describe the same unique circle: one of radius four centered around the origin. The two equations differ intensionally, but their extension is the same.

It seems strange to ask which of these two descriptions is the "right" description of a circle. They are different descriptions of the same thing. Some descriptions might be more useful than others for some purposes. It also interesting to ask what properties the circles have irrespective of a particular description. For instance the length of the perimeter and the area of a circle are certainly relatable to these descriptions, but they are also in a sense independent of the particulars. The perimeter and area depend on the radius but not the center, though both appear in the equations. This suggests that the radius is a more fundamental structure to a circle than its center, though both certainly matter.

The analogy I wish to draw is that rule-based and OT-theoretic formalisms are like the Cartesian and polar systems. The analogy is far from perfect, but it is instructive. Both rule-based and OT analyses provide descriptions of platonic, infinitely sized objects. In many cases, but not all, the two formalisms describe the same object, insofar as the empirical evidence allows.

What is this object? The transformations from underlying forms to surface forms can be thought of as a FUNCTION, in the mathematical sense of the word. Another word for function becoming prevalent in the phonological literature is MAP (Tesar 2014). There are three parts to a function. One, there is its domain, which is the set of objects the function applies to. Two, there is its co-domain, which is the set of objects to which the elements of the domain are mapped. Three, there is the map itself, which says which domain elements are transformed to which co-domain elements. Thus to specify a function, one needs to provide a description of its domain, its co-domain, and a description of which domain elements become which co-domain elements.

This lines up nearly perfectly with the fundamental questions of phonological theory. The underlying representations correspond to the domain. The surface representations are the co-domain. And the transformation from underlying to surface forms is the map from domain elements to co-domain elements. From this perspective, describing the phonology of a language requires describing aspects of this function, regardless of whether the function is described intensionally with SPE-style or OT grammars.

Further, in linguistic typology we are actually interested in the CLASS of such functions that correspond to POSSIBLE human phonologies. If the phonologies of languages are circles we would be interested in the universal properties of circles and the extent of their variation. Circles are pretty simple, so the answers are straightforward. All circles have a center and a radius, but their centers can be different points and their radii can have different lengths. What universal properties do phonological functions share? What kind of variation does the human animal permit in this function?

This is why computational approaches to language have much to offer. Studying the extensions of constraints and transformations through the lens of a computationally-grounded encyclopedia of categories helps us better understand the nature of phonological component of grammar.

3 Representing constraints and transformations

Ultimately, phonological grammars represent the functions mentioned earlier. However, unlike circles, phonologies are not described with single equations; instead, phonological grammars contain multiple, interacting parts. In OT grammars those parts are constraints. In rule-based grammars those parts are rules. In this section, we put these intensions aside and examine the extensions of phonotactic constraints and the extensions of phonological transformations. Then in the next sections we examine the computational nature of those extensions.

3.1 Phonotactic knowledge and markedness constraints

Halle (1978) gives phonotactic knowledge as an example of knowledge that is learned but not taught. He provides an experiment demonstrating this knowledge, whose results are shown in Table 5.1. I have informally conducted this experiment myself on dozens, if not hundreds of young adults, who are native speakers of English. When presented visually with orthographic representations of the words in Table 5.1 (but ungrouped), student reliably and uniformly identify *thole*, *plast* and *flitch* as the English words.[3] Just as circles are fruitfully thought of as an infinite set of points, phonotactic knowledge can likewise be thought of as an infinite set of strings. All possible English words are in the set; all logically

---

[3] A small minority of students suggest that *vlas* and *sram* might be English words but they agree they are less sure about these than the others. For more on gradient versus categorical distinctions in phonotactics, see Hayes & Wilson (2008) and Gorman (2013). In this chapter, we assume a categorical distinction for expositional purposes, but as discussed in Heinz (2010a) nothing really hinges on this.

Table 5.1: Words from Halle (1978).

possible English words	impossible English words
thole	ptak
plast	hlad
flitch	sram
	mgla
	vlas
	dnom
	rtut

possible, impossible words are out of the set. This is but one concrete way to see that "language makes infinite use of finite means"; generative grammars allow us to distinguish among infinitely many logically possible forms. One question linguists address is: What is the nature of this infinite set?

Markedness constraints in OT express phonotactic knowledge. Markedness constraints are said to prohibit marked structures so they distinguish well-formed structures from ill-formed ones. We will consider their extensions as follows: all surface forms with zero violations are in the set; all surface forms with nonzero violations are out of the set (cf. McCarthy 2003). Therefore, the extensions of these constraints can be interpreted as all and only those strings which are well-formed according to the constraint; they are those structures which DO NOT CONTAIN the marked structure as a sub-structure.

For example, consider the constraint *NÇ̬ (Pater 2001), which states that nasals followed by voiceless consonants are marked sequences. The extension of this constraint can be conceived as the set of strings not containing marked structure, some of which are explicitly shown in (3).

(3) {a, b, aba, anda, anba, ...}.

In fact every logically possible string which does not contain this marked substructure is in the extension of the *NÇ̬ constraint. As will be discussed in greater detail in Section 5.1, substrings like *n't* are sub-structures of strings.

Another example comes from syllable structure. It is widely held that codas are marked. Words with codas are said to violate the constraint NOCODA. Thus the well-formed structures picked out by this constraint are all and only those strings which do not contain codas as indicated by (4).

(4) {a, a.ba, pa.pa, ...}

The representations in (4) differ from those in (3) because they include a symbol for the syllable boundary. The available symbols, and the choice of representation more generally, is an important issue, to which I will return at the end of this chapter.

3.2 Transformations

Extensions of transformations can also be described as infinite sets. In this case the elements of the set are PAIRS: the first element of the pair represents the INPUT and the second element the OUTPUT. Such extensions have been called MAPS by Tesar (2014) and others.

As an example, consider the SPE-style rule shown in (5), which epenthesizes [ɨ] between stridents.

(5) Ø → ɨ / [+strident] __ [+strident]

The extension of this rule can be interpreted as every pair of strings (i, o) such that if i is the input to the rule o would be the output. The extension of (5) is shown in (6).

(6) { (wɪʃz, wɪʃɨz), (d͡ʒʌd͡ʒz, d͡ʒʌd͡ʒɨz), (dagz, dagz), ... }

Here is another example. Consider the rule in (7), which devoices word-final obstruents.

(7) [−sonorant] → [−voice] / __ #

This rule describes the infinite set of pairs, indicated in (8).

(8) { (rat, rat), (sap, sap), (rad, rat), (sab, sap), (sag, sat), (flugenrat, flugenrat), (flugenrad, flugenrat), ... }

OT descriptions of [ɨ]-epenthesis and word-final obstruent devoicing describe the SAME extensions. Baković (2013, Chapter 4) shows how to translate any rule of the form A→ B / C __ D into a core ranking where a markedness constraint like *CAD outranks those faithfulness constraints violated by A→B. As he explains, this ranking "is assumed to be embedded within a constraint hierarchy" whose other constraints must also be ranked a certain way.

In other words, the ranking in (9) is the core ranking necessary to describe the pairs of strings in (6).

(9) *[+STRIDENT][+STRIDENT] >> DEP(ɨ)

Obviously, if there is a candidate which does not violate *[+STRIDENT][+STRIDENT] but violates some other faithfulness constraint F, then F must outrank DEP(ɨ). These and other constraints are part of the presumed constraint hierarchy to which Baković refers.

Similarly, in order to describe the set of pairs in (8), the core ranking in (10) must be embedded in the constraint hierarchy.

(10) *[+VOICE,-SONORANT]# >> ID(VOICE)

Both OT grammars and rule-based grammars can be used to describe the same sets of pairs. In cases where they define the same extension, they are like the polar and Cartesian systems which can describe the same circles with different equations, which are interpreted differently according to the system they inhabit.

Here we have focused on simple transformations — ones that in rule-based theories could be described by a single rule. But phonologies in the world's languages are more complex than that. There are multiple, interacting factors. Still, both OT grammars and rule-based grammars ultimately generate pairs of strings like the ones in (6) and (8). They do this in different ways, but they do it nonetheless. Furthermore, the way phonology is taught, practiced and studied — both rule-based and constraint-based theories — is exactly by examining fragments of grammars and building up to larger and larger analyses.[4] The approach here is no different. Thus, the object of interest in both cases is these sets of pairs, which are the transformations from underlying to surface forms. As discussed earlier in (1), this is the basis for modern generative phonology. What is the nature of these maps?

4 Expressivity and restrictiveness

Before continuing, I would like to emphasize a common typological goal of every theory of phonology. A good theory must be both SUFFICIENTLY EXPRESSIVE to accurately describe the actual phonologies in the world's languages and MAXIMALLY RESTRICTIVE. It is clear enough why expressive adequacy matters. To be clear, by

---

[4] In fact, both rule-based and OT grammars predict there to be complete phonological grammars which only instantiate the process of inter-strident epenthesis or word-final devoicing. The fact no known phonology only contains a map which would correspond to a single traditional phonological rule has never been taken as a problem for either rule-based theories or OT.

"sufficiently expressive", I am referring to theories that, for every natural language phonology P, provide a descriptively adequate grammar for P. It may be less clear why maximal restrictiveness matters, but it does and no less so.

4.1 Why restrictiveness matters

There are three reasons why restrictiveness matters. First, it helps address the problem of how children quickly learn the phonology of their language (so it helps us reach an explanatorily adequate theory of phonology; cf. Chomsky 1965, Chapter 1).

Second, scientific hypotheses are stronger when they are more restrictive. The hypothesis that outlaws the most logically possible phonologies as humanly impossible can be said to be the strongest because it is the most readily falsifiable (Popper 1959). For a restrictive theory, it is possible to identify logically possible patterns, which would serve as a counterexample to the theory, if in fact it were found in the phonology of some language.

Third, it is easy to find a sufficiently expressive theory of phonology which is not restrictive. The widely held Church-Turing thesis states that anything that can be calculated or computed can be computed by Turing machines (and equivalently Church's lambda calculus). If phonologists believe their theories and models of phonology are computable (no matter how complex or intricate the computations) then there is already a sufficiently expressive theory of phonology available. The problem with this theory is that it is unrestrictive because it says everything that is computable is possible. The mere existence of a phonology will never be sufficient grounds for dismissing the Church-Turing Theory of Phonology. All of this is a way of saying that a theory not only needs to explain WHAT THERE IS, BUT ALSO WHAT THERE IS NOT.

The larger point is that expressiveness needs to be balanced against restrictiveness. Failure to be sufficiently expressive does not automatically disqualify a theory. It is enough for theories to be "nearly sufficiently expressive" to be viable. I say this because sometimes theories, especially when newly posited, are not sufficiently expressive (though they are very restrictive). For example, the Copernican theory of the solar system was originally not sufficiently expressive to predict the retrograde motion of the planets, at least as compared to the best Ptolemaic models at the time. Still the predictions were close. The Copernican theory was more restrictive however (since fewer types of retrograde motions were possible with the sun as the center of the system.) Closer to home, classic OT was not abandoned simply because of its inherent inability to represent opaque maps (see McCarthy 2008a; Baković 2007; Baković 2011 for discussion and examples of opaque maps in phonology). Instead, subsequent research focused on trying to modify the theory to make it more expressive.

Theories are rarely monolithic entities; they contain many parts working together. Ultimately, restrictiveness matters for the whole theory, as the sum of its parts, as opposed to the individual parts themselves. One aspect of the theory may overgenerate in an unrestricted manner, provided some OTHER COMPONENT of the theory excludes the problematic cases. Thus evaluating some aspect of the restrictiveness of a theory is by no means a straightforward affair: it means evaluation must occur with respect to other components which can be said to plausibly exclude the problematic cases.

There are degrees of expressivity and degrees of restrictiveness. Once we recognize the extensions of the constraints and transformations posited in phonological theories are infinite sets and functions, then we will see that the theory of computation naturally provides an encyclopedia of categories which measures these degrees of expressivity and restrictiveness. Furthermore, in this regard, the theory of computation is without peer.

4.2 The Chomsky Hierarchy

In this section, I will provide an overview of why the theory of computation provides a valuable way to examine the expressivity and restrictiveness of linguistic theories. Figure 5.1 shows the Chomsky Hierarchy which classifies stringsets according to the kind of grammars that generates them. Points in the space represent stringsets. The larger regions properly include the smaller ones so for instance all regular stringsets are context-free but not vice versa. As shown in the figure, linguistic generalizations (modeled as stringsets) have been argued to belong to certain regions and not others within the hierarchy.

(The issue of representation — whether we want to model linguistic forms with string structures, tree structures, autosegmental structures, or other kinds of graph structures is taken up in the discussion Section 8. There, I will argue that even if string structures are left behind, computational theory still provides an unmatched encyclopedia of categories for these other structures, analogous to the ones I discuss here for strings.)

At the top of the hierarchy is the "computably enumerable" region which includes everything. These are essentially the stringsets whose elements are computable.[5] This is the most expressive, but least restrictive class.

---

[5] More formally, it is decidable whether or a not any particular string belongs to the set. Interestingly, most logically possible sets of strings are *not* computably enumerable (Turing 1937).

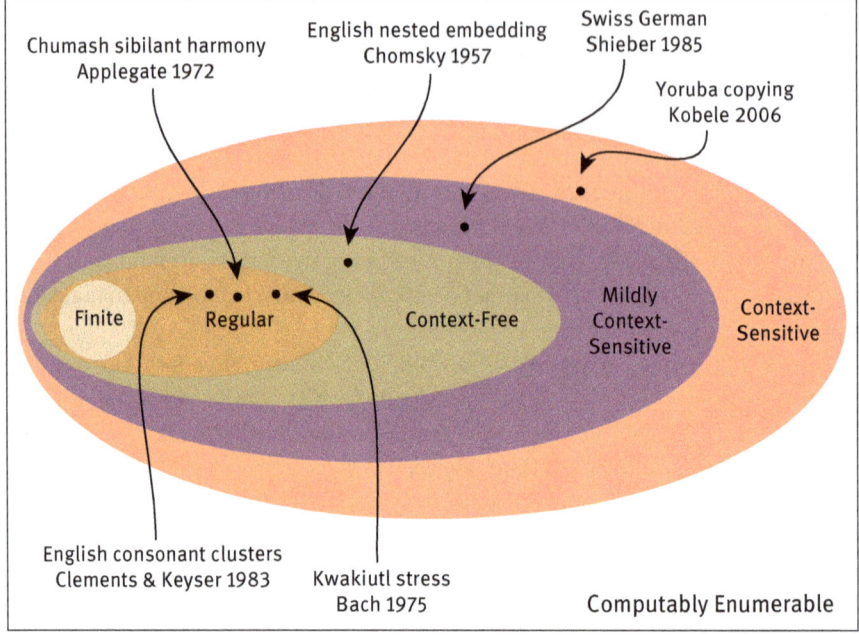

Figure 5.1: Natural language patterns in the Chomsky Hierarchy.

At the bottom of the hierarchy are the "finite stringsets". These stringsets are of finite cardinality. Unlike infinite sets, which require a generative grammar to generate or recognize them, elements of finite sets can be listed. In introduction to linguistics courses, we learn that linguistic generalizations cannot be modeled with finite sets because there is no principled upper bound on the length of possible words or sentences. The finite languages are the most restrictive, but least expressive class. In between the computably enumerable and finite classes are the regular, context-free and context-sensitive regions.

An important aspect of the hierarchy is that several regions have independently motivated, equivalent descriptions. Regular stringsets for instance can be defined with monadic second order logical formulae, finite-state acceptors, or regular expressions. Computer scientists Engelfriet and Hoogeboom explain: "It is always a pleasant surprise when two formalisms, introduced with different motivations, turn out to be equally powerful, as this indicates that the underlying concept is a natural one. Additionally, this means that notions and tools from one formalism can be made use of within the other, leading to a better understanding of the formalisms under consideration" (Engelfriet & Hoogeboom 2001: 216). At a high level of abstraction, the different characterizations can be thought of as different views on the same underlying object roughly in the same way different equations in different coordinate systems can describe the same circle. The more views we have, the better we can understand what it is we are looking at.

Also, each region X describes a linguistic hypothesis: linguistic generalizations must belong to X. Early work in generative grammar was interested in establishing evidence for or against such hypotheses in order to establish upper bounds on the nature of linguistic generalizations. The weakest scientific hypothesis is that they are computably enumerable, which is what I called the Church-Turing Theory of Phonology. As X moves down the hierarchy, the hypotheses become stronger, so the claim that the weak generative capacity of human syntax is a regular stringset is a strong scientific hypothesis. However, it is generally considered to be false (Chomsky 1956; Shieber 1985).

4.3 Phonology is Regular

The Chomsky Hierarchy is the best-known hierarchy in formal language theory, but it is not the only one. In fact there are several other hierarchies, some which only became well understood in recent decades, and others which are still being formed. Also, the Chomsky Hierarchy in Figure 5.1 classifies stringsets, but hierarchies exist (and are being developed) for sets of pairs of strings (relations/maps/functions) as well. It is important to distinguish hierarchies for one kind of set (e.g. stringsets) from another (e.g. sets of pairs of strings).

An important region in a hierarchy for relations (sets of pairs of strings) is also called Regular. It is called this because it shares much in common with the regular class of stringsets. For instance, one way to define the regular class of stringsets is with non-deterministic finite-state acceptors and one way to define the regular class of string-to-string maps is with non-deterministic finite-state *transducers*. Readers are referred to other texts for more information about finite-state grammars (Sipser 1997; Beesley & Kartunnen 2003; Roark & Sproat 2007; Jurafsky & Martin 2008; Hulden 2009).

The primary result in computational phonology to date is that the transformations from underlying to surface forms — these phonological maps — are in fact REGULAR. The argument goes something like this: Optional, left-to-right, right-to-left, and simultaneous application of SPE-style rules A→B/C_D (where A,B,C,D are regular stringsets) DESCRIBE REGULAR RELATIONS, provided the rule cannot reapply to the locus of its structural change (Johnson 1972; Koskenniemi 1983; Kaplan & Kay 1994). Rule ordering is functional composition (finite-state transducer composition). Regular relations are closed under composition (so the composition of two regular relations is also a regular relation). Rule-based grammars (finitely many ordered rewrite rules of the above type) can describe virtually all attested phonological patterns. This does not mean these grammars do so elegantly, that the rules correspond to psychologically real constructs, or that they have any other desirable trait. It just means that the input/output map is describable with such a grammar.

The above argument constitutes significant evidence for the following statement:

(11) (Regular Hypothesis) Phonological maps are regular relations.

If this is true, then it is true REGARDLESS of whether they are described with SPE, OT, or other grammar formalisms! Here are some other ways of saying the same thing:
- There are no non-regular phonological maps.
- A UNIVERSAL property of phonological maps is that they are regular.

Again, the fact that every rule-based grammar describes a regular relation, in addition to the fact that there is no counterexample to the hypothesis that phonological maps are regular, is strong evidence that the hypothesis in (11) is correct.

One consequence of this result is that finite-state grammars become a lingua franca for different phonological theories describing some aspect of the phonology of a language. Hence in addition to the work mentioned above which translates rule-based grammars into finite-state machines, there exists much work which shows how to translate OT grammars into finite-state machines (Frank & Satta 1998; Karttunen 1998; Gerdemann & van Noord 2000; Jäger 2002; Riggle 2004). Thus, for attested phonological patterns — just as with circles — there at several ways we can describe them. Those stringsets and maps can be described with rule-based grammars, OT grammars, finite-state machines, and other tools (e.g. logical formulae).

Another consequence of (11) follows from a theorem by Scott & Rabin (1959). This theorem establishes that the domain and image of regular relations are regular sets of strings. This means the set of possible underlying representations and the set of possible surface representations are also regular. In other words, phonotactic knowledge and markedness constraints describe regular stringsets. Or equivalently, every stringset defined by a markedness constraint has the property of "being regular".

4.4 The Subregular Hypothesis

"Being regular" is therefore plausibly a universal property of phonological patterns (both stringsets and maps). Furthermore, it is restrictive: there are many logically possible, NON-REGULAR patterns.

However, while "being regular" may be a necessary property, it is not restrictive enough. There are many logically possible, regular patterns that are still bizarre from a phonological perspective. We will encounter some of these strange creatures shortly.

There are many interesting SUBREGULAR classes of stringsets, as shown in Figure 5.2. Figure 5.2 shows a "close-up" view of the regular region shown in Figure 5.1. This will constitute the "encyclopedia of categories" and it will be explored in more detail in Section 5.2, though an overview will be given here.

The subregular hierarchies are bounded by the Regular region at the top and Finite region at the bottom. A region higher up in the diagram which is connected by a line to a region lower down in the diagram indicates the lower region is a subset of the higher region. So every generalization in the lower region is expressible in the higher one, but not vice versa.

There are two main branches in these hierarchies, the successor branch (+1) and the precedence branch (<) (for now the Tier-Based Strictly Local class can be ignored). The successor branch is also known as the Local branch, and the precedence branch is also known as the Piecewise branch. Along each branch, the regions are defined in logical terms. The Monadic Second Order regions are the most expressive and least restrictive. This is followed by (in order of decreasing

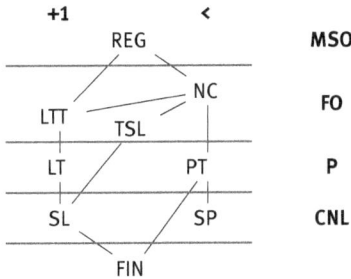

Names of the classes of stringsets			
REG	Regular	FIN	Finite
LTT	Locally Threshold Testable	NC	Non-Counting
LT	Locally Testable	PT	Piecewise Testable
SL	Strictly Local	SP	Strictly Piecewise
TSL	Tier-based Strictly Local		

Representational Primitives (order)		Logical Power	
+1	Successor	MSO	Monadic Second Order
<	Precedence	FO	First Order
		P	Propositional
		CNL	Conjunction of Negative Literals

Figure 5.2: Subregular hierarchies of stringsets.

expressivity/increasing restrictiveness) the First Order, Propositional regions and then the least expressive and most restrictive regions, the Conjunction of Negative Literals. While the hierarchy is presented here in logical terms these regions can also be defined in other ways and have multiple characterizations just like the regions in the Chomsky Hierarchy.

The Subregular Hypothesis refers to the idea that phonological patterns belong to small, well-defined regions of regular stringsets and maps. Thus the term "Subregular Hypothesis" on its own does not say much because it itself does not say WHICH subregular regions are at stake. To anticipate the remainder of this chapter, we distinguish between a strong and weak subregular hypothesis for constraints (a similar hypothesis will be put forward for maps). The "strong" subregular hypothesis is that phonological markedness constraints are Strictly Local and Strictly Piecewise (at the bottom of the hierarchy). The "weak" subregular hypothesis is that they are Tier-Based Strictly Local, which is a particular generalization of the Strictly Local class (inspired by phonological tiers). Both of these hypotheses are discussed explicitly in Sections 5.2.1 and 5.2.3.

5 Constraints

This section is devoted to markedness constraints. The primary purpose is to describe the Subregular Hierarchies in Figure 5.2, which constitutes the encyclopedia of categories, that I am arguing is important for understanding the nature of markedness constraints in phonology. To help motivate the discussion, and help make it more accessible, I will begin by discussing part of an encyclopedia of types (the actual constraints found in natural language).

5.1 The encyclopedia of types: Stringsets

In this section, I present some constraints known to be attested in the world's languages. These will be contrasted with constraints that are unattested. This is not intended to be an exhaustive or comprehensive encyclopedia of types. Only four types of markedness constraints are presented. This is intended to be sufficient to motivate the encyclopedia of categories, presented afterwards.

5.1.1 Four types of constraints

The first type of markedness constraint we encountered penalizes certain contiguous sequences of sounds (substrings). The impossible English words in Halle's

(1978) example all begin with illicit consonant clusters. We saw that *NÇ also penalizes substrings. This constitutes one kind of markedness constraint.

There are other kinds of constraints employed by phonologists which identify structures other than substrings as marked. For instance, if we were to ask native speakers of Samala (Applegate 1972, 2007) about the words in Table 5.2, they would reliably and uniformly distinguish them as shown in the table. How do Samala speakers know which of these words belong to different columns?[6] Well, it appears that Samala speakers know that words cannot contain both [+anterior] sounds like [s] and [-anterior] sounds like [ʃ].[7] Applegate (1972) modeled this knowledge as the result of a productive, regressive sibilant harmony process. In OT, this knowledge would be a consequence of a high ranking constraint of the form *[+strident,α anterior]. . . [+strident,$-\alpha$ anterior] (Hansson 2001; Rose & Walker 2004; Heinz 2010a). This constitutes a second type of attested markedness constraint in the world's languages.

Another logically possible type of constraint is illustrated with by speakers of a language I will call "Language X" (its true identity will be revealed momentarily), shown in Table 5.3. What constraint are the speakers of this language

Table 5.2: Phonotactic knowledge in Samala.

possible Samala words	impossible Samala words
ʃtojonowonowaʃ	stojonowonowaʃ
stojonowonowas	ʃtojonowonowas
pisotonosikiwat	pisotonoʃikiwat
nasipisotonosikiwa	naʃipisotonoʃikiwa

Table 5.3: Phonotactic knowledge in Language X.

possible words of Language X	impossible words of Language X
ʃotkoʃ	sotkoʃ
ʃoʃkoʃ	ʃotkos
ʃosokoʃ	ʃoʃkos
soʃokos	soskoʃ
sokosos	
pitkol	
pisol	
piʃol	

---

6 By the way, [ʃtoyonowonowaʃ] means 'it stood upright' (Applegate 1972).
7 The relevant feature could also be [distributed].

utilizing to reliably distinguish the logically possible words shown there? In this case, we observe speakers of Language X reject words that begin and end in sibilants that disagree in the feature [anterior]. Unlike the Samala example, sibilants interior to the word may disagree with edge-bound sibilants as evidenced by possible words like [soʃokos]. But if there are sibilants at word edges, they must agree in order for the word to be a possible word of Language X. This type of constraint is distinct type of constraint from the previous two types mentioned.

Next we consider Language Y. Table 5.4 shows how speakers of this language discriminate logically possible words. How do they do it? The two columns in Table 5.4 are distinguished as follows. Possible words have an EVEN NUMBER of sibilant sounds, but impossible words have an ODD NUMBER of sibilant sounds. So speakers of Language Y are sensitive to the even/odd parity of the number of sibilant sounds. This constitutes a fourth type of constraint, distinct from the ones mentioned earlier.

So far we have considered four logically possible kinds of constraints. What is the actual typology, the encyclopedia of types?

The actual typology of course looks like this. Attested phonotactic patterns include those which forbid substrings of words (such as *NÇ. They also include ones where words don't contain both sounds like ʃ and s (as in Samala). However, the logically possible phonotactic patterns represented by languages X and Y are unattested. There are no known phonotactic patterns where the last sound in a word depends in some fashion on its first sound (as in Language X). And there are no known phonotactic patterns where the right generalization is that words must contain an even number of members of a particular natural class (as in Language Y).

Table 5.4: Phonotactic knowledge in Language Y.

possible words of Language Y	impossible words of Language Y
ʃotkoʃ	ʃoʃkoʃ
sotkoʃ	ʃoskoʃ
ʃotkos	soʃkos
pitkol	ʃoʃkos
soʃkostoʃ	soskoʃ
	soksos
	piskol
	piʃkol

5.1.2 Explaining the typology

We would like to have an explanation for this fact. We would like our theory of markedness to explain why constraints like those found in English and Samala are possible, but the ones found in Language X and Language Y are not.

So what's the explanation? In OT, constraints like *#mgl and *[+strident,α anterior]...[+strident,−α anterior] structures would be part of CON. But constraints like *ODD-SIBILANTS or *#[+strident,α anterior]...[+strident,−α anterior]# would not be. The explanation in OT largely comes down to constraints that are present in CON and those that are absent from CON. (Whether complex markedness constraints can be derived via constraint interaction is a matter I take up later in Section 7.)

This is not controversial. The basic syllable typology is derived in OT by including the constraints NoCoda,Onset and excluding the constraints NoOnset,Coda. If the constraints NoOnset,Coda were included in CON, then it would not be possible to derive a typology where onsets may be required (but are never forbidden) and codas may be forbidden (but are never required).

In phonetically-based phonology (Hayes et al. 2004), the explanation would be that there are perceptual and/or articulatory reasons for constraints like *#mgl and *[+strident,α anterior]...[+strident,−α anterior]. But there would be no such reasons for constraints like *ODD-SIBILANTS or #[+strident,α anterior]... [+strident,−α anterior]#. More generally, this research program hypothesizes that constraints in CON are based on phonetic principles, and that certain rankings of these constraints are also fixed according to these principles. This is a significant improvement over stipulating certain constraints as belonging to CON to the exclusion of others.

However, we should carefully examine the proposed perceptual and/or articulatory reasons. Consider the case of the pattern in Language X. Following Lai (2012, 2015), let us now refer to this pattern as First/Last Harmony. We know long-distance assimilation is well-attested (Hansson 2001; Rose & Walker 2004) and arguments have been made for its perceptual basis (Gallagher 2010). We also know word edges in phonology are privileged positions (Fougeron & Keating 1997; Beckman 1998; Endress et al. 2009). So what theory of perception or articulation prevents there from being harmony only in privileged positions?[8] This is a case where the phonetic principles seem to overpredict the attested typology.

---

[8] Alan Yu also points out that there is a perceptually-motivated diachronic path to arriving at this language (pace Ohala 1981 and Blevins 2004). A language like Samala would be the precursor language to one with First/Last Harmony. Since interior sibilants in the precursor language

	[s]	[ʃ]
[s]	✓	✗
[ʃ]	✗	✓

[... — ... — ...]

	[s]	[ʃ]
[s]	✓	✗
[ʃ]	✗	✓

[# — ... — #]

Figure 5.3: Pattern templates for Sibilant Harmony (left) and First/Last Harmony (right).

We may also wonder to what extent memory requirements could explain the difference between the attested pattern in Samala and First/Last Harmony. In fact, however, it comes down to the pattern type, or template. This is because both types can be described simply by marking which pairs of sounds are permitted or forbidden in a given template as shown in Figure 5.3. The 2x2 cells for are identical — it is only the templates that differ.

As for the pattern in Language Y, it is plausible that perception or articulation should be able to explain the absence of even/odd parity constraints (or more generally constraints which count mod n) in phonology, but I haven't seen any explicit connection. Whatever the explanation may be, it SHOULD connect to the computational properties discussed here. More generally, if phonology is truly reducible ENTIRELY to phonetic principles then there ought to be research showing how the computational laws being posited in this chapter can be clearly derived from such phonetic principles.

This is not meant to deny any role to phonetic explanation in phonology. Instead this discussion is intended to make clearer some of the limits of those explanations and to persuade researchers in those areas that the computational principles discussed here are worth connecting their work to. At the very least, a complete theory of of phonology will refer to phonetic factors IN ADDITION TO the computational principles discussed here. I return to this issue in Section 7.3.

The computational explanation offered in this chapter is simply this. The extensions of constraints on substrings (like *NC̬) and constraints on subsequences (like [+strident, α anterior]... [+strident, $-\alpha$ anterior] in Samala) are Strictly Local and Strictly Piecewise stringsets respectively. With the exception of the finite languages, these are the most restrictive, least expressive regions in the Subregular Hierarchies shown Figure Table 5.2. On the other hand, First/Last Harmony and *ODD-SIBILANTS belong to the Locally Testable and Regular regions, respectively. In other words, the widely-attested constraints are the formally simple ones, where the measure of complexity is determined according to these hierarchies.

---

are not perceived as accurately as ones at word edges, some of them may change over time to disagreeing sibilants. This would result in a language whose words obey First/Last Harmony.

5.2 The encyclopedia of categories

In the last section, extensions of phonological constraints and transformations were introduced and it was argued that conceiving them as stringsets (formal languages), and string-to-string maps was reasonable and potentially insightful. In this section, we explain what the theory of computation has to say about this cast of characters. To do so requires some technical details. I will try to keep them light and only provide a sketch. Readers interested in the all the details are referred to Rogers et al. (2013), which also provides cognitive interpretations of the different regions.

We are going to explore LANGUAGE-THEORETIC and LOGICAL descriptions of stringsets and string-to-string maps from a generative perspective. The word "language" in "language-theoretic" refers to a formal language, what we have been calling a stringset. We may as well call it "stringset-theoretic". The idea behind language-theoretic descriptions is that they are completely independent of any grammatical description. In other words, these descriptions are statements that are simply true of the stringset itself (and not the grammar that generates it). They can therefore be thought of as essential properties of the stringsets. Examples will be provided shortly.

Logical descriptions are not agrammatical. Logical formulae are grammars in the sense that they generate stringsets as extensions. However, they are useful here because the expressive power of different logics is well understood. In the encyclopedia of categories — the Subregular Hierarchies — presented in Figure 5.2, there were four types of logic. As mentioned earlier, in order of strictly increasing expressive power, they are: conjunctions of negative literals (CNL), propositional logic (P), first order logic (FO), and monadic second order logic (MSO). The type of logic forms one parameter that is used to define the regions in the Subregular Hierarchies (Rogers & Pullum 2011).

There is one other parameter used to define the regions. This parameter specifies the kind of structures used to model strings. The parameter specifies the kind of relation used to handle the order of elements in the string. The relations that have been studied are SUCCESSOR (+1) and PRECEDENCE (<).

If strings are modeled so that the order of elements is handled by the successor relation, then SUBSTRINGS will be sub-structures of strings. On the other hand, if strings are modeled so that the order of elements is handled by the precedence relation, then SUBSEQUENCES will be sub-structures of strings. As an example, with the successor relation, **bcc** is a sub-structure of *a***bcc***ab*, but with the precedence relation, **aab** is a sub-structure of *a***a**bcc**b**.

We will now examine the consequences of the ordering relation in terms of the logical power.

5.2.1 Conjunctions of Negative Literals

Stating constraints as a "negative literal" is logical talk for what phonologists simply call marked structure. When conjunctions of such constraints are considered, we define stringsets which do not contain any of the marked structures. The order parameter (successor or precedence) tell us whether to interpret literals (the string structures) as substrings or subsequences.

Let us begin with successor, so the literals are interpreted as substrings. The negative literal $\neg aa$ is thus interpreted to mean the substring aa is a marked structure. So any string containing this marked structure violates the constraint and is not in the extension of the constraint.

Here is an example. I will use φ to stand for logical formulae, and $\mathbb{L}(\varphi)$ to stand for the stringset extension of φ. Following Rogers et al. (2013), I also will use ⋊ and ⋉ for the left and right word boundaries. The the formula below can be read as "Strings which do not begin with a b, do not contain aa as a substring, do not contain bb as a substring, and do not end with an a, are well-formed".

$$\varphi = (\neg \rtimes b) \wedge (\neg aa) \wedge (\neg bb) \wedge (\neg a \ltimes)$$

The extension $\mathbb{L}(\varphi)$ is easy to write since conjunction is interpreted as set intersection. A word about notation: Σ is a finite set of symbols (the alphabet); Σ^* means all logically possible strings one can write with this alphabet; and $\overline{S}$ means the complement of stringset S with respect to Σ^*. Thus, a term by term translation of φ above into its extension is shown below.

$$\mathbb{L}(\varphi) = \overline{b\Sigma^*} \cap \overline{\Sigma^* aa \Sigma^*} \cap \overline{\Sigma^* bb \Sigma^*} \cap \overline{\Sigma^* a}$$

It is not difficult to see that this is the same as the infinite set $\{ab, abab, ababab, \ldots\}$.

So now we can provide one definition of the Strictly Local stringsets. A Strictly k-Local (SL_k) stringset is one which can be defined as the conjunction of negative literals, where the literals are interpreted as substrings, and whose longest forbidden literal (substring) is of length k. The Strictly Local stringsets are those that are SL_k for some k.

If the order relation is precedence, then the literals are interpreted as subsequences. The negative literal $\neg aa$ is thus interpreted to mean the subsequence aa is a marked structure. So any string containing this marked structure violates the constraint and is not in the extension of the constraint.

Here is an example. The formula below can be read as "Strings which do not contain an a followed by an a nor a b followed by a c are well-formed". So here the literals aa and bc are interpreted as subsequences, and not as substrings.

$$\varphi = (\neg aa) \wedge (\neg bc)$$

A term by term translation of φ above into its extension is shown below.

$$\mathbb{L}(\varphi) = \overline{\Sigma^* a \Sigma^* a \Sigma^*} \cap \overline{\Sigma^* b \Sigma^* c \Sigma^*}$$

Strictly Piecewise stringsets are defined analogously to Strictly Local stringsets. A Strictly k-Piecewise (SL_k) stringset is one which can be defined as the conjunction of negative literals, where the literals are interpreted as subsequences, and whose longest forbidden literal (sub-sequence) is of length k. The Strictly Piecewise stringsets are those that are SP_k for some k.

That many attested markedness constraints define SL and SP stringsets is not in dispute. Clearly, constraints like *NÇ are SL and constraints like *[+strident, α anterior]... [+strident, $-\alpha$ anterior] are SP. The strong subregular hypothesis states that *all* markedness constraints are either SL or SP (Heinz 2010a).

(12) (Strong Subregular Hypothesis) Markedness constraints are SL or SP.

The one notable outstanding case Heinz (2010a) discusses is the set of surface forms derived from long-distance dissimilation. These appear to be Non-Counting but do not belong to any lower class (hence they are called 'Properly Non-Counting') (Heinz et al. 2011).[9] They are discussed further below.

Whether constraints like Onset are SL or not depends on the choice of representation. If syllable boundaries are included in string representations, which is a common practice, then constraints like Onset are SL since they can be represented this way: (¬ .V). The importance of representations will be further discussed in Section 8.

I would like to conclude the discussion of the "Strict" classes by providing their language-theoretic characterizations. This characterization for SL stringsets is provided in (13), which Rogers & Pullum (2011) name Suffix Substitution Closure.

(13) (Suffix Substitution Closure) A stringset L is SL if there is a k such that for all strings u_1, v_1, u_2, v_2, x with the length x equal to $k - 1$, it is the case that if $u_1 x v_1$ and $u_2 x v_2$ belong to L then $u_1 x v_2$ belongs to L as well.

---

[9] The Non-Counting class also goes by the names Star-Free and Locally Testable with Order (McNaughton & Papert 1971).

Suffix Substitution Closure is ultimately a Markovian principle: the well-formedness of the next symbol in the string depends only on the previous $k - 1$ symbols (given as x above). So if both v_1 and v_2 can follow x, what comes before x (u_1 and u_2) does not matter. This Markovian notion is important in generalizing SL stringsets to SL functions discussed in Section 6.

On the other hand, subsequence closure characterizes the SP class (Rogers et al. 2010).

(14) (Subsequence Closure) A stringset L is SP if for all u belonging to L, every subsequence of u also belongs to L.

What is remarkable about the language-theoretic characterizations above is not only that stringsets which have these properties are exactly the ones that can be defined as the conjunction of negative literals, but also that these characterizations DO NOT MENTION ANY SORT OF GRAMMAR AT ALL. In this way, they are more like definitions of circles which do not refer to either the Cartesian or polar coordinate system. They are characterizations which speak directly to the nature of the stringsets without getting bogged down in any particular grammatical formalism. Language-theoretic characterizations are about the SHAPE of the language to which any grammar must conform itself.

Another remarkable fact about these characterizations is that they immediately suggest INFERENCE procedures. If one is observing words from a language L THAT IS A PRIORI KNOWN to be SL_k and one observes u_1xv_2, u_2xv_2, one can immediately deduce that u_1xv_2 also belongs to L. Similarly, if one is observing words from a language L THAT IS A PRIORI KNOWN to be SP, and one observes the word u, one can immediately determine all subsequences of u also belong to L.

These facts lay at the basis of learning algorithms developed for the SL_k and SP_k classes. Garcia et al. (1990) first proved that the SL_k stringsets are identifiable in the limit from positive data. I have argued elsewhere that IDENTIFICATION IN THE LIMIT FROM POSITIVE DATA is a rigorous and insightful learning paradigm (Heinz 2016), and I will not review the arguments here. Heinz (2010a) shows how a similar algorithm provably identifies SP_k languages in the limit from positive data, and Heinz et al. (2010b) generalizes these ideas to a family of learning algorithms, a result which was generalized even further by Heinz et al. (2012).

If the strong subregular hypothesis is correct, these learning results provide a deep explanation of it. Constraints on phonological well-formedness are SL and SP because people learn phonology in the way suggested by these algorithms. More specifically, people generalize in accordance to inference procedures suggested by the closure properties in (13) and (14). But it is the inference procedures themselves that are basic which structure the SL$_k$ and SP$_k$ classes; the inference procedures are not auxiliaries to the classes.

5.2.2 Propositional Logic

Next we move up one level to the next kind of logic: propositional. Unlike the conjunction of negative literals, where all formulae had the form $(\neg l_1) \wedge (\neg l_2) \wedge \ldots \wedge (\neg l_n)$ for n literals (l_i), propositional logic allows any well-formed propositional formulae to generate a stringset. Not only is any combination/ordering of negation and conjunction now permitted, but disjunction ($\vee$) is also allowed. As a consequence, mainly familiar propositional connectives are also allowed, such as implication ($\rightarrow$) and the biconditional ($\leftrightarrow$). Propositional logic is therefore more expressive (and less restrictive) than the conjunction of negative literals.

For example, the following formula is a well-defined formula in propositional logic.

$$\varphi = b \vee (aa \rightarrow ac)$$

If these literals are interpreted with respect to the successor model of strings, then this formula translates to the following English: "Words are well-formed if they contain the substring b or if it is the case that if they contain the substring aa they also contain the substring ac." Below I provide the extension of φ under the successor interpretation of the literals.

$$\mathbb{L}(\varphi) = \Sigma^* b \Sigma^* \cup (\Sigma^* aa \Sigma^* ac \Sigma^* \cup \Sigma^* ac \Sigma^* aa \Sigma^*)$$

If these literals are interpreted with respect to the precedence model of strings, then this formulae translates to the following English: "Words are well-formed if they contain the subsequence b or if it is the case that if they contain the subsequence aa they also contain the subsequence ac." Here is the extension of φ under the precedence interpretation of the literals.

$$\mathbb{L}(\varphi) = \Sigma^* b \Sigma^* \cup (\Sigma^* a \Sigma^* a \Sigma^* c \Sigma^* \cup \Sigma^* a \Sigma^* c \Sigma^* a \Sigma^*)$$

I submit that both of these logically possible constraints seem more odd from a phonological perspective than the SL or SP constraints. At first glance, it seems strange to have a markedness constraint which requires that if one sub-structure is present another one must be present as well.

This is perhaps the most notable difference between the kinds of constraints permitted using propositional logic. Such constraints can REQUIRE sub-structures to be present in well-formed words (Rogers & Pullum 2011). The interpretation of the simple formulae $\varphi = b$ is that well-formed words must contain the sub-structure b. Such examples exist in the phonological literature. For instance, it is true that the constraint ONSET has this flavor. As we have mentioned with ONSET, however, the choice of representation matters: this can be construed as SL provided syllable boundaries are introduced as symbols in strings. Another constraint like this is what Hyman (2009) calls Obligatoriness, the requirement that all well-formed words bear an accent (or stress). Unlike ONSET, there is no straightforward representational "fix" for this constraint. I return to this issue in Section 5.3.

Now we can provide one definition of the Locally Testable stringsets. A Locally k-Testable (LT_k) stringset is one which can be defined with a formula in propositional logic, where the literals are interpreted as substrings, and whose longest literal (substring) is of length k. The Locally Testable stringsets are those that are LT_k for some k.

Similarly, a definition of the Piecewise Testable stringsets can be given. A Piecewise k-Testable (PT_k) stringset is one which can be defined with a formulae in propositional logic, where the literals are interpreted as subsequences, and whose longest literal (subsequence) is of length k. The Piecewise Testable stringsets are those that are PT_k for some k.

There are language-theoretic characterizations of these classes too. This characterization is given in (15) for the Locally Testable class.

(15) (Substring Equivalence) A stringset L is LT if there is a k such that for all strings u and v, if u and v have the same set of substrings of length k then either both u and v belong to L or both u and v do not belong to L.

In other words, Substring Equivalence means that membership in a LT stringset L only depends on the set of substrings of some length k. If two distinct strings have the same substrings up to some length k then no LT_k stringset is able to distinguish them.

A similar characterization is given in (16) for the Piecewise Testable class.

(16) (Subsequence Equivalence) A stringset L is PT if there is a k such that for all strings u and v, if u and v have the same set of subsequences of length k then either both u and v belong to L or both u and v do not belong to L.

Subsequence Equivalence means that membership in a PT stringset L only depends on the set of subsequences up to some length k. If two distinct strings have the same subsequences of some length k then no PT_k stringset is able to distinguish them.

Like the characterizations for the "Strict" classes, these characterizations naturally suggest inference procedures. If one is observing words from a language L THAT IS A PRIORI KNOWN to be LT_k and one observes u, one can immediately deduce that all words with the exactly the same substrings up to length k also belong to L. Similarly, if one is observing words from a language L THAT IS A PRIORI KNOWN to be PT_k, and one observes the word u, one can immediately determine all words with the exactly the same subsequences up to length k also belong to L.

That the PT_k and LT_k stringsets are identifiable in the limit from positive data was established by García & Ruiz (2004). Heinz et al. (2011) and Heinz et al. (2012) show there are learning algorithms for these classes which have much in common with the ones for the Strict classes. An interesting difference, however, between these algorithms and the ones for the Strict classes has to do with time-complexity: there is a clear computational sense in which learning these more expressive classes takes significantly longer than learning the Strict classes.

5.2.3 First Order Logic

The next rung up the logical hierarchy brings us to First Order (FO) Logic. The main differences between first order logic and propositional logic is that literals disappear and variables appear. It is not necessary in this chapter to provide the technical details regarding FO models of strings. For this, readers are referred to Rogers et al. (2013).

There are only three important items readers need to to understand. First, FO logic is strictly more powerful logic than Propositional logic. Second, as usual, whether the ordering relation is given as the successor relation or the precedence relation will determine the kinds of stringsets expressible with FO formulae. FO logic with the successor relation yields the class called the Locally Threshold Testable (LTT) class, and FO logic with the precedence relation yields the class called Non-Counting (NC). Third, successor is FO-definable from precedence, but not vice versa so the Non-Counting class properly includes the LTT class.

I will go straight to the language-theoretic properties. If the ordering relation is the successor, then the class of stringsets that is FO-definable is called the Locally Threshold Testable (LTT) class, and it properly includes the LT class.

One important difference between the FO-definable classes and the Propositional-definable classes is that the FO-definable classes are able to distinguish the presence of otherwise identical sub-structures. In this way, FO-definable classes can count the number of sub-structures up to some threshold.

On the other hand, the Propositional classes can only detect the presence or absence of sub-structures. So for a given sub-structure, Propositional logic can distinguish zero of them from one of them. FO logic, however, can detect up to some number n of sub-structures. So a limited ability to count is present at the FO-level. There is always some finite number n after which the number of sub-structures cannot be distinguished. FO-definable classes are not sufficiently expressive to be able to count indefinitely. Thus the difference between LTT and LT is that in the LTT class, the NUMBER of substrings can be counted, but only up to some threshold t (Thomas 1997).

(17) (Substring Threshold Equivalence) A stringset L is LTT if there is a k and a t such that for all strings u and v, if u and v have the same number, up to some threshold t, of substrings of length k then either both u and v belong to L or both u and v do not belong to L.

By now the reader may expect that language-theoretic characterization of FO-definable classes with the precedence relation is similar except that the number of subsequences up to some threshold is distinguishable. It is, however, in fact much simpler than that.

(18) (Non-Counting) A stringset L is NC if there is a k such that for all strings u, x, v if $ux^k v$ belongs to L then so does $ux^{k+1}v$.

The reason for this is that the Non-Counting class can do much more than count subsequences. This is partly because the successor ordering relation is FO-definable from precedence, but not vice versa.[10] Consequently, every stringset in the LTT region is also in the Non-Counting region, but not vice versa. NC is strictly more expressive than LTT. Thus, Figure 5.2 shows that the the NC class properly includes the LTT class. McNaughton & Papert (1971) comprehensively establish several other important characterizations of the Non-Counting class.

Are there markedness constraints that count up to some threshold? An example of such a constraint would be something like *3NÇ where words with zero, one or two NÇ substrings are considered well-formed, but words with three

---

[10] For those familiar with the FO formulae, here is the definition where $x \triangleleft y$ means y is a successor of x, and $x < y$ means x precedes y.

$$x \triangleleft y \stackrel{\text{def}}{=} x < y \land \neg(\exists z)[x < z \land z < y]$$

or more are ill-formed. Needless to say, such constraints do not seem like the kinds of constraints found in natural language.

On the other hand, there are constraints in natural language that have been argued to be properly Non-Counting. These are the stringsets that are definable from long-distance dissimilation (Heinz et al. 2011). Heinz et al. (2011) also show that such constraints belong to subclasses of the Non-Counting region they call Tier-based Strictly Local (TSL). These stringsets are defined with the common notion of phonological tier (Goldsmith 1976). Like the Strictly Local class, TSL stringsets can be defined with formulae that are conjunctions of negative literals, interpreted under the successor relation after non-tier elements are ignored. Thus the kind of long-distance behavior is limited in some kind of way. TSL stringsets are not as well understood as the other classes (there are not multiple characterizations), but Heinz et al. (2011) argue that every markedness constraint in natural language is describable with TSL constraints. Of course an important issue is here what the tier is. Jardine & Heinz (2016) show that the tier can be identified from positive data when the bound k on the size of the constraints are known a priori (the tier is *not* known a priori).

I will refer to the hypothesis that all markedness constraints are TSL as the weak subregular hypothesis.

(19) (Weak Subregular Hypothesis) Markedness constraints are TSL.

Whether the evidence favors the strong or weak subregular hypothesis will be addressed in Section 7.

5.2.4 Monadic Second Order Logic

The next rung up the logical hierarchy and the highest to which we attend is Monadic Second Order (MSO) Logic. The difference between first order and monadic second order logic is that variables over SETS of elements in the domain are allowed in addition to the variables which vary over individual elements (which FO logic allows). There are several interesting consequences of adding such variables, which I will now review.

First, the two branches in the subregular hierarchies merge at this point because precedence is MSO-definable from successor.[11] So the stringsets that are

---

11 For those familiar with MSO logic, here is a definition. Individual variables are denoted with x, y, and X denotes a set variable. $x \triangleleft y$ means y is a successor of x, and $x < y$ means x precedes y.

MSO-definable with successor are exactly the stringsets that are MSO-definable with precedence.

Second, this class of stringsets corresponds exactly to the class of stringsets definable with finite-state acceptors, i.e. the regular class of stringsets (Büchi 1960).

Third, this class is strictly more expressive than both the Non-Counting and Locally Threshold Testable class (McNaughton & Papert 1971; Thomas 1997). It can be shown that the stringset defined by the constraint *ODD-SIBILANTS (see Section 5.1) is not Non-Counting, but it is a regular stringset.[12]

5.3 Further evidence supporting the Subregular Hypotheses

So far in this section, we mentioned the most common types of attested markedness constraints. We did not provide an exhaustive encyclopedia of types in Humboldt's sense, but enough of one to motivate the encyclopedia of categories that was presented. The discussion was designed to convince readers that the markedness constraints found in natural language were present at the lowest levels of the hierarchy and that as one moves up the hierarchy, the kinds of constraints describable at these higher levels become less and less natural from a phonological point of view.

This helped motivate two hypotheses. The Strong Subregular Hypothesis (12) says that markedness constraints are SP or SL. The Weak Subregular Hypothesis (19) says that markedness constraints are TSL.

While these constraints were motivated by appealing to common types of constraints, readers may wonder whether the hypotheses have been subjected to more rigorous empirical investigation. I would like to now give further evidence for the Strong and Weak Subregular hypotheses. First I will discuss studies of stress patterns in terms of the Subregular Hierarchies.

Jim Rogers and his students examined the stress patterns in the stress typology in Heinz (2007, 2009) with respect to the Strictly Local languages. There are 109 distinct patterns in this typology from over 400 languages. Edlefsen et al.

$$\text{closed}(X) \stackrel{\text{def}}{=} (\forall x, y)[(x \in X \wedge x \triangleleft y) \rightarrow y \in X]$$

$$x < y \stackrel{\text{def}}{=} (\forall X)[(x \in X \wedge \text{closed}(X) \rightarrow y \in X]$$

12 To see why the set of strings L containing only an even number of sibilants is not Non-Counting, the characterization in (18) can be used. For any k, observe that os^{2k}o belongs to L, but os^{2k+1}o does not.

(2008) report that 72% (of the 109 patterns) are SL_k with $k \le 6$ and 49% are SL_3. The 28% are which are not SL_6 are unbounded stress patterns and are shown to not be SL for any k. Heinz (2014) studies the four simplest types of unbounded stress patterns and shows that these are SP_2 once Culminativity (every word contains exactly one stress) is factored out. Culminativity has been argued to be a universal property of stress languages (Halle & Vergnaud 1987; Hayes 1995) and therefore this LT constraint may be thought to come for free. While recently Hyman (2009) suggests a more nuanced view, it seems ill-advised at this point to view the result regarding Culminativity in Heinz (2014) as a rejection of the Subregular Hypotheses. Rogers et al. (2013) argue that the other unbounded stress patterns similarly factor into the conjunction of SL and PT constraints or SP and LT constraints. The other unbounded stress patterns continue to be the subject of current research.

Two potential counterexamples come from work by Thomas Graf. Graf (2010a) provides a formal analysis of the stress patterns of Creek and Cairene Arabic, as they have been characterized in the literature. According to Graf's analysis, these stress patterns are not Non-Counting and are properly regular. If the posited linguistic generalizations are correct, by Graf's analysis, these cases would constitute clear counterexamples to the Subregular Hypotheses. A critical aspect of the linguistic generalizations that Graf's result relies on is that there is no secondary stress in these languages. If the secondary stress were perceptible, however, the constraints needed to describe the pattern would become SL. Whether secondary stress is perceptible or not to speakers of these languages is not a settled issue, and so there is some question regarding the accuracy of the linguistic generalizations.

Thus, with only a couple of potential counterexamples meriting further study, the current understanding of the stress typology supports the Strong and Weak Subregular Hypotheses.

A second source of evidence in favor of these hypotheses comes from psycholinguistic experimentation (Lai 2012, 2015). In a series of artificial language learning experiments, Lai compared how well native English speaking young adults could internalize the phonotactic pattern expressed by a SP constraint like *[+strident, α anterior]. . . [+strident, $-\alpha$ anterior] and a LT constraint like First/Last Harmony (*#[+strident, α anterior]. . . [+strident, $-\alpha$ anterior] #). Subjects in these experiments participated in a training session followed by a test session. In the training session, they are told they are going to hear the words of a foreign language. In the test session, they are given two words and are asked which one more likely belongs to the language they just heard.

Subjects belonged to one of three conditions, which determined the kind of training received. In the "Sibilant Harmony" (SH) condition, they were exposed to words which were well-formed according to the constraint *[+strident, α anterior].

... [+strident, –α anterior]. In the "First/Last Harmony" (FL) condition, they were exposed to words which were well-formed according to the First/Last Harmony constraint. Subjects in the control condition received no training (and during test were asked which word they thought was a better word).[13] All subjects were given the same test items in the test session.

As reported in Lai (2015), the results of this experiment were unambiguous. As expected, subjects in the control condition behaved according to chance. In the test session, subjects in the SH condition behaved in a manner consistent with internalizing the SP constraint because they consistently chose words in the test session that did not violate the constraint. On the other hand, subjects in the FL condition did not consistently choose words in the test session that did not violate the constraint. In fact, they behaved just like subjects in the SH condition! This is despite the fact that they were exposed to words like [soʃos] in training, which violate the constraint *[+strident, α anterior]... [+strident, –α anterior].

In sum, the experiments of Lai (2012, 2015) show that subjects find it easier to learn SP (or TSL) stringsets as opposed to LT ones. This evidence is consistent with both the Strong and Weak Subregular Hypotheses, but as far as I am aware, no other theory explains these results.

5.4 Constraints: A summary

A summary of the foregoing section can be made very simply. Phonologists have identified many kinds of constraints on string representations. Stringsets can be classified according to two core computational parameters: the type of ordering relation (successor or precedence) and the type of logical power. Together, these provide a Constraint Definition Language in the sense of de Lacy (2011). With only a few potential exceptions meriting further empirical investigation, the stringsets corresponding to phonological constraints overwhelmingly belong to the SL, SP, and TSL regions in the encyclopedia of categories shown in Figure 5.2, which are arguably the simplest.

Readers may wonder whether it is necessary to allow both ordering relations to be sub-structures in words.[14] If only the successor relation is permitted, then it

---

13 Finley & Badecker (2009) found no difference between the absence of training and a control condition where the words in the training condition contained words which were well-formed and ill-formed according to each targeted constraint type.
14 Readers may also wonder why the sub-structure that picks out the first/last template [#—...—#] is not available. Here the reason is simple: both the successor and precedence relations allow

is not possible to describe constraints like *[+strident, α anterior]... [+strident, -α anterior] at the CNL, P, and FO levels. MSO logic is needed. MSO logic with successor, however, permits any regular stringset to be described. Similarly, if only the precedence relation is permitted, it is not possible to describe constraints like *NC̦ at the CNL, and P levels. FO logic is needed. In other words, the most restrictive theory is the Strong Subregular Hypothesis (12): phonological constraints are defined by banning substrings or subsequences.

Finally, we may wonder why this would be the case. If the Strong Subregular Hypothesis is correct, then the extensions of synchronic constraints are SL or SP stringsets (or conjunctions thereof). Why would this be? The idea expressed in Heinz (2010a) is that human learners generalize in particular ways — and the ways they generalize yield exactly these classes. Synchronic constraints are aspects of grammar, and grammars are learned. They are systems that grow and develop in response to environmental stimuli. The learning biases structure the classes; it is not the case that the nature of the class is independent of the learners. As Dresher (1999) and Heinz (2009) argue, this kind of explanation is not available to learners within OT settings.

6 Transformations

Now we turn to transformations. From an OT perspective, this section is about faithfulness constraints and the map derived from the interaction of all the OT constraints. It is also about the typology of maps generated from a given CON. From a rule-based perspective, this section is about the extensions of individual phonological rules and their composition.

The computational theory of subregular relations is not as well developed as the Subregular Hierarchies. For example, logical characterizations of string relations have not yet been fully carried out. Previous work on subclasses of subregular relations is primarily limited to two classes known as the LEFT SUBSEQUENTIAL and RIGHT SUBSEQUENTIAL. Essentially, these are classes of transformations with finite look-ahead; so they are "myopic" in the sense of Wilson (2003).

More will be said about these classes momentarily. I will keep the discussion at a high level and readers can find the definitions of them and other technical details in many different places, including Berstel (1979), Mohri (1997), Roche &

---

every word to have a model and for distinct words to have distinct models. This is not the case with the sub-structure indicated by the template [#—... — #] is used to model words.

Schabes (1997), Lothaire (2005), Sakarovitch (2009). A linguistically motivated treatment is given in Heinz & Lai (2013).

Much recent work at the University of Delaware has sought to develop a hierarchy for string relations that is analogous to the one for stringsets shown in Figure 5.2. The most notable advance in this regard has been work by Jane Chandlee (Chandlee 2014; Chandlee et al. 2014; Jardine et al. 2014; Chandlee & Heinz 2018), which establishes relational counterparts to the Strictly Local stringsets, discusses their significant coverage of empirical phenomena, and explains how they can be learned.

6.1 The encyclopedia of types: Maps

Phonologists are familiar with many ways in which underlying forms can differ from surface forms. Underlying segments may be deleted. Their order may be permuted (metathesis). The features composing the segments may change. Additionally, there may be elements in surface forms which were not present underlyingly (epenthesis).

Additionally, the contexts that trigger these changes are of different types. The contexts may be local to where the changes occur, by which I mean the distance between the trigger and the target falls within some fixed bound. A typical example is where the triggering context is adjacent to the change. For instance regressive nasal place assimilation is typically written in rule format as [+nasal] → [αplace] / __ [−sonorant, α place]. Alternatively, the triggers can be found arbitrarily far away, as found in examples of long-distance consonantal harmony (Hansson 2001; Rose & Walker 2004) and disharmony (Suzuki 1998; Bennett 2013). Unlike the local cases, there appears to be no fixed bound on the distance between the trigger and the target.

The long-distance cases are of special interest, so I will largely follow the analysis of vowel harmony from Heinz & Lai (2013) to motivate the encyclopedia of categories introduced in the next section. Vowel harmony is a well-studied phenomenon in phonology (van der Hulst & van de Weijer 1995; Baković 2000; Finley 2008; Nevins 2010; Walker 2011, and many others). Vowel harmony refers to a systematic pattern of pronunciation in which certain features of vowels which are different at the underlying level are the same at the surface level. Thus vowel harmony has been called a process of assimilation. One reason it has attracted interest is because the affected vowels are not strictly speaking adjacent since consonants may intervene between them.

Schematically, an example of harmony can be distilled to the following mapping: /+−/ ↦ [++]. We will read this mapping as follows. The underlying form and surface form each contain two vowels. The mapping shows the values of the feature F for each vowel. Virtually all features defining vowels (roundness, height, backness, advanced/retracted tongue root) have been shown to participate in harmony in some language, and F can be understood to be any of these features. At the underlying level, the values of the first and second vowel are /+/ and /−/, respectively. At the surface level, however, both vowels bear the value [+] for feature F. Since consonants are irrelevant, they are not shown, but it should be understood that the mapping above includes consonants which may precede or succeed any of the vowels.

Heinz & Lai (2013) analyze six types of logically possible vowel harmony maps discussed in the phonological literature. These will be discussed, along with two other types, all of which are summarized in Table 5.5.

Following terminology introduced in the OT literature, I will refer to faithful vowels as those whose value of feature F stays constant in the underlying and surface forms. Unfaithful vowels are ones whose value of the feature F is not constant across the two levels.

One logically possible — but unattested — VH map maintains that the unfaithful vowels are always fewer in number than the faithful ones. (In words with an equal number of faithful and unfaithful vowels, which feature values would change would be determined according to some default.) This map has been called been Majority Rules (MR) harmony. (20) shows some examples of this MR.

(20) (Majority Rules Harmony) { (+ + −, + + +), (+ − +, + + +), (− + +, + + +), (− − +, − − −), (− + −, − − −), (+ − −, − − −), ... }

As has been discussed in the OT literature, this map is the optimal outcome of two very simple constraints: a markedness constraint banning successive vowels with different values of feature F (AGREE(F)) outranking the faithfulness constraint IDENT(F). Baković (2000: 26) defines the term this way:

> When Agree[F] is dominant, it winnows the candidate set down to basically two candidates, one with all [αF] segments and the other with all [−αF] segments. If IO-Ident[F] gets the next crack at the evaluation process, it will choose the one of these candidates that is least deviant from the input, regardless of the stem/affix or +/− distinctions. In other words, what ends up mattering is the *relative percentages* of [αF] and [−αF] vowels in the input: the underlyingly greater number of [−αF] vowels in [a map where /+ − −/ ↦ [− − −]] gangs up on the lesser number of [αF] vowels, yielding the problematic effect that I call 'majority rule.' [emphasis in original]

As recognized by Baković, MR is unattested and considered phonologically bizarre. His solution adds certain locally conjoined constraints to CON, which he argues has the effect of ridding Majority Rules maps from the typology, and which he argues is independently needed for analyzing dominant/recessive types of vowel harmony. The point I wish to emphasize here however is that Majority Rules is a logically possible map, which is quite easy to generate in classic OT with a simple markedness constraint (depending on whether arbitrary many consonants may intervene between vowels determines whether Agree(F) is SL or TSL) and standard faithfulness constraints.

Another possible map is one where the first or last vowel determines the features of the other vowels in the word. This has been called progressive harmony (PH) and regressive harmony (RH), respectively. Examples of a PH map are shown in (21).

(21) (Progressive Harmony) { (++−, +++), (+−+, +++), (−++, −−−), (−−+, −−−), (− + −, − − −), (+ − −, + + +), ... }

The inclusion of neutral vowels alters this map only slightly. Neutral are vowels which resist harmonizing and either are skipped (in which case they are called transparent) or force subsequent vowels to harmonize with them (in which case they are called opaque). Following Heinz & Lai (2013), I will use the symbols [⊖] and [⊟] to represent [−F] vowels that are transparent and opaque, respectively, and the symbols [⊕] and [⊞] to represent [+F] vowels that are transparent and opaque, respectively. With this expanded alphabet, mappings like /+ ⊖ −/ ↦ [+ ⊖ +] and /+ ⊟ +/ ↦ [+ ⊟ −] would also belong to the PH map.

In contrast to the above, sometimes vowel harmony is bounded, in the sense that only the subsequent vowel is affected. I will call this Local Assimilation (LA) and (22) below illustrates this map where only the initial vowel is the trigger.[15]

(22) (Local Assimilation) { (+ −−, ++ −), (−++, −−+), (+ −+, +++), (−+ −, −−−),... }

Early analyses of vowel harmony analyzed the extension of many patterns like bounded or unbounded PH or RH (van der Hulst & van de Weijer 1995), but this type of analysis is present in recent work as well (Nevins 2010).

Another logically possible, but unattested type of vowel harmony process has been called "Sour Grapes" (SG) (Padgett 1995; Wilson 2003). Informally, SG is like progressive harmony except that later vowels only harmonize if no opaque vowels occur later in the word. If an opaque vowel occurs somewhere after the

---

[15] Bounded spreading may be more common with the feature nasal. For convenience, the bound here is assumed to be the next relevant segment, but in fact the syllable seems to be a natural domain (Odden 1994). See discussion in Nevins (2010, Chapter 5).

initial vowel, then non-neutral vowels between it and the initial vowel will not harmonize. (23) illustrates a SG map.

(23) (Sour Grapes) { (+--, +++), (+-⊟, +-⊟), (+---, ++++), (+--⊟, +--⊟), ... }

Like Majority Rules, Sour Grapes has been argued to be a phonologically bizarre vowel harmony process. In particular, Wilson (2003) argues that harmony processes never look ahead beyond immediately adjacent segments. Wilson refers to the absence of look-ahead as a kind of myopia, and characterizes spreading processes as "myopic". The Sour Grapes pattern disobeys Wilson's (2003) principle that phonological laws are myopic. In a Sour Grapes pattern, each vowel gets to "look ahead" arbitrarily far to the end of the word to see if there is an opaque vowel downstream, and only harmonizes if it does not find one.

Classic OT has no difficulty generating SG maps. Under a typical analysis, there is a markedness constraint against segments that are [+F] but share all other features with ⊟ (such as *⊞). Consequently, underlying /⊟/ can never surface as [⊞]. Finley (2008: 32) describes the rest of the OT analysis this way.

> Sour grapes harmony patterns occur when a blocker prevents spreading to vowels intervening between the source and the blocker. For the input [/+ - ⊟/] ... the output [[+ - ⊟]] will be optimal rather than the desired [+ + ⊟]. This type of pathology is produced when the harmony-inducing constraint [AGREE(F)] does not localize the violation of harmony. In both the sour grapes candidate [+-⊟] and the spreading candidate [+ + ⊟], there is only one locus of disagreement. [...] However, because the sour grapes candidate incurs no faithfulness violations, it will emerge as optimal.

Like MR, SG has received attention in the literature because it the optimal outcome of relatively simple constraints in OT (Wilson 2003; McCarthy 2004; Finley 2008).

Interestingly, in the domain of tone, there DO seem to be some patterns that exhibit Sour Grapes-like behavior. See Hyman (2007) and Kula & Bickmore (2015) for cases in Kuki Thaadow and Copperbelt Bemba, respectively, and Jardine (2016) for extensive analysis and discussion.

Other analyses of vowel harmony argue that the right generalization is that vowels in a word harmonize to a particular feature value, if it is present anywhere in the word. This analysis has been called dominant/recessive (DR) since the feature F appears to have a dominant value (the one that vowels harmonize with) and a recessive value (the one that vowels don't harmonize with). In the example DR map below, the [+] value is the dominant one; so any underlying representation containing the harmonizing feature with the value [+] will surface so that the harmonizing feature in all vowels will also be [+].

(24) (Dominant/Recessive) { (++−, +++), (+−+, +++), (−++, +++), (−−+, +++), (−+−, +++), (+−−, +++), (−−−, −−−), ... }

A similar analysis of VH patterns (shown in (25)) is one where the root vowel determines the features of the other vowels in the word. This kind of analysis has been termed "Stem Control" (SC). Here the feature that spreads is determined by its morphological status, and not its inherent vowel as in DR harmony. Typically vowels agree with the closest stem vowel. Following Baković (2000), I use the $\sqrt{+}$ and $\sqrt{-}$ to indicate root vowels that are +F and −F, respectively.

(25) (Stem Control) $(\sqrt{+}+−, \sqrt{+}++), (\sqrt{+}−+, \sqrt{+}++), (\sqrt{-}++, −−−),$
$(\sqrt{-}−+, −−−), (\sqrt{-}+−, −−−), (\sqrt{+}−−−, \sqrt{+}++), (−\sqrt{+−}+, +\sqrt{+−}−), ...$}

The last logically possible harmony pattern to be discussed I will call Circumambient Unbounded harmony (CU), following Jardine (2016). This pattern is also like dominant/recessive harmony in that only one value of the feature triggers the harmony. However, CU harmony requires *two* /+F/ triggers which must SURROUND the affected vowels, and which may be ARBITRARILY FAR from them. The examples in (26) illustrate.

(26) (Circumambient Unbounded) { (+−−, +−−), (++−, ++−), (+−+, +++), (+−−−, +−−−), (+−−+, ++++), (−+−−+, −++++), ... }

The term "circumambient" refers to two surrounding triggers and the term "unbounded" refers to the absence of a bound on the distance between the two triggers. Yaka is the only language which appears to have CU vowel harmony (Hyman 1998), though Jardine (2016) argues Sanskrit n-retroflexion is formally similar, and (Graf 2010a) provides a logical analysis of it. (As discussed further below in 6.3, unbounded high tone plateauing is a well-attested, a common tonal pattern which is circumambient unbounded (Hyman 2011; Jardine 2016).)

Table 5.5 is a reproduction of Table 5.3 from Heinz & Lai (2013), with the additions of local assimilation and circumambient unbounded harmony. It summarizes the encyclopedia of types outlined above. Phonological theory has posited maps like LA, PH, RH, DR, and SC, the consensus appears to be that MR and SG are not only unattested but bizarre. In fact they have been called pathological patterns in some works (Wilson 2003, 2004; Finley 2008). Lastly, setting aside tonal phonology for now, maps like CU are only marginally attested. As before, we ask the question: What principle or principles separate the linguistically-motivated generalizations (PH, RH, DR, SC) from the pathological ones (MR and SG) and the marginally attested ones (CU)?

Table 5.5: Example mappings of underlying forms (w) given by local assimilation (LA), progressive harmony (PH), regressive harmony (RH), dominant/recessive harmony (DR), sour grapes harmony (SG), majority rules harmony (MR), and circumambient unbounded harmony (CU). Symbols [+] indicates a [+F] vowel and [–] indicates a [–F] vowel where F is the feature harmonizing. Symbols [⊟] and [⊖] are [–F] vowels that are opaque and transparent, respectively. (From Heinz & Lai 2013: 57.)

	w	LA(w)	PH(w)	RH(w)	DR(w)	SG(w)	MR(w)	CU(w)
a.	/+ – –/	[+ + –]	[+ + +]	[– – –]	[+ + +]	[+ + +]	[– – –]	[+ – –]
b.	/– + +/	[– – +]	[– – –]	[+ + +]	[+ + +]	[– – –]	[+ + +]	[– + +]
c.	/– – –/	[– – –]	[– – –]	[– – –]	[– – –]	[– – –]	[– – –]	[– – –]
d.	/– + –/	[– – –]	[– – –]	[– – –]	[+ + +]	[– – –]	[– – –]	[– + –]
e.	/+ – ⊟/	[+ + ⊟]	[+ + ⊟]	[– – ⊟]	[+ + ⊟]	[+ – ⊟]	[– – ⊟]	[+ – ⊟]
f.	/+ ⊖ –/	[+ ⊖ –]	[+ ⊖ +]	[– ⊖ –]	[+ ⊖ +]	[+ ⊖ +]	[– ⊖ –]	[+ ⊖ –]
g.	/+ – +/	[+ + +]	[+ + +]	[+ + +]	[+ + +]	[+ + +]	[+ + +]	[+ + +]

6.2 An encyclopedia of categories: String-to-string maps

Hierarchies of string-to-string transductions are not as well studied nor understood as classes of stringsets. Part of the issue is that string-to-string maps are inherently more complex; they have more parts than a stringset because in fact they are two stringsets — the domain and co-domain — and a map from elements of one to the other. Consequently, properties that converge for stringsets can diverge for string-to-string maps. One example is the class of regular stringsets. Regular stringsets are exactly those describable with MSO logical formulae with successor, deterministic finite-state acceptors and non-deterministic finite-state acceptors. (Informally, a finite-state machine is deterministic only if there is at most one path through the machine for each input; if there are some inputs with more than one path, it is non-deterministic.) However when the corresponding classes of string-to-string maps are considered, these three classes are distinct (Engelfriet & Hoogeboom 2001).

The hierarchies of transductions that are known to exist, such as those described by Roche & Schabes (1997, Chapter 1) and Engelfriet & Hoogeboom (2001) focus on the more expressive regions. There is very little work on regions that make the kinds of distinctions made in the Subregular Hierarchies discussed in the previous section.

Therefore, current answers to the questions at the end of the preceding section at present are unlikely to satisfy all readers since they are incomplete.

In this section, I will not explicate all the known regions, but only those that I think are currently most relevant for phonology. These regions are shown in

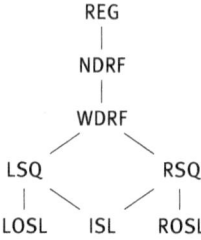

	Names of the classes of the sets of string pairs		
	Non-deterministic classes		
REG	Regular Relations		
NDRF	Non-Deterministic Regular Functions		
WDRF	Weakly Deterministic Regular Functions		
	Deterministic classes		
LSQ	Left Subsequential Functions	RSQ	Right Subsequential Functions
LOSL	Left Output Strictly Local	ROSL	Right Output Strictly Local
ISL	Input Strictly Local		

Figure 5.4: Subregular hierarchies of regular relations.

Figure 5.4. As before, lines connecting two regions indicate that the higher region properly includes the lower region. I will begin at the bottom and go up.

6.2.1 Input Strictly Local functions

Input Strictly Local functions generalize the notion of Strictly Local stringset. Recall the Strictly Local stringsets are Markovian in nature: the well-formedness of a string can be determined by examining the substrings of length k. Equivalently, this means that the well formedness of any position in the string can be determined by checking the $k - 1$ previous symbols. This is illustrated in Figure 5.5, for the case where $k = 2$.

Input Strictly Local functions are similarly Markovian. The idea is that every element in the input string corresponds to a STRING of symbols in the output

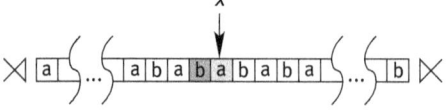

Figure 5.5: Schematic illustration of the Markovian nature of Strictly k-Local stringsets. Each element x of a string belonging to a strictly 2-local stringset depends only on the previous element. In other words, the lightly shaded cell only depends on the darkly shaded cell.

string. For any input symbol *x* its output string *u* will only depend on *x* and the previous *k* – 1 elements of *x* in the input string. Figure 5.6 illustrates, for the case where *k* = 2.

Local Assimilation (LA) is ISL with *k* = 3. Basically if the previous two elements are /⋈+/ (or /⋈−/) then if the current input element is a non-neutral vowel, the output string will be [+] (or [−]).

Chandlee (2014) shows that ISL functions can model a range of local phonological processes, including substitution, insertion, deletion, and synchronic metathesis. More generally, she shows that given a mapping describable with a rule of the form A → B / C __D where the set of strings in CAD is finite and the rule applies simultaneously then it is ISL for some *k*.

This result may seem counter-intuitive given the current discussion. A reader may wonder whether, especially given the diagram in Figure 5.6, how ISL functions can model any transformation triggered by any right context at all. As mentioned, every element in the input string corresponds to a STRING of elements in the output. These output strings can be any length, including length zero (the so-called "empty" string). The option to output the empty string allows the function to wait until it has enough information to decide what to output. But importantly, the amount of input it needs to see to make this decision is BOUNDED, by the specified value of *k*. For example consider regressive nasal place assimilation where underlying /inpa/→[impa]. Each row in Table 5.6 shows how the output string is determined by each input element *x* and the input element preceding *x*. Since the output string at each point is determined by a window whose size is bounded by *k*, ISL maps are myopic in Wilson's (2003) sense.

Chandlee also investigated the approximately 5500 phonological processes (from over 500 languages) reported in the P-Base database (v1.95 Mielke 2008). It was determined that over 95% of these patterns are ISL. Chandlee acknowledges

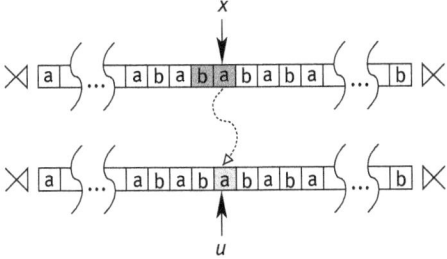

Figure 5.6: Schematic illustration of the Markovian nature of Input Strictly k-Local functions. For every Input Strictly 2-Local function, the output string *u* of each input element *x* depends only on *x* and the input element previous to *x*. In other words, the lightly shaded cell only depends on the darkly shaded cells.

Table 5.6: Illustrating why transformations with right contexts can still be ISL. The symbol λ represents the empty string (the string of length zero).

element preceding	input element	output string
x	x	u
⋊	i	i
i	n	λ
n	p	mp
p	a	a

that P-Base ought not be taken as representative of the cross-linguistic distribution of processes that target contiguous versus non-contiguous segments. However, given that it is the most comprehensive collection of processes of which we are aware, she deemed it necessary to survey.

Furthermore, Chandlee (2014) and Chandlee et al. (2014a) also show how ISL functions can be efficiently learned from finitely many examples in the sense of Gold (1967) and de la Higuera (1997). This stands in stark contrast to the class of regular functions which cannot be so learned. Remarkably, Jardine et al. (2014) generalize this result to obtain an even more efficient learning algorithm for this class of functions.

6.2.2 Output Strictly Local functions

A notable example of a map that Input Strictly Local functions are unable to model are ones like progressive harmony (PH) (21) above. Recall that a mapping like $/+----/\mapsto[++++]$ belongs to this map, and more generally for all numbers k, $/+-^k-/\mapsto[++^k+]$ and $/--^k-/\mapsto[--^k-]$. Such a map cannot be Input Strictly Local for any k. This is because whether the last input element surfaces as [+] or [−] depends on an INPUT element which is more than k input elements away.

Chandlee (2014) defines Left and Right Output Strictly Local functions (LOSL and ROSL) to address such maps. These capitalize on the output-oriented nature of many phonological processes (Kisseberth 1970; Prince & Smolensky 1993, 2004). They are Markovian like ISL functions, but this time the context is found in the output string, not the input string. Specifically for Left (Right) OSL functions, for any input element x, its output string u will only depend on x and the previous (following) $k-1$ elements of the output string. The idea is that a function is Left or Right, depending on whether the left or right context in the output string matters. Figures 5.7 and 5.8 illustrate Left and Right OSL functions, respectively, for the case where $k = 2$.

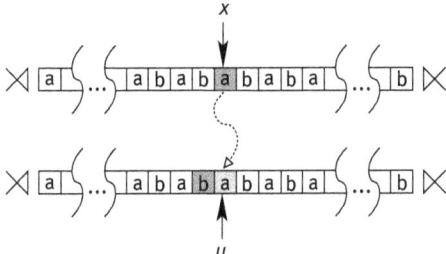

Figure 5.7: Schematic illustration of the Markovian nature of Left Output Strictly k-Local functions. For every Left Output Strictly 2-Local function, the output string u of each input element x depends only on x and the output element previous to u. As before, the lightly shaded cell only depends on the darkly shaded cells.

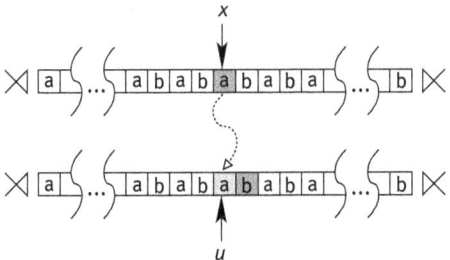

Figure 5.8: Schematic illustration of the Markovian nature of Right Output Strictly k-Local functions. For every Right Output Strictly 2-Local function, the output string u of each input element x depends only on x and the output element succeeding u. As before, the lightly shaded cell only depends on the darkly shaded cells.

Informally, Left and Right OSL functions can be thought of as characterizing the maps one can describe with rewrite rules that apply left-to-right or right-to-left (Howard 1972) (cf. the treatment of rule-application by Kaplan & Kay 1994). This appears to be approximately correct, though certain details are still being worked out. However, we can say with certainty that the map PH is LOSL and the map RH is ROSL. More generally, such functions capture spreading processes such as progressive and regressive nasal spreading.

Left and Right OSL functions can both be computed by subsequential transducers. For Right OSL functions, the input string must be processed right-to-left by the transducer and the resulting output will then be reversed. See Heinz & Lai (2013) for details.

6.2.3 Subsequential functions

In the abstract maps for vowel harmony discussed earlier, consonants were ignored. If arbitrary many consonants are allowed to intervene between the vowels then the PH and RH maps will not be LOSL nor ROSL, respectively. For the PH case, this means for all numbers k, $/+C^k-/\mapsto[+C^k+]$ and $/-C^k-/\mapsto[-C^k-]$. Such a map cannot be Left nor Right Output Strictly Local for any k because whether the last input element surfaces as [+] or [−] depends on an output element which is more than k output elements away. In a sense, at input element x, the functions cannot remember whether the preceding vowel in the output string was [+] or [−] because too many [C]s intervene.

We therefore move up the hierarchy in Figure 5.4. I note that as of yet there are no regions for string-to-string maps corresponding to the SP, LT, PT, TSL, or LTT stringsets.[16]

Informally, for Left (Right) Subsequential functions, each logically possible input string is classified as belonging to exactly one of finitely many regular stringsets. For any input element x, the output string u will only depend on x and the regular stringset to which its preceding input string belongs. Figure 5.9 illustrates left subsequential functions.

Even if arbitrary many consonants are allowed to intervene between the vowels then the PH and RH are in fact left and right subsequential, respectively. To see why, consider Table 5.7. Subsequential functions can "remember" up to finitely many pieces of information about the left context; in Table 5.7,

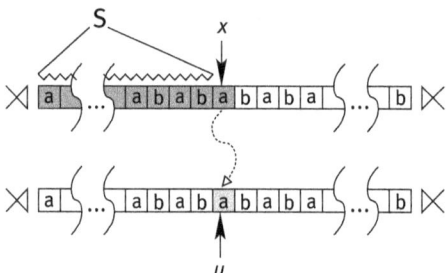

Figure 5.9: Schematic illustration of Left Subsequential functions. For every Left Subsequential function, the output string u of each input element x depends only on x and the stringset S to which the preceding input string belongs. As before, the lightly shaded cell only depends on the darkly shaded cells.

---

16 Some work exists that characterizes string-to-string maps which correspond to the NC stringsets (Lautemann et al. 2001). Also the author has work in progress characterizing string-to-string maps for each of these regions.

Table 5.7: Illustrating why PH is left subsequential even if arbitrarily many Cs intervene between vowels.

set to which string preceding x belongs	input element x	output string u
⋊	+	+
⋊ + C*	C	C
⋊ + C*	C	C
...	...	...
⋊ + C*	C	C
⋊ + C*	–	+

that the first vowel was [+F]. Thus even if k or more Cs then occur in the input string, the function simply outputs each C as it reads each C, without changing its memory state.

In the same way that ISL functions could "look ahead" by writing empty output strings, subsequential functions can do so do as well. However, like the ISL functions, there is a sense in which left subsequential functions can look into the right context of the input element ONLY some finite distance. There is a bound k on how far they can look ahead, which relates to the fact that it can only remember finitely much information about the input string. For this reason it is not possible to remember the EXACT preceding input string.

An example will help make this idea clear. The dominant/recessive (DR) map is neither left nor right subsequential. This is because, for all numbers k, $/-^k + -^k/ \mapsto [+^k + +^k]$ and $/-^k - -^k/ \mapsto [-^k - -^k]$. Such a map cannot be left subsequential because whether the first k input elements all surface as [+] or [–] depends whether the next element is [+] or not. Therefore, even though these functions might output the empty string for the first k input elements, if the [+] comes next, such functions would have to output k [+] symbols (and one more). But this is impossible because k can be ANY number and left subsequential functions can only classify the preceding input string into one of FINITELY many categories. Table 5.8 illustrates this conundrum. For this reason, left subsequential functions are myopic in the sense that they cannot look unboundedly far into the right context.

Right subsequential functions are similar except that input strings FOLLOWING the input element are categorized into finitely many regular stringsets. Also, right subsequential functions can only "look ahead" into the left context a finite distance (and an argument similar to the one made above shows why). It may be useful to think of right subsequential maps as the "reverse" of left subsequential maps: if L is a left subsequential map then there is a right subsequential map

Table 5.8: Illustrating why the dominant/recessive DR map is not left subsequential. The symbol λ represents the empty string. The problem is that the left subsequential function cannot remember exactly how many − symbols occurred before the first + (it cannot always correctly fill in the '. . . ').

set to which string preceding x belongs	input element x	output string u
λ	−	λ
−	−	λ
− −	−	λ
. . .	. . .	. . .
− − − . . .	−	λ
− − − . . . −	+	+ + + . . . + +

L^r such that $(w, v) \in L$ iff $(w^r, v^r) \in L^r$ (where x^r is the reverse of the string x so $(abc)^r = cba$). From a processing perspective, one could say that left subsequential functions process strings left-to-right, and right subsequential functions process strings right-to-left.

At the University of Delaware in 2010, the question was asked whether the transformations from underlying to surface forms are left or right subsequential. In other words, we investigated what I will call the Subsequential Hypothesis.

(27) (Subsequential Hypothesis) Phonological transformations are left or right subsequential.

With one interesting class of exceptions discussed below, this hypothesis appears to be well supported. This matters for two reasons. First, it is a stronger more restrictive hypothesis than the previously understood bound (phonology is regular, see Section 4.3). Second, it has been known for quite some time that left subsequential (and right subsequential) functions are learnable in a particular sense (Oncina et al. 1993). The algorithm presented there has even been adapted for use in phonology (Gildea & Jurafsky 1996). In other words, if phonological transformations are subsequential, then the computational nature of phonological transformations directly provides purchase on the learning problem.

So what is the evidence which favors (27)? I will use the term "subsequential" to mean either left or right subsequential. Chandlee (2014) proves that ISL, LOSL, and ROSL functions are subsequential; therefore, all the maps they cover are subsequential. Synchronically attested metathesis is also subsequential (Chandlee et al. 2012; Chandlee & Heinz 2012). Gainor et al. (2012) study the extensions of the vowel harmony maps in Nevins (2010) and conclude they are subsequential.

Since Nevins assumes a certain degree of underspecification, Heinz & Lai (2013) show that progressive and regressive vowel harmony with no underspecification pace OT (maps PH and RH above) are subsequential. Payne (2017) shows that long-distance consonant dissimilation maps described by Suzuki (1998) and Bennett (2013) are subsequential, and Luo (2017) shows that long-distance consonant assimilation maps described by Hansson (2008) and Rose & Walker (2004) are subsequential.

In some sense, these results are not too surprising because ultimately these results support Wilson's intuition that phonology is myopic. Nonetheless, if phonological myopia is best characterized as subsequentiality (or something stronger like ISL), then there is much concrete to gain: a theory which not only appears sufficiently expressive, but which is also more restrictive than previously entertained, and which has desirable learnability properties.

6.2.4 Weakly Deterministic functions

Weakly Deterministic functions are defined by Heinz & Lai (2013) as those maps that can be defined as the composition of a left subsequential and right subsequential function without the introduction of new alphabetic symbols. Heinz & Lai (2013) show that the dominant/recessive (DR) and stem-control (SC) maps are properly weakly deterministic. In fact the DR map is the composition of a map like progressive harmony (DR_P), which only spreads the dominant feature progressively, and a map like regressive harmony (DR_R), which only spreads the dominant feature regressively. Table 5.9 illustrates. Since DR_P and DR_R are left and right subsequential, respectively, their composition is weakly deterministic.

Heinz & Lai (2013) conjecture that sour grapes (SG) is NOT weakly deterministic. They explain that SG can be described as the composition of a left subsequential function and a right subsequential function, but that crucially the intermediate form requires the use of an additional alphabetic symbol which they write as [?]. Table 5.10 (adapted from their paper) illustrate the role an additional symbol plays in the decomposition. Essentially, [?] records the fact that this is a minus, which has a [+] in its left context. So the right subsequential function R will rewrite this as [−] or [+] depending on whether there is a [⊟] in the right context of the [?].

Table 5.9: Map DR_P converts every − after a + to + (like PH), and map DR_R convert every − before a + to + (like RH). As indicated, the composition of these two maps yields the DR map.

input		output
− − + − −	$\xrightarrow{DR_P}$ − − + + + $\xrightarrow{DR_R}$	+ + + + +

Table 5.10: Illustrations of the role of the new symbol [?] in the deterministic decomposition into a left subsequential function L and a right subsequential function R.

input		output
+---⊟ ↦ +$\overset{?}{-}\overset{?}{-}\overset{?}{-}$⊟ $\overset{R}{\mapsto}$		+---⊟
+---- $\overset{L}{\mapsto}$ +$\overset{?}{-}\overset{?}{-}\overset{?}{-}\overset{?}{-}$ $\overset{R}{\mapsto}$		+++++

While many theorists have argued in favor of dominant/recessive and stem-control analyses of vowel harmony(Baković 2000; Krämer 2003), this is not a settled debate (Nevins 2010). What Heinz & Lai (2013) show is that DR and SC maps are more computationally complex than PH and RH maps, and that SG maps are even more complex than these. If the debate is settled in favor of DR and SC maps then it means the subsequential hypothesis would be incorrect, and then the most restrictive hypothesis would retreat to the weakly deterministic region.

Jardine (2016) argues that circumambient unbounded (CU) maps are also not weakly deterministic. He shows that CU maps and SG maps are similar in that in both cases, the information which determines whether a vowel is unfaithful is located in two distinct places: one location is arbitrarily far before the vowel and the other location is arbitrarily far after the vowel. While both CU and SG maps are the same with respect to the first place (an earlier + is required), the CU map also requires a + in the second place but the SG map requires the ABSENCE of a ⊟.

Jardine's result is perhaps the most serious challenge to the Subsequential Hypothesis (or a revised Weakly Deterministic hypothesis) because the best characterization of Yaka vowel harmony seems to be that it is circumambient unbounded (Hyman 1998). However, this is the only known example of this type, and it is probably premature to reject the hypothesis on these grounds alone. I will return to this issue below.

6.2.5 Non-deterministic Regular functions and Regular relations

Non-deterministic Regular functions can be defined in at least two ways (Elgot & Mezei 1965). First, they can be defined as the composition of a left and right subsequential function, provided the intermediate string is allowed to use additional alphabetic symbols. As we have seen in the example of Sour Grapes (SG) in Table 5.10, these additional symbols allow certain types of information to become present in the string. Second, non-deterministic regular functions can be defined as those string-to-string functions that can be described with a non-deterministic finite-state transducer.

Both SG and CU maps thus properly belong to the non-deterministic regular function region (Heinz & Lai 2013; Jardine 2016).

Non-deterministic finite-state transducers are a grammatical formalism that can also describe transformations which have more than one output for each input. In fact the class of transformations describable with non-deterministic finite-state transducers are called regular relations. Beesley & Kartunnen (2003) and Hulden (2009) develop toolkits for manipulating regular relations for describing the phonology and morphology of languages.

The Majority Rules map cannot even be described with a non-deterministic finite-state transducer. It is in fact non-regular (Riggle 2004; Heinz & Lai 2013). According to the hierarchy presented here, it is the most complex kind of map under discussion.

Given that many phonological rules are optional, one may wonder whether it is appropriate to model individual transformations (as we have here) as functions instead of relations. There are two responses to this.

The first response is to say that the optionality is handled at a higher level of control than the individual transformation. This is essentially the position adopted in rule-based and constraint-based phonology. In rule-based phonology, the idea was that a rule was marked as optional. When deriving the output from an input and a rule marked as optional is encountered, additional, usually random, information is consulted (such as a coin flip) and the outcome determines whether the rule is applied or skipped. Thus the extension of the rule itself is still functional. Similarly, in stochastic OT (Boersma 1998; Boersma & Hayes 2001), a given constraint ranking has a functional extension, but a higher-level control process determines which particular constraint ranking will be utilized at any particular time.

The second response is to say that subclasses of regular relations are likely to follow the same lines developed here. Mohri (1997) establishes that as long as there is a bound on the amount of optionality, many properties of subsequential functions are preserved. More recently, Beros & de la Higuera (2014) also show how to generalize subsequential functions in a way that permits a degree of optionality. While subclasses of classes have not been studied the fact that they preserve important aspects of the underlying finite-state transducers and that classes like ISL have automata-theoretic characterizations based on subsequential transducers (Chandlee 2014; Chandlee et al. 2014a) strongly suggests that subclasses like ISL which permit a degree of optionality are only waiting to be discovered.

6.3 Further evidence

There is some psycholinguistic evidence which supports the hypothesis that phonological transformations are regular. In a series of artificial language learning experiments, Finley (2008) compared how well native English speaking young adults could learn a Majority Rules (MR) type map (which is non-regular) as compared to a Progressive Harmony (PH) type map (which is regular). Subjects were either assigned to the MR, PH, or control conditions. Each subject received a training session and then performed in a test session. The results clearly established that subjects learned the PH harmony pattern, but not the MR pattern.

Finley (2008) also conducted a series of experiments to investigate the learnability of the Sour Grapes (SG) map. This is one way to test the Subsequential Hypothesis. Here the results were inconclusive, probably due to an interference of neutral vowels in the particular paradigm (though see Finley 2015). However the subsequential hypothesis clearly predicts that SG should be more difficult to learn that PH, and so future research in this vein should be conducted to see whether the prediction is borne out.

An interesting source of evidence in favor of (a revised) Subsequential Hypothesis comes from work by Jardine (2016). Jardine studies Unbounded Tone Plateauing (UTP) (Kisseberth & Odden 2003; Hyman 2011) and concludes that such transformations are also circumambient unbounded. In UTP, a string of underlying low tones (or unmarked vowels) are realized as high only if there is a high tone at both the left and right edges of this string. Jardine makes a persuasive case for a typological asymmetry between tonal patterns and segmental patterns. Several well-documented cases of UTP exist in the literature, despite the absence of comprehensive typological surveys. On the other hand, despite the existence of several surveys on long-distance harmony, the only CU maps known to be present in segmental phonology come from Yaka vowel harmony and Sanskrit n-retroflexion. Furthermore, Jardine shows that the evidence that the segmental maps are truly unbounded is weaker than the evidence that the UTP cases are unbounded.

In other words, Jardine's work shows that UTP — because of its widespread and well documented existence — is a counterexample to the Subsequential Hypothesis (27). He suggests that it be revised as follows.

(28) (Revised Subsequential Hypothesis) Segmental transformations in phonology are left or right subsequential.

While Yaka vowel height harmony and Sanskrit n-retroflexion are arguably counterexamples to this revised hypothesis, I think it is prudent not to reject the hypothesis on these grounds. Unlike UTP, these cases are rare and the evidence that they are truly CU maps, while compelling, is not as strong as it is for the UTP cases. Future research may lead to a better understanding of these languages.

Thus, Jardine shows that tonal patterns are different from segmental patterns, since they are arguably more complex. Paraphrasing Hyman (2011), tonal phonology really can do more than segmental phonology!

6.4 Transformations: A summary

A summary of the foregoing section can be made very simply. Phonologists have identified many ways in which underlying forms are transformed into surface forms. The study of subregular string-to-string maps has not yet been as articulated as the one of subregular stringsets. Nonetheless, the study of the typology of the attested transformations in the light of the existing categories yields similar conclusions. With one interesting class of exceptions which is largely confined to tonal phonology (CU maps), segmental transformations appear to overwhelmingly belong to the simplest maps in the encyclopedia of categories shown in Figure 5.4.

Thus, even though an encyclopedia of categories for string-to-string maps as fine-grained as the one for stringsets does not yet exist, the work to date has nonetheless yielded important insights. The simplest maps are Markovian on the input or the output (ISL, LOSL, and ROSL), and very many phonological transformations belong to these classes. Transformations which are not Markovian in this sense involve long-distance harmony. Such patterns however are subsequential, which means they are still myopic in an important sense. This stands in contrast to the SG map which is not subsequential and the MR map, which is not even a regular relation. It is anticipated that other subregular regions for maps analogous to the SP or TSL regions will be developed that better characterize long-distance transformations.

The asymmetry between tonal CU maps and segmental CU maps noticed by Jardine (2015) is perhaps the most difficult to interpret. How can it be that some formal mechanism is available to one aspect of the grammar but not to another? Perhaps it is an indicator of the modularity of grammar (Heinz & Idsardi 2011, 2013). Jardine's work then can be understood as providing support for Hyman's thesis, that tonal phonology is in fact different from segmental phonology (Hyman 2011). As a separate module of the grammar, it has resources available to it that are not available everywhere else.

7 Summary and implications for the phonological component

In this section, I would like to review the main lessons for phonological theory to be taken from the computational analyses reviewed so far in this chapter.

7.1 Phonological generalizations have strong computational properties

From the computational perspective, most, if not all, phonological generalizations obey very strong computational laws. This is what typological analysis of phonological constraints and transformations that was reviewed in Sections 5 and 6 reveals. Phonological generalizations (both stringsets and maps) belong to small, well-defined regions WITHIN the region of regular stringsets and maps, and these regions are at the BOTTOM of the subregular hierarchies shown in Figures 5.2 and 5.4.

7.2 Problems with optimization

Current phonological theories do not account for these laws. Since Prince & Smolensky (1993), optimization has been a central feature of phonological theory including classical OT (Kager 1999), Stratal OT (Kiparsky 2000), Harmonic Grammar (Smolensky & Legendre 2006; Potts et al. 2008), Maximum Entropy (Goldwater & Johnson 2003; Hayes & Wilson 2008), and Harmonic Serialism (McCarthy 2008b). One of the most compelling features of optimization is the idea that complex patterns within and across languages arise from the interaction of simple constraints. The celebrated examples of syllabification in Berber (Dell & Elmedlaoui 1985), complex margin avoidance in Yokuts (Kisseberth 1970), and the many solutions to the international conspiracy *NÇ (Pater 2000) in terms of optimization all attest to this. However, if "complex patterns arising from the interaction of simple constraints" is optimization's greatest strength, it is also its greatest weakness.

As explained in Section 4.3, computational analysis has revealed that phonological transformations are regular. But even with regular constraints and a regular GEN, optimization can result in NON-REGULAR maps (Frank & Satta 1998). Optimization is very powerful because very complex patterns can indeed arise from simpler constraints. Majority Rules is a case in point (Riggle 2004; Heinz & Lai 2013).

This particular overgeneration problem is not specific to classical OT. It is a problem for Stratal OT, Harmonic Serialism and Maximum Entropy theories as well. This is not a controversial point. It is in fact just one more example of how "complex patterns arise from the interaction of simple constraints". It may be possible to add constraints to CON as in Baković(2000) to avoid generating MR type maps. Different types of constraints, such as targeted constraints (Wilson 2001; Baković & Wilson 2000; Baković 2004), or ones which operate over turbid structures (Finley 2008) may be invoked.

However, it is not enough to show that MR is avoided. One must show that all non-regular maps are avoided. Frank & Satta (1998) write: "It remains an open problem to characterize precisely the generative capacity [. . .] of [Optimality Systems]'s with other assumptions about the formal power of GEN and the constraints". While it still remains an open problem today, the markedness constraints involved in generating Majority Rule patterns are SL or TSL. In other words, even the simplest constraints under optimization can generate non-regular maps. Perhaps future research will show that there is an straightforward way to prevent non-regular maps from occurring in the factorial typology, but to me the prospects seem dim.

For even if it were possible to add new constraints (or constraint types) to CON to avoid deriving non-regular maps, there is a problem. These constraints would be in service of deriving a generalization that is already very simple to state: phonological transformations are regular. It means that in order for optimization to be the right theory of phonology that the constraints over which optimization operates have to be designed to blunt the power of optimization!

And these problems are just to avoid generating non-regular maps. The revised Subsequential Hypothesis limits the kinds of humanly possible segmental maps. The same kinds of problems mentioned above exist for developing a theory of CON which guarantees that segmental maps are always subsequential and avoid generating non-myopic maps like Sour Grapes (Jardine 2016a).

From a computational perspective then, optimization appears to be too powerful a tool. Critics of optimization have generally focused on the fact that OT undergenerates the typology with respect to opacity (Idsardi 1998, 2000; McCarthy 2007; Buccola 2013), but the overgeneration problem is equally pressing. In both cases, new constraint types or optimizing architectures are introduced with the ultimate purpose to make the optimal maps ones that conform to the computational generalizations stated in the present chapter.

Thus, from a computational perspective, with respect to the dual goals of developing both an adequately expressive theory and a maximally restrictive theory of phonology, optimization misses the mark. It is neither adequately expressive (because of opaque maps) nor sufficiently restrictive (because it generates non-regular maps like Majority Rules).

Of course the question can never be "Is Optimization the Right Theory?". After all, what is the alternative?

7.3 Organizing phonological theory around computational properties

One alternative suggested by the work reviewed in this chapter is that the computational properties highlighted here — and not optimization — be taken as the organizing principles of the phonological component of grammar. Constraints on surface forms are, with few exceptions, banning substrings and subsequences (Section 5). Phonological transformations which are intuitively "local" are also among the simplest types of logically possible maps (Section 6).

But is this theory adequately expressive? We have focused on maps which correspond to individual rules, so can the theory being suggested handle opacity? This is work in progress, but it appears so. Chandlee et al. (to appear) show that ISL functions can represent opaque maps. In fact, they show that every opaque map described in Baković (2007) is ISL (and as mentioned, Chandlee and her collaborators have established algorithms for learning the ISL functions).

Are there overgeneration problems as is the case with optimization-based theories? It is true that even the theory which adopts the strong subregular hypothesis (12) overgenerates in some sense. For instance, it is straightforward to write a grammar for a language which bans subsequences like *sg. This means words in this language are ill-formed if [g] occurs anywhere after [s]. So there is some overgeneration, though it is plausibly due to phonetic factors (see below). Joe Pater helpfully points out (p.c.) that when two theories overgenerate in different ways, it can be difficult to determine which overgenerates "less" or which is preferable along the dimension of overgeneration. I agree and this is another area where computational analysis has something to offer. The theory which overgenerates in a computationally simpler way ought to be preferred. Under this assumption, theories of phonology which adopt subregular properties overgenerate in a computationally simpler way as compared to theories organized around optimization. This is for the simple reason that they cannot possibly generate nonregular patterns like Majority Rules.

Another potential criticism is that computational properties highlighted here do not take into account phonetic substance. As mentioned, this means many possible subregular constraints and maps are not likely phonological ones because they are phonetically unnatural. I will put aside the important question of whether phonetically unnatural constraints and maps are phonologically possible and learnable, and just assume for the purposes of discussion that they are not.

In my view, it is a feature and not a bug that formal and substantive issues are separated. I am not so extreme as Hale & Reiss (2000) as to deny substance a role altogether, but I do think science proceeds by factoring complex systems. Ever since Chomsky & Halle (1968, Chapter 9), it has been clear that formal and substantive constraints on phonological systems are distinct. While details have not yet been worked out, substantive constraints on phonological systems would simply be IN ADDITION to the formal constraints being proposed here. This is really no different than the program offered by Chomsky & Halle (1968) or, for that matter, by Hayes et al. (2004), which adopts optimization as a formal system and ADDS substantive constraints to the nature of CON.

Finally, another argument that could be put in favor of optimization is that it readily lends itself to a theory of learning (Tesar 1995; Tesar & Smolensky 1998, 2000; Tesar 2014, and many others). This is a good argument. However, I have tried to highlight the fact that the subregular regions to which phonological patterns appear to belong ALSO readily lend themselves to a theory of learning (Oncina & Garcia 1991; Heinz 2007, 2010a,b; Chandlee 2014; Chandlee et al. 2014a; Jardine et al. 2014). Furthermore, if people generalize from data in the way suggested by these learning procedures, it explains the computational nature of the phonological patterns. This is in contrast to the learners in optimization-based theories (and variants thereof), where the nature of the phonological patterns is completely explained by what belongs and what does not belong to CON.

7.4 Next steps

If the computational properties highlighted in this chapter are taken seriously, there are many subsequent issues to attend to. There are several possibilities, but I will focus on the following four:
- better characterizing long-distance transformations;
- better understanding the role of abstractness;
- better understanding non-string representations of words; and
- testing the predictions of these hypotheses in imaginative ways.

Each of these is a current focus of research.

Chandlee (2014) provides a clear definition of locality and shows that many maps which are intuitively local (and some that are not) meet this definition. Her definition generalizes the notion of Strictly Local stringsets to maps. Strictly Piecewise stringsets (Rogers et al. 2010) can describe many long-distance constraints

(Heinz 2007, 2010a) as can Tier-Based Strictly Local stringsets (Heinz et al. 2011). What are the corresponding generalizations of the SP and TSL stringsets for maps and what range of the phonological transformations do they cover? Do they have learnability properties like the SP and TSL regions?

It is well known that deterministic regular functions are less expressive than non-deterministic functions (see Figure 5.4). Elgot & Mezei (1965) show a deep connection between non-determinism and abstractness: basically any non-deterministic function can be described as the composition of two deterministic functions provided the intermediate form is allowed to make use of symbols NOT IN THE INPUT ALPHABET. The fact that the "intermediate" alphabet contains symbols not in the input alphabet introduces a degree of abstractness (the extra symbols represent abstract information). This appears to be exactly the dividing line between dominant/recessive harmony patterns on one side and sour grapes harmony on the other. Better understanding the role of abstractness in maps and stringsets is important.

Another example of the interplay comes from a theorem by Medvedev (1964), which says that every regular language is the homomorphic image of strictly 2-local languages. In layman's terms this means every regular stringset, which can be used to model complex kinds of constraints, can be derived from a strictly 2-local stringset, which belongs to the lowest level of the Subregular Hierarchies. It suggests that what looks complex is actually very simple. But the trick is that the SL_2 language has a bigger alphabet and the latent information hidden in the more complex regular language is made explicit in the SL_2 language. Thus, by making our alphabet larger and more abstract we simplify constraints we may want to state. But the price is that the alphabet no longer represents observables (so one consequence is learning remains as difficult as before).

A related issue is non-string based representations. The main idea is that there is an interplay between the generative capacity of a formalism, the representation, and the power of logic. We have seen this already with respect to how order is represented. Representing order with successor and precedence has the following implication: if you want to represent *[+strident,α anterior]... [+strident,−α anterior] you will need MSO logic with successor, but only CNL logic with precedence. Another example is discussed in Section 8 below has to do with constraints on syllabic structure.

Finally, if these computational properties are to become part of the ontology of a theory of phonology, then much research is possible which tests the psychological validity of this ontology. The artificial language learning experiments by Finley (2008) and Lai (2012, 2015) are just one example of the kind of research that can be carried out. So far this work supports the hypotheses offered here. But currently there are more hypotheses than there are experiments testing them.

8 Representational issues

Before concluding, I would like to address the issue of representation. The above computational analysis appears to rest on the assumption that words must be modeled as strings. We modeled phonotactic knowledge and markedness constraints with infinite sets of STRINGS and we modeled the transformation from underlying to surface forms with infinite sets of STRING pairs. We argued that it is these objects whose nature we are interested in. The nature of these objects directly informs the questions in (2). As with circles (remember circles?), the nature of these objects is to some extent independent of the grammars used to describe them.

Phonologists are well aware that other representations of words exist, which are not based on strings and that phonological theories have employed many kinds of data structures. Nonlinear representations of words including autosegmental representations (Goldsmith 1976), the grid (Liberman & Prince 1977), feature-geometric representations (Clements 1985), and gestural scores (Browman & Goldstein 1992). Instead of strings, these theories employ graph-like data structures. Therefore, it is reasonable to wonder how much of the foregoing analysis depends on the string-based representations employed.

In this section, I would first like to explain that the extensions are not limited to string representations. The concept of "extension" of a grammar is much more general.

Then I would like to explain why the results in this chapter still matter, even though they use string-based representations. There are two parts to this. The first part reiterates the fact that string-based representations are in fact widely adopted in phonology and explains why they are widely adopted. Insofar as these reasons are compelling, the results in this chapter matter.

The second part argues that even if the right representations are not string-based, studies like the ones reviewed in this chapter are a necessary step for understanding the computational nature of phonological patterns. I will explain why subregular hierarchies like the ones presented in this chapter for strings exist for these other representational schemes for words, even if they have not yet all been discovered.

The main conclusion is that the interplay between the choice of representation and the computational principles presented here are likely to be fruitful areas of research in the coming decades.

8.1 Extensions without strings

In Section 3, I discussed the concept "extension of a grammar", and suggested that for constraints the extensions are infinite sets of strings and for transformations they are infinite sets of pairs of strings. More generally, the extension is an infinite set of objects, and the objects can be anything so long as it is well-defined.

For instance, a constraint like NOCODA could be defined so that the well-formed elements of its extension includes objects like the ones shown below.

(29)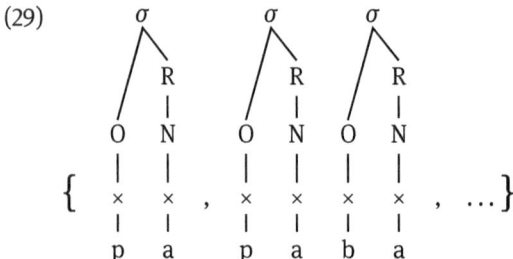

Non-linear representations such as these are common in phonological theory, and have brought much insight. Similarly, when discussing transformations from underlying to surface forms, the left and right elements in each pair can also be represented with a non-linear, graph-like representation similar to the ones shown in (29).

In order to think about the extensions of constraints and transformations, it is necessary to think about the representations of words. The constraint definition will determine which representations of the "logically possible" representations are well-formed and which are not. For instance, we may wonder whether the following representation is permitted by the theory and if so whether it violates NOCODA.

(30)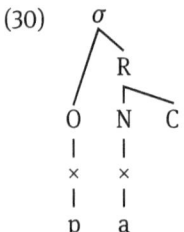

At issue of course is the marked structure(s) NOCODA, which is supposed to define when graph-like representations such as those in the preceding examples are adopted. There are several possibilities. Just having a node in the graph labeled with "C" for instance could be sufficient, in which case (30) would violate it. Or it may be necessary for the node labeled "C" to dominate a phonetic element (in which case (30) would not violate it). Or it may be that the labels in the preceding examples are just ornaments for phonologists for readability, and that what really matters is that there is consonantal material after the nucleus dominated by the same syllable node.

A more difficult question raises itself with these representations with respect to the constraint ONSET. At the very least this constraint REQUIRES an "O" node to be present. It does not ban a sub-structure, suggesting this constraint is at the Propositional level. Here again we see an interplay between the choice of representation and the power of the constraint. To state ONSET, this enriched representation requires a more complex constraint type than the string representation with the latent syllable boundary, which can define ONSET as the Strictly 2-Local constraint (*.V).

These are all interesting possibilities that have been explored to various degrees in the phonological literature. The point I wish to make is a fairly obvious one: representations of words matter when defining constraints or transformations. The extensions of the constraints and transformations will be in terms of these representations. String representations were used throughout this chapter, but some other representations could have been used, and computational analysis could have preceded on those representations instead.

8.2 Why string representations matter

Strings are one of the most basic data structures (Lothaire 1997, 2005). They are sequences of events. They are typically defined inductively with the primitive operation of concatenation and an alphabet: there is a unique string of zero length (the base case) and then if w is a string and there is a symbol a in the alphabet then the concatenation of w and a (written wa) is also a string (the inductive case). It is natural to think of phonological forms in terms of strings. The act of speech can be thought of as a sequence of articulatory or acoustic events. Writing systems are string-based representations of speech.

The most compelling reason to study string representations is that phonologists use them. One reason may be practical: it is more convenient to typeset strings than graph-like representations. But even from a theoretical perspective, the fact that representations were prominently debated at one point in the history of phonological theory (mainly during the 1970s and 1980s) does not mean that such issues are necessarily live today. As Hyman (2014) discusses, phonological theory has moved away from issues of representation (see also Anderson 1985). String-based representations are prominent nowadays, even in explaining long-distance harmony (Rose & Walker 2004; Walker 2011; Nevins 2010), a domain in which at one time autosegmental spreading analyses seemed particularly well suited (Hayes 1986). Tonal phonology is less amenable to string-based representations (for discussion, see also Marlo 2007), but even the principles governing autosegmental representations have yet to address every question posed by every language (Hyman 2014).

A second reason to work with strings is that the string is a fundamental data structure that has been well-studied (Lothaire 1997, 2005). This helps to make studying stringsets and string-to-string maps the easiest place to start. If we want to understand how computational principles play out with complicated data structures, we better first understand how they play out with simpler structures like strings.

The particular subregular hierarchies being established for strings are likely to have analogues for other data structures. For instance, Strictly 2-Local sets of tree structures have been studied and they can be used to describe context-free string sets (Rogers 1998). More generally, regular tree languages are also well-studied (Comon et al. 2007). While hierarchies as articulated as the ones for strings do not yet exist for these other data structures, they are in fact a focus in theoretical computer science (Rozenberg & Salomaa 1997).

Closer to issues in phonological theory, Kornai (1995) shows how autosegmental representations can be processed by finite-state automata for recognition and generation. Similarly, Jardine & Heinz (2015) show that autosegmental representations have important string-like properties and can be thought of as the concatenation of finitely many autosegmental primitives. Jardine (2016b) shows how Strictly Local autosegmental representations can be defined (and how in certain circumstances the No Crossing Constraint is a Strictly Local constraint).

In short, the methodological points being made in this chapter stand regardless of whether or not the representations are strings are something else. Computational principles provide a natural encyclopedia of categories with which the typology of phonological generalizations can be illuminated.

9 Conclusion

This has been a long chapter. Thankfully, the conclusion can be brief. Phonology is about how underlying lexical representations are transformed into surface ones. An important question asks about the cross-linguistic nature of these transformations. Grammars are typically conceived as generating patterns; these patterns are extensions of the grammar in the same way the extension of an algebraic equation is the set of points satisfying that equation. Computational analysis studies these EXTENSIONS, and such analysis of phonological generalizations is ongoing. Nonetheless, the results so far reveal that despite the cross-linguistic diversity, there are very strong, specific, universal computational properties shared by almost all phonological patterns. The few potential counter-examples are of special interest and deserve further study. Explaining these plausibly universal computational properties of phonological patterns is hard for theories that rely on optimization as a central organizing feature of the theory, but is straightforward if the computational properties highlighted within this chapter become the organizing principles themselves. These principles are natural for many reasons, only some of which could be covered here. Also, there is a clear sense in which these principles derive from principles of inference and learning. While there is still much work to do, a theory of phonology built around these computational principles promises to be sufficiently expressive, maximally restrictive, and learnable.

Acknowledgement: I am in indebted to Jane Chandlee, Rémi Eyraud, Bill Idsardi, Adam Jardine, Regine Lai, Jason Riggle, and Jim Rogers for invaluable discussion. I am also grateful to Jane Chandlee, Alex Cristia, Thomas Graf, Larry Hyman, and Lisa Pearl for helpful comments on an earlier draft. I also thank the students in my computational phonology course at the 2015 LSA Summer Institute, and the students in the Spring 2015 computational phonology seminar at the University of Delaware, in particular Hossep Dolatian, Hyun Jin Hwangbo, Huan Luo, Amanda Payne, Kristina Strother-Garcia, and Mai Ha Vu. Of course I assume full responsibility for flaws present in this chapter.

References

Anderson, Stephen R. 1985. *Phonology in the twentieth century*. Chicago: University of Chicago Press.
Applegate, Richard B. 1972. *Ineseño Chumash grammar*. Doctoral dissertation, University of California, Berkeley.
Applegate, Richard B. 2007. *Samala-English dictionary: A guide to the Samala language of the Ineseño Chumash people*. Santa Ynez, CA: Santa Ynez Band of Chumash Indians.
Bach, Emmon. 1975. Long vowels and stress in Kwakiutl. *Texas Linguistic Forum* 2. 9–19.
Baković, Eric. 2000. *Harmony, dominance and control*. Doctoral dissertation, Rutgers University, New Brunswick, NJ.
Baković, Eric. 2004. Unbounded stress and factorial typology. In John J. McCarthy (ed.), *Optimality Theory in phonology: A reader*. Oxford: Blackwell. ROA-244, Rutgers Optimality Archive, http://roa.rutgers.edu/
Baković, Eric. 2007. A revised typology of opaque generalizations. *Phonology* 24. 217–259.
Baković, Eric. 2011. Opacity deconstructed. In van Oostendorp et al. (eds.) *The Blackwell companion to phonology*, 2011.
Baković, Eric. 2013. *Blocking and complementarity in phonological theory*. Sheffield: Equinox.
Baković, Eric & Colin Wilson. 2000. Transparency, strict locality, and targeted constraints. In Roger Billerey & Brook Danielle Lillehaugen (eds.), *Proceedings of the 19th West Coast Conference on Formal Linguistics*, 43–56. Somerville, MA: Cascadilla Press.

Beckman, Jill. 1998. *Positional faithfulness*. Doctoral dissertation, University of Massachusetts, Amherst.

Beesley, Kenneth & Lauri Kartunnen. 2003. *Finite state morphology*. Stanford: CSLI.

Bennett, William. 2013. *Dissimilation, consonant harmony, and surface correspondence*. Doctoral dissertation, Rutgers University, New Brunswick, NJ.

Benua, Laura. 1995. Identity effects in morphological truncation. In Jill Beckman, Laura Walsh Dickey & Suzanne Urbanczyk (eds.), *Papers in Optimality Theory*, 77–136. Amherst, MA: GLSA Publications.

Benua, Laura. 1997. *Transderivational identity: Phonological relations between words*. Doctoral dissertation, University of Massachusetts, Amherst.

Beros, Achilles & Colin de la Higuera. 2014. A canonical semi-deterministic transducer. In Alexander Clark, Makoto Kanazawa, & Ryo Yoshinaka (eds.), *Proceedings of the 12th International Conference on Grammatical Inference (ICGI 2014)*, vol. 34, 33–148. JMLR: Workshop and Conference Proceedings.

Berstel, Jean. 1979. *Transductions and context-free languages*. Dordrecht: Springer.

Blevins, Juliette. 2004. *Evolutionary phonology*. Cambridge: Cambridge University Press.

Boersma, Paul. 1998. *Functional phonology: Formalizing the interactions between articulatory and perceptual drives*. Doctoral dissertation, Universiteit van Amsterdam. Published as LOT International Series 11. The Hague: Holland Academic Graphics.

Boersma, Paul & Bruce Hayes. 2001. Empirical tests of the gradual learning algorithm. *Lingustic Inquiry* 32. 45–86.

Browman, Catherine P. & Louis Goldstein. 1992. Articulatory phonology: An overview. *Phonetica* 49. 155–180.

Buccola, Brian. 2013. On the expressivity of Optimality Theory versus ordered rewrite rules. In Glyn Morrill & Mark Jan Nederhof (eds.), *Proceedings of Formal Grammar 2012 and 2013*, vol. 8306 of *Lecture notes in computer science*, 142–158. Berlin: Springer.

Büchi, J. Richard. 1960. Weak second-order arithmetic and finite automata. *Mathematical Logic Quarterly* 6. 66–92.

Chandlee, Jane. 2014. *Strictly local phonological processes*. Doctoral dissertation, University of Delaware.

Chandlee, Jane, Angeliki Athanasopoulou & Jeffrey Heinz. 2012. Evidence for classifying metathesis patterns as subsequential. In *Proceedings of the 29th West Coast Conference on Formal Linguistics*, 303–309. Somerville, MA: Cascadilla Press.

Chandlee, Jane, Rémy Eyraud & Jeffrey Heinz. 2014a. Learning strictly local subsequential functions. *Transactions of the Association for Computational Linguistics* 2. 491–503.

Chandlee, Jane & Jeffrey Heinz. 2012. Bounded copying is subsequential: Implications for metathesis and reduplication. In *Proceedings of the 12th Meeting of the ACL Special Interest Group on Computational Morphology and Phonology*, 42–51. Montreal: Association for Computational Linguistics.

Chandlee, Jane & Jeffrey Heinz. 2018. Strict locality and phonological maps. *Linguistic Inquiry* 49. 23–60.

Chandlee, Jane, Jeffrey Heinz & Adam Jardine. 2018. Input strictly local opaque maps. *Phonology*, to appear.

Chandlee, Jane, Adam Jardine & Jeffrey Heinz. 2014. Learning repairs for marked structures. Poster at the Annual Meeting of Phonology. MIT.

Chomsky, Noam. 1951. *Morphophonemics of Modern Hebrew*. Doctoral dissertation, University of Pennsylvania, Philadelphia. Published New York: Garland Press, 1979.
Chomsky, Noam. 1956. Three models for the description of language. *IRE Transactions on Information Theory* 113124. IT-2.
Chomsky, Noam. 1965. *Aspects of the theory of syntax*. Cambridge, MA: MIT Press.
Chomsky, Noam & Morris Halle. 1968. *The sound pattern of English*. New York: Harper & Row.
Clements, George N. 1985. The geometry of phonological features. *Phonology Yearbook* 2. 225–252.
Comon, Hubert, Max Dauchet, Rémi Gilleron, Florent Jacquemard, Denis Lugiez, Christof Löding, Sophie Tison & Marc Tommasi. 2007. *Tree automata techniques and applications*. http://www.grappa.univ-lille3.fr/tata (accessed 12 October 2007).
Dell, François & Mohamed Elmedlaoui. 1985. Syllabic consonants and syllabification in Imdlawn Tashlhiyt Berber. *Journal of African Languages and Linguistics* 7. 105–130.
Dresher, B. Elan. 1999. Charting the learning path: Cues to parameter setting. *Linguistic Inquiry* 30. 27–67.
Dresher, B. Elan. 2011. The phoneme. In van Oostendorp et al. (eds.) 2011, vol. 1, 241–266.
Edlefsen, Matt, Dylan Leeman, Nathan Myers, Nathaniel Smith, Molly Visscher & David Wellcome. 2008. Deciding strictly local (SL) languages. In Jon Breitenbucher (ed.), *Proceedings of the Midstates Conference for Undergraduate Research in Computer Science and Mathematics*, 66–73.
Elgot, C. C. & J. E. Mezei. 1965. On relations defined by generalized finite automata. *IBM Journal of Research and Development* 9. 47–68.
Endress, Ansgar D., Marina Nespor & Jacques Mehler. 2009. Perceptual and memory constraints on language acquisition. *Trends in Cognitive Science* 13. 348–353.
Engelfriet, Joost & Hendrik Jan Hoogeboom. 2001. MSO definable string transductions and two-way finite-state transducers. *ACM Transactions on Computational Logic* 2. 216–254.
Finley, Sara. 2008. *The formal and cognitive restrictions on vowel harmony*. Doctoral dissertation, Johns Hopkins University, Baltimore.
Finley, Sara. 2015. Learning non-adjacent dependencies in phonology: Transparent vowels in vowel harmony. *Language* 91. 48–72.
Finley, Sara & William Badecker. 2009. Artificial language learning and feature-based generalization. *Journal of Memory and Language* 61. 423–437.
Fougeron, Cécile & Patricia A. Keating. 1997. Articulatory strengthening at edges of prosodic domains. *Journal of the Acoustical Society of America* 101. 3728–3740.
Frank, Robert & Giorgo Satta. 1998. Optimality Theory and the generative complexity of constraint violability. *Computational Linguistics* 24. 307–315.
Gainor, Brian, Regine Lai & Jeffrey Heinz. 2012. Computational characterizations of vowel harmony patterns and pathologies. In *Proceedings of the 29th West Coast Conference on Formal Linguistics*, 63–71. Somerville, MA: Cascadilla Press.
Gallagher, Gillian. 2010. Perceptual distinctness and long-distance laryngeal restrictions. *Phonology* 27. 435–480.
García, Pedro & José Ruiz. 2004. Learning k-testable and k-piecewise testable languages from positive data. *Grammars* 7. 125–140.
García, Pedro, Enrique Vidal & José Oncina. 1990. Learning locally testable languages in the strict sense. In *Proceedings of the Workshop on Algorithmic Learning Theory*, 325–338. Tokyo.
Gazdar, Gerald & Geoffrey K. Pullum. 1982. Natural languages and context-free languages. *Linguistics and Philosophy* 4. 469–470.

Gerdemann, Dale & Gertjan van Noord. 2000. Approximation and exactness in finite state optimality theory. In *Proceedings of the 5th Meeting of the ACL Special Interest Group in Computational Phonology*, 34–45.

Gildea, Daniel & Daniel Jurafsky. 1996. Learning bias and phonological-rule induction. *Computational Linguistics* 24. 497–530.

Gold, E. Mark. 1967. Language identification in the limit. *Information and Control* 10. 447–474.

Goldsmith, John A. 1976. *Autosegmental phonology*. Doctoral dissertation, Massachusetts Institute of Technology, Cambridge, MA.

Goldwater, Sharon & Mark Johnson. 2003. Learning OT constraint rankings using a maximum entropy model. In Jennifer Spenader, Anders Eriksson & Östen Dahl (eds.), *Proceedings of the Stockholm Workshop on Variation within Optimality Theory*, 111–120. Stockholm: Stockholm University.

Gorman, Kyle. 2013. *Generative phonotactics*. Doctoral dissertation, University of Pennsylvania, Philadelphia.

Graf, Thomas. 2010a. Comparing incomparable frameworks: A model theoretic approach to phonology. *University of Pennsylvania Working Papers in Linguistics* 16, Article 10. http://repository.upenn.edu/pwpl/vol16/iss1/10.

Graf, Thomas. 2010b. *Logics of phonological reasoning*. Master's thesis, University of California, Los Angeles.

Graf, Thomas. 2013. *Local and transderivational constraints in syntax and semantics*. Doctoral dissertation, University of California, Los Angeles.

Hale, Mark & Charles Reiss. 2000. Substance abuse and dysfunctionalism: Current trends in phonology. *Linguistic Inquiry* 31. 157–169.

Halle, Morris. 1959. *The sound pattern of Russian*. The Hague: Mouton.

Halle, Morris. 1978. Knowledge unlearned and untaught: What speakers know about the sounds of their language. In Morris Halle, Joan Bresnan & George Miller (eds.), *Linguistic theory and psychological reality*, 294–303. Cambridge, MA: MIT Press.

Halle, Morris & Jean-Roger Vergnaud. 1987. *An essay on stress*. Cambridge, MA: MIT Press.

Hansson, Gunnar. 2001. *Theoretical and typological issues in consonant harmony*. Doctoral dissertation, University of California, Berkeley.

Hansson, Gunnar. 2008. Diachronic explanations of sound patterns. *Language and Linguistics Compass* 2. 859–893.

Hayes, Bruce. 1986. Assimilation as spreading in Toba Batak. *Linguistic Inquiry* 17. 467–499.

Hayes, Bruce. 1995. *Metrical stress theory*. Chicago: University of Chicago Press.

Hayes, Bruce, Robert Kirchner & Donca Steriade (eds.). 2004. *Phonetically-based phonology*. Cambridge: Cambridge University Press.

Hayes, Bruce & Colin Wilson. 2008. A maximum entropy model of phonotactics and phonotactic learning. *Linguistic Inquiry* 39. 379–440.

Heinz, Jeffrey. 2007. *The inductive learning of phonotactic patterns*. Doctoral dissertation, University of California, Los Angeles.

Heinz, Jeffrey. 2009. On the role of locality in learning stress patterns. *Phonology* 26. 303–351.

Heinz, Jeffrey. 2010a. Learning long-distance phonotactics. *Linguistic Inquiry* 41. 623–661.

Heinz, Jeffrey. 2010b. String extension learning. In *Proceedings of the 48th Annual Meeting of the Association for Computational Linguistics*, 897–906. Uppsala: Association for Computational Linguistics.

Heinz, Jeffrey. 2014. Culminativity times harmony equals unbounded stress. In Harry van der Hulst (ed.), *Word stress: Theoretical and typological issues*, 255–275. Cambridge: Cambridge University Press.

Heinz, Jeffrey. 2016. Computational theories of learning and developmental psycholinguistics. In Jeffrey Lidz, William Synder & Joe Pater (eds.), *The Oxford handbook of developmental linguistics*. Oxford: Oxford University Press.

Heinz, Jeffrey & William Idsardi. 2011. Sentence and word complexity. *Science* 333. 295–297.

Heinz, Jeffrey & William Idsardi. 2013. What complexity differences reveal about domains in language. *Topics in Cognitive Science* 5. 111–131.

Heinz, Jeffrey, Anna Kasprzik & Timo Kötzing. 2012. Learning with lattice-structured hypothesis spaces. *Theoretical Computer Science* 457. 111–127.

Heinz, Jeffrey & Regine Lai. 2013. Vowel harmony and subsequentiality. In András Kornai & Marco Kuhlmann (eds.), *Proceedings of the 13th Meeting on the Mathematics of Language (MoL 13)*, 52–63. Sofia, Bulgaria.

Heinz, Jeffrey, Chetan Rawal, & Herbert G. Tanner. 2011. Tier-based strictly local constraints for phonology. In *Proceedings of the 49th Annual Meeting of the Association for Computational Linguistics*, 58–64. Portland, OR: Association for Computational Linguistics.

Higuera, Colin de la. 1997. Characteristic sets for polynomial grammatical inference. *Machine Learning* 27. 125–138.

Howard, Irwin. 1972. *A directional theory of rule application in phonology*. Doctoral dissertation, Massachusetts Institute of Technology, Cambridge, MA.

Hulden, Mans. 2009. *Finite-state machine construction methods and algorithms for phonology and morphology*. Doctoral dissertation, University of Arizona, Tucson.

Hulst, Harry van der & Jeroen van de Weijer. 1995. Vowel harmony. In John A. Goldsmith (ed.), *The handbook of phonological theory*, 495–534. Oxford: Blackwell.

Humboldt, Wilhelm von. 1999. *On language*. Edited by Michael Losonsky. Translated by Peter Heath. Cambridge: Cambridge University Press. Originally published 1836.

Hyman, Larry M. 1998. Positional prominence and the "prosodic trough" in Yaka. *Phonology* 15. 41–75.

Hyman, Larry M. 2007. Kuki-Thaadow: An African tone system in Southeast Asia. *Berkeley Phonology Lab Annual Report*. University of California, Berkeley: Department of Linguistics.

Hyman, Larry M. 2011. Tone: Is it different? In John A. Goldsmith, Jason Riggle, & Alan C. L. Yu (eds.), *The handbook of phonological theory*, 2nd edn. 197–238. Oxford: Wiley-Blackwell.

Hyman, Larry M. 2014. How autosegmental is phonology? *The Linguistic Review* 31. 363–400.

Hyman, Larry M. 2009. How (not) to do phonological typology: The case of pitch-accent. *Language Sciences* 31. 213–238 (Data and Theory: Papers in Phonology in celebration of Charles W. Kisseberth).

Idsardi, William. 1998. Tiberian Hebrew spirantization and phonological derivations. *Linguistic Inquiry* 29. 37–73.

Idsardi, William J. 2000. Clarifying opacity. *The Linguistic Review* 17. 337–350.

Jäger, Gerhard. 2002. Some notes on the formal properties of bidirectional optimality theory. *Journal of Logic, Language, and Information* 11. 427–451.

Jardine, Adam. 2016a. Computationally, tone is different. *Phonology* 32. 247–283.

Jardine, Adam. 2016b. *Locality and non-linear representations in tonal phonology*. Doctoral dissertation, University of Delaware.

Jardine, Adam, Jane Chandlee, Rémi Eyraud & Jeffrey Heinz. 2014. Very efficient learning of structured classes of subsequential functions from positive data. In Alexander Clark, Makoto Kanazawa & Ryo Yoshinaka (eds.), *Proceedings of the 12th International Conference on Grammatical Inference (ICGI 2014)*, vol. 34, 94–108. JMLR: Workshop and Conference Proceedings.

Jardine, Adam & Jeffrey Heinz. 2015a. A concatenation operation to derive autosegmental graphs. In *Proceedings of the 14th Meeting on the Mathematics of Language (MoL 2015)*, 139–151. Chicago.

Jardine, Adam & Jeffrey Heinz. 2016. Learning tier-based strictly local languages. *Transactions of the Association for Computational Linguistics* 4. 87-98.

Johnson, C. Douglas. 1972. *Formal aspects of phonological description*. The Hague: Mouton.

Jurafsky, Daniel & James Martin. 2008. *Speech and language processing: An introduction to natural language processing, speech recognition, and computational linguistics*, 2nd edn. Upper Saddle River, NJ: Prentice-Hall.

Kager, René. 1999. *Optimality Theory*. Cambridge: Cambridge University Press.

Kaplan, Ronald & Martin Kay. 1994. Regular models of phonological rule systems. *Computational Linguistics* 20. 331–378.

Karttunen, Lauri. 1998. The proper treatment of optimality in computational phonology. In *FSMNLP'98*, 1–12. International Workshop on Finite-State Methods in Natural Language Processing, Bilkent University, Ankara.

Kiparsky, Paul. 2000. Opacity and cyclicity. *The Linguistic Review* 17. 351–366.

Kisseberth, Charles W. 1970. On the functional unity of phonological rules. *Linguistic Inquiry* 1. 291–306.

Kisseberth, Charles W. & David Odden. 2003. Tone. In Derek Nurse & Gérard Philippson (eds.), *The Bantu languages*, 59–70. London: Routledge.

Kobele, Gregory. 2006. *Generating copies: An investigation into structural identity in language and grammar*. Doctoral dissertation, University of California, Los Angeles.

Kornai, András. 1995. *Formal phonology*. Outstanding Dissertations in Linguistics. New York: Garland Publishing.

Koskenniemi, Kimmo. 1983. *Two-level morphology*. Publication no. 11, Department of General Linguistics. Helsinki: University of Helsinki.

Krämer, Martin. 2003. *Vowel harmony and Correspondence Theory*. Berlin: Mouton de Gruyter.

Kula, Nancy C. & Lee S. Bickmore. 2015. Phrasal phonology in Copperbelt Bemba. *Phonology* 32. 147–176.

Lacy, Paul de. 2011. Markedness and faithfulness constraints. In van Oostendorp et al. (eds.) 2011, Chapter 74.

Lai, Regine. 2012. *Domain specificity in phonology*. Doctoral dissertation, University of Delaware.

Lai, Regine. 2015. Learnable vs. unlearnable harmony patterns. *Linguistic Inquiry* 46. 425–451.

Lautemann, Clemens, Pierre McKenzie, Thomas Schwentick & Heribert Vollmer. 2001. The descriptive complexity approach to {LOGCFL}. *Journal of Computer and System Sciences* 62: 629–652.

Liberman, Mark & Alan Prince. 1977. On stress and linguistic rhythm. *Linguistic Inquiry* 8. 249–336.

Lothaire, M. (ed.). 1997. *Combinatorics on words*. Cambridge: Cambridge University Press.

Lothaire, M. (ed.) 2005. *Algebraic combinatorics on words*, 2nd edn. Cambridge: Cambridge University Press.

Luo, Huan. 2017. Long-distance consonant harmony and subsequantiality. *Glossa* 2, 52.

Marlo, Michael. 2007. *The verbal tonology of Lumarachi and Lunyala: Two dialects of Luluyia*. Doctoral dissertation, University of Michigan, Ann Arbor.

McCarthy, John J. 2003. OT constraints are categorical. *Phonology* 20. 75–138.
McCarthy, John J. 2004. Headed spans and autosegmental spreading. Unpublished manuscript, University of Massachusetts, Amherst.
McCarthy, John J. 2007. *Hidden generalizations: Phonological opacity in Optimality Theory.* London: Equinox.
McCarthy, John J. 2008a. *Doing Optimality Theory.* Oxford: Blackwell.
McCarthy, John J. 2008b. The gradual path to cluster simplification. *Phonology* 25. 271–319.
McNaughton, Robert & Seymour Papert. 1971. *Counter-free automata.* Cambridge, MA: MIT Press.
Medvedev, Yu. T. 1964. On the class of events representable in a finite automaton. In Edward F. Moore (ed.), *Sequential machines: Selected Papers*, 215–227. Boston: Addison-Wesley. Originally published in Russian in *Avtomaty*, 1956, 385–401.
Mielke, Jeff. 2008. *The emergence of distinctive features.* Oxford: Oxford University Press.
Mohri, Mehryar. 1997. Finite-state transducers in language and speech processing. *Computational Linguistics* 23. 269–311.
Nevins, Andrew. 2010. *Locality in vowel harmony.* Cambridge, MA: MIT Press.
Odden, David. 1994. Adjacency parameters in phonology. *Language* 70. 289–330.
Ohala, John J. 1981. The listener as a source of sound change. In C. S. Masek, R. A. Hendrik & M. F. Miller (eds.), *Papers from the Parasession on Language and Behavior, Chicago Linguistics Society*, 178–203. Chicago: CLS.
Oncina, José & Pedro García. 1991. Inductive learning of subsequential functions. Technical Report DSIC II-34, University Politécnia de Valencia.
Oncina, José, Pedro García & Enrique Vidal. 1993. Learning subsequential transducers for pattern recognition tasks. *IEEE Transactions on Pattern Analysis and Machine Intelligence* 15. 448–458.
Oostendorp, Marc van, Colin J. Ewen, Elizabeth Hume & Keren Rice (eds.). 2011. *The Blackwell companion to phonology.* 5 volumes. Oxford: Blackwell.
Padgett, Jaye. 1995. Partial class behavior and nasal place assimilation. In Keiichiro Suzuki & Dirk Elzinga (eds.), *Proceedings of the 1995 Southwestern Workshop on Optimality Theory*. University of Arizona: Coyote Papers.
Pater, Joe. 2000. *NC. In Kiyomi Kusumoto (ed.), *Proceedings of the 26th Annual Meeting of the North East Linguistics Society*, 227–239. Amherst, MA: GLSA.
Pater, Joe. 2001. Austronesian nasal substitution revisited: What's wrong with *NC (and what's not). In Linda Lombardi (ed.), *Segmental phonology in Optimality Theory: Constraints and representations*, 159–182. Cambridge: Cambridge University Press.
Payne, Amanda. 2017. All dissimilation is computationally subsequential. *Language* 93. e353–e371.
Popper, Karl. 1959. *The logic of scientific discovery.* New York: Basic Books.
Potts, Christopher, Joe Pater, Rajesh Bhatt & Michael Becker. 2008. Harmonic grammar with linear programming: From linear systems to linguistic typology. Rutgers Optimality Archive ROA-984.
Potts, Christopher & Geoffrey K. Pullum. 2002. Model theory and the content of OT constraints. *Phonology* 19. 361–393.
Prince, Alan & Paul Smolensky. 1993. *Optimality Theory: Constraint interaction in generative grammar.* Technical Report 2, Rutgers University Center for Cognitive Science.
Prince, Alan & Paul Smolensky. 2004. *Optimality Theory: Constraint interaction in Generative Grammar.* Oxford: Blackwell.

Riggle, Jason. 2004. *Generation, recognition, and learning in finite state Optimality Theory*. Doctoral dissertation, University of California, Los Angeles.
Roark, Brian & Richard Sproat. 2007. *Computational approaches to morphology and syntax*. Oxford: Oxford University Press.
Roche, Emmanuel & Yves Schabes. 1997. *Finite-state language processing*. Cambridge, MA: MIT Press.
Rogers, James. 1998. *A descriptive approach to language-theoretic complexity*. Stanford: CSLI Publications.
Rogers, James, Jeffrey Heinz, Gil Bailey, Matt Edlefsen, Molly Visscher, David Wellcome & Sean Wibel. 2010. On languages piecewise testable in the strict sense. In Christian Ebert, Gerhard Jäger, & Jens Michaelis (eds.), *The mathematics of language*, vol. 6149 of *Lecture notes in Artifical Intelligence*, 255–265. Dordrecht: Springer.
Rogers, James, Jeffrey Heinz, Margaret Fero, Jeremy Hurst, Dakotah Lambert, & Sean Wibel. 2013. Cognitive and sub-regular complexity. In Glyn Morrill & Mark-Jan Nederhof (eds.), *Formal grammar*, vol. 8036 of *Lecture notes in computer science*, 90–108. Dordrecht: Springer.
Rogers, James & Geoffrey K. Pullum. 2011. Aural pattern recognition experiments and the subregular hierarchy. *Journal of Logic, Language and Information* 20. 329–342.
Rose, Sharon & Rachel Walker. 2004. A typology of consonant agreement as correspondence. *Language* 80. 475–531.
Rozenberg, Grzegorz & Arto Salomaa (eds.). 1997. *Handbook of formal languages: Beyond words*, vol. 3. Dordrecht: Springer.
Sakarovitch, Jaques. 2009. *Elements of automata theory*. Cambridge: Cambridge University Press. (Translated by Reuben Thomas from the French original, Paris: Vuibert, 2003.)
Scott, Dana & Michael Rabin. 1959. Finite automata and their decision problems. *IBM Journal of Research and Development* 5. 114–125.
Shieber, Stuart. 1985. Evidence against the context-freeness of natural language. *Linguistics and Philosophy* 8. 333–343.
Sipser, Michael. 1997. *Introduction to the theory of computation*. Boston: PWS Publishing.
Smolensky, Paul & Géraldine Legendre. 2006. *The harmonic mind: From neural computation to Optimality-Theoretic grammar*. Cambridge, MA: MIT Press.
Suzuki, Keiichiro. 1998. *A typological investigation of dissimilation*. Doctoral dissertation, University of Arizona, Tucson.
Tesar, Bruce. 1995. *Computational Optimality Theory*. Doctoral dissertation, University of Colorado at Boulder.
Tesar, Bruce. 2014. *Output-driven phonology*. Cambridge: Cambridge University Press.
Tesar, Bruce & Paul Smolensky. 1998. Learnability in Optimality Theory. *Linguistic Inquiry* 29. 229–268.
Tesar, Bruce & Paul Smolensky. 2000. *Learnability in Optimality Theory*. Cambridge, MA: MIT Press.
Thomas, Wolfgang. 1997. Languages, automata, and logic. In Rozenberg & Salomaa (eds.) 1997, 389–455.
Turing, Alan. 1937. On computable numbers, with an application to the Entscheidungsproblem. *Proceedings of the London Mathematical Society* 2. 230–265.
Walker, Rachel. 2011. *Vowel patterns in language*. Cambridge: Cambridge University Press.

Wilson, Colin. 2001. Consonant cluster neutralization and targeted constraints. *Phonology* 18. 147–197.

Wilson, Colin. 2003. Analyzing unbounded spreading with constraints: Marks, targets, and derivations. Unpublished manuscript, UCLA.

Wilson, Colin. 2004. Experimental investigation of phonological naturalness. In *Proceedings of the 22nd West Coast Conference on Formal Linguistics*, 534–546. San Diego: University of California.

Anthony Brohan and Jeff Mielke
Frequent segmental alternations in P-base 3

Abstract: P-base (Mielke 2008) is a large typological database of several thousand phonological rules and distributions in 537 languages. In this chapter we demonstrate how it can be applied to a wide range of questions in phonological typology, making use of several new features of version 3. This includes possible follow-up studies to many of the other chapters in the volume. As a starting point, we show that the crosslinguistic frequency of segments in segment inventories are largely similar to UPSID (Maddieson 1984; Maddieson & Precoda 1990), a similarly-sized genetically balanced database of segment inventories. Second, we show that a considerable number of the phonological patterns in P-base fall into a small number of categories defined in terms of the classes of segments involved, the features changing, and the position of the trigger relative to the target. For instance, regressive preconsonantal nasal place assimilation accounts for 4.54% of the sound patterns, and because place changes are quite rare, this constitutes more than half of all cases of place assimilation. Other types of sound patterns are shown to be distributed in ways that are consistent with phonetic accounts of phonological typology, e.g., consonant epenthesis is dominated by glottals and glides, particularly in contexts that have been argued to be the locus of epenthesis as a sound change.

1 Introduction

Much of what is currently known about phonological typology is based on the UCLA Phonological Segment Inventory Database (UPSID), compiled by Ian Maddieson and colleagues. The UPSID database was published with 317 languages in Maddieson's 1984 book *Patterns of sounds*, later expanded to 451 inventories (Maddieson & Precoda 1990), and now being expanded as LAPSyD (Maddieson 2014). The availability of UPSID has meant that studies of phonological universals have preferentially favored segment inventories (Lindblom & Maddieson 1988; Hyman 2008) over phonological alternations. Crosslinguistic databases of phonological alternations have often involved custom databases of particular types of phonological patterns such as lenition (Lavoie 2001; Kirchner 2001) and metathesis (Hume 2004). P-base (Mielke 2008) is a general database of phonological alternations in several hundred languages, but until recently it was organized in terms of classes of sounds, making it difficult to use to study phonological patterns more generally. We report a study of frequent phonological patterns in a newly reorganized version of P-base.

2 P-base

P-base was compiled from descriptions available on library stacks at the Ohio State University and Michigan State University. It was originally collected to test models of natural classes (Mielke 2005, 2008), and was structured according to classes involved in phonological patterns (6170 classes involved in alternations, and about 3000 others involved in phonotactic restrictions. These alternations include general phonological patterns as well as morphologically conditioned patterns.

We report on a reorganized P-base that is structured according to phonological alternations and distributional restrictions. As an example of this reorganization, (1) shows how Japanese high vowel devoicing (Vance 1987) was entered in the original P-base as two phonologically active classes, and (2) shows how the same phonological pattern is entered in P-base 3, as a single phonological pattern involving two classes of sounds.

(1) Japanese high vowel devoicing in P-base 1:
   JAPA0.0   {i, ɯ}   "Target,X → vls / C[-vc] __ {C[-vc], #}"
   JAPA1.0   {p,t,k,s,ʃ,h}   "Trigger,high vowels → vls / X __ {X, #}"

In the P-base 1 version, a user could easily query the classes of sounds involved in patterns such as this one, but the details of the alternation were stored in text strings, leaving it up to the user to perform keyword searches in order to identify similar patterns, and even to associate these two entries (the target and the trigger) with one another.

(2) Japanese high vowel devoicing in P-base 3:
   jpn 6795   {i,ɯ} → {i̥,ɯ̥}/{p,t,k,s,ʃ,h} __ $\begin{Bmatrix} p,t,k,s,ʃ,h \\ \# \end{Bmatrix}$

P-base 3 is a MySQL database with a web interface.[1] It contains phonological patterns from 630 language varieties, corresponding to 537 distinct ISO639.3 codes, and matched to AUTOTYP family trees (Bickel & Nichols 1996). Sound pattern

---
[1] http://pbase.phon.chass.ncsu.edu

entries contain fields for input, output, segmental context, prosodic domain, morphological effects, prosody, and optionality.

Automated querying of sound pattern properties is enhanced with feature analysis, which is implemented by associating each of the 1274 distinct IPA transcriptions with a vector of feature values in one of several feature systems. P-base currently supports seven feature systems: a descriptive feature system, the systems described in *Preliminaries to the analysis of speech* (Jakobson, Fant & Halle 1952), *The sound pattern of English* (Chomsky & Halle 1968), *Problem book in phonology* (Halle & Clements 1983), and three versions of Unified Feature Theory (Clements & Hume 1995). Mielke et al. (2011) compares the performance of six of these systems in characterizing the phonologically active classes of sounds in P-base. This example and the rest of this chapter use the familiar Halle & Clements (1983) feature system.

IPA symbols are used to explicitly represent the segments that undergo, condition, and result from phonological patterns. Types of sound patterns such as assimilation are recognized by converting the segment-based description to a feature-based description. A feature analysis of the pattern in (2) is shown in (3). The feature analysis is computed automatically by P-base, meaning that the user can symbolically search for patterns involving various segments, features, and types of changes.

(3) P-base 3 feature analysis:
$$\begin{bmatrix} +\text{syllabic} \\ +\text{high} \\ -\text{long} \end{bmatrix} \rightarrow [-\text{voice}] / [-\text{voice}] \_\_ \begin{Bmatrix} [-\text{voice}] \\ \# \end{Bmatrix}$$
Assimilation: [–voice]

Associating each of the segments in (2) with its feature representation automates a big part of the process of analyzing and classifying the alternation. An algorithm determines common features between each cell of the structural description, allowing the sound patterns to be described in terms of natural classes. This natural class analysis is instantiated on a given language's inventory, so we are able to query for patterns which target a particular natural class given a particular language. The feature analysis also determines which features in an alternation are implicated in a change by looking for differences between the common features of the input and output.[2] Comparing the set of changes detected with

---

[2] This procedure works well for parallel patterns, but fails at detecting a common feature change in chain shift alternations.

common features in the environment can detect assimilations. So, although the change (devoicing) is not explicit in (2), this information is easily extracted by observing that output segments differ from the input segments only by being devoiced. Assimilation is recognized similarly, by observing that the feature value that describes the change is shared by the left or right context, or both.

This automated feature analysis is available through P-base 3's online query tool, and here it contributes to classifying 4560 phonological alternations in the database. In addition, there are approximately 1300 distributional patterns in P-base 3 that we are not considering here. P-base 3 entries for an additional 1000 or so phonological alternations from P-base 1 remain to be completed. These are mostly patterns that do not easily fit the basic segmental pattern template (e.g., metathesis, coalescence, prosodic patterns). The purpose of this chapter is to describe the most frequent patterns, so these are not very consequential here.

3 Database comparison and sampling

When considering questions about what properties of phonological systems are crosslinguistically frequent and why, it is useful to be able to determine whether a feature is frequent because of essentially universal forces that shape sound systems, or due to shared inheritance within a particularly well-attested language family, or to areal factors. In UPSID, shared inheritance has been dealt with by only including languages that are sufficiently distant from languages that are already included.

The phonological patterns in P-base are the result of an exhaustive search of descriptive grammars available in a large university library. As such, it is not a genetically balanced sample, and its bias toward better-described language families is discussed in Mielke (2008: 47–48). An UPSID-like inclusion criterion would reduce the number of included languages considerably. Our approach has been to include all available language descriptions and then take genetic balance into account when interpreting results. LAPSyD (Maddieson 2014) has followed a similar approach in expanding upon UPSID, by including more closely related languages in the database and allowing the user to employ appropriate criteria for considering their relationships.

Since the 451-language version of UPSID (Maddieson & Precoda 1990) includes about the same number of languages as P-base, and is genetically balanced, we turn to segment inventories as a basis for comparison between the samples of the two databases, before considering the role of genetic sampling in a typological survey of phonological patterns. Figure 6.1 provides an overview of

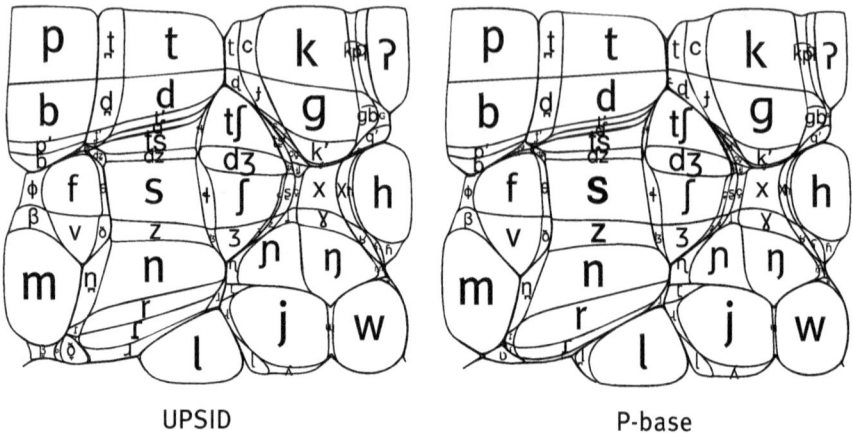

Figure 6.1: Frequency counts of basic consonants in UPSID and P-base inventories.

the distribution of consonants in UPSID and P-base. These are density-equalizing maps (Gastner & Newman 2004) of a chart of basic consonants (Mielke 2017), where the area of each cell reflects the number of languages having the sound in their inventories. The two charts tell similar stories about frequent and infrequent consonants. [m] is the most frequent consonant in both samples, followed by [k] and [j]. Differences that are apparent include the higher frequency of approximants such as [β] and [ð̞] in UPSID (which may really be a difference in the methods for selecting representative IPA symbols), and the higher frequency of [r] and voiced stops in P-base.

Since the genetic relationships between the languages in both samples are known (or at least posited), it is possible to compensate for genetic imbalances by applying a sampling algorithm such as G-sampling (Bickel 2008). The frequencies depicted in Figure 6.1 are not adjusted for genetic relationships, meaning that the frequency of a segment in a sample is literally the number of languages in the sample that have that segment. This technique does not distinguish between a case where a segment has been innovated many times in many different language families, and a case where a segment has been innovated once in one family and all the instance of that segment are found in that family. UPSID minifies this concern by not sampling closely related languages, but it is still vulnerable to over-counting segments found in large families.

In short, G-sampling works by descending a language family tree and counting only the number of subgroups where the presence or absence of a linguistic feature is significantly skewed in comparison to the higher level. If all the members

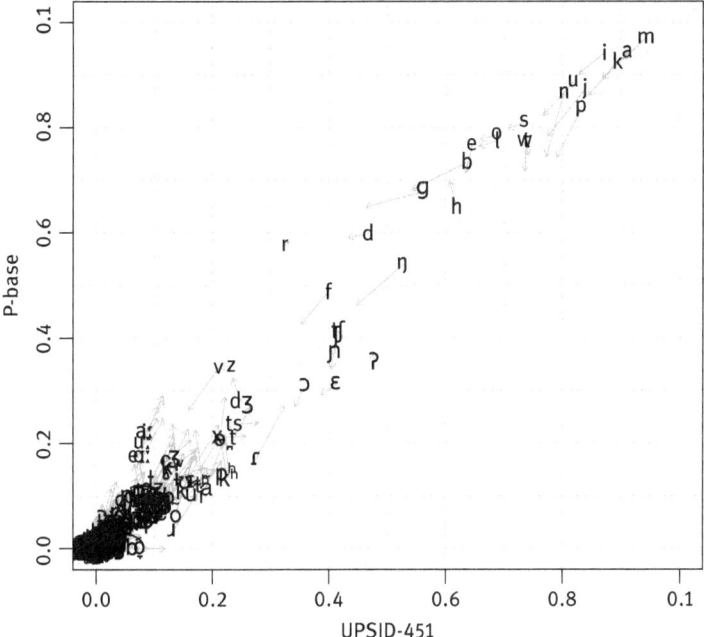

Figure 6.2: Effects of G-sampling on segment frequencies.

of a language family have a particular segment, it is counted once for that family. If only one language in a large family has a particular segment, it is counted once for that language, and the rest of the family (if it is significantly skewed relative to the other language families, would be counted once as not having the segment). See Bickel (2008: 7–8) for a more explicit statement of the algorithm.

Figure 6.2 shows the result of applying G-sampling to the UPSID and P-base samples of inventories. The coordinates of each IPA symbol in the figure represent the proportion of P-base and UPSID inventories containing the segment. The gray arrow originating from each IPA symbol represents the effect of G-sampling: an arrow pointing down and to the left means that G-sampling reduced the proportion of languages having the segment (indicating that frequent occurrence in particular language families led to its higher raw numbers). The fact that the segments are close to the diagonal indicates that they are generally similar in both databases. The vast majority of distinct IPA transcriptions are attested in only a handful of languages in either sample. Segments appearing substantially above the diagonal are more frequent in P-base, and segments appearing substantially below the diagonal are more frequent in UPSID. Where they diverge, UPSID can be considered to be more reliable, because the primary difference is the sampling techniques.

A major effect of G-sampling is to move everything closer to the middle, along the diagonal. If G-sampling were having the effect of reconciling differences between the UPSID and P-base samples, the arrows would be pointing closer to the diagonal, not parallel to it. The two databases are the most divergent on [r], and G-sampling indicates that this is not due to sampling. On the other hand, [v] and [ɾ] both occur in about 25% of languages, but G-sampling affects them in opposite ways, that are similar across the two databases, suggesting that the frequency of [v] is overestimated due shared inheritance, while the frequency of [ɾ] is underestimated due to language families that lack it.

The rest of this chapter is concerned with phonological alternations, for which there is no other database to compare to. The fact that segment frequencies in P-base are similar to UPSID, which was collected with genetic balance in mind, lead us to be less concerned about genetic balance in our interpretation of other patterns in the P-base language sample. While it would be possible to apply G-sampling to our counts of phonological alternations, we elect not to, on the basis of the inventory comparison, and because G-sampling works best for phenomena whose presence or absence is easily counted.

Counting the absence of a feature is where phonological patterns become challenging to genetic sampling techniques. It is reasonable to expect language descriptions to report binary features such as verb-object vs. object-verb word order in a consistent way, and only a little less reasonable to expect phonological descriptions to indicate in similar terms whether a particular type of phonological segment is present or absent in the inventory of a language. By comparison, descriptions of phonological alternations and distributional restrictions vary widely in their exhaustiveness, and it is much harder to interpret a pattern that is unreported as truly absent from the language. A detailed phonological description may include a range of postlexical rules that require some phonetic sophistication to recognize, and the fact that such a pattern is not included in a description of a related language is not conclusive.[3] To be confident enough in the absence of a pattern to conclude that it is innovative in a related language would require

---

[3] All the usual caveats about studies of phonological inventories apply to studies of phonological alternations. A phoneme inventory and a phonological rule are both very high-level descriptions, and many steps intervene between the numbers reported in this paper, and the linguistic descriptions they are based on. The criticisms of UPSID put forth by Simpson (1999: 349) apply equally to the segment inventories in P-base, and the phonological alternations that this paper is mainly concerned with are subject to similar issues. In general, these have been taken as described from the grammars in which they appeared, except when contradicted by available data. The aggregate data presented here is expected to highlight many facts about phonological patterns that are interesting to typologists, and also to reflect some conventions in how phonological patterns are typically described.

going and looking for each pattern in each language where it wasn't reported. We have not done this.

4 Overview of segmental changes

Figure 6.3 provides an overview of all the changes involving basic consonants and vowels. Input-output mappings between pairs of segments are indicated by arrows. The size of the arrow represents how many time each input-output mapping is observed. The arrows are superimposed on a density-equalized IPA chart, where cell area indicates the G-sampled frequency of occurrence in P-base inventories. Vowels and consonants have been placed in the same chart, with front unrounded vowels aligned to palatal consonants and back rounded vowels aligned to labiovelar consonants. Cells and arrows in Figure 6.3 are colored by

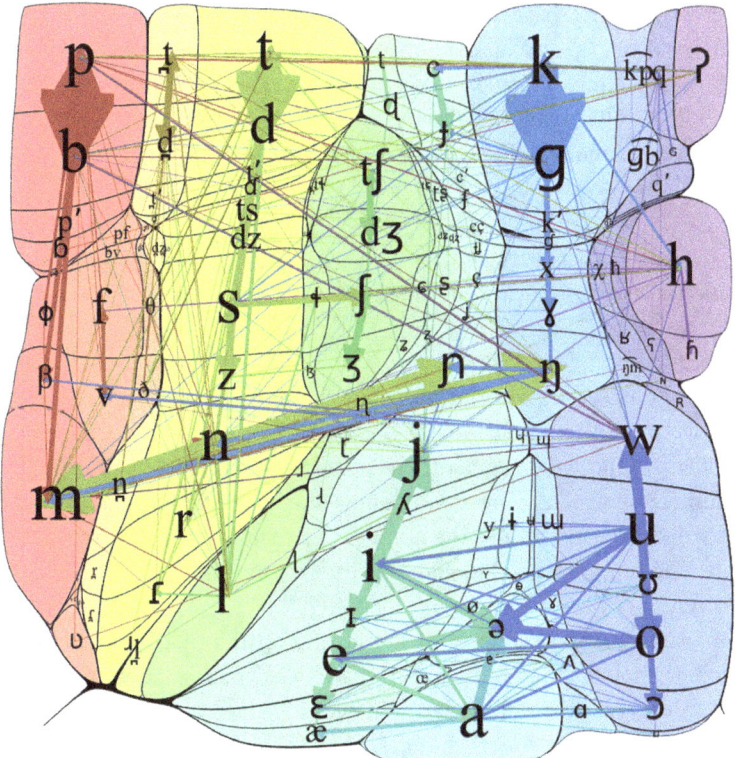

Figure 6.3: All input-output mappings colored by place.

place of articulation. Arrows reflect the properties of the input, so arrows that extend over a region of a different color indicate changes of place of articulation.

A striking observation from Figure 6.3 is that there are few kinds of frequent place changes (represented by horizontal or diagonal arrows passing over a different color). The most salient manner changes represent voicing and devoicing of obstruents, spirantization of stops, nasalization of voiced stops, /ɾ/, and /l/, gliding of high vowels, and height changes among vowels. The most frequent place changes involve nasal changing into other nasals, palatalization of the consonants /s k g/, debuccalization, including /k/ spirantizing to [h], and vowels changing backness and rounding, especially by changing to [ə].

Another set of place changes requires comment: /w/ is involved in many place changes with bilabial stops and voiced labial fricatives. This reflects the arbitrary choice of putting labiovelar /w/ near the velars instead of the labials. Additionally, we do not have much articulatory evidence for how many instances of /w/ really involve a velar constriction, and how many should really be transcribed as /β/ and placed in the bilabial column. UPSID has transcribed more approximants as /β/ than P-base has. /k/ → [h] is notable because most instances of spirantization do not involve place changes, but /k/'s fricative counterpart /x/ is considerably less frequent than /h/ in segment inventories. Reinterpretation of /k/ lenition as /k/ → [h] in languages with /h/ but no /x/ is consistent with the principle of structural analogy (Blevins 2004: 154):

> In the course of language acquisition, the existence of a (non-ambiguous) phonological contrast between A and B will result in more instances of sound change involving shifts of ambiguous elements to A or B than if no contrast between A and B existed.

The input-output mappings of Figure 6.3 are summarized in Figures 6.4 and 6.5. In both figures, the background color indicates the place or manner/voicing of the output segment, and color of the outer ring of the balloon indicates the place or manner/voicing of the input segment. The area of each colored outer ring represents the number of structure preserving input-output mappings, and the area of each inner white circle represents the number of structure changing input-output mappings. The numbers used to generate the balloons are segment counts, not pattern counts.

The manner mappings in Figure 6.4 are mostly off the diagonal, meaning that there are few changes that do not affect manner or voicing. These are dominated by the categories involved in place changes observed above (nasals, palatalization of obstruents, and vowel changes). All of these are about evenly split between structure changing and structure preserving. The leading (off-diagonal) manner changes include obstruent voicing, which is mostly structure changing,

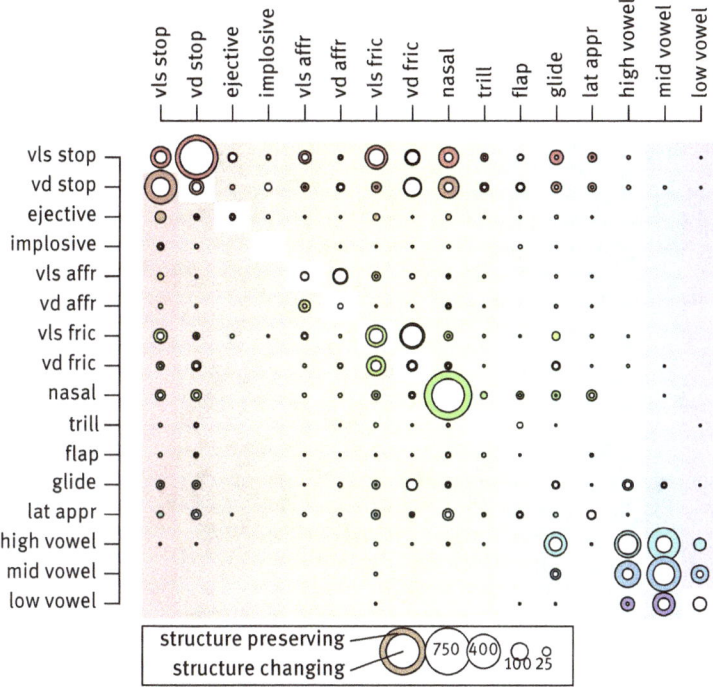

Figure 6.4: Changes by manner of articulation and voicing. Input is on the left and output is on the top. Area of colored outer ring represents the number of structure preserving changes in the category. Area of inner white circle represents the number of structure changing changes in the category.

and obstruent devoicing, which is mostly structure preserving. This asymmetry can potentially be explained entirely in terms of the rarity of voiced obstruents without voiceless counterparts.

Vowel height changes are abundant, especially between high and mid vowels, and are more likely to be structure preserving than non-height changes. High vowels frequently turn into glides, and the converse is less frequent. Stops change manner in many different ways, and a salient fact is that stop changes that result in a fricative, flap, implosive, or ejective are typically structure changing, but stop changes that result in a nasal, trill, glide, or lateral approximant are more likely to be structure preserving.

The place mappings in Figure 6.5 mostly fall into one of three types. First, many are on the diagonal, meaning place is unchanged (as seen above in Figure 6.4). Second, many involve pairings of bilabial, alveolar, palatal, and velar, which are by far the most frequent nasal places of articulation (as can be seen

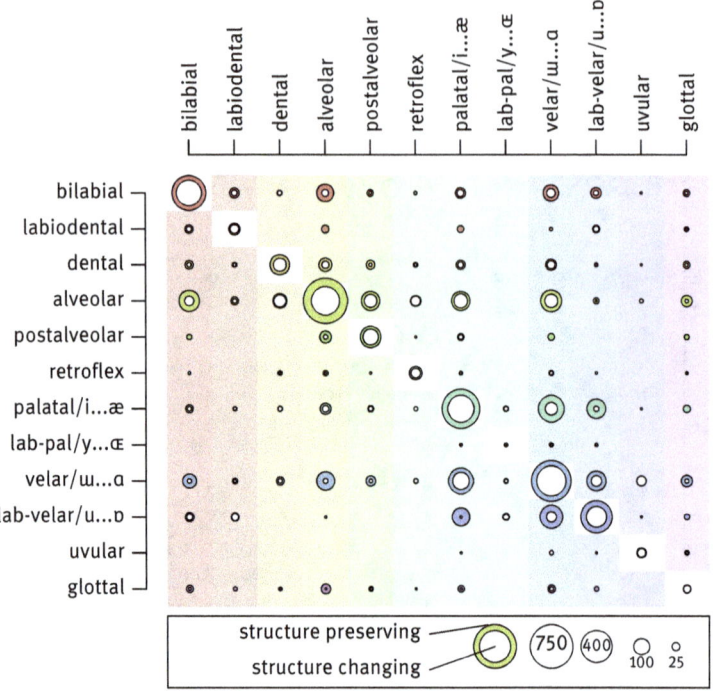

Figure 6.5: Changes by place of articulation. Input is on the left and output is on the top. Area of colored outer ring represents the number of structure preserving changes in the category. Area of inner white circle represents the number of structure changing changes in the category.

in Figure 6.3, and abovein Figure 6.1). This is because nasal place assimilation accounts for a large portion of place changes. Third, there are many vowel backness/rounding changes, which in this figure are overlaid on palatal, labial-palatal, velar, and labial-velar. The infrequency of changes involving labial-palatal/front rounded segments reflects the rarity of these segments to begin with. Similarly, the fact that place changes resulting in bilabial or alveolar outputs are mostly structure preserving reflects the fact that almost all inventories contain /m/ and /n/, so nasal place assimilation to these places of articulation is almost never structure changing.

Changes from velar to glottal place are mostly structure preserving, consistent with the idea that /k/ → [h] often appears as a structure preserving alternative to /k/ → [x]. /k/ → [ʔ] is also usually structure preserving, and so are most other place changes resulting in glottals. The most frequent of the rest is alveolar-glottal, which is mostly /s/ → [h][4]. Blevins (2008b) draws a connection between structure preservation and different outcomes of preconsonantal /s/ weakening in Romance languages, mediated by the role of contrast in the perceptibility of [h]: s > h / __C is a recurrent sound change, seen in many varieties of Spanish, which has /h/ as a phoneme. French, which does not have /h/, instead underwent the sound change s > Ø / __C (Hall 1949). This is consistent with the finding that h ~ Ø is highly confusable for speakers of languages that lack the contrast, especially in preconsonantal position (Mielke 2003).

This analysis of input-output mappings has illustrated that some changes are far more frequent than others. A logical next step to understanding these facts is to examine the types of sound patterns these segmental changes are involved in.

5 Top-down analysis

We will analyze the phonological alternations in P-base in two ways. The first one involves labeling the patterns according to established phonological criteria and finding the most frequently co-occurring labels. The second one will involve clustering the patterns in order to induce categories that may not be detected through expected labels.

5.1 Methods

The 4560 phonological alternations were partitioned according the criteria listed in Tables 6.1–6.3 on the basis of the automated phonological feature analysis provided by P-base, in order to count the most frequently-occurring patterns.

All 4560 patterns under consideration meet the criteria for Rule (having an input-output mapping), and do not meet the criteria for Distribution (describing what can or cannot occur in a particular context) so we omit these criteria.[5]

---

[4] Other voiceless fricatives also turn to [h], but not as often as /s/ does, which is consistent with /s/ being very frequent in inventories. Corresponding changes such as /z/ → [ɦ] are not observed.

[5] For the purpose of these definitions, place features = [anterior], [coronal], [back], [high], or [labial]; nasals = $\begin{bmatrix} +\text{nasal} \\ -\text{continuant} \end{bmatrix}$; liquid = $\begin{bmatrix} +\text{vocalic} \\ +\text{consonantal} \end{bmatrix}$; high vowel = $\begin{bmatrix} +\text{syllabic} \\ +\text{high} \end{bmatrix}$; mid vowel = $\begin{bmatrix} +\text{syllabic} \\ -\text{high} \\ -\text{low} \end{bmatrix}$; low vowel = $\begin{bmatrix} +\text{syllabic} \\ +\text{low} \end{bmatrix}$; obstruent stop = $\begin{bmatrix} -\text{sonorant} \\ -\text{continuant} \end{bmatrix}$. glottal = based on [ʔ h ɦ]; vocalic glide = $\begin{bmatrix} -\text{vocalic} \\ -\text{consonantal} \end{bmatrix}$ but not glottal, e.g., [β̞ ð̞ j ɥ w]; palatized = having the palatalization

Table 6.1: Phonological pattern labels for contexts

Label	Definition	Count	Percent
Word-initial	context includes # __	215	4.71%
Word-final	context includes __ #	454	9.96%
Prevocalic	context includes __ [+syl] (not [+syl] __)	829	18.18%
Postvocalic	context includes [+syl] __ (not __ [+syl])	399	8.75%
Intervocalic	context includes [+syl] __ [+syl]	442	9.69%
Preconsonantal	context includes __ [+cons] (not [+cons] __)	1069	23.44%
Postconsonantal	context includes [+cons] __ (not __ [+cons])	493	10.81%
Interconsonantal	context includes [+cons] __ [+cons]	89	1.95%

Tables 6.1–6.3 show the labels used to classify phonological patterns, and the number of matching patterns for each label. These labels were selected in order to systematize what we as phonologists expect to be frequent, and what we find to be frequent on the basis of our experience querying P-base. Most phonological alternations in P-base fall into more than one of the categories, and in the next section we will examine the co-occurrence of labels. To select label co-occurrences to report, we conducted a chi-squared test for the combinations of each process label with every other label, in order to identify pairs of labels that co-occur more than chance.

An example is shown in (4), comparing the co-occurrence of the labels Deletion and I=h.

(4)

	Observed				Expected		
	I=h	I≠h	Total		I=h	I≠h	Total
Deletion	62	712	774	Deletion	19	755	774
not Deletion	47	3739	3786	not Deletion	90	3696	3786
Total	109	4451	4560	Total	109	4451	4560

For this test, $\chi^2(1) = 123.31$, exceeding 6.635, which is the critical value for $\alpha = 0.01$. This captures the fact that the 62 cases of /h/ deletion are more than would be expected if the two labels co-occurred at random. Rather, /h/ is the input for 2.4% of all patterns, but it is the input for 8.0% of all deletion patterns, and /h/ deletion

---

diacritic [ʲ]. Palatalization has been excluded from assimilation in the reporting of these results. There is overlap of 69 patterns between Progressive Assimilation and Regressive Assimilation because some patterns operate in both directions but do not require both at the same time (which would be Bidirectional Assimilation).

Table 6.2: Phonological pattern labels for inputs and outputs

Label	Definition	Count	Percent
C →	input consists only of consonants	2794	61.27%
→ C	output consists only of consonants	2368	51.93%
V →	input consists only of vowels	1383	30.33%
→ V	output consists only of vowels	970	21.27%
Stop →	input is obstruent stops	994	21.80%
Nasal →	input is nasals	498	10.92%
Liquid →	input is liquids	169	3.71%
Glide →	input is glides	220	4.82%
Glottal →	input is glottals	163	3.57%
ʔ →	input is [ʔ]	36	0.79%
h →	input is [h]	109	2.39%
High Vowel →	input is high vowels	352	7.72%
Mid Vowel →	input is mid vowels	11	0.24%
Low Vowel →	input is low vowels	148	3.25%
i →	input is [i]	95	2.08%
u →	input is [u]	39	0.86%
ə →	input is [ə]	58	1.27%
a →	input is [a]	102	2.24%
→ Stop	output is obstruent stops	626	13.73%
→ Nasal	output is nasals	495	10.86%
→ Liquid	output is liquids	157	3.44%
→ Glide	output is glides	360	7.89%
→ Glottal	output is glottals	174	3.82%
→ ʔ	output is [ʔ]	83	1.82%
→ h	output is [h]	60	1.32%
→ High Vowel	output is high vowels	274	6.01%
→ Mid Vowel	output is mid vowels	3	0.07%
→ Low Vowel	output is low vowels	124	2.72%
→ i	output is [i]	52	1.14%
→ u	output is [u]	43	0.94%
→ ə	output is [ə]	58	1.27%
→ a	output is [a]	102	0.70%
Other	not matching any named processes	895	19.63%

accounts for 57% of all occurrences of /h/ as input. Trivial co-occurrences were omitted (e.g., I=Nasal implies I=C, and I=Nasal is not expected to be independent from O=Nasal) and labels which imply the same subset of labels were compared on that subset (e.g., Vowel Raising and I=a were compared on the basis of the 1383 V→patterns, not all 4560 patterns, because both labels imply that the input is a vowel).

Table 6.3: Phonological pattern labels for processes

Label	Definition	Count	Percent
Epenthesis	input is Ø	326	7.15%
Deletion	output is Ø	774	16.97%
Assimilation	changing feature shared with environment	1631	35.77%
... Progressive	... shared with left environment only	479	10.50%
... Regressive	... shared with right environment only	971	21.29%
... Bidirectional	... shared with left and right environment	273	5.99%
... Place	place feature assimilates	369	8.09%
... Total	output is exactly the same as environment	99	2.17%
Palatalization	output is palatalized or change is $\begin{bmatrix}-\text{ant}\\+\text{dist}\end{bmatrix}$	145	3.18%
Spirantization	Input is [−son] and change includes [+cont]	228	5.00%
Gemination	Input is [+cons] and change is [+long]	39	0.86%
Degemination	Input is [+cons] and change is [−long]	4	0.09%
Gliding	V→ and output is a vocalic glide	116	2.54%
Debuccalization	input is non-glottal C & output is glottal	82	1.80%
Voicing	change includes [+voice]	394	8.64%
Devoicing	change includes [−voice]	248	5.44%
Lenition	Degemination, Spirantization, Debuccalization, Voicing, or Vowel Shortening	628	13.77%
V Shortening	V→V and change is [−long]	184	4.04%
V Lengthening	V→V and change is [+long]	102	2.24%
V Raising	V→V and change is [+high] or [−low]	131	2.87%
V Lowering	V→V and change is [−high] or [+low]	119	2.61%
V Tensing	V→V and change is [+tense]	121	2.65%
V Laxing	V→V and change is [−tense]	123	2.70%
V Fronting	V→V and change is [−back]	88	1.93%
V Backing	V→V and change is [+back]	69	1.51%
V Rounding	V→V and change is [+round]	85	1.86%
V Nasalization	V→V and change is [+nasal]	87	1.91%

5.2 Results by pattern type

Figures 6.6, 6.7, 6.10, and 6.12 illustrate some of the patterns in the structure of the label counts in Tables 6.1–6.3. Each circle's area represents the number of patterns matching one or more labels. The rectangular nodes are broad categories of patterns, and edges connect groups that are in a subset-superset relationship. The purpose of displaying them this way is for the relative size of the circles to provide a visual gestalt impression of what the bulk of phonological patterns are.

From Tables 6.1–6.3, above, a few facts are apparent, each investigated more closely below. Deletion is 2.4 times as frequent as epenthesis, and glides and glottals make up a disproportionately large portion of the cases of epenthesis, as compared to deletion. Assimilatory and non-assimilatory changes each make up a little over a third of phonological patterns in the sample. Among assimilatory changes, regressive assimilation is more frequent than progressive assimilation. Regressive assimilation accounts for more than twice as many patterns as progressive assimilation. These asymmetries between formally symmetrical processes such deletion and epenthesis and between progressive and regressive assimilation are an important contribution of phonological typology to phonological theory: an important goal of phonological theory is to account for why some things happen more often than other things, whether it is because of markedness, the role of sound change, or something else.

5.2.1 Epenthesis and deletion

Figure 6.6 illustrates some major patterns for epenthesis. About one third of epenthesis patterns in P-base involve epenthetic vowels, and 64% of these are one of the vowels [i u ə]. Among many factors thought to contribute to epenthetic vowel quality, (e.g., Hume & Bromberg 2005), it has often been observed that epenthetic vowels tend to be short and otherwise perceptually non-salient. High vowels are often shorter than lower vowels (Catford 1977; Maddieson 1997), so epenthetic high vowels are consistent with the general idea that phonological repairs make minimal changes (Steriade 2001). [i u] are likely the shortest underlying vowels in the inventories of many languages in P-base, and while [ə] occurs in fewer inventories than [i u], [ə] epenthesis accounts for the majority of vowel epenthesis patterns that are structure-changing with respect to segments (i.e., [ə] epenthesis in languages without /ə/).[6]

There are 210 cases of epenthesis of glides, glottals, and other consonants. Of these, 43.7% are glide epenthesis, 33.3% are glottal epenthesis, and all other types of consonants combined amount to 24.0%. This is consistent with two recent accounts of the typology of consonant epenthesis. Vaux (2002) showed that consonant epenthesis is not restricted to a few default consonants, but that nearly every familiar consonant is epenthetic in at least one language, and that many of the more obscure epenthetic consonants (such as [ɹ] in some varieties of English) are due to restructuring of deletion patterns. Blevins (2008a) argued that the record of sound changes supports two basic sources of epenthetic consonants:

---

[6] Since /i/ and /u/ occur in such a large number of inventories, there is very little opportunity to observe structure changing epenthesis involving these vowels.

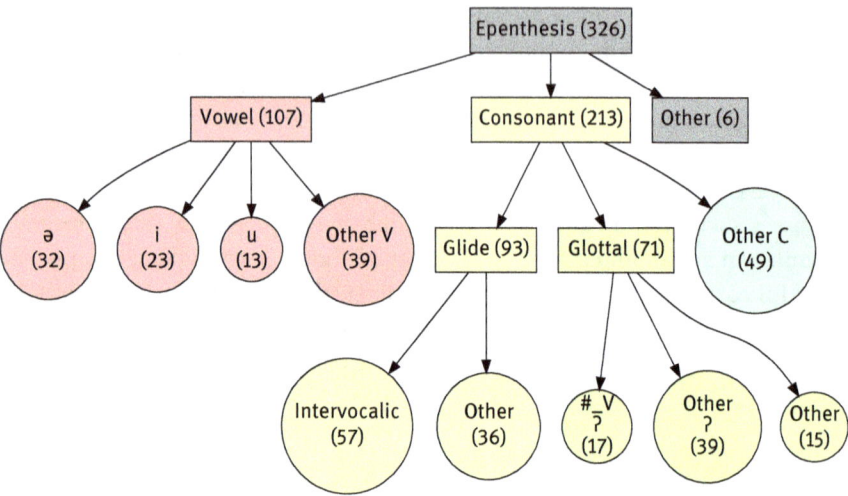

Figure 6.6: Summary of epenthesis patterns.

reinterpretation of vowel-vowel sequences as vowel-glide-vowel, and the phonologization of naturally occurring irregular phonation at prosodic boundaries (Pierrehumbert & Talkin 1992) as glottal consonants. Blevins attributes epenthetic consonants other than glides and glottals to complex and/or unnatural sources such as subsequent glide fortition and the restructuring of consonant deletion patterns. Blevins' account predicts that non-glide/non-glottal epenthesis will be sparse, because they require telescoping or restructuring of existing patterns, and the particular epenthetic consonant involved is dependent on fortition and deletion patterns occurring in any particular language, which are likely not to be nearly as specific as the sources of epenthetic glides and glottals. The contexts in which glottals and glides are epenthesized in P-base is also consistent with the historical account. 61% of glide epenthesis is intervocalic, and most of the rest is either prevocalic or postvocalic. It generally is not sensitive to word boundaries. On the other hand, only the word-initial prevocalic context is significantly associated with glottal epenthesis, accounting for 33% of [ʔ] epenthesis.

Figure 6.7 illustrates some major patterns for deletion. 37% of deletion patterns involve vowels, which is slightly higher than the proportion of epenthesis patterns involving vowels. A major difference between vowel epenthesis and vowel deletion is that epenthesis often involves a single default vowel, while deletion may target particular vowels or all of the vowels. Low vowels play a bigger role in deletion than in epenthesis. Unsurprisingly, wholesale vowel deletion typically occurs next to vowels, especially before other vowels, and word-finally.

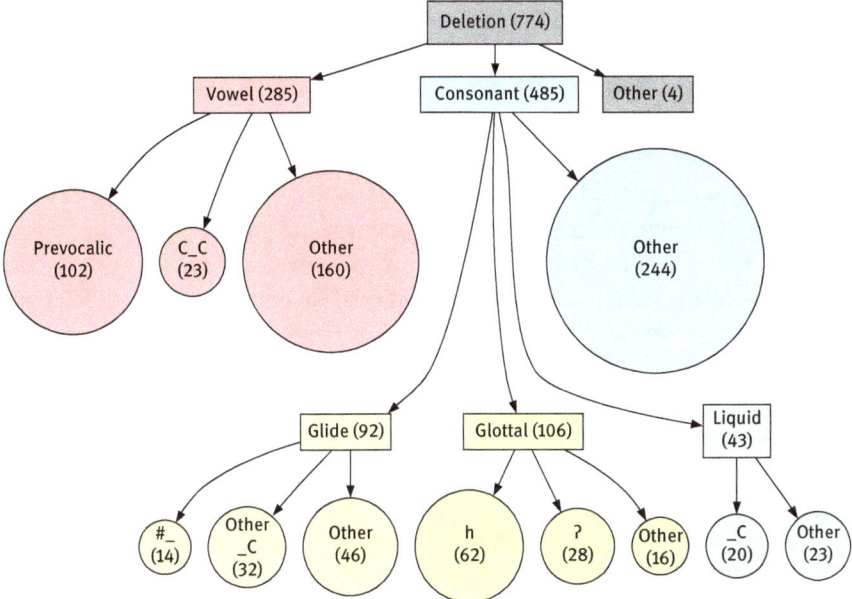

Figure 6.7: Summary of deletion patterns.

The biggest difference between consonant deletion and consonant epenthesis is that non-glide/nonglottal consonants get deleted in large numbers. Much of this applies to large groups of consonants, particularly in consonant clusters or between vowels, and word-finally. Stops,[7] nasals, and glottal consonants are each specifically targeted by 10% of deletion patterns, and glides account for 12%. Nasals and stops are lumped together with other consonants as "Other" because they are not significantly more frequent as deletion targets than they are as targets in general, but the distribution of nasal and stop deletion can be seen below in Figure 6.8.

Glide deletion is triggered by an adjacent vowel 43% of the time and triggered by an adjacent consonant 35% of the time. This is relevant for considering multiple ways for deletion and epenthesis contexts to be associated: they can be unrelated, such as when there is a specific phonetic source for deletion or epenthesis with, they can be opposite, as in the case of vowels (deleted next to vowels and epenthesized next to consonants), or they can be the same, because deletion

---

[7] Here and elsewhere, "stops" is used to mean obstruent stops, not including [ʔ], which typically has very different phonological behavior, and has often been treated as a glide by phonologists (e.g., Chomsky & Halle 1968).

and epenthesis both involve the same phonological or phonetic ambiguity (i.e., XY and Y are confusable, so X is deleted before Y in some languages and inserted before Y in some languages). Glide deletion appears to be a mixture of at least two of these. Vowel-adjacent glide deletion could involve the same phonological ambiguity that enables glide epenthesis, and consonant-adjacent glide deletion could involve completely independent factors.

Like glides, glottals are deleted only about as frequently as they are epenthesized (unlike all other consonants and vowels), which is still quite frequent. However, while [ʔ] dominates glottal epenthesis, [h] dominates glottal deletion. This is understandable in terms of the phonetic bases for [ʔ] epenthesis and /h/ deletion. Glottal gestures at prosodic boundaries provide fodder for phonological [ʔ] epenthesis, and probably bear less resemblance to [h], but /h/ is a deletion target due to its perceptual weakness, both in terms of its tendency to be reduced in production and its weak acoustic cues even when produced successfully (e.g., Mielke 2003).

Figure 6.8 shows the distribution of epenthesis and deletion across contexts. Consistent with the greater frequency of deletion overall, the norm is for epenthesis to be less frequent then deletion in each specific case, with notable exceptions mostly discussed above, such as glottal epenthesis at prosodic boundaries and glide epenthesis next to vowels. The most important environment for stop and nasal deletion is preconsonantal, which is broadly consistent with consonant clusters as a locus for consonant change, and with perceptual accounts of consonant cluster simplification (Côté 2000; Steriade 2001). Vowel deletion is triggered both by consonants and vowels, probably for very different reasons.

Deletion generally targets segments that are present in lexical representations, and by definition it is structure preserving in the segmental sense, because

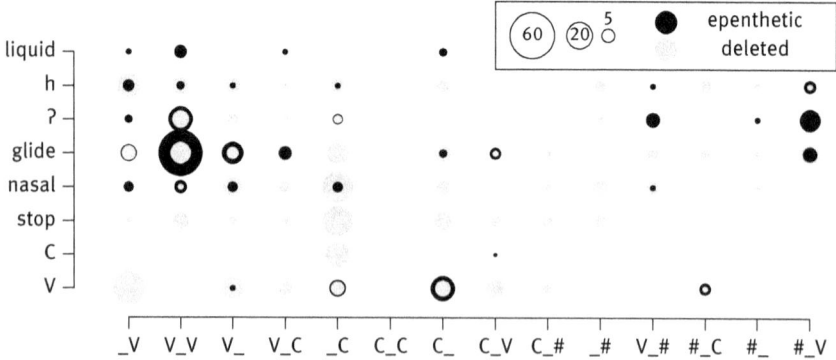

Figure 6.8: Epenthesis and deletion by segment and context.

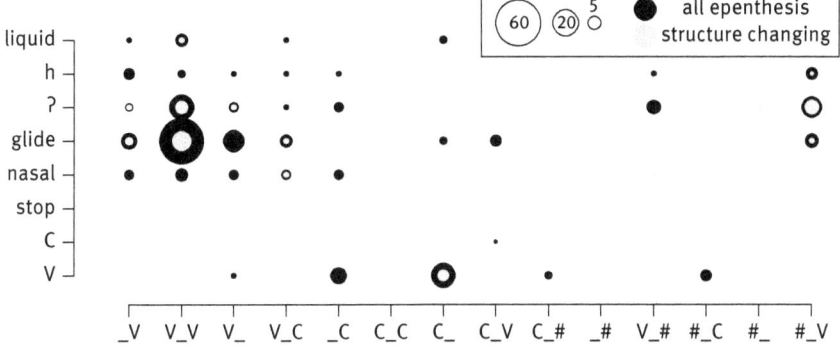

Figure 6.9: Structure-changing epenthesis by segment and context.

while it may produce novel sequences, it cannot produce novel segments (because it produces no segments). Epenthesis, on the other hand, may be either structure preserving or structure changing, and it is useful to examine which kinds of epenthesis are most likely to result in novel segments in the language where they occur. This is illustrated in Figure 6.9[8].

Among the glottals, [ʔ] epenthesis is frequently structure changing, but [h] is rarely structure changing. Glide epenthesis is structure changing at a similar rate across context, and the two main contexts where it is always structure preserving (V_ and C_V) may reflect a tendency to describe glide epenthesis in these contexts as diphthongization and palatalization, respectively. Most of the cases of structure changing vowel epenthesis involve epenthetic [ə], which is consistent both with the idea that an epenthetic vowel will have a neutral vowel quality if it is not being interpreted as a lexical vowel, and that most languages already have /i/ and /u/, so there are few opportunities for them to be introduced to a language by epenthesis.

5.2.2 Assimilation

Figure 6.10 illustrates some major patterns for assimilation, which accounts for 35.8% of the sound patterns in P-base, or a little more than half of the segmental changes (phonological alternations that are not deletion or epenthesis). 24.2% of assimilation patterns change vowels into other vowels, and 24.6% of these are

---

[8] In these balloon plots, frequency is indicated by area, and the epenthesis and deletion balloons are superimposed (e.g., vowel deletion is slightly more frequent than vowel deletion in the C_C context). In Figure 6.9, the balloons are superimposed, but the "all epenthesis" balloons are by definition as large or larger than the subset of epenthesis that is structure changing.

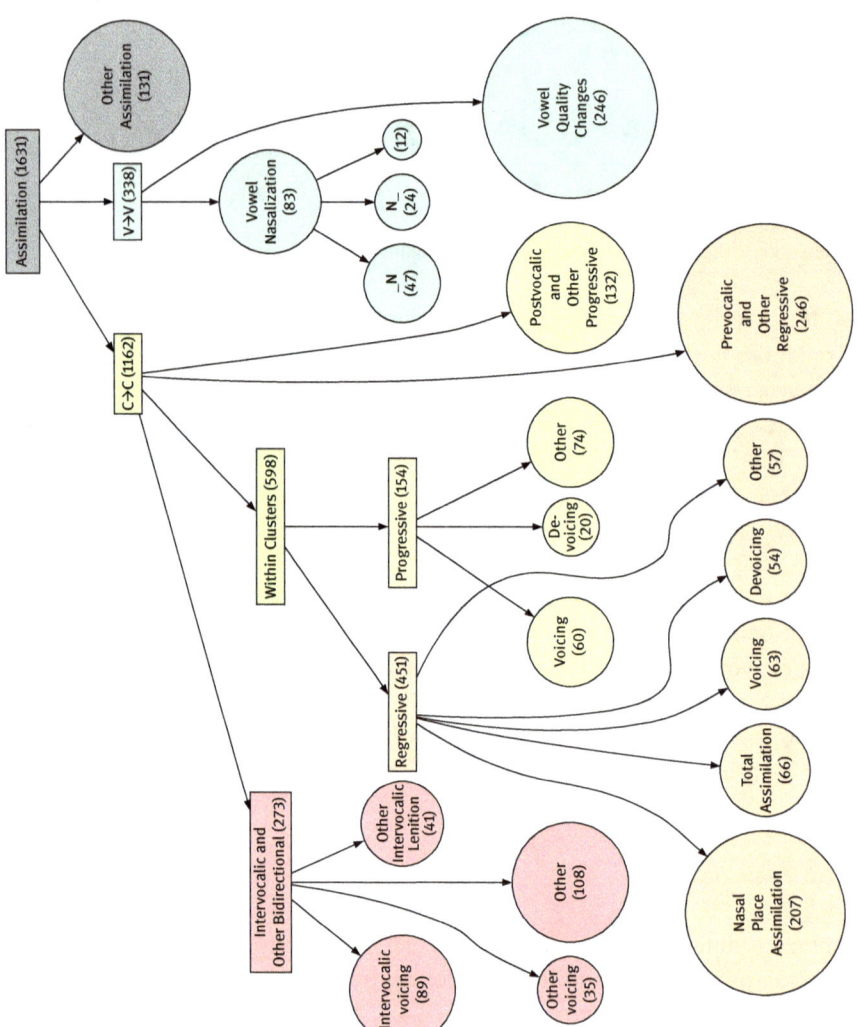

Figure 6.10: Summary of assimilation patterns.

nasalization. The rest are vowel quality changes that are predominantly conditioned by other vowels. 51.4% of consonant assimilation patterns occur within consonant clusters, which is reminiscent of consonant deletion.

Consonant-consonant assimilation patterns are even more biased toward regressive assimilation (2.9 times as many regressive than progressive CC assimilations, vs. a ratio of 2.0 for assimilations in general). The elephant in the room for regressive vs. progressive CC assimilation is regressive nasal place assimilation, which accounts for 46.4% of all regressive CC assimilation. While this is consistent with the perceptual account of CC repair strategies, it can also be attributed in part to nasal-consonant clusters simply being more frequent than consonant-nasal clusters. Total assimilation accounts for 14.6% of regressive CC assimilation, and a negligible part of progressive CC assimilation. Nasal place assimilation and total assimilation account for much of the directional asymmetry in CC assimilation. If nasal place assimilation is excluded, the ratio of regressive to progressive assimilation in consonant clusters drops from 2.9 to 1.7.

Voicing and devoicing together account for 32.9% of CC assimilation. Devoicing is biased toward regressive (with a ratio of 2.7) while voicing is not. In addition to consonant cluster assimilation, intervocalic voicing accounts for 32.3% of bidirectional assimilation patterns, and it is the largest recognizable subgroup within prevocalic and postvocalic assimilatory consonant changes, although it is not significantly more frequent in those contexts. Palatalization and lenition are ill-served by the split into assimilatory and non-assimilatory patterns, because only some of each is formally assimilation in the feature system we are using. We have excluded palatalization from the assimilation analysis (because we are using a feature system that does not readily capture it as assimilation) and included it below in Figure 6.12 with other miscellaneous patterns. If included here, palatalization would increase the number of prevocalic regressive assimilation among consonants. Many intervocalic lenition patterns are assimilatory, and these are included in both figures

Figure 6.11 shows assimilatory changes by feature and context. Unlike the previous balloon plots, the [+] and [–] values are not superimposed, and the visible area of the black outer ring represents the number of times the [–] value of the feature spreads.

5.2.3 Other recurrent changes

Figure 6.12 illustrates some major types of sound patterns not addressed in the preceding sections. Lenition (including voicing, spirantization, and debuccalization) accounts for 628 patterns (13.77%), many of which are also classified as

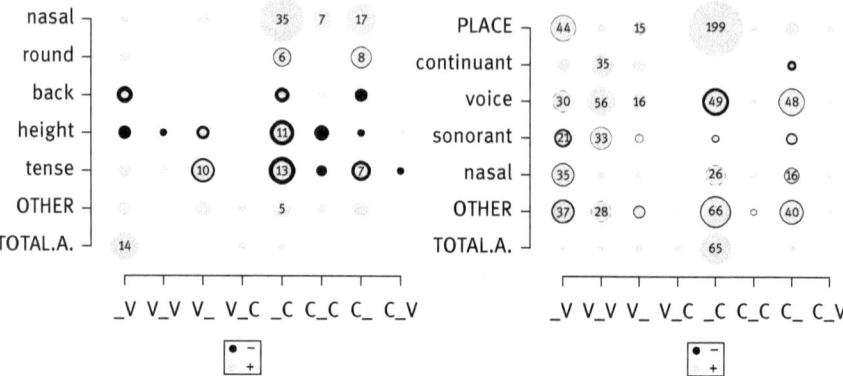

Figure 6.11: Vowel (left) and consonant (right) assimilation by feature and context.

assimilation. Word-final devoicing occurs 48 times (1.05%). Final devoicing can be considered to be assimilatory in utterance-final position, and word-final devoicing has been analyzed as a generalization of utterance-final deletion (see, e.g., Vennemann 1974; Blevins 2006; Myers 2010, 2012). A possible connection between devoicing in clusters and at edges is that assimilatory final devoicing is regressive, and in consonant clusters, regressive devoicing assimilation is quite a bit more frequent than progressive devoicing assimilation, while voicing is symmetrical.

Palatalization (defined in terms of the change, not the trigger) has 145 occurrences (3.18%), and 82 of these are prevocalic. Many of these are triggered specifically by front and/or high vowels, as expected. While we did not code for subsets of vowels in this analysis, this is certainly relevant for palatalization. There are 116 cases of vowel gliding, where a vowel becomes a vocalic glide (or 2.54% of all patterns). For comparison, there are only 17 instances where glides become vowels. 73% of vowel gliding instances occur prevocalically and 66% involve only high vowels.

In the top-down analysis, the label "Lenition" has been used to characterize a set of pre-determined changes (Degemination, Spirantization, Debuccalization, Voicing, Vowel Shortening). We can instead unpack this notion of lenition and look at changes which occur intervocalically, which involve changes of the feature [sonorant], [voice], and [continuant]. Below is a view of the feature changes, highlighting common pathways of intervocalic lenition (Figure 6.13).

Common paths which emerge from this picture are the attestation of stop voicing, voiced and voiceless stop spirantization, and voiced stop flapping. Other changes along this lattice (gliding of voiceless stops (e.g., /p/ → [w] / V__V)) are also seen to be represented. This lattice illustrates that most of these lenition patterns typically make a minimal feature change.

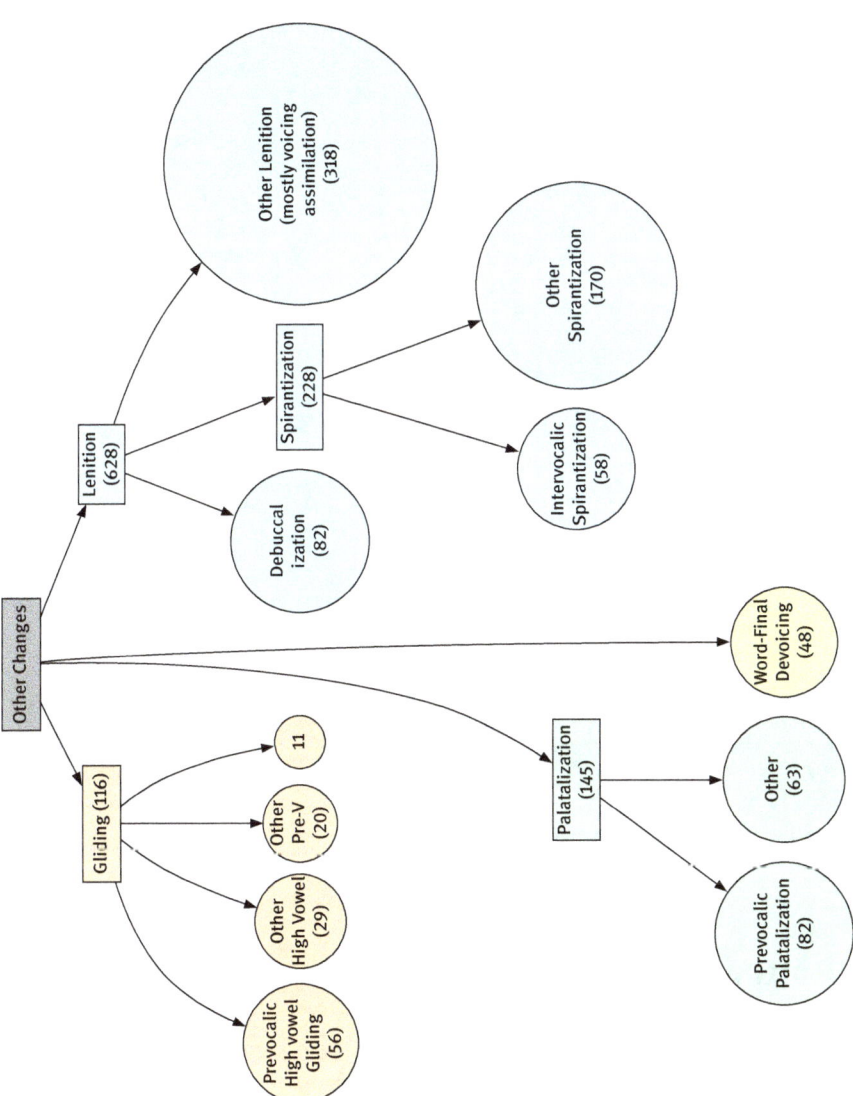

Figure 6.12: Other recurrent processes.

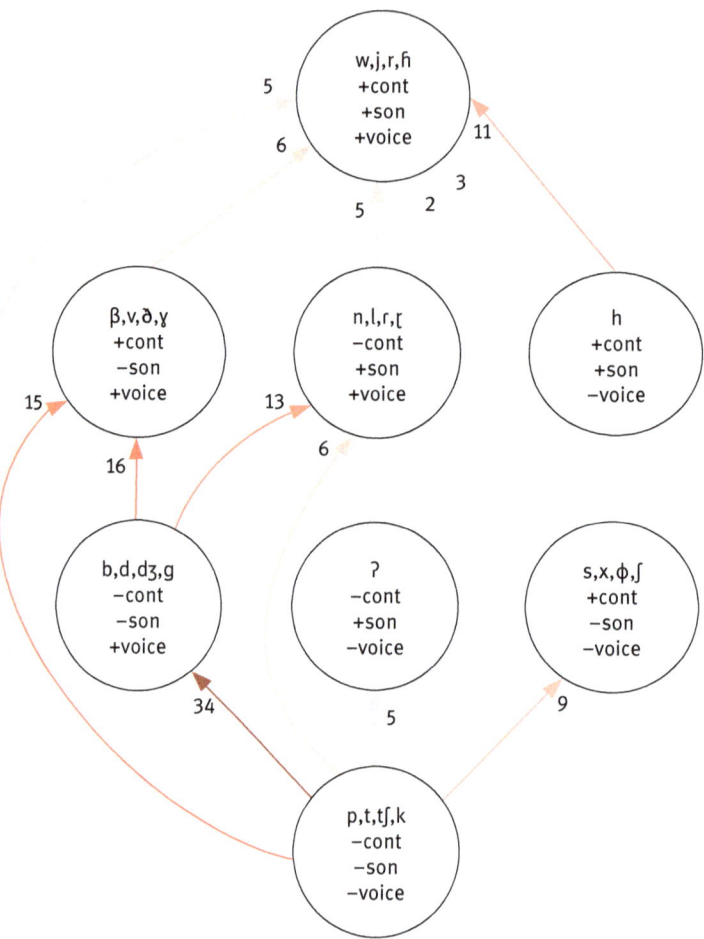

Figure 6.13: Changes involved in intervocalic lenition.

6 Bottom-up analysis

A bottom-up analysis of the patterns in P-base was conducted to determine whether there were significant groupings of features patterning together that our top-down analysis was missing. The bottom-up analysis generates generalizations based on the data, and induces potential categories of patterns from the observed set of phonological patterns.

6.1 Methods

We employed Multiple Correspondence Analysis, a technique of vector space reduction for multinomial data. This technique summarizes a large set of variables with a small number of factors (similar to Principal Components Analysis). This essentially can be used to reduce the data set into a smaller number of factors, which can be inspected to see how features pattern together. Patterns which are associated with each other show up with similar weightings in their factors, for instance features like [±tense] and [±ATR] generally group together in their behavior; so they have a similar weighting in the factor space.

Each factor can be interpreted as summarizing a dimension along which the set of phonological rules vary. The first factor splits the set of patterns into left-triggered and right-triggered rules. We can inspect the grouping of features in this factor space to see what relations exist between features, with the idea that features which are close to each other generally pattern together. We achieve this by running a hierarchical cluster analysis on a trimmed set of features (features with a low factor loading have little predictive value in the MCA analysis – they don't pattern with other features in a predictable manner). Hierarchical clustering works to identify features which are close together in the factor loading space; which effectively yields a tree of features which tend to co-occur with each other.

Two analyses were undertaken, the first takes binary features referring to P-base's feature analysis of the input, output, change, environment and detected assimilations (to the left and right).[9] Here the number of features is tremendous (46 possible values in 7 possible positions), and after filtering features which are farther away than 1.2 in our factor loadings we have the following cluster dendrograms.

6.2 Results

With this set of data, the primary axis of variation is between left-triggered and right-triggered rules (Figures 6.14 and 6.15). Inspecting the diagram yields predictable clumps of features which pattern together generally around triggering context, and a number of processes tend to cluster (such as lenition) together. Sensible labels were attached to groups of clusters based on querying P-base and seeing how these features which describe patterns tend to group together in terms of set of patterns described.

---

[9] I: Input, O: Output, C: Change, ER: Environment right, EL: Environment Left, AR: Assimilated Right, AL: Assimilated Left

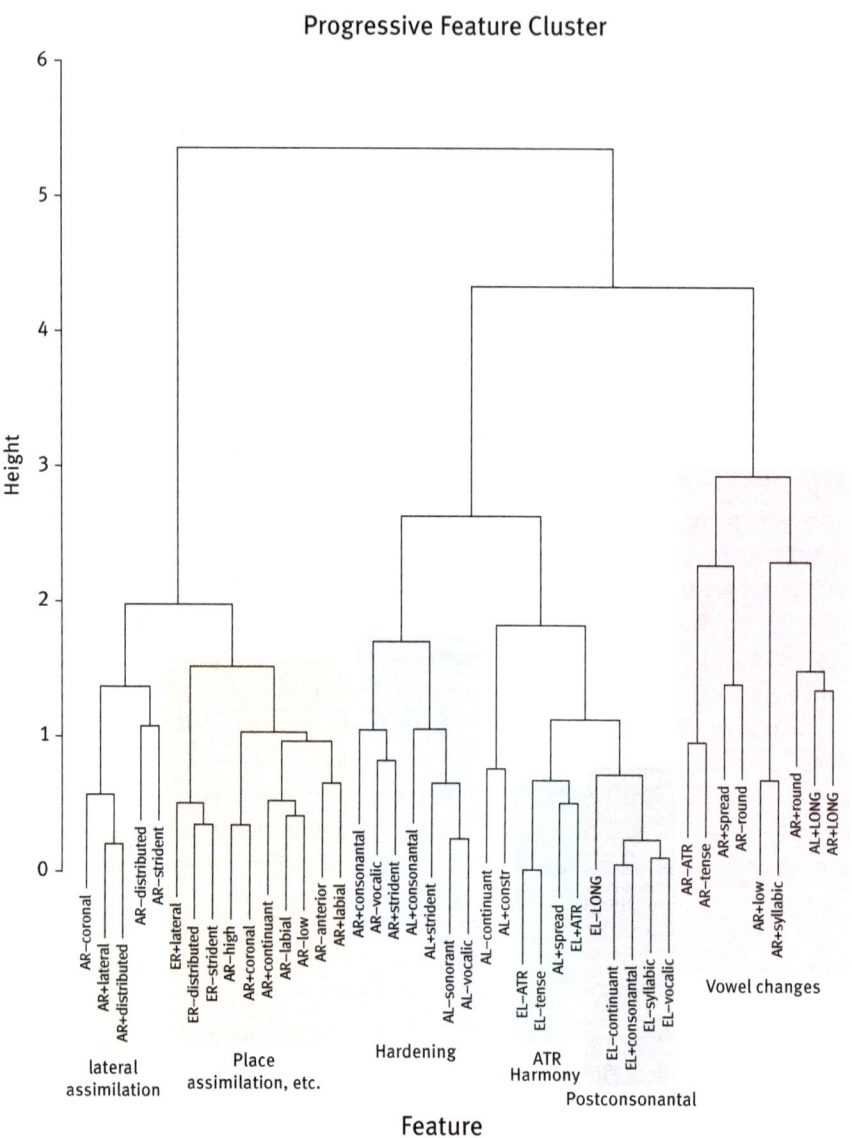

Figure 6.14: Progressive Feature Cluster Dendrogram.

Multiple correspondence analysis seeks to build factor weights based on the predictive quality of features, so this approach tends to under-emphasize the size of particular groupings which have been seen in the top-down labeling to be rather significant groupings. A feature such as ER-[+lateral] would tend to get a significant weighting along an axis if it had a narrow predictive value (there are

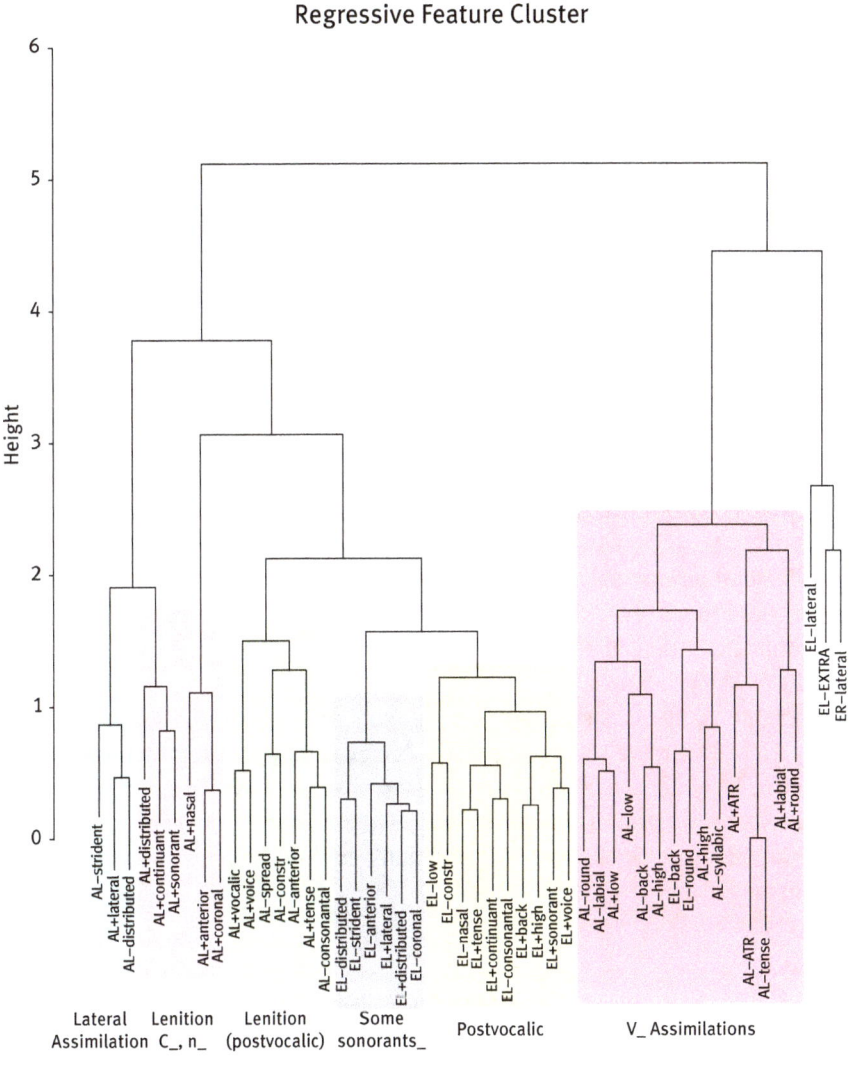

Figure 6.15: Regressive Feature Cluster Dendrogram.

only a small number of processes (deletion, total assimilation)), then it would get a higher factor weighting with other processes which match the same predictive value (occur with deletion, total assimilations).

A second analysis considered only the binary features referring to P-base's feature analysis of the features changed in each described rule. The intention of this analysis is to consider what clustering around particular processes we should expect. This approach has the benefit of being more interpretable as there are fewer features (46 features) in the analysis, so more can be visualized in the dendrogram (Figure 6.16).

This second set of analyses are intended to determine features which group together in terms of their changes. Here the dependence of features on each other is being predicted. We have a similar grouping of features which pattern together ([+round]/[+labial]) in terms of the changes, but there seem to be significant groupings representing changes associated with sonorant/glide hardening, gliding, debuccalization, and a complex of changes associated with vowels.

The interpretability of this dependence between feature changes is a little loose, and somewhat dependent on the predictability of one feature change given another, or the representation of changes in the database. We see that a commonly changed feature [+voice] is not represented in this set because it occurs in so many different contexts and doesn't often pattern with any one particular feature.

This bottom-up analysis has provided associations between features which either describe a rule's environment, assimilations, or changes. Common environments and common change processes end up grouping together under the cluster dendrograms.

Common processes such as place assimilation are unable to be captured under this dendrogram-type approach because they are represented as the change of several place-related features. Other processes which are triggered in a diverse set of triggering contexts (intervocalic/pre-sonorant) voicing don't show up as having good predictive value and don't end up significantly populating a certain factor.

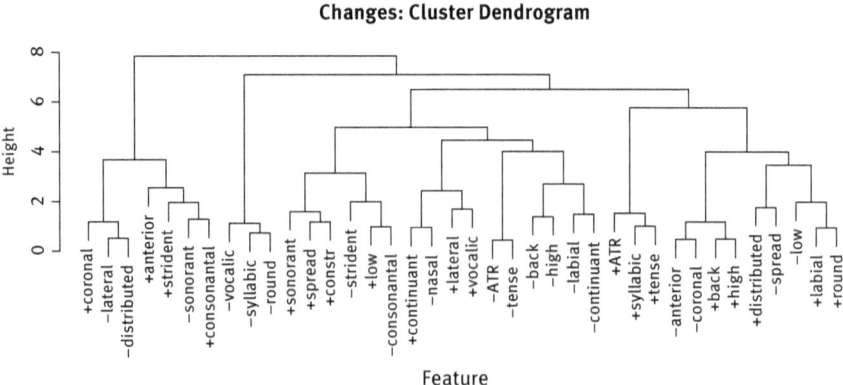

Figure 6.16: Changes.

7 Discussion

Phonological alternations are clearly a diverse set of phenomena, often reflecting idiosyncratic, arbitrary facts about the particular language in which they occur. A major goal of phonological typology is to determine what is frequent and why, and a major recurring theme in this exploration of P-base has been that certain very specific types of phonological alternations are extremely frequent, and their frequency is not predictable on the basis of the frequency of their parts. It is useful to interpret the very frequent patterns in terms of potential phonetic and structural sources, i.e., in terms of phonetic factors that could drive sound change and independent linguistic or cognitive factors that could drive learners to learn sound patterns in a particular way.

7.1 Highly frequent patterns

A small number of sound patterns with quite specific descriptions are very frequent. The most striking is preconsonantal regressive nasal place assimilation, whose 207 cases account for 4.54% of the 4560 sound pattern entries and 56% of all place assimilation. Most of the rest of place assimilation is also in the preconsonantal context. Place changes are very rare otherwise. Place assimilation has played a central role in the development of distinctive feature systems, especially in feature geometry (e.g., Clements 1985; Sagey 1986[1990]; Clements & Hume 1995; Halle et al. 2000). It is clear that phonological theory needs a system for representing place assimilation, but it is interesting to know that it is called upon primarily for a narrow range of frequent patterns and only sporadically otherwise.

The distribution of place assimilation patterns recalls the claims made recently by Vaux and Blevins, which are superficially opposite but compatible: Vaux (2002) argued that almost any consonant can be epenthetic, and Blevins (2008a) argued that glottals and glides are the only epenthetic consonants generated in great numbers by sound change. Here we have seen a wide range of assimilation patterns but only regressive nasal place assimilation is observed in huge numbers. This and some of the other patterns we have reported in this chapter showcase what Moreton (2008) terms "channel bias": phonological typology reflects a bias that has an explanation in recurrent sound change, and human language competence can apparently handle a wide range of sound patterns that rarely occur, for historical reasons. It is our hope that future research will examine P-base more closely for patterns that reveal Moreton's analytic bias, i.e., sound patterns that have a clear phonetic basis like glide epenthesis and nasal place assimilation, but nevertheless are rare in the record of synchronic phenomena, due to bias in the system of phonological representations or the learning process.

7.2 Nasal place assimilation

Preconsonantal regressive nasal place assimilation stands out as our prototypical highly specific highly frequent sound pattern whose frequency is not accounted for by the frequency of its parts. The imbalance between nasals and oral stops in the frequency of place assimilation has been known for a long time, and a lot of work has been devoted to accounting for why nasals undergo place assimilation more frequently than oral stops (e.g., Cho 1990). While a perceptual explanation is intuitive (because nasalization interferes with formant transitions that provide cues to place, exacerbating perceptual weaknesses associated with being preconsonantal), Winters (2003) showed that perceptibility does not account for the asymmetry. We offer a potential articulatory basis for the asymmetry. Gick et al. (2013) and Chiu & Gick (2013) have recently shown that nasals differ from oral stops in the forcefulness of the closure, e.g., lip compression is weaker in [m] than in [b]. This is thought to be because the lingual or labial closure for an oral stop needs to withstand an increase in intraoral pressure, but the closure in a nasal consonant does not, and the constrictions are executed differently. We speculate that a consequence of this less forceful closure at the place of articulation for nasal consonants makes them more susceptible to being reduced, providing an articulatory basis for NC clusters being heard as homorganic at the place of articulation of the second consonant, without any appeal to misperception.

7.3 Conclusions

This study of frequent sound patterns in P-base has been deliberately incomplete. We have avoided focusing a lot of attention on types of sound patterns that have been the focus of a lot of crosslinguistic work already (but could be revisited), and certainly we have overlooked interesting types of sound patterns that have not been well studied before. We encourage readers who have been intrigued by any of these possibilities, or by questions raised in other chapters in this volume, to follow up with their own P-base queries at http://pbase.phon.chass.ncsu.edu.

References

Bickel, Balthasar. 2008. A refined sampling procedure for genealogical control. *Sprachtypologie und Universalienforschung* 61. 221–233.
Bickel, Balthasar & Johanna Nichols. 1996. The AUTOTYP database. http://www.spw.uzh.ch/autotyp/, electronic database.
Blevins, Juliette. 2004. *Evolutionary phonology*. Cambridge: Cambridge University Press.

Blevins, Juliette. 2006. A theoretical synopsis of Evolutionary Phonology. *Theoretical Linguistics* 32. 117–165.
Blevins, Juliette. 2008a. Consonant epenthesis: Natural and unnatural histories. In Jeff Good (ed.), *Linguistic universals and language change*, 79–107. Oxford: Oxford University Press.
Blevins, Juliette. 2008b. Natural and unnatural sound patterns: A pocket field guide. In Klaas Willems & Ludovic de Cuypere (eds.), *Naturalness and iconicity in language*, 121–148. Amsterdam: Benjamins.
Catford, J. C. 1977. *Fundamental problems in phonetics*, volume 1. Edinburgh: Edinburgh University Press.
Chiu, Chenhao & Bryan Gick. 2013. Producing whole speech events: Anticipatory lip compression in bilabial stops. *Proceedings of Meetings on Acoustics* 19. 060252. http://asa.scitation.org/doi/abs/10.1121/1.4800579
Cho, Young-Mee. 1990. *Parameters of consonantal assimilation*. Ph.D. thesis, Stanford University. (Published München: Lincom, 1999.)
Chomsky, Noam & Morris Halle. 1968. *The sound pattern of English*. New York: Harper and Row.
Clements, G. N. 1985. The geometry of phonological features. *Phonology Yearbook* 2. 225–252.
Clements, G. N. & Elizabeth V. Hume. 1995. The internal organization of speech sounds. In John Goldsmith (ed.), *The handbook of phonological theory*, 245–306. Oxford: Blackwell.
Côté, Marie-Hélène. 2000. *Consonant cluster phonotactics: A perceptual approach*. Ph.D. thesis, Massachusetts Institute of Technology. https://rucore.libraries.rutgers.edu/rutgers-lib/38478/
Gastner, Michael T. & M. E. J. Newman. 2004. Diffusion-based method for producing density-equalizing maps. *Proceedings of the National Academy of Sciences of the United States of America* 101. 7499–7504.
Gick, Bryan, I. Ian Stavness & C. Chenhao Chiu. 2013. Coarticulation in a whole event model of speech production. *Proceedings of Meetings on Acoustics* 19, 060207. http://asa.scitation.org/doi/abs/10.1121/1.4799482.
Hall, Robert A. 1949. The linguistic position of Franco-Provençal. *Language* 25. 1–14.
Halle, Morris & George N. Clements. 1983. *Problem book in phonology*. Cambridge, MA: MIT Press.
Halle, Morris, Bert Vaux & Andrew Wolfe. 2000. On feature spreading and the representation of place of articulation. *Linguistic Inquiry* 31. 387–444.
Hume, Elizabeth V. 2004. The indeterminacy/attestation model of metathesis. *Language* 80. 203–237.
Hume, Elizabeth & Ilana Bromberg. 2005. Predicting epenthesis: An information-theoretic account. Paper presented at 7èmes journées internationales du réseau français de phonologie, Aix-en-Provence. https://www.researchgate.net/publication/228973329_Predicting_epenthesis_An_Information-theoretic_account
Hyman, Larry M. 2008. Universals in phonology. *The Linguistic Review* 25. 83–137.
Jakobson, Roman, C. Gunnar M. Fant & Morris Halle. 1952. *Preliminaries to speech analysis: The distinctive features and their correlates*. Massachusetts Institute of Technology, Acoustics Laboratory, Technical Report No. 13; 2nd printing with additions and corrections.
Kirchner, Robert M. 2001. *An effort based approach to consonant lenition*. New York: Routledge.
Lavoie, Lisa M. 2001. *Consonant strength: Phonological patterns and phonetic manifestations*. New York: Garland.
Lindblom, Björn & Ian Maddieson. 1988. Phonetic universals in consonant systems. In Larry M. Hyman & Charles N. Li (eds.), *Language, speech, and mind: Studies in honour of Victoria Fromkin*, 62–78. London: Routledge.

Maddieson, Ian. 1984. *Patterns of sounds*. Cambridge: Cambridge University Press.
Maddieson, Ian. 1997. Phonetic universals. In William J. Hardcastle & John Laver (eds.), *The handbook of phonetic sciences*, 619–639. Oxford: Blackwell.
Maddieson, Ian. 2014. *LAPSyD: Lyon-Albuquerque Phonological Systems Database*, CNRS, Lyon, France. http://www.lapsyd.ddl.ish-lyon.cnrs.fr/lapsyd/
Maddieson, Ian & Kristin Precoda. 1990. Updating UPSID. *UCLA Working Papers in Phonetics* 74. 104–111.
Mielke, Jeff. 2003. The interplay of speech perception and phonology: Experimental evidence from Turkish. *Phonetica* 60. 208–229.
Mielke, Jeff. 2005. Ambivalence and ambiguity in laterals and nasals. *Phonology* 22. 169–203.
Mielke, Jeff. 2008. *The emergence of distinctive features*. Oxford: Oxford University Press.
Mielke, Jeff. 2017. Visualizing phonetic segment frequencies with density-equalizing maps. *Journal of the International Phonetic Association*, https://doi.org/10.1017/S0025100317000123.
Mielke, Jeff, Lyra Magloughlin & Elizabeth Hume. 2011. Evaluating the effectiveness of Unified Feature Theory and three other feature systems. In John Goldsmith, Elizabeth Hume & Leo Wetzels (eds.), *Tones and features: In honor of G. Nick Clements*, 223–263. Berlin: Mouton de Gruyter.
Moreton, Elliot. 2008. Analytic bias and phonological typology. *Phonology* 25. 83–127.
Myers, Scott. 2010. Regressive voicing assimilation: Production and perception studies. *Journal of the International Phonetic Association* 40. 163–179.
Myers, Scott. 2012. Final devoicing: Production and perception studies. In Toni Borowsky, Shigeto Kawahara, Mariko Sugahara & Takahito Shinya (eds.), *Prosody matters: Essays in honor of Elisabeth Selkirk*, 148–180. London: Equinox Press.
Pierrehumbert, Janet & David Talkin. 1992. Lenition of /h/ and glottal stop. In G. J. Doherty & D. R. Ladd (eds.), *Papers in laboratory phonology*, vol. 2: *Gesture, segment, prosody*, 90–117. Cambridge: Cambridge University Press.
Sagey, Elizabeth C. 1986. *The representation of features and relations in non-linear phonology*. Ph.D. dissertation, Massachusetts Institute of Technology. (Published New York: Garland, 1990.)
Simpson, Adrian P. 1999. Fundamental problems in comparative phonetics and phonology: Does UPSID help to solve them? In *Proceedings of ICPhS XIV*, Berkeley, CA, 349–352. http://www.personal.uni-jena.de/~x1siad/papers/icphs99_fund.pdf
Steriade, Donca. 2001. Directional asymmetries in place assimilation: A perceptual account. In Elizabeth Hume & Keith Johnson (eds.), *Perception in phonology*, 219–250. New York: Academic Press.
Vance, Timothy J. 1987. *An introduction to Japanese phonology*. Albany, NY: State University of New York Press.
Vaux, Bert. 2002. Consonant epenthesis and the problem of unnatural phonology, Paper presented at Yale University Linguistics Colloquium.
Vennemann, Theo. 1974. Words and syllables in natural generative phonology. In A. Bruck, R. Fox & M. L. Galy (eds.), *CLS 10: Parasession on natural phonology*, 364–374. Chicago: Chicago Linguistic Society.
Winters, Stephen J. 2003. *Empirical investigations into the perceptual and articulatory origins of crosslinguistic asymmetries in place assimilation*. Ph.D. dissertation, Ohio State University, Columbus, OH. https://etd.ohiolink.edu/pg_10?0::NO:10:P10_ACCESSION_NUM:osu1054756426

Aditi Lahiri
Predicting universal phonological contrasts

Abstract: FUL (*Featurally Underspecified Lexicon*) assumes that a handful of features will account for the phonological systems in the world's languages. Such an assumption would not be unusual. However, FUL makes several other assumptions including the following: (i) consonants and vowels share place features which are not represented on separate tiers; (ii) features are monovalent; (iii) there are no feature dependencies; (iv) CORONAL and PLOSIVE are always underspecified in representation but present on the surface, which in turn presupposes that both these features must occur in all languages; (v) phonological activity is not the only way to determine feature contrast. These assumptions are based on synchronic, diachronic, and experimental evidence. Detailed case studies examine whether these hypotheses hold in instances where the opposite claims have been made.

1 Introducing FUL

In a landmark work, Jakobson, Fant, & Halle (1952, henceforth JFH) proposed a set of 21 distinctive features for describing phonological systems. Well defined acoustic and articulatory correlates were identified for their features, and the same features were employed to classify place of articulation for vowels and consonants. An example would be the feature ACUTE: front vowels (such as [i y e ø æ]) and fronted consonants (e.g., alveolars and palatals) were classified as ACUTE and characterised as having high frequency energy. First proposed in 1999, the FUL system (short for *Featurally Underspecified Lexicon*) endorsed these two fundamental assumptions of JFH's. The following considerations, some differing from JHF, are especially highlighted in FUL: (i) phonological features form a hierarchical system; (ii) all features are monovalent; (iii) the contrasts established by this set of features should account for phonological alternations across the languages of the world; (iv) a small set of features are universally underspecified, and these features should therefore always be part of the inventory; (v) there are no feature dependencies; (vi) underlying phonological representations, as part of the mental lexicon, govern production and comprehension, with underspecification, thus, implying asymmetries in processing; (vii) feature specification and building the feature tree during acquisition initially follow a universal pattern; (viii) feature specification and underspecification should also play a part in language change.

Notions from the JHF tradition such as "markedness", "specificity", "redundancy", and "activity" have in one way or another been widely used by phonologists. No one has ever assumed that all features have the same "weight", and most phonologists do not specify non-contrastive features. Chomsky & Halle (1968) engaged in detailed discussions about markedness combined with redundancy to obtain the right phonological alternations. In the early eighties, underspecification was hotly debated (cf. Archangeli 1988), particularly with respect to coronality (Paradis & Prunet 1991), and the concept was indeed frowned upon (McCarthy 1988). Halle et al. (2000) emphasise that full specification for contrastive features should be the norm. Despite the unease, there is no doubt that asymmetries and markedness differences exist across feature distributions and directions of the output of phonological rules, and various methods have been employed to handle them. Calabrese (1995) distinguished different types of feature representations such as contrastive, marked, and full, which in turn were interspersed in the ordering of rules. Mohanan (1993) favoured what he called "fields of attraction" and "dominance", which allowed him to express degrees of markedness. Clements (2001) proposed a complex model combining both specification and underspecification, which allowed non-contrastive features to be specified if they were "active" in phonology. He distinguished between "active" features (which may form natural classes) and "prominent" features (which, for instance, play a role in spreading).

Against this historical backdrop, this chapter sets out the FUL view of underspecification and asymmetry, and specifically addresses two questions:
(i) How do FUL's features and their hierarchical organisation account for the phonological contrasts of the languages of the world?
(ii) To what extent are (UNDER)SPECIFICATION and (IN)ACTIVITY correlated?

Through examining several test cases bearing on these issue in especially challenging ways, we seek to further strengthen the case for the FUL approach. Particular emphasis will be on the feature CORONAL, the focus of a lot of attention in past decades. In the course of a brief historical overview, Section 2 compares several approaches to coronals. Section 3 highlights the specifics of FUL in relation to other models, in particular the Contrastive Hierarchy proposed by Dresher and colleagues and Clements' system of underspecification. Finally, Section 4 returns to monovalent features, in particular to account for complex vowel alternations like those of Kàlɔ̀ŋ analysed in Hyman (2003). The typological moral is that coronal contrasts and alternations involving coronal triggering on the face of it show a great deal of variation, but analysis – along lines dictated by a particular theoretical model, FUL – reveals fundamental unity of phonological grammar behind crosslinguistic diversity.

2 Towards FUL: [coronal] vs. [–back]

A decade after JFH, articulatorily oriented features were in the ascendancy in *The sound pattern of English* (Chomsky & Halle 1968, SPE), being supposedly better suited to describe phonological patterns of the world's languages. A major change was the establishment of separate place features for vowels and consonants. Vowels, for example, were all [–anterior], while consonants could be both [+anterior] and [–anterior]; vowels were characterised by [±back] and were always [–coronal]. Thus, there was no way to pair [coronal] consonants like dentals and palatoalveolars with [–back] vowels. A subset of features considered by SPE (1968: 407, adapted from Table 3) for various main places of articulation (and not including secondary articulations such as palatalised labials), is given in (1):[1]

(1) SPE feature composition for place of articulation

	anterior	coronal	high	low	back
CONSONANTS					
labials	+	–	–	–	–
dentals	+	+	–	–	–
palato-alveolars	–	+	+	–	–
does not exist	–	–	–	–	–
palatals	–	–	+	–	–
velars	–	–	+	–	+
uvulars	–	–	–	–	+
pharyngeals	–	–	–	+	+
VOWELS & GLIDES					
high front	–	–	+	–	–
high back	–	–	+	–	+
mid front	–	–	–	–	–
mid back	–	–	–	–	+
low front	–	–	–	+	–
low back	–	–	–	+	+

The eighties led the way to grouping features into natural classes rather than listing them arbitrarily (e.g., Clements 1985, 1989; Sagey 1986; Clements & Hume

---

1 Notwithstanding the move towards articulatorily oriented features in phonology, the acoustics of features continued to be investigated by Stevens, Blumstein and colleagues (cf. Stevens & Blumstein 1978; Blumstein & Stevens 1980; Lahiri, Gewirth, & Blumstein 1984), the goal being to locate invariant acoustic cues for distinctive features rather than for segments, which had proved to be impossible (cf. Lahiri et al. 1984 for cues to distinguish CORONAL and LABIAL diffuse stops).

1995; McCarthy 1988). Although controversies raged over the precise grouping, one assumption remained unchanged: vowels and consonants did not share all place features. The DORSAL node dominated vowels which were largely distinguished by [±back]. This had the unwanted consequence of segregating front vowels ([−back], [−coronal] [−anterior]) from dentals, alveolars, and palatoalveolars, which were grouped under [coronal]. Additionally, the height features [±high], [±low] were dominated by [dorsal]. The feature tree in (2) gives the general idea (see further Lahiri & Reetz 2010):[2]

(2) Established class nodes (after Clements 1985; McCarthy 1988)

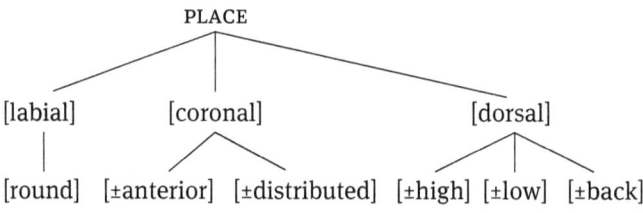

Consonants: [labial], [coronal], [dorsal]
All vowels: [dorsal], except for [round]

In a novel proposal, Clements (1989) argued that, similar to JFH, vowels and consonants ought to be brought together if the notion of constriction of the vocal tract with the parameters of degree and location was to be taken seriously. However, although the place features were accordingly the same, the place nodes for vowels and consonants would be on separate tiers.

(3) Feature tree following Clements & Hume (1995)
    (a) CONSONANTS – PLACE only

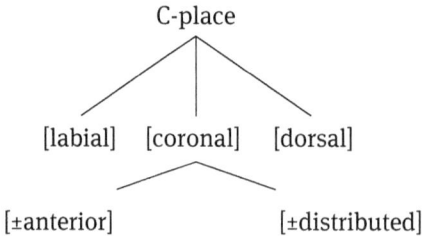

---

2 The tier structures in the feature trees (1)–(4) are not relevant for the present discussion.

(b) VOCOIDS – PLACE only

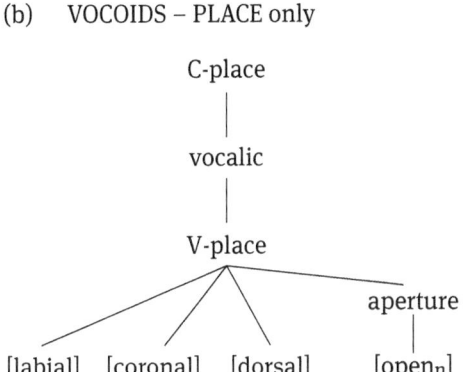

[labial]: labial consonants, rounded vowels
[coronal]: coronal consonants, front vowels
[dorsal]: dorsal consonants, back vowels

A fundamental difference from earlier models is that [coronal] here entirely replaced [±back]. In response to Clements' unified theory, Halle et al. (2000) proposed to dispense with dependencies, such that [back] [high] [low] were no longer dependents of DORSAL.[3] Thus, any fronting that would spread [dorsal] would not necessarily spread [–back]. Nevertheless, vowels and consonants remained distinct in terms of place features. The PLACE node proposed by Halle et al. (2000) is as in (4):

(4) Feature organisation as in Halle et al. (2000)

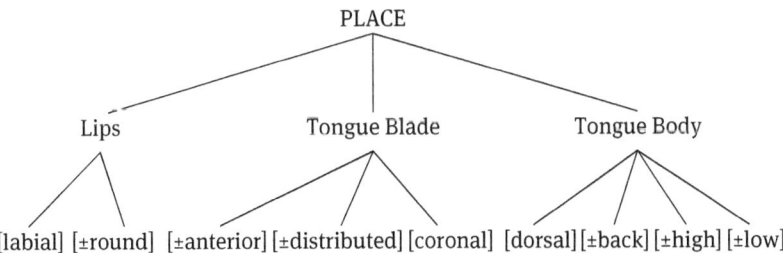

Taking JFH's view of combining all consonantal and vocalic features seriously, Lahiri & Evers (1991) and Lahiri & Reetz (2002) (cf. also Lahiri 2000; Ghini 2001a)

---

3 The feature tree given in Halle et al. (2000: 389) does not indicate +/− values. However, from their discussion of Irish assimilation it is obvious that as before the features HIGH, LOW, DISTRIBUTED, ROUND, ANTERIOR, BACK are binary.

pointed out that there was no necessity to duplicate the V-place node for vowels and secondary articulations, and that the aperture node was not only relevant for vowels but also for consonants. Thus, the constriction relevant on the horizontal dimension along the vocal tract was determined by the ARTICULATORS, and on the vertical dimension was characterised by the height of the tongue. Consequently, as seen in (5), the PLACE node dominated separate nodes ARTICULATOR and TONGUE HEIGHT, as well as the TONGUE ROOT features, with the PLACE features thus identical for vowels and consonants. Although, to honour tradition, we have kept the basic articulatory names, each feature has well defined acoustic cues as well. The features and feature organisation we will defend are based on universal principles of phonological alternations as well as production and perceptual mechanisms. The features are the same for production and perception (cf. Lahiri & Reetz 2010; Lahiri 2010; Plank & Lahiri 2015). Furthermore, the FUL processing model has clear-cut processes of matching from the signal to the representation and the other way around.

(5)   Feature tree for FUL

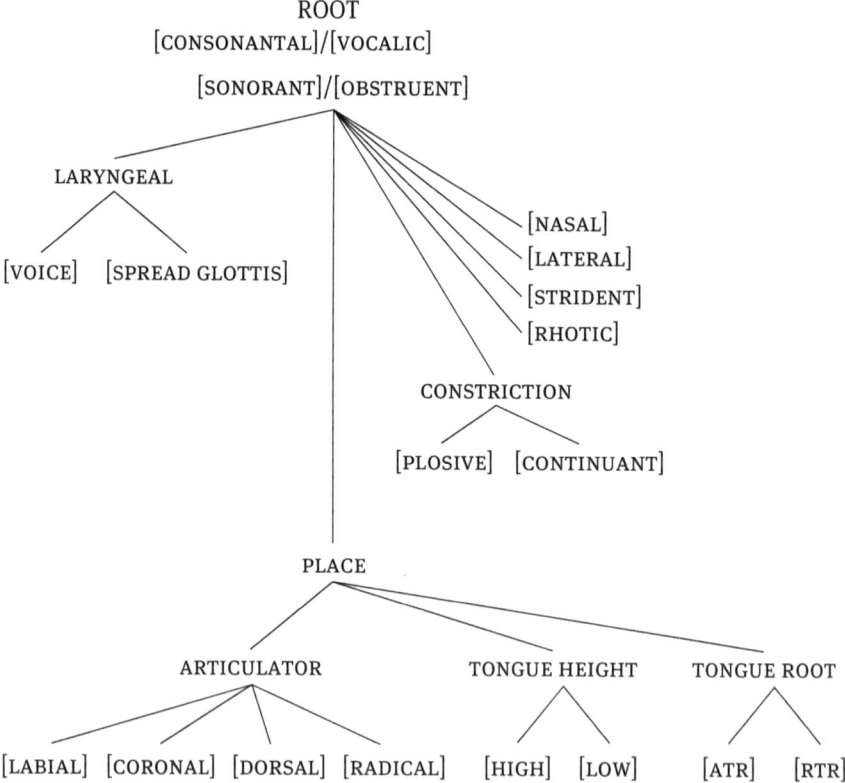

A subset of the phonemes grouped under each feature (vowels and consonants) are given in (6).

(6) Features and segments
    [LABIAL]   labial consonants, rounded vowels
    [CORONAL]   front vowels, dental, palatal, palatoalveolar, retroflex consonants
    [DORSAL]   back vowels, velar, uvular consonants
    [RADICAL]   pharyngealised vowels, glottal, pharyngeal consonants
    [HIGH]   high vowels, palatalised consonants, retroflex, velar, palatal, pharyngeal consonants
    [LOW]   low vowels, dental, uvular consonants
    [ATR]   palatoalveolar consonants, tense vowels
    [RTR]   retroflex consonants, lax vowels

Two pairs of opposing features – CONSONANTAL/VOCALIC and SONORANT/OBSTRUENT – are the major class features available in all languages. All phonemes must be either CONSONANTAL or VOCALIC and SONORANT or OBSTRUENT. The members of each pair are conflicting – i.e., CONSONANTAL implies not VOCALIC and vice versa. The nodes LARYNGEAL, CONSTRICTION, PLACE, TONGUE HEIGHT, TONGUE ROOT, RADICAL are always present, although they may be empty if there are no contrastive phonemes in the language concerned, as discussed below. All features are monovalent; therefore, they are either present or absent, and unlike in Halle et al. (2000) and Clements (2001), there is no mixture of some binary (e.g., [±back]) and some monovalent features (e.g., [dorsal]). Further, in contrast to earlier approaches – for instance, in Clements (2001: 114, 47) [±posterior] is dominated by [coronal] – no features dominate other features in FUL.

A number of assumptions fall out from the feature tree and we take them in turn.

First, the features under each node are mutually exclusive. An exception is the LARYNGEAL node, where [VOICE] and [SPREAD GLOTTIS] can co-occur, as attested in only a few languages (among them Bengali and Hindi).[4] Thus, [NASAL/LATERAL/RHOTIC/STRIDENT], [CONTINUANT/PLOSIVE], [LABIAL/CORONAL/DORSAL/GLOTTAL], [HIGH/LOW], [ATR/RTR] are mutually exclusive for consonants. For vowels, [LABIAL] may combine with [CORONAL] and [DORSAL].

Second, the only dependencies we assume are universal implications such as [NASAL] ⇒ [SONORANT] or [STRIDENT] ⇒ [OBSTRUENT].

---

4 It is possible that the features under the LARYNGEAL node should be independent and not be subsumed under a single node.

Third, underspecification is fundamental to FUL. However, there are only two features which are universally underspecified: [CORONAL] and [PLOSIVE]. The reasons are based on contrast sensitivity and typological prominence.

Fourth, only those features that are necessary to maintain contrasts between the phonemes of a language are used. This is similar to Dresher's (2009) contrastivity, with the exception that there is no "activity" requirement in FUL. Feature specifications are independent of whether or not the features play an "active" role in phonological processes – as to be discussed in the context of a case study in the next section.

Fifth, feature trees are built in language acquisition based on the universal principle of PLACE-first (Ghini 2001b), where ARTICULATOR contrasts precede TONGUE HEIGHT contrasts. For the ARTICULATOR contrasts, [CORONAL] is the universal default: all languages must have this feature. Since [CORONAL] is underspecified, the assumption is that when during acquisition, a non-coronal phoneme is enountered, it becomes specified. For instance, Levelt (1995) and Fikkert & Levelt (2008) observed that a contrastive feature like [LABIAL] becomes specified first. For TONGUE HEIGHT, we believe that the feature [LOW] will be assigned first.

These assumptions are fairly restrictive and we are aware that they are in conflict with many assumptions made in the literature. Three issues are especially critical and will be addressed presently:

(i) How can languages be accounted for where [CORONAL] is supposed to be active?
(ii) If no dependent features such as [±anterior] and [±distributed] are permitted, how can various sets of sounds be accounted for which were classified by these features?
(iii) Does [CORONAL] always exist?

3 Underspecification of [CORONAL] and "activity"

3.1 Coronal activities

It has variously been proposed that it is essential that [CORONAL] is "active" and therefore needs to be specified. We will discuss two relevant case studies in some depth: palatalisation in Inuit dialects as analysed in Compton & Dresher (2001, henceforth C&D), and Tahltan vowel harmony as analysed in Clements (2001). In both instances, the presence of [CORONAL] is indispensible.

3.2 Development of Proto-Eskimo vowels and palatalisation

Proto-Eskimo had four vowels */i u a ə/ and in most Inuit dialects /ə/ merged with reflexes of */i/. Traditional descriptions distinguish between "strong *i*" from original */i/, which triggers palatalisation, and "weak *i*" from original */ə/, which fails to trigger palatalisation. In C&D's story, features are ordered according to a Contrastive Hierarchy as established by the Sucessive Division Algorithm. Only features which are "active" are on the top of the hierarchy. Based on various processes, it can be shown that [LOW], [LABIAL], and [CORONAL] are active in Proto-Eskimo and are treated as the marked values and the opposites are unmarked. The hierarchy for Proto-Eskimo is given in (7).

(7) Proto-Eskimo contrastive hierarchy for vowels: [LOW] > [LABIAL] > [CORONAL]

(a) Contrastive hierarchy

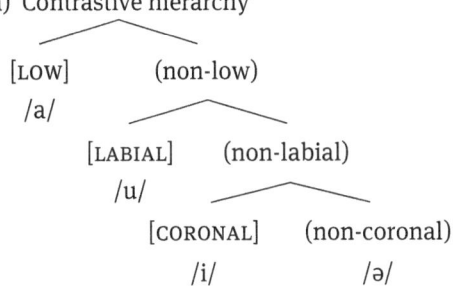

(b) Feature contrast table of the 4-vowel system

/i/	/u/	/a/	/ə/
[CORONAL]	[LABIAL]	[LOW]	[—]

The hierarchy begins with [LOW], this being the first division by Jakobson & Halle (1956) on the grounds of highest sonority. The next cut follows the common pattern of place-next. The most important aspect is that /i/ is [CORONAL] and this is the feature that is required to trigger palatalisation. All four-vowel systems of this family have the strong *i* as coronal. The three-vowel systems /i u a/, however, do not have /ə/, neither is palatalisation being triggered. Thus, these vowel systems (again beginning with [LOW]) are organised as follows:

(8) 3-vowel system

(a) Feature tree

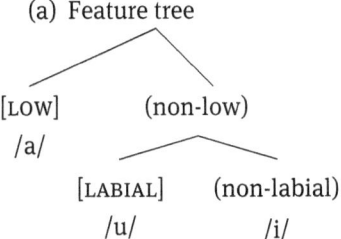

(b) Feature contrast table
/i/   /u/   /a/
[−]   [LABIAL] [LOW]

This is an elegant analysis which produces the pattern of alternations set out in (9). Weak *i* alternations show no effect of the feature CORONAL, while strong *i* alternations do, since /i/ is specified for CORONAL. Strong *i* leads to palatalisation with surface [tʃ] and [ʎ].

(9) Palatalisation present and absent
Barrow Inupiaq weak and strong *i* (C&D (5) based on Kaplan 1981)

	stem	gloss	3SG.INTR /-tuq/	3SG.SUBJ /-luni/	Proto-Eskimo
(weak *i*)	isiq-	enter	isiqtuq	isiʁluni	*itəʁ-
(strong *i*)	isiq-	be-smoky	isiqsuq	isiʁʎuni	*əðiʁ-
(weak *i*)	makit-	stand up	makittuq	makilluni	*makət-
(strong *i*)	tikitʃ	arrive	tikittʃuk	tikiʎʎuni	*təkit-

Although FUL agrees that the vowel /i/ is [CORONAL], it faces several problems with the assumption that CORONAL alone triggers palatalisation. The assumption in FUL is that palatalisation would normally occur with the additional feature [HIGH]; certainly the vowel /i/ is involved, but not the main place feature. Second, [CORONAL] would be underspecified, and thus will not play an active role. How could it work under these assumptions and would such an analysis be in any way preferable? We provide an alternative below.

First, the Inuit palatalisations affect all places of articulation; a summary from C&D's data is in (10).

(10) Surface outputs in Inuit due to palatalisation
n → ɲ
l → ʎ
k → tʃ
t → s

Note that the obstruents become strident, which would be the phonetic enhancement of the palatalisation process. It is actually not evident from C&D's analysis why [CORONAL] is the active feature relevant for palatalisation, since the inputs /t l s/ are all [CORONAL] to begin with. The only change in place of articulation is /k/ → /s/. All relevant features in FUL are tabulated in (11); the consonants [ʎ ɲ s tʃ] are listed for convenience, but they are in parentheses since they are derivatives of /l n t k/ in the context of /i/.

(11) FUL features for vowels (4-vowel system)

	i	u	a	ə
ART	COR	DORSAL	DORSAL	
TH	HIGH	HIGH	LOW	

(12) Features for relevant CORONAL consonants

	l	(λ)	t	(s)	n	(ɲ)	k	(tʃ)
ART	COR	COR	COR	COR	COR	COR	DOR	COR
TH		HIGH					√	√
				STRID				STRID

Although the tables show the distribution of features, a proper tree diagram is necessary to show the precise nature of the underlying representations and how the palatalisation process should work. On our analysis, the underlying representations of four contrasting vowels and consonants, /i u k l/, are as follows:

(13) Underlying representation of /i/ /u/ /k/ /l/

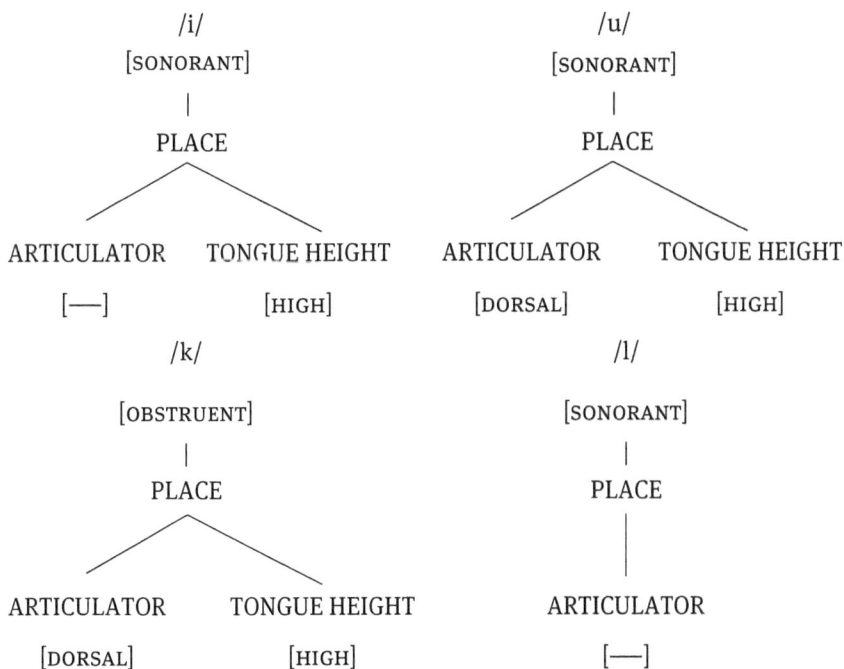

We distinguish between UNDERSPECIFIED features, which are marked as [—] with the relevant node (e.g., ART [—] for /i/), and NOT SPECIFIED such as the empty cell for ARTICULATOR for /ə/. We will see presently that the underspecified features will eventually have specific features filled in by production rules, while those that are not specified or redundant will be more variable. Thus, /ə/ will have a PLACE node but no ARTICULATOR node properly assigned; it may, therefore, obtain different features in production.

Palatalisation is triggered by /i/, which is ARTICULATOR-free but specified for TONGUE HEIGHT [HIGH]. Two processes are involved in the way /i/ "fronts" /k n l/, a not uncommon way to describe palatalisation. The first entails ensuring that the sequence of ARTICULATOR features do not mismatch, leading to [DORSAL] being deleted in the context of ARTICULATOR-free /i/. The second, where the ARTICULATOR features of the consonants /n l/ are unspecified, involves the spreading of [HIGH] to non-[HIGH] coronal consonants making them palatals and thereby [HIGH]. Both are illustrated in (14).

(14) Palatalisation

(a) /k/ → [tʃ]: deletion of [DORSAL]

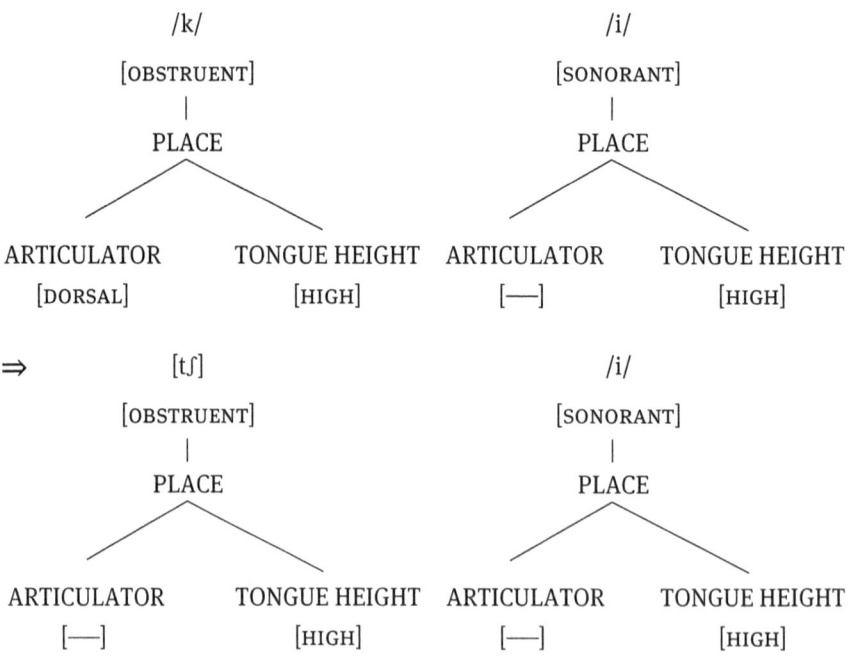

(b) Palatalisation of /l/ → [ʎ]: spreading of [HIGH]

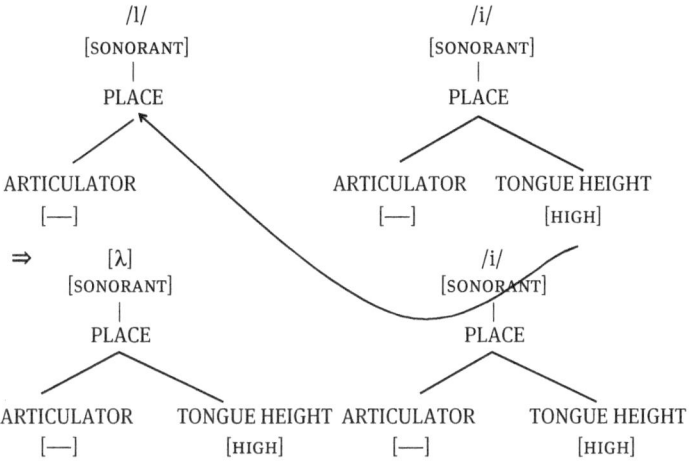

There is a third palatalisation which is an assibilation process, where /t/ does not change the place of articulation, but becomes a strident [s]. To account for this, [STRIDENT] is incorporated as a fill-in surface rule as an effect of the spreading of [HIGH], as in (15). Languages differ in the way /t/ becomes a sibilant; in English, for instance, [HIGH] leads to /t/ becoming a /tʃ/, as in *don't you* → *don*[tʃ]*you*.

(15)   Assibilation: /t/ → [s]

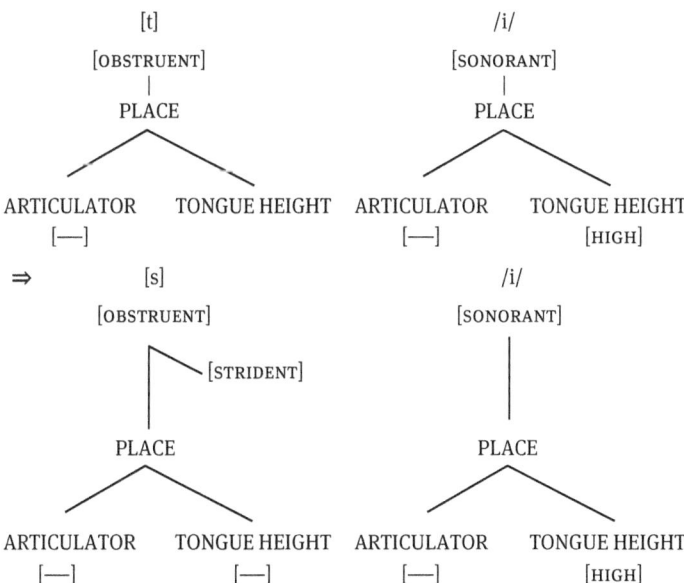

To obtain the correct surface forms we need further steps, viz., rules which fill in features for production (cf. Lahiri 2010; Plank & Lahiri 2015). An ARTICULATOR-free consonant will be provided with [CORONAL] as in (16). This will also include the addition of [STRIDENT] for /t/ in the context of /i/.

(16)   Surface production rules for vowels
       ART [−] → [CORONAL]
       ART [DORSAL] & TH [HIGH] → ADD [LABIAL]

There are a few additional points to be made. First, we are able to account for palatalisation even if [CORONAL] is unspecified. However, why would this analysis be preferred over that of C&D, who assume that the [CORONAL] specification of /i/ can account for all the palatalisation processes? They elegantly connect the presence and absence of palatalisation and the specification of [CORONAL] for /i/. We do not deny that /i/ is [CORONAL] nor that it plays a significant role. However, C&D do not discuss the various ways in which [CORONAL] should affect the other consonants and in fact they do not show how palatalisation is actually realised. For instance, why is it that /l/ becomes /ʎ/ when [CORONAL] from /i/ spreads? Is /l/ not [CORONAL]? What about other coronal consonants such as /n/? Why does the addition of [CORONAL] from /i/ alone lead to palatalisation? Is it the vocalic element that is crucial and [CORONAL] from consonants has no effect?[5] For /k/-palatalisation, it is obvious that the place feature of the consonant changes. In our analysis, this is treated as an assimilation process whereby the ARTICULATOR features merge; this can be achieved by spreading or deletion. However, in our view palatalisation of the other consonants which are inherently all [CORONAL] is different. Thus, we crucially distinguish between palatalisations which affects back consonants and those which share the place feature with /i/. It is not clear how this is accounted for in C&D.

Second, the main aim of C&D's analysis is to confirm that the four-vowel and three-vowel systems have different feature distributions. Accordingly, for them the difference lies in the four-vowel systems requiring [CORONAL] to be specified for /i/, which triggers palatalisation, while it is unspecified in the three-vowel system (see above (7), (8)). Can our analysis account for this contrast, given that [CORONAL] is always underspecified and will always be filled in in the surface representation because it has an empty ARTICULATOR node? The answer is yes. Recall that in FUL it is not coronality *per se* which triggers palatalisation: it is [HIGH] that plays a crucial role. We compare the four- and three-vowel systems in FUL:

---

5   We are assuming that these consonants should be [CORONAL] in C&D based on the rest of their analysis.

(17) FUL features for vowels in Inuit dialects (3- and 4-vowel systems)
(a) 3-vowel system

	i	u	a
ART	[—]	DORSAL	DORSAL
TH			LOW

(b) 4-vowel system

	i	u	a	ə
ART	[—]	DORSAL	DORSAL	
TH	HIGH	HIGH	LOW	

Unlike C&D, it is not the presence or absence of coronality which is of central concern, but the TONGUE HEIGHT contrasts. In the three-vowel system, [HIGH] is not required, since the ARTICULATOR features are enough to distinguish /i/ and /u/. The first height feature is always [LOW]. If that is sufficient, there is no further need for [HIGH]. In the four-vowel system, the presence of a fourth vowel /ə/ requires [HIGH] to be specified. Since [HIGH] is essential for /i/ to trigger either fronting or assibilation, the three-vowel systems do not cater to palatalisation. Consequently, the lack of specification of [CORONAL] universally does not prevent us from accounting for the presence and absence of palatalisations.

3.3 Tahltan coronal harmony

Palatalisation in Inuit dialects directly leads us into a discussion of vowel harmony where coronal consonants differ in terms of their transparency, thereby either blocking or permitting harmony. Tahltan coronal harmony was analysed in Shaw (1991: 144–152), reconsidered in Clements (2001), and further discussed in Lahiri & Reetz (2010, henceforth L&R). In Shaw's account, Tahltan, an Athapaskan language, has a series of five coronal obstruents, and coronal harmony is only applicable across three sets — apical, laminal, and palatoalveolar consonants. The process involves fricatives of these places of articulation, which assimilate to all coronal place features, and stridency of any following coronal obstruent of one of these three sets. The simple and lateral series are transparent to this harmony process. Tahltan has four series of affricates and fricatives. The only true stops belong to the simple series.

Even in the lateral series, the consonants are not sonorants, but obstruent affricates and fricatives.

We compare Clements' analysis to L&R. The coronal obstruents and the relevant features proposed by Clements are given in (18) along with the corresponding features from FUL. Only the crucial features are listed.

(18)   Tahltan coronal obstruents and their features (Clements' features: lat lateral, strid strident, distr distributed, ant anterior, apic apical, post posterior)

simple	lateral	apical	laminal	palatoalveolar
d	dl	dʑ	dð	dʒ
t	tɬ	ts	tθ	tʃ
t'	tɬ'	ts'	tθ'	tʃ'
	ɬ	s	θ	ʃ
	l	z	ð	ʒ

	Clements					FUL				
	ROOT					ROOT				
	lat	coronal							ARTICULATOR	TONGUE HEIGHT
		strid	apic	post						
d					PLOSIVE			[−]	
dl	+					LAT		[−]	
s, dʑ		+					STRID	[−]	LOW
θ, dð			−				STRID	[−]	
ʃ, dʒ				+			STRID	[−]	HIGH

In Clements (2001), the features [strident], [apical], and [posterior] are dominated by the [coronal] node, and only the marked feature values are specified, namely [+strident], [−apical], and [+posterior]. Thus, of the five coronal sets of a consonants, two are not specified for [coronal], but the others are. Stridency is a property only of coronal consonants; i.e., strident is dependent on coronal. The simple and the lateral series are unmarked for coronal, which is neither lexically specified nor active, and hence absent for these consonants. Thus, only the specified coronal consonants are engaged in harmony, but the others are transparent for harmony. In FUL, however, ALL coronal consonants, including the simple and the lateral consonants, are unspecified for the ARTICULATOR node and [STRIDENT] is independent of the ARTICULATOR node. An important assumption in FUL is that all fricatives and obstruent affricates in Tahltan are [STRIDENT]. Before we discuss the actual harmony process, we will look at some examples.

(19) Tahltan coronal harmony (Shaw 1991) (target within square brackets and trigger underlined)

(i) /-s/ '1SG subject marker' /s/ → /θ/, /ʃ/

(a)	mɛθɛ/s/ɛθ	mɛθɛ[θ]ɛθ	I'm wearing (on feet)	*fricative trigger*
(b)	na/s/t̪θ'ɛt	na[θ]t̪θ'ɛt	I fell off (horse)	*affricate trigger*
(c)	dɛ/s/kʷʊθ	dɛ[θ]kʷʊθ	I cough	*intervening syllable*
(d)	xaʔɛ/s/t'aθ	xaʔɛ[θ]t'aθ	I'm cutting the hair off	*intervening simple t'*
(e)	ɛ/s/dʒɪni	ɛ[ʃ]dʒɪni	I'm singing	*voiced affricate trigger*
(f)	ya/s/tɬɛtʃ	ya[ʃ]tɬɛtʃ	I'm singing	*intervening lateral tɬ*
(g)	ɛ/s/dan	ɛ[s]dan	I'm drinking	*no change*

(ii) /-θ/ '1DUAL subject marker' /θ/ → /s/, /ʃ/

(h)	u/θ/idʒɛ	u[ʃ]idʒɛ	we are called	*voiced affricate trigger*
(i)	dɛ/θ/it'as	dɛ[s]it'as	we are walking	*intervening simple t'*
(j)	xa/θ/i:dɛts	xa[s]i:dɛts	we plucked it	*intervening simple d*

The differences between the first set, with /s/ changing to /θ/ /ʃ/, and the second set, with /θ/ changing to /s/ and /ʃ/, depend on the target: an apical (or perhaps dental) strident /s/ changes to the palatoalveolar or interdental in the respective contexts, while interdental /θ/ changes to palatoalveolar /ʃ/ or dental /s/.

In Shaw's rule for harmony, the rightmost specified coronal node spreads leftwards with the concomitant delinking of the previous coronal specification of the target (cf. Lahiri & Reetz 2010 for a detailed analysis). The target is an immediately adjacent specified coronal node. Since both trigger and target need to be specified coronal nodes, the lateral and simple series are unaffected by the spreading and cannot block harmony. Clements accomplishes consonantal harmony with a single AGREE constraint which ensures that all coronal nodes containing the marked feature values must be identical within the word. This means that the coronal laterals and plosives remain untouched while the others are involved in harmony. Both Shaw and Clements need to separate the lateral and plosives from the other consonants in terms of coronal specification. They achieve the harmony process by ensuring that the simple [d] and the lateral [dl] series are free of the coronal node, while the other series require features which are dominated by the coronal node.

How does it work in FUL? Under our analysis, harmony is restricted to obstruents specified for STRIDENT; as mentioned before, [CORONAL] will surface, but is unspecified in the underlying representation. Moreover, the plosives and the laterals do not have the feature [STRIDENT].

(20) Tahltan harmony in FUL: for a sequence of [STRIDENT] obstruents, TONGUE HEIGHT features spread regressively within a word when no other [STRIDENT] obstruent intervenes

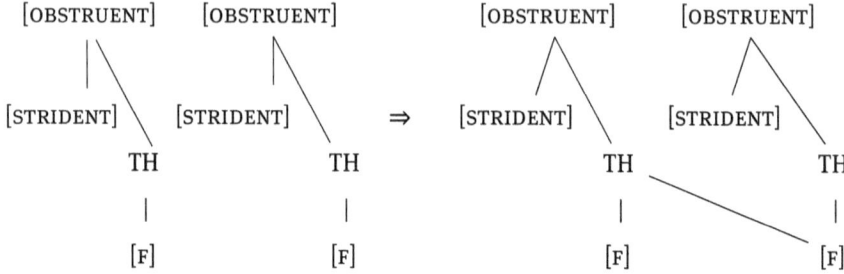

(21) Harmony examples in FUL with and without intervening consonants (intervening segments in bold and trigger underlined)

(i)	θ	d	t͡ʃ	→	ʃ	d	t͡ʃ
	[–]		[HIGH]		[HIGH]		[HIGH]
	[STRID]		[STRID]		[STRID]		[STRID]
(ii)	s	tɬ'	t͡ʃ	→	ʃ	tɬ'	t͡ʃ
	[LOW]		[HIGH]		[HIGH]		[HIGH]
	[STRID]		[STRID]		[STRID]		[STRID]
		[LATERAL]				[LATERAL]	
(iii)	θ	d	ts	→	s	d	ts
	[–]		[LOW]		[LOW]		[LOW]
	[STRID]		[STRID]		[STRID]		[STRID]
(iv)	s	d	θ	→	θ	d	θ
	[LOW]		[–]		[–]		[–]
	[STRID]		[STRID]		[STRID]		[STRID]

In (i) and (ii), [HIGH] dominates, turning both /θ/ and /s/ to /ʃ/, while in (iii) [LOW] spreads and /θ/ becomes /s/. For (iv), since assimilation is progressive, the TONGUE HEIGHT feature [LOW] of /ts/ is deleted to agree with the unspecified TONGUE HEIGHT feature of /θ/. The TONGUE HEIGHT features spread across the laterals (e.g., /tɬ'/) and plosives (e.g., /d/) which are both independent of the TONGUE HEIGHT node and does not block any feature spreading. No other feature is altered.

Thus, for Tahltan, in both Shaw and Clements' analyses, some of the coronal consonants could not be specified for coronality to obtain correct results for harmony. For both analyses, stridency was an additional complication since the distinguishing features for the various places of articulation with coronal consonants as well as the feature [STRIDENT] were dependent on [CORONAL]. Consequently, to prevent some of the coronal consonants from undergoing harmony or to be transparent to harmony, they were prevented from having the coronal feature or in Clements' terms, "coronal was not active". FUL does not have that choice. The feature CORONAL is always there and is always underspecified. Furthermore, since there are no features dependent on CORONAL, to obtain the other contrasts, different features are employed.

4 Lack of dependent features and CORONAL contrasts

4.1 Ways of accounting for CORONAL contrasts

As mentioned above, FUL disallows dependent features. Although this has positive aspects, we still need to be able to distinguish many places of articulation which are all [CORONAL]. Since SPE, the features [±anterior] and [±distributed] have been used to distinguish between the various coronal affricates and fricatives. The traditional SPE feature combinations (cf. (1)) for coronal consonants made by the tip and blade of the tongue are as follows:

(22)   SPE features used to distinguish various coronal consonants

	dentals	[+anterior] [+distributed]
	alveolar	[+anterior] [−distributed]
	retroflex	[−anterior] [−distributed]
	palatoalveolar	[−anterior] [+distributed] [−back]
cf.	palatal	[−coronal] [−anterior] [+distributed]

In FUL, both palatal and retroflex consonants are [CORONAL] and [HIGH], and therefore are not distinguishable by these two features. These types of consonantal contrasts could be potential problems: palatal versus retroflex stops /c ʈ/ and nasals /ɲ ɳ/, and palatoalveolar versus retroflex sibilants /ʃ ʂ/.

Lahiri & Reetz (2010) maintain that it is extremely rare (if attested at all) that phonemic contrast occurs between dentals and alveolars on the one hand and retroflex and palatals on the other. For example, Malayalam has been claimed to have both alveolar and dental stops. However, the alveolar stop is always derived from a rhotic and the minimal pairs that can be obtained are via gemination. The rhotic, when geminated, becomes an alveolar (Lahiri et al. 1984). Palatals are definitely coronal (Lahiri & Blumstein 1984; Keating & Lahiri 1993), but we propose that a palatal versus retroflex underlying contrast in stops is only possible if the palatal stop is affricated or is an "alveopalatal" consonant, both of which would be [STRIDENT] (cf. Hall 1997), or if one is derived from the other. In Malayalam, which has both retroflex and palatal stops, only retroflex stops occur in the underlying inventory. The palatal stops are derived in specific morphological environments from intervocalic velars when preceded by front vowels. Mohanan & Mohanan (1984: 589) also suggest that, given the complex conditioning of the palatalisation rule, "[p]erhaps the right solution is to say that Palatalization is blocked when the segment has some ad hoc diacritical feature [–P]". Mohanan & Mohanan also make a distinction between UNDERLYING and LEXICAL alphabet, the latter being derived by rules in the lexicon. Their claim is that the lexical alphabet "has significant consequences for human perception of speech sounds" (1984: 598). Possibly Mohanan & Mohanan's lexical contrasts and our underlying contrasts are the same. A further possibility is that, like the dental/alveolar contrast, the feature [HIGH] is specified in one case and not in the other.

If a language has both palatal and retroflex nasals, FUL predicts that they are not truly contrastive. Either the palatal nasal /ɲ/ is an assimilated variant of an alveolar or dental /n/ in the context of a palatal or palatoalveolar stop, or the retroflex nasal is derived, or it consists of a nasal-plus-glide sequence. Again, Malayalam is a good example since it has seven phonetic nasals derived from three underlying ones which are labial, dental, and velar /m n ŋ/ (Mohanan & Mohanan 1984: 583–586, 596–598). Mohanan & Mohanan show that palatal and retroflex nasals are derived by a homorganic nasal assimilation rule in the context of following palatal and retroflex stops, and the palatal stops are in turn derived from velars. Thus, the feature contrast for a language like Pitta-Pitta, which has been claimed to have a series including dentals, alveolar, palatal, and retroflex stops and nasals (from Hall 1997) would be as follows.[6]

---

[6] In Hall's terminology, rather confusingly, traditional "palatals" are called "alveolopalatals", and they differ in their coronality: "The term 'palatals' will used here to refer to true palatals, such as German [ç j] and not to sounds like Hungarian [c ɟ], which are alveolopalatal" (1997: 70, §2.6). According to Hall, alveolopalatals are coronal whereas true palatals are not; thus, "alveopalatals" [c ɟ ɲ ɕ ʑ] are [+coronal], "true palatals" [ç j] are [–back, +dorsal]; also, he assumes that a four-way contrast among a single series of [+coronal –cont] is maximal (1997: 88, (4)). Since [±back] is not an option, in FUL all of these consonants are [CORONAL]. Hall also states, and here

(23) Pitta-Pitta [CORONAL] segments in FUL
      t̪   t   ṭ   c
      n̪   n   ṇ   ɲ
      [LOW] [−] [ATR] [HIGH]

So far we have not considered secondary articulations, although we have discussed palatalisation and the spreading of the feature [HIGH] of coronal vowels. In the next section we compare the fronting of velars with the palatalisation of other coronal consonants.

4.2 Palatalised consonants and palatalisation

In Bhat's seminal work (1978: 60–61), three types of palatalisation have been shown to recur across languages: (i) fronting of velars (24a); (ii) change of place within coronal consonants, with alveolar/dental becoming palatoalveolar/palatal (24b); and (iii) addition of secondary articulation to any place of articulation (24c); the context is invariably high front vowel /i/ and glide /j/ and sometimes the front vowel /e/.

(24) Results of palatalisation
      (a) k, x   →   tʃ, ç
      (b) t, s   →   tʃ, ʃ
      (c) p, t   →   pʲ, kʲ

Examples of (23a) include Slavic languages where [k g x] became [tʃ, dʒ, ʃ] (SPE, 421–422). Polish is known to have palatalisations as in (23b) where coronal consonants [t d s z r n l] become pre-palatal consonants before front vowels and glides (Rubach 1984: 60). English alveolars such as [t d] become [tʃ dʒ] in the context of [j]. Finally "secondary palatal" articulation occurs involving "raising the central part of the tongue while keeping the main articulator intact" (Bhat 1978: 67). Secondary palatalisation of this sort occurs in Dutch diminutive formation, to be discussed in more detail below. Two issues need to be addressed: palatalised

---

we agree, that no language contrasts alveolopalatals [ɕ] and palatoalveolars like [ʃ], and in fact the same holds true for palatals and palatalised velars – which is why, in his model, they have the same features. However, no language contrasts alveopalatal [ɕ] and palatal [c] either, and moreover there cannot be stops in both positions: one of the consonants has to be a continuant (cf. Lahiri & Blumstein 1984).

consonants, and particularly palatalised velars such as [kʲ] vs. [c] or [ç], and palatalisation as a process.

There have been many discussions of palatalised consonants, succinctly summarised and discussed in Hall (1997). In our view, as argued above (cf. also Lahiri & Evers 1991; Lahiri & Reetz 2010), palatalisation is triggered by [CORONAL] and [HIGH]; to set the scene for its defense, let us look at a few notable alternatives.

To repeat, the crucial features traditionally implicated were [±anterior] and [±back]. The pertinent consonants had the following features:

(25) Differentiating front and back vowels and consonants

Dental-Alveolar	Palatoalveolar	Velar	Front vowels and [j]
Coronal	Coronal	Dorsal	Dorsal
[+anterior]	[−anterior]	[+back]	[−back]

Palatalisation: [k] → [tʃ] / —[i]⁷

k	i	tʃ	i/j
Dorsal	Dorsal	Coronal	Dorsal
[+back]	[−back]		[−back]

Thus, a change from [k] to [tʃ] in the context of [i] or [j] would involve a change in the primary change of articulation of dorsal to coronal in the context of [−back], which was dominated by dorsal. This problem was addressed in detail by Clements and taken up by Hume, leading to the feature set we discussed above.

In the analysis of Clements (1989), the structure of palatalisation would involve the following features:

(26) Palatalisation according to Clements (1989)

	k	−	j	→	kʲ	→	tʃ
C-place							
[coronal]							+
[dorsal]	+				+		
V-place							
[coronal]					+		+
[dorsal]							

---

[7] The change leads most often to a [HIGH] consonant such as [ç tʃ ʃ]. Sometimes /t/ also becomes /s/ in a similar context, but that is more of an assibilation whereby the stop becomes a sibilant fricative, again in the context of a high vowel or glide.

The first step involves a palatalised [kʲ], which has a C-place dorsal as well as a V-place coronal. This in turn undergoes tier promotion, complex segment formation, and concomitant affrication to become [tʃ]. This was a remarkable proposal, suggesting for the first time that [j] led to palatalisation because of its coronal status. Our view is similar, except that we do not have the independent tiers. However, before we delve into FUL's proposal, we briefly discuss Hall's take on this.

According to Hall (1997), palatals ("alveopalatals" in his terminology) differ from "true" palatals such as German [ç]. His features for these consonants would be as follows.

(27) Hall's features for palatalised consonants

	alveolar/dental	alveopalatal	palatal	palatalised velar	velar
	s	ɕ/ʃ	ç	xʲ	x
[coronal]	+	+			
[dorsal]			+	+	+
[anterior]	+	−			
[back]		−	−	−	+

This differs from the Clements & Hume's feature set:

(28) Features for palatalised consonants in Clements & Hume (1995)

	alveopalatal	palatal	palatalised velar	velar
	ɕ	ç	xʲ	x
CONS	+	+		
[coronal]			+	+
[dorsal]				
VOC	+		+	
[coronal]				

Hall argues that, in his terminology, the features deliberately do not contrast [ç] and [xʲ], because these two sounds never co-occur. The crucial point here is that under Hall's analysis, unlike Clements & Hume's, palatalisation is governed by a feature [+P], which is essentially [−back].

However, as seen above, [−back] would normally be dominated by [dorsal]. Under Hall's analysis, the palatalisation feature [+P] must, therefore, come under both [coronal] and [dorsal]. This is because under his analysis palatal [ç] is [dorsal] but unlike Sagey-Halle's analysis, front vowels and glides are coronal and not dorsal (1997: 79–83). In (29) we reproduce Hall's analysis of a velar and alveolar palatalisation, with velar [x] to [ç] being a regular phenomenon in German.

(29) Palatalisation of [x] > [ç], [s] > [ʃ] according to Hall (1997: 83 (73), 78 (63))

(a)　　　i　　　　　x　　　–>　　i　　　　ç
　　　[place]　　[place]　　　　[place]　　[place]
　　　[+coronal]　[+dorsal]　　　[+coronal]　[+dorsal]
　　　　│　　　　　　　　　　　　　 \　　　 /
　　　[+P]=[−back]　　　　　　　　　　[+P]

(b)　　　s　　　　　i　　　–>　　ʃ　　　　　　　i
　　　[place]　　[place]　　　　[place]　　　　[place]
　　　[+coronal]　[+coronal]　　[+coronal]　　　[+coronal]
　　　　　　　　　│　　　　　　　　 \　　　　　/
　　　　　　　[+P]=[−back]　　　　　　　[+P]

(c)　　　　　[+P]
　　　　　／　　＼
　　　[+coronal]　[+dorsal]

As Hall states, [+P] as [−back] presents an apparent formal problem, because it requires this feature to be located under both [+coronal] and [+dorsal] (1997: 83–84).

(30) Definition of the palatalisation feature [+P] (Hall 1997: 83)
"the segments that are marked [+P] include (a) front vowels like [i e æ], (b) palatoalveolars [ʃ ʒ], (c) alveolopalatals [ɕ ʑ], (d) palatals [ç j], and (e) palatalized segments (e.g. pʲ bʲ tʲ dʲ kʲ gʲ). The property shared by all of these segment types in (a)-(e) is a fronted tongue body (see Sagey 1986: 278)"

Consequently, since front vowels are coronal (like in FUL), Hall's analysis dispenses with the awkwardness of having a dorsal [k] becoming a coronal palatoalveolar in the context of dorsal [i] or [j] via [−back], which too is dominated by dorsal. However, since the palatals are still dorsal (unlike FUL), the [+P] feature has to be dominated by BOTH coronal and dorsal.

Instead of this rather complex analysis, we follow Clements' assumptions that all palatals and palatoalveolars and front vowels and glides are coronal, and thus palatalisation which causes a fronting of velar consonants is an assimilation to a coronal place of articulation and by a coronal. However, as noted above, palatalisation involves also the "backing" of dentals/alveolars [t d] to [tʃ dʒ] or [ʃ ʒ] as well as adding secondary articulations. We turn to this below.

We have argued elsewhere (i) that neither fronted velars and palatals, nor palatalised velar and regular velar in the context of [i] may contrast in any single language (Keating & Lahiri 1993), and (ii) that alveopalatal and palatal stops do not co-occur in the same language (Lahiri & Blumstein 1984). Thus, features for these various coronal consonants as compared to a velar would be as in (31).

(31) Strident, fronted, palatalised, and velar consonants in FUL

		dental/ alveolar	palato- alveolar	palatal	palatalised velar	velar
		s	ɕ/ʃ	ç/c	xʲ/kʲ/c̠	x/k
ART						
	[CORONAL]	√	√	√		
	[DORSAL]				√	√
TH						
	[LOW]	√				
	[HIGH]		√	√	√	

Note that FUL's features for alveopalatal and palatal sounds are the same: if there is a contrast it has to be via [STRIDENT]. In FUL, the palatalisation of velars, as for example [k] → [ç] in German or [k] → [tʃ] in Slavic, would always have to be as follows:

(32) Velar palatalisation in FUL

(a) [k] → [ç]   i   x   →   i   ç
                  VOC   OBSTR   VOC   OBSTR
                             CONTINUANT   CONTINUANT
                  ART TH   ART   ART TH   ART
                  [−] [HIGH] [DOR]   [−] [HIGH]   [−]

(b) [k] → [tʃ]   k   i   →   tʃ
                  OBSTR   SON   OBSTR
                                                 STRIDENT
                  ART   ART TH   ART
                  [DOR]   [−] [HIGH]   [−]

Earlier, in Lahiri & Evers (1991, henceforth L&E), where we permitted dependent features, palatal and palatoalveolar consonants were distinguished by [−anterior]. Thus, the various coronal consonants were distinguished as follows:

(33) Differentiating front and back vowels and consonants (A = Articulators, TP = Tongue Position, αF = mnemonic of different values for high and low] (adapted from L&E, 90, 11)

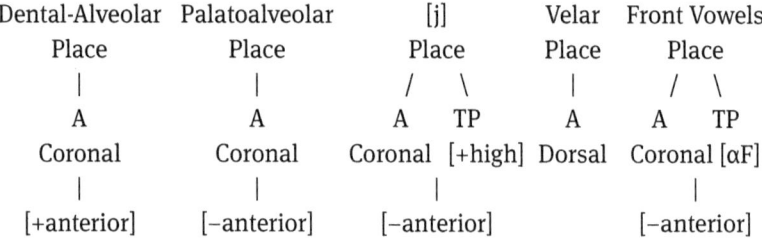

Despite allowing both binary features and dependency, in L&E palatalisation of velars was a change of dorsal to coronal and crucially [+high] and not [−anterior]. However, [±anterior] played a crucial role in converting dental-alveolar consonants into palatoalveolars:

(34) L&E (a) velar palatalisation vs. (b) dental palatalisation

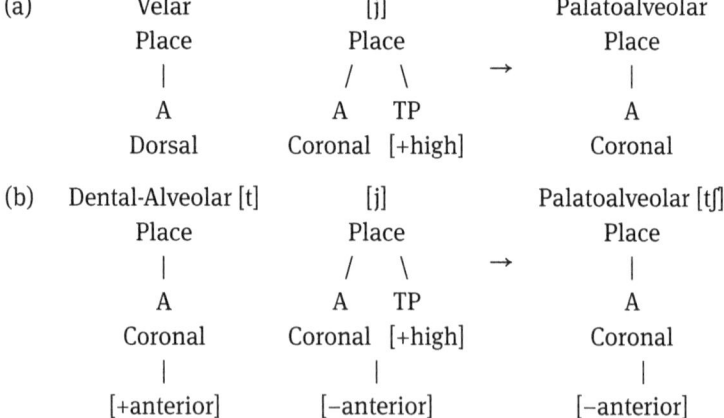

We believe this was not the correct approach. In the FUL model, Lahiri & Reetz (2010) argued that the contrasts enabled by [±anterior] and [±distributed] were adequately dealt with by TONGUE HEIGHT [HIGH] & [LOW] features along with [ATR] and [RTR]. Within FUL, a move from dental to palatoalveolar or palatal would not be a change in main articulators. It would be more of a change to stridency lead by a combination of the feature [HIGH] and [CORONAL], both enhancing high frequency energy. Thus, the usual dental/alveolar change can lead to [ʃ] or [tʃ], i.e., a change to fricative or an affricate, both of which must be [STRIDENT]. Stridency comes as a concomitant change because, as argued earlier in Lahiri & Blumstein (1984), the palatoalveolar place of articulation cannot be articulated without fricativisation. Clements (1986, 2001) came to the same conclusion that there is concomitant affrication. Thus, dental palatalisation would be formalised as follows:

(35) Dental palatalisation in FUL

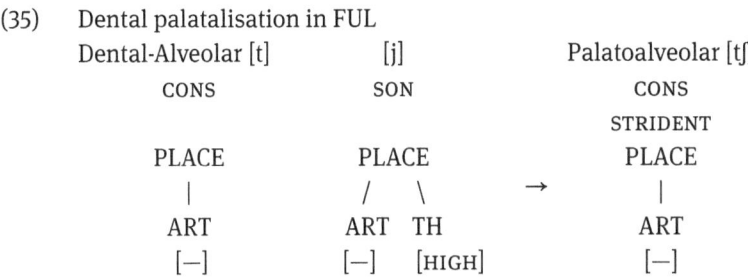

What about secondary articulations involving palatalisation? We will argue that these do not involve any ARTICULATOR feature, but only the feature [HIGH].

For L&E, secondary palatalisations were NOT caused by a change of any ARTICULATOR feature but by height features. In FUL, the palatalised versions of all places of articulation likewise have a non-redundant [HIGH].

(36) Palatalised /k/ in FUL

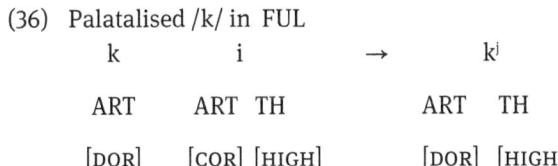

The contrast for other palatalised consonants as in the Finno-Ugric language Ter Lapp would also be marked by [HIGH]:

(37) Palatalised and non-palatalised consonants
       p   pʲ   v   vʲ
    [LAB] [LAB] [HIGH] [LAB] [LAB] [HIGH]

An analysis of the Dutch diminutive (Trommelen 1984; Gussenhoven & Jacobs 2011, partially also discussed in L&E) sheds more light on palatalisation where alveolars become palatoalveolars. Labials and velars have a secondary articulation with devoiced [j].

(38) Dutch diminutives: underlying form /tjə/ (following Gussenhoven & Jacobs):

(a) [t]-deletion + [jə]
    i.   lɑp   lɑpʲə   'rag'
    ii.   buk   bukʲə   'book'

(b) place assimilation and [jə]
    iii.   raːm   raːmpʲə   'window'
    iv.   koːniŋ   koːniŋkʲə   'king'

(c) [t]-deletion & palatalisation leading to [c], [ʃ]
    v.   pɑs   pɑʃə   'step'
    vi.   faːs   faːʃə   'vase'
    vii.   fut   fucə   'foot'
    viii.   lint   liɲcə   'ribbon'
    ix.   fœyst   fœyʃə   'fist'

(d) palatalisation
    x.   zeː   zeːcə   'sea'
    xi.   mɑːn   mɑːɲcə   'moon'
    xii.   paːl   paːlcə   'post'
    xiii.   oːr   oːrcə   'ear'

(e) degemination of [t] in coda cluster
    xiv.   kaft   kafʲə   'book-cover'
    xv.   bɔχt   bɔχʲə   'bend'

(f) [ə] insertion and palatalisation
    xvi.   bɔm   bɔməcə   'bomb'
    xvii.   pɑn   pɑnəcə   'pot'
    xviii.   bɑl   bɑləcə   'ball'

The underlying form of the diminutive is assumed to have a coronal stop [t] for two reasons. First, when the stem is disyllabic or contains a long vowel and ends in a non-coronal sonorant such as [m] or [ŋ], the underlying [t] assimilates in place, resulting in forms such as (38b iii, iv). Second, when the stem contains a short vowel followed by a sonorant (38f), an [ə] is inserted and the [t] becomes a palatalised stop [c]. Palatalisation is more obvious in (38c) and (38d). The [t] of the diminutive is deleted after a stem ending in an obstruent (38a). In (38c), after [t] is deleted, the stem-final coronal obstruent ([s] or [t]) becomes [ʃ] or [c] respectively. The examples in (xii) and (xiii) are particularly interesting because when there is a sequence of two [t]s, one deletes and the remaining palatalises.

Gussenhoven & Jacobs (2011, 2017) state that the underlying form is /tjə/ and the palatalised stop [c] is defined as [−anterior, −distributed] stop.[8] For our purposes, since both /t/ and /j/ are placeless, we could simply assume that there is only a CV morpheme. L&V analysed the diminutive suffix in a similar fashion with an empty obstruent root followed by a floating [−anterior] [+high] segment unspecified for any other feature and a schwa.

(39) Dutch diminutive suffix in L&E (with [±anterior]; R obst = ROOT [OBSTRUENT])
R obst   Place   ə (schwa)

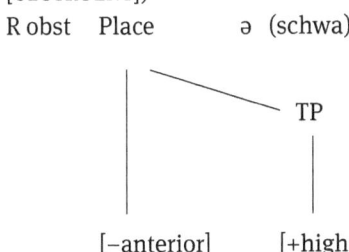

[−anterior]   [+high]

However, given that all palatalised segments in FUL are represented by the ARTICULATOR node with a [HIGH] under TONGUE HEIGHT, we could represent the diminutive morpheme as in (40), with the features of the relevant consonants in (41).

(40) Dutch diminutive morpheme in FUL
```
     OBSTR    CONS    VOC
       |      / \      |
      ART   ART  TH   [ə]
      [−]       [HIGH]
```

---

8 L&E assumed that the palatalisation of [t] lead to an affricate [tʃ]. This was an incorrect assumption, as Carlos Gussenhoven points out, because it ought to be more like [c], which is a stop. However, the second author of L&E, Vincent Evers, finds that the diminutive of *plaats* 'place' ends up as [plaːtʃə] and is, thus, not very different from the diminutive of *plaat* 'plate'. What is important here is that for FUL, both are [CORONAL], differing in affrication.

Palatalisation for the diminutive involves [s] becoming [ʃ] and [t] becoming [c]. For FUL, both involve adding [HIGH]. To illustrate, we show the features of the relevant consonants in Dutch.

(41) Features of consonants involved in palatalisation in the Dutch diminutive

			t	s	ʃ	c	j
ROOT							
	[OBSTRUENT]		√	√	√	√	
	[SONORANT]						√
	[CONTINUANT]			√	√		
ARTICULATOR							
	[CORONAL]		√		√	√	
TONGUE HEIGHT							
	[HIGH]				√	√	√

In (42) we state the rules which are required to obtain the diminutive forms. The point we would like to make here is that the high front glide [j] which is part of the diminutive morpheme has the feature [HIGH] which in turn requires the obstruents [t s] to become [c ʃ] respectively. Since ALL consonants in question are [CORONAL], there is nothing else that is required. The only other relevant process is place assimilation where the place-underspecified [t] acquires the place of the final consonant in words like [raːmpʲə] from /raːm – tjə/. Sample derivations are added in (43).

(42) Diminutive formation in FUL
(i)   [ə] insertion: V [SONORANT] — DIMINUTIVE suffix
(ii) [t] deletion. [OBSTRUENT]$_{\text{DIMINUTIVE}}$ > Ø/ [OBSTRUENT] —
(iii) PLACE ASSIMILATION: spread specified features to the ARTICULATOR node
(iv) PALATALISATION: spread feature [HIGH], delete feature [CONS]

(43)   Sample derivations (the rule numbers refer to those in (42))

	lint – tjə	raːm – tjə	fut – tjə	faːs – tje	bɔm – tjə
(i)	—	—	—	—	bɔmə - tjə
(ii)	lint – Øjə	—	fut – Øjə	faːs – Øje	bɔmə - tjə
(iii)	—	raːmpjə	—	—	—
(iv)	lincə	—	fucə	faːʃə	bɔməcə
Output	lincə	raːmpə	fucə	faːʃə	bɔməcə

As for secondary palatalisation in forms such as [rɔkʲə] 'skirt-DIM', the crucial point we have made is that there is no real necessity to mark palatalised segments with special sets of features or as complex segments. Secondary palatalisation need not involve a change in place; thus, palatalised [k], which is [kʲ], would be represented as as ART[DORSAL], TH[HIGH], without change of ARTICULATOR. But dental consonants can change place of articulation. Palatalised dentals often undergo a change of place of articulation such as the Dutch [t] becoming [c]. Under our conception this can happen only if the context includes a high front vowel or a glide, not any front vowel. The general process of assimilation invoves the spreading of [HIGH]. Palatalised coronal stops can often also become strident affricates or fricatives because a combination of [CORONAL] and [HIGH] would provide a greater energy in the higher frequencies, a characteristic of strident segments. The addition of [STRIDENT] comes as a "free ride" since the unmarked articulation of all obstruents in the palatoalveolar region is with stridency (Lahiri & Blumstein 1984: 142).[9]

Second, it has been claimed that non-high front vowels can trigger secondary palatalisation for example in Nupe and Kinyarwanda (Sagey 1986: 209–218, 227–240). In these languages, secondary palatalisation is triggered not only by [i], but also by [e]. As in other languages, these consonants are phonetically produced by an offglide. We would argue (as in L&E, p. 95) that in these cases this glide could also be present phonologically as an onglide of the vowel such that [e] would be underlyingly [je]. If this is the case, it would predict that in the course of time the [j] triggering the palatalisation would be absorbed by the vowel and the consonant survives with a single major ARTICULATOR plus a TONGUE HEIGHT feature [HIGH]. This can be reflected in the orthography as in Russian, where the palatalisation mark of the consonant rests on the following vowel. Note that the fronting of velars is a matter of place change whereby a [DORSAL] [k] becomes a [CORONAL] consonant. Here, the context need not always be a high front vowel, but it could be any front vowel: it is [CORONAL] status that matters. However, as always, [i] and [j] are favoured.

5 Morphophonological alternation and language-specific underspecification

FUL accepts only monovalent and privative features along with underspecification of [CORONAL] and [PLOSIVE]. Consequently, minus features are not allowed. Since the mid to late eighties, the main articulator features LABIAL, CORONAL,

---

9 This comment has also been made by many phonologists including Sagey as well as in SPE.

DORSAL have been assumed to be monovalent. The question we ask is whether it is possible to account for complex analyses which may involve language-specific underspecification. This section is based on Hyman's analysis of vowel harmony in Kàlɔ̀ŋ, and what we would like to show is that despite the sparse nature of the FUL system, the complex set of alternations involving both specified and underspecified place features for vowels can be accounted for.

In Hyman's analysis of Kàlɔ̀ŋ, a Mbam language (Niger-Congo) of Cameroon, the stem-affix alternations are governed by a limited set of features, and there are three types of harmony: ATR, FRONT, and ROUND harmony. First, we examine the vowel /a/ and its realisations in different contexts. These realisations are summarised in (44).

(44) Realisations of affix /a/ adapted from Hyman (2003: 90 (7))[10]

	Prefix /a-/		Root Vowel		Suffix /-a/		
(i)	e-		i	u	-e		a → ə → e /i a → ə → e /u
(ii)	e-	o-	e	o	-e	-o	a → e /e a → o / o
(iii)	ɛ-	ɔ-	ɛ	ɔ	-ɛ	-ɔ	a → ɛ / ɛ a → ɔ / ɔ
(iv)	a-		a		-a		/a/ remains unchanged

The affix /a/ remains unchanged when the root also contains /a/ (iv). When the root has a high vowel, /a/ becomes /e/ (i), while it takes on the features of the root if they contain mid vowels /e ɛ o ɔ/.

The underlying features of the relevant vowels in Hyman's analysis are given in (45).

(45) Kàlɔ̀ŋ underlying features (Hyman 2003: 94)

	i	u	e	o	ɛ	ɔ	a	ə [e]
ATR	x	x	x	x				x
FRONT	x		x		x			
ROUND		x		x		x		
OPEN			x	x	x	x	x	x

---

10 When the root has the "abstract" vowels /I U/, which in turn surface as [i~e] or [u~ɔ], the suffix remains /a/. Our focus is not on the abstract vowels, which as Hyman shows are entirely transparent and predictable, but on the first three contexts.

Like Dresher and Clements, Hyman invokes the notion of "activity" and argues that only the "active" four features that are necessary to account for the data should be relevant. Using a system like that of Clements, ATR and OPEN fall under a single APERTURE node. The vowel [ə] does not surface, but is assumed to be the intermediate fronted vowel of /a/ when the root has a high vowel /i u/.

Examples for the first three harmony cases are given in (46).

(46) Alternations with the RECENT PAST prefix /a/ (adapted from Hyman 2003: 93 (14); the English glosses are ours)

    a. root /i u/
        ù-sà-tínìt > ù-sè-tínìt il a couru he ran/he has run
        ù-sà-tûm > ù-sè-tûm il a commencé he started/he has started

    b. root /e ɛ o ɔ/
        ù-sà-télèmit > ù-sè-télèmit il s'est levé he got up/he has got up
        ù-sà-nɛ́ŋɛ̀ > ù-sɛ̀-nɛ́ŋɛ̀ il a nagé he swam/he has swum
        ù-sà-yòsòn > ù-sò-yòsòn il a regardé he watched/he has watched
        ù-sà-tɔ́ŋɔ̀ > ù-sɔ̀-tɔ́ŋɔ̀ il a chanté he sang/he has sung

    c. ù-sà-sàŋâ > ù-sà-sàŋâ il a mangé he ate/he has eaten

The features ATR, FRONT, and ROUND participate actively in the harmony process and the last two are "parasitic" on FRONT (Hyman 2003: 90). Our interest here is in the vowel /a/, which changes to [e] not only in the context of /i/, but also in the context of /u/ where, in a parallel scenario, it ought to change to [o]. Hyman argues that "the fronting of /a/ under ATR harmony is a secondary development, the primary one being to lower its F1". That is, /a/ "first converts to a [+ATR] central vowel, here symbolised as schwa", which in turn becomes /e/ (44(i)). Why should this be so in a perfectly regulated harmony system? Why does the spreading of ATR ignore the place features for the high vowels? We turn to FUL for an answer. (47), including a tree diagram representation, gives the features that FUL would assign on universal principles; note that CORONAL remains underspecified.

(47) Kàlɔŋ vowels in FUL: Underlying representation (shading indicates underspecification)

	i	u	e	o	ɛ	ɔ	a
PLACE	•	•	•	•	•	•	•
ARTICULATOR	•	•	•	•	•	•	
CORONAL	√		√		√		
LABIAL		√		√		√	
TONGUE ROOT	•	•	•	•	•	•	•
ATR	√	√	√	√			
TONGUE HEIGHT	•	•	•	•	•	•	•
LOW				√	√	√	√

```
    /i/         /u/         /e/         /o/         /ɛ/         /ɔ/         /a/
   PLACE       PLACE       PLACE       PLACE       PLACE       PLACE       PLACE
   /|\         /|\         /|\         /|\         /|\         /|\          /\
ART TR TH   ART TR TH   ART TR TH   ART TR TH   ART TR TH   ART TR TH      TR TH
 |  |  |     |  |  |     |  |  |     |  |  |     |  |  |     |  |  |        |  |
 — ATR —    LAB ATR —   — ATR LOW   LAB ATR LOW  — LOW      LAB — LOW       — LOW
```

A clear distinction needs to be made between the underspecified CORONAL and the lack of an ARTICULATOR node. As always, CORONAL is not specified in the representation, but if the vowel has an ARTICULATOR node, it will get the feature on the surface by a fill-in rule. Thus, /a/ will not get a CORONAL specification, but /i e ɛ/ will. A futher lack of feature specification involves TONGUE HEIGHT (TH) as well as TONGUE ROOT (TR) features: /i u/ are not specified for height, but they do have the TH node and /ɛ ɔ a/ are not specified for TR. The feature filling rules, which determine the surface features, are as follows:

(48) Surface feature filling rules
   (i) LABIAL ⇒ DORSAL; any surface LABIAL vowel will get a DORSAL feature
   (ii) Unfilled ARTICULATOR nodes will be assigned CORONAL; i.e., /i e ɛ/ will be assigned CORONAL
   (iii) Unfilled TONGUE ROOT nodes will be assigned RTR; i.e., /ɛ, ɔ, a/ will be assigned RTR

Thus, /a/ has the feature LOW without precise place features suggesting that phonetically it can be in between.

Under this representational hypothesis, it is clear why, when ATR spreads from /i u/, the suffix /a/ will automatically become /e/: /a/ and /e/ share the feature [LOW] and nothing else. Thus, spreading [ATR] from /i, u/ to /a/ turns it into /e/. The difference between /a/ and /e/ is that /a/ does not have an ARTIC-ULATOR node. This gets filled in on the surface where it will then emerge as /e/ since ATR has spread. Consequently, unlike in Hyman's analysis, /a/ > [e] does not require an intermediate analysis which produces [ə] (49i). The harmony processes for high and mid vowels look different because of the mismatch between the TH features. These are spelt out with relevant examples below.

(49) Harmony processes
 (a) ATR harmony: Mismatching TH between root and suffix

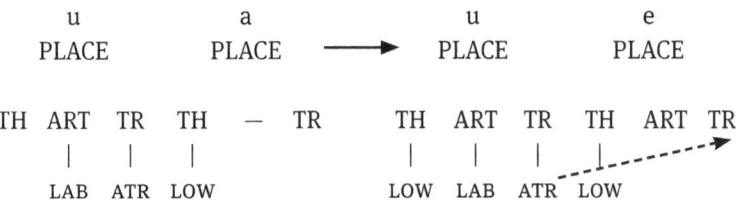

 (b) ARTICULATOR and ATR spreading: Matching TH between root and suffix

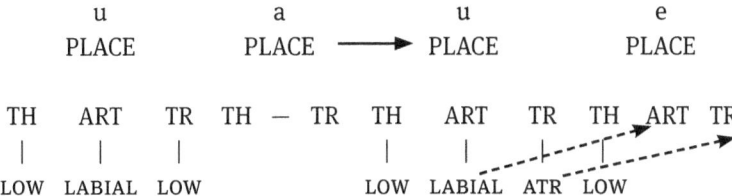

Hyman mentions another interesting harmony process that includes two different underlying vowels which sometimes surface as [i u] but not always:

(50) /i, u/ vs. /I, U/ (cf. Hyman, (5))

Roots /I, U/ with /i~ɛ, u~ɔ/ in open and closed syllables

closed σ	open σ – suffix /-a/	
/lÍk/ kù-lêk	kù-lík-à	'désirer'
		*kù-lík-è (no ATR harmony for final /a/)
/lɛ̀k/ kù-lêk	kù-lɛ́k-ɛ̀	'lecher'
		final /a/ assimilates to root
/lÙk/ kù-lɔ̀k	kù-lùk-à	'nommer'
		*kù-lùk-è (no ATR harmony for final /a/)
/lɔ̀k/ kù-lɔ̀k	kù-lɔ́k-ɔ̀	'abîmer'
		final /a/ assimilates to root

Underlying /I U/ are realised as /ɛ ɔ/ in closed syllables and as /i u/ in open syllables. With the suffix /-a/, underlying /I U/ are not realised as *kù-lík-è and *kù-lùk-è, since underlying /a/ does not undergo ATR harmony, but underlying /ɛ ɔ/ remain in open syllables and /a/ assimilates to them. Consequently, Hyman analyses the vowels /I U/ as having only the features FRONT and ROUND; neither ATR nor OPEN are specified, which accounts for several distributions:

(51) Hyman's analysis of /I, U/ compared with /i u/

	i	u	I	U
ATR	x	x		
FRONT	x		x	
ROUND		x		x
OPEN				

- Each V has one feature specification
- /I U/ acquire ATR in open syllables, merging with /i u/
- /I U/ acquire OPEN in closed syllables, merging with /ɛ ɔ/
- The aspectual suffix /-a/ does not undergo ATR harmony with these root vowels

Lack of ATR and OPEN, then, ensue in the lack of harmony alternations.

(52) Consequences of the analysis

    (a) /I, U/ do not condition ATR harmony   /I, U/ lack ATR
    (b) /I/ never conditions FRONT harmony   /I/ lacks the OPEN feature
    (c) /U/ never conditions ROUND harmony   /U/ lacks the OPEN feature
    (d) /I, U/ become [i, u] by ATR harmony   /I, U/ differ from /i, u/ only in ATR
    (e) /I, U/ are transparent to FRONT/ROUND harmony   /I, U/ lack the OPEN feature

Is it possible to account for this complex situation in FUL, where not only CORONAL is underspecified, but the vowels /I U/ must lack height as well as ATR features? Our proposal is outlined in (53).

(53) FUL features for all vowels

	i	u	e	o	ɛ	ɔ	a	I	U
PLACE	•	•	•	•	•	•	•	•	•
ARTICULATOR	•	•	•	•	•	•		•	•
CORONAL	√		√		√		√		
LABIAL		√		√		√			√
TONGUE ROOT	•	•	•	•	•	•	•	•	•
ATR	√	√	√	√					
TONGUE HEIGHT	•	•	•	•	•	•	•	•	•
LOW			√	√	√	√	√		

Tree diagrams for /I U/ and their variants /i u ɛ ɔ/ and suffixal /a/

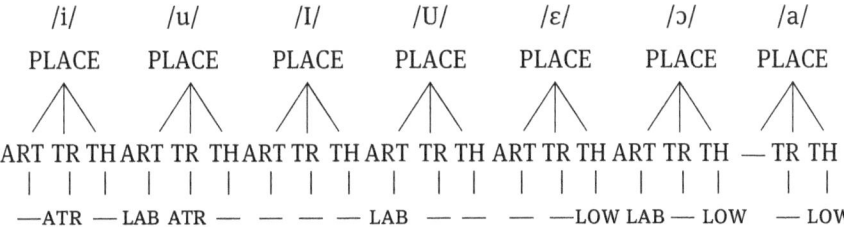

Thus, in closed syllables, the addition of [LOW] for unspecified TH of /I U/ would give /ɛ ɔ/, while in open syllables they would receive the feature [ATR].

(54) Surface variants of /I U/
    closed syll open syll
    /lÍk/   kù-lêk   kù-lík-à
    [–] →   add LOW add ATR

    /lÙk/   kù-lɔ̂k   kù-lùk-à
    [LAB] →   add LOW add ATR
              [LAB, LOW] [LAB, ATR]

We have seen, then, that the underspecification of [CORONAL] does not prevent FUL from accounting for such complex patterns as vowel harmony in Kàlɔ̀ŋ in a principled way. What is additionally required here is the lack of specification of ATR and OPEN (i.e., height) features, not a problem in the FUL framework: the raising and fronting of /a/ to [e] can then be achieved without an intermediate step.

6 Moving on

To sum up, FUL provides a set of monovalent features, along with underspecification of [CORONAL] and [PLOSIVE], which are intended to be universal. Thus, binary features like [±high] or [±voice] are not acceptable and the automatic consequence is that negative features cannot form natural classes. However, it is possible to refer to a node which does not contain a fully specified feature. Thus, ARTICULATOR remains empty for CORONAL, which gets filled in on the surface. Rules like English aspiration of voiceless consonants (under the assumption that underlying stops are unaspirated) could be realised as below:

(55) Aspiration in English (adding SPREAD GLOTTIS)

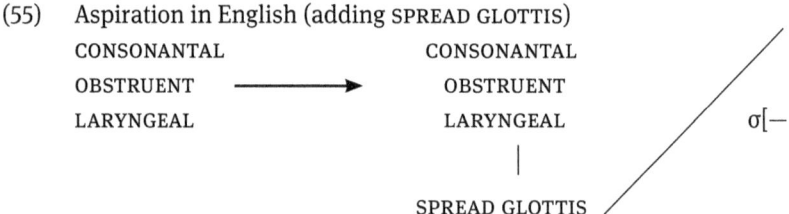

The rule of aspiration says that when the LARYNGEAL node is "empty" and does not contain either SPREAD GLOTTIS or VOICE, the feature SPREAD GLOTTIS would be added. When, on the other hand, the feature VOICE is part of the LARYNGEAL node, then SPREAD GLOTTIS would not be added. Thus, in a word like /pɪn/, the initial consonant has no laryngeal feature and acquires SPREAD GLOTTIS in syllable-initial position, but since the LARYNGEAL node for /b/ (in words like /bɪn/) are already specified with the feature VOICE, no other feature can be added. Consequently, /b/ remains without aspiration.

In fleshing out a model like FUL, a host of further questions need to be tackled. We will only broach three here: they are ones where significant progress has been or is being made. First, since unlike contrastive theories that assume activation we assume that universal features are acquired first and always establish a contrast, then how do the other features become part of the system? Second, if CORONAL and PLOSIVE are always underspecified, then they must always be available in natural languages; but are they? Finally, we have claimed that underspecification has consequences for processing: but to what extent do we have evidence supporting this?

With respect to **acquisition**, if CORONAL must always be present, then the first cut is CORONAL vs. something else. Following Ghini (2001a), we maintain that PLACE-first is a universal principle. The acquisition literature suggests that LABIAL is produced first (cf. Jakobson 1941; Levelt 1995; Fikkert & Levelt 2008). Fikkert & Levelt find that words are undifferentiated with respect to features and the word node itself has LABIAL, with vowels and consonants sharing the same feature. Our assumption is that CORONAL is underspecified but present, and in fact the LABIAL vs. CORONAL contrast is the first one to be manifest on the surface. We also assume that all languages have PLOSIVES – not necessarily all places of articulation, but at least one. This tallies with Hyman (2008) who argues that two of the valid universals about phonological inventories are that all have oral stops and all have coronals. But CORONAL phonemes need not be PLOSIVES; they could be CONTINUANT for instance. Thus, in acquisition, we would first find a contrast of underspecified CORONAL vs. some other ARTICULATOR (in all probability LABIAL) and PLOSIVE vs. probably CONTINUANT. Recall that FUL assumes that vowels and consonants share PLACE. Thus, for vowels as well, the first cut is probably CORONAL vs. LABIAL. It could be the case that the LABIAL vowels are also DORSAL.

We have also suggested that in terms of TONGUE HEIGHT, [LOW] is acquired first. But we do not believe that this needs to be underspecified universally, because a language might only have one vowel, with no necessity to specify any height contrast. Thus, other features are built very much on the basis of contrast. The question is whether contrasts depend entirely on "activity" or on distribution. The answer is probably both. Initially, infants are not going to be exposed to lots of alternations which would conclusively establish activity. However, distribution is something they inevitably enounter right away.

Challenging the assumption of the **universality** of coronals, Blevins (2009) has suggested that Northwest Mekeo lacks CORONAL obstruents, though it may acquire them via language contact. All Mekeo dialects, however, have coronal sonorants; /l/ occurs in other Mekeo dialects and Northwest Mekeo itself has a palatal glide /y/ (Blevins' notation) which alternates with /ɛ/. Blevins argues that /l/ can be seen as primarily lateral with redundant coronal specification. That is not an assumption made by FUL, where PLACE is primary. Consequently, it is not the case that this universal "bites the dust": CORONAL is very much present even in Northwest Mekeo, albeit perhaps not in obstruents. In Blevins' own terms, CORONAL appears on the surface via assimilation, and with /i/.

(56) Palatalisation in Mekeo dialects (Blevins 2009: 267; combining her examples (6) and (7))

Northwest Mekeo	/g/ → [dʑʲ] / _ i	[gina][11]
West Mekeo	/g/ → [dʑʲ, dʒ] / _ i	[dʒina]
North Mekeo	/k/ → [tsʲ, dʒ] / _ i	[tʃina]
East Mekeo	/k/ → [tsʲ, tʃ] / _ i (optional)	[kina]
		'sun, day'

---

[11] Blevins provides these examples. If, however, /g/ > [dʒ] in Northwest Mekeo in the context of /i/ it is not obvious to us where the example *gina* comes from.

This fits in with FUL's assumptions perfectly. In FUL /i/ is CORONAL (underspecified, with only the ARTICULATOR node), and in its context, as we have seen earlier for palatalisation, DORSAL consonants will lose their feature. Our analysis is in (57).

(57) Mekeo palatalisation

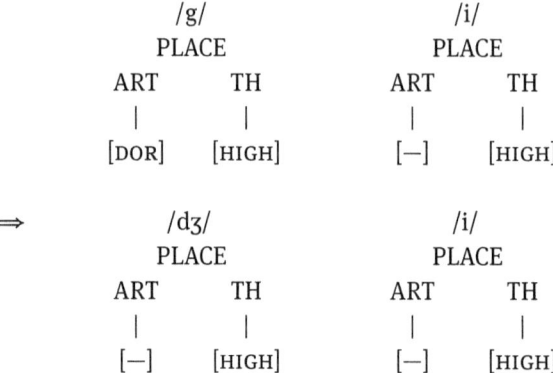

Whether the result is an affricate or is pronounced with a palatalised affricate is a matter of phonetic implementation. The crucial point is that /g/ loses its DORSAL feature in the CONTEXT of a CORONAL underspecified HIGH vowel.

Finally, in the FUL approach, underspecification in representations is intended to have consequences for **processing**. What is the evidence? We have shown in several experimental studies that CORONAL underspecifiation predicts asymmetries. For example, in an MMN (mismatch negativity) paradigm in an EEG experiment in German, when listeners were saturated with the nonsense syllable [egi] (played several times) and were then provided with a deviant stimulus [edi], the surface coronal feature from /d/ was found to mismatch with the DORSAL representation of /g/, triggering a high negative peak. However, the negative peak was significantly lower when the presentation of stimuli was reversed: when [edi] was the standard (surface CORONAL, mapping onto an underspecified representation) and was followed by deviant [egi], then the surface DORSAL was tolerated by the underspecified representation. The same asymmetric pattern is found with underspecified [PLOSIVE] and specified [NASAL]. This is illustrated in (58) and (59).

(58) CORONAL~DORSAL asymmetry in MMN (Cornell et al. 2013; Lahiri 2012; Lahiri & Kotzor 2017)

| Acoustic stimulus (standard) | [edi] CORONAL | Representation [—] *underspecified* |
| Acoustic stimulus (deviant) | [egi] DORSAL | NO-MISMATCH = low MMN |

| Acoustic stimulus (standard) | [edi] DORSAL | Representation [DORSAL] |
| Acoustic stimulus (deviant) | [edi] CORONAL | MISMATCH = higher MMN |

(59) PLOSIVE~NASAL asymmetry in MMN (Cornell et al. 2013; Lahiri 2015; Lahiri & Kotzor 2017)

Acoustic stimulus (standard)	[edi] PLOSIVE	Representation [—] *underspecified*
Acoustic stimulus (deviant)	[eni] NASAL	NO-MISMATCH = lower MMN
Acoustic stimulus (standard)	[eni] NASAL	Representation [NASAL]
Acoustic stimulus (deviant)	[edi] PLOSIVE	MISMATCH = higher MMN

Aymmetries have also been observed in several other experimental designs such as lexical decision tasks with semantic priming (Roberts et al. 2013; Lahiri & Reetz 2010; Eulitz & Lahiri 2004).[12]

Typologically, FUL's general goal is to define and regulate a set of features which can cover all possible contrasts and alternations in the languages of the world; the ability to account for acquisition and processing are important added bonuses. Our focus here was on the CORONAL node where the largest set of contrasts needs to be accommodated; but, naturally, other contrasts, such as pharyngeal ones coming under the RADICAL node, would equally be taken care of along similar lines. Insofar as contrasts and alternations, however crosslinguistically diverse, fall into just those patterns that are dictated by a particular theoretical model, FUL, and not into any others conceivable, fundamental unity is revealed behind diversity.

---

[12] Hybrid models which allow both abstract and episodic representations (Pierrehumbert 2016) are hard to test. FUL does not deny that native listeners are especially sensitive to familiar voices; surely one's mother's voice is easier to identify in a noisy environment than the voice of a salesperson. Nor do we disregard the fact that different dialects can cause hiccups in processing or that hearing an unfamiliar dialect for many days at a time leads to familiarisation. Nevertheless, we believe that individual lexical representations are abstract and do not contain details of individual voices or dialects. Certainly representations can change and become more flexible, but our claim is that basic contrasts and feature representations along with concomitant processing implications are universal.

Acknowledgement: This work was partially supported by the ERC Advanced Research Grant MORPHON 695481, PI Aditi Lahiri.

References

Archangeli, Diana. 1988. Aspects of underspecification theory. *Phonology* 5. 183–207.

Bhat, D. N. S. 1978. A general study of palatalization. In Joseph H. Greenberg, Charles A. Ferguson, & Edith Moravcsik (eds.), *Universals of language, vol. 2: Phonology*, 47–92. Stanford: Stanford University Press.

Blumstein, Sheila & Kenneth Stevens. 1980. Perceptual invariance and onset spectra for stop consonants in different vowel environments. *Journal of the Acoustical Society of America* 67. 648–662.

Blevins, Juliette. 2009. Another universal bites the dust: Northwest Mekeo lacks coronal phonemes. *Oceanic Linguistics* 48. 264–273.

Calabrese, Andrea. 1995. A constraint-based theory of phonological markedness and simplification procedures. *Linguistic Inquiry* 26. 373–463.

Chomsky, Noam & Morris Halle. 1968. *The sound pattern of English*. New York: Harper & Row.

Clements, George N. 1985. The geometry of phonological features. *Phonology Yearbook* 2. 225–252.

Clements, G. Nick. 1989. A unified set of features for consonants and vowels. Unpublished, Cornell University, Ithaca, NY.

Clements, G. Nick. 2001. Representational economy in constraint-based phonology. In Hall (ed.) 2001, 71–146.

Clements, George N. & Elizabeth V. Hume. 1995. The internal organization of speech sounds. In John A. Goldsmith (ed.), *The handbook of phonological theory*, 245–306. Oxford: Blackwell.

Compton, Richard & B. Elan Dresher. 2011. Palatalization and "strong *i*" across Inuit dialects. *Canadian Journal of Linguistics* 56. 203–228.

Cornell, Sonia A., Carsten Eulitz, & Aditi Lahiri. 2013. Inequality across consonantal contrasts in speech perception: Evidence from mismatch negativity. *Journal of Experimental Psychology: Human Perception and Performance* 39. 757–772.

Dresher, B. Elan. 2009. *The contrastive hierarchy in phonology*. Cambridge: Cambridge University Press.

Eulitz, Carsten & Aditi Lahiri. 2004. Neurobiological evidence for abstract phonological representations in the mental lexicon during speech recognition. *Journal of Cognitive Neuroscience* 16. 577–583.

Fikkert, Paula & Clara Levelt. 2008. How does Place fall into place? The lexicon and emergent constraints. In Peter Avery, B. Elan Dresher, & Keren Rice (eds.), *Contrast in phonology: Theory, perception, acquisition*, 231–270. Berlin: Mouton de Gruyter.

Ghini, Mirco. 2001a. *Asymmetries in the phonology of Miogliola*. Berlin: Mouton de Gruyter.

Ghini, Mirco. 2001b. Place of articulation first. In Hall (ed.) 2001, 71–146.

Gussenhoven, Carlos & Haike Jacobs. 2011. *Understanding phonology*. 3rd edn 2017. London: Hodder Education.

Hall, T. Alan. 1997. *The phonology of coronals*. Amsterdam: Benjamins.

Hall, T. Alan (ed.). 2001. *Distinctive feature theory*. Berlin: Mouton de Gruyter.

Halle, Morris, Bert Vaux, & Andrew Wolfe. 2000. On feature spreading and the representation of place of articulation. *Linguistic Inquiry* 31. 387–444.

Hyman, Larry M. 2003. "Abstract" vowel harmony in Kàlɔ̀ŋ: A system-driven account. In Patrick Sauzet & Anne Zribi-Hertz (eds.) *Typologie des langues d'Afrique et universaux de la grammaire*, vol. 1, 85–112. Paris: L'Harmattan.

Hyman, Larry M. 2008. Universals in phonology. *The Linguistic Review* 25. 83–137.

Jakobson, Roman. 1941. *Kindersprache, Aphasie und allgemeine Lautgesetze*. Uppsala: Almqvist & Wiksell.

Jakobson, Roman, Gunnar Fant, & Morris Halle. 1952. *Preliminaries to speech analysis: The distinctive features and their correlates* (Technical Report No. 13). Cambridge, MA: MIT, Acoustics Laboratory.

Jakobson, Roman & Morris Halle. 1956. *Fundamentals of language*. The Hague: Mouton.

Kaplan, Lawrence D. 1981. *Phonological issus in North Alaskan Inupiaq*. Fairbanks: Alaska Native Language Center.

Keating, Patricia & Aditi Lahiri. 1993. Fronted velars, palatalized velars, and palatals. *Phonetica* 50. 73–101.

Kotzor, Sandra, Allison Wetterlin, & Aditi Lahiri. 2017. Symmetry or asymmetry: Evidence for underspecification in the mental lexicon. In Aditi Lahiri & Sandra Kotzor (eds.), *The speech processing lexicon*, 85–106. Berlin: De Gruyter Mouton.

Lahiri, Aditi. 2000. Hierarchical restructuring in the creation of verbal morphology in Bengali and Germanic: Evidence from phonology. In Aditi Lahiri (ed.), *Analogy and markedness: Principles of change in phonology and morphology*, 71–123. Berlin: Mouton de Gruyter, paperback 2003.

Lahiri, Aditi. 2012. Asymmetric phonological representations of words in the mental lexicon. In Abigail C. Cohn, Cécile Fougeron, & Marie Huffman (eds.), *The Oxford handbook of laboratory phonology*, 146–161. Oxford: Oxford University Press.

Lahiri, Aditi & Sheila E. Blumstein. 1984. A re-evaluation of the feature 'coronal'. *Journal of Phonetics* 12. 133–145.

Lahiri, Aditi & Vincent Evers. 1991. Palatalization and coronality. In Paradis & Prunet (eds.) 1991, 79–100.

Lahiri, Aditi, Letitia Gewirth, & Sheila E. Blumstein. 1984. A reconsideration of acoustic invariance for place of articulation in diffuse stop consonants: Evidence from a cross-language study. *Journal of the Acoustical Society of America* 76. 391–404.

Lahiri, Aditi & Henning Reetz. 2002. Underspecified recognition. In Carlos Gussenhoven & Natasha Warner (eds.), *Labphon 7*, 637–676. Berlin: Mouton de Gruyter.

Lahiri, Aditi & Henning Reetz. 2010. Distinctive features: Phonological underspecification in representation and processing. *Journal of Phonetics* 28. 44–59.

Levelt, Clara. 1995. Segmental structure of early words: Articulatory frames or phonological constraints. In Eve V. Clark (ed.), *The Proceedings of the Twenty-seventh Annual Child Language Research Forum*, 19–27. Stanford: CSLI.

McCarthy, John. 1988. Feature geometry and dependency: A review. *Phonetica* 43. 84–108.

Mohanan, K. P. 1993. Fields of attraction in phonology. In John Goldsmith (ed.), *The last phonological rule: Reflections on constraints and derivations*, 61–116. Chicago: University of Chicago Press.

Mohanan, K. P. & Tara Mohanan. 1984. Lexical phonology of the consonant system in Malayalam. *Linguistic Inquiry* 15. 575–602.

Paradis, Carole & Jean-François Prunet (eds.). 1991. *The special status of coronals* (Phonetics and Phonology 2). San Diego: Academic Press.

Paulian, Christiane. 1986. Les voyelles en nù-kàlùŋè: Sept phonèmes, mais ... *Cahiers du Lacito* 1986/1. 51–65.

Pierrehumbert, Janet B. 2016. Phonological representation: Beyond abstract versus episodic. *Annual Review of Linguistics* 2. 33–52.

Plank, Frans & Aditi Lahiri. 2015. Macroscopic and microscopic typology: Basic Valence Orientation, more pertinacious than meets the naked eye. *Linguistic Typology* 19. 1–54.

Roberts, Adam, Allison Wetterlin, & Aditi Lahiri. 2013. Aligning mispronounced words to meaning. *The Mental Lexicon* 8. 140–163.

Rubach, Jerzy. 1984. *Cyclic and lexical phonology: The structure of Polish*. Dordrecht: Foris.

Sagey, Elizabeth C. 1986. *The representation of features and relations in non-linear phonology*. Doctoral dissertation, MIT, Cambridge, MA.

Shaw, Patricia. 1991. Consonant harmony systems: The special status of coronal harmony. In Paradis & Prunet (eds.) 1991, 125–157.

Stevens, Kenneth & Sheila E. Blumstein. 1978. Invariant cues for place of articulation in stop consonants. *Journal of the Acoustical Society of America* 64. 1358–1368.

Trommelen, Mieke. 1984. *The syllable in Dutch*. Dordrecht: Foris.

B. Elan Dresher, Christopher Harvey, and Will Oxford
Contrastive feature hierarchies as a new lens on typology

Abstract: We propose a way of looking at phonological typology that is based on a fundamental distinction between a phonetic and phonological analysis of the sound systems of languages. We build on approaches to phonology pioneered by Sapir and the Prague School (Jakobson and Trubetzkoy), instantiated within a generative grammar. We view phonemes as being composed of contrastive features that are themselves organized into language-particular hierarchies. We propose that these contrastive feature hierarchies shed light on synchronic and diachronic phonological patterns, and therefore offer a new lens on phonological typology. Thus, on this view the subject matter for typological investigation is not a phonetic sound (e.g., [i]) or a phoneme (/i/), or even a phonemic inventory (/i, a, u/), but an inventory generated by a feature hierarchy: for example, /i, a, u/ generated by the hierarchy [low] > [round]. This yields a different set of representations from the same terminal symbols generated by the hierarchy [round] > [low].

We will illustrate this approach to phonological representations with a synchronic analysis of Classical Manchu, and then show how it accounts for the results of typological surveys of rounding harmony in Manchu-Tungusic, Eastern Mongolian, and Turkic, and for the distribution of palatalization in Yupik-Inuit dialects. We will then propose that contrast shift should be recognized as a type of phonological change, and show how it applies to diachronic developments of the Algonquian and Ob-Ugric vowel systems. We find that feature hierarchies can be relatively stable, but contrast shifts do occur, for various reasons, and these can result in dramatic differences in patterning. Harvey's analysis of Ob-Ugric also shows that elements of feature hierarchies can spread and be borrowed, like other aspects of linguistic structure. As Sapir (1925) proposed, languages whose phonemes line up in similar ways (i.e., have similar contrastive feature hierarchies) show similar phonological patterning, though they may differ considerably in their phonetic realizations. We conclude that contrastive feature hierarchies provide an interesting level of representation for typological research.

1 Introduction

This article addresses a question raised in the proposal for the Workshop on Phonological Typology (Oxford University, August 2013): Phonological typology vs. phonetic typology – same or different? We will propose a way of looking at phonological

https://doi.org/10.1515/9783110451931-008

typology that is clearly DIFFERENT from phonetic typology. In particular, we will propose that CONTRASTIVE FEATURE HIERARCHIES offer a new lens on typology, while also shedding light on synchronic and diachronic phonological patterns.

We will begin in Section 2 with some general remarks on typology, phonological contrast, and contrastive feature hierarchies. Section 3 illustrates the relation between contrast and phonological activity, as exemplified by the Classical Manchu vowel system. We then show how contrastive hierarchies can lend insight to synchronic, diachronic, and areal typology, with examples drawn from a typological survey of rounding harmony and the relative ordering of features [round] and [front] (Section 4), the diachrony of Algonquian vowel systems (Section 5), and areal typology of Ob-Ugric vowel systems (Section 6), respectively. Section 7 is a brief conclusion.

2 Typology, phonological contrast, and contrastive feature hierarchies

2.1 Phonological typology and contrast

Following Hyman (2007), the kind of typology we will be concerned with is "an underlying one, based on phonological analysis, not on surface inventories". Hyman cites Vajda's (2001) view of phonological typology: "it is possible to classify languages according to the PHONEMES they contain [...] Typology is the study of STRUCTURAL FEATURES across languages. Phonological typology involves comparing languages according to the NUMBER OR TYPE OF SOUNDS they contain" [emphasis added]. We will build on this view by advancing a specific notion of the terms "phonemes", "structural features", and "number or type of sounds".

In the same article, Hyman (2007) cites Sapir's (1925: 43) "intrinsically typological" idea that "two languages, A and B, may have identical sounds but utterly distinct phonetic [read: phonological] patterns". Sapir also constructs two languages C and D that illustrate the converse situation: phonetically their sounds are different, but their "pattern alignments" are isomorphic. Sapir (1925) arranges the phonemes as in (1).

(1) Different phonetics, similar patterning (Sapir 1925)
    a. Pattern of C

a		ε	i		u	
aː		εː				
	h		w	j	l	m n
p	t	k	q			
b	d	g	G			
f	s	x	χ			

b. Pattern of D

æ		e	i		y		
æː		eː					
	h		v	ʒ	r	m	ŋ
pʰ	tʰ		kʰ	qʰ			
ß	ð		ɣ	ʁ			
f	ʃ		ç	ħ			

The phonemes /v/ and /ʒ/ appear to be out of place in the chart of language D, but Sapir justifies their positions by their phonological behaviour, in that their places in the pattern are parallel to those of language C's /w/ and /j/, respectively. Sapir (1925: 47–48) allows that the "natural phonetic arrangement" of sounds is a useful guide to how they pattern, but he goes on: "And yet it is most important to emphasize the fact, strange but indubitable, that a pattern alignment does not need to correspond exactly to the more obvious phonetic one."

The isomorphic alignments in C and D can be understood as indicating that corresponding phonemes have the same CONTRASTIVE values. The chart in (2) represents one possible way of suggesting what the contrastive specifications might be for the consonants in (1). In each cell, the first sound is from C, the second from D. The differences between them do not involve contrastive specifications.

(2) Contrastive specifications suggested by the charts in (1)

			Labial	Coronal	Dorsal	Post-dorsal
Obstruent	Voiceless	Stop	p/ pʰ	t/ tʰ	k/ kʰ	q/ qʰ
		Spirant	f/f	s/ʃ	x/ç	χ/ ħ
	Voiced		b/ß	d/ð	g/ɣ	ɢ/ʁ
Sonorant		Nasal	m/m		n/ŋ	
		Liquid		l/r		
		Glide	w/v	j/ʒ		h/h

It was observed that the language D phonemes /v/ and /ʒ/ appear to be in the "wrong place", which in (2) translates into their having incorrect specifications. In generative grammar, this mismatch can be resolved by assigning them different underlying specifications, matching those of their counterparts. These types of examples have been much discussed in connection with how abstract Sapir's theory of phonology was (cf. McCawley 1967). Less attention has been paid to the other examples, which do not appeal to abstractness, but which show the importance of establishing the contrastive properties of segments. For example, the obstruents in the third row in (2) are contrastively voiced and redundantly stops or spirants. No abstractness is at issue here, but we have to distinguish between contrastive and non-contrastive properties.

It follows that for Sapir the pattern alignment of a phoneme amounts to its contrastive status, which is not determined by its phonetics, but is a function of its phonetic and phonological behaviour. Thus, a synchronic analysis of the phonology should, among other things, give an account of the contrastive features of each phoneme.

Turning to diachrony, Prague School phonologists have argued that the contrastive properties of phonemes also play an important role in phonological change. The insight that phonological change may involve a reorganization of the phonemes of a language goes back to an article by Roman Jakobson first published in 1931 (Jakobson 1972 [1931]): "Once a phonological change has taken place, the following questions must be asked: What exactly has been modified within the phonological system? [. . .] has the structure of individual oppositions [contrasts] been transformed? Or in other words, has the place of a specific opposition been changed [. . .]?"

It should be noted that phonological theories that put the emphasis on contrast have not been unproblematic. In pre-generative structuralist theories, synchronic grammars were composed of contrasting elements locked into systems of oppositions. If one takes too literally Saussure's (1972 [1916]: 166) dictum that "dans la langue il n'y a que des différences [. . .] sans termes positifs" then grammars become incommensurable, and one has no way to relate successive stages of a language, or even closely related dialects (Moulton 1960). Generative grammar (Chomsky & Halle 1968) solves this problem by construing phonology as a system of rules that mediate between underlying (lexical) and surface (phonetic) forms. Now, grammar change takes the form of the addition, loss, reordering, or restructuring of rules.

Kiparsky (1965) demonstrated that a series of sound changes in Armenian dialects, shown in (3), can be understood in terms of the spreading of three rules, described informally in (4). Kiparsky (1965) points out that these sound changes spread from one dialect to another, regardless of how many contrasts they contained. If we were to classify the dialects in terms of oppositions, we would arrive at meaningless groupings for explaining any synchronic or diachronic facts. He writes:

> An incidental feature of the present example is that it highlights the pointlessness of a structural dialectology that [. . .] distinguishes dialects according to points of structural difference rather than according to the innovations through which they diverged [. . .] If in the present example we were to divide the dialects into those with two stop series and those

with three, we would be linking together dialects that have nothing to do with each other and separating dialects that are closely related. (Kiparsky 1965: 17)

(3) Armenian dialects (Kiparsky 1965)

Old Armenian	th	t	d	Contrasts	Sound changes
East Central	th	t	dh	2	Aspiration
West Central	th	d	dh	2	Voicing, aspiration
Northern	th	t	d	2	———
Eastern	th	t	t	1	Devoicing
Western	th	d	d	1	Voicing
Northwestern	th	d	th	1	Voicing, aspiration
Southern	th	d	t	2	Voicing, devoicing

(4) Armenian sound changes (Kiparsky 1965)
  a. Aspiration: /d/ aspirates to [dh] (or [th]) in the Central and Northwestern dialects.
  b. Voicing: /t/ voices to [d] in the Western, West Central, Northwestern, and Southern dialects.
  c. Devoicing: /d/ devoices to [t] in the Eastern and Southern dialects.

The above considerations show the inadequacy of a phonology that deals only in structural points of contrast ("differences"), without also including substantive properties ("positive terms"), including features and a system of rules or constraints. However, we believe that generative grammar went overboard in jettisoning the structuralist notion of language-particular contrast. We will argue that contrast plays a crucial role in synchronic and diachronic phonology, and hence in phonological typology.

2.2 A theory of phonological contrast

To implement contrast in an explicit theory, we assume first that contrastive features are assigned hierarchically, using a method that was called "branching trees" in the literature of the 1950s and 60s (Jakobson, Fant, & Halle 1952; Jakobson & Halle 1956), stated in (5). We call it the Successive Division Algorithm (Dresher 1998, 2003, 2009), given informally in (6):

(5) The contrastive feature hierarchy (based on Jakobson, Fant, & Halle 1952, among others):
Contrastive features are assigned by language-particular feature hierarchies.

(6) The Successive Division Algorithm:
Assign contrastive features by successively dividing the inventory until every phoneme has been distinguished

As a first approximation we assume further that phonology computes only contrastive features, in keeping with the Contrastivist Hypothesis in (7).

(7) The Contrastivist Hypothesis (Hall 2007):
The phonological component of a language L operates only on those features which are necessary to distinguish the phonemes of L from one another.

That is, only contrastive features can be PHONOLOGICALLY ACTIVE, where feature activity is defined as in (8):

(8) Phonological activity (adapted from Clements (2001: 77):
A feature can be said to be active if it plays a role in the phonological computation; that is, if it is required for the expression of phonological regularities in a language, including both static phonotactic patterns and patterns of alternation.

If the Contrastivist Hypothesis is correct, (9) follows as its corollary.

(9) Corollary to the Contrastivist Hypothesis:
If a feature is phonologically active, then it must be contrastive.

This corollary suggests a working heuristic: Assume that active features are contrastive, and find, if possible, a feature ordering that fits the observed patterns of activity. We believe that this heuristic represents the practice of many descriptive phonologists, minus the requirement that all active features are necessarily contrastive. That is, phonologists typically limit their analyses to those features that are RELEVANT to the workings of the language, and these active features also serve as the contrastive features, as far as possible.

A further assumption is that features are binary, and that every feature has a MARKED and UNMARKED value. We assume, as in (10), that markedness is language particular (Rice 2003, 2007) and accounts for asymmetries between the two values of a feature, where these exist.[1] Where the asymmetry is substantial, a feature may appear to act in a privative manner, so that the unmarked value may

---

[1] We do not exclude the possibility that there may be universal tendencies concerning markedness; for example, we do not know of a language where [−nasal] is marked. However, Rice (2003, 2007) shows that a number of presumed universals of markedness are not empirically supported. Therefore, we adopt the conservative position that all markedness relations are language specific. We are prepared to modify this view where evidence exists in favour of a stronger position.

appear to be absent. In other cases, both values of a feature may be referred to by the phonology (Mackenzie 2011, 2013). We will designate the marked value of a feature F as [F], and the unmarked value as (*non-F*).[2]

(10) Feature markedness:
Each feature F has a marked value, [F], and an unmarked value, (*non-F*). Where these values function asymmetrically, the marked value is the more active one.

Finally, this theory of contrast does not need to make any assumptions as to where features come from: the Successive Division Algorithm works equally well if features are universal, as supposed by Chomsky & Halle (1968), or emergent, as suggested by Mielke (2008) and Samuel (2011). Dresher (2014) observes that the contrastive hierarchy itself ensures that phonological representations across languages will look rather similar even in the absence of a universal set of features.

To illustrate the workings of the feature hierarchy and the Contrastivist Hypothesis, consider a hypothetical vowel inventory /i, u, a/. The Successive Division Algorithm requires that an inventory of three phonemes must be characterized by exactly two features, though both the choice of features and their ordering may vary. In (11), we illustrate two possible contrastive hierarchies that use the features [back] and [low]; in (12), we give two more hierarchies using the features [front] and [round]. Other combinations of features are also possible, but these examples should suffice to illustrate the concept.

(11) Two contrastive hierarchies for /i, u, a/ based on [back] and [low]

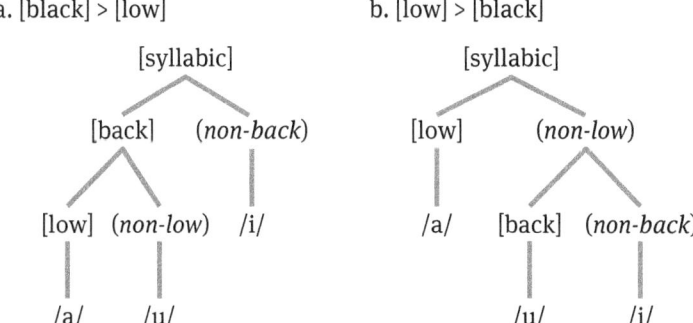

---

2 Markedness considerations thus dictate whether we name a feature [back] or [front]: if a language has backing triggered by a back vowel but no fronting triggered by a front vowel we call the harmony feature [back]; conversely, we attribute fronting or palatalization to a feature [front]. In some cases the phonetic ranges of vowels might influence the choice of label.

(12) Two more contrastive hierarchies for /i, u, a/, based on [front] and [round]

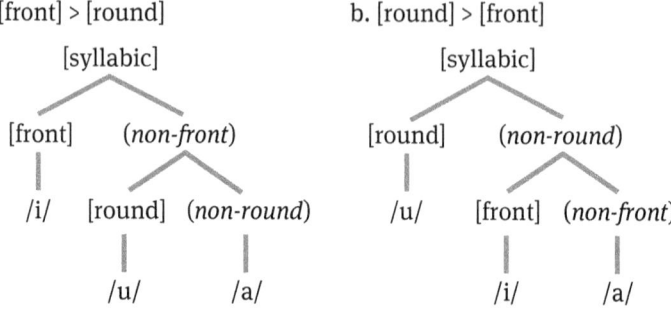

a. [front] > [round]　　　　　　b. [round] > [front]

The feature hierarchy constrains phonological activity in a number of ways. First, it follows from (7) that both /a/ and /u/ can potentially trigger backing in (11a), because both are contrastively [back]; in (11b), only /u/ is contrastively [back], so that is the only potential phoneme that could cause backing. In (12), the feature [back] is not contrastive in the vowel system at all, and we do not expect any vowel to cause backing.

Second, the hierarchy constrains neutralization and merger: we make the hypothesis in (13). In (11a) and (12a), we expect that /u/ could merge with /a/, whereas in (11b) it would more likely merge with /i/. Note that this restriction does not apply to ordinary synchronic processes. For example, in both languages in (12) /i/ is contrastively [front] and /u/ is contrastively [round]; therefore, both languages may have harmony processes whereby /a/ is fronted in the environment of /i/ and rounded in the environment of /u/, whether or not /a/ is a contrastive sister of /i/ or /u/. Though /a/ can alternate synchronically with both /i/ and /u/, depending on position, it can only merge diachronically with one of these vowels.[3]

(13) Hypothesis concerning diachronic mergers:
　　　Mergers affect phonemes that are CONTRASTIVE SISTERS.

The typological generalizations we will be discussing can thus not be found by looking at inventories alone (say, /i, a, u/), or at individual phonemes (say, /a/), or phones ([a]), without also considering the relevant contrastive feature hierarchy. Notice also that a consequence of this hierarchical method for assigning contrastive features is that a contrastive specification need not be unpredictable. For example, in (11a) /a/ is the only [low] vowel, so its [back] feature is predictable; but it is still contrastive, for it distinguishes between /a, u/ and /i/.

---

[3] For example, in dialects descending from Proto-Eskimo that retain a four-vowel system (either overtly or in underlying representations), the reflex of Proto-Eskimo */ə/ can assimilate to different vowels depending on context, but diachronically this vowel has only merged with Proto-Eskimo */i/; see Compton & Dresher (2011) and Section 4.2 below.

3 Example of contrast and activity: The Classical Manchu vowel system

In this section we will illustrate the connection between contrast and phonological activity, taking as an extended example the Classical Manchu vowel system, following the analysis of Zhang (1996) and Dresher & Zhang (2005). Classical Manchu has six vowel phonemes, as shown in (14).

(14)　Classical Manchu vowel system (Zhang 1996)
　　　　/i/　　　　　/u/
　　　　　　　　　　/ʊ/
　　　　　　/ə/
　　　　　　　　　　/ɔ/
　　　　　　/a/

3.1 Contrastive feature hierarchy for Classical Manchu

Based on the phonological patterning of the Classical Manchu vowels, Zhang (1996) proposes the feature hierarchy in (15), which yields the marked feature representations in (16).[4]

(15)　Classical Manchu vowels (Zhang 1996): [low] > [front] > [round] > [ATR]

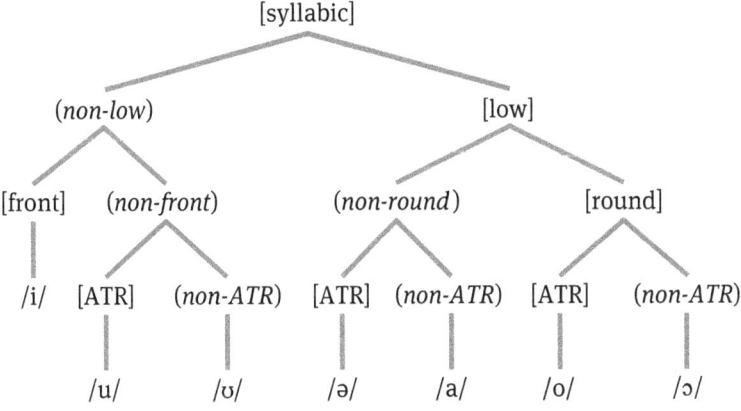

---

4 Zhang (1996) labels the features [labial] rather than [round], and [coronal] rather than [front]. For our purposes these names are interchangeable and do not imply any differences in the substance of these features.

(16) Classical Manchu vowels: Marked contrastive featural representations

/i/	/u/	/ʊ/	/a/	/ə/	/ɔ/
[front]	[ATR]		[low]	[low]	[low]
				[ATR]	[round]

The three most notable kinds of phonological activity involving vowels are ATR harmony, rounding (labial) harmony, and palatalization. We will briefly discuss them in turn, and show how the patterns of activity motivate the hierarchy in (15).

3.2 ATR harmony

The vowels /ə/ and /u/ trigger ATR harmony within a word: /ə/ alternates with /a/ (17a) and /u/ alternates with /ʊ/ (17b).

(17) ATR harmony
    a. /ə/ alternates with /a/

	[ATR]	xəxə	'woman'	xəxə-ŋgə	'female'
	(non-ATR)	aɢa	'rain'	aɢa-ŋɢa	'of rain'

    b. /u/ alternates with /ʊ/

	[ATR]	xərə-	'ladle out'	xərə-ku	'ladle'
	(non-ATR)	paqt'a-	'contain'	paqt'a-qʊ	'internal organs'

An apparent exception is caused by the fact that /ʊ/ changes to [u] everywhere except after dorsal (velar ~ uvular) consonants; however, the underlying contrast between /ʊ/ and /u/ emerges in the way they participate in ATR harmony (17): underlying /u/ co-occurs with ATR vowels (18a), underlying /ʊ/ co-occurs with non-ATR vowels (18b).

(18) ATR harmony and the neutralization of /u/ and /ʊ/
    a. Underlying /u/: ATR harmony

	[ATR]	susə	'coarse'	susə-tə-	'make coarsely'
	[ATR]	xət'u	'stocky'	xət'u-kən	'somewhat stocky'

    b. Underlying /ʊ/: non-ATR vowels

	(non-ATR)	tulpa	'careless'	tulpa-ta-	'act carelessly'
	(non-ATR)	tat'ṣun	'sharp'	tat'ṣu-qan	'somewhat sharp'

The vowel /i/ is neutral and co-occurs in stems with both ATR (19a) and non-ATR vowels (19b). Similarly, suffix /i/ freely occurs with both types of vowels (19c).

(19) /i/ is neutral with respect to ATR harmony
a. /ə/ ~ /a/ suffix
[ATR] pəki 'firm' pəki-lə 'make firm'
(non-ATR) paqtʂ'in 'opponent' paqtʂ'i-la- 'oppose'
b. /u/ ~ /ʊ/ suffix
[ATR] sitərə- 'hobble' sitərə-sxun 'hobbled; lame'
(non-ATR) panjin 'appearance' panji-sχun 'having money'
c. /i/ suffix
[ATR] əmt'ə 'one each' əmt'ə-li 'alone; sole'
(non-ATR) taχa- 'follow' taχa-li 'the second'

Perhaps unexpectedly, when /i/ is in a position to trigger harmony, it occurs only with non-ATR vowels (20).

(20) Stems with only /i/ co-occur with non-ATR vowels
a. /ə/ ~ /a/ suffix
(non-ATR) ili- 'stand' ili-χa 'stood'
(non-ATR) fili 'solid' fili-qan 'somewhat solid'
b. /u/ ~ /ʊ/ suffix
(non-ATR) tʂ'ili- 'to choke' tʂ'ili-qʊ 'choking'
(non-ATR) sifi- 'stick in the hair' sifi-qʊ 'hairpin'

The evidence from activity, therefore, is that /ə/ and /u/ have an active feature in common, that we are calling [ATR], that is not shared by the other vowels; by hypothesis, this feature must be contrastive. The same is evidently not the case with /i/, though /i/ is phonetically ATR. In the representations proposed in (15) and (16), /ə/ and /u/, but not /i/, are contrastively [ATR].

3.3 Round (labial) harmony

Two successive /ɔ/ vowels cause a suffix /a/ to become /ɔ/ (21a); a single /ɔ/, short or long, does not trigger rounding (21b).[5] Note that /u/ and /ʊ/ do not trigger round harmony (22).

---

[5] Various proposals have been offered to account for why a single /ɔ/ does not cause rounding harmony; a similar restriction occurs in Oroqen (Zhang & Dresher 1996; Walker 2001, 2014). Based on the observation that a single irregular stem-internal /ɔ/ does cause harmony in Baiyinna Oroqen (Li 1996; Walker 2014), Dresher & Nevins (2017) propose that the restriction may actually be that a low suffix vowel may obtain a [round] feature from a stem-internal /ɔ/, but not from an /ɔ/ that is stem-initial.

(21) Round (labial) harmony
    a. Two successive /ɔ/ vowels trigger round harmony
        ɔ...ɔ   pɔtʂ'ɔ 'colour'   pɔtʂ'ɔ-ŋGɔ 'coloured'
        Compare aGa   'rain'   aGa-ŋGa   'of rain'
    b. A single /ɔ/, short or long, does not trigger rounding
        Single ɔ   tɔ-   'alight (birds)' tɔ-na- 'alight in swarm'
        Single ɔɔ   tɔɔ-   'cross (river)'   tɔɔ-na- 'go to cross'

(22) No round harmony triggered by high vowels
    a. After /u/
        gulu   'plain'   gulu-kən   'somewhat plain'
        kumun 'music'   kumu-ŋgə 'noisy'
    b. After /ʊ/ (/ʊ/ becomes [u] except after a back consonant)
        χʊtun   'fast'   χʊtu-qan 'somewhat fast'
        tursun   'form'   tursu-ŋGa 'having form'

The evidence from activity here, then, is that /ɔ/ must have an active, therefore contrastive, feature that causes rounding, which we are calling [round]; the same is not the case with /u/ and /ʊ/, though they are also phonetically rounded. The feature ordering in (15) has the result that /ɔ/ is contrastively [round], but /u/ and /ʊ/ are not.

3.4 Palatalization

The vowel /i/ uniquely causes palatalization of a preceding consonant, which suggests that it alone has a contrastive triggering feature we call [front]. There is no evidence that it has any other active features.

3.5 Height contrast

The alternations /ə/ ~ /a/ ~ /ɔ/ and /u/ ~ /ʊ/ are limited to a height class, and we still need to distinguish /ə/ from /u/ and /a/ from /ʊ/. It is simplest to assume one height contrast, which we call [low] (as there are only two height classes, [high] would also be possible here). As shown in (15), no more features are required in ordered to make each vowel distinct from every other, and there is no evidence that any other feature is active in this vowel system.

4 Synchrony: Typology with contrastive feature hierarchies

Contrastive feature hierarchies allow us to update Sapir's approach to phonological systems and view phonological typology in a new way. Rather than considering only the number of segments in an inventory, or their geometrical arrangement, we can look at inventories in terms of their active/contrastive features and how they are ordered. As with Sapir's languages A–D, this approach reveals unexpected similarities between inventories that do not superficially look very similar; conversely, inventories that look quite similar may turn out to have different patterns of phonological activity because they have different contrastive hierarchies.

To illustrate, we will consider a number of vowel systems which have contrasts between front and back round vowels. Two features that could potentially play a role in such inventories are [front] and [round]. We have seen that both of these features are contrastive and active in Classical Manchu vowels, but in asymmetrical ways: whereas /i/ is contrastively [front], [round] is restricted to /ɔ/, and is not contrastive in /u/ and /ʊ/. This is a result of ordering [front] > [round]; if the ordering were [round] > [front], then /u/ and /ʊ/ would be contrastively [round], and /i/ would not be assigned [front]. If the orderings of these features is allowed to vary cross-linguistically, we expect to find vowel systems that manifest each ordering. What the specific consequences of these orderings are in any given language depends on the number of segments in the inventory, and the ordering of other contrastive features.

4.1 Vowel systems with [front] > [round]

Contrastive feature hierarchies shed new light on the results of typological surveys of rounding (labial) harmony in Manchu-Tungusic, Mongolian, and Turkic (Korn 1969; Kaun 1995). We have seen that round harmony in Classical Manchu is limited to the [low] vowels. On our account, only the low vowel /ɔ/ is contrastively [round] in this inventory, because of the ordering of [front] > [round]. The same holds for most Manchu-Tungusic languages, which have similar vowel inventories. A Tungusic example is Oroqen (Zhang 1996), shown in (23): again, only low vowels are triggers (in the solid box) and targets (in the dashed box) of harmony. Oroqen has both ATR and non-ATR low vowels. We assume it has the same feature hierarchy as Classical Manchu (plus a length contrast that we omit from the tree), as shown in (24).

(23) Oroqen (Tungusic) vowel system (Zhang 1996)

				/u/	/uu/
/i/	/ii/			/ʊ/	/ʊʊ/
/e/		/ə/	/əə/	/o/	/oo/
/ɛ/		/a/	/aa/	/ɔ/	/ɔɔ/

(24) Oroqen vowels: [low] > [front] > [round] > [ATR]

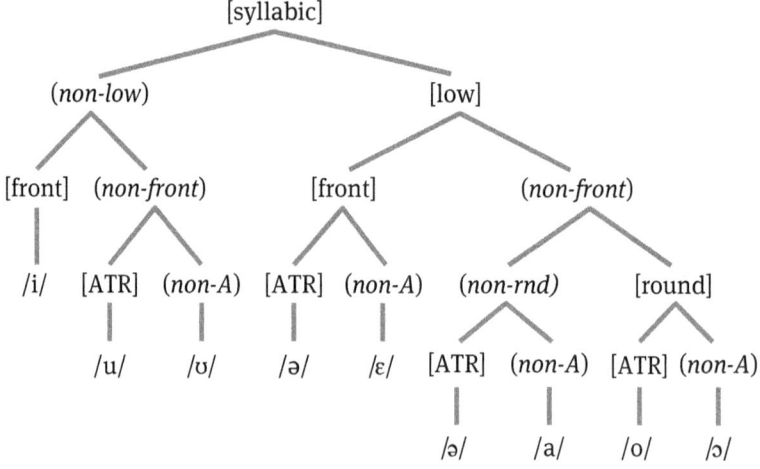

The schematic representation of the Oroqen vowel system in (23) might suggest a different explanation for the fact that [round] is active only in the [low] part of the inventory. One might suppose that one could simply read off this display that rounding is not contrastive in the high vowels, because there is no /ɨ/ in the inventory. That is, one might think that the contrasts between /o, oo, ɔ, ɔɔ/ and /ə, əə, a, aa/ are more minimal than the ones between /u, uu, ʊ, ʊʊ/ and /i, ii/. The notion of "minimal contrast" or "minimal difference" (Padgett 2003; Calabrese 2005; Campos-Astorkiza 2009; Nevins 2010) or "crowding" (Kaun 1995) has been proposed as the principle governing contrast. This approach is correct in one direction: if there is only one phonetic property that distinguishes between two phonemes, then that property MUST be contrastive. However, the converse does not hold: a feature may still be contrastive in a phoneme even if it is not the only phonetic property that distinguishes that phoneme from any other. Minimal contrast has been shown to be incorrect on both conceptual and empirical grounds (Archangeli 1988; Dresher 2009, 2015, 2016); the latter will become apparent when we look at Yowlumne Yokuts in the next section. One of the merits of the hierarchical approach to contrast is that it can operate smoothly even when minimal phonetic differences between phonemes are lacking, as they often are.

Eastern Mongolian languages have round harmony, that, as in the majority of Manchu-Tungusic languages, is limited to low vowels. A typical example is Khalkha Mongolian (Svantesson 1985; Qinggertai 1982), with the vowel inventory in (25). We assume that they have similar feature hierarchies as most of the Manchu-Tungus languages (26). In these languages, harmony triggers are non-high because only non-high vowels are contrastive for [round], a limitation that follows from the fact that [front] (as well as a height feature) is higher in the hierarchy than [round].

(25) Khalkha Mongolian vowels (Svantesson 1985; Qinggertai 1982)

/i/		/u/
		/ʊ/
	/ə/	/o/
	/a/	/ɔ/

(26) Khalkha Mongolian vowels (Dresher & Zhang 2005): [low] > [front] > [round] > [ATR]

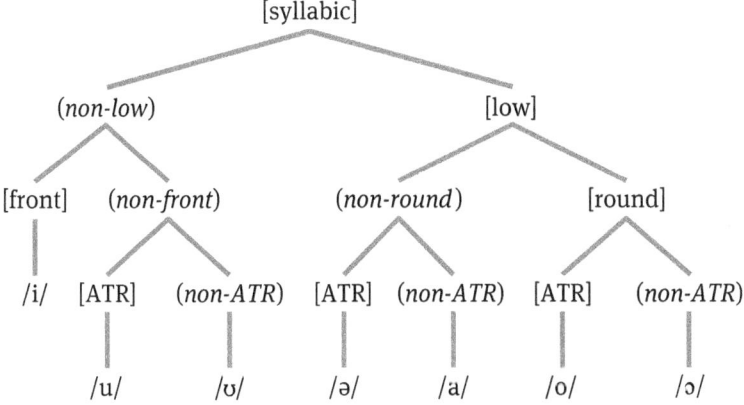

4.2 Vowel systems with [round] > [front]

It is interesting to compare the above languages with Yowlumne Yokuts (Southwestern USA; Newman 1944), which has an underlying vowel inventory whose basic configuration looks similar (minus the ATR contrasts); but it is a completely different type of language. In Yokuts, BOTH /u/ and /ɔ/ trigger height-bounded round harmony: /u/ rounds only /i/, and /ɔ/ rounds only /a/ (27). Why can /u/ trigger harmony here, but not in Manchu-Tungusic and Eastern Mongolian?

(27) Yowlumne Yokuts vowel system (Newman 1944)

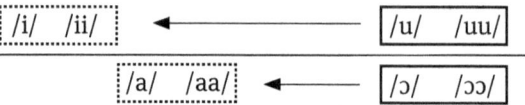

A simple solution is available in terms of the contrastive hierarchy: in Yowlumne, [round] is ranked over [front]. Hence, both /u/ and /ɔ/ are [round], and [front] is not a contrastive feature in this language, as shown in (28) (we omit the length contrast in the tree).

(28) Yowlumne Yokuts vowels: [high] > [round]

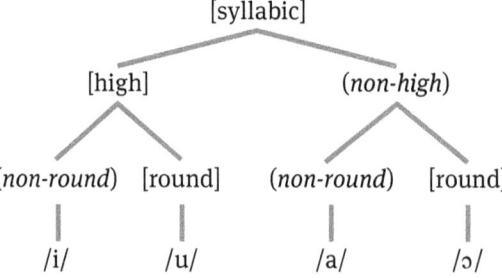

In support of this analysis, we note that /i/ in Yowlumne is phonologically inert, and serves also as the epenthetic vowel. This is in sharp contrast to the [front] /i/ in Manchu-Tungusic and many Mongolian languages.

Another language family in which [round] is typically ordered ahead of [front] are the Yupik and Inuit languages that descend from Proto-Eskimo, which is reconstructed to have vowels */i/, */a/, */u/, and a fourth vowel assumed to be */ə/ (Fortescue et al. 1994). In most dialects this vowel has merged with /i/. In some of these dialects merger is total, resulting in a three vowel system; other dialects retain a trace of the distinction between */i/ and */ə/.

Original */i/ could cause palatalization of consonants, and some Inuit dialects show palatalization (or traces of former palatalization) (Dorais 2003: 33). In parts of Baffin Island, for example, the word 'foot' is pronounced [isiɣak], where *i* has caused a following original *t* to change to *s* (29a). This assibilation is the most common manifestation of palatalization in Inuit. In such dialects, it is traditional to distinguish between "strong *i*", which descends from */i/ and causes palatalization (29a), and "weak *i*", which descends from */ə/ and does not (29b). In some dialects the two types of *i* exhibit other kinds of distinct behaviour as well.

(29) "Strong" and "weak" *i* in some Inuit dialects
    a. Strong *i*   *itəyaʁ   >   isiyak   'foot'
    b. Weak *i*   *ətəmaɣ   >   itimak   'palm of hand'

Compton & Dresher (2011) observe the generalization in (30) about dialects in which /i/ causes or once caused palatalization:

(30) Generalization about Inuit palatalization (Compton & Dresher 2011): Inuit /i/ can cause palatalization (assibilation) of a consonant ONLY in dialects where there is evidence for a (former) contrast with a fourth vowel; where there is no contrast between strong and weak *i*, /i/ does not trigger palatalization.

This generalization follows if we assume that the feature hierarchy for Inuit and Yupik is [low] > [round] > [front] as in (31). When the fourth vowel is in the underlying inventory, /i/ has a contrastive [front] feature that enables it to cause palatalization (31a). But in the absence of a fourth vowel, [front] is not a contrastive feature (31b).

(31) Inuit and Yupik vowels (Compton & Dresher 2011): [low] > [round] > [front]
    a. Contrastive feature hierarchy: Four underlying vowels

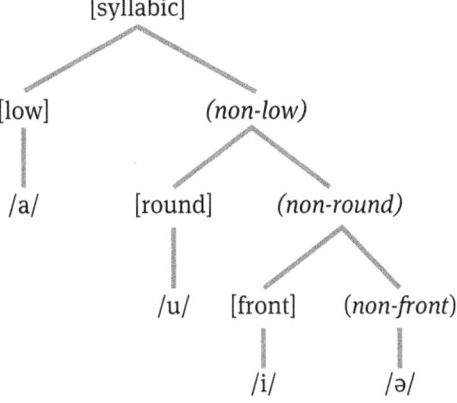

    b. Contrastive feature hierarchy: Three underlying vowels

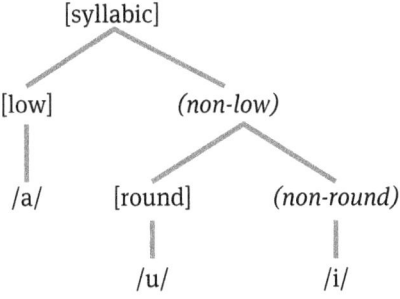

4.3 Vowel systems where ordering of [round] and [front] is not crucial

Turkic languages have symmetrical inventories. They are typically analyzed with three features: one height feature and two place features, as in (32) (see Kabak 2011 for Turkish). Here, every feature specification is contrastive in any order; the vowels completely fill the eight-cell vowel space defined by three binary features. A possible ordering of the features of Turkish is given in (33); however, the same contrastive specifications would result from any ordering of these three features.[6] We predict, therefore, that all round vowels could potentially be triggers of round harmony in such languages. This prediction is correct, though harmony observes limitations that are not due to contrast, but to other factors.

(32) Turkish vowel system

	[front]		(non-front)	
	(non-round)	[round]	(non-round)	[round]
[high]	/i/	/ü/	/ɨ/	/u/
(non-high)	/e/	/ö/	/a/	/o/

(33) Contrastive feature hierarchy for Turkish vowels: [high] > [front] > [round]

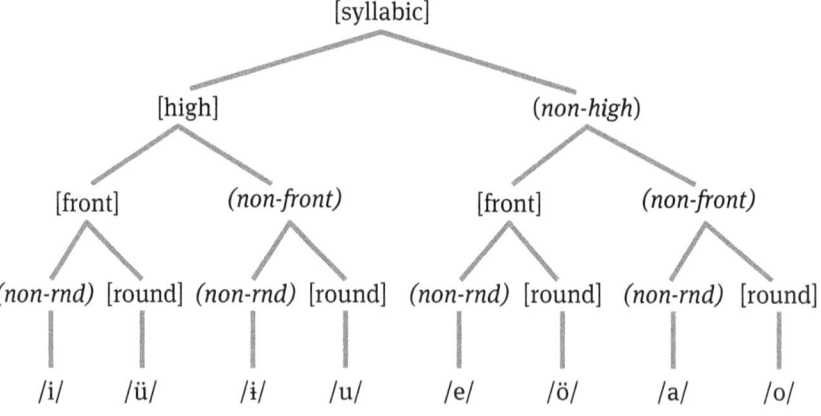

---

6 This is not to say that there can be no other empirical evidence, for example from synchronic alternations or diachronic mergers, that can choose between these orderings.

In Turkish, harmony triggers can be high or low, but targets are typically limited to high vowels (34). In Kachin Khakass (Korn 1969), both triggers and targets of round harmony must be high (35), the opposite of the Manchu-Tungus-Eastern Mongolian pattern. Because all vowels have contrastive [round] and [front] features, however they are ordered, these restrictions cannot be due to considerations of contrast, but to other factors.

(34) Turkish round harmony triggers and targets

/i/	/ü/	/ɨ/	/u/
/e/	/ö/	/a/	/o/

(35) Kachin Khakass round harmony triggers and targets

/i/	/ü/	/ɨ/	/u/
/e/	/ö/	/a/	/o/

This way of classifying phonological systems allows us to account for two Manchu languages that are notable exceptions to the prevailing Manchu-Tungusic pattern of round harmony. Spoken Manchu and Xibe are modern Manchu languages in which [ATR] has been lost and /ə/ has become a *(non-low)* vowel (Zhang 1996; Dresher & Zhang 2005). The vowel system of Xibe, for example, is given in (36). The reclassification of /ə/ as a *(non-low)* vowel necessitates a new contrastive feature to distinguish it from /u/. The most natural modification is to extend the feature [round], already in the system, to /u/.

(36) Xibe (based on Li & Zhong 1986)

/i/	/y/	/ə/	/u/
/ɛ/	/œ/	/a/	/ɔ/

Evidence that /u/ is in fact contrastively [round] in Xibe can be found in the creation of new phonemes /y/ and /œ/. The latter derives from sequences of /ɔ/ and /i/, where the [front] feature derives from /i/ and the [round] feature from /ɔ/. Similarly, the new phoneme /y/ derives from sequences of /u/ and /i/, showing that /u/ had acquired a [round] feature. More evidence that /u/ is contrastively [round] in Xibe comes from a new form of round harmony that arose in Xibe, whereby /ə/ alternates with /u/ in suffixes: /u/ occurs if the stem-final vowel is round, /ə/ occurs otherwise.

The participation of /u/ in triggering round harmony, rare in the Manchu-Tungusic family, is accounted for by the extension of the contrastive [round] specification to /u/. The phonological patterning of the vowels in Xibe points to a contrastive hierarchy and branching tree as in (37). This tree very closely resembles the Turkish feature hierarchy in (33).

(37) Contrastive feature hierarchy for Xibe vowels (Zhang 1996): [low] > [front] > [round]

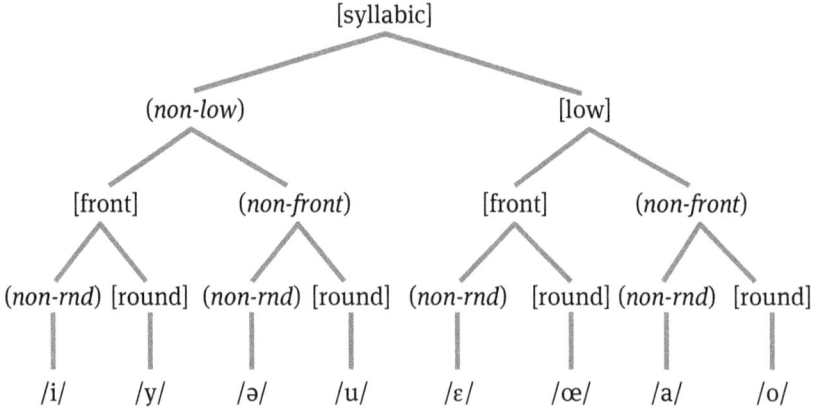

4.4 Summary

To sum up, we can classify languages into types based on the contrastive scopes of the vowel features [front] and [round] as in (38). Whether a feature is contrastive on a given vowel depends on the feature hierarchy and the size and structure of the phonological inventory.

(38) Typology of contrastive [front] and [round]
 a. If [front] > [round], /i/ can cause palatalization, but /u/ may or may not trigger round harmony.
 b. If [round] > [front], /u/ may trigger round harmony, but /i/ may or may not cause palatalization.
 c. In languages where [round] and [front] are contrastive for all vowels, both these features may be active in all vowels.

5 The diachrony of Algonquian vowel systems: Contrast shift as a type of change

Understanding the role of contrastive hierarchies in phonological patterning allows us to implement the program for diachronic phonology set out by Jakobson (1972 [1931]), which we alluded to in Section 2. That is, when a phonological change occurs in a language we need to look at what effect the change has had on the system of contrasts.

For example, we have seen a number of differences between the vowel system of Classical Manchu (Section 3.1) and that of Xibe (Section 4.3); on the assumption that Xibe descends from a language whose vowel system is essentially the same as that of Classical Manchu, we can assume that the Xibe vowel system derives from the Classical Manchu one by a series of phonological changes (Zhang 1996; Dresher & Zhang 2005). Some of the changes are overt at a phonetic level, such as the loss of /ʊ/ and the raising of /ə/. These phonetic changes are accompanied by a change in phonological features, namely, the loss of [ATR] as a contrastive feature and change of /ə/ from a [low] vowel to a (*non-low*) vowel. Less overt, but just as consequential for the phonological patterning of Xibe, is the change in contrastive status of /u/ from lacking a specification for [round] in Classical Manchu to being [round] in Xibe.

We will designate as a CONTRAST SHIFT any change in the contrastive feature hierarchy or in the contrastive status of a phoneme. A contrast shift can involve a reordering of features, or a change of features. A contrast shift may come about as a result of an overt phonetic change, such as the loss of a phoneme or a change in its phonetic realization. Of particular interest are "silent" changes like the one involving Xibe /u/, whereby a segment that does not appear to change phonetically from one synchronic stage to the next nevertheless takes on different contrastive features, with consequences for its synchronic patterning.

We propose that contrast shift is an important type of diachronic phonological change that can have far-reaching effects on the phonology of a language.[7] As should by now be evident, contrast shift can only be understood with reference to a particular feature hierarchy.

5.1 The vowel system of Proto-Algonquian

In a survey of the historical development of Algonquian vowel systems, Oxford (2012a, 2015) identifies persistent patterns in vowel changes. In an attempt to

---

[7] Analyses that exploit the contrastive hierarchy in accounting for diachronic change include: Zhang (1996) and Dresher & Zhang (2005) on Manchu; Barrie (2003) on Cantonese; Rohany Rahbar (2008) on Persian; Dresher (2009: 215–225) on East Slavic; Compton & Dresher (2011) on Inuit; Gardner (2012), Roeder & Gardner (2013), and Purnell & Raimy (2013) on North American English vowel shifts; Purnell & Raimy (2015) and Dresher (2017) on Old English; and large-scale studies by Harvey (2012) on Ob-Ugric, Ko (2010, 2011, 2012) on Korean, Mongolic, and Tungusic, and Oxford (2011, 2012a, 2015) on Algonquian.

make sense of these patterns, Oxford posits the feature hierarchy in (39) for Proto-Algonquian (the length contrast is omitted for ease of exposition).

(39) Proto-Algonquian vowels (Oxford 2015): [round] > [front] > [low]

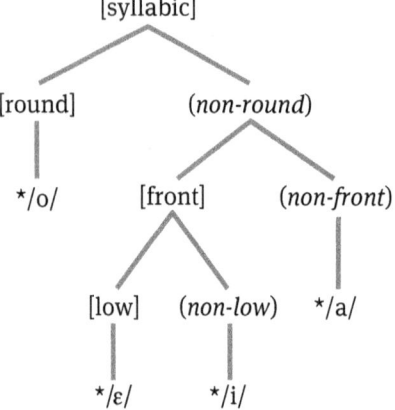

The hierarchy in (39) is motivated by feature activity that can be recovered as having been present in Proto-Algonquian. Thus, */o/ triggers rounding, an indication that it has an active, hence contrastive, [round] feature. Similarly, */i/ triggers palatalization, indicating a contrastive feature we call [front]. Patterns of partial neutralization relate */ɛ/ and */i/, suggesting that they are contrastive sisters by (13). Finally, */a/ does not trigger any processes, consistent with its being assigned no positive (marked) contrastive features. This evidence is summarized in (40).[8]

(40) Proto-Algonquian feature activity
    a. */o/ is [round]: triggers rounding
    b. */i/ is [front]: triggers palatalization
    c. */i, ɛ/ are sisters: partial neutralization
    d. */a/ has no marked contrastive features: is never a trigger

5.2 The Central Algonquian languages and Blackfoot

The Proto-Algonquian vowel feature hierarchy continues unchanged in the Central Algonquian languages and in Blackfoot. It accounts for two recurring

---

[8] See Oxford (2015) for the sources of these observations.

patterns: (a) palatalization always includes */i/ as a trigger; and (b) */ɛ/ regularly merges with */i/. Examples of these processes are listed in (41). The patterns in (41a) support the view that palatalization is triggered by a contrastive [front] feature, and favours vowels that are (*non-low*); the mergers in (41b) are consistent with the idea (13) that mergers tend to involve terminal nodes in the feature tree.

(41) Central Algonquian and Blackfoot feature activity
    a. Palatalization always includes */i/ as a trigger
        i. Proto-Algonquian */t, θ/-palatalization is triggered by */i, iː/;
        ii. Innu */k/-palatalization is triggered by */i, iː, ɛː/;
        iii. Betsiamites Innu /t/-palatalization is triggered by /iː/;
        iv. Blackfoot */k/-assibilation is triggered by PA */i, iː/;
        v. Blackfoot /t/-assibilation is triggered by Blackfoot /i, iː/.
    b. */ɛ/ regularly merges with */i/
        i. Partial or complete mergers of short */ɛ/ > /i/ occur in Fox, Shawnee, Miami-Illinois, Cree-Innu, Ojibwe, and Blackfoot;
        ii. long */ɛː/ > /iː/ in Woods Cree, Northern Plains Cree, and Blackfoot.

5.3 The Eastern and Western Algonquian languages

On the eastern and western edges of the Algonquian area, developments diverge from the predictions of the Proto-Algonquian hierarchy: in particular, the high vowels, derived from Proto-Algonquian */o/ and */i/, begin to pattern together. In the east, Proto-Eastern Algonquian lost the length contrast only in the high vowels (i.e., the reflexes of */o/, */i/), and in the west, Proto-Arapaho-Atsina and Pre-Cheyenne merged */o, oː/ with */i, iː/.

Under the hierarchy inherited from Proto-Algonquian, however, [high] is not a contrastive feature, and the old height feature, [low], is ordered at the bottom of the vowel feature hierarchy. The result is that the high vowels derived from */o/ and */i/ are not a natural class. If the hierarchy constrains patterning, then a new height contrast with the feature [high] must have come to outrank the place contrasts. That is, the Proto-Algonquian feature [low] is reinterpreted as [high] and moves to the top of the hierarchy, creating the new hierarchy and contrastive feature tree in (42).

(42) Eastern and western proto-languages (Oxford 2015): [high] > [round] > [front]

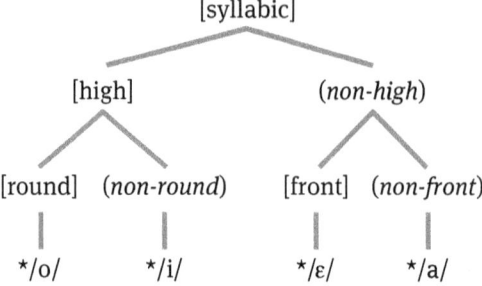

Subsequent developments in the eastern and western daughter languages follow the predictions of the new hierarchy. The patterns consistently differ from those of Central Algonquian: (a) palatalization in these languages is triggered by */ɛ/ but EXCLUDES */i/; and (b) */ɛ/ merges with or shifts to */a/ (not */i/). Instances of these processes are listed in (43).

(43) Eastern and Western Algonquian feature activity
    a. Palatalization is triggered by */ɛ/ but excludes */i/
        i. Massachusett */k/-palatalization is triggered by Proto-Eastern Algonquian */ɛː/ but not */iː/;
        ii. Cheyenne "yodation", where */k/ > /kj/, is triggered by */ɛ(ː)/ only.
    b. */ɛ/ merges with or shifts to */a/
        i. Partial or complete mergers of PA short */ɛ/ and */a/ occur in Abenaki, Mahican, Mi'kmaq, and Maliseet-Passamaquoddy;
        ii. Proto-Eastern Algonquian long */ɛː/ shifts to /aː/ in Massachusett and merges with */a/ in Western Abenaki;
        iii. long and short */ɛ(ː)/ shift to /a(ː)/ in Cheyenne;
        iv. vowel harmony involves */ɛ(ː)/ and */a(ː)/ in Arapaho.

Again, these patterns support the view that palatalization is triggered by a contrastive [front] feature: only /ɛ/ is contrastively [front] in these languages.[9]

---

[9] However, they are a counterexample to a proposed implicational universal to the effect that "in a given language, low and mid front vowels apparently only trigger palatalization if high front vowels trigger it too" (Kochetov 2011). Kochetov notes, however, that "Bhat (1978) mentions some cases where mid front vowels palatalize velars to the exclusion of high front vowels". The typological rarity of such cases may be due to the rarity of feature hierarchies like (42). More

The mergers in (43b) follow from the sisterhood of */ɛ/ and */a/ under the new hierarchy. A single contrast shift thus accounts for the patterning of a large number of phonological changes across the Algonquian family.

6 Areal isoglosses: Borrowing contrast shifts in the Ob-Ugric Mansi and Khanty languages

The Algonquian languages have relatively simple vowel systems, and the types of phonological activity we observed follow from the contrastive trees in a rather straightforward manner. To see how alternations work in the context of more complex and asymmetric feature trees, we need to look at languages with larger vowel systems. Harvey (2012) shows that the principles of contrast shift can be used to describe the sound changes which have occurred over time in the vowel systems of the Ob-Ugric languages, from the reconstructed Proto-Ob-Ugric up until modern times, starting approximately 3,400 years ago when Hungarian split from Ob-Ugric. Moreover, he shows that contrastive shifts in the Ob-Ugric Mansi and Khanty languages show clear isoglosses and are borrowed between languages.

The Ob-Ugric languages are found in central Russia, to the east of the Ural mountains along the Ob river system. The two branches of Ob-Ugric are the Mansi languages, in the southwest, and the Khanty languages, to the east and north. The Ob-Ugric languages inherited a complex vowel system: Proto-Ob-Ugric has been reconstructed to have nineteen vowel phonemes (Harvey 2012, based on Sammallahti 1988). Also characteristic of Ob-Ugric was a pervasive front-back vowel harmony that affected all vowels; we assume that the relevant feature is [front].

6.1 Proto-Mansi

We will focus here on Mansi. Starting from the Proto-Mansi first-syllable vowel system reconstructed by Steinitz (1955), and taking into account the phonological patterning attributed to that period, Harvey (2012) posits the Proto-Mansi contrastive hierarchy in (44).

---

expected is the fact that the palatalizations in question involve dorsal consonants, which, according to Kochetov (2011), are "almost exclusively targeted by /i/ and other front vowels", unlike coronals which may be targeted by high vocoids.

(44) Proto-Mansi (Harvey 2012): [long] > [front] > [high] > [round] > [low]
   a. Contrastive feature hierarchy for the (non–long) vowels

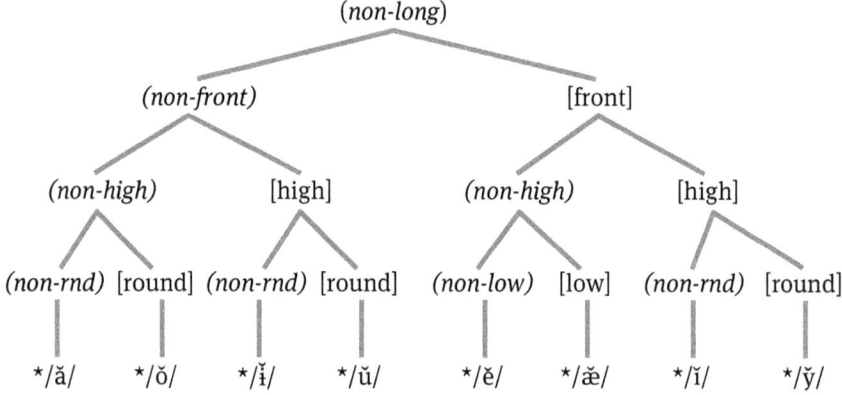

   b. Contrastive feature hierarchy for the [long] vowels

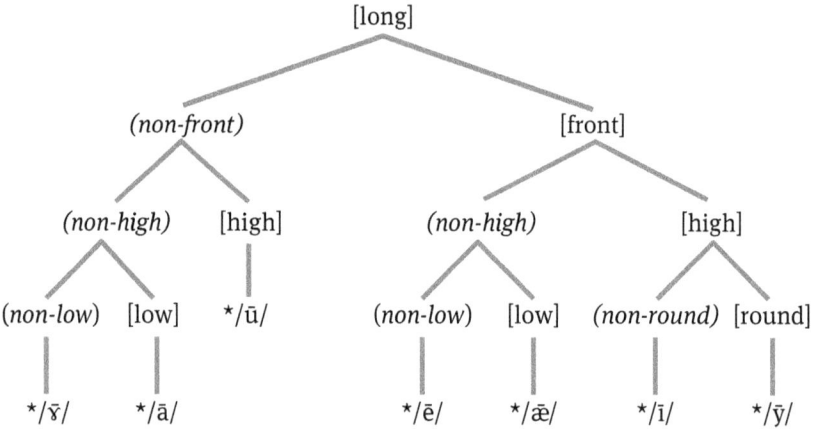

A major type of phonological activity that provides evidence for this hierarchy is front vowel harmony (45a), which we suppose to be governed by the feature [front]. The Ob-Ugric languages have no neutral vowels, therefore all vowels must have a contrastive value for this feature. Proto-Mansi also had a system of productive ablaut-like root-vowel alternations (Honti 1988a:149, 1988b:174), where a certain set of suffixes causes roots with long vowels to shorten, as in the Western Mansi examples in (45b).

(45) Feature activity reconstructed for Proto-Mansi
   a. Front vowel harmony
      Suffix vowels harmonize with root vowels in the feature [front]; thus, the vowel in the 1st person future suffix in Southern Mansi is front or back depending on the root vowel: e.g., *jām-ăm* 'I will go' ~ *wēr-ĕm* 'I will make'.
   b. Root-vowel alternations
      A [long] vowel in a monosyllabic root becomes (*non-long*) when it occurs with specific lexically-defined inflectional or derivational suffixes, as well as appearing in certain compound environments: e.g., Western Mansi *tyœls* 'I will sit down' ~ *tałt-* 'put into (a boat)', where WM /yœ/ ~ /a/ derives from Proto-Mansi */ǣ/ ~ */ǣ̆/; *wɣ̄ɣm* 'I see' > *wăj* 'he/she sees'.

Both front vowel harmony and root-vowel alternations have been reconstructed for the proto-languages (Honti 1988a:149, 1988b:174). Any contrastive hierarchy for Proto-Mansi must account for both of these processes. Moreover, changes to the hierarchies leading from Proto-Ob-Ugric to the modern languages must remain consistent with them in languages where they remain productive. That is, the features active in harmony and vowel alternation must remain contrastive.

The examples in (45) also illustrate the importance of markedness in the operation of these alternations. In front vowel harmony (45a), the suffix *-ăm* changes to *-ĕm*. Simply changing *ă* to be [front] yields the features (*non-long*), [front], (*non-high*), (*non-round*), a combination that does not exist in (44). In the branch of the tree under (*non-long*), [front], and (*non-high*), there is no contrastive (*non-round*); rather, we must choose between *non-low* */ĕ/ and [low] */ǣ̆/. The correct outcome is obtained by choosing the unmarked branch, */ĕ/. In (45b), the alternation */ǣ/ ~ */ǣ̆/ is straightforward (as is a similar alternation */ī/ ~ */ĭ/), but */ɣ̄/ ~ */ă/ again shows the effects of choosing the unmarked value of an unspecified feature; in this case, we choose (*non-round*) */ă/ rather than [round] */ŏ/.

One might question the inclusion of [long] as a feature in the hierarchy in (44). A currently widespread view represents the difference between long and short vowels in structural terms, rather than as a feature: a short vowel associates to a single timing unit, and a long vowel associates to two such units (see Odden 2011 for discussion). However, the long/short contrast interacts with other features, and therefore has to be represented somewhere in the contrastive tree.[10] Moreover, Oxford (2012b) shows how a length contrast can be easily reinterpreted as a tense ~ lax contrast, which is often represented in featural terms, depending on where in the feature hierarchy the relevant contrast is located. Therefore, including [long] in a contrastive feature hierarchy does not preclude representing length differences in structural terms.

6.2 Western Mansi

Early Western Mansi (~600 ybp) has been reconstructed to have thirteen vowels (Steinitz 1955:154; Sammallahti 1988:504; Honti 1998: 330). Harvey (2012) details the changes by which the Proto-Mansi vowel system in (44) evolved into that of Early Western Mansi. In addition to some mergers, at the Proto-Eastern-Western Mansi stage a new feature [contour] becomes contrastive for two vowels. Then in Early Western Mansi, [round] is promoted one step above [high]. These changes cause [low] to be non-contrastive, and yield the hierarchy in (46), where [contour] is realized as a diphthong (as with Proto-Mansi, the hierarchies are for vowels in initial syllables, which exhibit the full range of contrasts).

(46) Early Western Mansi (Harvey 2012): [long] > [front] > [round] > [high] > [contour]
    a. Contrastive feature hierarchy for the (*non-long*) vowels

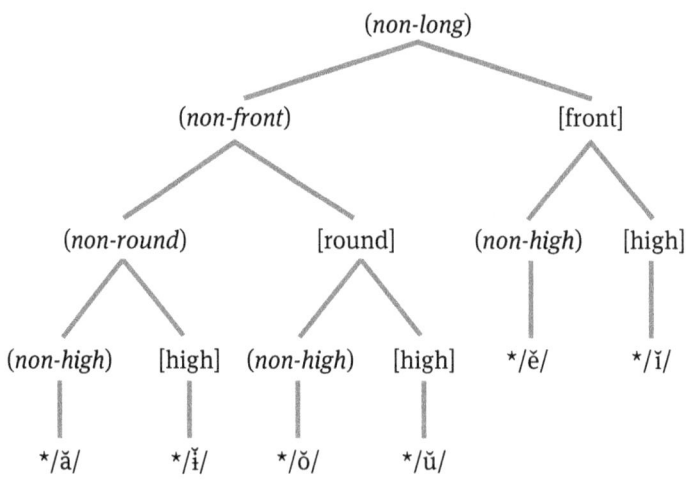

---

10 See, for example, analyses of Lithuanian vowel length in Campos-Astorkiza (2009) and Dresher (2009).

b. Contrastive feature hierarchy for the [long] vowels

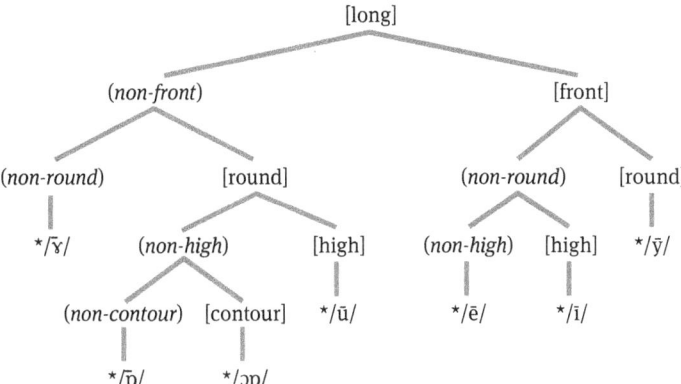

At some point a contrastive shift occurred whereby [front] dropped to the bottom of the hierarchy (47). As a result, five vowels, over one third of the inventory, no longer contrast for [front]. This change had important consequences for phonological activity in Western Mansi. The first consequence is that front harmony is lost. Ob-Ugric front/back harmony does not have neutral vowels: either all vowels participate in harmony, or none do. The loss of the front/back contrast in a significant portion of vowels thus caused the demise of harmony.

Second, the shift rearranges the pairs of vowels that participate in root-vowel alternations. Previously, */ï/ could alternate with */ĭ/ by changing [long] to (non-long). Now, however, there are two short counterparts of */ï/ with features (non-round) and [high]; of these, */ĭ/, not */ĭ/, is unmarked. One would predict that root-vowel alternation would be lost as a productive process when a pair like Southern Mansi ʎīχ 'wedge'~ ʎĭχt 'wedges' is no longer derivable by the phonology. Loss of productivity indeed occurs in the modern language.

(47)   Western Mansi (Harvey 2012): [long] > [round] > [high] > [contour] > [front]

a. Contrastive feature hierarchy for the (non-long) vowels

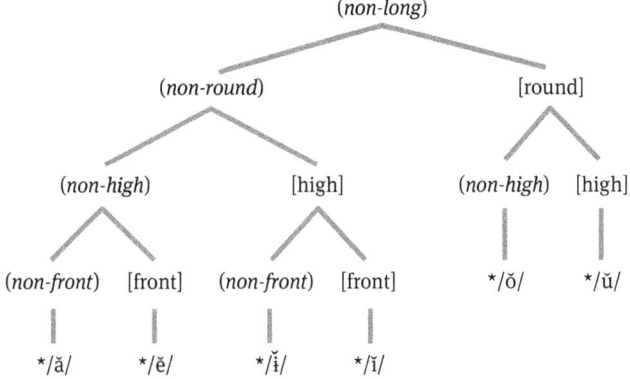

b. Contrastive feature hierarchy for the [long] vowels

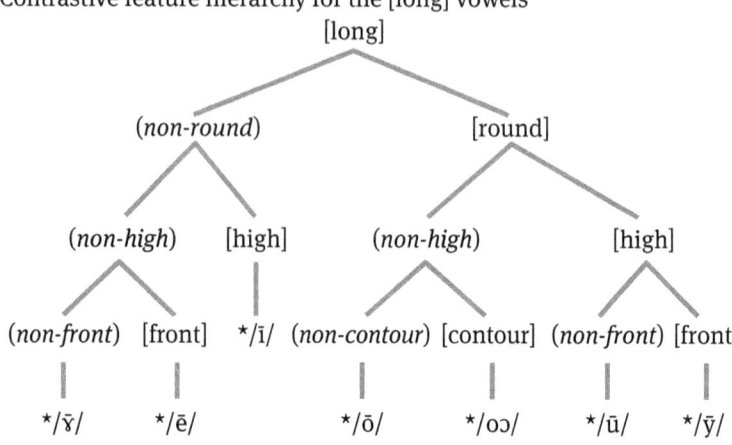

A third consequence has to do with sub-phonemic drift. This can be illustrated by the diachronic changes that vowels with contrastive [contour] underwent. The (non-contour) vowel */ō/ in (46b) developed from an earlier */ā/, and the [contour] vowel */ɔʊ/ developed from earlier */ǣ/. Both vowels underwent rounding, an ENHANCEMENT of their contrastive features (Stevens, Keyser, & Kawasaki 1986; Hall 2011). The addition of phonetic rounding may have contributed to the promotion of [round] as a contrastive feature, with the consequence that [low] is no longer contrastive. Lacking [low] the vowels are free to raise to */ō/ and */ɔʊ/, respectively. When [front] is demoted as in (47), it no longer constrains the vowels' contrastive space. The result is that */ɔʊ/ is able to front to /øœ/ (e.g., Modern Western Mansi /øœmp/ 'dog'), while */ō/ is also fronted, though not as far (/o̧tər/ 'prince').

6.3 Northern Mansi

Northern Mansi has reduced phonological complexity more than any other Mansi dialect group, to the extent that front harmony and productive root-vowel alternations have been completely lost. As in the Western dialect, all vowels in Early Northern Mansi were contrastive for [front], and as in that dialect, [front] was demoted over time. Starting from the Proto-Mansi vowel system in (44), Harvey (2012) posits that [long] dropped to the bottom of the hierarchy, and [round] was demoted below [low], yielding the tree in (48).

(48) Early Northern Mansi (Harvey 2012): [front] > [high] > [low] > [round] > [long]
   a. Contrastive feature hierarchy for the (non–front) vowels

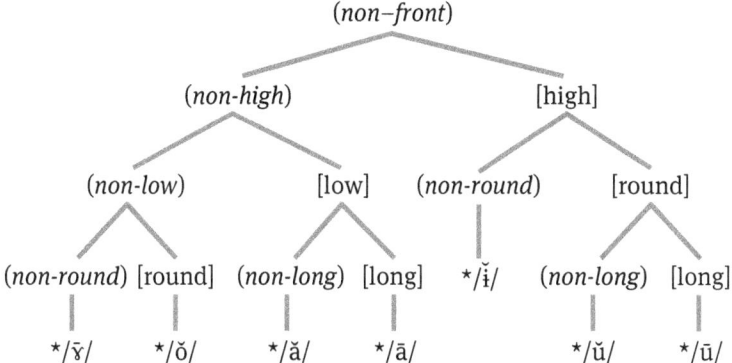

   b. Contrastive feature hierarchy for the [front] vowels

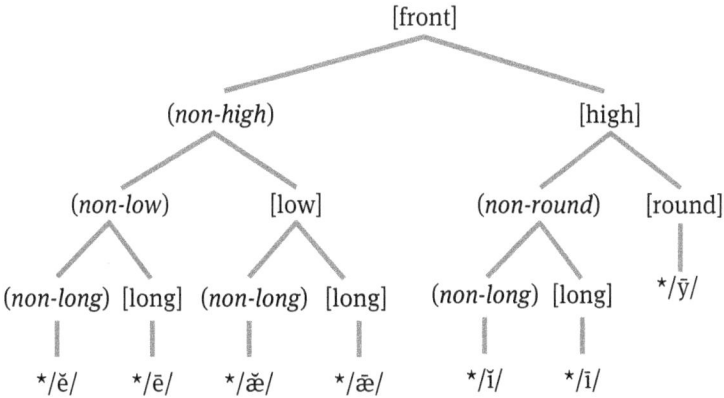

At a stage just prior to the modern Northern Mansi dialects, [front] was demoted as in (49).

(49) Pre-Modern Northern Mansi (Harvey 2012): [high] > [round] > [long] > [front]
a. Contrastive feature hierarchy for the (*non-high*) vowels

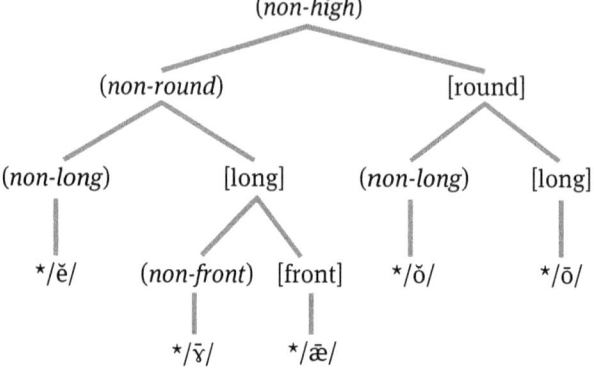

b. Contrastive feature hierarchy for the [high] vowels

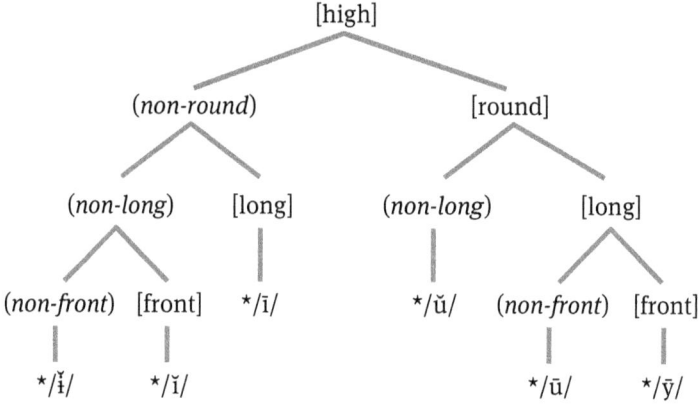

When the front feature is dropped to the lowest rank, about half of the vowels lose their contrastive [front] feature. In the next stage the three remaining [front] vowels are merged to their back counterparts: */ǽ/ > */ɤ̆/, */ĭ/ > */ɨ̆/, and */ȳ/ > */ū/. Once complete, these mergers leave no vowels with a contrastive [front] feature at all. As expected, front harmony is no longer viable, and has disappeared from Northern Mansi.

We also expect that root-vowel alternation would become untenable. For instance, in Proto-Mansi, /ū/ alternated with /ŭ/. After */ȳ/ has merged with */ū/, there is no way for a speaker of the modern language to tell which /ū/ should alternate and which should not. As predicted, vowel alternation has almost completely vanished in Northern Mansi.

Although the evolution of the vowel systems of Western and Northern Mansi differ in their details, in both the feature [front] was demoted, and in both front harmony and root-vowel alternations were adversely affected. Interestingly, the dropping of [front] has also produced two very different results. In Western Mansi, front dropping has caused some back vowels to become more front; in Northern Mansi, the loss of the same contrast has caused some front vowels to merge with their back counterparts.

6.4 Contrastive isoglosses

The dropping of [front] occurred in three of the four Mansi languages, and all three have lost front harmony. However, [front] dropping did not occur in the early history of Mansi. It can be shown that the shift occurred later in the daughter languages, as illustrated in (50), where X indicates when [front] dropping occurred.

(50) Chronology of [front] dropping in the Mansi languages

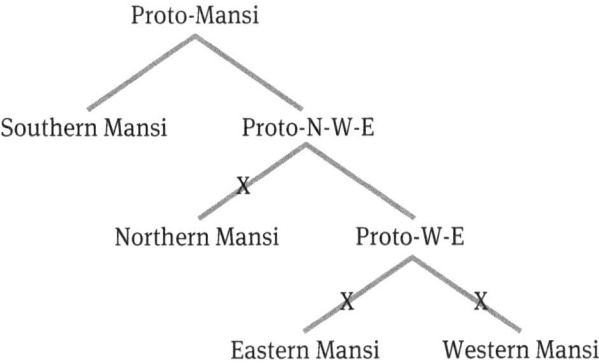

If [front] dropping is not a genetic inheritance common to the non-Southern Mansi languages, could it have been spread by areal diffusion? That is, can contrast shift show areal patterning, like other elements of linguistic systems? To investigate this question, Harvey (2012) plotted a number of contrast shifts on a map, and the results are shown in Figure 8.1. It is clear that the contrast shifts have occurred in a way that is not at all random.

Figure 8.1 shows the Ob-Ugric language area, in central Russia to the east of the Ural mountains along the Ob river system. A key to the dialect groupings and language name abbreviations is given below the map. Mansi languages (M) are in the southwest, and the Khanty languages (K) are east and north. The dashed

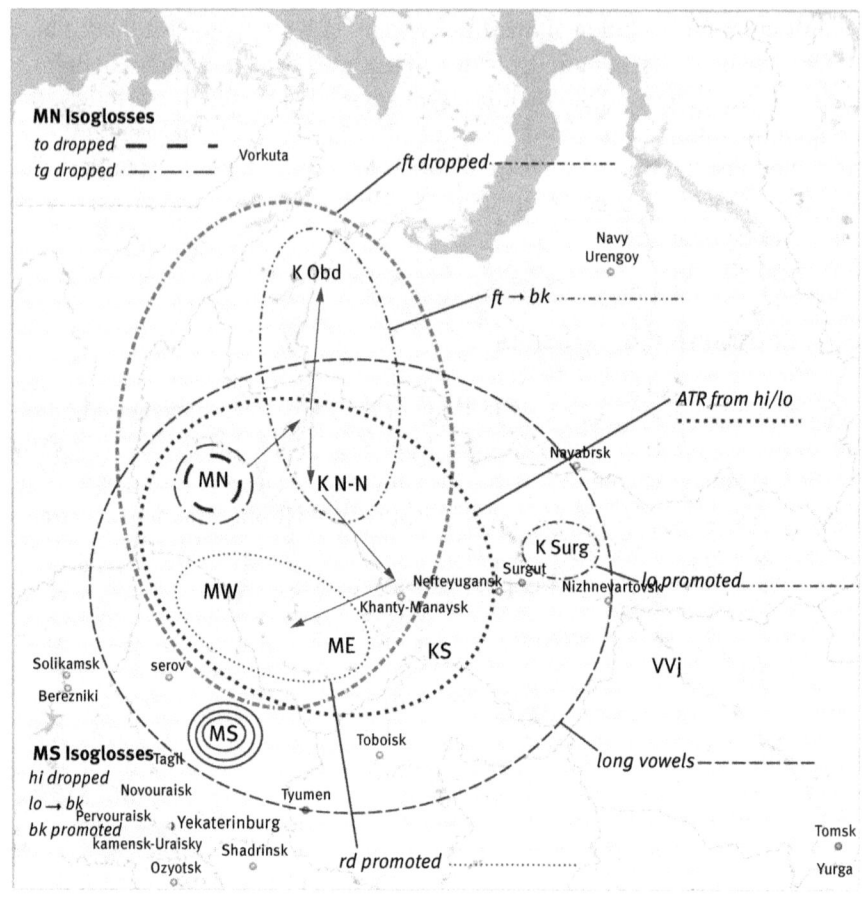

Figure 8.1: Ob-Ugric isoglosses of feature contrasts and contrast shifts (Harvey 2012)

Key to dialect groups and abbreviations

    KN: Northern Khanty   MN: Northern Mansi
        K Obd: Obdorsk
        K N-N: Kazym   MW: Western Mansi
    KE: Eastern Khanty
        K Surg: Surgut   ME: Eastern (Konda) Mansi
        VVj: Vach-Vasjugan
    KS: Southern (Irtysh) Khanty   MS: Southern (Tavda) Mansi

line labelled *ft dropped* shows all the languages which had the [front] dropping contrast shift.

It appears that the innovative dialect from which [front] dropping radiated is Northern Mansi. Northern, Western, and Eastern Mansi all participate in the shift. Interestingly, two of the Khanty languages, Kazym and Obdorsk Khanty, also had a phase where [front] dropped. Those languages that are geographically and culturally farther away from the likely innovation centre have not borrowed the shift. The arrows indicate the Ob river and its tributaries, which are the main routes for cultural contact and communication.

We conclude that there a pattern to these contrastive changes: they follow routes of cultural contact. Contrast shifts show clear isoglosses and can be borrowed between languages. The contrastive analysis of the Ob-Ugric languages presented here is also consistent with earlier dialect studies (Honti 1998; Steinitz 1955), and matches earlier observations about which dialects are conservative or innovative.

7 Conclusions

The approach to phonological typology we have sketched here is based on a fundamental distinction between a phonetic and phonological analysis of the sound systems of languages. This view builds on approaches to phonology pioneered by Sapir and the Prague School (Jakobson and Trubetzkoy), instantiated within a generative grammar. More specifically, it views phonemes as being composed of contrastive features that are themselves organized into language-particular hierarchies. Because of the hypothesized connection between contrast and activity, we expect languages with similar hierarchies and inventories to exhibit similar patterns.

In some of the language families we have surveyed here, feature hierarchies appear to be relatively stable, as exemplified by Manchu-Tungusic, Eastern Mongolian, Yupik-Inuit, and branches of Algonquin. Contrast shifts can occur, however, for various reasons, and these can result in dramatic differences in patterning, as shown by the modern Manchu languages, Eastern and Western Algonquin as compared with Central, and extensive changes in Ob-Ugric vowel systems viewed over a relatively long period of time. Finally, Ob-Ugric shows that elements of feature hierarchies can spread and be borrowed, like other aspects of linguistic structure.

We have seen that, like Sapir's languages C and D, languages with similar contrastive structures may show varying phonetic realizations. For example, the breakdown of the front-back contrast had different phonetic results in Western and Northern Mansi: in the former it resulted in some back vowels fronting, and in the latter a series of vowels that used to be front retracted and merged with back vowels. What the two dialects have in common is the dropping and subsequent loss of [front] as a contrastive feature; thus, it no longer constrained the phonetic ranges of the vowels. In Algonquian, the various palatalizations and mergers show phonetic differences, and the phonetic descriptions of the vowels vary from dialect to dialect. But dialects sharing the same contrastive hierarchy show similar patterns at that level.

We hope to have demonstrated that contrastive feature hierarchies provide an interesting and fruitful level of representation for typological research in phonology.

Acknowledgements: This article is a revised and expanded version of Dresher, Harvey, & Oxford (2014). For comments we are grateful to Larry Hyman, and to audiences at the CRC Summer Phonetics/phonology Workshop, University of Toronto, July 2012; NELS 43, CUNY Graduate Center, October 2012; the GLOW 36 Workshop on Diachronic Workings in Phonological Patterns, Lund University, April 2013; the annual meeting of the CLA, Victoria, B.C., June 2013; and the Workshop on Phonological Typology, Somerville College, University of Oxford, August 2013. We would also like to thank members of the project on Markedness and the Contrastive Hierarchy in Phonology at the University of Toronto (Dresher & Rice 2007): http://homes.chass.utoronto.ca/~contrast/. This research was supported in part by grants 410-2003-0913 and 410-08-2645 from the Social Sciences and Humanities Research Council of Canada.

References

Archangeli, Diana. 1988. Aspects of underspecification theory. *Phonology* 5. 183–207.
Barrie, Mike. 2003. Contrast in Cantonese vowels. *Toronto Working Papers in Linguistics* 20. 1–19.
Bhat, D. N. S. 1978. A general study of palatalization. In Joseph H. Greenberg, Charles A. Ferguson, & Edith A. Moravcsik (eds.), *Universals of human language,* vol. 2: *Phonology,* 47–92. Stanford: Stanford University Press.
Calabrese, Andrea. 2005. *Markedness and economy in a derivational model of phonology.* Berlin: Mouton de Gruyter.
Campos-Astorkiza, Judit Rebeka. 2009. *The role and representation of minimal contrast and the phonology – phonetics interaction.* München: Lincom Europa.
Chomsky, Noam & Morris Halle. 1968. *The sound pattern of English.* New York: Harper & Row.
Compton, Richard & B. Elan Dresher. 2011. Palatalization and "strong *i*" across Inuit dialects. *Canadian Journal of Linguistics/Revue canadienne de linguistique* 56. 203–228.

Dorais, Louis-Jacques. 2003. *Inuit uqausiqatigiit: Inuit languages and dialects (second, revised edition)*. Iqaluit: Nunavut Arctic College.
Dresher, B. Elan. 1998. On contrast and redundancy. Paper presented at the annual meeting of the Canadian Linguistic Association, May, Ottawa. Ms., University of Toronto.
Dresher, B. Elan. 2003. Contrast and asymmetries in inventories. In Anna-Maria di Sciullo (ed.), *Asymmetry in grammar*, vol. 2: *Morphology, phonology, acquisition*, 239–257. Amsterdam: John Benjamins.
Dresher, B. Elan. 2009. *The contrastive hierarchy in phonology*. Cambridge: Cambridge University Press.
Dresher, B. Elan. 2014. The arch not the stones: Universal feature theory without universal features. *Nordlyd* 41(2). 165–181, special issue on Features, ed. by Martin Krämer, Sandra Ronai, & Peter Svenonius. University of Tromsø – The Arctic University of Norway.
Dresher, B. Elan. 2015. The motivation for contrastive feature hierarchies in phonology. *Linguistic Variation* 15. 1–40.
Dresher, B. Elan. 2016. Contrast in phonology 1867–1967: History and development. *Annual Review of Linguistics* 2. 53–73.
Dresher, B. Elan. 2017. Contrastive feature hierarchies in Old English diachronic phonology. *Transactions of the Philological Society*, doi:10.1111/1467-968X.12105.
Dresher, B. Elan, Christopher Harvey, & Will Oxford. 2014. Contrast shift as a type of diachronic change. In Hsin-Lun Huang, Ethan Poole, & Amanda Rysling (eds.), *NELS 43: Proceedings of the Forty-Third Annual Meeting of the North East Linguistic Society, The City University of New York*, vol. 1, 103–116. Amherst, MA: GLSA.
Dresher, B. Elan & Andrew Nevins. 2017. Conditions on iterative rounding harmony in Oroqen. *Transactions of the Philological Society* 115. 365–394.
Dresher, B. Elan & Keren Rice. 2007. Markedness and the contrastive hierarchy in phonology. http://homes.chass. utoronto.ca/~contrast/.
Dresher, B. Elan & Xi Zhang. 2005. Contrast and phonological activity in Manchu vowel systems. *Canadian Journal of Linguistics/Revue canadienne de linguistique* 50. 45–82.
Fortescue, Michael, Steven A. Jacobson, & Lawrence D. Kaplan. 1994. *Comparative Eskimo dictionary with Aleut cognates*. Fairbanks: Alaska Native Language Center.
Gardner, Matt Hunt. 2012. Beyond the phonological void: Contrast and the Canadian Shift. Ms., Department of Linguistics, University of Toronto.
Hall, Daniel Currie. 2007. The role and representation of contrast in phonological theory. Doctoral dissertation, University of Toronto.
Hall, Daniel Currie. 2011. Phonological contrast and its phonetic enhancement: Dispersedness without dispersion. *Phonology* 28. 1–54.
Harvey, Christopher. 2012. Contrastive shift in Ob-Ugric vowel systems. Ms., University of Toronto.
Honti, László. 1988a. Die ob-ugrischen Sprachen I: Die wogulische Sprache. In Sinor (ed.) 1988, 147–171.
Honti, László. 1988b. Die ob-ugrischen Sprachen II: Die ostjakische Sprache. In Sinor (ed.) 1988, 172–196.
Honti, László. 1998. Ob Ugrian. In Daniel Abondolo (ed.), *The Uralic languages*, 327–357. London: Routledge.
Hyman, Larry M. 2007. Where's phonology in typology? *Linguistic Typology* 11. 265–271.
Jakobson, Roman. 1972 [1931]. Principles of historical phonology. In Allan R. Keiler (ed.), *A reader in historical and comparative linguistics*, 121–138. New York: Holt, Rinehart

and Winston. Translation of Prinzipien der historischen Phonologie. *Travaux du cercle linguistique de Prague* 4. 247–267. Copenhagen, 1931.

Jakobson, Roman, C. Gunnar M. Fant, & Morris Halle. 1952. *Preliminaries to speech analysis*. MIT Acoustics Laboratory, Technical Report, No. 13. Reissued by MIT Press, Cambridge, Mass., 11th printing, 1976.

Jakobson, Roman & Morris Halle. 1956. *Fundamentals of language*. The Hague: Mouton.

Kabak, Barış. 2011. Turkish vowel harmony. In van Oostendorp et al. (eds.) 2011.

Kaun, Abigail Rhoades. 1995. *The typology of rounding harmony: An Optimality Theoretic approach*. Doctoral dissertation, University of California, Los Angeles.

Kiparsky, Paul. 1965. *Phonological change*. Doctoral dissertation, MIT.

Ko, Seongyeon. 2010. A contrastivist view on the evolution of the Korean vowel system. In Hiroki Maezawa & Azusa Yokogoshi (eds.), *MITWPL 61: Proceedings of the Sixth Workshop on Altaic Formal Linguistics*, 181–196.

Ko, Seongyeon. 2011. Vowel contrast and vowel harmony shift in the Mongolic languages. *Language Research* 47. 23–43.

Ko, Seongyeon. 2012. *Tongue root harmony and vowel contrast in Northeast Asian languages*. Doctoral dissertation, Cornell University.

Kochetov, Alexei. 2011. Palatalization. In van Oostendorp et al. (eds.) 2011.

Korn, David. 1969. Types of labial vowel harmony in the Turkic languages. *Anthropological Linguistics* 11. 98–106.

Li, Bing. 1996. *Tungusic vowel harmony*. The Hague: Holland Academic Graphics.

Li, Shulan & Qian Zhong. 1986. *Xiboyu jianzhi* [A brief introduction to the Xibe language]. Beijing: Minzu Chubanshe.

Mackenzie, Sara. 2011. Contrast and the evaluation of similarity: Evidence from consonant harmony. *Lingua* 121. 1401–1423.

Mackenzie, Sara. 2013. Laryngeal co-occurrence restrictions in Aymara: Contrastive representations and constraint interaction. *Phonology* 30. 297–345.

McCawley, James D. 1967. Edward Sapir's "phonologic representation". *International Journal of American Linguistics* 33. 106–111.

Mielke, Jeff. 2008. *The emergence of distinctive features*. Oxford: Oxford University Press.

Moulton, William G. 1960. The short vowel systems of Northern Switzerland: A study in structural dialectology. *Word* 16. 155–182.

Nevins, Andrew. 2010. *Locality in vowel harmony*. Cambridge, MA: MIT Press.

Newman, Stanley. 1944. *Yokuts language of California* (VFPA 2). New York: The Viking Fund Publications in Anthropology.

Odden, David. 2011. The representation of vowel length. In van Oostendorp et al. (eds.) 2011.

Oostendorp, Marc van, Colin J. Ewen, Elizabeth Hume, & Keren Rice (eds.). 2011. *The Blackwell companion to phonology*. Oxford: Blackwell.

Oxford, Will. 2012a. "Contrast shift" in the Algonquian languages. In A. McKillen & J. Loughren (eds.), *Proceedings from the Montreal-Ottawa-Toronto (MOT) Phonology Workshop 2011: Phonology in the 21st Century: In Honour of Glyne Piggott. McGill Working Papers in Linguistics* 22 (1).

Oxford, Will. 2012b. On the contrastive status of vowel length. Presented at the MOT Phonology Workshop, University of Toronto, March 2012. http://home.cc.umanitoba.ca/~oxfordwr/papers/Oxford_2011_MOT. pdf.

Oxford, Will. 2015. Patterns of contrast in phonological change: Evidence from Algonquian vowel systems. *Language* 91. 308–357.

Padgett, Jaye. 2003. Contrast and post-velar fronting in Russian. *Natural Language & Linguistic Theory* 21. 39–87.
Purnell, Thomas & Eric Raimy. 2013. Contrastive features in phonetic implementation: The English vowel system. Presented at the CUNY Phonology Forum Conference On The Feature, January 2013.
Purnell, Thomas & Eric Raimy. 2015. Distinctive features, levels of representation, and historical phonology. In Patrick Honeybone & Joseph Salmons (eds.), *The handbook of historical phonology*, 522–544. Oxford: Oxford University Press.
Qinggertai (Chingeltei). 1982. Guanyu yuanyin hexielü [On the vowel harmony rule]. *Zhongguo Yuyanxue Bao* 1. 200–220.
Rice, Keren. 2003. Featural markedness in phonology: Variation. In Lisa Cheng & Rint Sybesma (eds.), *The second Glot International state-of-the-article book: The latest in linguistics*, 387–427. Berlin: Mouton de Gruyter.
Rice, Keren. 2007. Markedness in phonology. In Paul de Lacy (ed.), *The Cambridge handbook of phonology*, 79–97. Cambridge: Cambridge University Press.
Roeder, Rebecca & Matt Hunt Gardner. 2013. The phonology of the Canadian Shift revisited: Thunder Bay and Cape Breton. *University of Pennsylvania Working Papers in Linguistics: Selected Papers from NWAV 41*, 19 (2). 161–170.
Rohany Rahbar, Elham. 2008. A historical study of the Persian vowel system. *Kansas Working Papers in Linguistics* 30. 233–245.
Sammallahti, Pekka. 1988. Historical phonology of the Uralic languages. In Sinor (ed.) 1988, 478–554.
Samuels, Bridget D. 2011. *Phonological architecture: A biolinguistic perspective*. Oxford: Oxford University Press.
Sapir, Edward. 1925. Sound patterns in language. *Language* 1. 37–51. Reprinted in Martin Joos (ed.), *Readings in linguistics I*, 19–25. Chicago, IL: University of Chicago Press, 1957.
Saussure, Ferdinand de. 1972 [1916]. *Cours de linguistique générale. Publié par Charles Bally et Albert Sechehaye; avec la collaboration de Albert Riedlinger. Éd. critique préparée par Tullio de Mauro.* Paris: Payot.
Sinor, Denis (ed.). 1988. *Handbuch der Orientalistik: Handbook of Uralic studies*, vol. 1: *The Uralic languages*. Leiden: E. J. Brill.
Steinitz, Wolfgang. 1955. *Geschichte des wogulischen Vokalismus*. Berlin: Akademie-Verlag.
Stevens, Kenneth N., Samuel Jay Keyser, & Haruko Kawasaki. 1986. Toward a phonetic and phonological theory of redundant features. In Joseph S. Perkell & Dennis H. Klatt (eds.), *Symposium on invariance and variability of speech processes*, 432–469. Hillsdale, NJ: Lawrence Erlbaum.
Svantesson, Jan-Olaf. 1985. Vowel harmony shift in Mongolian. *Lingua* 67. 283–327.
Vajda, Edward. 2001. Test materials dated August 17, 2001. Posted at http://pandora.cii.wwu.edu/vajda/ling201/test2materials/Phonology3.htm.
Walker, Rachel. 2001. Round licensing and bisyllabic triggers in Altaic. *Natural Language & Linguistic Theory* 19. 827–878.
Walker, Rachel. 2014. Nonlocal trigger-target relations. *Linguistic Inquiry* 45. 501–523.
Zhang, Xi. 1996. *Vowel systems of the Manchu-Tungus languages of China*. Doctoral dissertation, University of Toronto.
Zhang, Xi & B. Elan Dresher. 1996. Labial harmony in written Manchu. *Saksaha: A Review of Manchu Studies* 1. 13–24.

Ellen Broselow
Laryngeal contrasts in second language phonology

Abstract: This chapter investigates the acquisition of obstruent laryngeal contrasts in foreign language acquisition. The goal is to determine the alignment between the putative universal markedness relationships established through cross-linguistic investigation and the patterns found in second language phonology, particularly those patterns that appear to be independent of both the native and the foreign language systems.

Cross-linguistic research has revealed that obstruent laryngeal contrasts are more common in nonfinal than in final positions; that when contrast is limited in final position, voiceless obstruents are the preferred segment type; and that the preferred repair for underlying voiced obstruents in final position is devoicing of the obstruent rather than any of the logically possible alternatives such as post-obstruent vowel insertion. A survey of studies on the acquisition of foreign language laryngeal contrasts supports a hierarchy of difficulty in the acquisition of foreign structures that is consistent with the principles established by typological investigation: learners from a wide range of native language backgrounds show earlier success in mastering final voiceless than final voiced obstruents, even when the native language has neither and the foreign language has both, while the opposite order of acquisition is not attested. Furthermore, devoicing is frequently found in second language phonology even in the absence of a phonological devoicing process in either the native or the foreign language.

However, second language learners do exhibit some tendencies that are not predicted by established typological generalizations, such as effects of word size and of manner and/or place of articulation on the likelihood of obstruent devoicing. We consider possible explanations for these tendencies as well as the question of whether these tendencies ever become phonologized as categorical processes in established native language grammars.

1 Introduction

Among the strongest candidates for typological universals in phonology are three generalizations that pertain to laryngeal contrasts. The first generalization refers to favored contrast position: a language that exhibits laryngeal contrasts in final position (whether syllable-final, word-final, or phrase-final) will exhibit laryngeal contrast in initial positions as well. The second generalization concerns favored segment type: where a language limits or suppresses laryngeal contrasts in final position, the obstruents most likely to surface in this position are voiceless. And the third generalization addresses favored repair: languages that ban voiced obstruents in final position typically enforce this ban by devoicing underlyingly voiced obstruents, despite the in-principle availability of alternative strategies such as consonant deletion, vowel insertion, and nasalization (see Blevins 2004 and Steriade 2001/2008, among many others).

If these generalizations are true universals, we expect them to meet the criteria defined by Blevins (2010), following Kiparsky (2008):

(1) Prerequisites for true phonological universals
   a. Phonological universals should have no exceptions.
   b. Phonological universals should constrain change.
   c. Phonological universals should emerge spontaneously within grammars (e.g., as in the final devoicing often associated with children's L1 English productions).
   d. Learners will not construct grammars that violate universals.
   e. Universals are part of every grammar.

Potentially fruitful test cases for criteria (1c) and (1d) involve new linguistic systems, among them the patterns of speakers acquiring a novel language. Typological markedness has frequently been invoked to explain the emergence of patterns in second language (L2) phonology that appear to have no basis in either the native or the foreign language grammars (e.g., Eckman 1977, 1984). A surprising number of L2 studies have reported that for speakers of native languages that lack final laryngeal contrasts, or that lack any final obstruents, the mastery of final voiceless obstruents precedes the mastery of final voiced obstruents. This finding has served as a veritable poster child for arguments that second language learning is guided by universal principles, even in the absence of direct supporting evidence in the input to the learner.

The goal of this chapter is to survey the literature on the second language acquisition of laryngeal contrasts, in order to determine, first, the extent to which L2 patterns align with typological generalizations, and second, whether the second language data can shed light on the nature and source of these typological generalizations. To begin, we distinguish two opposing views (along a broad spectrum) concerning the nature of typological asymmetries. On one view, typology reflects what Moreton (2008) calls "channel bias": factors based in articulation and perception make certain structures less likely to survive in the transmission of language across generations (Blevins 2004 and Ohala 1981, among many others), and listeners' imperfect perception of more fragile contrasts ultimately results in phonologization of a system lacking these contrasts (Hyman 1976). The numerous aerodynamic and acoustic factors that make voicing difficult to maintain and to perceive in final positions (reviewed in Blevins 2004, 2006 and Myers 2012) make the typological generalizations concerning laryngeal contrasts very strong candidates for this sort of explanation. However, some L2 evidence has been argued to support the view that at least some typological generalizations reflect what Moreton calls "analytic bias", defined as "cognitive biases which facilitate the learning of some phonological patterns and inhibit that of others" (Moreton 2008: 84). On this view, language learners simply will not entertain the hypothesis that the system they are learning fails to conform to the relevant typological generalization. In surveying the second language literature, we will consider the fit of the second language data, particularly the finding that L2 learners frequently master some L2 structures earlier than other equally novel structures, with typological generalizations. We will consider explanations of the L2 patterns ranging from the articulatory and perceptual difficulty of particular structures (channel bias effects) to learning biases potentially rooted in universal grammatical constraints (analytic bias effects).

Before proceeding, a caveat is in order regarding the scope of this survey. First, in considering the acquisition of final obstruents, we will consider only single obstruents in final position, since the introduction of consonant clusters introduces additional factors that cloud the debate. Second, the term "second language acquisition" casts a wide net, including learners ranging from children to adults, with varying levels of proficiency and exposure, and situations ranging from naturalistic learning to formal instruction. Furthermore, the studies in the second language literature below include a wide range of methodologies which makes comparison across studies difficult. We will see, however, that certain patterns emerge across a wide range of subject populations and methodologies.

Section 2 reviews the typological claims concerning the favored positions for laryngeal contrasts in native language systems, as well as favored segment types in different positions. In Section 3 we will see that studies of speakers from a wide range of native languages show more success in mastering the typologically more natural structures, and we will consider possible explanations of individual cases. Section 4 focuses on the question of whether the preferred repair strategy for those learners who fail to successfully produce final voiced obstruents is devoicing of the obstruent, as predicted by Steriade's (2001/2008) proposal. Here we will consider the interaction of devoicing with speaker-dependent factors such as proficiency as well as linguistic factors such as word size and the manner and place of articulation of the target final obstruents. We conclude by discussing the implications of the second language data for theories of typology.

2 Preferred position of contrast and preferred segment type

The typological literature on laryngeal contrasts presents convincing evidence for two generalizations: (i) laryngeal contrasts in nonfinal positions are more common than such contrasts in final positions; and (ii) when contrast is absent or actively suppressed in final position, voiceless obstruents are the likely survivors. Of the 51 languages surveyed by Keating et al. (1983), 18 displayed "at least some neutralization of voicing-related contrasts among stops" in final position (Westbury & Keating 1986: 160).

However, the facts demand more fine-grained distinctions than simply final vs. nonfinal positions. Contrasting word-final and word-internal syllable-final positions, both Wetzels & Mascaró (2001) and Myers (2012) argue that devoicing in syllable-final position implies devoicing in word-final position, but not vice versa. Thus, Myers (2012) presents examples of languages in which devoicing affects only word-final obstruents (e.g., Russian, Walloon, and Uyghur) as well as languages in which syllable-final obstruents, both within and at the end of words, are voiceless (e.g., Takelma, Breton, and Malay). However, languages with devoicing only in word-internal syllable-final position appear to be unattested. A further distinction between word-final and utterance-final positions is made by Westbury & Keating (1986), who argue that "some effects commonly reported as 'word' effects are in fact constrained by pause – i.e. they are utterance effects" (Westbury & Keating 1986: 161). Blevins (2006) and Myers (2012), reviewing the factors that favor devoicing in prepausal position, provide convincing arguments for a diachronic scenario in which both word-final and subsequent syllable-final devoicing develop from the generalization of utterance-final devoicing. Consistent with this proposal, Myers & Padgett (2015) provide evidence that participants exposed in artificial language learning experiments to utterance-final obstruent devoicing extended devoicing to utterance-medial word-final coda obstruents (though the converse did not hold: participants exposed to utterance-final voicing did not extend devoicing to utterance-internal syllable codas).

In addition to position in the syllable, word, and utterance, preceding and following segmental context are crucially important factors for laryngeal contrast. Thus, even heterosyllabic obstruents within a cluster frequently assimilate in voicing (see, e.g., Lombardi 1995 for a set of grammatical constraints meant to reflect the typological possibilities). Steriade (1999) argues that the relevant factor determining the possibility of voicing contrasts is not prosodic structure *per se* but rather the extent to which specific contexts allow the realization of acoustic cues that signal the contrast (for example, the possibility of release). Steriade proposes the hierarchy below (adapted here from Gordon's 2007 summary), in which the possibility of contrast in one position on the hierarchy implies the possibility of contrast in all positions to the left (examples of languages along the hierarchy appear below each cutoff point):

(2) Implicational hierarchy (after Steriade 1999, Gordon 2007)

Voicing contrasts preferred   Voicing contrasts dispreferred

Intersonorant....presonorant.....word-finally.....preobstruent....all positions

Totontepec, Mixe   Lithuanian   Hungarian   Arabic   Khasi

The question of preferred member of contrasting laryngeal sets also demands finer-grained distinctions than those embodied in the common assumption that voiceless obstruents are less marked than voiced obstruents; the choice of preferred laryngeal specification is related both to the position in which the obstruent appears and to the nature of the laryngeal contrast in individual languages. The term "voicing contrast" as used in both the typological literature and the second language phonology literature often conflates two distinct types of contrast: voicing contrasts, which oppose voiceless and voiced consonants (short lag VOT vs. prevoiced), and aspiration contrasts, which oppose aspirated and unaspirated consonants (long lag vs. short lag VOT). These differences have typological consequences in terms of preferred segment type. In final position, the favored member of a voiceless-voiced contrast is typically the voiceless member, while in languages relying on a contrast between voiceless aspirated and unaspirated pairs, aspirated stops may emerge as the output of neutralization (Westbury & Keating 1986; Vaux & Samuels 2005). Cross-linguistic study reveals interactions between contrast type and contrast position; Keating et al. (1983) argue that languages with a true initial voicing contrast (such as Arabic, Dutch, and Japanese) generally show the same contrast possibilities in initial and medial positions, while languages with an initial aspiration contrast (such as Gaelic, Mandarin, and Swedish) frequently show deaspiration and/or voicing of intervocalic medial stops.

The phonological specifications that best characterize the different types of laryngeal contrast are a matter of some debate, rooted in larger debates concerning binary vs. unary features, the role and extent of of underspecification, and the notion of universal markedness hierarchies implying a single least marked member of a series. Voiceless unaspirated stops are characterized as [-voice] by Wetzels & Mascaró (2001), who argue for binary specification of voicing, but as lacking any specified laryngeal features by Lombardi (1995), who argues for privative [voice] and [aspiration], with voiceless unaspirated stops representing the unspecified (and least marked) value. However, Vaux, & Samuels (2005) argue that the universal output of laryngeal neutralization in stops is a segment that is underspecified for laryngeal features, and that languages vary in the surface realization of the underspecified stop, which may be either aspirated or unaspirated. Arguments for full specification are provided by Beckman et al. (2011), who claim that the two-way laryngeal contrast in Swedish is best characterized as a contrast between fully specified [spread glottis] and [voiced]). Iverson & Salmons (2011) present a typology of final laryngeal neutralization that provides ten options defined in terms of insertion or deletion of the features [voice], [spread], and [constricted] – of which at least seven are, they argue, attested. The possibility that languages might differ not only in the phonetic realization of a contrast but also in the phonological specification of what might appear to be similar contrasts across languages highlights the difficulty of deciding at what level a typological generalization must hold in order to be considered universal (a point made in detail in Hyman's 2008 discussion of the distinction between "descriptive universals" and "analytical universals"). An additional complication comes from disagreement in the correct analyses of individual languages – see, for example, the disagreement between Blevins (2004, 2006, 2010) and Yu (2004), who argue for the existence of productive final voicing, and Kiparky (2008), who argues that closer inspection of the putative voicing languages does not support the existence of final obstruent voicing as a true phonological process.

Despite disagreements of analysis, however, some cross-linguistic generalizations about the preferred position of voicing contrasts and the preferred output of contrast suppression have emerged as relatively uncontroversial: final position is the most likely position to exhibit impoverished contrast, and the presence of final voiced obstruents implies the presence of voiceless obstruents in final position. These generalizations therefore serve as a starting point for the investigation of the acquisition of voicing contrasts in second language learning. As we will see below, numerous studies have documented that L2 learners tend to master the typologically less marked laryngeal structures more readily than the more marked structures, even when both are equally novel for the learner.

3 Hierarchy of difficulty in L2 voicing contrasts

Not surprisingly, the second language literature contains no studies of L2 production that have manipulated and controlled every positional variable that may affect the realization of obstruent laryngeal contrasts (position in the word and the utterance; context in terms of word and sentence stress and intonation; and preceding and following segmental contexts). Nonetheless, studies using a variety of methods and a variety of contexts have converged on the finding of a hierarchy of difficulty (Broselow & Kang 2013): L2 learners are more successful in producing novel voicing contrasts in typologically less marked (i.e., nonfinal) positions, and are more successful in producing final voiceless than voiced obstruents. We consider the results on the acquisition of L2 final laryngeal contrasts in terms of the learners' native language backgrounds: languages with no final obstruents; languages with only voiceless final obstruents; languages with a final laryngeal contrast; and languages that lack a voicing contrast even in nonfinal positions.

3.1 L1 has no final obstruents

Perhaps the most well documented cases of laryngeal contrast acquisition involve speakers of a native language with no final obstruents whose target language contains both voiceless and voiced final obstruents. For these speakers, both classes of final obstruent are equally novel, so asymmetry in the mastery of one class over the other cannot, at least at first glance, be ascribed to either the native or the target language. Yet numerous studies have documented greater accuracy in the production of English final voiceless than voiced obstruents by native speakers of Mandarin (Eckman 1981; Flege & Davidian 1984; Weinberger 1987; Wang 1995; Yavas 2009), Tswana (Wissing & Zonneveld 1996), the Tibeto-Burman languages Angami and Ao (Wiltshire 2006), and Japanese (Eckman 1981; Edge 1991; Yavas 2009) – all languages that lack word-final (and, in many cases, syllable-final) obstruents. Despite large differences across studies in the rates of target-like productions, final voiceless obstruents still show substantially higher accuracy than final voiced obstruents. In Wang's (1995) word production task, for example, 19% of final voiceless stops produced by Mandarin speakers in English pseudowords were identified as target-like, as opposed to only 2% of final voiced stops. For Wissing & Zonneveld's (1996) Tswana speakers, percentages of target-like final obstruents were much higher overall, but the difference between voiceless vs. voiced final obstruents was still large (74% vs. 52%). The earlier mastery of final voiceless stops is of course in line with typological generalizations, and the literature reveals no reports of learners who are more successful in producing final voiced than voiceless obstruents.

All of the studies mentioned above involve English as the target language. Unfortunately, a study of Mandarin speakers learning Swedish (Abrahamsson 2003) focused only on changes in rates of epenthesis and deletion over time; productions with voicing change were coded as correct, and no report was made of individual error rates for final voiceless and voiced obstruents. The paucity of studies addressing the acquisition of final-contrast languages other than English is a lamentable gap in the second language acquisition literature, and without such studies it is difficult to distinguish English-specific effects from more general effects.

3.2 L1 has only voiceless final obstruents

Earlier mastery of final voiceless than voiced obstruents is expected among speakers whose native language limits final obstruents to voiceless, and this pattern is well attested, both for speakers of languages with productive voicing alternations (German, Smith et al. 2009; Dutch, Simon 2009, 2010; Polish, Flege & Davidian 1984; Catalan, Cebrian 2000) and for speakers of languages that lack such alternations but nonetheless restrict final obstruents to voiceless (Cantonese, Edge 1991, Peng & Ann 2004; Taiwanese Mandarin, Wang 1995; Japanese, Edge 2004; and Thai, Hancin-Bhatt 2000).

Greater accuracy in the production of final voiceless obstruents has been found not only for learners of English, but also for Cantonese-speaking learners of French (Cichocki et al. 1993) and German-speaking learners of Swedish (Hammarberg 1990). While we cannot eliminate the native language as the (possibly sole) source of this asymmetry, it is important to note that final voicing is realized very differently in French and Swedish than in English. In French and Swedish, closure voicing in final stops is a major cue to the final voicing contrast (Blevins 2004; Helgason & Ringen 2008), whereas in English, final obstruents are often at least partially devoiced, and voicing during closure does not appear to be a necessary cue for English speakers to identify a final stop as voiced (Hillenbrand et al. 1984). Thus, these studies suggest that the asymmetric mastery of final voiceless vs. voiced obstruents in second language acquisition cannot be ascribed solely to facts about the way this contrast is realized in English.

3.3 L1 has a final voicing contrast

The assumption that L2 learners take their native language system as their starting point predicts that speakers of languages with only final voiceless obstruents will show greater difficulty in producing L2 voiced than voiceless final obstruents. Similarly, where both the L1 and the L2 employ laryngeal contrasts in final position, we might reasonably expect learners to be equally proficient in producing L2 voiceless and voiced final obstruents. In fact, however, devoicing of English final obstruents has been noted among native speakers of two languages that are reported to have a two-way laryngeal contrast in final position, Farsi (Eckman 1984) and Hungarian (Altenberg & Vago 1983). These findings are unexpected if the native language grammar serves as the starting point for second language acquisition, and are perhaps equally surprising if we approach the problem as one of cross-language differences in phonetic implementation; since Hungarian final stops are reported to have significant voicing during closure (Gosy & Ringen 2009), transfer of the L1 articulatory routines would seem to suggest that Hungarian speakers' final stops in English should sound, if anything, even more fully voiced than native speakers' final English stops. We will return to possible explanations of this phenomenon in Section 3.5.

3.4 L1 has no voice contrast

An ideal testing ground for a hierarchy of difficulty involving position of laryngeal contrast is provided by learners whose native languages lack laryngeal contrast not only in final position but in any position. For speakers of such languages, L2 contrasts in final and nonfinal positions are equally novel. While there do not seem to be any studies of this ideal combination (L1 lacking laryngeal contrasts in all positions and L2 allowing both final and nonfinal laryngeal contrasts), Hansen (2004) studies English learners of Vietnamese, a language in which she reports that laryngeal contrast, even in initial position, is possible only for coronal stops and for labiodental and velar fricatives. Hansen carried out a longitudinal study of two Vietnamese speakers learning English, including three lengthy interviews and word list reading tasks spaced over one year. While the focus of her study was on the speakers' production of English codas, she does informally report that accuracy was consistently higher for onsets than for codas, supporting a hierarchy of difficulty effect for position. Hansen's data also provide additional support for a hierarchy of difficulty for voiceless vs. voiced final obstruents. Although in Vietnamese neither voiced nor voiceless fricatives occur in final position, where the only possible consonants are voiceless stops, nasals, and glides, she reports that "voiceless consonants emerged before their voiceless counterparts [. . .] a finding consistent for every voiceless-voiced pair" (Hansen 2004: 113). This asymmetry held for both participants, in both the interview data and the word list task.

A language that lacks a voicing contrast in any position is Korean. Although Korean does employ a three-way laryngeal contrast among tense, aspirated, and plain voiceless stops in nonfinal positions, voicing *per se* is never contrastive; unaspirated stops are predictably voiced in intersonorant positions, voiceless elsewhere. Major & Faudree (1996) investigated Korean speakers' productions of English obstruents in initial, intervocalic medial, and final positions. In a word list reading task, Major & Faudree found no positional effect for voiceless obstruents, 98% of which were judged as target-like in all three positions. For voiced obstruents, however, productions in final position were significantly less target-like (38%) than those in initial or medial positions (98% or above for both). Since voiced obstruents do not occur in either word-initial or word-final position in Korean, this result is not readily attributable to the native language, but is consistent with the typological generalization that voicing contrasts are more marked in final position than in presonorant positions.

Major & Faudree's (1996) study was designed to investigate the claim of Eckman (1977) that the presence of voicing contrast in final position implies a contrast in medial position, which in turn implies initial contrast. This claim conflicts with Steriade's (1999) hierarchy, which identifies intersonorant position as the most favored position for voicing contrasts (with the implication that intersonorant contrast implies initial contrast). The fact that the Korean speakers' productions of voiceless stops were judged equally target-like in medial and initial positions, despite the native language process of intersonorant voicing, might be taken as support for Steriade's claim that intersonorant position is the most favored for voicing contrasts, since this is the position where native language effects could make voiceless obstruents difficult to produce. However, an alternative explanation is that the Korean speakers identified the English stops with their native language aspirated stops, which do not undergo intersonorant voicing. This is consistent with the adaptation of voiceless stops in English words borrowed into Korean, which are typically adapted as aspirated (e.g., [pʰoːkʰa] 'poker'), even when the original stop is unaspirated in English (Oh 1996; Kenstowicz 2005).

3.5 Possible explanations of the difficulty hierarchies

The studies reviewed above provide evidence for hierarchies of difficulty consistent with typological generalizations: L2 learners show evidence of greater accuracy in producing voicing contrasts in nonfinal than in final positions, and greater accuracy in producing final voiceless than voiced obstruents. These asymmetries are particularly interesting when they appear to be emergent – that is, when neither the native nor the target language provides evidence for the asymmetry. There are essentially three categories of explanations for learners' relative lack of success in producing final voiced obstruents, which can be summarized as follows:

(3) Possible explanations of failure to produce final voiced obstruents in L2
    a. Perception-based: Non-native speakers perceive voiced final obstruents as voiceless.
        L2 speaker's output target = voiceless;
        L2 productions perceived by native speakers as voiceless.

b. Articulation-based: Non-native speakers produce non-target-like voiced obstruents.
L2 speaker's output target = voiced;
L2 productions perceived by native speakers as voiceless.
c. Grammatically-based: Non-native speakers' (interlanguage) grammars ban final voiced obstruents.
L2 output target = voiceless;
L2 productions perceived by native speakers as voiceless.

These accounts are not, of course, necessarily mutually exclusive. Blevins (2006) reviews multiple factors that make final voiced obstruents difficult both to produce and to perceive: laryngeal spreading or closing at phrase boundaries, which interferes with the maintenance of voicing; phrase-final lengthening, which may obscure durational cues to voice contrasts; and the absence of audible release in final position. Learners' difficulties in producing target-like final voiced obstruents have been demonstrated in various studies; e.g., Flege, McCutcheon, & Smith (1987) found that Mandarin speakers' voicing during the closure of English final voiced stops was significantly shorter than that of native speakers, and Wissing & Zonneveld (1996) found that Tswana speakers differed significantly from native speakers both in voicing into closure and in the lengthening of vowels before voiced obstruents, a major cue to voicing in final position in English (Raphael 1972).

Difficulties in perception are also in evidence in the L2 literature, though in some cases production has been shown to lag perception. For example, Wissing & Zonneveld's Tswana speakers correctly identified 70% of English final voiced stops as voiced in a forced choice task, but produced only 52% of English final voiced stops as target-like. For speakers of Dutch, where final obstruents are devoiced, Broersma (2005) found categorization accuracy for both voiced and voiceless English final obstruents comparable to that of native speakers of English, though Dutch speakers are not necessarily entirely successful in producing English-like final voicing contrasts (Simon 2009, 2010). A considerable body of literature on cross-language perception indicates that even where speakers perform well on tests of their ability to perceive contrasts, they may be using different cues than are used by native speakers; for example, Flege & Wang (1989) found that removing burst cues from English final stop stimuli resulted in a significant worsening of discrimination by Cantonese speakers but not by native speakers of English. Thus, perception and production are crucially intertwined: listeners need to both recognize and produce the cues that the target language relies on to signal a contrast.

Approaches that locate L2 patterns in the developing L2 grammar have long appealed to markedness, defined as typologically-based preferences for less marked over more marked structures (e.g., Eckman 1977). In versions of Optimality Theory that directly connect typology and acquisition by encoding typologically-motivated constraints as part of every grammar, such hierarchies of difficulty can be analyzed as the effect of markedness constraints, the effects of which become visible only when the target language provides learners with novel structures that violate these constraints (Broselow, Chen, & Wang 1998; Hancin-Bhatt 2000; Eckman 2004; Peng & Ann 2004; Wiltshire 2006; Cardoso 2007, among others). Thus, the existence of languages like Mandarin and Tswana motivates a universal (but violable) constraint banning all final obstruents (*FINALOBSTRUENT). The existence of languages like German and Catalan, which restrict final obstruents to voiceless, motivates a universal (though violable) constraint *FINALVOICEDOBSTRUENT, which will be ranked low in languages like English but high in languages like German (see, e.g., Lombardi 1995) – and, by default, in Mandarin, on the assumption that markedness constraints rank as high as is consistent with the data of the target language (e.g., Smolensky 1996). On this view, Mandarin speakers' more successful production of final voiceless than voiced obstruents can be seen as reflecting an intermediate stage between the native and target language grammars, in which the constraint banning final obstruents of any type has been demoted, but the constraint banning final voiced obstruents remains highly ranked.

(4) Proposed Grammars (Broselow et al. 1998)
    a. Mandarin Grammar:
       *FINALVOICEDOBSTRUENT, *FINALOBSTRUENT, >> Faithfulness
    b. English Grammar:
       Faithfulness >> *FINALVOICEDOBSTRUENT, *FINALOBSTRUENT
    c. Interlanguage Grammar (Mandarin-speaking learners of English):
       *FINALVOICEDOBSTRUENT >> Faithfulness >> *FINALOBSTRUENT

Broselow (2004) argues that the intermediate ranking falls out of the Gradual Learning Algorithm approach (Boersma & Hayes 2001), in which the rate of constraint demotion is an effect of the frequency of input tokens that violate the constraint. Since the constraint banning all final obstruents will of necessity be violated more frequently than the constraint banning only voiced final obstruents, the general constraint is demoted more rapidly than the more specific constraint. Another application of the Gradual Learning Algorithm approach, in which constraint rankings are stochastic and variable across different speech events, is to predict variation; Cardoso (2007) uses the GLA to model the variable productions he finds in his study of Brazilian Portuguese learners of English.

While the constraint-based approach appears to be compatible with the earlier mastery of L2 voiceless than of voiced final obstruents for speakers of languages like Mandarin (with no final obstruents) or like German (with only voiceless final obstruents), this approach faces a challenge from the cases of asymmetry mentioned above involving speakers of languages with final voicing contrasts. Speakers of Hungarian (Altenberg & Vago 1983) and Farsi (Eckman 1984), which allow both voiced and voiceless final obstruents, should approach the L2 with a native language grammar that has the same constraint ranking as English. To account for these learners' greater success in producing English voiceless than voiced final obstruents, a proponent of the grammar-based approach might argue that while the grammars of Hungarian and Farsi permit final voiced obstruents, the phonetic realization of voiced targets is sufficiently different from the realization of voicing in English that the learners' attempts to produce voiced stops are not recognized as such by native English speakers. However, this explanation faces the difficulty that in Hungarian, final voiced stops are actually more fully voiced than are their English counterparts (Gosy & Ringen 2009), a fact that might lead us to expect that transfer of native language articulatory routines should make final voicing easy to hear. An alternative explanation could appeal to a difference in the phonological feature specifications that define the laryngeal contrasts in English vs. in the other languages. If, as proposed in Iverson & Salmons (1995), Jessen & Ringen (2002), Vaux & Samuels (2005), and many others, the relevant feature distinguishing stops is [spread glottis] for aspirating languages like English but [voice] for voicing languages like Hungarian, then the grammars of Hungarian and Farsi may not in fact be identical to that of English. The validity of these approaches can only be evaluated in the context of detailed study of the acoustics of the relevant languages, explicit analyses of the grammars of the two languages, and explicit theories of phonological specification.

An additional explanation for the developmental asymmetry that should be considered is the possibility of asymmetries in the data available to the learner. If final voiceless obstruents are significantly more frequent in the target language than are final voiced obstruents (that is, if input to the learners contains significantly more tokens of final voiceless than voiced obstruents), this could explain why learners might acquire the former before the latter, with no recourse to markedness considerations. As Broselow & Xu (2004) point out, the order in which new English structures are mastered by Mandarin-speaking learners does not correlate in any obviously way with the frequency of different English coda types as outlined by Kessler & Treiman (1997), though systematic studies of frequency in learner input are lacking.

In summary, the second language data provides convincing evidence for hierarchies of difficulty: for learners from a variety of native language backgrounds, L2 final voiced obstruents seem to be harder to successfully produce than either L2 nonfinal voiced or final voiceless obstruents. We now examine the nature of L2 learners' unsuccessful productions of final voiced obstruents.

4 L2 repair of final voiced obstruents: Too many solutions?

Steriade (2001/2008) identifies the "too many solutions" problem in Optimality Theory: the theory predicts that languages will vary in their strategies for realizing underlying structures that are banned on the surface, but all or most languages seem to converge on a single repair for particular prohibited structures. This problem arises from the assumptions that the choice of repair in a language is a function of the ranking of faithfulness constraints defining preferred input-output correspondence relationships, along with the assumption that constraints are freely rankable across languages. We do indeed find cross-linguistic differences in the repair of many structures: for example, structures containing vowel hiatus are variously realized by deletion of a vowel, coalescence of the two vowels into a single vowel or a diphthong, gliding of a vowel, or insertion of a consonant between the vowels. Yet, although speakers have in principle a number of options for repairing structures containing final voiced obstruents (deletion of the obstruent; epenthesis of a vowel following the obstruent; sonorization of the obstruent), Steriade argues that the only productive repair found across languages is final devoicing.

Steriade proposes to solve this problem by assuming that faithfulness constraints are not necessarily freely rankable; she argues that the ranking of some constraints is set by the P-Map, which defines the perceptual distance between different structures (Steriade 2001/2008). Rankings that produce the maximal perceptual similarity between input and output structures are favored by the P-Map. Her claim is that devoicing is the chosen repair for final voiced obstruents because devoicing produces an output that is perceptually more similar to the input – for example, input /Vb/ is more similar to output [Vp] than it is to [VbV], [V], or [Vm]. The universal ranking of faithfulness constraints penalizes other changes more harshly than a change in voicing:

(5) Ranking of faithfulness constraints favoring devoicing
 MAX(C), DEP(V) >> IDENT(VOICE)

Since Steriade's claim is based in typology, we would expect the preference for devoicing over other repairs to be instantiated in second languages phonology as well as in first languages. However, before considering whether the preference for final devoicing holds for second language phonological data, we note that the typological facts are not entirely straightforward, since languages using strategies other than final devoicing are attested. One example is adduced by Kiparsky (2008), who points out, citing Cahill (1999), that vowel epenthesis is used to prevent the creation of a voiced obstruent in coda position in Konni (northern Ghana). This language has a productive voicing assimilation process whereby an obstruent assimilates in voicing to a following obstruent. However, where voicing assimilation would give rise to a voiced coda obstruent, assimilation is blocked by the insertion of a vowel between the obstruents:

(6) Konni (Kiparsky 2008, citing Cahill 1999)
    a. /tig-ka/   *tikka*   'the village'
    b. /biis-bu/   *biisibu*   'the breast' (*biiz-bu)

These facts do not directly contradict Steriade's claim that final devoicing is the universally preferred strategy for transforming final voiced obstruents to some other structure, since in Konni, vowel insertion functions not to remove an underlying voiced obstruent, but rather to block the creation of a new voiced obstruent in coda position. However, if perceptual similarity is the major motivation for choice of repair, Steriade must argue that in this case, the output *biisibu* is more similar to input /biisbu/ than would be the output *biizbu.

A stronger challenge to the universality of final devoicing is posed by the facts of Noon, a Cangin language of Senegal. Merrill (2015) provides evidence that Noon systematically nasalizes voiced stops that are brought into coda position by morpheme concatenation:

(7) Northern Noon (Merrill 2015)

	bare verb	perfect -*in*	
a.	nasal-final		
	tam	tam-in	'be hot'
	an	an-in	'drink'
	daŋ	daŋ-in	'be viscous'
b.	stop-final		
	tam	tab-in	'be forbidden'
	man	mad-in	'resemble'
	daŋ	dag-in	'be taut'

Merrill argues that the nasalization process arose from two earlier processes: at an earlier stage, all voiced stops were prenasalized; subsequently, prenasalized stops became plain stops in onset position but became nasals in coda. Although the nasalization pattern arose through separate sound changes, it seems to have become established in the synchronic grammar by learners who have not been exposed to the separate stages that gave rise to this pattern. This disqualifies the preference for final devoicing for the status of true phonological universal, according to Kiparsky's criteria (reviewed in Section 1), which include the claim that learners will never construct grammars that violate a true universal.

Nonetheless, it is clear that the overwhelming majority of languages do choose final devoicing as the preferred option. A weaker version of Steriade's claim would be to ascribe the preference for final devoicing to a default, initial-state ranking which holds in the absence of evidence to the contrary, but which could be adjusted when learners are exposed to evidence contradicting this ranking. On this view, the responsibility to explain the rarity of repairs other than final devoicing would rest with channel bias effects, rather than on the formal grammar.

However, attempts to investigate channel bias effects in repair of final voiced obstruents are not entirely consistent with the perceptual similarity hypothesis. Kawahara & Garvey (2010), in an online experiment, elicited direct judgments of perceptual similarity by asking participants to compare forms with final voiced obstruents (e.g., *ab*) with possible correponding forms (e.g., *am, a, aba, ap*) and to rate the similarity of each pair. In trials that involved orthographic presentation of forms, the devoicing option was chosen as most similar to the final-obstruent form, consistent with Steriade's claim. But when forms were presented auditorily, the form with final epenthetic schwa was judged most similar to the final-obstruent form. Kawahara & Garvey note that the final obstruents in the auditory stimuli were released, and although the release was spliced off, sufficient information may have remained to bias listeners toward the vowel insertion form. These facts suggest that determining the closest perceptual match may rely on a complex combination of subtle phonetic details.

With these facts in mind, we now turn to the question of whether learners' non-target-like productions provide evidence for devoicing as the preferred (if not necessarily universal) repair. We consider the relative proportions of different repairs (consonant deletion, vowel insertion, and final devoicing) in various studies, and the effect on choice of repair of several factors: learner proficiency, task, and grammatical context; the existence of an active devoicing process in the native language; word size and stress; and manner and place of articulation.

4.1 Learner proficiency, task effects, and grammatical context

While the second language literature contains numerous reports of devoicing of final obstruents, it also contains many examples of vowel insertion and consonant deletion. This is not in itself a counterexample to Steriade's claim that final devoicing is the preferred option, since devoicing is only a possibility if the learner can produce some sort of obstruent in final position. A more serious problem for Steriade would be cases in which final voiced obstruents were systematically nasalized by learners, while voiceless obstruents were produced faithfully. I am not aware of such patterns in the second language literature.

The interesting question from the standpoint of Steriade's proposal is whether it is the case that once speakers begin to acquire final obstruents, devoicing becomes the norm. Devoicing is indeed a common phenomenon, though we find a good deal of variation in devoicing rates across different studies, even for speakers of the same native language; for example, Wang's (1995) Mandarin speaker participants, who had been in the US less than one year, had a devoicing rate of 9%, while Flege & Davidian's (1984) Mandarin participants, with five or more years in the US, show a devoicing rate of 29.5%. The lower devoicing found among the less advanced learners correlated with higher rates of consonant deletion and vowel epenthesis, consistent with the course of development suggested by Abrahamsson (2003) for speakers of native languages without final obstruents : consonant deletion > vowel epenthesis > feature change (devoicing) > target value.

Choice of repair is also clearly affected by the experimental task. For example, Edge (1991) found that in a word list reading task, Japanese speakers produced 30% of the word-final voiced obstruents with an epenthetic vowel, but that the rate of epenthesis dropped to less than 5% in tasks involving connected speech. It is not surprising that reading tasks, in particular, might favor epenthesis.

Another factor that may affect both accuracy and choice of repair is the grammatical status of the final consonant. Hansen (2004) found much higher accuracy for past tense /d/ (43%) than for stem-final /d/ (11%), although for some reason, similar effects did not obtain for plural vs. stem-final /z/.

4.2 Native language devoicing

Speakers whose native language has an active devoicing process can be expected to transfer this process to a second language, and indeed, many do; Cebrian (2000) reports 97.8% devoicing in prepausal forms by Catalan speakers; Flege & Davidian (1984) report a devoicing rate of 48.3% for Polish speakers; and Hammarberg (1990) reports that almost all the errors of the Swedish-learning German speakers involved devoicing. However, speakers of a language with alternations that support a productive devoicing process do not necessarily devoice L2 forms more often than speakers whose language lacks such a process – or even than learners with no native language final obstruents. Comparison across studies is problematic, given differences in methodology, proficiency of subjects, etc., but Flege & Davidian's study involved native speakers of three typologically distinct languages: Mandarin (no final obstruents), Polish (active final devoicing), and Mexican Spanish (final obstruents limited in occurrence; voiced stops spirantize following continuants). The devoicing rates of the three groups (29.5%, 48.3%, and 43%) were not significantly different, though there was a high degree of within-group variation. The three native language groups in Flege & Davidian's study were chosen to investigate the extent to which native language processes affected the production of the second language; thus, the comparison of Spanish speakers, with an active spirantization process, and Polish speakers, with an active devoicing process, is instructive. While the likelihood of L2 devoicing was not significantly higher for Polish speakers than for the other two groups, the rate of final stop spirantization was much higher for the Spanish speakers (19.3%) than for either Polish (1.2%) or Chinese (0.8%) speakers. Thus, while the likelihood of L2 spirantization correlated with the existence of a native language spirantization process, L2 devoicing appeared even when unsupported by the native language.

4.3 Word size and stress

For speakers of a language which (like Mandarin) disallows obstruent codas, deletion of a final obstruent and insertion of a vowel are equally valid strategies for creating possible native language syllable types. Several studies have presented evidence that the English of Mandarin-speaking learners shows evidence of a correlation between repair strategy and output word size, with a preference for disyllabic words as the determining factor (Heyer 1986; Weinberger 1987; Wang 1995; Steele 2002). For example, Wang (1995) found that the size of the source word had a significant effect on the learners' choice of repair of pseudoword forms, with a preference for vowel insertion in monosyllables but deletion in disyllables:

(8) Mandarin speakers' repair by word size (Wang 1995)

input size	C deletion	V insertion	C devoicing	Target-like
monosyllable	8%	72%	10%	10%
disyllable	63%	18%	8%	11%

Wang also investigated the effect of word stress on the choice of deletion vs. insertion. Her disyllabic forms were equally divided between those with initial stress and those with final stress. Epenthesis was more likely in the final-stress disyllables than in the initial-stress disyllables, suggesting that in the absence of word size effects, stress did have an effect. However, in a comparison of monosyllables with final-stress disyllables, the overall rate of epenthesis was still significantly higher for monosyllables than for final-stress disyllables.

Additional evidence of word size effects comes from Cardoso's (2007) study of six speakers of Brazilian Portuguese, a language in which the only possible coda obstruent is /s/. The speakers in this study either produced coda stops correctly, or inserted a vowel following the coda stop (which he argues is a productive native language strategy for syllabifying stops, though he notes that devoicing has been reported in other studies of Brazilian Portuguese-English interlanguage). Cardoso's study included learners at three levels, and while the lowest level speakers produced almost no codas successfully (i.e., inserted a following vowel), the intermediate and advanced learners were far more likely to produce coda stops in polysyllabic words (37% and 59%, respectively), than in monosyllables (16% correct production for intermediate and 31% correct production for advanced learners). As Cardoso notes, Brazilian Portuguese contains a number of highly frequent monosyllables, as does English, though in English, monosyllabic content words must arguably be bimoraic. He argues that "the language learner opts for minimal word disyllabicity, a structure that is enforced neither in BP nor in English, over bimoraicity, which represents the target-like structure" (Cardoso 2007: 227).

Thus, while devoicing is extremely common in second language phonology, it is not necessarily the favored strategy, even for learners who have the ability to produce obstruents in final position. These facts are consistent with the view that the choice of final devoicing over other repairs represents at most a strong preference rather than an absolute universal, and one that may interact with other universal preferences. In fact, the word size effects are reconcilable with Steriade's claim that the universal preference for final devoicing represents a default ranking of faithfulness constraints, given the architecture of Optimality Theory grammars. So long as the faithfulness constraints are outranked by markedness constraints demanding a disyllabic word minimum, vowel insertion will be chosen over deletion or devoicing for final obstruents in monosyllables, even when the ranking of faithfulness constraints defines devoicing as the generally preferred option. This is illustrated in the tableau below (where D indicates any voiced obstruent):

(9) Word size effect ranking

/CVCVD/	MinWord	*FinalVoiced Obstruent	Dep(V)	Ident(voice)
a. CVCVD		*!		
☞ b. CVCVT				*
c. CVCVDv			*!	

/CVD/	MinWord	*FinalVoiced Obstruent	Dep(V)	Ident(voice)
a. CVD		*!		
b. CVT	*!			*
☞ c. CVDv			*	

In this ranking (essentially that proposed in Broselow et al. 1998 to describe the Mandarin learners' patterns) the constraint banning vowel insertion, Dep(V), outranks Ident(voice), the constraint forbidding devoicing, consistent with Steriade's proposed ranking. However, the higher-ranked MinWord (words must be at least disyllabic) will rule out the devoicing option for monosyllables.

Thus, a grammar that adheres to Steriade's proposed ranking of faithfulness constraints need not necessarily entail that devoicing will be the only choice in every context. This brings us back to the typological question: if this is a possible grammar, then we should expect to find native languages in which the L2 pattern of insertion in monosyllables and devoicing in polysyllables has become grammaticalized. One language in which devoicing is related to word size is Turkish, where Becker et al. (2011) demonstrate that monosyllables are more likely than longer words to preserve voiced obstruents in final position (e.g., [ad] 'name'). However, the resistance to devoicing in these forms does not change word size; Becker et al. attribute the preservation of voice to a cross-linguistic tendency toward greater faithfulness to word-initial syllables. At this point the tendency toward epenthesis in monosyllables and devoicing in polysyllables seen in the English of native speakers of Mandarin and Brazilian Portuguese does not appear to have been grammaticalized in any language – though it is possible that such a pattern, if it did arise, might be unstable, since the next generation of learners might be led to reanalyze the originally monosyllabic forms as underlying disyllabic.

4.4 Manner effects

Final devoicing typically affects both stops and fricatives, despite differences in the realization of voicing in these two classes. Thus, it is interesting to see whether voiced stops and fricatives pattern similarly in second language phonology.

An asymmetry between stops and fricatives emerges in Simon's (2009, 2010) investigation of Dutch speakers' productions: though all obstruents are devoiced in final position in Dutch, the Dutch speakers in her study produced English final voiced stops significantly more successfully than final voiced fricatives (the respective rates of devoicing were 76% for fricatives vs. 49% for stops). As Simon points out, this pattern is consistent with the cross-linguistically greater rarity of voiced fricatives than voiced stops, which can be explained by the fact that the glottal opening required for frication is antithetical to the cross-glottal pressure differential required to sustain voicing (Ohala 1983). Voiced stops and fricatives differ in terms of perceptibility as well; Myers (2012) found a tendency for English speakers to identify utterance-final voiced fricatives as voiceless, while a similar tendency was not found for utterance-final voiced stops.

A pattern that appears to be the reverse of the Dutch pattern is attested in Hansen's (2004) study of two Vietnamese speakers' productions. Hansen includes all voicing errors in the category of feature change errors, but her discussion makes it clear that the normal feature change for stops was devoicing. While 49% of final voiced stops underwent feature change, only 4% of final fricatives did (the opposite of the Dutch pattern, in which fricatives were more likely to be devoiced):

(10) Vietnamese speakers' choice of repair (Hansen 2004)

		Target-like	Deletion	Epenthesis	Feature Change
voiceless stops	/p/	88%	0	12%	0
	/t,k/	52%	29%	15%	2%
voiceless fricatives	/f, s/	59%	23%	12%	6%
voiced stops	/b,d,g/	19%	24%	3%	49%
voiced fricatives	/v, z/	19%	47%	25%	4%

A closer look at the choice of repair for stops and fricatives is intriguing. The rate of target-like productions was the same for voiced stops and voiced fricatives; the major difference lies in the higher rates of deletion and epenthesis for voiced fricatives (72% combined) vs. voiced stops (27% combined). This may be a native language effect: Vietnamese has no final fricatives, but does have final stops (albeit only voiceless ones). Thus, the higher rate of devoicing for stops than fricatives may simply reflect the fact that devoicing is not an option for final fricatives, since these speakers cannot yet successfully produce fricatives in final position. However, it is puzzling that for voiceless stops and fricatives, the rates of target-like productions were comparable (leaving out the surprisingly high rates for /p/). Thus, while the Vietnamese data provide clear support for a difficulty hierarchy involving voiceless vs. voiced final fricatives, their significance with respect to the relationship between manner and the likelihood of devoicing is less clear.

If we take the Dutch pattern – greater likelihood of devoicing of final fricatives than final stops – as representative of phonetically-grounded factors disfavoring voiced fricatives, it seems likely that we should find languages in which the pattern of devoicing final fricatives but not final stops has become phonologized. Myers (2012) addresses this question in the context of his proposal that word-final and syllable-final devoicing processes arise historically from the generalization of utterance-final devoicing: "One might expect from this that utterance-final fricative devoicing should be the most common version of the pattern of final devoicing [. . .] But it certainly does not seem as if such cases are more common than [. . .] devoicing of all obstruents including stops" (Myers 2012: 173). Myers cites only one language, Gothic, where final devoicing is limited to fricatives. Thus, while the Dutch speakers' L2 patterns are congruent with aerodynamic and perceptual factors that appear to make a final voicing contrast in stops more natural than one in fricatives, it does not seem to be the case that this asymmetry has become widely grammaticalized. If such an asymmetry emerges frequently in second language phonology but never as a pattern in a first language, it might provide an argument for an analytic bias against a grammar that allows devoicing for one set of obstruents but not another, although at this point the evidence from second language production is too limited to support this claim. A related question is whether the same or different feature specifications govern laryngeal contrasts for stops and fricatives, and whether stop devoicing and fricative devoicing should be treated as different processes in grammars. (See Vaux 1998 for the proposal that the unmarked opposition for voiceless and voiced fricatives is [+spread glottis] vs. [-spread glottis], and van Oostendorp 2007 for the proposal that for at least some Dutch dialects, the fricative contrast is better explained in terms of length rather than laryngeal features.)

4.5 Place of articulation

Another factor related to voicing is place of articulation: because voicing requires that supraglottal pressure be lower than air pressure below the glottis, a smaller oral cavity makes voicing more difficult to sustain. Thus, velar stops tend to be less fully voiced than stops made farther front (Ohala 1983; Maddieson 1984). Despite the connection between constriction location and difficulty of sustaining voicing, there seem to be no languages that, say, devoice final velar stops but maintain voicing contrasts for coronals and labials. Nor are there clear examples of such patterns in second language phonology, although there is evidence for differences in degree of voicing across place of articulation. Yavas (2009) studied the production of final English bilabial, coronal, and velar stops by native speakers of Mandarin, Japanese, and Portuguese, and found that although the amount of closure voicing did not differ significantly by place of articulation, there was an interaction between the place of the stop and the height of the preceding vowel: velars were significantly less voiced, but only when they followed high vowels:

(11) Mean percentage of closure voicing (Yavas 2009)

	bilabial	alveolar	velar
after high vowel	28.2%	24.2%	18%
after low vowel	30.1%	28.9%	27%

Native speakers also showed less voicing in the high vowel-velar case than in other cases, but their percentage of voicing was, for each vowel-consonant combination, significantly higher than that of native speakers (e.g., 65.5% voicing during a velar closure following a high vowel).

While it makes sense that the smaller oral cavity associated with velars and the narrower constriction of high vowels should have an additive effect on voicing, this does not appear to be a phonologized pattern in languages; Moreton (2008) argues that few languages show systematic interactions of vowel height and voicing, and those interactions that are attested take the form of the raising of vowel height before voiced consonants and the lowering of vowel height before voiceless consonants (though see Yu 2011 for a different interpretation of Moreton's data). Thus, place and vowel height effects, though they appear in the phonetic detail of both native and non-native speakers, appear not to have been grammaticalized in either first language or interlanguage phonology. Again, this is an area where research is relatively sparse.

5 Conclusion

We set out to determine first, whether the facts of second language phonology are compatible with typological generalizations, and second, whether the second language facts can shed light on the source of typological generalizations.

We found numerous cases supporting a difficulty hierarchy for final voiceless vs. voiced stops in second language phonology, and this difficulty hierarchy aligns with the typological generalizations on preferred segment type.

Across a range of native languages, including those with no final obstruents, those with only voiceless final obstruents, and those with a final laryngeal contrast, speakers successfully produced L2 final voiceless obstruents before final voiced obstruents. In no case was there evidence of speakers acquiring the more marked structure (final voiced obstruents) before the less marked structure (final voiceless obstruents). Whether these facts reflect articulatory and perceptual factors or the effects of formal grammatical constraints is difficult to resolve – since the structural constraints of Optimality Theory are generally grounded in articulatory and perceptual considerations, there is considerable overlap between the approaches. However, we note that locating the difficulty of final voiced obstruents in articulatory and perceptual difficulty alone predicts that the likelihood of a difficulty hierarchy emerging in second language acquisition should be a function of the phonetic robustness of the contrast in the target language; for example, languages in which final stops are uniformly released should provide the learner with more cues to the voicing contrast than languages without such release. Systematic study of the productions of both native and second language speakers across a range of languages is necessary to address this question.

We also found that final devoicing was quite common in second language phonology, although it was by no means the only strategy used. Since speakers must be able to produce obstruents in final position before they can devoice them, the fact that vowel insertion and consonant deletion were also common repairs of L2 forms does not in itself invalidate Steriade's (2001/2008) claim that final devoicing is the only solution to the final obstruent problem. We did, however, find evidence that some speakers exhibit a systematic relationship between choice of repair and preferred word size. It is intriguing that this pattern was found for speakers of two different languages, Mandarin and Brazilian Portuguese, but is not clearly attested in any native language system.

Effects of aerodynamic factors that contribute to the difficulty of sustaining voicing appeared in some studies, at the level of relatively fine phonetic detail: Dutch speakers' final fricatives were less voiced than stops (Simon 2010), and Mandarin, Japanese, and Portuguese speakers' velars were less voiced than alveolars and bilabials, though only after high vowels (Yavas 2009). On the channel bias account, we might expect these differences to give rise to systems in which the phonetic asymmetries become phonologized. Yet such systems seem either rare or unattested; Myers (2012) cites only one language, Gothic, in which fricatives, but not stops, are regularly devoiced.

A reasonable place to look for systems that have phonologized the effects found in second language phonology is in regionalized varieties of English, where what generally began as a second language has now become standardized.

A striking number of regional Englishes show evidence of at least some final devoicing. In a survey of English varieties of Africa, South Asia, and Southeast Asia, Mesthrie (2004) reports final devoicing in St. Helens English, Cape Flats English, Black South African English, Nigerian English, Ghanaian English, Cameroon English, Cameroon Pidgin, Singapore English, and Malaysian English. Final devoicing is also reported in Fiji English (Tent & Mugler 2004), Tok Pisin (Smith 2004), and Liberian Settler English (Singler 2004). The prevalence of final devoicing suggests that speakers did indeed converge on this repair as their systems stabilized. It is notable that none of these descriptions identify epenthesis or deletion as regular productive processes targeting single final voiced obstruents, and no systems are identified as showing different treatment of final stops and fricatives or systematic effects of place of articulation that are independent of the substrate language. Thus, at least some of the well-founded phonetic effects that emerge in second language phonology fail to acquire the status of regular phonological processes.

Acknowledgements: I am grateful to audiences at Oxford, CUNY, and Stony Brook and particularly to Larry Hyman for comments that have improved this paper.

References

Abrahamsson, Niclas. 2003. Development and recoverability of L2 codas: A longitudinal study of Chinese-Swedish interphonology. *Studies in Second Language Acquisition* 25. 313–349.

Altenberg, Evelyn & Robert Vago. 1983. Theoretical implications of an error analysis of second language phonology production. *Language Learning* 33. 427–448.

Becker, Michael, Nihan Ketrez, & Andrew Nevins. 2011. The surfeit of the stimulus: Analytic biases filter lexical statistics in Turkish laryngeal alternations. *Language* 87. 84–125.

Beckman, Jill, Pétur Helgason, Bob McMurray, & Catherine Ringen. 2011. Rate effects on Swedish VOT: Evidence for phonological overspecification. *Journal of Phonetics* 39. 39–49.

Blevins, Juliette. 2004. *Evolutionary phonology: The emergence of sound patterns*. Cambridge: Cambridge University Press.

Blevins, Juliette. 2006. A theoretical synopsis of Evolutionary Phonology. *Theoretical Linguistics* 32. 117–166.

Blevins, Juliette. 2010. Phonetically-based sound patterns: Typological tendencies or phonological universals? In Cécile Fougeron, Barbara Kühnert, Mariapaola D'Imperio, & Nathalie Vallée (eds.), *Papers in Laboratory Phonology 10: Variation, phonetic detail and phonological modeling*, 201–224. Berlin: Mouton de Gruyter.

Broersma, Miriam. 2005. Perception of familiar contrasts in unfamiliar positions. *Journal of the Acoustical Society of America* 117. 3890–3901.

Broselow, Ellen. 2004. Unmarked structures and emergent rankings in second language phonology. *International Journal of Bilingualism* 8. 51–65.

Broselow, Ellen, Su-I Chen, & Chilin Wang. 1998. The emergence of the unmarked in second language phonology. *Studies in Second Language Acquisition* 20. 261–280.

Broselow, Ellen & Yoonjung Kang. 2013. Second language phonology and speech. In Julia Herschensohn & Martha Young-Scholten (eds.), *The Cambridge handbook of second language acquisition*, 529–554. Cambridge: Cambridge University Press.

Broselow, Ellen & Zheng Xu. 2004. Differential difficulty in the acquisition of second language phonology. *International Journal of English Studies* 4 (special issue: Advances in Optimality Theory). 13–163.

Cahill, Michael. 1999. *Aspects of morphology and phonology of Konni*. Ph.D. dissertation, Ohio State University.

Cardoso, Walcir. 2007. The variable development of English word-final stops by Brazilian Portuguese speakers: A stochastic Optimality Theory account. *Language Variation and Change* 19. 219–248.

Cebrian, Juli. 2000. Transferability and productivity of L1 rules in Catalan-English interlanguage. *Studies in Second Language Acquisition* 22. 1–26.

Cichocki, Wladyslaw, Anthony B. House, A. Murray Kinloch, & Anthony C. Lister. 1993. Cantonese speakers and the acquisition of French consonants. *Language Learning* 43. 43–68.

Eckman, Fred. 1977. Markedness and the contrastive analysis hypothesis. *Language Learning* 27. 315–330.

Eckman, Fred. 1981. On the naturalness of interlanguage phonological rules. *Language Learning* 31. 195–216.

Eckman, Fred. 1984. Universals, typology, and interlanguage. In William E. Rutherford (ed.), *Language universals and second language acquisition*, 79–105. Amsterdam: John Benjamins.

Eckman, Fred. 2004. From phonemic differences to constraint rankings: Research on second language phonology. *Studies in Second Language Acquisition* 26. 513–549.

Edge, Beverly. 1991. The production of word-final voiced obstruents in English by L1 speakers of Japanese and Cantonese. *Studies in Second Language Acquisition* 13. 377–393.

Flege, James Emil & Richard D. Davidian. 1984. Transfer and developmental processes in adult foreign language speech production. *Applied Psycholinguistics* 5. 323–347.

Flege, James Emil, Martin J. McCutcheon, & Steven C. Smith. 1987. The development of skill in producing word-final English stops. *Journal of the Acoustical Society of America* 82. 433–447.

Flege, James Emil & Chipin Wang. 1989. Native-language phonotactic constraints affect how well Chinese subjects perceive the word-final English /t/-/d/ contrast. *Journal of Phonetics* 17. 299–315.

Gordon, Matthew. 2007. Typology in Optimality Theory. *Language and Linguistics Compass* 1. 750–769.

Gosy, Maria & Catherine Ringen. 2009. Everything you always wanted to know about VOT in Hungarian. Talk presented at the International Conference on the Structure of Hungarian 9. Debrecen, Hungary.

Greenberg, Joseph, Charles Ferguson, & Edith Moravscik (eds.). 1978. *Universals of human language*. Volume 2: Phonology. Stanford, CA: Stanford University Press.

Hammarberg, Björn. 1990. Conditions on transfer in phonology. In Allan R. James & Jonathan Leather (eds.), *New sounds 90: Proceedings of the 1990 Symposium on the Acquisition of Second-Language Speech*, 198–215. Dordrecht: Foris.

Hancin-Bhatt, Barbara. 2000. Optimality in second language phonology: Codas in Thai ESL. *Second Language Research* 16. 201–232.

Hansen, Jette G. 2004. Developmental sequences in the acquisition of English L2 syllable codas. *Studies in Second Language Acquisition* 26. 85–124.
Helgason, Pétur & Catherine Ringen. 2008. Voicing and aspiration in Swedish stops. *Journal of Phonetics* 36. 607–628.
Heyer, Sarah. 1986. English final consonants and the Chinese learner. Unpublished master's thesis, Southern Illinois University Edwardsville.
Hillenbrand, James, Dennis R. Ingrisano, Bruce L. Smith, & James E. Flege. 1984. Perception of the voiced-voiceless contrast in syllable-final stops. *Journal of the Acoustical Society of America* 76. 18–26.
Hyman, Larry. 1976. Phonologization. In Alphonse Juillard (ed.), *Linguistic studies offered to Joseph Greenberg,* volume 2, 407–418. Saratoga, CA: Anna Libri.
Hyman, Larry. 2008. Universals in phonology. *The Linguistic Review* 25. 83–137.
Iverson, Gregory & Joseph Salmons. 1995. Aspiration and laryngeal representation in Germanic. *Phonology* 12. 369–396.
Iverson, Gregory & Joseph Salmons. 2011. Final devoicing and final laryngeal neutralization. In Marc van Oostendorp, Colin Ewen, Elizabeth V. Hume, & Keren Rice (eds.), *The Blackwell companion to phonology*, volume 3, 1622–1643. Oxford: Blackwell Publishing.
Jessen, Michael & Catherine Ringen. 2002. Laryngeal features in German. *Phonology* 19. 189–218.
Kawahara, Shigeto & Kelly Garvey. 2010. Testing the P-map hypothesis: Coda devoicing. Rutgers Optimality Archive.
Keating, Patricia, Wendy Linker, & Marie Huffman. 1983. Patterns in allophone distribution for voiced and voiceless stops. *Journal of Phonetics* 11. 277–290.
Kenstowicz, Michael. 2005. The phonetics and phonology of loanword adaptation. In S.-J. Rhee (ed.), *Proceedings of ECKL 1: Proceedings of First European Conference on Korean Linguistics*, 316–340. Seoul: Hankook Publishing.
Kessler, Brett & Rebecca Treiman. 1997. Syllable structure and the distribution of segments in English syllables. *Journal of Memory and Language* 37. 295–311.
Kiparsky, Paul. 2006. The amphichronic program vs. evolutionary phonology. *Theoretical Linguistics* 32. 217–236.
Kiparsky, Paul. 2008. Universals constrain change; change results in typological generalizations. In Jeff Good (ed.), *Language universals and language change*, 23–53. Oxford: Oxford University Press.
Lombardi, Linda. 1995. Laryngeal neutralization and syllable well-formedness. *Natural Language and Linguistic Theory* 13. 39–74.
Maddieson, Ian. 1984. *Patterns of sounds*. Cambridge: Cambridge University Press.
Major, Roy & Michael Faudree. 1996. Markedness universals and the acquisition of voicing contrasts by Korean speakers of English. *Studies in Second Language Acquisition* 18. 69–90.
Merrill, John. 2015a. Nasalization as a repair for voiced obstruent codas in Noon. Talk presented at the Annual Meeting of the LSA, January, 2015.
Merrill, John. 2015b. Nasalization as a repair for voiced obstruent codas in Noon. *LSA Annual Meeting Extended Abstracts.* http://journals.linguisticsociety.org/proceedings/index.php/ExtendedAbs/article/view/3014
Mesthrie, Rajend. 2004. Synopsis: The phonology of English in Africa and South and Southeast Asia. In Schneider et al. (eds.) 2004, 1099–1110.
Moreton, Elliott. 2008. Analytic bias and phonological typology. *Phonology* 25. 83–127.
Myers, Scott. 2012. Final devoicing: Production and perception studies. In Toni Borowsky, Shigeto Kawahara, Takahito Shinya, & Mariko Sugahara (eds.), *Prosody matters: Essays in honor of Elisabeth Selkirk*, 148–180. London: Equinox.

Myers, Scott & Jaye Padgett. 2015. Domain generalisation in artificial language learning. *Phonology* 31. 399–434.
Oh, Mira. 1996. Linguistic input to loanword phonology. *Studies in Phonetics, Phonology, and Morphology* 2. 117–126.
Ohala, John. 1981. The listener as a source of sound change. In Carrie S. Masek, Roberta A. Hendrick, & Mary Frances Miller (eds.), *CLS: Papers from the parasession on language and behavior*, 178–203. Chicago: Chicago Linguistic Society.
Ohala, John. 1983. The origin of sound patterns in vocal tract constraints. In Peter MacNeilage (ed.), *The production of speech*, 189–216. New York: Springer.
Oostendorp, Marc van. 2007. Exceptions to final devoicing. In Jeroen van de Weijer & Erik Jan van de Torre (eds.), *Voicing in Dutch: (De)voicing – phonology, phonetics, and psycholinguistics*, 81–98. Amsterdam: John Benjamins,
Peng, Long & Jean Ann. 2004. Obstruent voicing and devoicing in the English of Cantonese speakers from Hong Kong. *World Englishes* 23. 535–564.
Raphael, Lawrence. 1972. Preceding vowel duration as a cue to the perception of the voicing characteristic of word-final consonants in American English. *Journal of the Acoustical Society of America* 51. 1296–1303.
Schneider, Edgar, Kate Burridge, Bernd Kortmann, Rajend Mesthrie, & Clive Upton (eds.). 2004. *A handbook of varieties of English*. Berlin: Mouton de Gruyter.
Simon, Ellen. 2009. Acquiring a new second language contrast: An analysis of the English laryngeal system of native speakers of Dutch. *Second Language Research* 25. 377–408.
Simon, Ellen. 2010. Phonological transfer of voicing and devoicing rules: Evidence from NL Dutch and L2 English conversational speech. *Language Sciences* 32. 63–86.
Singler, John. 2004. Liberian Settler English: Phonology. In Schneider et al. (eds.) 2004, 874–884.
Smith, Geoff. 2004. Tok Pisin in Papua New Guinea: Phonology. In Schneider et al. (eds.) 2004, 710–728.
Smolensky, Paul. 1996. On the comprehension/production dilemma in child language. *Linguistic Inquiry* 27. 720–731.
Steele, Jeffrey. 2002. L2 learners' modification of target language syllable structure: Prosodic licensing effects in interlanguage phonology. In Allan R. James & Jonathan Leather (eds.), *New sounds 2000: Proceedings of the 4th International Symposium on the Acquisition of Second Language Speech*, 315–324. Klagenfurt: University of Klagenfurt.
Steriade, Donca. 1999. Phonetics in phonology: The case of laryngeal neutralization. *UCLA Working Papers in Phonology* 3. 25–146.
Steriade, Donca. 2001/2008. The phonology of perceptibility effects: The P-Map and its consequences for constraint organization. In Kristin Hanson & Sharon Inkelas (eds.), *The nature of the word*, 151–179. Cambridge: MIT Press.
Tent, Jan & France Mugler. 2004. Fiji English: Phonology. In Schneider et al. (eds.) 2004, 750–779.
Vaux, Bert. 1998. The laryngeal specification of fricatives. *Linguistic Inquiry* 29. 497–511.
Vaux, Bert & Bridget Samuels. 2005. Laryngeal markedness and aspiration. *Phonology* 22. 395–346.
Wang, Chilin. 1995. *The acquisition of English word-final obstruents by Chinese speakers*. Unpublished doctoral dissertation, Stony Brook University.
Weinberger, Steven. 1987. The influence of linguistic context on syllable simplification. In Georgette Ioup & Steven H. Weinberger (eds.), *Interlanguage phonology: The acquisition of a second language sound system*, 401–417. Rowley, MA: Newbury House.

Westbury, John & Patricia Keating. 1986. On the naturalness of stop consonant voicing. *Journal of Linguistics* 22. 145–166.

Wetzels, Leo & Joan Mascaró. 2001. The typology of voicing and devoicing. *Language* 77. 207–244.

Wiltshire, Caroline. 2006. Word-final consonant and cluster acquisition in Indian Englishes. In David Bamman, Tatiana Magnitskaia, & Colleen Zaller (eds.), *Online proceedings supplement, Boston University Conference on Language Development* 30.

Wissing, Daan & Wim Zonneveld. 1996. Final devoicing as a robust phenomenon in second language acquisition: Tswana, English and Afrikaans. *South African Journal of Linguistics* 14. 3–23.

Yavas, Mehmet. 2009. Factors influencing the VOT of English long lag stops in interlanguage phonology. In M. A. Watkins, A. S. Reuber, & B. O. Baptista (eds.), *Recent research in second language phonetics/phonology: Perception and production*, 244–255. Newcastle-upon-Tyne: Cambridge Scholars Publishing.

Yu, Alan C. 2004. Explaining final obstruent voicing in Lezgian: Phonetics and history. *Language* 80. 73–97.

Yu, Alan C. 2011. On measuring phonetic precursor robustness: A response to Moreton. *Phonology* 28. 491–518.

Tomas Riad
The phonological typology of North Germanic accent

Abstract: The dialects of Swedish and Norwegian frequently exhibit a tonal contrast within the intonational prominence that is superimposed on primary stressed syllables. Realizational and distributional properties are largely shared such that a rather tightly constrained typology is in evidence. The aim of this article is to show that the linguistic properties that form the basis of the North Germanic tonal accent typology are structural in nature, relating to phonological representation in terms of value of the lexical tone as high/H or low/L, tonal association patterns in compounds, and spreading behaviour. The main type of structure to compare between dialects is the long compound (several TBU's, regularly assigned accent 2), given that the accent distinction is privative, and that accent 2 is the marked member of the distinction. Several previous typologies have been based on phonetic categories (e.g., number of tonal peaks, presence/absence of a separate focus gesture) and often also include functional notions like focus. I argue that such typologies fail to capture several generalizations, once we look at all major dialect types, and that they also tend to overgenerate in their predictions of possible dialect types. The secondary aim of the article is to provide an updated and coherent account of the major dialect types. To bring out the typological variables, I make pairwise comparisons of minimally different dialects on particular variables, and provide illustrating examples from natural speech.

The typology of closely related varieties gives us an idea of the frame for variation, which in turn allows for the formulation of what constitutes a likely or less likely diachronic change. The North Germanic tonal typology is very coherent with regard to structure, geographic distribution of features, and also shared history. A relevant analysis will reveal the prosodic relationship between dialects, and allow us to formulate hypotheses regarding the relative structural distance between tonal varieties. From there we can adduce arguments for the reconstruction of diachronic developments.

1 Introduction

Many of the dialects of Swedish and Norwegian exhibit a tonal contrast within the intonational prominence that is superimposed on a syllable carrying primary stress. Many properties of these so-called accents are shared between dialects, but the tonal variation makes the dialects sound quite different from one another, and this constitutes the main source for the man-in-the-street's recognition of the major dialect areas. This article is concerned with laying bare the linguistic properties that form the basis of the typology. My main point is that they are all structural in a quite concrete sense, relating to phonological representation in terms of value of the lexical tone as high/H or low/L, tonal association patterns in compounds, and spreading behaviour. Several previous typologies have been based on more phonetic and/or functional categories (e.g., number of tonal peaks, presence/absence of a separate focus gesture) which may describe parts of the typology well, but which are ultimately too superficial. They tend either to be insufficient when the typology is extended to all major dialect types or to overgenerate in their predictions of possible dialect types. The importance of identifying the most relevant structural categories for typology in the tonal domain is emphasized below. Following from this, I also hope to provide an updated and coherent account of the major dialect types.

Varieties of Germanic that exhibit a lexical tonal contrast occur not only in North Germanic (NGmc), but also in the Central Franconian varieties spoken in and around the Rhine delta (West Germanic). There too, the tonal distinction is superimposed on stressed syllables. If we look more widely, we find this type of system also in, for instance, Bosnian/Croatian/Serbian, varieties of Basque, Latvian and Lithuanian. The North Germanic system is differently constituted from the Franconian and Baltic ones, e.g., in requiring two syllables for the expression of one of the tonal categories (accent 2). There is also an organic relationship between the NGmc tonal varieties and the Danish stød system (Gårding 1977; Ringgaard 1983; Riad 2000a, 2000b, 2009b), but the typology given below will not include Danish in a principled way, as there are outstanding issues regarding the representation and status of Danish stød.[1]

The identification of parameters for microvariation is of course always of interest, descriptively as well as comparatively. In the case of the typology of very closely related varieties, the interest is enhanced by the fact that one has a chance of getting a handle on the general frame for variation. Depending on the unity of the system as a whole, the access of relatively rich linguistic information might allow for the formulation of what constitutes a likely or less likely change. The North Germanic typology is very coherent with regard to tonal structure, geographic distribution of features, and also shared history. A good analysis should reveal the prosodic relationship between dialects, and allow us to formulate hypotheses regarding the relative structural distance between tonal varieties, in its

---

[1] For instance, scholars do not agree on whether stød is a tonal configuration or a separate phonological type of object.

turn a prerequisite for the reconstruction of diachronic developments within the tonal system.

It is our task, then, to identify the properties that best describe the variation and thereby the individual varieties. My claim is that phonology provides the most relevant level at which to formulate these things. In particular, we must view phonetic and functional categories with scepticism. While phonetics will provide a lot of relevant information, it is the typology at the phonological/grammatical level that best explains relationships between varieties.[2]

2 Previous typologies

There are a number of earlier typological treatments of NGmc accent. The ground-breaking study of Meyer (1937, 1954) provides accent contrasts in chiefly disyllabic simplex forms for some one hundred informants from various locations around Scandinavia, with most recordings made in the Central Swedish and Dala regions, a fair amount from the Göta region (West Swedish, WSw), some recordings from North Swedish (NSw) and scattered items from Finland, Estonia, and Denmark. Meyer's materials form an initial basis for the description of dialects in terms of the number of tonal peaks, i.e., as one- or two-peaked realizations of accent 2 (cf. (1) below). This material was also used as basis for a hypothesis known as the "Scandinavian accent orbit" by Öhman (1967), where varieties were lined up according to the phonetic timing of peaks. In the phonetic tradition of Norway, there are the studies of Fintoft (1970), Mjaavatn (1978), and Fintoft, Mjaavatn, Møllergård, & Ulseth (1978), where four types of tonal contour are identified (the same set for both accent 1 and accent 2). These are then paired to get the various dialect areas. In Norway, tradition refers to dialect types via the first tone of the accent 1 contour, as "high-tone" and "low-tone" dialects.

In the Swedish tradition it is customary to talk about single peak dialects and double peak dialects (or one- and two-peak dialects). This refers exclusively to the accent 2 contour, as accent 1 invariably has only one peak (Gårding & Lindblad 1973; Bruce & Gårding 1978). This terminology remains in later work by Bruce (2005, 2007), where the typology is more refined and more clearly extended to the

---

[2] This is not to say that there are no important distinctions of a finer kind. Meyer's (1937) average contours exhibit small timing differences between dialects, employed by Öhman (1967) in his "Scandinavian accent orbit", and Dalton & Ní Chasaide (2007) have shown how systematic such differences can be between varieties within what is considered the same dialect of Irish. The exact boundary, if any, between phonology and phonetics in this regard is ultimately a matter of model and interpretation.

broader intonation. Below is the basic typology currently assumed for disyllabic simplex words in citation form (given in Bye 2004, based on Gårding & Lindblad 1973), illustrated with Meyer's tonal contours.³

(1) The typology of Gårding & Lindblad (1973)

Type	Accent 1	Accent 2	Region
0			Finnmark, Finland, North Sweden, South Denmark
1 1A	**One peak** early in stressed syllable	**One peak** late in stressed syllable	South Sweden, West Norway
1B	late in stressed syllable	early in post-stress syllable	Gotland, Bergslagen (Sweden)
2 2A	**One peak** late in stressed syllable	**Two peaks** one in each syllable	Central Sweden, West Nyland, Southwest Norway
2B	in post-stress syllable	one in each syllable	Göta, East Norway

The general problem with this type of phonetic typology is overgeneration. The reference points mentioned admit several types that are not attested (e.g., a variant of 2A but with accent 1 having EARLY timing of the peak, or a type

---

3 Bruce (2007, 2010) adds an interesting and important discussion of North Swedish, which we return to in Section 5.4.

combining accent 1 of 1A with accent 2 of 1B), without articulating expectations or reasons for why they should be excluded (or not). Some answers to this type of problem will come out of a segmentation of the tonal contours into constituent tones (Bruce 1977, 2004).

Proper phonological typologies, where reference is made to phonological categories, e.g., by breaking down the global contour into a string of constituent tones, are given in work by Lorentz (1995), Riad (1998b, 2006), Bye (2004), and Bruce (2005, 2007). In Lorentz (1995), for instance, the contour is divided into lexical tone, prominence tone, and boundary tone. It must be noted, however, that beyond the lexical tone, the functional aspects are not reliably tied to individual tones (Riad 2006). For one thing, there appears to be a bias to use H tones for the prominence function, whether it is a separate tonal gesture or a boundary tone (cf. Section 7).

The phonological typologies vary in geographic coverage (as well as in analysis), but have in later years come to heed the broader area of North Germanic tonal dialects, including both Norway and Sweden, and sometimes also the few remaining tonal dialects of Finland (Lorentz 1995; Riad 1998b; Bye 2004). In addition, these systems can then be put in relation with Danish stød, which is clearly related historically (as is evident from lexical distributional patterns), but which also clearly stands out within the linguistic area.

Part of the background assumptions made by Gårding & Lindblad (1973), Bruce (2005) and others is that two peaks would never occur in accent 1, at least not to the exclusion of two peaks in accent 2. Another (related) fact is that accent 2 always has the richer tonal structure, e.g., by requiring one more tonal feature than accent 1. Beside these things, which have implications for the representation of accentual contours, there are distributional facts of which scholars have different interpretations. For instance, tradition has often considered accent 2 as the typical accent of disyllabic forms with initial stress, a fact supported by sheer type and token frequencies. In phonological analyses this has sometimes been interpreted as grounds for assuming accent 2 as the default accent of disyllables (Kock 1878; Danell 1937: 51; Malmberg 1970: 157; Öhman 1966; Teleman 1969: 187; Nyström 1997; Lahiri et al. 2005; Wetterlin 2010). On the other hand, accent 2 correlates robustly with a large class of suffixes, inviting a quite different analysis where accent 2 results from lexically represented information in those suffixes (Riad 2009a, 2012, 2014, 2015). This type of difference will not be settled in this article.[4] Instead, we shall make a number of basic assumptions explicit and then move on to the typological comparison.

---

4 For a general discussion of the analytical history of Scandinavian accent, see Naydenov (2011).

3 The tonal accent system and the crucial forms

The terms "accent 1" and "accent 2" are usually used with reference to the entire tonal contour of words in citation form, hence in a focused context. This means that lexical and intonational tonal material is not distinguished until further segmentation is made. (2) provides an overview of the segmentation in Central Swedish, for the two prominence levels in which the accent distinction is realized. We will refer to the higher prominence level as the "big" accent, and the lower prominence level as the "small" accent (Myrberg & Riad 2015). This keeps the terminology free from functional implications, and directs attention to the phonological shape, without tying it to a particular dialect.[5] There is thus a categorical prominence level distinction between big accent and small accent, and the lexical distinction is realized in both of them. For the purposes of the typology, it will suffice to look at the big accent, which (largely) includes the tonal material of the small accent.[6] Bolded tones are lexical, all other tones are postlexical. The accent distinction is privative.

(2) Prominence levels and accents of Central Swedish (Myrberg 2010; Myrberg & Riad 2015, 2016)

prominence level	accent 1	accent 2	accent 2 in compounds	typical functions
big accent	L*H	**H***LH	**H***L*H	focus, contrastive topic, initiality accent
small accent	HL*	**H***L	H*L	given material, second occurrence focus (post-focally), new material (non-final in the phrase), stressed words generally (except e.g. verbs in lexicalized phrases and auxiliaries)

The initial H* tone of the accent 2 contour is what distinguishes the big accent contours for accent 1 and accent 2, respectively. The rise in the big accent (LH) is

---

[5] Bruce (1977) called these "sentence accent" and "word accent". Later they have been referred to as "focus/focal accent" and "word accent", "focal accent" and "non-focal accent" (e.g., Bruce 2007), or "prominence level 2" and "prominence level 1" (Myrberg 2010). For a fuller discussion of the reasons for adopting the terms "big" and "small", see Myrberg & Riad (2015).
[6] The small accent is HL in both instances, but with different associations, yielding the difference in timing (Bruce 1977). The leading H in accent 1 is sometimes in evidence also in the big accent (hence HL*H), but the phonological status of this tone is disputed. It is more stable in the small accent (Bruce 1977), and its presence in the big accent is related to articulatory emphasis, and thereby the height of the trailing H (Fant & Kruckenberg 2008). Engstrand (1995, 1997) has argued that the leading H in the big accent is predictable from ambient intonation.

common to both accent 1 and 2, and is purely intonational (hence postlexical). We will refer to it as the "prominence tone". The tonal sequence is the same in the two cases of accent 2, but the initial H tone has different sources. In simplex accent 2, the initial H tone (bold) is lexical (in a root or a suffix), whereas in compound accent 2, this tone is postlexical. This postlexical accent 2 tone is assigned by a rule which is sensitive to the number of stresses, and which overrules lexical specifications.[7] Any tones of accent 1 are assigned postlexically. We will use the term "lexical tone" or "(post)lexical tone" in reference to the first tone in the accent 2 contour (bolded). This tone is what instantiates the marked member of the accentual opposition, and accent 1 consequently consists of just intonation tones. The lexical tone is invariably associated to the primary stressed syllable. The next tone is the "prominence tone". In accent 1, it is associated to the primary stressed syllable, while in accent 2, it is displaced to the right by the lexical tone which occupies the stressed syllable. A lexical tone thus always has precedence to the stressed syllable (= TBU), which will only host a single, associated tone. In citation forms the prominence tone is followed by the "boundary tone", usually L%. The boundary tone is not associated to a TBU, but is aligned with the end of the phrase. The three terms are used in the overview in (9).

Let us now have a look at the privative contrast in simplex forms. In the following panels the big accent (on ¹¹*Allan* and ²¹*Anna*, respectively) is followed by a small accent (on *ï*¹¹*går* 'yesterday'). The presence of the small accent here creates a stable endpoint for the big accent, allowing us to compare the realization of the shared part of the big accent contour in the two accents. The (small accent) HL* is coordinated with the beginning of the stressed vowel of *ï*¹¹*går* in each panel.

(3) Accent 1, simplex, big accent, *Allan* (name) (female SM, elicited)

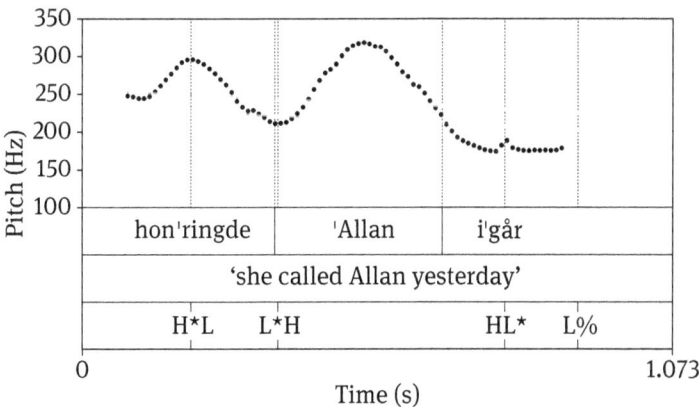

---

[7] The tonal identity between lexical accent 2 and postlexical accent 2 is no coincidence, but the result of a diachronic change, from postlexical to lexical (Riad 1998a).

(4) Accent 2, simplex, big accent, *Anna* (name) (female SM, elicited)

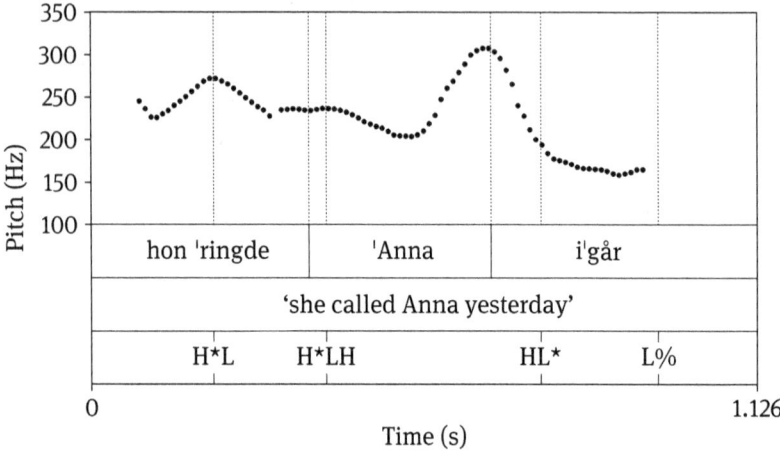

The distinction between the two accents thus lies in the initial part of the contour, where accent 2 contains an extra tone. The rest of the big tonal contour of accent 2 is identical to all of the accent 1 contour and constituted by intonation tones only. We can illustrate this fact by matching the two contours as in (5), where the lexical tone of accent 2 is to the left of the first vertical line. In the right-hand panels, the contour of accent 1 is compressed and the identity of the intonational part of the contour is evident. The tonal sequences for accent 2 and accent 1 are given above and below, respectively.

(5) The identity of the intonational part of the contour

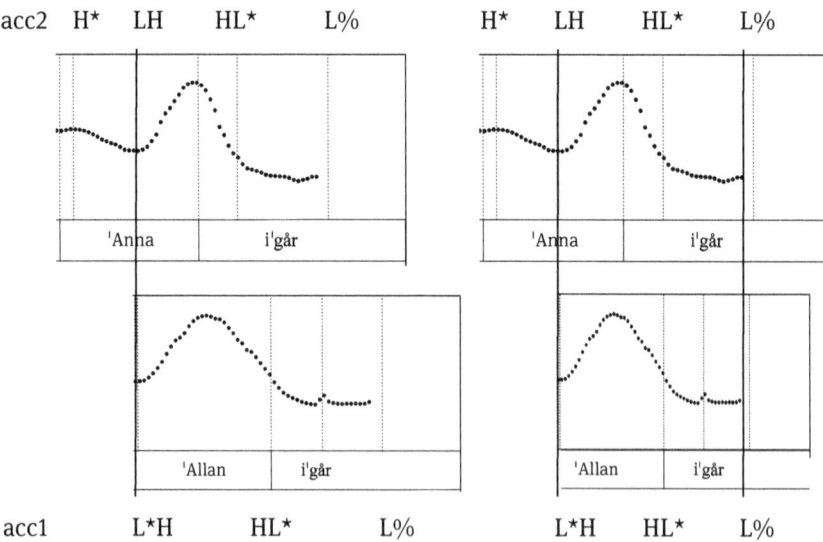

The shared part of the contour is delayed in accent 2, due to the presence of the lexical tone. For the big accent 1 there is, then, more space for the prominence tone (L*H), and the low target of the following small accent (HL*) is reached earlier in *igår* than following a big accent 2.

Simplex forms typically only contain a single association point since minimal prosodic words in Swedish can contain only a single stressed syllable, unlike, e.g., English and German (Riad 2014). Whenever there are more stresses, more minimal prosodic words are created, and the structure as a whole receives what we shall call "compound accent".[8] Compound accent is melodically the same as accent 2, but the first tone is postlexical rather than lexical, cf. (2). Accent is here sensitive to the number of stresses in a form, and this holds of Central Swedish and several other dialects (Dala, Narvik, Göta).[9] The fact that more TBU's become available in compounds also makes it possible for the prominence tone to associate, to the last stress of the compound (or other similar forms containing two stresses, formal compounds or derivations with a stressed suffix, cf. (24)). This is illustrated in (6).

(6) Accent 2, compound, *talespersonerna* 'the spokespersons' (male NN, sr)[10]

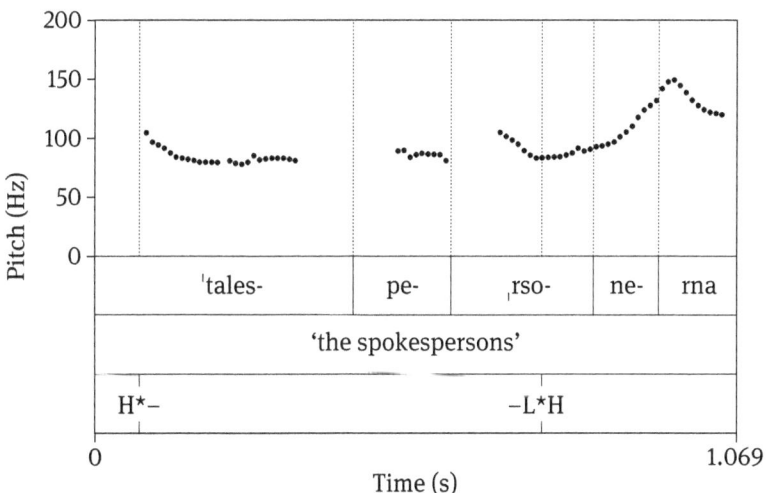

---

[8] Compound accent occurs in any form that contains two stresses, predominantly but not exclusively compounds, cf. (24) below.
[9] Several dialects admit either accent in compounds and thereby do not have a "compound rule". This is discussed in Section 5.3. In the comparisons we make we shall use instances of accent 2 in compounds.
[10] The orthographic form is divided into syllables according to retroflexion in the phonetic form which is [ˈtʰɑːlɛspæˌʂuːnɛɳa]. Unknown speakers are coded as 'NN', known ones with initials.

This contour shows how the postlexical H* associates to the first stress and the prominence L*H associates to the second and last stress. The trailing H of the prominence tone floats and does not exhibit stable timing (Bruce 1987). Indeed, it may in some dialects drift to the right of the focused word (Bruce 2003; Myrberg 2010).[11] The example in (6) is cut out from the middle of a phrase, so there is no final boundary L%, a fact that might motivate the relatively late realization of the floating H. The fact that it is the last stress that is the target for the secondary association is clear from forms that contain several stressed syllables. This is illustrated in (7).

(7) Accent 2, long compound, *uppmärksamhetssplittring* 'attention split' (female NN, sr)

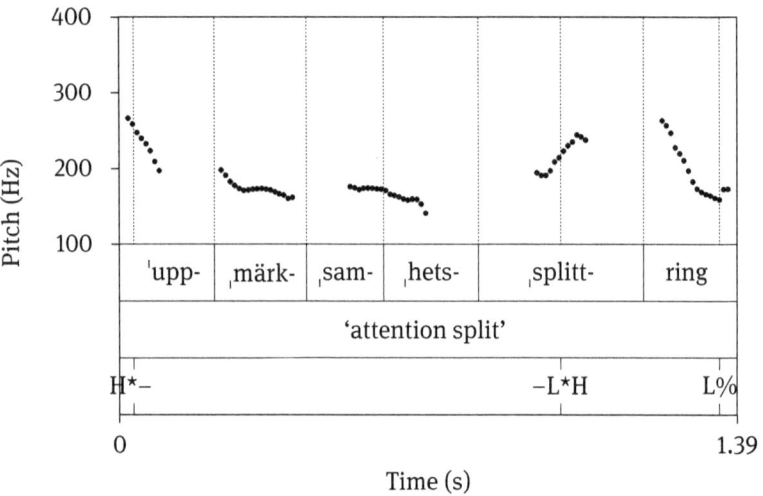

Longish compounds in focus position (i.e., exhibiting the big accent) that carry accent 2 is the single most relevant type of data to use in dialect comparison, since they exhibit more properties of the tonal grammar than any other form. Unlike simplex forms, otherwise the typical data used in typologies of North Germanic accent, long compounds show whether or not there is a secondary association to a later TBU, as well as if there is spreading or interpolation between association points. Both of these things prove to be important parameters of the

---

11 It has, however, not been reported that there would be a stable association point in the following word, as has for example been reported for Standard Greek (Arvaniti 2002; Grice et al. 2000).

tone accent typology.¹² We comment on compounds with accent 1 separately, in Section 5.3.

The lexical accent distinction in terms of minimal pairs is of no particular interest to the typology as such. The distinction carries a very marginal functional load, and alleged minimal pairs are often not "clean", i.e., they are often constituted by inflected forms where the uninflected forms do not form a minimal pair (8a). Also, it is incidental changes like vowel reductions and consonant assimilations that determine whether there are relatively many minimal pairs (Norwegian, around 3000, Leira 1998) or not (Swedish, about 350, Elert 1972), cf. (8b). Furthermore minimality is seldom instantiated by forms of the same grammatical category, (8c). The many flaws of minimal pairs, however, do not mean that there is no unpredictable lexical distinction. Monomorphemic word pairs like those in (8d) show that lexical tones are real. These forms are also semantically close to each other.

(8) The tonal accent distinction
    a. ¹'and-en   'the duck'   ²'ande-n   'the spirit'
        ¹'steg-en   'the steps'   ²'stege-n   'the ladder'
    b. Nw ¹'bønd-er   'farmers'   ²'bønne-r   'prayers'
        [bøn:ər]   [bøn:ər]
        Sw ¹'bönd-er   'farmers'   ²'bön-er   'prayers'
        [bønˑdɛr]   [bøːnɛr]
    c. ¹'bur-en   'the cage, n.' ²'bur-en   'carried, p.ptcp'
    d. ¹'syrak   'angry'   ²'elak   'mean'
        ¹'ketchup   'ketchup'   ²'senap   'mustard'

It is the near-minimal pairs in (8d) that establish the lexical contrast, rather than the alleged minimal pairs in (8a) and (8c).

4 One typology

The tonal dialects form a coherent typology by virtue of sharing some basic properties. For one thing the realization of accent 2 requires two syllables (disregarding the few apocopating dialects; Lorentz 2008), whereas accent 1 requires only

---

12 The secondary association here is motivated by the availability of TBU's. Grice, Ladd, & Arvaniti (2000) discuss cases of secondary association of phrase accents (corresponding to the separate focus gesture in Bruce's terminology) in Hungarian, Greek, and Cypriot Greek. Intonation tones may then associate to a stressed syllable in the following word (Greek) or another syllable down the line, depending on prosodic context.

a single syllable. This is indeed the first argument for the privative nature of the contrast. Since accent 2 requires more space, there should be more tonal material in that contour.[13]

The fact that accent 2 requires so much space has an interpretation in terms of tone bearing unit, which is the stressed syllable in Swedish and Norwegian. Tones associate to primary stressed syllables in all dialects, and in some dialects they associate to secondary stresses, too. This understanding of the TBU coupled with the common assumption of one-tone-per-TBU rather predicts the synchronic requirement of two or more syllables for the occurrence of accent 2. If the TBU were the mora, as for example in most eastern Central Franconian varieties (Peters 2007: 171), there would be nothing in the way of a contrast in monosyllables.

Another thing that makes the typology coherent is the tonal alternation, which means that there are no challenges to the Obligatory Contour Principle (OCP). While it has been proposed that there are OCP-induced tonal epentheses (Lorentz 1995), the simplest analysis is achieved by simply segmenting the tonal contour into three basic parts: lexical tone (if any), prominence tone, and boundary tone, where each tone is (or begins with) the opposite value of the preceding tone. The lexical tone is invariably a single tone, and that seems to be the case also with the boundary tone, though the issue has not been systematically studied. The prominence tone may be single or complex. The apparent generalization here (which we return to in Section 7) is that a prominence tone must contain an H tone, unless the boundary tone is H% and employed for the expression of focus (East Norwegian). At any rate, there is no need to postulate tonal epenthesis. The more conservative view that there are no epenthetic tones also has a restrictive effect on the typology as such, as it reduces the variational space, and also has something to say for the structural similarity between dialects irrespective of tonal values.

Further support for the coherence of the typology comes from the lexical distribution of the accents, which is very stable across dialects. Accent 2 shows up with the same set of unstressed, posttonic suffixes (Sw *-ar*, *-or*, *-are*, *-ing*, *-nad*, *-lig*, *-ig*, *-a*, among others, and corresponding Norwegian suffixes), a fact that points at both a morphological anchoring of lexical tone and a shared origin.

Another shared property is the fact that the postlexical generalization of accent in compounds is always in the direction of accent 2. No dialect that has a tonal contrast exhibits prosodically motivated assignment of accent 1 in compounds. Most dialects, however, exhibit some prosodic assignment of accent

---

13 Unlike the case in Central Franconian and Lithuanian, where there is a basic requirement of two sonorant moras for the tonal distinction to be realized, there is no sonority requirement in Swedish and Norwegian that affects the tonal contour. The situation for Danish stød resembles that of Central Franconian and Lithuanian in this regard (Basbøll 2005: 272).

2, usually at least in the core set of stem compounds containing a clash (South Swedish; Strandberg 2014) and in recently formed formal compounds arising from initial stress insertion (*protes*¹'*tere* > ²'*protes*ˌ*tere* 'to protest'; e.g., East Norwegian; Kristoffersen 2000: 165). Often, accent 2 is broadly generalized to any form containing two stresses (e.g., Central Swedish, Dala, Göta, North Norwegian).[14]

Finally, the geographic contiguity of the tonal systems obviously points at a common historical core. Although some developments have taken place – yielding the variation we study as a typology here – there are no indications of a tonal variety that is radically different from that of any other dialect. With Danish stød, however, there is reason to believe that a radical change has taken place, as some basic conditions are different there: beside the different phonetic exponent, there is the sonority requirement in stressed syllables ("stød basis"), the possibility of more than one stød in a single compound, and the largely (but not completely) inverse distribution of stød compared with accent 2.[15] The historical affinity is not in question, but neither is the typological distance.

5 The variables and the dialects

A number of variables instantiate the typological variation and in this section we go through them. Recall that we shall look only at compounds carrying big accent 2, since most of the basic properties of the tonal system are contained in, and therefore derivable from, that type of form.

First, the value of the lexical tone: H or L. The first tone in accent 2 is either lexical or postlexical (compounds). It is invariably the same tone value in simplex forms as in compounds, and it also behaves consistently, associating to the primary stressed syllable.

Second, the number of associations for accent 2 in compounds: two or one. Dialects differ with respect to whether or not they admit a second association beside that of the initial postlexical tone. If a secondary association occurs (in a system with generalized accent 2 in compounds), it is at the last stressed syllable

---

[14] To make this point clear, the alternative to prosodically motivated accent assignment is lexically motivated accent assignment, which looks at the properties of the first compound member in free form.

[15] Some Central Franconian dialects, too, exhibit the possibility of more than one accent within compounds or compound-like forms (Peters 2006: 120). This points at a difference regarding culminativity, between, on the one hand, NGmc tonal dialects, where there is invariably one accent per (maximal prosodic) word, always with association to the primary stressed syllable, and on the other hand, Danish and Central Franconian dialects of the Hasselt type, where there can be more than one accents in a word, hence in both primary and secondary stressed syllables.

of the compound. Dialects which only admit a single association in compounds assign tonal accent the same way in simplex as in compounds, i.e., they exhibit no "compound rule".

Third, the shape of transitions: spreading or interpolation. In dialects that admit two associations in compounds, the transition from the (post)lexical tone to the prominence tone may have a characteristic profile that suggests backwards spreading of the prominence tone, or else that there is phonetic interpolation between the two. To some extent, there is also some variation in the transition from the prominence tone to the boundary tone.

There is a fourth potential variable that concerns the big accent (in focal contexts), specifically whether the big accent is expressed by enhancement of the small accent (southern varieties, Dala), or by the addition of a separate focus gesture (Central Swedish, Göta) to the small accent (Bruce 2004). We will return to this potential variable later (Section 7), and suggest that while it is phonetically reasonable, it does not constitute a relevant phonological parameter. Rather it is dependent on, and derivable from, more general properties of the melodic make-up of the tonal contour.

Let us first take a look at a map of Sweden and Norway, indicating the general distribution of some of these variables. In the following subsections we go through the variables one at a time and illustrate how they instantiate typological variation by pairwise comparing dialects which differ minimally on one or the other variable (Figure 10.1).

5.1 Value of the lexical tone: H or L

In (9) we have divided the melody of compounds in each dialect into three segments, called "(post)lexical tone", "prominence tone", and "boundary tone".[16]

(9) Tones of the accent 2 contour in compounds in several dialects

Lexical	Prominence	Boundary	Dialect
H*	L*H	L%	Central Swedish, Stockholm, North Sw
L*	H*	L%	Dala, Narvik, Färnebo
H*	L*H	L%	Göta 1, West Swedish
H*	L*	H%	Göta 2, West Swedish
H*	L	H%	East Norwegian, Oslo
L*	HL	L%	South Swedish, Skåne, Bergen
H*	LH	L%	Stavanger, Southwest Norwegian

---

[16] The actual prominence FUNCTION is sometimes carried by the boundary tone, when H%, cf. Section 7.

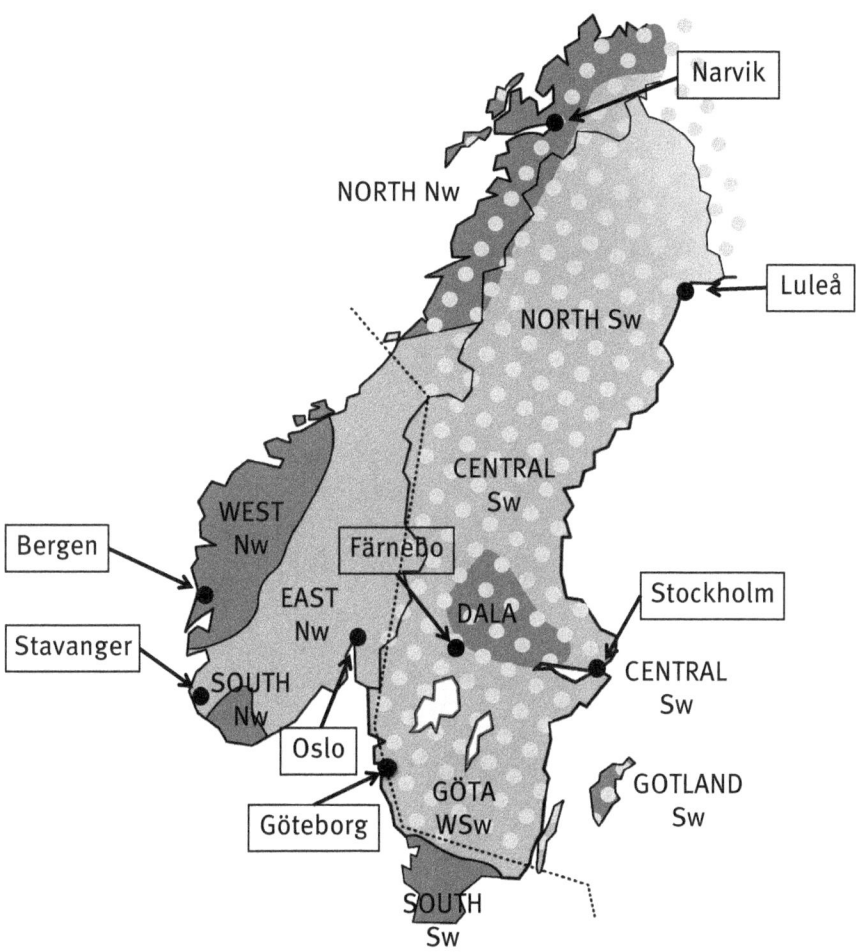

Figure 10.1: Map of Scandinavia, with some important locations indicated. Darker areas have an L*, and lighter areas an H*, as (post)lexical tone. The isogloss (dotted line) indicates the boundary between dialects that have two (east, north) or one (west, south) association points in compounds.

As can be seen, the lexical tone varies between H* and L*. All tones in the first column are marked with a star to indicate that the (post)lexical tone is invariably associated. We shall now make the comparison between a CSw variety (Stockholm) and a Dala variety (Norberg). These varieties differ primarily with respect to the value of the lexical tone. Grammatically, they are otherwise the same, i.e., with regard to tonal associations and spreading pattern. We use the word *sommarledigheten* 'the summer holidays' as our sample word. This word contains three stresses and will have accent 2 in all dialects, either by virtue of a prosodic compound rule, or by virtue of the first morpheme *sommar* 'summer' being lexically accent 2. In Figure 10.2, autosegmental representations are provided for both dialects compared, above and below the sample word, and also stylized contours.

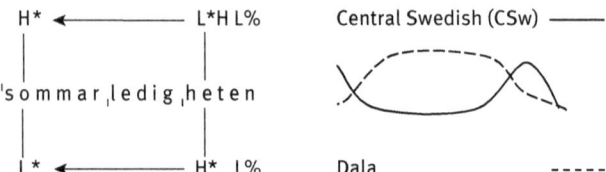

Figure 10.2: Schematic comparison of CSw and Dala. These dialects differ primarily on tonal value of the (post)lexical tone.

We look first at two examples from CSw. The previous panels that we have looked at were all taken from this variety. The compounds in (10) and (11) both contain three minimal prosodic words each, hence three stresses. The (post)lexical tone associates to the first and the prominence tone associates to the last.

(10) Central Swedish (Stockholm), compound, accent 2, *samhällskroppen* 'the body of society' (male GE, sr)

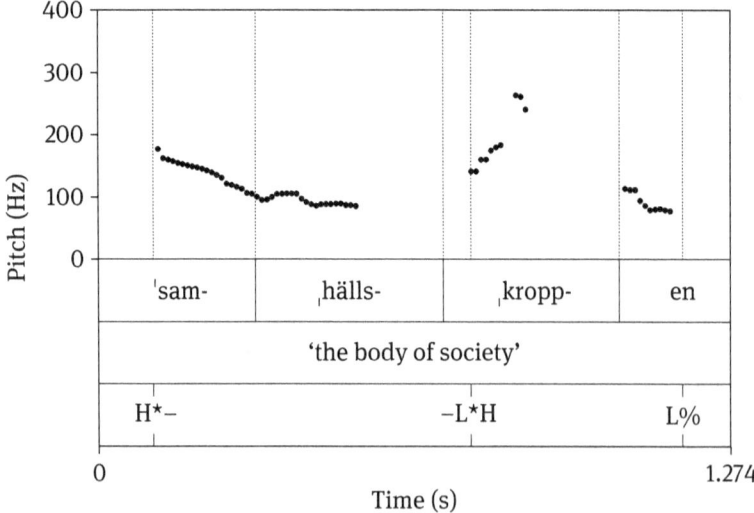

(11) Central Swedish (Stockholm), compound, accent 2, *samarbeta* 'cooperate' (male JH, sr)

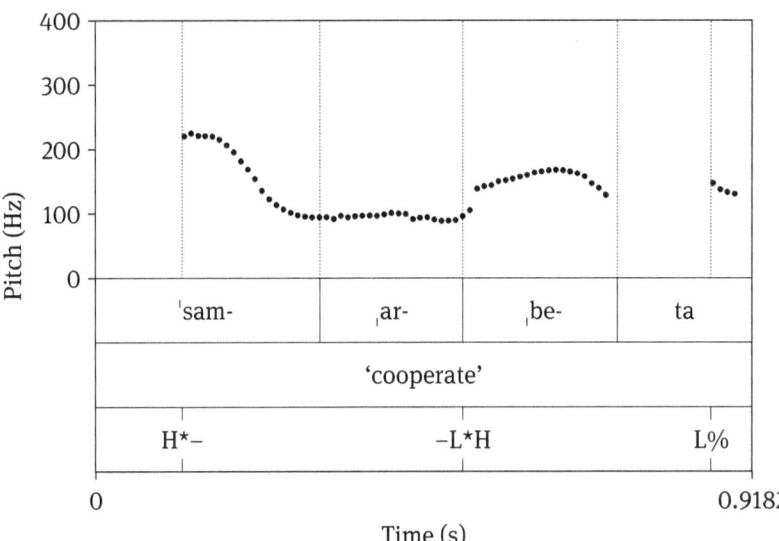

These CSw contours should now be compared with Dala. The two contours are from speakers from Norberg and Dala-Järna.

(12) Dala (Norberg), compound, accent 2, *manshatare* 'man hater' (female LG, sr)

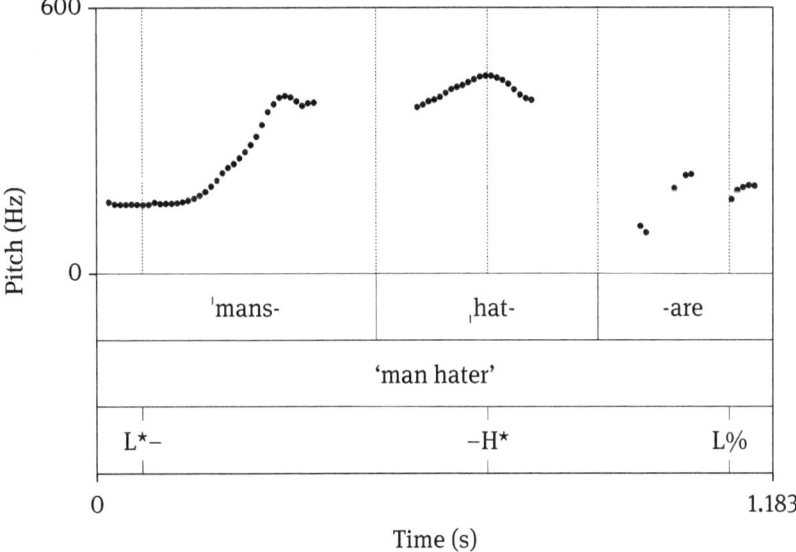

(13) Dala (Dala-Järna), compounds, accent 2, *vallhund* 'shepherd's dog', *arbetstid* 'working time' (male NN, sr)

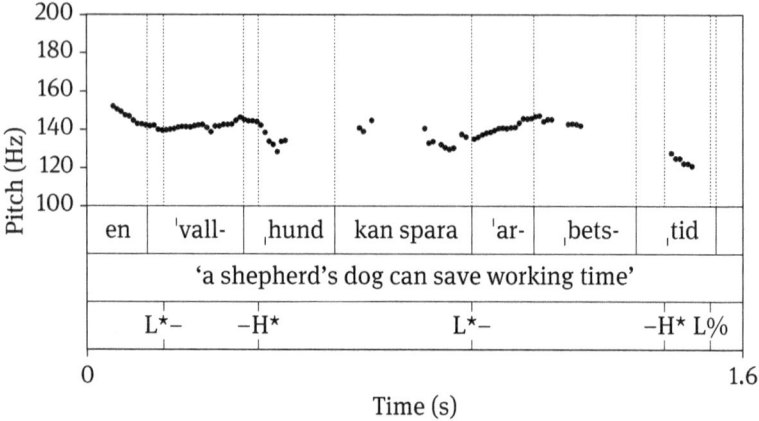

In the analysis of both of these dialects the prominence tone spreads back from the last stressed syllable to the (post)lexical tone. In the CSw variety this means a tonal floor from the last stress back to right after the (post)lexical H*. In Dala varieties this means a high plateau from the prominence H* in the last stress back to the (post)lexical L* on the primary stress.

The value of the (post)lexical tone is readily identified from panels like these, and we maintain that this tone is also a phonologically relevant category, therefore useful for typological concerns. As we saw in (5), the lexical tone is quite easy to isolate, by simple comparison of accent 1 and accent 2 forms, where the accent 2 forms will contain an extra tone before the intonational tones that are common to both accents.[17]

Let us look at another example of a minimal contrast on tonal value. This time we compare East Norwegian (ENw) with South Swedish (SSw), shown in Figure 10.3. These dialects have parallel association patterns, but each tone contrasts. H and L tones do not fulfill functional purposes in exactly the same way, there being a bias for H tones to serve as markers of prominence. In Norwegian it has long been maintained that the boundary tone also carries the function of

---

[17] In the Norwegian tradition, where one distinguishes "high-tone" dialects from "low-tone" dialects, the terminology refers to the value of the PROMINENCE tone (i.e., the first tone of accent 1). This is a rather unfelicitous choice of category, since it does not necessarily single out a phonological unit. In CSw the prominence tone is L*H, i.e., a bitonal unit. Calling this a "low-tone" dialect would refer to just half of the phonological category.

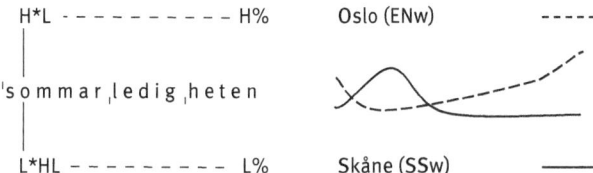

Figure 10.3: Schematic comparison of ENw and Skåne. These dialects differ primarily regarding the tonal value of the (post)lexical tone.

focus (Fretheim & Nilsen 1989; Kristoffersen 2000: 278).[18] This does not affect the tonal grammar, however, which is parallel. Panels exemplifying these dialects are given in (14) and (15), below for ENw, and in (20) for SSw.

5.2 Number of associations in compounds: Two or one

The second column of the table in (9) indicates whether or not a dialect admits a secondary association in compounds. The second tone (usually carrying the prominence function) is star-marked if it associates to the last stressed syllable of a compound. Geographically this property defines an isogloss cutting through the Scandinavian peninsula, as marked in Figure 10.1. The independence of this variable is demonstrated by the fact that there are dialects with H and L lexical tone on either side of the isogloss. The dialects to the north and east of this isogloss are sometimes referred to as "connective" dialects since compounds exhibit a particular prosodic pattern which connects the beginning and end of the compounds. It is invariably the case in these dialects that the prominence tone goes to the last stress. On the other side of the isogloss compounds are partly assigned accent according to the lexical specification (or its absence) in the first compound member. The pattern is sometimes called "non-connective". These dialects also often exhibit a prosodic rule assigning accent 2, in the narrow context of word initial stress clash, i.e., where the first morpheme is monosyllabic and directly followed by the stress of the second element. There are also morphological requirements that further constrain the application of this prosodic rule (cf. Strandberg 2014 for South Swedish). It looks like stress clash is the original context for postlexical accent 2, and it has been argued that this is also the context in which accent 2 arises (Riad 1998a). The connective pattern to the east and north of the isogloss should thereby be understood as an innovation,

---

[18] The boundary H% can also be followed by another boundary tone L%, which we disregard here.

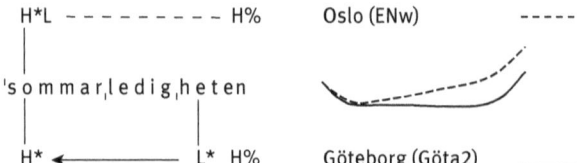

Figure 10.4: Schematic comparison of ENw (Oslo) and Göta/WSw (Göteborg). These dialects differ primarily on the secondary association in compounds.

spreading from Central Swedish dialects, and perhaps independently in the very north (Strandberg 2014: 174).

The dialects that we will first compare regarding a secondary association are East Norwegian (Oslo) and West Swedish/Göta (Göteborg), which have the same tonal make-up but which differ crucially on the issue of a secondary association, as shown in Figure 10.4.

A secondary association occurs in WSw, which keeps the contour down until the last stress. Thereafter the contour rises to the final H%, which is aligned with the end of the word. In ENw, by contrast, there is no secondary association and the tonal contour begins to rise directly after the H*L at the primary stress. We begin with ENw, where the focus function is in fact placed on the boundary H%, often referred to as the focal H (Fretheim & Nilsen 1989; Kristoffersen 2000: 278).

(14) ENw (Oslo), compound, accent 2, *granskingsrapportene* 'the examination reports' (female NN, nrk)

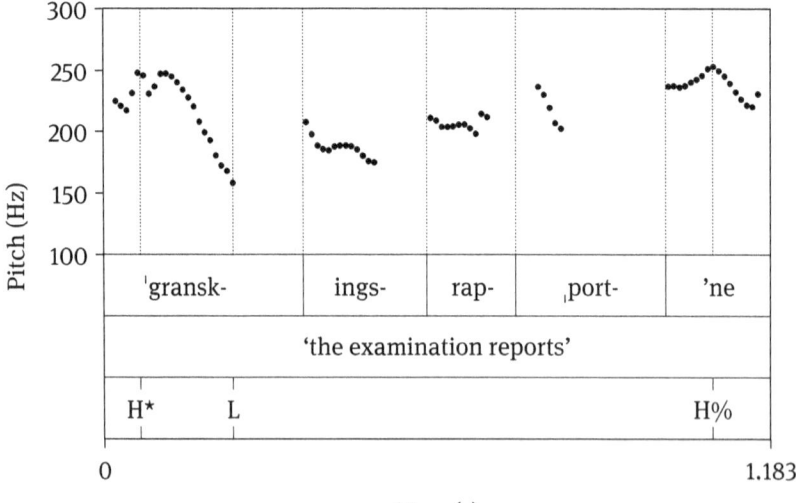

(15) ENw (Oslo), compound, accent 2, *ordførerspørsmålet* 'the chairman issue' (female NN, nrk)

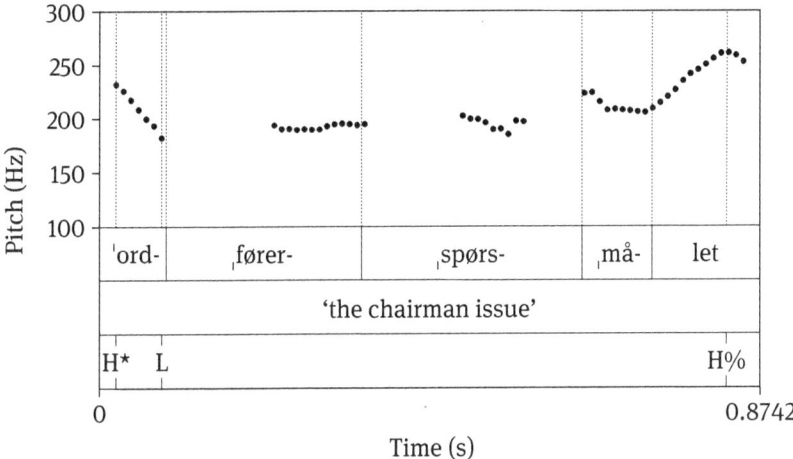

The lowest point in the ENw contours is right after the initial H*. From there there is a steady rise until the end. The WSw contours, by contrast, have the lowest point at the last stress of the compound.

(16) WSw, Göta 2 (Göteborg), compound, accent 2, *åsidosatta* 'slighted' (male NG, sr)

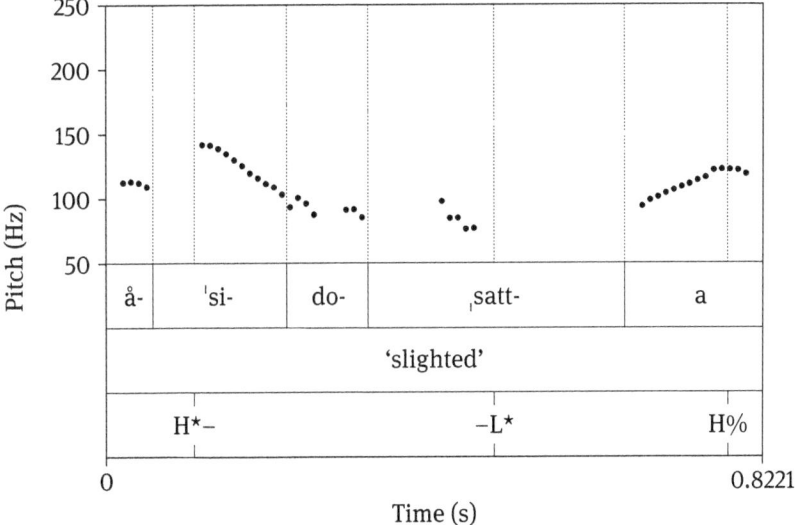

(17) WSw, Göta 2 (Göteborg), compound, accent 2, *fotbollsfamiljen* 'the football family' (male BG, sr)

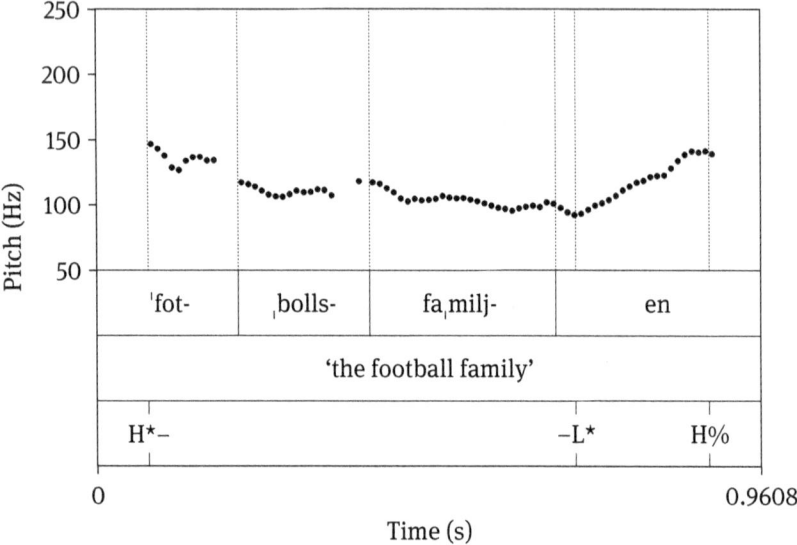

We shall have a look at another example of the same type of alternation between dialects. This time we look at two dialects of the two-peaked type, namely Central Swedish and Stavanger in southwest Norway, compared in Figure 10.5.

The Stavanger variety has been investigated by Hognestad (2012) and the panels below are based on his recordings. The intonation system of this dialect has clearly begun to change in the last couple of generations.[19] The panels in (18) and (19) are taken from a (young) speaker who exhibits the system of the older generation in careful, elicited speech.[20] This is where the contrast vis-à-vis Central Swedish is the clearest. The tones after the initial H* have been separately coordinated with the following low and high points.[21]

---

[19] For instance, speakers have developed a sensitivity to a secondary association. Hognestad proposes that this ongoing change might lead to generalized connective accent 2 in compounds. At this stage, there is not (yet) a "compound accent", and all speakers still exhibit both accent 1 and accent 2 in compounds. The shape of accents with sensitivity to the final secondary stress contains an early second peak followed by a characteristic high plateau (rather than the low floor that occurs in Central Swedish, which has the same tonal make-up). An example of such a high plateau occurs in the accent 1 compound in (22).
[20] In informal conversation this informant exhibits a pattern more like the other informants his age.
[21] The analyses of the three Stavanger forms do not necessarily agree with those given by Hognestad (2012).

The phonological typology of North Germanic accent — 363

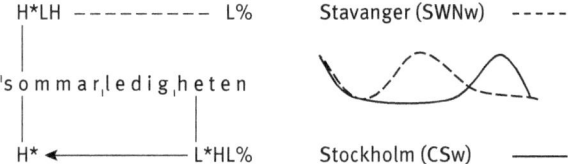

Figure 10.5: Schematic comparison of SWNw (Stavanger) and CSw (Stockholm). These dialects differ primarily on the secondary association in compounds.

(18) Stavanger (SWNw), compound, accent 2, *femtenårsjubileum* 'fifteen year jubilee' (male OLVI 7124, elicited)

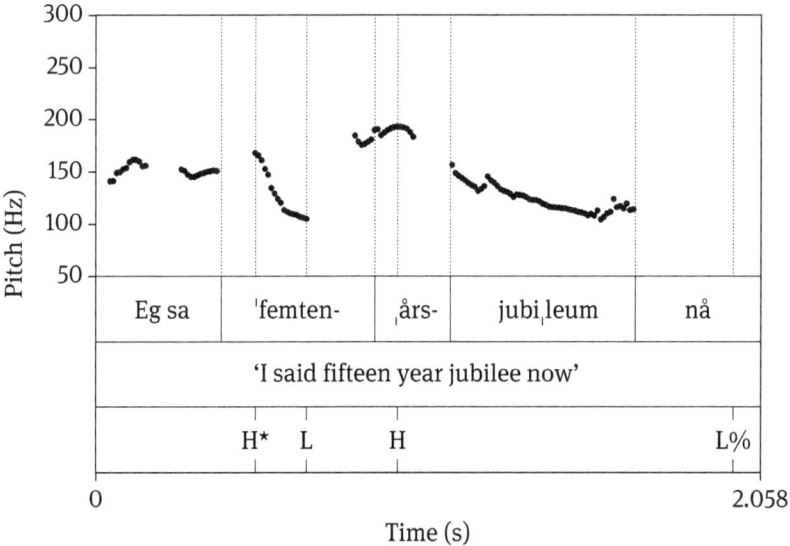

In this example we can clearly see how the second H tone occurs relatively close to the left edge, certainly not at the last stress. It might look as if it were associated to the second stress, but that is not in fact the case. This is clear from the next example where the peak is in an unstressed syllable.

(19) Stavanger (SWNw), compound, accent 2, *delingsmodellene* 'the sharing models' (male OLVI 7110, elicited)

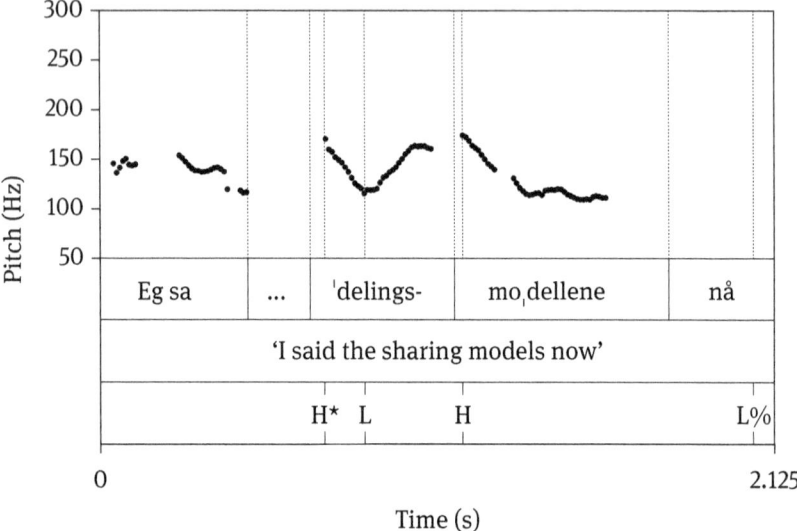

These contours should be compared with the ones given for Central Swedish above, such as (7), (10), and (11), where a secondary association at the rightmost stress is clearly in evidence in a dialect with the same tonal sequence.

Our third comparison regarding tonal association involves Dala and South Swedish (Skåne). These varieties have the same tonal make-up but differ regarding secondary association, as represented in Figure 10.6.

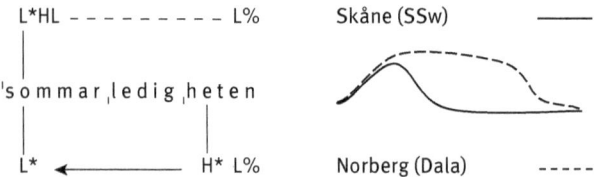

Figure 10.6: Schematic comparison of SSw (Skåne) and Dala (Norberg). These dialects differ primarily regarding the secondary association in compounds.

We have already seen examples of Dala (items (12) and (13), above). From Skåne we have the following utterance, which contains two compounds with the accent 2 contour.

(20) Skåne (SSw), compounds, accent 2, *uppgifter* 'tasks' and *tydliggöras* 'be clarified' (male SG, sr)

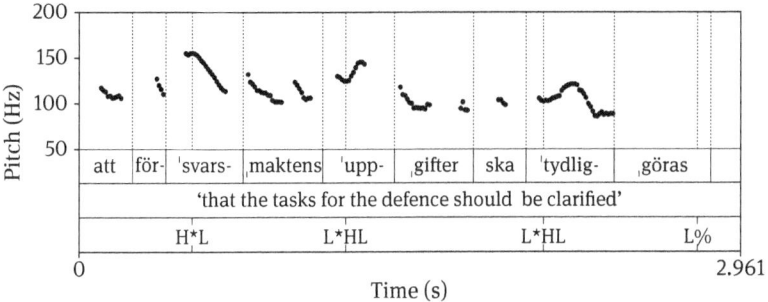

The tonal accent 2 contour is L*HL, where the (post)lexical tone is L*. We have registered the peak and the immediate drop as an HL prominence tone. The status of the L tonal segment is somewhat unclear, e.g., whether it is part of the prominence tone, or if it represents some kind of default. Further research on SSw varieties is needed to clarify the issue.

5.3 Consequences of the association patterns

The dialects that allow only a single association in compounds assign tonal structure in the same way in compounds as in simplex forms. While there may be a limited prosodic rule that applies in compounds (and compound-like structures), there will not be a representational difference in terms of tonal association in these forms. This structural fact allows us to (correctly) predict that the single-association (non-connective) dialects should admit BOTH accents in compounds, as a matter of principle. Below are panels that contain accent 1 compounds from the dialects we have looked at that have a single association point: ENw, SWNw, and SSw.

(21) ENw (Oslo), compound, accent 1, *nyhetssak* 'news item' (male JA, nrk)

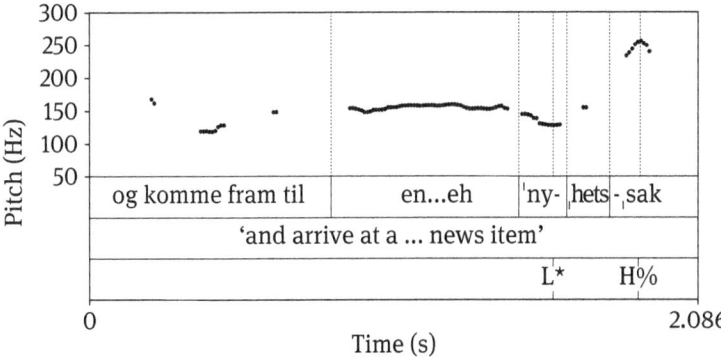

(22) SWNw (Stavanger), compound, accent 1, *fordelingsmodellene* 'the distribution models' (male FAØV 6926, elicited)

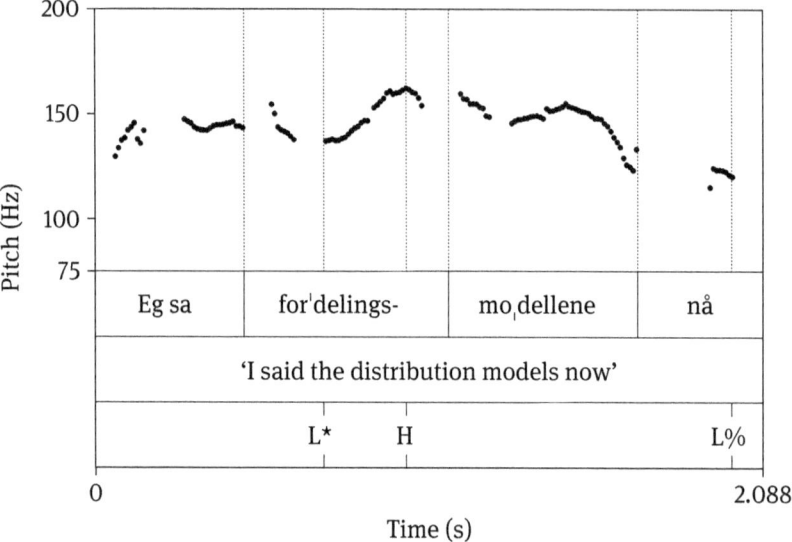

For Skåne we take a cut-out from the previous example (20). In this dialect accent 1 is H*L, which amounts to the prominence tone.

(23) SSw (Skåne), compound, accent 1, *försvarsmaktens* 'the defense force's' (male SG, sr)

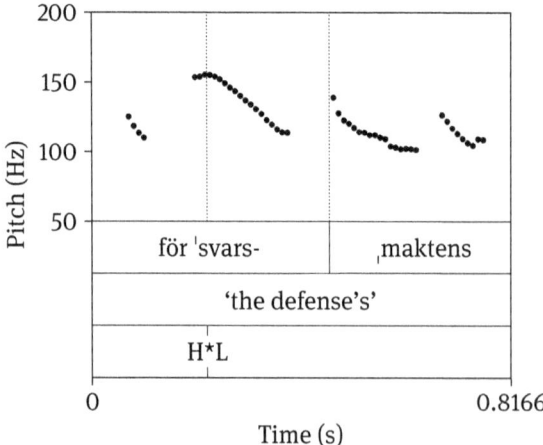

The dialects that require two association points in compounds always have a realization of accent 2 in this type of form. Thus, no dialect has generalized accent 1 in compounds (while still maintaining a distinction in simplex forms). This fact should ideally follow from representation, and we would propose that it is the combination of which tonal segments there are and the identification of the relevant TBU that actually predicts the pattern. If the dialect allows association to more than one TBU, then there must also be more than one tone that COULD associate. In the privative analysis of the distinction, only accent 2 has more than one tonal segment (the (post)lexical tone and the prominence tone), and so we can predict that there could be no such thing as a connective realization of accent 1.[22]

Furthermore, the connective accent 2 pattern is not limited to the morphological category of compounds. Rather, the generalization concerns forms that contain more than one stress. This obviously complicates the notions of "simplex" and "compound" such as we have used them up to now. The "compound rule" has a purely prosodic basis, rather than a morphological one. The tonal representation results from the presence of two stresses (not from the presence of a morphological object as such). Thus, when we say that there is a "compound rule", it is important to note that this is in fact a statement about phonological representation, triggered by prosodic information. The same thing goes for the notion of "simplex", again normally a morphological notion. The typical prosodic shape of simplex forms will be that of a minimal word, with one stress and a single syllabification domain (Riad 2014). But there are also morphological simplex forms that are prosodically like compounds. The three types of forms that are targeted by the compound rule, which assigns postlexical accent 2, are listed in (24).

(24) Targets of the "compound rule", CSw
Proper compounds: ²¹sommar₁dag 'summer day', ba²¹nan₁skal 'banana peel', ²¹under₁söknings₁domare 'examining magistrate'
Formal compounds: ²¹även₁tyr 'adventure', ²¹para₁dis 'paradise', ²¹ar₁bete 'work', ²¹geni₁tiv 'genitive'
(Some) derivations: ²¹sjuk₁dom 'illness', ²¹kraft₁full 'forceful', ²¹under₁bar 'wonderful'

---

[22] There have been proposals that there are dialects that have very nearly the same tonal makeup in accent 1 and accent 2 (Kristoffersen 2007 for Oppdal, Segerup 2004 for Göteborg). These things would be expected to have a phonetic explanation in terms of realization, under the analysis pursued here, and not lend themselves to immediate phonological translation as identical melodies. Otherwise, there should be nothing in the way of a generalized, connective accent 1 in compounds, which is unattested.

Derivations form a sort of middle category between compounds and typical simplex forms. Diachronically, this is not unreasonable since derivations typically stem from compounds in Germanic languages. Synchronically, the situation is that many derivational suffixes are unstressed. Nearly all of them induce accent 2 lexically. Several derivational suffixes are (still) stressed, however, like those exemplified in (24). These suffixes induce accent 2 via the postlexical, "compound rule". The data in (24) point very clearly in the direction of structural properties determining both the fact that only accent 2 could occur with double associations, and that it is the number of TBU's that determine the occurrence of a connective accent pattern, not the morphological category of the form.

5.4 Shape of transitions 1: Spreading or interpolation

We turn now to the third parameter of variation, which is whether dialects have a phonological spreading rule from the prominence tone back to the (post)lexical tone, or whether phonetic interpolation takes place. Dialects of northern Sweden are traditionally considered to be prosodically closely related to those of CSw, since they have the same tonal make-up with a two-peaked realization of accent 2. In simplex forms and short compounds, where the stresses are adjacent, the similarity is obvious (Bruce 2007: 135). There are some contrasts, however, one of which is revealed when we look at longer compounds, as in Figure 10.7, where the transition from the postlexical tone to the prominence tone can be studied (Riad 2006; Bruce 2007).

In many varieties of North Swedish the fall from the postlexical H* to the following L is much flatter than the corresponding fall found in CSw, where it is steep (cf. (7) above). The effect of this dynamic is that the initial H* in NSw tends to sound less prominent than the prominence L*H at the end of the compound. Indeed, the phenomenon is usually described as STRESS on the last member of compound (Bruce 1982). We would maintain that it is really just the perception of the tonal contour that

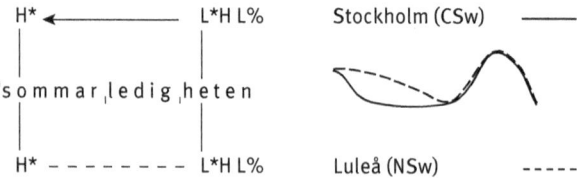

Figure 10.7: Schematic comparison of CSw (Stockholm) and NSw (Luleå). These dialects have the same tonal composition and association patterns, but differ in the transition between the postlexical tone and the prominence tone.

gives this impression (Riad 2006). The phonological interpretation of the contrast that we propose is that CSw exhibits backward spreading of the low tone of the L*H prominence tone, creating a floor between the two anchor points, while NSw lacks the spreading rule and instead exhibits phonetic interpolation, as a gradual fall. This analysis is in line with the segmentation of the contour into two elements, H* and L*H. The pattern in Figure 10.7 is in evidence only in long compounds, with minimally one syllable between the association points. Two examples are given below. They should be contrasted with the CSw items (6), (7), (10) and (11) above.

(25) NSw (Luleå), compound, accent 2, *lärarmöte* 'teachers' meeting' (male NN, sr)

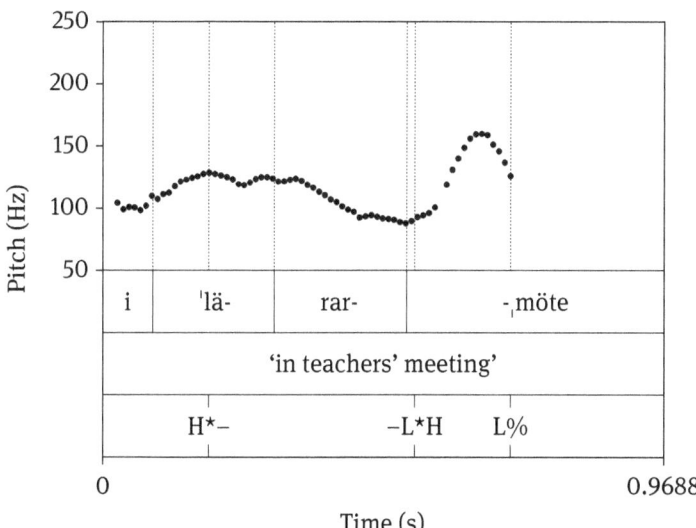

(26) NSw (Luleå), compound, accent 2, *gärningsmän* 'offenders' (male NN, sr)

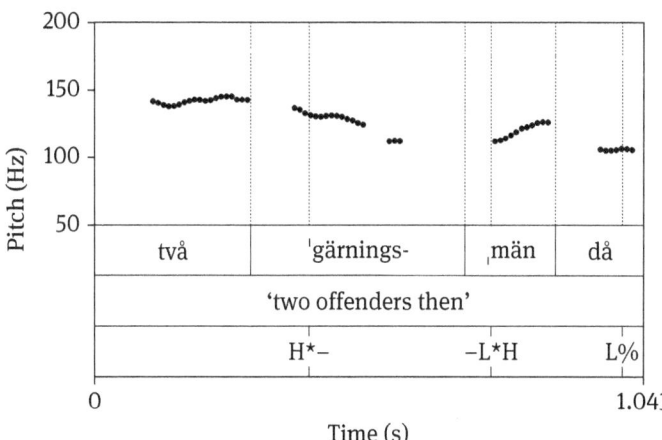

The same contrast is also found with dialects that have a (post)lexical L* in accent 2. The contrast is then between Dala, which exhibits a high plateau by spreading, and East Färnebo-north, which has a rising contour, shown in Figure 10.8.

```
L* ---------- H* L%        East Färnebo-north  -----
|              |
'sommar‚ledig‚heten
|              |
L* ←---------- H* L%        Norberg (Dala)      ———
```

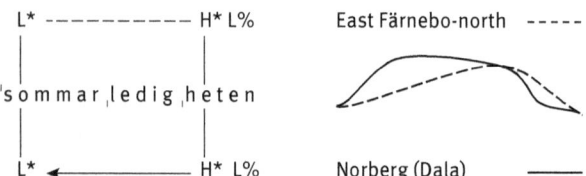

Figure 10.8: Schematic comparison of Dala (Norberg) and East Färnebo-north. These dialects have the same tonal composition and association patterns, but differ regarding the transition between the postlexical tone and the prominence tone.

East Färnebo is described by Kallstenius (1902). The area is on the border between Dala and Göta varieties (cf. Figure 10.1), where the northern part is more like Dala and the southern is more like Göta, i.e., WSw. We have two examples of compounds from the SweDia 2000 materials (Bruce, Engstrand, & Eriksson 1998), from Gåsborn in the Färnebo area. Unfortunately, they both have adjacent stresses, and are therefore not ideal for showing the rising slope.

(27) East Färnebo-north (Gåsborn), compound, accent 2, *husbonden* 'the master' (male Gåsborn, om, SweDia)

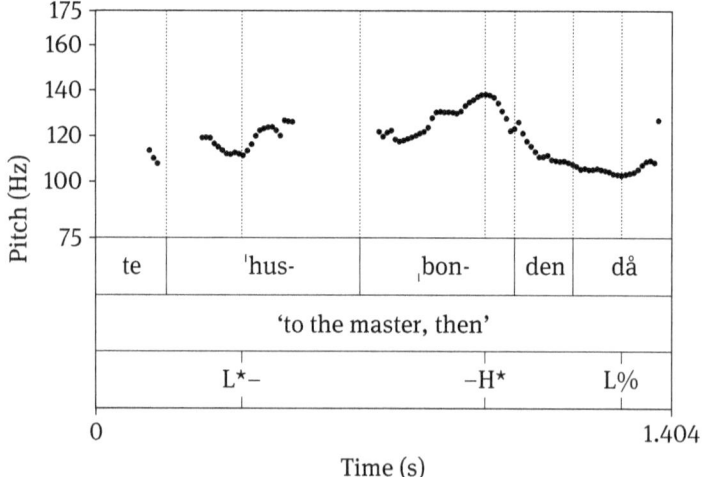

(28) East Färnebo-north (Gåsborn), compound, accent 2, *avrättad* 'executed' (male Gåsborn, om, SweDia)

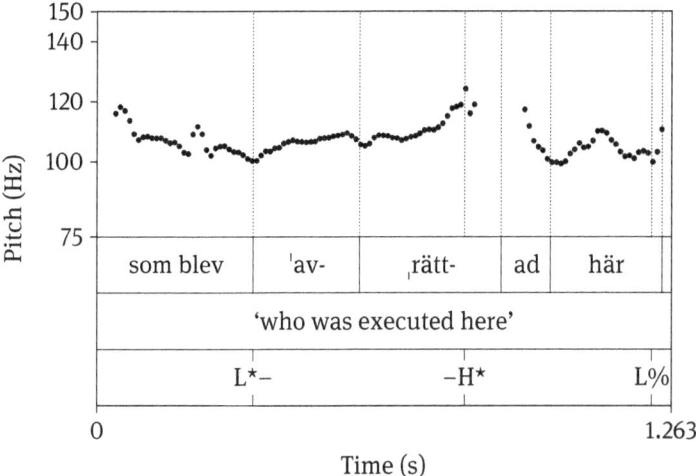

These panels should be compared with the Dala items that we looked at in (12) and (13), above. Closer study of the East Färnebo type is required to establish the structure more firmly.

6 Transitions and dialect change

We shall now look at a couple of other contrasts that provide key information on diachronic relationships between dialects. We will not make a full diachronic argument here, but rather point to variations in tonal alignment that make sense in terms of transitions between tonal varieties.

6.1 Floating H in Central and West Swedish

The first contrast is not obviously structural and concerns the timing of an unassociated tonal segment in otherwise very similar dialects. This type of phonetic variation is likely to be important for changes in the phonological structure. We look at the contrast between CSw and two varieties of WSw which we will call Göta 1 and Göta 2. It is well-known that the unassociated H of the prominence tone L*H in CSw may occur at a variable distance from the associated L* (Bruce 1987). Things like the size of the word carrying accent and the sentential context surely have an influence, but the matter has not been fully investigated. However, it is clear that the timing varies between dialects, too. A comparison of items (6) and (7) illustrate the variation within CSw, where *talespersonerna* 'the spokespersons' in (6) is phrase medial (late H), and *uppmärksamhetssplittring* 'attention split' in (7) is phrase final (earlier H). In the Göta dialects the timing of the trailing H is routinely later, in all contexts.[23] This is seen in items (16) and (17), which are exponents of Göta 2. In these forms, the boundary tone appears to be H%, just like in ENw (items (14) and (15)). But there are also pronunciations in the Göta region where the final boundary tone is L% just as in closely related CSw. This form we shall call Göta 1 in contrast with Göta 2 illustrated in (16) and (17) above. The comparison we are considering is given in Figure 10.9.

Here is an example of an emphatic pronunciation in what we call Göta 1, however without making claims for this being a separate dialect type, rather than an alterative pronunciation in one and the same variety.

(29) WSw, Göta 1 (Göteborg), compound, accent 2, *betydelseassociationen* 'the semantic association' (male LGA, sr)

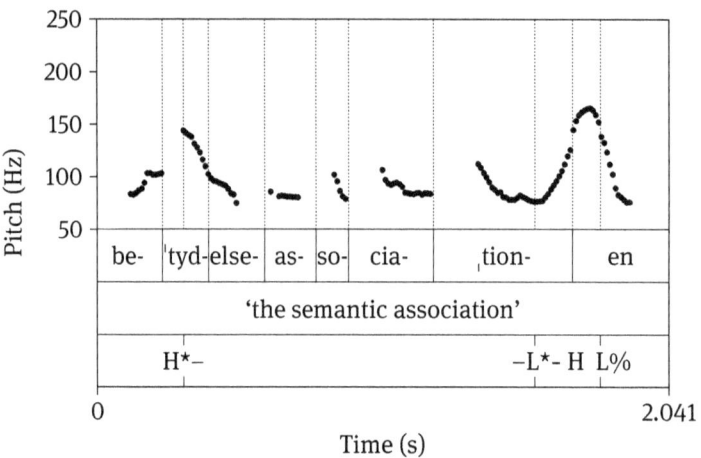

Comparing with CSw item (7) and Göta 2 item (17) above, we see clearly that the floating H of L*H is timed later in Göta 1 compared with CSw, but earlier than in Göta 2, where the H looks like it is also the boundary tone. The invited conclusion to draw from this is that these variant realizations represent possible developmental

---

23 Bruce (2003: 246) states that the focus gesture, i.e., the second rise, is not coordinated with the secondary stress in compounds in the Göta varieties. However, Riad & Segerup (2008) found that the L*H was systematically associated in the last (secondary) stress in compounds. It is the trailing H of L*H which is not obviously timed with that syllable.

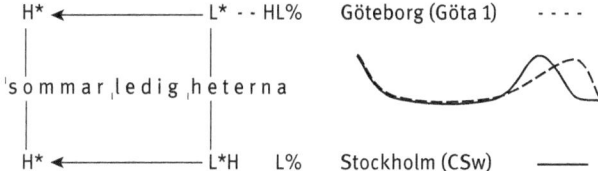

Figure 10.9: Schematic comparison of CSw (Stockholm) and Göta 1 (Göteborg). These dialects have the same tonal composition and association patterns, but differ regarding the transition between the associated and floating tonal segments of the prominence tone.

stages. Moving one dialect to the west of WSw, i.e. into ENw, the typological difference is simply the absence of a secondary association, as described in Section 5.3.

6.2 Boundary L% and displacement: Stockholm and Eskilstuna

We will touch briefly on another difference regarding tonal transition occurring within the CSw area where it borders on the Dala area. The issue here is the fall from the prominence L*H tone to the boundary L%. In the Stockholm area, this fall is relatively smooth and adjusted to the space available. If space is limited, it is not always the case that an L target is reached before the end of the phrase. In the Eskilstuna area, to the west of Stockholm, by contrast, the L target of the boundary tone is reached with much greater regularity. Indeed, the boundary tone is often pulled into the last or even penultimate syllable. This gives rise to a phenomenon called the Eskilstuna curl (Bleckert 1997; Riad 2000a, 2000b, 2009b), which involves a sharp tonal drop followed by creaky voice or a full glottal stop (phonetically much like Danish stød). This prosodic event is accompanied by a characteristic diphthongization. The contrast we shall look at is depicted in Figure 10.10.

An example of a contour from Eskilstuna-east is given in (30), where the tonal contour is HLHL just as in Stockholm, but where the alignment of tonal segments at the end of the contour is partly different. The panels in (30) and (31)

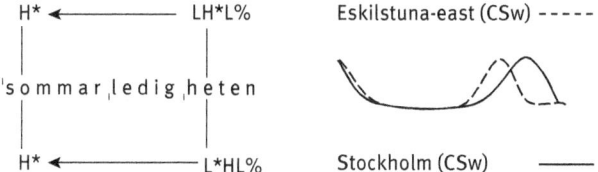

Figure 10.10: Schematic comparison of CSw (Stockholm) and Eskilstuna-east (CSw). These dialects have the same tonal composition, but differ regarding the association of the prominence tone and the realization pattern for the boundary L%.

are taken from Nordberg's recordings in Eskilstuna in the 1960s (Nordberg 1970, 1972, 1985).

(30) CSw, Eskilstuna-east, compound, accent 2, *syateljé* 'sewing studio' (female E147)

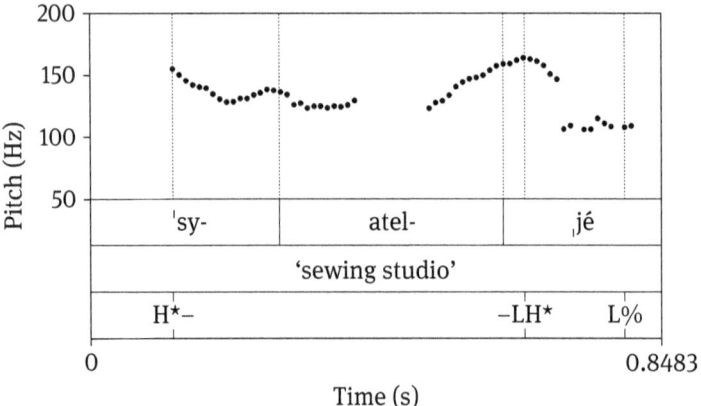

The (post)lexical tone is in the primary stressed syllable, but the following L occurs *before* the last stressed syllable, in contrast with Stockholm where it is normally associated in the stressed syllable. Instead, the H tone of LH is associated in Eskilstuna. The reason for this behaviour is to be found at the very end of the contour, where the L% boundary tone is pulled firmly into the stressed syllable, leaving little room for all of the prominence tone L*H. In this situation, the prominence contour is pushed back, the H segment associating (H*) while the preceding L becomes a leading tone to H*. The sharp fall from H* to L% in the last stressed syllable causes phonetic stød in this case, as can in fact be seen in the contour in (30). Many other recordings exhibit creaky voice in the corresponding place. At the segmental level there is some centralizing diphthongization (Bleckert 1997).

The association of an H* at the last stress of compounds is in fact a step toward the system found in Dala (cf. Section 5.1). And a further step in that direction is found in the northwestern side of the city of Eskilstuna.[24] In this variety, which we will call Eskilstuna-west, compounds no longer exhibit an H* (post)lexical tone on the first stressed syllable. Instead, the (post)lexical tone is now L*. This contrast is schematically illustrated in Figure 10.11, still in comparison with CSw, though a comparison with Dala would be equally warranted.

---

[24] Thanks to Bengt Nordberg who pointed out (p.c.) that there appears to be a dialect boundary cutting through the city of Eskilstuna.

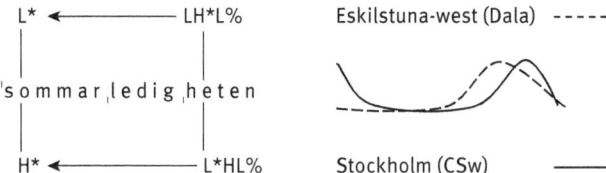

Figure 10.11: Schematic comparison of CSw (Stockholm) and Eskilstuna-west (CSw/Dala). Eskilstuna-west has an L* (post)lexical tone and is hence closer to Dala than to CSw.

The proposed analysis here is that the leading L of LH* spreads backwards to the initial stress, where it gets reinterpreted as the (new) lexical tone. Viewing this as a phonological change, the context for reinterpretation is likely to be simplex forms where the space is limited, especially in accent 1. In accent 1 monosyllables (or final stressed syllables) L*HL% would change into H*L% as an effect of the boundary tone target *within* the syllable. The parallel change in accent 2 simplex would entail a change from H*LHL% to L*HL%. The tonal structures of accents 1 and 2 are never more than one tone off from each other, in any dialect, which means that phonological changes in timing never happen in one condition only.

Here is now an example of a compound from Eskilstuna-west, illustrating the situation depicted in Figure 10.11. Notice that the lexical tone is L* and that there is a rising tone within the final stressed syllable, indicating the spreading behaviour of the leading L tone of the LH* prominence tone.[25]

(31) Dala, Eskilstuna-west, compound, accent 2, *paltbrödskaka* 'palt bread loaf' (female E8)

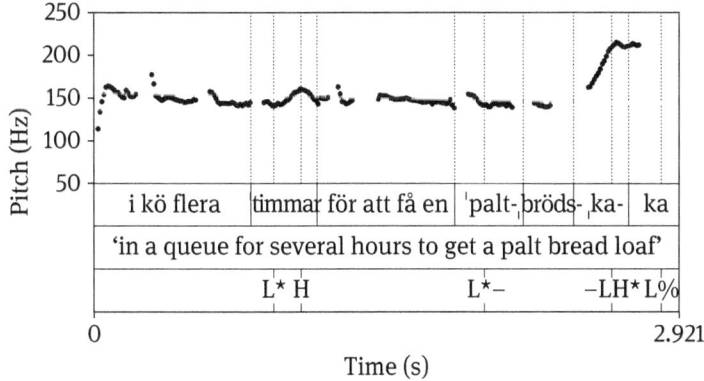

---

[25] It is not entirely clear that the association pattern for the prominence is LH* rather than L*H. Closer investigation is required.

The boundary L% tone is realized in creaky voice following the sharp fall from LH* to L% (therefore not visible in (31)). The next dialect over will be of the Dala type that we saw in (12) and (13), i.e., with an immediate rise after the initial (post) lexical L*. The Dala variety thus shows that the prominence tone is now reduced to just the H*, which spreads backwards until the (post)lexical L*.

Note that the grammar of these systems does not really change: the associations remain the same. It is only the tonal values that change, apparently as a function of a leftward shift of tones, in turn due to the curl behaviour of the boundary L%.

There are other changes related to Eskilstuna-curl in the area, which provide further clues also for the reconstruction of how stød might have become phonologized and the markedness patterns reversed between a tonal system of the Central Swedish and a stød system like that found in Danish Sjælland (Riad 2000a, 2000b, 2009b).

6.3 Observations

The spreading and interpolation behaviours provide evidence of alignment tendencies to the left and to the right (Riad 1998b). Any dialect that has two association points in compounds, and which hence has accent 2 as a rule in compounds and other forms with two stresses, show association to the first and the last stressed morpheme. This should be interpreted as a solution to the double desiderata on the part of tones. Leftward alignment is primary and all dialects have the main stress as an obligatory association point, whereas rightward alignment comes to the surface only when a secondary association point is sought out. Given a secondary association, dialects may then differ in how the transition between the two association points is realized. Backwards spreading is a sign of the grammaticalized "desire" of the prominence tone to be at the left edge, simultaneously with being associated at the right edge. This leads to a tonal floor (Central Swedish, Göta) or a plateau (Dala, Narvik). Interpolation is the case when no backwards spreading takes place, a fact that could be interpreted as the action of a constraint against (the markedness of) spreading (Riad 1998b). In dialects that allow only one association point, it is invariably the first TBU which receives a tonal mark. In this way, we can account for the fact that there is no systematic association to any medial stresses in long compounds.

7 The shape of the big accent

The shape of the big accent has been subjected to typologization in work by Bruce (e.g., 2005), concerning the dialects of Sweden. The general observation is that the big accent is taken to be an enhanced version of the small accent contour in the dialects of Dala and South Swedish, whereas in Central Swedish and the Göta dialects (WSw) the big accent involves a separate tonal gesture, which is added linearly to the small accent contour. A diagram depicting this for accent 2 is given in Figure 10.12, cited from Bruce (2005: 421).

As can be seen, the SSw and Dala varieties have the same shape for both the big and the small accent, where the big accent peaks are simply higher than the small accent peaks in the same position. The CSw and Göta varieties, by contrast, exhibit differences in the overall shape of the contours for small and big accents. This is very clear in CSw where the separate tonal gesture of the big accent is in evidence in both positions, respectively, forming a plateau in 1st focus and a narrower peak in 2nd focus. In Göta the separate peak of 1st focus merges with the following lexical peak, but in 2nd focus there is a clearly separate tonal gesture.

This might look as if there were a simple typological difference between varieties that have a separate tonal gesture and those that do not, in their respective big accents, compared to their small accents. But this contrast can in fact be derived from a single generalization that concerns all dialect types (and both accents). Notice first that the dialects that have a separate tonal gesture in their big accent 2 also have a lexical H* tone, while those that exhibit enhancement only have a lexical L* tone. This property generalizes to other dialects that are not included in the diagram.

The broader generalization that we can formulate based on this observation is that the big accent requires an H tone, and that a (post)lexical H* cannot serve this

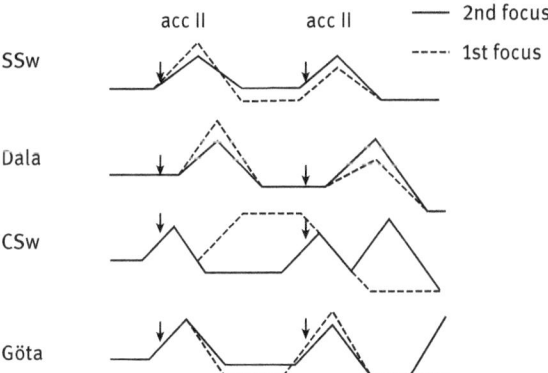

Figure 10.12: Accent realization for four prosodic dialect types. The pitch contours schematically represent a phrase consisting of two simplex accent 2 words, with narrow focus on either the first (1st focus, big accent) or second (2nd focus, big accent) word. Arrows indicate the CV-boundary of stressed syllables. An example of a possible text here is *långa NUNNOR*, vs. *LÅNGA nunnor* 'tall nuns'.

task. Just in case a dialect has the tone value H for the (post)lexical tone, another H must be available to get a proper prominence tone in place. This is done either by adding a secondary peak as part of the prominence tone (L*H, CSw, Göta 1), or by recruiting an H% boundary tone for the purposes of prominence (ENw, Göta 2). If the (post)lexical tone is L*, all is good, as the prominence tone will then predictably be H (by OCP). It would thus appear to be a general property of all North Germanic dialects that an H tone must be available somewhere after the (post) lexical tone for the instantiation of a big accent. This is hardly a surprising fact, as peaks typically are associated with prominence, but it also allows us to derive the typological difference in phonological shape of the big accent from one single source. To see this consider Figure 10.13, where the dialects that we have looked at are depicted. Some varieties which we have not looked at specifically but which share properties with other dialects have been listed together in types.

The five types in the upper half of Figure 10.13 have a (post)lexical H* tone and the three types in the lower half have a (post)lexical L*. In all varieties, the remaining tones of the big accent include an H tone. A good way of illustrating the generality of this H tone is to look at accent 1. Bruce (2005) does not discuss the presence of a separate focus gesture in accent 1, but there is an indirect reference

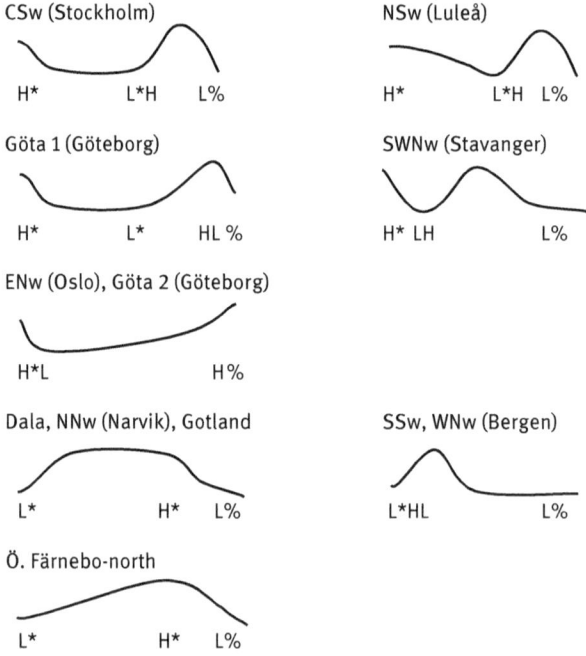

Figure 10.13: Big accent 2 in long compounds in schematic representation.

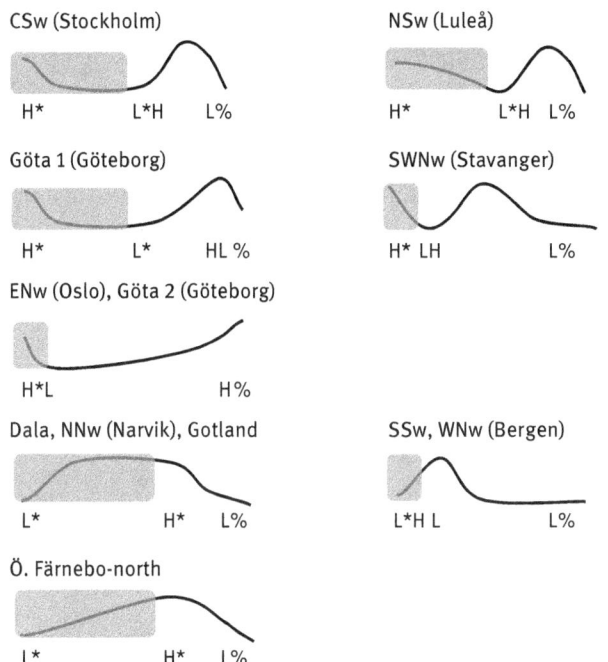

Figure 10.14: Removing the (post)lexical tone, leaving the contour of big accent 1. All instances of accent 1 contain an H tone.

to it in Bruce (2003). Clearly though, the null hypothesis must be that the focus gesture generalizes across big accent in both accent 1 and accent 2. In Figure 10.14 the (post)lexical part of the big accent 2 contour has been shaded over, leaving the big accent 1 contour unshaded. As can be readily seen, each dialect has a remaining H tone that can be engaged for prominence purposes.

The inclusion of accent 1 in the comparison explains why the (post)lexical H*, part only of accent 2, is not available for the expression of prominence. The requirement of an H tone for prominence purposes is a condition on intonation generally. If all dialects have the same type of privative accent distinction, as per our analysis above, then it follows that (post)lexical H* should not be available for intonational prominence purposes.[26]

---

[26] One could have imagined that the (post)lexical H* would have been employed for prominence purposes in some dialect, in parallel with what we see for the boundary H% in East Norwegian. However, that would have predicted the possibility of a contrast between accent 2 as H*L and accent 1 as L*H, but this has not been reported for any dialect. This adds weight to the generality of the privative nature of the accent distinction.

East Norwegian and Göta 2 employ the boundary H% tone as part of their big accent. This fact also supports the superordinate status of the H tone required for prominence purposes within the big accent. The notion of a "separate tonal gesture" should thus not be interpreted as the necessary ADDITION of a gesture. What is already there can also be employed for this purpose.

The asymmetry between dialects concerning the presence or absence of a separate tonal gesture is visible also in another fact. The tonal contours for the big accent 2 that we have seen contain either three or four tones. Given the variable tonal values, this would predict four possible contours under OCP.

(32) Four possible contours for big accent 2
       H LH L   ~~L HL H~~
       H L H   L H L   (or L HL L^{27})

However, we only find four alternating tones if the first tone, the (post)lexical tone, is H. The absence of LHLH now follows from the generalization that an H tone must be regularly available for prominence purposes in the big accent. In fact it narrows this generalization to "exactly one H tone".

Our conclusion is that "separate tonal gesture" vs. "enhancement" are surface observations that depend on other things, rather than proper typological features. A prediction for diachrony would be that we should not expect to see tonal behaviours that appear to preserve the separate tonal gesture as such (e.g., in the transition from CSw to Dala, via Eskilstuna). But we should expect to see preservation of an H tone in the big accent contour. As shown by Myrberg (2013, 2016), enhancement is related to function and information structural status in Central Swedish. This is likely to generalize to many, perhaps all, dialects, and would thereby not be a structural typological property either.

8 North Germanic and Central Franconian: Comparative notes

The typology of the North Germanic tonal accents is strikingly strict, employing just a few variables, which can be identified and demarcated by studying structural properties within a dialect, and by looking at comparable structures across dialects. The strictness found could possibly be due to some element of simplicity

---

[27] As mentioned, it is not clear whether there is a strict separation between the two consecutive L's in South Swedish.

in the model of analysis, or to our current lack of detailed knowledge of intonation in several of the dialects. At the same time, however, there is a robustness both to intuitions regarding which dialects are similar and which are different, and to the tonal behaviours that we have looked at, which are all readily manifest on the surface, such as tonal values and the presence of a secondary association. At this junction, then, it seems fair to assume that there are fundamental, shared properties that make the tonal typology relatively coherent.

Another Germanic tonal system which is by now rather well-studied is Central Franconian (Schmidt 1986; de Vaan 1999; Gussenhoven & van der Vliet 1999; Gussenhoven 2000, 2007, 2012; Peters 2006, 2007; Köhnlein 2011, 2016). The Central Franconian accentual contrast is often mentioned as typologically similar to the North Germanic one. Here, we shall make some comparative notes that profile some differences between them.

One fundamental property of the NGmc accents is the dependence on morphology, which keeps the lexical distribution rather constant between dialects. The stable classes of words that occur with accent 2 in all dialects contain posttonic suffixes ($^{2|}läk$-are 'doctor', $^{2|}fäng$-$else$ 'prison', etc.). Such words also have higher token frequencies, compared with monomorphemes with accent 2, which tend to vary in accent between dialects, e.g., $^{1/2|}senap$ 'mustard', $^{1/2|}Anders$ (name) (Bruce 1998: 50). Our analysis of this situation is that it is the posttonic suffixes that carry the tonal information (hence -are_2, -$else_2$, etc.), which is assigned and realized in the preceding stressed syllable (Riad 2014). This connects the patterning of accent 2 to morphology and also accounts for the often observed fact that accent 2 only occurs in polysyllabic words.[28] It also harmonizes with the greater tonal richness of accent 2 compared with accent 1, see (5).

In Central Franconian, by contrast, the lexical tone contrast is fully contained within the stressed syllable, such that the contrast can be expressed in a pair of monosyllabic morphemes, e.g., ^{1}man 'basket' vs. ^{2}man 'man' (dialect of Mayen; Schmidt 1986). The situation with accent being assigned from a suffix to the root therefore does not occur in Franconian. Still, morphological factors do influence the contours. The marked accent tends to occur in morphologically more complex forms than the unmarked accent, often as the diachronic result of apocope, e.g., unmarked $^{2}stain$ 'stone, SG' vs. marked $^{1}stain$ 'stone, PL' (dialect of Arzbach; Köhnlein 2011).

Importantly, the lexical distribution of the tonal contrast in Franconian varies between dialects based on segmental factors, concerning both vowel type in the stressed syllable and local environment (e.g., de Vaan 1999: 26ff.;

---

[28] If the argumentation starts from the number of syllables as basic to accent 2, the morphological patterning is left unexplained.

Köhnlein 2011: 219ff.). This segmental dependence represents a major constitutional difference between NGmc tone (discounting Danish stød), where there is no segmental dependence whatsoever, and Central Franconian. This difference is clearly of importance for the understanding of typology as well as tonogenesis.

A second fundamental property relates to the TBU. In NGmc, the TBU is the stressed syllable, a typical situation in languages with accents of the North Germanic kind (Gussenhoven 2007), that is, languages where a tonal contrast is only ever found in stressed syllables. Also, the normal situation (in any tonal system) is that only one tone is associated to the TBU, a fact that is strictly obeyed in most tonal dialects of NGmc. This puts a limit on the possible tonal variation within stressed syllables. If one assumes a less typical TBU, such as the syllable (stressed or unstressed) or the mora, then that will admit a more fine-grained typology, but it is unlikely to refute the generalizations found for NGmc. Rather, such an assumption is likely to overgenerate and predict the existence of dialects that may never be found. We have thus taken a conservative view from which it may be possible to diversify (given clear evidence), rather than starting from an overly rich structure, from which it may be hard to retreat.

In Central Franconian, the TBU is either the mora in stressed syllables, as roughly in the tonal dialects in the Netherlands, or the stressed syllable, as roughly in the tonal dialects in Belgium (Gussenhoven 2007; Peters 2007). This distinction of TBU defines a rather clear isogloss. With a TBU the size of a mora, an association system is going to have more phonological options within the stressed syllable, in principle, for tones stemming from the lexical contrast or from intonation (e.g., as in the dialect of Helden; Gussenhoven & van den Beuken 2012).

A third property, related to the above, is the absence of a sonority restriction on syllables that carry tone in the NGmc system. Accent 2 can be assigned in a word like $^{2\prime}pappa$ 'dad' just as well as in $^{2\prime}mamma$ 'mom', and accent 1 works as well in $^{1\prime}taxi$ as in $^{1\prime}mammon$. In NGmc, the absence of a sonority restriction seems to be part and parcel of the space requirement for accent 2, which in turn seems to be one reason why the dialect variation is so regimented.

The Central Franconian dialects that have the stressed syllable as TBU are similar to NGmc regarding the lack of a sonority restriction. However, unlike NGmc, these dialects admit a contrast within a single syllable, regardless of the sonority of the segments in that syllable. An example of this is the dialect of Hasselt (Peters 2006). In such dialects, the tonal contrast can thus be realized in more types of words than in dialects with a sonority restriction in the stressed syllable. In the latter type of dialect a consonant must be sonorant in order for a tonal contrast to be realized. The mora-based varieties of Central Franconian are of this type (e.g., the dialect of Venlo; Gussenhoven & van der Vliet 1999), and so is Lithuanian, and also the Danish stød system, which has developed from an earlier tonal system. Such systems are analysed as having the (sonorant) mora as TBU, though the requirement of a stressed syllable remains.

Furthermore, in systems of the Lithuanian and Central Franconian type there is a stronger inclination for there to be durational and/or segmental effects that covary with tonal constellations. A tonal contrast may be (partly) dependent on a segmental property (Franconian) and vice versa (Lithuanian). In some such dialects, the primacy of tone over and above vowel quality/quantity is harder to ascertain and is sometimes questioned. In at least some varieties of East Aukštaitian Lithuanian, the tonal distinction has been replaced by one relating to vowel duration and quality (Hualde & Riad 2014).[29]

A fourth fundamental property that likely has a constraining effect on the variation within the NGmc tone system is the stability of realization of tones across syntactic and pragmatic contexts. This is to say that an instance of, say, big accent 2 will have basically the same shape in declaratives, interrogatives, imperatives, etc. For example, there is no dedicated interrogative tonal contour in Swedish, although an optional rise may occur (House 2002, 2004). Although this is an understudied area for many NGmc dialects, the typical situation is that accents are recognized as similar in various intonational contexts.

This is not the situation in Central Franconian where the realization of tonal contours often varies a lot between different intonational contexts, within the same dialect (Gussenhoven 2000, 2012; Köhnlein 2011). To some extent, this may be due to the intonational tones themselves being more varied in Franconian compared with NGmc. But the interaction of tone with intonation in Franconian must also be handled in a more flexible tonal grammar, given that even the ordering between a lexical tone and an intonational tone can vary between contexts (dialect of Roermond; Gussenhoven 2000). Such phenomena have not been reported for Swedish and Norwegian.

9 Conclusion

The presentation of data and the discussion in this chapter has aimed at laying bare a number of properties that are important in any account of the typology of North Germanic accent. The contention is that the relevant level is phonological,

---

[29] There is clearly a connection between the mora-based tonal assignment, the sonority restriction and the segmental dependence, though the exact typological implications, also with respect to tonal systems of the South East Asian types, remain to be worked out.

pertaining to representation and grammatical behaviour of phonological units, in this case tones. The basic shapes of big accents within the typology are definable in just these terms: value of (post)lexical tone, secondary association (or not), and tonal spreading (or not). Functional properties like information structural concerns will influence the realization of the big accent (e.g., scaling, local alignment), but not define it. Phonetic variation will be important for identifying minor variation within a type (e.g., timing of floating H, sharpness of falls), and this will play a role in accounting for dialect transitions, i.e., diachronic change. But we cannot rely on phonetic variation for the systematic typology, as it does not properly constrain it.

Acknowledgements: Feedback from Sara Myrberg and Jan Hognestad during the preparation of this paper is gratefully acknowledged.

Sources of the data here analysed are identified by these abbreviations: BG = Bert Göteborg; JA = Jon Almaas; JH = Jonas Hallberg; LG = Lotta Gröning; LGA = Lars-Gunnar Andersson; NG = Niklas Göteborg; NN = unknown speaker; SG = Sverker Göransson; OLVI and FAØV = Stavanger informants from Hognestad (2012); nrk = Norsk Rundkringkasting (Norwegian Radio and TV); om = older male (SweDia); sr = Sveriges Radio (Swedish Radio and TV).

References

Arvaniti, Amalia. 2002. The intonation of yes-no questions in Greek. In M. Makri-Tsilipakou (ed.), *Selected papers on theoretical and applied linguistics*, 71–83. Thessaloniki, Department of Theoretical and Applied Linguistics, School of English, Aristotle University.
Basbøll, Hans. 2005. *The phonology of Danish*. Oxford: Oxford University Press.
Bleckert, Lars. 1987. *Centralsvensk diftongering som satsfonetiskt problem* (Skrifter utgivna av institutionen för nordiska språk vid Uppsala universitet 21). Uppsala.
Bruce, Gösta. 1977. *Swedish word accents in sentence perspective* (Travaux de l'institut de linguistique de Lund 12). Lund: CWK Gleerup.
Bruce, Gösta. 1982. Reglerna för slutledsbetoning i sammansatta ord i nordsvenskan. In Claes-Christian Elert & Sigurd Fries (eds.), *Nordsvenska*, 123–148. Umeå University.
Bruce, Gösta. 1987. How floating is focal accent? In Kirsten Gregersen & Hans Basbøll (eds.), *Nordic prosody* 4, 41–49. Odense: Odense University Press.
Bruce, Gösta. 1998. *Allmän och svensk prosodi* (Praktisk Lingvistik 16). Lund University.
Bruce, Gösta. 2003. Late pitch peaks in West Swedish. *Proceedings of ICPhS* 15, Barcelona, 245–248.
Bruce, Gösta. 2004. An intonational typology of Swedish. *Speech Prosody 2004*, Nara, Japan, 175–178.

Bruce, Gösta. 2005. Intonational prominence in Swedish revisited. In Sun-Ah Jun (ed.), *Prosodic typology: The phonology of intonation and phrasing*, 410–429. Oxford: Oxford University Press.

Bruce, Gösta. 2007. Components of a prosodic typology of Swedish intonation. In Riad & Gussenhoven (eds.) 2007, 113–146.

Bruce, Gösta. 2010. *Vår fonetiska geografi: Om svenskans accenter, melodi och uttal*. Lund: Studentlitteratur.

Bruce, Gösta & Eva Gårding. 1978. A prosodic typology for Swedish dialects. In Gårding et al. (eds.), 219–228.

Bruce, Gösta, Olle Engstrand, & Anders Eriksson. 1998. De svenska dialekternas fonetik och fonologi år 2000 (SweDia 2000) – en projektbeskrivning. *Folkmålsstudier* 39. 33–54.

Bye, Patrik. 2004. Evolutionary typology and Scandinavian pitch accent. Manuscript, University of Tromsø.

Dalton, Martha & Ailbhe Ní Chasaide. 2007. Melodic alignment and micro-dialect variation in Connemara Irish. In Riad & Gussenhoven (eds.), 293–316.

Danell, Gideon. 1937. *Svensk ljudlära*. 4th edition. Stockholm: Svenska bokförlaget, Norstedt & söner.

Elert, Claes-Christian. 1972. Tonality in Swedish: Rules and a list of minimal pairs. In Evelyn S. Firchow, Kaaren Grimstad, Nils Hasselmo, & Wayne O'Neil (eds.), *Studies for Einar Haugen*, 151–173. The Hague & Paris: Mouton.

Engstrand, Olle. 1995. Phonetic interpretation of the word accent contrast in Swedish. *Phonetica* 52. 171–179.

Engstrand, Olle. 1997. Phonetic interpretation of the word accent contrast in Swedish: Evidence from spontaneous speech. *Phonetica* 54. 61–75.

Fant, Gunnar & Anita Kruckenberg. 2008. Multi-level analysis and synthesis of prosody with applications to Swedish. Manuscript, Kungliga Tekniska Högskolan.

Fintoft, Knut. 1970. *Acoustical analysis and perception of tonemes in some Norwegian dialects*. Oslo: Universitetsforlaget.

Fintoft, Knut., P. E. Mjaavatn, E. Møllergård, & B. Ulseth. 1978. Toneme patterns in Norwegian dialects. In Gårding et al. (eds.), 197–206.

Fretheim, Thorstein & Randi Alice Nilsen. 1989. Terminal rise and rise-fall tunes in East Norwegian intonation. *Nordic Journal of Linguistics* 12. 155–182.

Gårding, Eva. 1977. *The Scandinavian word accents* (Travaux de l'institut de linguistique de Lund 11). Lund: CWK Gleerup.

Gårding, Eva & Per Lindblad. 1973. Constancy and variation in Swedish word accent patterns. *Working Papers* 7. 36–110. Dept. of Linguistics, Lund University.

Gårding, Eva, Gösta Bruce, & Robert Bannert (eds.). 1978. *Nordic prosody: Papers from a symposium* (Travaux de l'institut de linguistique de Lund 13). Lund University.

Grice, Martine, D. Robert Ladd, & Amalia Arvaniti. 2000. On the place of phrase accents in intonational phonology. *Phonology* 17. 143–185.

Gussenhoven, Carlos. 2000. The lexical tone contrast of Roermond Dutch in Optimality Theory. In Merle Horne (ed.), *Prosody: Theory and experiment*, 129–167. Dordrecht: Kluwer.

Gussenhoven, Carlos. 2007. Intonation. In Paul de Lacy (ed.), *The Cambridge handbook of phonology*, 253–280. Cambridge: Cambridge University Press.

Gussenhoven, Carlos. 2012. Asymmetries in the intonation system of Maastricht Limburgish. *Phonology* 29. 39–79.

Gussenhoven, Carlos & Peter van der Vliet. 1999. The phonology of tone and intonation in the Dutch dialect of Venlo. *Journal of Linguistics* 35. 99–135.

Gussenhoven, Carlos & Frank van den Beuken. 2012. Contrasting the high rise and the low rise intonations in a dialect with the Central Franconian tone. *The Linguistic Review* 29. 75–107.

Hognestad, Jan K. 2012. *Tonelagsvariasjon i norsk: Synkrone og diakrone aspekter, med særlig fokus på vestnorsk*. PhD dissertation, University of Agder.

House, David. 2002. Intonational and visual cues in the perception of interrogative mode in Swedish. *Proceedings of ICSLP 2002*, 1957–1960. Denver, Colorado.

House, David. 2004. Final rises and Swedish question intonation. *Proceedings of Fonetik 2004*, 56–59. Stockholm University.

Hualde, José Ignacio & Tomas Riad. 2014. Word accent and intonation in Baltic. In N. Campbell, D. Gibbon, & D. Hirst (eds.), *Speech Prosody 7*, 669–671. Dublin.

Kallstenius, Gottfrid. 1902. *Värmländska Bärgslagsmålets ljudlära*. Stockholm: Norstedt & Söner.

Kock, Axel. 1878. *Språkhistoriska undersökningar om svensk akcent*. Lund: Gleerup.

Köhnlein, Björn. 2011. *Rule reversal revisited: Synchrony and diachrony of tone and prosodic structure in the Franconian dialect of Arzbach*. PhD dissertation, University of Leiden.

Köhnlein, Björn. 2016. Contrastive foot structure in Franconian tone-accent dialects. *Phonology* 33. 87–123.

Kristoffersen, Gjert. 2000. *The phonology of Norwegian*. Oxford: Oxford University Press.

Kristoffersen, Gjert. 2007. Dialect variation in East Norwegian tone. In Riad & Gussenhoven (eds.), 91–111.

Lahiri, Aditi, Allison Wetterlin, & Elisabet Jönsson-Steiner. 2005. Lexical specification of tone in North Germanic. *Nordic Journal of Linguistics* 28. 61–96.

Leira, Vigleik. 1998. Tonempar i bokmål. *Norskrift* 95. 49–86.

Lorentz, Ove. 1995. Tonal prominence and alignment. *Phonology at Santa Cruz* 4. 39–56.

Lorentz, Ove. 2008. Tonelagsbasis i norsk. *Maal og Minne* 1. 50–68.

Malmberg, Bertil. 1970. *Lärobok i fonetik*. Lund: Gleerup.

Meyer, Ernst A. 1937. *Die Intonation im Schwedischen I: Die Sveamundarten*. Helsingfors: Fritzes bokförlags AB. Mercators tryckeri.

Meyer, Ernst A. 1954. *Die Intonation im Schwedischen II: Die norrländischen Mundarten* (Stockholm Studies in Scandinavian Philology 11). Uppsala: Almqvist & Wiksell.

Mjaavatn, Per Egil. 1978. Isoglosses of toneme categories compared with isoglosses of traditional dialect geography. In Gårding et al. (eds.), 207–216.

Myrberg, Sara. 2010. *The intonational phonology of Stockholm Swedish* (Stockholm Studies in Scandinavian Philology 53). Stockholm University.

Myrberg, Sara. 2013. Focus type effects on focal accents and boundary tones. *Proceedings of Fonetik 2013*, 53–56. Linköping University.

Myrberg, Sara. 2016. Second occurrence focus in Stockholm Swedish. Manuscript, Stockholm University.

Myrberg, Sara & Tomas Riad. 2015. The prosodic hierarchy of Swedish. *Nordic Journal of Linguistics* 38. 115–147.

Myrberg, Sara & Tomas Riad. 2016. On the expression of focus in the metrical grid and in the prosodic hierarchy. In Caroline Féry & Shinichiro Ishihara (eds.), *Oxford handbook of information structure*, 441–462. Oxford: Oxford University Press.

Naydenov, Vladimir. 2011. *Issues in the phonology of the tonal accents in Swedish and their Norwegian and Danish counterparts*. PhD dissertation, University of Sofia.

Nordberg, Bengt. 1970. *Språket som socialt kännetecken: Rapport om ett språksociologiskt försök*. Uppsala, FUMS report 7.
Nordberg, Bengt. 1972. *Morfologiska variationsmönster i ett centralsvenskt stadsspråk*. Uppsala, FUMS report 23.
Nordberg, Bengt. 1985. *Det mångskiftande språket: Om variation i nusvenskan*. Malmö: Liber Förlag.
Nyström, Staffan. 1997. Grav accent i östra Svealands folkmål. In Maj Reinhammar (ed.), *Nordiska dialektstudier:* Föredrag *vid femte nordiska dialektkonferensen*, 215–222 (Skrifter utgivna av Språk- och folkminnesinstitutet genom dialektenheten i Uppsala. Ser. A:27). Uppsala: Språk- och folkminnesinstitutet.
Öhman, Sven. 1966. Generativa regler för det svenska verbets fonologi och prosodi. In Sture Allén (ed.), *Svenskans beskrivning* 3, Göteborg.
Öhman, Sven. 1967. Word and sentence intonation: A quantitative model. *Speech Transmission Laboratory Quarterly Progress and Status Report* (STL-QPSR) 2–3. 20–54. Dept. of Speech Transmission, Royal Institute of Technology, Stockholm.
Peters, Jörg. 2006. The dialect of Hasselt. *Journal of the International Phonetic Association* 36. 117–124.
Peters, Jörg. 2007. A bitonal lexical pitch accent in the Limburgian dialect of Borgloon. In Riad & Gussenhoven (eds.), 167–198.
Riad, Tomas. 1998a. The origin of Scandinavian tone accents. *Diachronica* 15. 63–98.
Riad, Tomas. 1998b. Towards a Scandinavian accent typology. In Wolfgang Kehrein & Richard Wiese (eds.), *Phonology and morphology of the Germanic languages*, 77–109. Tübingen: Niemeyer.
Riad, Tomas. 2000a. The origin of Danish stød. In Aditi Lahiri (ed.), *Analogy, levelling and markedness: Principles of change in phonology and morphology*, 261–300. Berlin: Mouton de Gruyter.
Riad, Tomas. 2000b. Stöten som aldrig blev av – generaliserad accent 2 i Östra Mälardalen. *Folkmålsstudier* 39. 319–344. Helsingfors.
Riad, Tomas. 2006. Scandinavian accent typology, *Sprachtypologie und Universalienforschung* 59. 36–55.
Riad, Tomas. 2009a. The morphological status of accent 2 in North Germanic simplex forms. In Martti Vainio, Reijo Aulanko, & Olli Aaltonen (eds.), *Nordic prosody: Proceedings of the 10th Conference, Helsinki 2008*, 205–216. Frankfurt am Main: Peter Lang.
Riad, Tomas. 2009b. Eskilstuna as the tonal key to Danish. *Proceedings Fonetik 2009*, 12–17. Stockholm University.
Riad, Tomas. 2012. Culminativity, stress and tone accent in Central Swedish. *Lingua* 122. 1352–1379.
Riad, Tomas. 2014. *The phonology of Swedish*. Oxford: Oxford University Press.
Riad, Tomas. 2015. *Prosodin i svenskans morfologi*. Stockholm: Morfem förlag.
Riad, Tomas & Carlos Gussenhoven (eds.). 2007. *Tones and tunes I: Studies in word and sentence prosody*. Berlin: Mouton de Gruyter.
Riad, Tomas & My Segerup. 2008. Phonological association of tone: Phonetic implications in West Swedish and East Norwegian. *Proceedings Fonetik 2008*, 93–96. Göteborg.
Ringgaard, Kristian. 1983. Review of Liberman (1982). *Phonetica* 40. 342–344.
Schmidt, Jürgen Erich. 1986. *Die mittelfränkischen Tonakzente (Rheinische Akzentuierung)*. (Mainzer Studien zur Sprach- und Volksforschung 8). Stuttgart: Steiner.

Segerup, My. 2004. Gothenburg Swedish word accents: A fine distinction. *Proceedings Fonetik 2004*, 28–31. Stockholm University.

Strandberg, Mathias. 2014. *De sammansatta ordens accentuering i Skånemålen*. PhD dissertation, Uppsala University.

Teleman, Ulf. 1969. Böjningssuffixens form i svenskan. *Arkiv för nordisk filologi* 84. 163–208.

de Vaan, Michiel. 1999. Towards an explanation of the Franconian tone accents. *Amsterdamer Beiträge zur älteren Germanistik* 51. 3–44.

Wetterlin, Allison. 2010. *Tonal accents in Norwegian: Phonology, morphology and lexical specification*. Berlin: Mouton de Gruyter.

Carlos Gussenhoven
Prosodic typology meets phonological representations

Abstract: Universally, phonological grammars have three structural features. First, there are segments (vowels, consonants, tones); second, there are constituents that contain them (the prosodic hierarchy); and third, there are two ways in which segments are anchored in constituents (phonological alignment and association). The specific segments and constituents a language has are not necessarily shared with other languages. There are three points that arise from this conceptualization. First, while word stress is a constituent (a foot), sentential prominence is derivative and not to be represented in terms of additional mechanisms like metrical grids or trees. Second, association appears to have been overused at the expense of the simpler concept of phonological alignment, to the detriment of descriptions of intonation. Third, the much-discussed word prosodic concepts of tone, stress, and accent turn out to belong to each of the three very different structural features of phonological grammars: tone is a segment, stress a prosodic constituent, and accent an instruction for association. As such, they will not easily fit into a single typological taxonomy.

1 Introduction

Like Christmas presents, phonological grammars are best typologized under three structural headings. First, there is the contents, the actual present, or equivalently, the phonological features and segments that make up the segmental strings. Next, there are the containers, the box, the wrapping paper, and the ribbon, equivalent to a suite of constituents in the prosodic hierarchy (Selkirk 1981; Nespor & Vogel 1986; Selkirk & Lee 2015). Finally, there are ways of anchoring the present inside the box, airbags or polystyrene beads perhaps, equivalent to phonological alignment and segmental association (Goldsmith 1976; McCarthy & Prince 1993). The purpose of this article is, first, to point out that tone, stress, and accent are not easily typologized within a single taxonomy, since they are instantiations of each of these three very disparate aspects of grammars, respectively. The second goal is to draw attention to two aspects in prosodic descriptions that do not fit this model. One is the burgeoning of representations of prominence above the word level. The second is the imbalance in the employment of phonological alignment and phonological association, where phonological alignment has been underused and phonological association overused, to the detriment of our understanding of phonological representations of intonation.

2 Segments

In this section, I defend two positions. First, all languages have phonological segments (Section 2.1), and second, there is no systematic phonetic representation in the sense of Chomsky & Halle (1968) (Section 2.2). A claim that there are no phonological segments is refuted in Section 2.3. In Section 2.4, I point out that the "suprasegmental" view of phonological structure has blurred the segmental status of tones, with a detrimental effect on typological discussions of word prosody.

2.1 Vowels, consonants, and tones

Vowels, consonants, and tones are the three featurally specified phonological constituents providing phonological content. Linearly arranged segments and specific features in them may form parallel autosegmental tiers (Goldsmith 1976; Pierrehumbert 1980; McCarthy 1985). All languages have segments, but a language's specific segments ultimately result from varyingly probable responses to ergonomic conditions in speech production and perception (Flemming 1995; Boersma 1996; Clements & Ridouane 2011). That is, if [a] occurs in all languages, it is because conditions on its inclusion are highly favorable, but a language without low vowels may well be encountered any time from now. Tones are often excluded from the meaning of the term "segmental", which in its narrower sense only refers to vowels and consonants. Hyman (2011) brings out the segmental status of tones particularly clearly, showing that they are segments *par excellence* in displaying more versatile behavior than vowels and consonants. In addition to representing morphemes by themselves, being autosegmental, causing and undergoing assimilation, only tones are routinely associated with numerous adjacent association units, interact with other tones over large distances, are displaced over large distances, and are frequently retained in the representation without association (floating tones).

2.2 Segments and phonetic implementation

The phonology-phonetics interface which is assumed here is that of Pierrehumbert (1980), in which the surface configuration of discrete phonological constituents is translated into an analogue representation, exemplified in her dissertation by a target-interpolation model for the translation of tones into English f0 contours. Regardless of the particular conception of phonetic implementation (target interpolation, as in Pierrehumbert 1980, a gestural score, as in Browman & Goldstein 1986, exemplars, as in Pierrehumbert 2002), this process is unlikely to leave behind a one-to-one correspondence between phonological segments and chunks in the signal. For instance, a nasalized vocoid represents no segment if it is a context-dependent nasalization of a long oral vowel, as in English [kʰɑ̃ːm̃] /kɑːm/ 'calm'. It corresponds to one segment if it results from a contrastively nasalized vowel, as in French /kã/, occurring twice in *cancan*, while it results from two segments in Frisian [ĩfɔlə] 'to substitute for', where /in/ is realized as [ĩ] before fricatives (compare [indɑmə] 'to contain').

Arguing against the existence of a systematic phonetic representation, Pierrehumbert (1990) brings up the case of the "segment" between /p/ and /l/ in *police* in a token of the word in which a brief interval occurs between the release of [p] and the contact for [l]. On the basis of the phonetics, no principled choice is possible between schwa or the release of the plosive. (See also Ladd 2014: Ch. 2, who extensively discusses the illusory nature of a systematic phonetic representation.) As a result, speech signals can be transcribed in many ways without any one of them having a superior claim to correctness, as in the case of [bʱa], [bʱa̠], [ba̤], [ba̱] [bà], etc. for an utterance [ba] pronounced with breathy voice. This situation differs sharply from phonological transcriptions, only one of which is correct for any given pronunciation of a linguistic expression and for which, moreover, no signal is required for a transcriber who knows the language, as evidenced by pronunciation dictionaries (Gussenhoven 2007; see also Abercrombie's 1964: 17; 1967: 128 discussion of "impressionistic" and "systematic" transcriptions).

2.3 Refuting a claim of segmentless phonology

One view that rejects segments altogether is represented by Port & Leary (2005), who claim that the assumption of a segmental structure has been 'a fundamental mistake of the generative paradigm'. Their point is that 'phonetic segments are not formal symbol tokens', whereby we should bear in mind that their objection is directed at the (presumed) existence of phonological segments, since there is agreement on the non-existence of phonetic segments (Section 2.2). It is important to see that the non-existence of phonetic segments provides no basis for deciding the status of phonological segments. As Ladd (2014: 22) points out, cursive writing shows many contextual effects on the shapes of letters and does not present obvious segmentation points between letters, much in the way that a phonetic signals blurs the segments that they express, but that does not invalidate the reality of the set of discrete letters that are realized (cf. Hyman 2015b). Port & Leary present three main arguments. First, there is no evidence of a segment-based processing of speech. Second, speakers are unable to list the phonemes of their language with the same ease as they can list the letters used to represent the language. Third, people are inconsistent in writing transcriptions. A response to the first argument must ignore the overwhelming evidence of segment manipulations in deletion, insertion, spreading processes in phonological grammars, since these might not fall under empirical evidence for Port & Leary (2005) and probably fall outside their definition of processing. However, it can be weakened by evidence from segment-based language change. The Dutch diphthongs /εi œy ʌu/, as in *bijt* 'bite 1SG', *buit* 'loot', *bout* 'bolt', have recently lowered to [æi œy au] in Netherlandic Dutch (Jacobi 2009: 66; van der Harst 2011: 298). However, this lowering does not apply to monophthongal /ε ʏ ɔ/ in *bed* 'bed', *put* 'water well', and *bot* 'bone', whose phonetic qualities before the change were close to those of the starting points of the diphthongs, particularly in the case of /ε/, which has undergone raising in recent years. This can be explained if the diphthongs are phonological segments that are distinct from segments that are phonetically similar to their beginning and end points. The argument can be widened to phonological change over longer time spans, including the Neogrammarian reconstruction work on Indo-European. McQueen et al. (2006) provide experimental evidence that makes the same point. They showed that listeners' adaptation to a spectral change in either [s] or [f] affects the perceptual boundary between these segments throughout the lexicon, not just in the test items, which finding can only be explained if words are made up of segments. In addition, speech error research strongly suggests that representations are segmental as well as syllabic (Fromkin 1973; Nooteboom & Quené 2017).

The second argument touches on the tacit nature of human cognitive functioning and the limited domains in it that become available for awareness. Language is notoriously tacit, but some differentiation does exist, in part depending on the structure of the language. For many languages, syllables are relatively close to awareness, but segments, intonation, and tone much less so. The fact that people find it easy to count visible objects, like letters, punctuation marks, and Arabic digits, would appear to be unrelated to the relative difficulty of achieving full awareness of the segmental structure of one's native language.

Third, the fact that people are bad at transcribing words segmentally and show interference from the morphology and the orthography (Strange 1995) testifies – again – to an incomplete process of segmental awareness as well as interference of other aspects of the linguistic structure and of the orthography. Total segmental awareness may perhaps not have been achieved whenever the analysis of languages has remained controversial, as in the case of the German affricate /ts/, which is more generally assumed to be a segment in initial and final position (e.g., *Zeit* 'time', *Herz* 'heart') than when it straddles a syllable boundary, as in *Katze* 'cat'. Sequences like /ps/ have also been argued to be single segments (Wiese 1996: 13, 265). Still, many people do acquire the ability to produce pronunciation dictionaries, and with it, the ability to count the segments of their language. Uncertainties may remain for less accessible aspects, like complexity of segments, syllabic affiliation, and over decisions about whether or not to include predictable assimilations. However, these aspects do not undermine the otherwise strong evidence that segmental representations are relatively easily introduced into a speaker's awareness.

2.4 The distorting lens of the suprasegmental view

The traditional classification into three types of segments (vowels, consonants, and tones) competes with an alternative conceptualization of phonological structure, one based on the even older division into segmental and suprasegmental phenomena, whereby tones are divorced from a more narrowly defined "segmental" class of vowels and consonants (e.g., Lehiste 1970). While endorsing the idea that suprasegmental features may encompass whole strings of spectrally defined units (vowels and consonants), Lehiste motivated the suprasegmental status of f0, intensity, and duration by observing that only spectrally defined units can have values for each of those three parameters, unlike any of those three themselves. That is, intensity cannot be said to have an f0, say. Table 11.1 shows the

Table 11.1: Four suprasegmental phonetic parameters and the phonological phenomena most closely cued by them, dividing the segmental grouping of vowels, consonants, and tones and classifying tones with prosodic constituents (i.e., feet, the representation of stress).

Segmental		Suprasegmental	
spectrum	vowels, consonants	fundamental frequency	lexical tones, intonational tones, stress
		intensity	stress
		duration	quantity, stress

classic four phonetic parameters in the first column in each partition and the phonological phenomena that are cued by them in the second. The multiple cues to stress are an indication of a more general spread of cues involved in the realization of phonological constituents.

The view in Table 11.1 goes against the three-segment view defended here in grouping tones together with a prosodic constituent, the foot, into a class of entities that are NOT vowels or consonants. This has had a detrimental influence on the typology of word prosody. Together with a poorly defined notion "accent", their grouping has blurred the tripartite division into three aspects of phonological grammars identified in the introduction. In addition, the metaphor of prosody as an overlay on vowels and consonants ("suprasegmental") has reified inappropriate notions of stress as being a relational concept that needs another syllable for it to exist (Trager & Smith 1951: 36; Liberman & Prince 1976), and perhaps also of intonation as sets of utterance-wide melodies.

3 Prosodic constituents

In this section, I argue that in all languages segments are contained in a hierarchically arranged set of otherwise empty constituents, with higher ones encompassing lower ones (Selkirk 1981; Nespor & Vogel 1986; Selkirk & Lee 2015). Prosodic constituents constrain the distribution of segments. For instance, an English sequence like /pk/ can only occur across a syllable boundary, as in *napkin*, because inside the syllable, there is no legitimate way in which they can be located in that order. Similarly, they may forbid specific mixes of segments. Pharyngealized and contrastively plain consonants do not occur in the same syllable in Zwara Berber (Gussenhoven 2017), and nasal and non-nasal segments may not occur in the same phonological word in some languages (Walker 2011). They may also restrict their number, like the single voiced obstruent in Japanese words (Itô & Mester 1986) and the single glottalized consonant in the Indo-European syllable (Hopper 1973; Gamkrelidze & 1973).

The specific suite of constituents is language-specific. First, constituents with identical ranks may take different forms in different languages, and second, languages do not have identical suites of prosodic constituents. The first point in particular is true for syllables and feet, as discussed in Sections 3.1 and 3.2. The second point would appear to be true of feet, as discussed in Section 3.3, phonological words (Schiering et al. 2010), and accentual phrases. The situation becomes more varied at the higher end of the hierarchy. For instance, only six out of the 14 chapters in Jun (2014) with descriptions of (groups of) languages postulate an accentual phrase, a constituent somewhat

Table 11.2: Indonesian and Japanese syllable structures with disyllabic examples /salak/ 'Salacca zalacca' and /nikoN/ 'brand name'.

	Indonesian	Japanese
Syllable structure	σ onset — rhyme 　　　peak　coda 　　(nucleus)	σ μ μ C V X
Disyllabic example	ω σ σ μ μ s a　l a k	ω σ σ μ μ μ n i　k o N

larger than the word (Basque, Bengali, Dalabon, Georgian, Japanese, and Mongolian). Section 3.4 emphasizes that in the interest of conceptual clarity, stress is to be equated with word stress, i.e., foot structure. Headedness of higher prosodic constituents than the foot and the Pword is less obvious and the ways in which higher-level prominence has been recruited to explain phonological phenomena have not been successful in improving our understanding of prosodic phenomena.

3.1 Syllables

Mainstream analyses of syllable structure have assumed a binary division into subconstituents.[1] One such analysis is the majority onset-rhyme type, as exemplified for Indonesian, and another the Japanese type, where the first cut is between the onset plus the vowel in the first mora vs. the segment in the second mora (Kubozono 1999). Table 11.2 illustrates these, together with disyllabic examples.

The difference in Table 11.2 suggests that syllables emerge from data. At the same time, if associations are universal, so will be the phonological constituent that provides the elements with which segments are associated, and the syllable will therefore have to be universal too. As was clear in Section 2.3, linguists have two ways of deciding if a constituent exists. In theoretical linguistics, their existence depends on their role in the grammar. If no distributional

---

[1] An exception is Clements & Keyser (1981), who worked with multiply branching syllables.

generalization of any kind refers to a specific constituent, it has no reason for figuring in the grammar of that language. For instance, Labrune (2012) proposed that Japanese equates syllables with moras, thus denying the existence of heavy syllables. As it happens, in this case such evidence is found in the fact that the syllable is the domain of word accent, while there is at least one syllable-based generalization about accent placement in longer loanwords (Kubozono 2011; Kawahara 2016). In addition, unaccented word-initial syllables have high pitch if they are long, but low pitch if they are short in Tokyo Japanese, a difference that is hard to capture without the syllable (e.g., Pierrehumbert & Beckman 1988). The other way is to provide behavioral evidence. For most linguists, Kawahara's (2016) review of durational evidence for the rhyme in the Japanese syllable would be enough to refute Labrune's (2012) claim. Conversely, Hyman (2015a) shows that reference to the syllable can be avoided altogether in Gokana, but that is the extent of the claim. A demonstration that the language has no syllables would have to await the negative results of phonetic and behavioral research.

3.2 Feet

The obligatory status of stress as well as its syllable-based nature (Hyman 2006) follow from the fact that feet are headed and directly dominate syllables. That is, if prosodic constituents are obligatory and words are parsed into feet, stess is obligatory if the language has feet. Stress thus has no phonological substance. There will typically be a hyperarticulation of the stressed syllable, often leading to greater duration, more even spectral balance and relatively little undershooting of targets. Also, many languages have developed different segmental profiles for stressed and unstressed syllables, like English. However, there is in principle no problem with languages that have feet which do not obviously lead to measurable properties.

Compared to the shapes of syllables, those for the foot are more varied still. In addition to the distinction between trochees and iambs, trochees come in many shapes, depending on the language. Thus, there is the syllabic trochee ([σ σ]), the even moraic trochee ([μ.μ] or [μμ]) (Hayes 1995), and the uneven moraic trochee ([μμ. μ], [μ. μ] or [μμ]), as widely used in the analysis of Germanic languages (Zonneveld et al. 1999). And there is the Germanic foot, which can have a disyllabic strong branch (indicated by parentheses) and ranges across the structures [μμ.μ], [μ.μ], [(μ.μμ) μ], [(μ.μ) μ] and [μμ], as in /wor.du/ 'words', /lo.fu/ 'praises', /ky.niŋ.ga/ 'king', /we.ru.du/ 'troops' and /sel/ 'hall' (Dresher & Lahiri 1991). Like syllable structure, foot structure evidently emerges on the basis of language input.

3.3 Languages without feet

Not all languages have stress. Perception experiments in which Indonesian listeners had to choose between pronunciations with f0 obtrusions on different syllables showed that two of the three regionally defined groups had no clear preference, which was interpreted to mean that their language had no word stress, but marked intonation phrases with the help of a boundary accent (Goedemans & van Zanten 1993). Maskikit & Gussenhoven (2016) established the Pearson correlations between the time stamps of the f0 peak and six syllable-related landmarks in an Ambonese Malay corpus of one trisyllabic and seven disyllabic words with varied segmental structures recorded in a variety of prosodic conditions. The aim was to see if the segmental landmark that best predicts the location of the f0 peak was located in the putatively stressed syllable. Most probably, this would have to be the beginning of the rhyme or the end of that syllable. We found a steady increase of the correlation as the landmark was later in the word, the best value being the beginning of the rime of the last syllable. Since descriptions have claimed that the PENULTIMATE syllables of these words have word stress (van Minde 1997), the putatively stressed syllable appeared to play no role in the alignment of the f0 peak. Other phonetic measures equally failed to single out the penultimate syllable as having stress. Tellingly, segmentally equivalent Dutch data with penultimate stress did show the highest correlation with the beginning of the penultimate rime, which coefficient differed significantly from that between the f0 peak and the beginning of the penultimate syllable. Clearly, the attribution of stress in Ambonese Malay, and by a justifiable extension in Indonesian, has been due to the perception of stress caused by the phrase-final intonation contour by speakers of languages with stress.

Ambonese Malay thus has no stress. Additionally, there is independent evidence that it has no feet, though it does have syllables and Pwords. Maskikit & Gussenhoven (2016) investigated the durational coherence of the beginnings and endings of successive syllable rhymes in the same words as used for predicting the location of the f0 peak, on the assumption that absence of metrical structure might reveal itself in low correlations among these landmarks. Table 11.3 gives the results of a Principal Component Analysis showing greater coherence among the landmarks in Dutch than in Ambonese Malay, as expressed in the percentage explained variance by the two orthogonal variables (aka "components") which were extracted from the six segmental timing variables. Both are higher in the Dutch data, meaning that overall the temporal coherence of the Dutch words is higher than of the Ambonese Malay words. And to return to the first point, the prediction of the location the f0 peak, it is best predicted in Ambonese Malay by

Table 11.3: Explained and cumulative explained variance of the six landmarks by the first two components obtained from a Principal Component Analysis (columns 2 and 3) and the explained variance in the time stamp of the f0-peak by the time stamp of the best a single landmark (column 4) and by the combination of the two components (column 5) in a corpus of Ambonese Malay and Dutch words.

	Explained variance among 6 landmarks		Explained variance of f0 peak	
	Component 1	+ Component 2	Best single landmark	Two components
Ambonese Malay	64%	80%	67%	71%
Dutch	70%	92%	81%	77%

using THE TWO COMPONENTS, indicating the diffuseness of the variation in the peak location relative to the syllabic landmarks. For Dutch, a SINGLE LANDMARK, the beginning of the penultimate rhyme, predicts it best, other landmarks being less relevant.

Our investigation indicated that Ambonese Malay does have Pwords. There is an evident contrast between a reduplicated monosyllabic word and a disyllabic word. This is due to the placement of the f0 peak within the domain of the Pword, whereby the reduplicant is a separate Pword. A declarative pronunciation of (1a), a non-reduplicated form (van Minde 1997: 29), has the peak around the boundary between the two syllables, but the reduplicated form (1b) will have it centrally in the second syllable. Significantly, this phrasal minimal pair will wrongly impress speakers of languages like Dutch and English as showing contrastive stress. In combination with the data showing the absence of stress and feet in the language, these examples show that Pwords need not be headed, and can exist without containing feet.

(1) a. (goŋ.goŋ)$_\omega$ 'to bark'
    b. (goŋ)$_\omega$ (goŋ)$_\omega$ 'gongs'

Distributional properties also indicate that the language has syllables, as evidenced by its rejection of complex onsets, non-nasal word-internal codas and word-internal insertion of glottal stops to separate identical vowels. The case of Ambonese Malay does not exclude languages that demonstrably have no stress, but still have feet. Their existence could reveal itself in the way the foot constrains the distribution of segments.

3.4 Questionable extensions of word stress to the phrasal domain

Headed feet and headed Pwords predict that words maximally have primary and secondary stress, as in English ˈsala͵mander and ͵saluˈtation. The discrete view of stress espoused here contrasts with a conception of stress as graded levels of prominence extending beyond the level of the word. For English, these have been used to account for pitch accent distributions in the sentence (Chomsky & Halle 1968 and Liberman & Prince 1976, *inter alia*). Of the three mechanisms that have been used to represent continuous prominence, one has been widely rejected, the *n*-ary feature [stress] of Chomsky & Halle (1968). The other two do not fit into my Christmas-present model, the metrical tree and the metrical grid (Liberman & Prince 1976). Elsewhere I have argued that these metrical representations have failed to provide successful generalizations to account for the postlexical "Rhythm Rule" or "Stress Shift" (Gussenhoven 2010, 2015). By contrast, a representation with prosodic constituents, notably the phonological phrase, in combination with "accent" in the sense of syllables that are to be provided with an intonational pitch accent (see 4.4) does provide full coverage. Since other generalizations governing the distribution of accents are morphosyntactic, the only remaining roles for a metrical representation are the representation of utterance rhythm, of prominence and the provision of matching templates in textsetting to respect poetic meter (cf. Giegerich 1983).

None of these tasks requires the presence of a metrical grid or tree. First, even though they are quite capable of speaking is tune with some poetic meter, speakers do not normally speak rhythmically at all (Nolan & Jeon 2014). And while we can redundantly derive degrees of prominence from a surface representation like (2) (from Gussenhoven 2015), it is not clear how adding that information facilitates the phonetic implementation of either speech rhythm or prominence.

(2) {[The (**top**)] [in (**ROOF**) (**top**)]} {[is (**NOT**)] [the (**same**) (**top**)] [as (**that**) in
 %L   H*L   H% %L   H*L
 (**TABLE**) (**top**)]}
 H*L   L%

Finally, while we can represent (2) in terms of a metrical score and point out structural similarities between music and language (Lerdahl & Jackendoff 1983), it is not the case that all sentences fit at least a single meter; neither do we need a grid or tree to establish what utterances do fit a given meter, assuming we know the conventions. In (2), bold print is used for stressed syllables and small capitals for accented syllables; Pwords are in parentheses, phonological phrases in square brackets and intonational phrases in accolades. The point is that (2) gives all the information needed to generate a flawless, canonical utterance.

4 Alignment and association

In Sections 4.1 and 4.2, I briefly discuss the two anchoring devices that represent the third structural aspect of phonological grammars. In Section 4.3, I discuss the ways in which association and alignment are contrastive and how higher-ranking constraints may prevent expected associations or alignments, citing data from Japanese and varieties of Dutch. Next, in the spirit of Section 3.4, Section 4.4 critically discusses the semantic extensions that 'association' has undergone in the intonational literature. Finally, in Section 4.5 I discuss and defend the notion of accent, the device which is used to enforce the association of a tone.

4.1 Alignment

All linguistic constituents are aligned with one or more other constituents (McCarthy & Prince 1993). Alignments minimally amount to the coincidence of an edge of one (prosodic or segmental) constituent with an edge of another. One implication is that no constituent can be demanded to make an appearance in random locations in linguistic expressions. A second implication is that infixation is oriented towards the beginning or the end of a constituent, as in the well-known case of Tagalog verbal *um*. The suffix's left edge aligns with the left edge of the derived verb, but because demands on syllable structure prevent it from appearing word-initially if the base begins with a consonant, it only ever aligns left on the surface with vowel-initial hosts. Thus, /um/+/alis/ gives [umalis] 'to leave', but /um/+/sulat/ gives [sumulat] 'to write'. In both cases, the prefix is leftmost in the word, while respecting the minimization of onsetless syllables (Schachter & Otanes 1972; Prince & Smolensky 1993).

Alignment of segments is particularly relevant for tones. If we disregard the autosegmental behavior of vowels and consonants with respect to each other in the phonology of Semitic languages (McCarthy 1985), vowels and consonants typically appear in single strings in morphemes, even in quite lengthy ones. Like plain-clothed policemen at a fancy ball or clowns in a crowded village square, tones tend to be sparser on their tier compared to vowels and consonants on theirs, making their alignments more conspicuous. Examples of the less common situation of more tones than vowels are given in (3a) and (3b). The lax vowel in the vocative chant in (3a) is given as long, following the observation in Hayes & Lahiri (1991a) that they neutralize with long vowels under this intonation contour. Example (3b) has a lax vowel spanning four tones in an intonation contour. In (3c), finally, the more typical situation is given of tones spanning stretches of vowels and consonants. The L-tone spans the stretch between the preceding H* and following H%, approximately coinciding with /əv ðəʊz pʊl/.

(3)

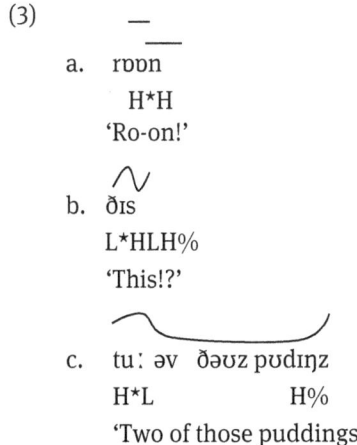

   a.   rʊɒn
         H*H
         'Ro-on!'

   b.   ðɪs
         L*HLH%
         'This!?'

   c.   tuː əv ðəʊz pʊdɪŋz
         H*L   H%
         'Two of those puddings?'

These segmental timings have been described as lengthening (of vowels) in (3a, b) and "spreading" or "control" by the L-tone of the post-accentual stretch in (3c) (Beckman & Pierrehumbert 1986). Both the beginning and the end of the stretch show up as targets, spectral change in (3a, b) and pitch elbows in (3c) in the f0 contour.

4.2 Association

Association is a temporal integration between segments (or features) with either rhymes or moras, the tone bearing units (TBUs) (Howie 1974; Hyman 1985). The motivation for TBUs is (i) the relatively constant phonetic timing of a tone's target in relation to a location in the TBU and (ii) the implication that strings of tones will be regularly distributed over strings of TBUs. For the first aspect, Pierrehumbert

(1980: 44) observed that the target of the accented tone (T*) of English was timed in a fairly constant fashion relative to an accented syllable, but that the following "phrase accent", by which she meant the tone after T*, showed "a fair amount of variation" in a location near the end of the nuclear word. This point is shown graphically in (4), with transcripion following e.g. Gussenhoven (2016).

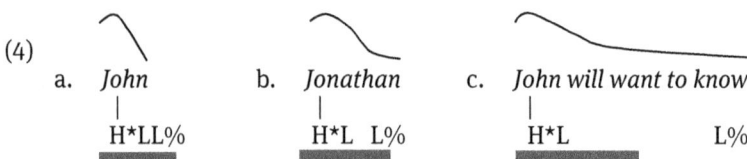

(4) a. *John* b. *Jonathan* c. *John will want to know*
         | | |
      H*LL%   H*L L%   H*L   L%

The timing of L is related to its distance from H* and is not governed by the syllable structure of the post-accentual stretch, as shown for English by Barnes et al. (2010). To a limited extent, the timing and scaling of associated tones are affected by contextual factors, like tone crowding and the nature of adjacent tones. Thus, in (4a), the target of H* occurs earlier than in (4b, c), because it needs to make room for the targets of the following L-tones. In (4b, c), the distance of H* to L is greater than that in (4a), because despite accommodating the L-tone by being earlier, the target of H* is close enough to the final boundary for LL% to be squeezed up to it. Observe that the graphs are distorted because they are projected onto the orthographic examples; an impression of their utterance durations is provided by the horizontal bars.

The second motivation for TBUs is the way the strings of tones are distributed over them, which figured emphatically in work by Leben (1970, 1973) and Goldsmith (1976). This is shown, for instance, by the different distributions of LH in Mende words like /lèlèmá/ 'praying mantis' and /ndàvúlá/ 'sling', where L is associated with the first two syllables in the first word, but only with the first in the second word, other syllables having H. Unlike the situation illustrated in (3), the synchronization of the target of L with its syllables is of the same order of precision as that between H and its syllables (see also Beckman & Pierrehumbert 1986: 281). That is, the Mende contrast cannot be reproduced in (4).

4.3 Alignment and association are contrastive and violable

ALIGNMENT is contrastive in two senses. First, a tone can be aligned with edges of different prosodic constituents. An H-tone, for example, may be aligned with the right edge of an intonation phrase or with the right edge of a syllable. When the right edges of these constituents do not themselves coincide, the alignment contrast is evident from the fact that the two tones are in different locations, as shown in (5a, b). However, the same contrast occurs when the two prosodic constituent edges do coincide, as in (6a, b), where the edge immediately above the H-tone is the edge with which it aligns. As a result, the H-tones will be treated differently by the phonetic implementation rules.

(5) a.)$_\sigma$...)$_\iota$ b.)$_\sigma$...)$_\iota$
         H   H

(6) a.)$_\iota$ b.)$_\iota$
)$_\sigma$ H
       H   )$_\sigma$

A case in point concerns H* and H$_\alpha$ in Tokyo Japanese. Its accentual phrase (α) begins with L$_\alpha$H$_\alpha$, while an interrogative utterance ends in H%, as seen in (7a).

(7) a. { (hi) }   b. { (hi) }
         | |
       L$_\alpha$ H$_\alpha$H%   L$_\alpha$ $\boxed{\text{H}_\alpha}$H*$\boxed{\text{L}}$H%
       'Day?/Sun?'   'Fire?'

The two tones in the Tokyo Japanese pitch accent H*L associate with the first mora in the accented syllable and the next mora, if there is one, respectively (Pierrehumbert & Beckman 1988). In (7b) this is possible only for H*, there being no second mora available for L. Each of the members of this minimal pair now consists of a sequence of two H-tones, H$_\alpha$ in (7a) and H* in (7b), where the second is the floating interrogative H%. Since the boxed tones in (7b) are deleted for lack of a TBU, the difference between (7a) and (7b) is that H$_\alpha$ (7a) left-aligns with the left edge of the accentual phrase, while H* in (7b) left-aligns with the left edge of the rhyme of the accented syllable, as expressed by the diacritics α and *, respectively. For those speakers who maintain this contrast,[2] the pitch

---

[2] Many speakers neutralize the word accent contrast on word-final monomoraic accented syllables in monosyllabic (cf. (5a) and (5b)) and disyllabic words, as in /hana/ 'nose' vs. /haná/ 'flower' in utterance-final declarative and interrogative contexts (cf. Vance 1995). In words of more than two syllables, the contrast is reliably preserved in declarative intonation (L%), due to the presence of a preceding syllable with Hα. In the unaccented case, the pitch falls from peninitial Hα to mid pitch at the word end, but in the accented case, it rises towards H* and then falls to mid in the last part of the final syllable (Warner 1997). In questions, the situation in trisyllabic words is similar to that in the disyllabic cases, so that the prediction is that trisyllabic minimal pairs are not distinct when spoken with question intonation in the speech of speakers who neutralize disyllables and monosyllables. I am not aware of experimental work on this question.

movement in (7a) is lower than that in (7b). Thus, while these forms have identical phonological tones, LHH, in which the first H is associated with the one available mora, the alignments of that first H are not identical, leading to a phonetic distinction (Gussenhoven 2004: 187). A similar case was earlier reported by Hayes & Lahiri (1991b), who noted that the IP-final string LHL in Bengali had a systematically higher and later f0 peak when H is aligned with the IP, in which case it signals a question (L* $H_\iota L_\varphi$), than when it aligns with the phonological phrase, in which case it signals a narrow-focus declarative (L* $H_\varphi L_\varphi$).

A second sense in which alignment is contrastive arises from OT, which holds that alignment constraints are ranked amongst each other. When two tones with different alignments compete for the same position, the order they appear in will depend on their ranking. In (8a), the right-edge alignment of H% to the right edge of the intonation phrase is ranked above a constraint that aligns the right edge of a lexical H to the right edge of the syllable, a situation is found in Venlo Limburgish interrogatives (Gussenhoven & van de Vliet 1999).

(8) a. ... kniin) } b. ... kniin) }
       H H%   L% H
       'Rabbit?'   'Rabbit?'

By contrast, the ranking is reversed in the dialect of Roermond Limburgish, as in (8b) (Gussenhoven 2000). In (8b), L% is aligned as close to the edge of the intonation phrase as it can be, while granting a rightmost position to the lexical H, just as H is as close to the edge of its syllable as it can be, while granting a rightmost position for H% in (8a). (The parenthesis stands for the right edge of the syllable and the curly bracket for that of the IP.) Importantly, the spatial orientation of } to the right of) is a metaphor for HIGHER CONSTITUENCY, not for distance or time. Hume (1998) gave the same analysis for Leti metathesis, where underlying VC# is CV# phrase-finally, except that she could use the more encompassing LINEARITY constraint instead of a constraint aligning C with the right word edge.

ASSOCIATION contrasts with non-association. To return to Tokyo Japanese, observe that both (7b) and (9b) are accented by means of the H*L pitch accent.

(9) a. { [san] }   b. { [san] }
       L_α H_αH% L_α $\boxed{H_\alpha}$ H*L H%
       'Three?'   'Acid?'

In word-final monomoraic accented syllables like (7b), the trailing L (boxed) cannot associate, since there is no mora available for it and the language disallows the association of more than one tone to a TBU. As a result, the floating lexical tone, identified through its left-edge alignment with the right edge of H* (cf. CONCATENATE in Riad 1998), is deleted. Because in (9b) a second mora is available, [n], L can associate here. As a result, the interrogative contours for the two monosyllables are notably different, a mid-to-high rise in (7b) and a fall-rise in (9d). The interrogative contours for unaccented (9a) and accented (9b) are highly salient as a result, quite unlike the more vulnerable contrast between (7a) and (7b). Non-crucially, floating H_α is deleted in both (7b) and (9b) (Gussenhoven 2004: 188).

Both alignment and association are VIOLABLE. Alignment is violated in Giryama, where the last lexical H-tone aligns right with the right edge of the IP, regardless of the location of its sponsoring morpheme, which can be a considerable distance from the phrase end (Volk 2011). However, instead of associating with the last syllable, it associates with the penult. The constraint that outranks it will either be one that locates a boundary tone on that last syllable, rendering it unavailable for H, or one that attracts H to a stressed penult. A similar frustration of right-edge alignment occurs in a number of European languages (4.3).

Similarly, an expected association of an intonational tone may be frustrated by the presence of a lexical tone in the accented syllable, as in Hasselt Limburgish (Peters 2008).

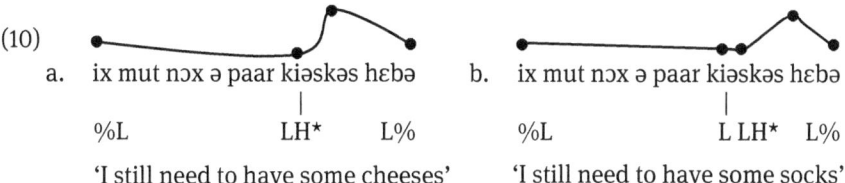

(10)
    a. ix mut nɔx ə paar kiəskəs hɛbə   b. ix mut nɔx ə paar kiəskəs hɛbə
                      | |
        %L   LH*   L%   %L   L LH* L%
      'I still need to have some cheeses'   'I still need to have some socks'

In (10a), H* associates with the accented syllable /kiəs/ in the word for 'cheeses', while in (10b), a lexical L is associated with that syllable in the word for 'socks'. As a result, H* in (10b) needs to forgo its absolute left-edge alignment in the accented syllable as well as its association, in favor of the lexical tone. While this analysis is identical to that in Peters (2008), I have not adopted his convention of attaching the star to the tone that associates, intonational H* in (10a) and lexical L (Peters' L*) in (10b). While '*' is an instruction to associate the segment bearing it to an accented TBU, it is not equivalent to association, which is symbolized by an association line. In (10b), the intonational pitch accent LH* aligns left with the lexical tone, where it fails to associate its H*, due to the pre-emptive association of L in the lexicon with the TBU that is designated as accented postlexically.

4.4 Experimental support

Phonetic research has established the existence of variation between floating and associated post-T* tones among varieties of West Germanic in the Netherlands. In Roermond Limburgish, right-hand boundary tones associate with stressed syllables (Gussenhoven 2000), while tones in equivalent positions in Dutch remain floating (van de Ven & Gussenhoven 2013). The first situation was shown for the post-focal stressed syllables in /ɛin(dələk)/ *eindelik* 'at last', /klɔɔʁ/ *klaor* 'ready', and /ɣɛt/ 'something', in which the beginning of the rhyme is increasingly close to the right boundary of the IP. Its association is reflected in the beginning of the f0 fall in the interrogative melody L* HL%, as shown in Figure 11.1. The high plateau illustrates a case of two-edge alignment, which creates two targets with approximately the same f0 between which the pitch is interpolated. In the Roermond case, the left-edge alignment does not, but the right-edge alignment does result in an association. For more discussion of associating post-T* tones see Grice et al. (2000).

By contrast, the timing of both the first and second targets of the medial low level stretch in a Dutch H*L H% contour has been investigated by Peters et al. (2012) and by van de Ven & Gussenhoven (2013), respectively. The second target is shown in Figure 11.2 by the downward arrow. The data is based on two

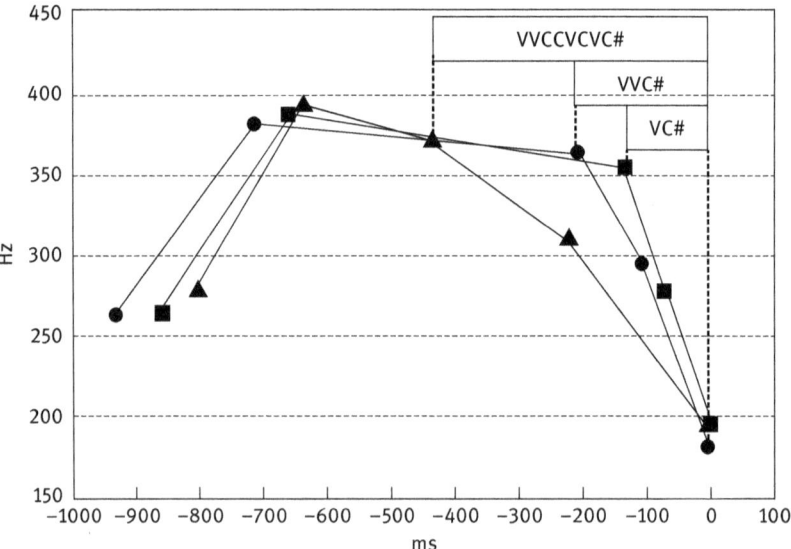

Figure 11.1: Synchronization of the beginning of the f0 fall in Roermond Limburgish with the beginning of the rhyme of the last stressed syllable in the intonation phrase.
▲ = antepenultimate stressed /ɛin(dələk)/, ● = final stressed /klɔɔʁ/; ■ = final stressed /ɣɛt/.
N = 24.

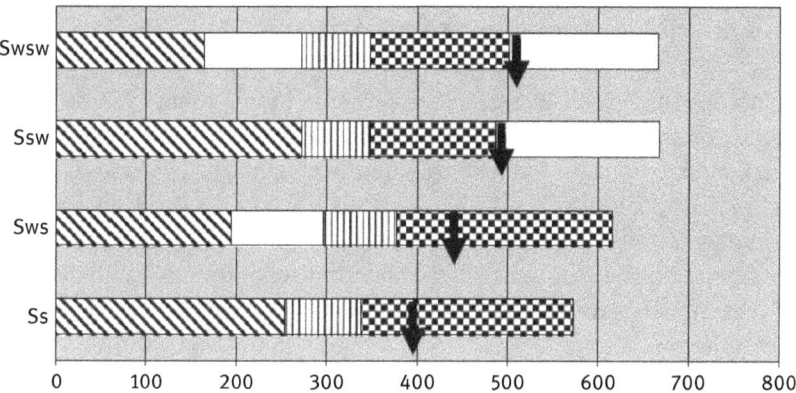

Figure 11.2: Synchronization of the pre-final f0 rise in Dutch with the end of the intonation phrase.
▨ = Word1; ▭ = unstressed syllable; ▦ = stressed rhyme; ▥ = onset consonant.
N= 432. Design after Lickley et al. (2005).

unaccented words in final position in IP, which varied from monosyllabic to disyllabic, with initial stress. The horizontal bars give durations of onsets and rhymes and are aligned at the beginning of the first word. From top to bottom, the words are two disyllables, a monosyllable plus a disyllable, a disyllable plus a monosyllable, and two monosyllables. The only effect on the timing of the low target is the end of the intonation phrase. Such insensitivity to the phonological structure indicates a lack of association. The alignment of this L is identical to that of the associated H of the Roermond dialect, shown in Figure 11.1.

Two-edge alignment offers a principled solution to a phenomenon that has been described as "spreading" of Pierrehumbert's (1980) phrase accent in English, reanalyzed as the final boundary tone of the intermediate phrase (Beckman & Pierrehumbert 1986). This is the low level stretch due to their L-, as occurring between H* and H% in cases in which the accented (nuclear) syllable is located at some distance from the end of the intonation phrase, as in (3c). By allowing a segment to align with two edges, we can describe the way in which the realization of a single tone fills up the space between two flanking targets as an interpolation between two targets. While effectively this creates the effect of tone copying, including such a rule would frequently run counter to the tonal grammar of the language, which may apply the OCP without exception. Characterizing two edge-alignment as spreading directly contradicts the findings showing that L- floats. Spreading is equivalent to one of the four possible configurations predicted by two-edge alignment, the one where an association exists at both ends (and by implication all TBUs in between). Spreading thus retains its usual meaning of multiple associations of the same tone.

4.5 Questionable extensions of association

There have been proposals to extend the concept of association to TBUs other than rhymes or moras. Notably, Pierrehumbert & Beckman (1990: 158) described Japanese boundary tones as associating with the phonological constituent with whose edge they align with, as shown in Figure 11.3, where the first L and the last H associate with the utterance node, while that same L additionally associates with the first mora. The edge at which the boundary tone appears was derived by a set of percolation conventions that were meant to deal with cases of constituents with tones at one edge.

This extension of association to higher constituents was widely adopted, because it came with the related notion of SECONDARY ASSOCIATION. Its motivation was the need to describe the contrastive association of a boundary tone in Japanese to the first TBU of the accentual phrase, like the first L in (11). In (11a), Hα associates with the first mora, a feature of bimoraic long rhymes, as noted in Section 3.2, whereas initial $L_α$ has a free mora it can associate with in (11a). Pierrehumbert & Beckman (1988: 26ff.) document the systematic and substantial phonetic effect of this difference and called the phonetic interpretation of the associated $L_α$ its strong allophone and that of the floating one its weak allophone. Parallel situations readily cropped up after the publication of their book, as in

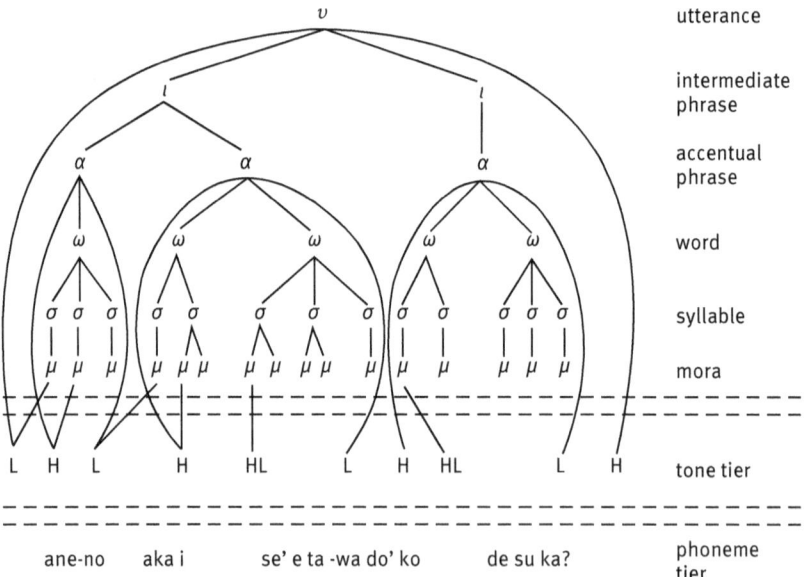

Figure 11.3: Associations of tones to moras and high prosodic constituents for *Ane-no akai seetaawa doko desuka?* 'Where is big sister's red sweater?' (from Pierrehumbert & Beckman 1988).

Grice (1995) and Gussenhoven & van der Vliet (1999), *inter alia*. In terms of the assumptions in this contribution, both (11a) and (11b) show the left edge alignment of floating H_α with the accentual phrase, but only in (11b) will it associate.

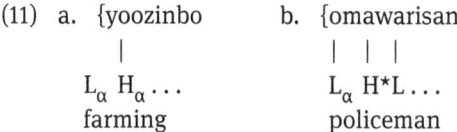

(11) a. {yoozinbo
         |
      L_α H_α ...
      farming

   b. {omawarisan
       | | |
      L_α H*L ...
      policeman

For cases like (11), association to a higher node looks like a complicated way of describing alignment. Describing alignment as association in the specific way in which Pierrehumbert & Beckman (1988: 154) interpret this also leads to the false prediction that distinctions like (8a, b) cannot exist. Observe that the nodes to which tones associate do not form a single tier in the way strings of moras or rhymes do. As a result, depending on whether Figure 11.3 is a two-dimensional object, as it appears on the page, or a three-dimensional object, in which node ι does not lie in the same plane as node α, for instance, the interpretation of the NO CROSSING CONSTRAINT (Goldsmith (1976) varies. Pierrehumbert & Beckman (1988: 154) in effect take the two-dimensional interpretation when proposing that boundary tones are sequenced so as to mirror their rank, with the tone at the highest edge occurring outermost in the tone string.

The resulting diffuseness of the meaning of association led to additional interpretations. For instance, Prieto et al. (2005) proposed that tones might associate with edges of these constituents by way of secondary association, doubling down on the ambiguity between association and alignment. Ladd (2004, 2006) instead argued that phonetic implementation rules should be available for fine-tuning the synchronization of tone targets with the syllabic, moraic, and CV-segmental structure. The concept of tone-to-node association further gave rise to the notational convention of showing the boundary tones as linked to the boundary bracket by means of an association line (Hayes & Lahiri 1991b). I blithely took over that practice in my (2004) book, but only up to Chapter 9. When formulating the optimality-theoretic descriptions of Northern Bizkaian Basque and Japanese, the meaning of constraints demanding association became intractable, for which reason I reverted to the original notation of Pierrehumbert (1980), announcing the change in Section 8.4 (p. 155).

Extensions of tone-to-TBU association at the tonal end were considered and rejected in Arvaniti et al. (2000), who showed that the prenuclear rise in Athenian Greek has its beginning synchronized with the end of the pre-accentual vowel and its ending at the beginning of the post-tonic vowel, thus embracing the consonants around the vowel of the accented syllable. Because neither tone therefore had a privileged temporal relation with the accented syllable, they briefly considered and rejected the option of labelling the LH-pitch accent as accented, rather than either L or H, in the spirit of a proposal of a dominating tonal node for the H*L pitch accent of Japanese by Pierrehumbert & Beckman (1988). Arvaniti et al. (2000) argued that this move would undermine the tenet of autosegmental phonology which derives f0 movements from interpolations of level targets. Within the terms of this contribution, the only option is to assign a star to one of the tones in the pitch accent. For Japanese, this is clearly H, but that decision is harder in the Greek case.[3]

The difference between alignment and association is in principle applicable to other segments, too. An association difference well may account for the phonetic behavior of "impure s" in Italian. As shown by Hermes et al. (2000), initial /s/ in onset clusters, as in *stella* 'star', is neither a separate syllable nor part of the onset, being durationally independent in a way that /b/ is *brilla* 'is shining' is not. Since association is potentially contrastive for all types of segments, the representation of "impure s" may lack an association to the onset, making /s/ in *stella* a word-initial floating consonant. In spirit, this is what Gierut (1999) and Barlow (2001) intended to achieve when characterizing impure /s/ as extrasyllabic. To be sure, despite a similarity in notation, association lines and lines indicating tree structures of prosodic constituents are distinct concepts. Absence of an association line neither implies non-parsing nor a parsing outside the syllable, as suggested by the term "extrasyllabic". That is, impure /s/ is just as much part of its syllable as a floating boundary tone is part of the constituent it aligns with. While consonants associate with onsets (or syllables, if no onset node exists, e.g., Hayes 1995) and moras, syllables do not ASSOCIATE with feet, but are dominated by them, or contained within them, in the metaphor of Section 1. A conceptual blurring of association lines and lines in tree structures may wreak havoc with notions like "spreading" and "improper bracketing". Segments can spread, i.e., associate with more than one of its segment-bearing units, while prosodic constituents ideally behave according to the Strict Layer Hypothesis. The TBUs for tones are moras or rhymes, VBUs for vowels are moras, while CBUs are onsets and moras. Just as vowels and tones may show multiple associations, so may consonants, which as a result may well be ambisyllabic. To quote Kessler (1998):

---

[3] The prenuclear pitch accent might be H*L, with L being aligned rightmost, as in my descriptions of English and Dutch, with somewhat delayed pronunciation of H*. This is in tune with the fact that the L-target is undershot under tone crowding. The motivation for LH as opposed to HL would appear to be the closer proximity of the two tones, but since there is no constant timing relation between them, that motivation is slim.

A major objection is that [ambisyllabicity] violates proper bracketing, or specifically, the prosodic hierarchy, which teaches that elements at one prosodic level are properly included in a single parent construct (Selkirk 1982: 355). To this one may well ask why segments should be considered part of the prosodic hierarchy; or why geminates, which autosegmental phonologists agree are typically single melodic constituents shared by two syllables, are not an equally big problem.

4.6 Accent

Accent is neither phonological content, like a segment, nor is it a prosodic constituent, like a foot. It amounts to a dual marking of a TBU and a tone (or other segment, but there have been no proposals of accented consonants or vowels), an instruction that the tone is to be associated with the TBU (Goldsmith 1976: 47, 87). When a melody appears in different locations in different words or expressions, it stands to reason to separate off the melody and mark its location as an address label on the TBU concerned in each word, i.e., to mark accent. Japanese and English are obvious examples. Gomez-Imbert & Kenstowicz (2000) present the instructive case of Barasana, which has the tone structures in (12).

(12) a. jai / H 'jaguar'   b. hee || HL 'ancestral'   c. wai || LH 'fish'   d. cai |\ LHL 'catfish'

These examples do not obviously suggest that the right analysis is one that assumes two melodies, H and HL, plus a lexical accent mark on the first or second mora, Barasana's TBU, rather than the four melodies H, HL, LH, and LHL of (12). One argument for the accentual analysis is based on the way pronouns impose their tone pattern on the following noun, whose original tones are deleted.

(13) a. ín à   3PL   jáí   'jaguar' – ín à jáì   'their jaguar'
     b. mání   1PL   mìnì   'pet'   – mání míní   'our pet'
     c. jɨ́ɨ̀   1SG   mìnì   'pet'   – jɨ́ɨ̀ míní   'my pet'
     d. mání   wɨ̀híbò   'tray'   – mání wɨ̀híbó 'our tray'
     e. ín à   bàbářá   'friends' – ín à bàbářà   'their friends'
     f. jɨ́ɨ̀   wɨ̀híbò   'tray'   – jɨ́ɨ̀ wɨ̀híbó   'my tray'

In (13a), the HL of [ín à] is copied onto [jáí], which loses its H, while in (13b) the doubly linked H of [mání] 'my' is copied onto [mìnì] 'pet', which loses its HL melody. Unexpectedly, however, the LH melody of [jɨ́ɨ̀] copies as H onto [míní], suggesting that the initial L does not count for the tone copy rule. This suspicion is confirmed in (13d), where the initial L of [wɨhíbò] is preserved when H of is copied from of [mání] to create [wɨhíbó] as opposed to ill-formed *[wɨhíbó]. Apparently, an L on the first mora is exempt from being copied as well as from being overwritten. Example (13e) confirms this, because [ínà] only manages to copy its HL on the second and third moras of [bàbáɾá], which loses its H on those moras. Finally, the H of [jɨɨ] is seen on the final two TBUs of [wɨhíbó].

The words in (12) now look like (14), where ★ over a vowel indicates the accented mora. The empty first moras in (14c, d) receive a default L. This analysis is supported by other processes, like the compound rule, which deletes the accent on the second constituent, causing the tones of the first constituent to spread through it, this time of course ignoring the accent location in the second constituent.

(14) a. ja̋i b. he̋e c. wa̋i d. ca̋i
        | || /   ∧
        ★   ★   ★   ★
        H   HL   H   HL

Importantly, accent belongs to the third aspect of our barebones concept of phonological grammars. That is, it concerns the anchoring of phonological content inside prosodic constituents. There are thus no necessary implications of the presence of a star for prominence or stress; neither are there necessary implications of distributional limitations per morphological word, phonological word, or accentual phrase. These features are frequently attested, as in English, where only stressed syllables can be accented, and which has led to the assumption that T★ is somehow metrically strong in and of itself (e.g., Prieto et al. 2005), or Japanese and Northern Bizkaian Basque, where accent is limited to one per domain.⁴ Such correlations of course require explanations, which might be sought in the segmentally privileged status of foot heads (e.g., English) and the fact that melodies are frequently longer than the extent of one TBU.⁵

---

4 English has a vacuous restriction of one per foot, as in *Cálifórnia* (Pierrehumbert 1980), by virtue of its TBU, the stressed syllable, but Japanese for instance routinely has more TBUs in the domain in which only one accent may occur.
5 The analytical approach to the nature of accent has no implications for its status in the grammar. In Gussenhoven (2004: 42), I drew a distinction between analytical concepts like "word melody" and "accent", which are based on distributional considerations, from phonological concepts like segments and prosodic constituents, which typically have measurable properties, with no implication that one type of concept is somehow superior to the other. On this, van der Hulst (2012: 1519) commented that '[CG] sees accent as an analytic device, suggesting that it is the "invention" of the linguist, adopted in order to organize data, and that therefore it is not as "real" as an H tone or "stress", which we can "hear".' To clarify, if a language were to have foot-based

5 Discussion and conclusion

After attending a class during a course on intonation I taught in 2009, Donca Steriade asked how it was that phonological representations of intonation need to provide tones with diacritics, like H*, H-, and H%, so as to alert the phonetic implementation rules to any special aspects of their scaling or timing. Isn't one H the same phonological entity as any other, the way lexical H-tones in Mende are of a kind? A more coherent answer than I gave at the time is that the diacritic notation is a stand-in for edge alignment, just as the association line is a representation of association. The point has implicitly been part of the work by Pierrehumbert (1980) and Pierrehumbert & Beckman (1988), even though their interpretation of the two phonological anchoring mechanisms changed. This is why there are no diacritics in the tone string in Figure 11.3 and why Pierrehumbert (1980) only provided association lines for the starred tone in English intonation, as in (4).

The conservative position defended in this article has considered the interpretations of a number of phonological concepts in detail. I have argued that, together, those interpretations make for a coherent conceptualization of a universal structure of phonological grammars. It consists of three structural aspects. First, there is a vacancy for phonological substance in the form of featurally specified tones, vowels, and consonants, whereby languages differ in the features and segments they have. Second, there is a prosodic hierarchy which provides the vacancy, the prosodic constituents that contain the segments, whereby languages differ in the specific prosodic constituents they have. And third, there are two ways in which segments are anchored in the prosodic constituents, (i) association to syllabic constituents, a relation which is unique to segments or features and moras or rhymes, and (ii) alignment, a form of anchoring that applies to all linguistic constituents. Finally, as an important byproduct of this exercise, each of three word-prosodic concepts that often appear together in typological discussions turned out to belong to these three very different aspects of the grammar. TONES are segments, STRESS is a prosodic constituent, while ACCENT is a diacritic indicating a segmental association in grammatical processes. It should be no surprise that they will not easily fit into a single taxonomy.

---

generalizations, while at the same time failing to reveal foot heads in the phonetic record, the foot would be an analytical notion, i.e., one based on distributional facts only, but it would still be a prosodic constituent of that language.

Acknowledgements: Parts of this article were presented at the 25th Manchester Phonology Meeting (25–27 May 2017), at the UCL Phonology Seminar (12 June 2017), at the conference on Approaches to Phonology and Phonetics (APAP) in Lublin (23–25 June 2017), and at the 2nd quinquennial Lahiri Fest at Eardisland Manor, Herefordshire (14 July 2017). I thank Jean Lekeneny for advice on data, Anna Balas for the reference to Port & Leary's article, and Larry Hyman and Aditi Lahiri for commenting on an earlier version.

References

Abercrombie, David. 1964. *English phonetic texts*. London: Faber and Faber.
Abercrombie, David. 1967. *Elements of general phonetics*. Edinburgh: Edinburgh University Press.
Arvaniti, Amalia, D. Robert Ladd, & Ineke Mennen. 2000. What is a starred tone? Evidence from Greek. In Broe & Pierrehumbert (eds.) 2000, 119–131.
Barlow, Jessica A. 2001. A preliminary typology of initial clusters in acquisition. *Clinical Linguistics and Phonetics* 15. 9–13.
Barnes, Jonathan, Nanette Veilleux, Alejna Brugos, & Stefanie Shattuck-Hufnagel. 2010. Turning points, tonal targets, and the English L-phrase accent. *Language and Cognitive Processes* 25. 982–1023.
Beckman, Mary E. & Janet B. Pierrehumbert. 1986. Intonational structure in Japanese and English. *Phonology* 3. 255–309.
Boersma, Paul. 1998. *Functional phonology: Formalizing the interactions between articulatory and perceptual drives*. The Hague: Holland Academic Graphics.
Broe, Michael B. & Janet B. Pierrehumbert (eds.). 2000. *Papers in Laboratory Phonology*, vol. 5: *Acquisition and the lexicon*. Cambridge: Cambridge University Press.
Browman, Catherine P. & Louis M. Goldstein. 1986. Towards an articulatory phonology. *Phonology Yearbook* 3. 219–252.
Chomsky, Noam & Morris Halle. 1968. *The sound pattern of English*. New York: Harper and Row.
Clements, N. George & Samuel Jay Keyser. 1981. *A three-tiered theory of the syllable*. Occasional Paper No. 19. The Center for Cognitive Science, MIT, Cambridge, MA.
Clements, G. Nick & Rachid Ridouane (eds.). 2016. *Where do phonological features come from? Cognitive, physical and developmental bases of distinctive speech categories*. Amsterdam: Benjamins.
Dresher, Elan B. & Aditi Lahiri. 1991. The Germanic foot: Metrical coherence in Old English. *Linguistic Inquiry* 22. 251–286.
Flemming, Edward. 2002. *Auditory representations in phonology*. Abington and New York: Routledge.
Fromkin, Victoria A. (ed.). 1973. *Speech errors as linguistic evidence*. The Hague: Mouton.
Gamkrelidze, Thomas & Vyacheslav Ivanov. 1973. Sprachtypologie und die Rekonstruktion der gemeinindogermanischen Verschlüsse. *Phonetica* 27. 150–156.
Giegerich, Heinz J. 1983. On English sentence stress and the nature of metrical structure. *Journal of Linguistics* 19. 1–28.

Gierut, Judith A. 1999. Syllable onsets: Clusters and adjuncts in acquisition. *Journal of Speech, Language, and Hearing Research* 42. 708–726.
Goedemans, Rob & Ellen A. van Zanten. 2007. Stress and accent in Indonesian. In Vincent J. van Heuven & E. A. van Zanten (eds.), *Prosody in Indonesian languages* (LOT Occasional Series 9), 35–62. Utrecht: Netherlands School of Linguistics.
Goldsmith, John A. 1976. *Autosegmental phonology*. Doctoral dissertation, MIT, Cambridge, MA. Bloomington, IN: Indiana University Linguistics Club.
Gomez-Imbert, Elsa & Michael Kenstowicz. 2000. Barasana tone and accent. *International Journal of American Linguistics* 66. 419–463.
Grice, Martine. 1995. *The intonation of interrogation in Palermo Italian: Implications for intonation theory*. Tübingen: Niemeyer.
Grice, Martine, D. Robert Ladd, & Amalia Arvaniti. 2000. On the place of phrase accents in intonational phonology. *Phonology* 17. 143–185.
Gussenhoven, Carlos. 2000. The boundary tones are coming: On the nonperipheral realization of boundary tones. In Broe & Pierrehumbert (eds.) 2000, 132–151.
Gussenhoven, Carlos. 2004. *The phonology of tone and intonation*. Cambridge: Cambridge University Press.
Gussenhoven, Carlos. 2007. Wat is de beste transcriptie voor het Nederlands? *Nederlandse Taalkunde* 12. 331–350.
Gussenhoven, Carlos. 2011. Sentential prominence in English. In van Oostendorp et al. (eds.) 2011, 2778–2806.
Gussenhoven, Carlos. 2015. Does phonological prominence exist? *Lingue e Linguaggio* 14. 7–24.
Gussenhoven, Carlos. 2016. The analysis of intonation: The case of MAE-ToBI. *Laboratory Phonology* 7. 1–35.
Gussenhoven, Carlos. 2017. Zwara (Zuwārah) Berber. *Journal of the Association for Laboratory Phonology* 7. 1–17. DOI: http://doi.org/10.5334/labphon.30
Harst, Sander van der. 2011. *The vowel space paradox: A sociophonetic study on Dutch*. Utrecht: LOT.
Hayes, Bruce. 1995. *Metrical stress theory: Principles and case studies*. Chicago: Chicago University Press.
Hayes Bruce & Aditi Lahiri. 1991a. Durationally specified intonation in English and Bengali. In Johan Sundberg, Lennart Nord, & Rolf Carlson (eds.), *Music, language, speech and brain* (Wenner-Gren Center International Symposium Series), 78–91. London: Palgrave.
Hayes, Bruce & Aditi Lahiri. 1991b. Bengali intonational phonology. *Natural Language and Linguistic Theory* 9. 47–96.
Hermes, Anne, Doris Mücke, & Martine Grice. 2013. Gestural coordination of Italian word-initial clusters: The case of Italian "impure s". *Phonology* 30. 1–25.
Hopper, Paul J. 1973. Glottalized and murmured occlusives in Indo-European. *Glossa* 7. 141–166.
Howie, J. M. 1974. On the domain of tone in Mandarin: Some acoustic evidence. *Phonetica* 30. 129–148.
Hulst, Harry van der. 2012. Deconstructing stress. *Lingua* 122. 1494–1521.
Hume, Elizabeth. 1998. Metathesis in phonological theory: The case of Leti. *Lingua* 104. 147–186.
Hyman, Larry M. 1985. *A theory of phonological weight*. Dordrecht: Foris.
Hyman, Larry M. 2006. Word-prosodic typology. *Phonology* 23. 225–257.

Hyman, Larry M. 2011. Tone: Is it different? In John Goldsmith, Jason Riggle, & Alan C. L. Yu (eds.), *The handbook of phonological theory*, 197–239. 2nd edn, Oxford: Wiley-Blackwell.
Hyman, Larry M. 2015a. Does Gokana really have syllables? A postscript to Hyman 2011. *Phonology* 32. 303–306.
Hyman, Larry M. 2015b. Why underlying representations? *UC Berkeley Phonology Lab Annual Report* (2015): 210–226. Published in *Journal of Linguistics* 54.
Itô, Junko & Armin Mester. 1986. The phonology of voicing in Japanese: Theoretical consequences for morphological accessibility. *Linguistic Inquiry* 17. 49–73.
Jacobi, Irene. 2009. *On variation and change in diphthongs and long vowels of spoken Dutch*. Doctoral dissertation, University of Amsterdam.
Jun, Sun-Ah. 2014. *Prosodic typology II*. Oxford: Oxford University Press.
Kawahara, Shigeto. 2016. Japanese has syllables: A reply to Labrune. *Phonology* 33. 169–194.
Kessler, Brett. 1998. Ambisyllabicity in the language of the Rigveda. http://spell.psychology.wustl.edu/ambisyll-sanskrit/Last change 27-08-2004
Kiparsky, Paul. 1982. Lexical morphology and phonology. In In-Seok Yang (ed.), *Linguistics in the morning calm: Selected papers from SICOL*, 3–91. Seoul: Hanshin.
Kubozono, Haruo. 1999. Mora and syllable. In Natsuko Tsujimura (ed.), *The handbook of Japanese linguistics*, 31–61. Malden, MA: Blackwell.
Kubozono, Haruo. 2011. Japanese pitch accent. In van Oostendorp et al. (eds.) 2011, 2879–2907.
Labrune, Laurence. 2012. Questioning the universality of the syllable: Evidence from Japanese. *Phonology* 29. 113–152.
Ladd, D. Robert. 2004. Segmental anchoring of pitch movements: Autosegmental phonology or speech production? In Hugo Quené & Vincent J. van Heuven (eds.), *On speech and language: Studies for Sieb G. Nooteboom*, 123–132. Utrecht: LOT.
Ladd, D. Robert. 2006. Segmental anchoring of pitch movements: Autosegmental association or gestural coordination? *Italian Journal of Linguistics* 18. 19–38.
Ladd, D. Robert. 2014. *Simultaneous structure in phonology*. Oxford: Oxford University Press.
Leben, William R. 1970. The representation of tone. In Victoria A. Fromkin (ed.), *Tone: A linguistic survey*, 177–219. New York: Academic Press.
Leben, William R. 1973. *Suprasegmental phonology*. Doctoral dissertation, MIT, Cambridge, MA.
Lehiste, Ilse. 1970. *Suprasegmentals*. Cambridge MA: MIT Press.
Lerdahl, Fred & Ray Jackendoff. 1983. *A generative theory of tonal music*. Cambridge, MA: MIT Press.
Liberman, Mark & Alan Prince. 1977. On stress and linguistic rhythm. *Linguistic Inquiry* 8. 249–336.
Lickley, Robin, Astrid Schepman, & D. Robert Ladd. 2005. Alignment of "phrase accent" lows in Dutch falling rising questions: Theoretical and methodological implications. *Language and Speech* 48. 157–183.
Maskikit-Essed, Raechel & Carlos Gussenhoven. 2016. No stress, no pitch accent, no prosodic focus: The case of Ambonese Malay. *Phonology* 33. 353–389.
McCarthy, John J. 1985. *Formal problems in Semitic phonology and morphology*. New York: Garland.
McCarthy, John J. & Alan Prince. 1993. Generalized alignment. In Geert Booij & Jaap van Marle (eds.), *Yearbook of morphology*, 79–154. Berlin: Springer.
McQueen, James M., Anne Cutler, & Dennis Norris. 2006. Phonological abstraction in the mental lexicon. *Cognitive Science* 30. 1113–1126.
Minde, Don van. 1997. *Malayu Ambong: Phonology, morphology, syntax*. Doctoral dissertation, University of Leiden.

Nespor, Marina & Irene Vogel. 1986. *Prosodic phonology*. Dordrecht: Foris.
Nolan, Francis & Hae-Song Jeon. 2014. Speech rhythm: A metaphor? *Philosophical Transactions of the Royal Society B: Biological Sciences* 369 (1658): 20130396. DOI: 10.1098/rstb.2013.0396.
Nooteboom, Sieb & Hugo Quené. 2007. The SLIP technique as a window on the mental preparation of speech: Some methodological considerations. In Maria-Josep Solé, Pamela S. Beddor, & Manjari Ohala (eds.), *Experimental approaches to phonology*, 339–350. Oxford: Oxford University Press.
Oostendorp, Marc van, Colin J. Ewen, Elizabeth Hume, & Keren Rice (eds.). *The Blackwell companion to phonology*. Oxford: Wiley-Blackwell.
Peters, Jörg. 2008. Tone and intonation in the dialect of Hasselt. *Linguistics* 46. 983–1018.
Peters, Jörg, Judith Hanssen, & Carlos Gussenhoven. 2015. The timing of nuclear falls: Evidence from Dutch, West Frisian, Dutch Low Saxon, German Low Saxon, and High German. *Laboratory Phonology* 6. 1–52.
Pierrehumbert, Janet B. 1980. *The phonology and phonetics of English intonation*. Doctoral dissertation, MIT, Cambridge, MA.
Pierrehumbert, Janet. 1990. Phonological and phonetic representation. *Journal of Phonetics* 18. 375–394.
Pierrehumbert, Janet B. 2002. Word-specific phonetics. In Carlos Gussenhoven & Natasha Warner (eds.), *Laboratory phonology vol. 7*, 1001–1039. Berlin: Mouton de Gruyter.
Pierrehumbert, Janet B. & Mary E. Beckman. 1988. *Japanese tone structure*. Cambridge, MA: MIT Press.
Post, Mark W. 2009. The phonology and grammar of Galo "words": A case study in benign disunity. *Studies in Language* 33. 934–974.
Port, Robert & Adam Leary. 2005. Against formal phonology. *Language* 81. 927–964.
Prieto, Pilar, Mariapaola D'Imperio, & Barbara Gili-Fivela. 2005. Pitch accent alignment in Romance: Primary and secondary associations with metrical structure. *Language and Speech* 48. 359–396.
Prince, Alan & Paul Smolensky. 1993. *Optimality Theory: Constraint interaction in Generative Grammar*. Rutgers University Center for Cognitive Science Technical Report 2.
Riad, Tomas. 1998. Towards a Scandinavian accent typology. In Wolfgang Kehrein & Richard Wiese (eds.), *Phonology and morphology of the Germanic languages*, 77–109. Tübingen: Niemeyer.
Schachter, Paul & Fe T. Otanes. 1972. *Tagalog reference grammar*. Berkeley: University of California Press.
Schiering, René, Balthasar Bickel, & Kristine A. Hildebrandt. 2010. The phonological word is not universal, but emergent. *Journal of Linguistics* 46. 657–709.
Selkirk, Elisabeth. 1981. On prosodic structure and its relation to syntactic structure. In Thorstein Fretheim (ed.), *Nordic prosody* 2, 111–114. Trondheim: Tapir.
Selkirk, Elisabeth. 1982. Syllables. In Harry van der Hulst & Norval Smith (eds.), *The structure of phonological representations*. Part 2, 337–383. Dordrecht: Foris.
Selkirk, Elisabeth & Seunghun J. Lee. 2015. Constituency in sentence phonology: An introduction. *Phonology* 31. 1–18.
Strange, Winifred. 1995. Cross-language studies of speech perception: A historical review. In Winifred Strange (ed.), *Speech perception and linguistic experience: Issues in cross-language speech research*, 3–45. Timonium, MD: York.
Trager, George L. & Henry Lee Smith. 1951. *An outline of English structure*. Washington: American Council of Learned Societies.

Vance, Timothy. J. 1995. Final accent vs. no accent: Utterance-final neutralization in Tokyo Japanese. *Journal of Phonetics* 23. 487–499.
Ven, Marco van de & Carlos Gussenhoven. 2011. The timing of the final rise in falling-rising intonation contours in Dutch. *Journal of Phonetics* 39. 225–236.
Volk, Erez. 2011. *Mijikenda phonology*. Doctoral dissertation, Tel Aviv University.
Walker, Rachel. 2011. Nasal harmony. In van Oostendorp et al. (eds.) 2011, 1838–1865.
Warner, Natasha. 1997. Japanese final-accented and unaccented phrases. *Journal of Phonetics* 25. 43–60.
Wiese, Richard. 2000. *The phonology of German*. Oxford: Oxford University Press.
Zonneveld, Wim, Mieke Trommelen, Michael Jessen, Curtis Rice, Gösta Bruce, & Kristján Árnason. 1999. Word stress in West-Germanic and North-Germanic languages. In Harry van der Hulst (ed.), *Word prosodic systems in the languages of Europe*, 477–603. Berlin: Mouton de Gruyter.

Subject Index

abstractness 7, 48, 55, 57, 59–60, 74, 76, 91, 97, 98, 128–129, 138, 170, 181–182, 260, 269, 275–276
accent 10–14, 16, 28, 38, 60, 82, 88, 152, 341–388, 389, 394, 396–397, 399–413
  see also pitch accent; stress
acquisition 43, 64, 80, 127, 98, 136, 204, 229, 236, 266–267, 269
  see also artificial language learning; learnability; second language acquisition
active (of a contrast/feature) 13, 60, 63, 67, 79, 197–198, 229–230, 236–247, 261, 266–267, 274, 278–280, 281–284, 285–286, 294–299, 301, 307
alignment 371, 373, 376, 384, 389–390, 397, 400–413
analogy 55, 68–69, 204
apocope 90, 351, 381
artificial language learning 157–158, 176, 182, 315
aspiration 3–5, 74, 78, 97, 266, 277, 316–317, 320–321, 324
assimilation 9, 59, 63, 66, 67, 93–97, 107, 145, 149, 160, 162, 164–165, 167, 173, 196, 198–199, 206–208, 210–211, 215–218, 221–226, 233, 242–243, 246, 248, 252, 256, 258–259, 263–264, 267, 280, 315, 326, 351, 390, 393
association 341, 342, 346, 349–351, 353–355, 358–359, 360, 362–364, 365–370, 373–376, 381, 382, 384, 389–390, 395, 400–411, 413
autosegment(al) 46, 57, 58, 137, 183, 185–186, 356, 390, 400, 410–411

borrowing 55, 68, 70, 82, 273, 297–307, 321
  see also loanword

clicks 12, 27, 36
coarticulation 63, 64, 77, 94, 96, 98
colour (vowels) 9, 57–58, 65, 84, 91, 93, 94, 96, 108

complexity 8, 28, 40–44, 49, 52, 63–65, 72–74, 79–80, 86, 92, 97n, 107, 115–116, 126–195, 212, 302
consonant cluster 15, 48, 86–87, 138, 143, 213–214, 216–218, 226, 256, 314, 315, 410
consonant (dis)harmony 138, 143, 145–146, 157–158, 160
constraint-based phonology see Optimality Theory
contact 14, 22, 267, 307
contrast privative, equipollent, or gradual 4, 13–14, 230, 259–260, 278, 316, 341, 346–347, 367, 379
contrast shift 273, 292–307
contrastive hierarchy 230, 237, 273–311
coronal 93, 107, 222–224, 229–259, 261–262, 264–269

databases 7, 35–36, 55, 112, 196, 202
  see also UPSID/LAPSyd database; P-base
deletion, of
– consonant 71–72, 94, 96, 160, 167, 208, 210–218, 223, 257–258, 313, 318, 325, 327–330, 332, 335–336
– feature 240, 242, 246, 258
– tone 403, 405, 411–412
– vowel 72–73, 76, 89, 95–96, 160, 167, 212, 214–215, 325
diachrony 16, 22, 29–30, 34, 48, 54–56, 68–70, 89–90, 98, 145n–146n, 196, 207, 211–212, 225, 229, 273, 276–277, 290–292, 292–297, 297–307, 313, 333, 341–343, 353, 371–376, 380, 392
diffusion (areal) see borrowing
diphthongization 63, 95–96, 215, 300, 325, 373–374, 392
dispersion 54–56, 64–65, 67–68, 93, 98
dissimilation 149, 155, 173

economy 56, 57, 59–60, 62–64, 67, 230, 240, 255, 267, 276, 399
enhancement 61, 63, 64, 67, 238, 302, 354, 377, 380

epenthesis 58–59, 76, 83–86, 88–90, 134–135, 160, 196, 210–215, 225, 288, 318, 325–328, 330–332, 336, 352

features distinctive or contrastive 61–64, 66–68
features monovalent/unary, bivalent/binary, or scalar 4, 60–61, 88, 96, 202, 221, 223, 235, 254, 259–260, 266, 278, 290, 316
feature geometry 67, 183, 225, 229, 232–236, 285, 297
final devoicing 5, 48, 62, 71, 134–135, 218–219, 313, 315, 325–331, 333, 335–336
  see also voicing contrast
floating tone 13, 350, 371–373, 384, 390, 403, 405–410
foot 50, 74, 77, 79, 88, 389, 393–399, 411–413
frequency (of occurrence, distribution) 12–13, 16, 56, 66, 79, 118, 120, 196–228, 312, 315–316, 323–324, 330, 333, 390, 407, 412

geminate 62, 82, 411
gemination/degemination 107, 210, 218, 248, 256
geography and phonology 117–123
glottalization 3, 394

hiatus 78, 79, 86, 212, 325

intonation 11–12, 27, 51, 317, 341, 344, 346–348, 358, 362, 379, 381–383, 389–390, 392–394, 397, 399–407, 413

labialization 57–58, 68, 95
laryngeal contrast see voicing contrast
learnability 52, 132, 150, 153, 159–160, 168, 172–173, 180–182, 187, 225, 323–324
  see also acquisition
lengthening see quantity contrast
lenition 107, 196, 204, 210, 216–221, 223
lexical/postlexical phonology 51, 56–60, 63, 64, 69–72, 76, 78n, 88, 96–97, 202, 346–347, 349–350, 352–353, 359, 370, 405

loanword 69, 70, 75, 81, 91, 396
  see also borrowing

markedness 63–67, 72, 76, 80–81, 126, 129–134, 140–145, 148–149, 151, 154–156, 163, 175–176, 179, 183–184, 211, 230, 237, 240, 244–245, 252, 255, 278–279, 281–282, 294, 299, 312–313, 316–318, 323–324, 330, 341, 347, 376, 381
merger 58n, 62, 69, 236, 280, 288, 290n, 295–297, 300, 304–305, 308
metathesis 35, 160, 167, 172, 196, 199, 404
meter (poetic) 50, 55, 399
mora 13, 50, 73, 76–82, 330, 352, 382–383, 395–396, 401, 403–405, 408–413
mora-timing see rhythm
morphophonology 12, 41, 55, 59–60, 66–67, 71, 73, 90, 92, 95, 259–265

nasalization 3, 5, 9–10, 39, 71–72, 81, 204, 210, 216–217, 226, 313, 326–328, 391
natural class 144, 197–198, 230–231, 266, 295
naturalness 56, 181, 314, 333
neutralization 5, 58–64, 67, 94, 280, 282, 294, 315–317, 401, 403n

Optimality Theory (OT) 6, 8, 50, 54, 56, 58, 61, 63, 67, 69, 80, 83, 86–88, 96–98, 127–136, 140, 143, 145, 159, 161–163, 173, 175, 178–179, 323, 325, 330, 335, 409

P-base 167, 196–228
palatalization 57–58, 62–63, 65n, 95, 204, 207n, 208n, 210, 215, 217–219, 231, 235, 236–243, 248–259, 267–268, 273, 279n, 282, 284, 288–289, 292, 294–297, 308
pharyngealization 63, 235, 394
phonemic level of representation 2–4, 54–106, 129, 273–274, 392
phonetics in relation to phonology 3–6, 8–11, 13, 16, 23, 31, 40n, 55–59, 64, 67, 69–71, 77, 88–93, 96–97, 107–125, 128, 145–146, 180–181, 196, 213–214, 225, 229, 231–232, 238, 248, 259, 262,

268, 273–276, 283–284, 286, 293, 307–308, 317, 319, 324, 327, 333–336, 341–344, 354, 367n, 368–369, 371, 384, 390–392, 394, 396–410, 413
phonetic implementation *see* phonetics in relation to phonology
phonological alternations 66, 69, 76–79, 196–228, 229–230, 234, 238, 259–265, 280, 282, 284, 290n, 297–299, 301–305, 319, 329, 352
phonological change *see* diachrony
phonologization 3, 9, 55, 63, 68–69, 212, 312, 314, 333–335, 376
phonotactics 28, 32, 35, 39, 48, 61, 76–77, 79–80, 129–130, 132–134, 140, 142–145, 157–158, 180, 183, 197, 278, 330
pitch accent 10–14, 16, 50, 51, 60, 78, 341–388, 399, 403–405, 410
play languages 54–55, 70–72, 75, 78
Prague School 3–5, 9, 13, 31–32, 44, 46, 55–57, 62, 69, 273, 276, 307
prosodic hierarchy 107, 389, 394, 411, 413
prosodic morphology 74, 75, 78, 80
prosody 3, 9, 10–11, 13, 27–28, 39, 50–51, 57–59, 64, 74–75, 77–78, 80–81, 97, 198–199, 212, 214, 315, 341–342, 349, 389–418

quantity contrast 48, 63, 69, 74, 80n, 94, 210, 218, 298, 322, 383, 393, 401

reconstruction 2, 3, 7, 14, 29–30, 39, 42, 64, 68, 236–238, 280, 288, 293, 300, 302, 304–305, 341, 343, 376, 392
redundancy *see* economy
reduplication 74–75, 78, 80, 398
rhythm 12, 38, 51, 107, 110–115, 119, 121, 399

sampling 16, 25, 35, 42, 51–52, 93n, 109–114, 116, 122, 199–202, 211
second language acquisition 312–340
segment inventories 9, 27–28, 32, 36–38, 42, 48, 55–57, 67–68, 98, 115–116, 196–207, 229, 248, 267, 273–274, 285
shortening *see* quantity contrast
song and chant 75–76, 78–79, 401

Sound Pattern of English (SPE) 5, 14, 46, 77, 83n, 108, 128–129, 181, 198, 213n, 230–231, 276, 279, 390, 399
speech perception 39, 55, 58, 62–64, 70, 107–108, 112, 145–146, 157, 207, 211, 214, 217, 226, 234, 248, 313–314, 321–322, 325–327, 323–333, 335, 368, 390, 392, 397
speech processing 107, 172, 229, 234, 266, 268–269, 392
speech production 3, 55, 58, 62–64, 107, 145–146, 185, 214, 226, 229, 231, 234, 240, 242, 313, 318–325, 327, 329–330, 332–335, 346n, 390, 396
spirantization 204, 210, 217–219, 329
spreading (features) 57–58, 64, 69n, 162–164, 169, 173, 185, 217, 222–224, 230, 233, 235, 240–242, 245–246, 249, 258–259, 261, 263, 350, 354, 358, 368–371, 375–376, 392, 394, 401, 407, 410, 412
stability (diachronic) 22, 55, 63, 64, 66, 91, 273, 307, 331, 346, 352, 381
stød 342, 345, 352–353, 373–374, 376, 382–383
stress 10, 13–14, 16, 27, 35, 48, 50–51, 56, 60, 73–75, 78, 88, 107, 110–111, 138, 152, 156–157, 317, 327, 329–330, 341–388, 389, 393–399, 405–407, 412–413
see also accent; rhythm
stress-timing *see* rhythm
suprasegmental 58, 390, 393–394
syllable 3, 12, 14, 28, 48, 50, 55–61, 63, 65, 69, 72–82, 83–90, 96–98, 107, 110, 117–121, 133–134, 145, 149, 152, 162n, 178, 182, 185, 263–265, 300, 315, 329–331, 341–345, 351–353, 359, 367, 381–383, 392–400, 402–413
syllable-timing *see* rhythm
syllable weight 78, 79, 82, 96, 110, 396
see also mora

tone 3–4, 10–14, 27–28, 35, 37, 39, 42, 48, 50, 60, 70, 74, 83n, 107, 116, 163–164, 176–177, 186, 341–388, 389–394, 400–413
see also floating tone

typology defined 1–2, 6–8, 12–13, 15, 16, 21–22, 44, 97–98, 108–110, 131, 145, 211, 225, 274

underspecification 9, 75, 83, 90, 96n, 173, 229–230, 236–247, 257, 258, 259–265, 266–269, 299, 316–317
UPSID/LAPSyD database 4n, 9, 35, 55, 56n, 66, 94, 122, 196, 199–202, 204

voicing contrast 3–5, 62–63, 66, 70–71, 121, 133, 135, 197–200, 204–205, 207n, 210, 216–220, 223–224, 235, 256, 266, 275–277, 312–340, 373–374, 391, 394
see also final devoicing
vowel harmony 3, 9, 12, 28, 48, 68, 160–165, 168, 170, 172–174, 176–177, 182, 185, 222, 236, 243–247, 260–265, 273, 274, 279–292, 296–305
vowel reduction 12, 64–65, 89, 95, 110, 121, 351
vowel systems 9, 11, 54–59, 64–72, 82–98, 236–243, 260–267, 273–274, 279–297–308

Language Index

Abenaki 296
Alawa 9
Alemannic 43n
Aleut 47
Algonquian 273, 274, 292–297, 308
Angami 318
Ao 318
Arabic 10, 49, 51, 63, 91, 97, 157, 316, 392
Arapaho 295, 296
Armenian 89, 276, 277
Arrernte 54, 55, 65n, 72–76, 81

Bambara 5
Basaá 3–4
Basque 10, 26, 42, 342, 395, 409, 412
Bella Coola 10
Bengali 51, 235, 395, 404
Berber 62, 89, 178, 394
Bininj Gun-Wok 41
Blackfoot 295
Breton 315

Campa 66
Cantonese 293n, 319, 322
Catalan 49, 89, 112, 113, 114, 319, 323, 328
Cheyenne 295, 296
Chichewa 49n
Chickasaw 51
Chinese (see Mandarin, Cantonese)
Chukchi 122
Chumash 138
Cree 295
Cree, Northern Plains 295
Czech 115

Danish 49n, 342, 345, 352n, 353, 353n, 373, 376, 382, 383
Desano 5
Doutai 5
Dutch 49, 112, 113, 249, 256, 257, 258, 259, 316, 319, 322, 323, 333, 335, 392, 397, 398, 400, 406, 407, 410n

Ekagi 122
English 3, 4, 5, 10, 11, 40, 41, 42, 46, 47, 50, 51, 63, 65n, 67, 69, 70, 75, 78, 78n, 85n, 90, 91, 109, 110, 111, 112, 113, 114, 115, 132, 132n, 133, 138, 142, 145, 151, 157, 176, 198, 211, 231, 241, 249, 261, 266, 293n, 313, 318, 319–324, 329, 330, 331, 332, 335, 336, 349, 384, 391, 394, 396, 398, 399, 402, 407, 410, 411, 412, 413
Eskimo (Proto) 236, 237, 238, 280n, 288
Eskimo 47, 236, 237, 238, 280n, 288
Estonian 113

Faroese 49
Farsi 51, 319, 324
Finnish 10, 73, 78, 79
Fox 295
Franconian (Central) 342, 352, 352n, 353n, 380–383
French 4, 10, 11, 51, 60, 71, 91, 110–115, 207, 319, 391

German 5, 11, 24n, 41, 43n, 49, 62, 89, 113, 114, 115, 138, 248n, 251, 253, 268, 319, 323, 324, 328, 349, 393
Germanic 50, 112, 114, 341–384, 396, 406
Gokana 54, 76, 79–81, 82, 396
Gothic 333, 335
Greek 27, 60, 108, 110, 111, 113, 350n, 351n, 409, 410
Greenlandic 26

Haruai 90
Hindi 235
Hungarian 49, 248n, 297, 316, 319, 320, 324, 351n

Icelandic 49
Igbo 10
Ik 10
Ikwere 5
Ilocano 47

Indonesian 10, 395, 397
Inuit 236, 238, 241, 243, 273, 288, 289, 293n, 307
Inupiaq (Barrow) 238
Irish 65n, 233n, 343n
Italian 63n, 74n, 110, 111, 112, 115, 410

Japanese 10, 11, 76, 81, 81n, 82, 97n, 110, 111, 112, 113, 114, 197, 316, 318, 319, 334, 335, 394, 395, 396, 400, 403, 404, 408, 409, 410, 411, 412n
Jaqaru 9
Jimi 68

Kabardian 43, 54, 56, 65, 65n, 90–94
Kachin Khakass 291
Kalam 59, 82–90
Kàlɔŋ 230
Karen (Sgaw) 122
Khanty 297, 305, 306
Kinyarwanda 259
Kom 10
Konni 326
Korean 3, 4, 5, 10, 51, 94, 293n, 320, 321
Koromfe 41
Kuki-Thaadow 10
Kune 41
Kunwinjku 41
Kwakiutl 138

Latvian 342
Lithuanian 300n, 316, 342, 352n, 383

Mahican 296
Malagasy 66
Malay 113, 315, 397–398
Malayalam 247, 248m
Maliseet-Passamaquoddy 296
Manchu (Classical) 281–284
Mandarin (Chinese) 11, 49, 70, 77, 113, 316, 318, 322, 323, 324, 328, 329, 331, 334, 335
Mansi 297–305
Maori 122
Marshallese 65, 94–97
Massachusett 296
Maung 122

Mayá 10
Mayali 41
Mazatec 66
Mekeo 267–268
Menomini 41, 66–69
Mi'kmaq 296
Miami-Illinois 295
Mixtec 10, 122
Mlabri 41
Moloko 57–59, 60, 64, 68
Mongolian 89, 273, 285, 287, 288, 291, 307, 395

Nahuatl 66
Nenets (Tundra) 76n
Nez Perce 122
Nimboran 9
Noon 326
Norwegian 10, 341, 351, 352, 352n, 354, 358, 360, 379n, 383, 384
Nunggubuyu 9
Nupe 259
Nzadi 42

Ob-Ugric 273, 274, 293n, 297, 298, 299, 301, 305, 306, 307
Ojibwe 295
Oroqen 283n, 285, 286

Pitta-Pitta 248, 249
Pohnpeian 122
Polish 25, 78, 112, 113, 114, 249, 319, 328, 329
Portuguese 41, 71, 91, 111, 324, 331, 334, 335

Qawasar 9, 66
Qiang 122

Romance 24, 27, 112, 114, 207
Russian 10, 42n, 62, 63, 70, 259, 315

Salishan 89
Samala 143, 144, 145, 145n, 146
Sanskrit 60, 77n, 78, 108, 164, 176
Semitic 27, 400
Serbo-Croatian 10, 78, 342
Shawnee 295

Sheko 122
Skou 10
Slave 41
Slavic 249, 253, 293n
Somali 10
Spanish 11, 49, 63, 78n, 110, 111, 112, 113, 114, 207, 329
Sundanese 47
Swedish 10, 51, 316–319, 328, 341, 343, 346, 349, 351, 352, 352n, 354, 356–360, 362, 362n, 364, 368, 371, 376, 377, 380, 383, 384

Tacana 66
Tahltan 243–247
Takelma 41, 315
Tashlhiyt (Berber) 77n
Teleéfoól 47
Thaayore 122
Thai 3, 113, 319
Totontepec (Mixe) 316
Towa 122

Tswana 318, 322, 323
Tungusic, Tungus 273, 285, 287, 288, 291, 293, 307
Turkic 273, 285, 290
Turkish 10, 24, 28, 91, 94, 290, 291, 292, 331

Usarufa 10
Uyghur 94, 315

Vietnamese 24, 47, 320, 332

Walloon 315
Welsh 49, 113
Wichita 65n

Xibe 291, 292, 293

Yaka 164, 174, 176
Yessan-Mayo 9
Yokuts (Yowlumne) 178, 286, 287, 288
Yoruba 10, 138
Yupik 273, 288, 289, 307

Author Index

Abercrombie, David 110, 123, 391, 414
Abitov, M. L. 91, 98
Abrahamsson, Niclas 318, 328, 336
Abry, Christian 105
Aikhenvald, Alexandra Y. 7, 18
Aissen, Judith 7, 17
Alber, Birgit 60, 98
Altenberg, Evelyn 319, 324, 336
Andersen, Henning 90, 99
Anderson, Stephen R. 47n, 53, 67, 77, 99, 117, 185, 187
Ann, Jean 323, 339
Aoun, Joseph 49
Applebaum, Ayla 91, 93n, 94, 99, 101
Applegate, Richard B. 138, 143, 143n, 187
Archangeli, Diana 230, 270, 286, 308
Árnason, Kristján 49, 418
Aronoff, Mark 46
Arvaniti, Amalia 113, 123, 350n, 351n, 384, 385, 409, 410, 414, 415
Atkinson. Quentin 115, 116, 124
Auer, Peter 12, 17
Austin, Peter 49, 82, 99

Bach, Emmon 138
Badecker, William 158n, 189
Bagov, P. M. 91, 99
Bailey, Gil 194
Baker, Mark 46
Baković, Eric 134, 135, 136, 160, 161, 164, 174, 179, 180, 187
Balas, Anna 414
Balkarov, B. X. 99
Bannert, Robert 385
Barlow, Jessica A. 410, 414
Barnes, Jonathan 402, 414
Barreteau, Daniel 82, 83, 99
Barrie, Mike 293, 308
Basbøll, Hans 49, 352, 384
Beauzée, Nicolas 26, 26n
Becker, Michael 193, 331, 336
Beckman, Jill 145, 188, 317, 336
Beckman, Mary E. 11, 17, 396, 401, 402, 403, 407, 408, 409, 410, 413, 414, 417

Bedell, George 97, 99
Beesley, Kenneth 139, 175, 188
Bender, Byron W. 94, 95, 96, 97, 98, 99
Bennett, William 160, 173, 188
Benua, Laura 129n, 188
Bergsland, Knut 47
Bermúdez-Otero, Ricardo 47n, 52, 53, 61, 69, 99
Beros, Achilles 175, 188
Berstel, Jean 159, 188
Bhat, D. N. S. 249, 270, 296n, 308
Bhatt, Rajesh 193
Bickel, Balthasar 7, 15, 17, 197, 200, 201, 226, 417
Bickmore, Lee S. 163, 192
Blake, Barry J. 36
Bleckert, Lars 373, 374, 384
Blevins, Juliette 48n, 83, 145n, 188, 204, 207, 211, 212, 218, 225, 226, 227, 267, 270, 313, 314, 315, 317, 319, 322, 336
Bloch, Bernard 62, 67, 99
Bloomfield, Leonard 41, 42n, 47, 66, 69, 99
Blumenfeld, Lev 60, 99
Blumstein, Sheila 231n, 248, 249n, 253, 255, 259, 270, 271, 272
Boas, Franz 41
Boë, Louis-Jean 105
Boersma, Paul 175, 188, 323, 390, 414
Booij, Geert 49, 416
Borowsky, Toni 61, 64, 75n, 99, 338
Borsley, Robert 49
Bossong. Georg 7, 17
Breen, Gavan 72, 75n, 99, 106
Bresnan, Joan 49, 82, 99, 104, 190
Broe, Michael B. 414, 415
Broersma, Miriam 322, 336
Brohan, Anthony v, viii, ix, **196–228**
Bromberg, Ilana 211, 227
Broselow, Ellen v, viii, ix, **312–340**
Browman, Catherine P. 183, 188, 391, 414
Bruce, Gösta 343, 344, 345, 346n, 350, 354, 368, 370, 371, 372n, 376, 377, 378, 379, 381, 384, 385, 418
Brugos, Alejna 414

Buccola, Brian 179, 188
Buckley, Eugene 6, 17
Bulmer, Ralph 59, 82, 83, 88, 100, 105
Burnett, James (Lord Monboddo) 28, 29
Burzio, Luigi 73, 99
Butcher, Andrew 106
Bybee, Joan L. 12, 17, 38, 46
Bye, Patrik 344, 345, 385
Bynon, Theodora 32n, 53

Cahill, Michael 326, 337
Calabrese, Andrea 101, 230, 270, 286, 308
Campanella, Tommaso 24, 25, 29, 36
Campos-Astorkiza 286, 300n, 308
Cardoso, Walcir 323, 324, 330, 337
Carstairs, Andrew 46
Casali, Roderic F. 55, 99
Catford, J. C. 91, 99, 100, 108, 124, 211, 227
Cebrian, Juli 319, 328, 337
Chakraborti, Paromita 12, 17
Chandlee, Jane 160, 167, 168, 172, 175, 180, 181, 187, 188, 191
Chen, Su-I 323, 336
Chiu, C. Chenhao 226, 227
Cho, Young-Mee 226, 227
Choi, John D. 91, 96n, 100
Chomsky, Noam 5, 14, 17, 43, 46, 52, 53, 67, 77, 83n, 100, 108, 124, 126, 127, 128, 129, 136, 137, 138, 139, 142, 181, 189, 198, 213n, 227, 230, 231, 270, 276, 279, 308, 390, 399
Cichocki, Wladyslaw 319, 337
Cinque, Guglielmo 46
Clairis, Christos 66, 100
Clark, Mary 14, 17
Clements, G. N. 5, 16, 17, 67, 79, 100, 138, 183, 189, 198, 225, 227, 228, 230–236, 243–247, 250–252, 255, 261, 270, 278, 390, 395n, 414
Cohn, Abigail 5, 18, 271
Colarusso, John 65n, 91, 91n, 92, 93, 93n, 100
Comon, Hubert 186, 189
Compton, Richard 236, 270, 280n, 289, 293n, 308
Comrie, Bernard 15, 36, 38, 41, 49, 82, 90, 100

Cope, Dana 124
Cornell, Sonia A. 268, 269, 270C
Côté, Marie-Hélène 227
Coupé, Christophe 119, 122, 124
Crane, Thera M. 42
Crawford, Penny 62, 105
Cristofaro, Sonia 37
Croft, William 8, 18, 36, 39, 124
Currie-Hall, Kathleen 63n, 100
Cutler, Anne 416

d'Andrade, Ernesto 49n
D'Imperio, Mariapaola 336, 417
Dauchet, Max 189
Dauer, Rebecca 110, 111, 121, 124
Davidian, Richard D. 318, 319, 328, 329, 337
DeCamp, David 62n, 100
Delisi, Jessica L. 89, 100
Dell, François 89, 100, 178, 189
Dellwo, Volker 113, 114, 115, 124
Dinnsen, Daniel A. 62, 100
Dixon, R. M. W. 7, 18
Dolatian, Hossep 187
Donegan, Patricia 12, 18
Donohue, Mark 3, 18
Dorais, Louis-Jacques 288, 309
Downing, Laura J. 73, 100
Dresher, B. Elan *viii*, *ix*, 50, 52, 55, 56n, 99, 100, 105, 129, 159, 189, 230, 236, 261, 270, **273–311**, 396, 414
Dressler, Wolfgang U. 16, 18
Dryer, Matlthew S. 7, 18, 38, 104
Duanmu, San 49
Durand, Jacques 49

É. Kiss, Katalin 49
Easterday, Shelece 121, 124
Ebeling, C. L. 63, 69, 100
Eckman, Fred 313, 318, 319, 321, 323, 324, 337
Edge, Beverly 318, 319, 328, 337
Edlefsen, Matt 156, 189, 194
Elert, Claes-Christian 351, 384, 385
Elgot, C. C. 174, 182, 189
Elmedlaoui, Mohamed 178, 189
Ember, Carol R. 118, 119, 124
Ember, Marvin 118, 119, 124

Endress, Ansgar D. 145, 189
Engelfriet, Joost 138, 165, 189
Engstrand, Olle 346n, 370, 385
Eulitz, Carsten 269, 270
Evans, Nicholas 3, 8, 18, 38, 39, 41, 42n, 55, 72, 90, 100
Evers, Vincent 233, 250, 254, 257n, 271
Ewen, Colin J. 18, 19, 20, 193, 310, 338, 417
Eyraud, Rémy 187, 188, 191

Fant, C. Gunnar M. 63, 83n, 102, 198, 227, 229, 271, 277, 310, 346n, 385
Fast, P. W. 82, 100
Faudree, Michael 320, 338
Feuillet, Jack 17, 37
Fikkert, Paula 236, 266, 270
Finley, Sara 158n, 160, 163, 164, 176, 179, 182, 189
Fintoft, Knut 343, 385
Firth, John Rubert 42n
Flämig, Walter 41
Flavier, Sébastien 124
Flege, James Emil 318, 319, 322, 328, 329, 337, 338
Flemming, Edward 64, 93, 100, 390, 414
Fortescue, Michael 288, 309
Foss, Donald J. 3, 18
Fougeron, Cécile 25n, 101, 145, 189, 271, 336
Fought, Carmen R. 118, 119, 120, 122, 124
Fought, John R. 118, 119, 120, 122, 124
Frank, Robert 140, 178, 189
Franzen, Vivan 105
Fretheim, Thorstein 359, 360, 385, 417
Fromkin, Victoria A. 227, 392, 414

Gabelentz, Georg von der 22, 26, 27, 29, 30, 36, 38, 51, 53
Gainor, Brian 172, 189
Gallagher, Gillian 145, 189
Gamkrelidze, Thomas 394, 414
García, Pedro 150, 181, 189, 193
Gårding, Eva 342, 343, 344, 345, 385, 386
Gardner, Matt Hunt 293n, 309, 311
Garvey, Kelly 327, 338
Gastner, Michael 200, 227
Gazdar, Gerald 127, 189

Genetti, Carol 42
Gerdemann, Dale 140, 190
Gewirth, Letitia 231n, 271
Ghini, Mirco 233, 266, 270
Gick, Bryan 226, 227
Giegerich, Heinz J. 399, 414
Gierut, Judith A. 410, 415
Gildea, Daniel 172, 190
Gili-Fivela, Barbara 417
Gilleron, Rémi 189
Girard, Gabriel 25
Goedemans, Rob 19, 397, 415
Gold, E. Mark 168, 190
Goldsmith, John A. 17, 19, 46, 155, 183, 190, 191, 227, 228, 270, 271, 389, 390, 402, 409, 411, 415, 416
Goldstein, Louis 103, 183, 188, 391, 414
Goldwater, Sharon 178, 190
Gomez-Imbert, Elsa 411, 415
Good, Erin M. 124
Gordon, Matthew K. viii, 6, 6n, 8, 18, 43, 91, 93n, 94, 99, 101, 316, 337
Gorman, Kyle 132n, 160
Gosy, Maria 320, 324, 337
Gouskova, Maria 2, 18
Grabe, Esther 112, 113, 114, 124
Graf, Thomas 127, 128n, 157, 164, 187, 190
Gravina, Richard 57, 59, 68, 101
Green, Jenny 65n, 101
Greenberg, Joseph H. 1, 3, 7, 8, 18, 32, 37, 55, 101, 270, 308, 337, 338
Grice, Martine 350n, 351n, 385, 406, 409, 415
Grimm, Jakob 30
Guimarães, Maximiliano 71, 101
Gussenhoven, Carlos viii, ix, 11, 18, 19, 45, 52, 78, 83n, 101, 124, 256, 257, 257n, 270, 271, 381, 382, 383, 385, 386, 387, **389–418**

Haarmann, Harald 36
Hagège, Claude 6, 19, 32n
Hale, Mark 75, 101, 181, 190
Hall, Daniel Currie 56n, 100, 309
Hall, Robert A. 207, 227
Hall, Tracy Alan 61, 100, 101, 248, 248n, 250, 251, 252, 270, 278, 302

Halle, Morris 5, 14, 16, 17, 19, 42n, 63, 67, 77, 83n, 91, 91n, 92, 100, 101, 102, 108, 124, 128, 129, 132, 133, 157, 181, 189, 190, 198, 213n, 225, 227, 229, 230, 231, 233, 235, 237, 270, 271, 276, 277, 279, 308, 310, 390, 399, 414
Hammarberg, Björn 319, 328, 337
Hammond, Michael 8, 19
Hancin-Bhatt, Barbara 319, 323, 337
Hannahs, S. J. 49
Hansen, Jette G. 320, 328, 332, 337
Hansson, Gunnar 143, 145, 160, 173, 190
Harnad, Stevan 108, 123, 124
Harrington, Jonathan 62, 103
Harris, James 78, 101
Harris, John 61, 64, 101
Harris, Zellig 57
Harst, Sander van der 392, 415
Harvey, Christopher *viii, ix,* **273–311**
Haspelmath, Martin 3, 19, 38, 45, 46, 104, 106, 108, 115, 124
Haudricourt, André-Georges 32
Havers, Wilhelm 47
Hayes, Bruce 16, 19, 46, 50, 132, 145, 157, 175, 178, 181, 186, 188, 190, 323, 396, 401, 404, 409, 410, 415
Healey, P. 47
Heidolph, Karl Erich 41, 47
Heine, Bernd 10, 17, 19
Heinz, Jeffrey *viii, ix,* 43, 52, 53, **126–195**
Helgason, Pétur 319, 336, 337
Hermes, Anne 410, 415
Heyer, Sarah 329, 338
Higuera, Colin de la 168, 175, 188, 191
Hildebrandt, Kristine A. 417
Hillenbrand, James 319, 338
Hjelmslev, Louis 42
Hockett, Charles F. 9, 19, 41, 99, 108, 124
Hognestad, Jan K. 362, 384, 386
Honey, P. J. 47
Honeybone, Patrick 47, 52, 53, 99, 103, 311
Honti, László 298, 299, 300, 307, 309
Hoogeboom, Hendrik Jan 138, 165, 189
Hopper, Paul J. 394, 415
House, Anthony B. 337
House, David 383, 386
Householder, Fred 47

Howard, Irwin 161, 191
Howie, J. M. 401, 415
Hsieh, Feng-Fan 70, 101
Hualde, José Ignacio 14, 19, 42, 63, 101, 383, 386
Huang, James 49, 309
Huber, Brad R. 119, 124
Huffman, Marie 271, 338
Hulden, Mans 139, 175, 191
Humboldt, Wilhelm von 26, 126, 191
Hume, Elizabeth 18, 19, 20, 193, 196, 198, 211, 225, 227, 227, 231, 232, 250, 251, 270, 310, 338, 404, 415, 417
Hwangbo, Hyun Jin 187
Hyde, Brett 60, 181
Hyman, Larry M. *i, iii, v, viii, ix,* **1–20**, 23, 31n, 38, 42, 42n, 44n, 50, 52, 53, 76, 77, 79, 80, 98, 101, 102, 152, 157, 163, 164, 174, 176, 177, 185, 186, 187, 191, 196, 227, 230, 260, 261, 263, 264, 267, 271, 274, 308, 309, 314, 336, 338, 390, 392, 396, 401, 414, 415, 416

Idsardi, William 43, 52, 53, 177, 179, 187, 191
Ineichen, Gustav 36
Ingrisano, Dennis R. 319, 338
Isidore of Seville 27
Itô, Junko 81, 82, 102, 394, 416
Ivanov, Vyacheslav 414
Iverson, Gregory 317, 324, 336

Jackendoff, Ray 399, 416
Jacobi, Irene 399, 416
Jacobs, Haike 45, 105, 256, 257, 270
Jacobson, Steven A. 309
Jäger, Gerhard 191, 194
Jakobson, Roman O. 1, 32, 42, 55, 59, 63, 83, 102, 198, 227, 229, 237, 266, 271, 273, 276, 277, 292, 307, 309, 310
Jakovlev, N. F. 91, 102, 106
Janda, Richard D. 63, 69, 102
Janker, Peter M. 62, 105
Jardine, Adam 155, 160, 163, 164, 168, 174, 175, 176, 177, 179, 181, 186, 187, 188, 191, 192
Jenkins, James J. 3, 18
Jeon, Hae-Song 399, 417

Jespersen, Otto 41, 42, 108, 124
Jessen, Michael 324, 338, 418
John, Tina 62, 103
Johnson, C. Douglas 139, 140, 192
Johnson, Keith 228
Johnson, Mark 178, 190
Jönsson-Steiner, Elisabet 140, 386
Jun, Sun-Ah 50, 385, 394, 416
Jung, Dagmar 12, 17
Jurafsky, Daniel 139, 172, 190, 192
Jurgec, Peter 89, 102

Kabak, Barış 290, 310
Kager, René 60, 102, 178, 192
Kahl, Thede 37
Kahn, Daniel 77, 83, 102
Kaisse, Ellen M. 78, 99, 101
Kallstenius, Gottfrid 370, 386
Kang, Yoonjung 317, 337
Kaplan, Abby 65, 102
Kaplan, Lawrence D. 238, 271, 309
Kaplan, Ronald 139, 169, 192
Karlsson, Anastasia M. 105
Kartunnen, Lauri 139, 175, 188
Karvonen, Dan 74, 102
Kaschube, Dorothea 3, 18
Kasprzik, Anna 191
Kaufmann, Stefan 81
Kaun, Abigail Rhoades 285, 286, 310
Kawahara, Shigeto 76, 102, 228, 327, 338, 396, 416
Kawasaki-Fukumori, Haruko 77, 104, 302, 311
Kay, Martin 138, 169, 192
Keating, Patricia 145, 189, 248, 253, 271, 315, 316, 338, 339
Kenstowicz, Michael 6, 19, 70, 101, 102, 321, 338, 411, 415
Kessler, Brett 77n, 102, 324, 338, 410, 416
Ketrez, Nihan 336
Keyser, Samuel Jay 63, 103, 105, 138, 302, 311, 395, 414
Kibrik, A. E. 41
Kim, Susan 61, 87, 103
Kinloch, Murray 337
Kiparsky, Paul v, viii, ix, 6, 16, 19, 52, **54–106**, 178, 192, 276, 277, 310, 313, 326, 338, 416

Kirchner, Robert M. 190, 196, 227
Kisseberth, Charles W. 6, 19, 127, 168, 176, 178, 191, 192
Kleber, Felicitas 62, 103
Ko, Seongyeon 293n, 310
Kobele, Gregory 127, 138, 192ko
Kochetov, Alexei 296n, 297n, 310
Kock, Axel 345, 386
Kodzasov, S. V. 41
Kohler, Klaus J. 77, 103
Köhnlein, Björn 381, 382, 383, 386
Kolly, Marie-José 124
König, Ekkehard 38
Korhonen, Mikko 63, 69, 103
Korn, David 285, 291, 310
Kornai, András 186, 191, 192
Koskenniemi, Kimmo 139, 192
Kötzing, Timo 191
Krämer, Martin 192, 309
Kristoffersen, Gjert 353, 359, 360, 367, 386
Kruckenberg, Anita 346, 385
Kuaševa, T. X. 99
Kubozono, Haruo 76, 81, 82, 102, 103, 395, 396, 416
Kuipers, Aert H. 91, 92, 103
Kula, Nancy C. 163, 192
Kumaxov, M. A. 91, 99, 103

Labov, William 62, 103
Lacy, Paul de 19, 102, 158, 192, 311, 385
Ladd, D. Robert 63, 103, 228, 351, 385, 391, 392, 409, 414, 415, 416
Ladefoged, Peter 108, 124
Lahiri, Aditi ii, v, viii, ix, 50, 52, **229–272**, 345, 386, 387, 396, 401, 404, 409, 414, 415
Lai, Regine 145, 157, 158, 160, 161, 162, 164, 165, 169, 173, 174, 175, 178, 182, 187, 189, 191, 192
Lautemann, Clements 170, 192
Lavoie, Lisa M. 196, 227
Laycock, D. C. 82, 103
Lazard, Gilbert 32
Leary, Adam 391, 392, 417
Leben, William R. 402, 416
Lee, Seunghun 192, 389, 394, 417
Leeman, Dylan 189

Leemann, Adrian 124
Lehiste, Ilse 393, 416
Leira, Vigleik 351, 386
Lekeneny, Jean 414
Lerdahl, Fred 399, 416
Levelt, Clara 236, 266, 270, 271
Levinson, Stephen C. 18, 55, 72, 90, 100
Li, Bing 283n, 310
Li, Shulan 291, 310
Liberman, Anatoly 63, 69, 103
Liberman, Mark 183, 192, 394, 399, 416
Lickley, Robin 407, 416
Lieber, Rochelle 45
Lightfoot, David 49
Lindblad, Per 343, 344, 345, 385
Lindblom, Björn 64, 103, 196, 227
Linhartova, Vendula 124
Linker, Wendy 338
Lister, Anthony C. 337
Lloyd James, Arthur 110, 124
Lombardi, Linda 104, 193, 315, 323, 338
Lorentz, Ove 345, 351, 352, 386
Lothaire, M. 160, 185, 186, 192
Louriz, Nabila 70, 102
Low, E. L. 112, 113, 114, 124
Luo, Huan 173, 187, 192

McCarthy, John J. 8, 20, 75, 80, 104, 133, 136, 163, 178, 179, 187, 193, 230, 232, 271, 389, 390, 400, 416
McCawley, James D. 81, 104, 276, 310
McCutcheon, Martin J. 332, 337
McKenzie, Pierre 192
MacMahon, April M. S. 61, 64, 104
McNaughton, Robert 149, 154, 156, 193
McQueen, James 392, 416
Mackenzie, Sara 279, 310
Maddieson, Ian v, viii, ix, 4, 9, 19, 38, 55, 91, 94, 104, **107–125**, 196, 199, 211, 227, 228, 333, 338
Magloughlin, Lyra 228
Major, Roy 320, 321, 338
Mallinson, Graham 36
Manaster-Ramer, Alexis 69, 104
Marlo, Michael 186, 192
Marsico, Egidio 124
Martin, James 139, 192

Martin, Samuel 82, 104
Martinet, André 1, 4, 42, 62, 104
Martínez-Gil, Fernando 66, 104
Mascaró, Joan 315, 316, 339
Maskikit-Essed, Raechel 397, 416
Matasović, Ranko 91, 104
Mateus, Maria Helena 49
Matthews, Peter 46
Mchombo, Sam 49
Medvedev, Yu. 182, 193
Mehler, Jacques 125, 189
Melville, Herman 24
Mennen, Ineke 414
Merrill, John 326, 338, 338
Mesgnien-Meninski, François (de) 25, 28, 36
Mester, Armin 81, 82, 102, 394, 416
Mesthrie, Rajend 336, 338, 339
Metzeltin, Michael 37
Meyer, Ernst A. 343, 386
Mezei, J. E. 174, 182, 189
Mielke, Jeff v, viii, ix, 167, 193, **196–228**, 279, 310
Minde, Don van 397, 398, 416
Mithun, Marianne 38
Mjaavatn, Per Egil 343, 385, 386
Mohanan, K. P. 82, 104, 230, 248, 271
Mohanan, Tara 248, 271
Mohri, Mehryar 159, 175, 193
Møllergård, E. 343, 385
Moravcsik, Edith A. 36, 37, 52, 101, 270, 308, 385
Moreton, Elliot 225, 228, 313, 314, 334, 338, 340
Morpurgo Davies, Anna 29, 53
Motsch, Wolfgang 41
Mou, Xiaomin 70, 101
Moulton, William G. 276, 310
Moure, Teresa 37
Mücke, Doris 415
Mugler, France 336, 339
Munroe, R. H. 125
Munroe, Robert L. 117, 124, 125
Myers, Nathan 189
Myers, Scott 218, 228, 314, 315, 332, 333, 335, 338
Myrberg, Sara 346, 346n, 350, 380, 384, 386

Nagarajan, Hemalatha 82, 104
Naydenov, Vladimir 345, 386

Nedjalkov, Vladimir P. 32
Nespor, Marina 125, 189, 389, 394, 417
Nevins, Andrew 71, 73, 101, 106, 160, 162, 162n, 172, 173, 174, 185, 193, 283, 286, 309, 310, 336
Newman, M. E. J. 200, 227
Newman, Stanley 287, 288, 310
Newmeyer, Frederick J. 15, 20
Ní Chiosáin, Máire 65, 104
Nichols, Johanna 1, 7, 20, 38, 197, 226
Nilsen, Randi Alice 359, 360, 385
Nolan, Francis 399, 417
Noord, Gertjan van 140, 190
Nooteboom, Sieb 392, 416, 417
Nordberg, Bengt 374, 374n, 387
Norris, Daniel 416
Nyström, Staffan 345, 387

Ó Siadhail, Mícheál 65n, 104
O'Dell, Michael 62, 105
Odden, David 45, 74, 104, 162n, 176, 192, 193, 299, 310
Oestereicher, Wulf 38
Oh, Mira 321, 338
Ohala, John J. 77, 103, 104, 145, 193, 313, 332, 333, 339
Öhman, Sven 343, 345, 387
Olovjannikova, I. P. 41
Oncina, José 172, 181, 189, 193
Oostendorp, Marc van 2, 18, 19, 20, 187, 189, 192, 193, 310, 333, 338, 339, 415, 416, 417
Osu, Sylvester 5, 17, 35, 104
Otanes, Fe T. 400, 417
Oxford, Will v, viii, ix, **273–311**

Padgett, Jaye 63, 65, 104, 162, 193, 286, 311, 315, 338
Pāṇini 77n
Papert, Seymour 149n, 154, 156, 193
Paradis, Carole 230, 271, 272, 367
Parker, Aliana 89, 105
Pater, Joe 133, 178, 180, 191, 193
Paulian, Christiane 272
Pawley, Andrew 59, 82, 83, 88, 100, 105
Payne, Amanda 173, 187, 193
Pellegrino, François 124
Peng, Long 319, 323, 339

Pensalfini, Rob 72, 76, 99, 105
Peters, Jörg 352, 353, 381, 382, 387, 405, 406, 417
Pierrehumbert, Janet 212, 228, 269, 272, 390, 391, 396, 401, 402, 403, 407, 408, 409, 410, 412n, 413, 414, 415, 417
Pike, Kenneth L. 42n, 47, 110, 125
Piroth, Hans Georg 62, 105
Plank, Frans i, iii, v, viii, ix, 3, 7, 12, 20, **2–53**, 126, 234, 242, 272
Popper, Karl 136, 193
Port, Robert F. 62, 105, 360, 391, 392, 414, 417
Post, Mark W. 417
Pott, August Friedrich 26n
Potts, Christopher 128n, 178, 193
Precoda, Kristin 4n, 9, 19, 55, 104, 196, 199, 228
Prieto, Pilar 409, 412, 417
Prince, Alan 6, 20, 61, 75, 80, 99, 104, 105, 127, 128, 129, 133, 168, 178, 183, 192, 193, 389, 394, 399, 400, 416, 417
Prunet, Jean-François 230, 271, 272
Pullum, Geoffrey K. 127, 128, 147, 149, 152, 189, 193, 194
Purnell, Thomas 293, 293n, 311

Qinggertai (Chingeltei) 287, 311
Quené, Hugo 392, 416, 417

Rabin, Michael 140, 194
Raible, Wolfgang 38
Raimy, Eric 106, 293, 293n, 311
Ramat, Paolo 37
Ramus, Franck 111, 112, 113, 114, 121, 125
Raphael, Lawrence 332, 339
Rask, Rasmus 30
Rawal, Chetan 191
Reetz, Henning 232, 233, 234, 243, 245, 247, 250, 254, 269, 271
Reiss, Charles 181, 190
Rennison, John R. 41
Riad, Tomas v, viii, ix, 52, **341–388**, 405, 417
Rialland, Annie 16, 17
Rice, Curtis 418
Rice, Keren 18, 20, 41, 99, 105, 193, 270, 278, 278n, 308, 309, 310, 311, 338, 417
Ridouane, Rachid 62, 77, 101, 105, 390, 414

Riggle, Jason 17, 19, 140, 175, 178, 187, 191, 194, 416
Ringen, Catherine 319, 320, 324, 336, 337, 338
Ringgaard, Kristian 342, 387
Rischel, Jørgen 41
Roark, Brian 139, 194
Roberts, Adam 269, 272
Roberts, Ian 49
Robins, R. H. 47
Roca, Iggy 61, 105
Roche, James 159, 165, 194
Roeder, Rebecca 293, 311
Rogers, James 127, 147, 148, 149, 152, 153, 156, 157, 181, 186, 187, 194
Rogova, G. B. 99
Rohany Rahbar, Elham 293, 311
Rood, David S. 65n, 105
Rose, Sharon 143, 145, 160, 173, 185, 194
Rozenberg, Grzegorz 186, 194
Rubach, Jerzy 63, 105, 249, 272
Ruiz, José 153, 189
Ryan, Kevin 73, 105

Sagey, Elizabeth C. 225, 228, 231, 251, 252, 259, 272
Šagirov, A. K. 91, 105
Sakarovitch, Jacques 160, 194
Salmons, Joseph 91, 103, 311, 317, 324, 338
Salomaa, Arto 186, 194
Samedov, D. S. 41
Sammallahti, Pekka 297, 300, 311
Samuels, Bridget 20, 93n, 106, 311, 316, 324, 339
Sapir, Edward 3, 8, 20, 41, 42, 273, 274, 275, 276, 307, 311
Satta, Giorgio 140, 178, 179, 189
Saussure, Ferdinand de 42, 311
Schabes, Yves 160, 165, 194
Schachter, Paul 400, 417
Scheibman, Joanne 12, 17
Schepman, Astrid 416
Schiering, René 394, 417
Schmidt, Jürgen Erich 381, 387
Schwartz, Geoffrey 73n, 105
Schwartz, Jean-Luc 55, 105
Schwentick, Thomas 192
Scobbie, James M. 57, 63, 63n, 69, 105

Scott, Dana 140, 194
Segerup, My 367, 372n, 387, 388
Seiler, Hansjakob 20, 32
Selkirk, Elisabeth 228, 338, 389, 394, 411, 417
Shattuck-Hufnagel, Stefanie 414
Shaw, Patricia 243, 245, 246, 272
Shibatani, Masayoshi 32, 53
Shieber, Stuart 127, 138, 139, 194
Shopen, Timothy 20, 38
Siewierska, Anna 38
Silander, Megan 117, 125
Simon, Ellen 319, 322, 332, 335, 339
Simpson, Adrian P. 202n, 228
Singler, John 336, 339
Sipser, Michael 139, 194
Siptár, Péter 49
Skalička, Vladimír 31
Slobin, Dan 7, 20
Smith, Adam 29, 53
Smith, Bruce L. 319, 338
Smith, Geoff 336, 339
Smith, Henry Lee 394, 417
Smith, Nathaniel 189
Smith, Neil 49
Smith, Norval 17, 41, 417
Smith, Steven C. 337
Smith, Tony 82
Smolensky, Paul 6, 20, 61, 105, 127, 128, 129, 133, 168, 178, 181, 193, 194, 323, 339, 400, 417
Sommer, Bruce A. 73, 105
Song, Jae Sung 37, 38
Spencer, Andrew 46
Sproat, Richard 139, 194
Stampe, David 12, 18
Stavness, I. Ian 227
Steinitz, Wolfgang 297, 300, 307, 311
Steriade, Donca 77, 105, 190, 211, 214, 228, 313, 315, 316, 325, 326, 328, 339, 413
Stevens, Kenneth N. 63, 103, 105, 108, 125, 231, 231n, 270, 272, 302, 311
Strandberg, Mathias 353, 359, 360, 388
Strange, Winifred 393, 417
Strother-Garcia, Kristina 187
Stuart-Smith, Jane 57, 63, 63n, 69, 105
Suzuki, Keiichiro 160, 173, 193, 194
Svantesson, Jan-Olof 89, 105, 287, 311

Sweet, Henry 40, 108, 125
Tabain, Marija 72, 106
Talkin, David 212, 228
Tallerman, Maggie 45, 49
Talmy, Leonard 7, 20
Tangi, Oufae 89, 100
Tanner, Herbert G. 191
Teleman, Ulf 345, 388
Tent, Jan 336, 339
Tesar, Bruce 131, 134, 181, 194
Thomas, Wolfgang 154, 156, 194
Thráinsson, Höskuldur 49
Timm, Jason 124
Topinzi, Nina 73, 73n, 106
Törkenczy, Miklós 49
Trager, George 394, 417
Trask, R. L. 12, 20
Trommelen, Mieke 256, 272, 418
Trubetzkoy, Nikolaj S. 1, 4, 5, 9, 20, 32, 42n, 55, 62, 91, 99, 106, 108, 125, 273, 307
Tsagov, M. 91, 106
Tsendina, Anna 105
Tukumu, Simon Nsielanga 42
Turčaninov, G. 91, 106
Turing, Alan 136, 137, 139, 194
Turpin, Myfany 75, 106

Ulseth, B. 343, 385
Urbina, Jon Ortiz de 42

Vaan, Michiel de 381, 388
Vago, Robert 319, 324, 336
Vajda, Edward 6, 20, 274, 311
Vallée, Nathalie 105, 336
Vance, Timothy J. 197, 228, 403, 418
Vanhove, Martine 39
Vaux, Bert 78, 89, 93, 186, 211, 225, 227, 228, 271, 316, 324, 333, 339
Veilleux, Nanette 414
Velupillai, Viveka 37
Ven, Marco van de 406, 418
Venditti, Jennifer J. 11, 17, 19
Vennemann, Theo 77, 106, 218, 228
Vergnaud, Jean-Roger 16, 19, 157, 190
Verner, Karl 30
Versteegh, Kees 97, 106
Vidal, Enrique 189, 193

Visscher, Molly 189, 194
Vliet, Pete van der 381, 383, 386, 404, 409
Vogel, Irene 389, 394, 417
Vollmer, Heribert 192
Vu, Mai Ha 187

Walker, Rachel 143, 145, 160, 173, 185, 194, 283, 311, 394, 418
Wang, Chilin 318, 319, 322, 323, 329, 330, 336, 337, 339
Watson, Janet 49
Weijer, Jeroen van de 160, 162, 191, 339
Weinberger, Steven 318, 329, 339
Wellcome, David 189, 194
Wells, John 64, 106
Westbury, John 315, 316, 339
Wetterlin, Allison 271, 272, 345, 386, 388
Wetzels, Leo 101, 228, 315, 316, 339
Whaley, Lindsay J. 20, 37
Wheeler, Max 49, 89
Whorf, B. L. 47
Wibel, Sean 194
Wiese, Richard 49, 89, 106, 387, 393, 417, 418
Wilson, Colin 132n, 159, 162, 163, 164, 178, 179, 187, 190, 195
Wiltshire, Caroline 318, 323, 340
Winteler, Jost 43
Winters, Stephen J. 125, 226, 228
Wissing, Daan 318, 322, 340
Wolfe, Andrew 78, 106, 227, 271
Wood, Sidney 91, 106
Wurzel, Wolfgang 41, 46, 106

Xolodovič, Aleksandr A. 32
Xrakovskij, Viktor S. 32
Xu, Zheng 324, 337

Yavas, Mehmet 318, 334, 335, 340
Yu, Alan C. 17, 19, 145, 191, 193, 317, 334, 340, 416

Zagona, Karen 49
Zanten, Ellen van 19, 397, 415
Zhang, Xi 281, 283, 285, 286, 287, 291, 292, 293, 293n, 309, 311
Zonneveld, Wim 318, 322, 340, 396, 418
Zwart, Jan-Wouter 49
Zwicky, Arnold M. 46